PERGAMON INTERNATIONAL LIBRARY
of Science, Technology, Engineering and Social Studies
The 1000-volume original paperback library in aid of education,
industrial training and the enjoyment of leisure
Publisher: Robert Maxwell, M.C.

An Annotated Reader in Environmental Planning and Management

THE PERGAMON TEXTBOOK
INSPECTION COPY SERVICE

An inspection copy of any book published in the Pergamon International Library will gladly be sent to academic staff without obligation for their consideration for course adoption or recommendation. Copies may be retained for a period of 60 days from receipt and returned if not suitable. When a particular title is adopted or recommended for adoption for class use and the recommendation results in a sale of 12 or more copies, the inspection copy may be retained with our compliments. The Publishers will be pleased to receive suggestions for revised editions and new titles to be published in this important International Library.

An Annotated Reader in Environmental Planning and Management

Edited by

Timothy O'Riordan and R. Kerry Turner

School of Environmental Sciences
University of East Anglia

PERGAMON PRESS

OXFORD · NEW YORK · TORONTO · SYDNEY · PARIS · FRANKFURT

UK	Pergamon Press Ltd., Headington Hill Hall, Oxford OX3 0BW, England
USA	Pergamon Press Inc., Maxwell House, Fairview Park, Elmsford, New York 10523, USA
CANADA	Pergamon Press Canada Ltd., Suite 104, 150 Consumers Rd., Willowdale, Ontario M2J 1P9, Canada
AUSTRALIA	Pergamon Press (Aust.) Pty. Ltd., P.O. Box 544, Potts Point, NSW 2011, Australia
FRANCE	Pergamon Press SARL, 24 rue des Ecoles, 75240 Paris, Cedex 05, France
FEDERAL REPUBLIC OF GERMANY	Pergamon Press GmbH, Hammerweg 6, D-6242 Kronberg-Taunus, Federal Republic of Germany

First edition 1983

Library of Congress Cataloging in Publication Data
Main entry under title:
An Annotated reader in environmental planning and management.
(Urban & regional planning series; v. 30) (Pergamon international library of science, technology, engineering, and social studies)
1. Environmental protection — Social aspects — Addresses, essays, lectures. I. O'Riordan, Timothy. II. Turner, R. Kerry. III. Series: Urban and regional planning series; v. 30. IV. Series: Pergamon international library of science, technology, engineering, and social studies.
TD170.3.A56   1982   333.7'2   82-7569

British Library Cataloguing in Publication Data
An Annotated reader in environmental planning and management. — (Urban and regional planning series; v. 30). — (Pergamon international library)
1. City planning   2. Regional planning
I. O'Riordan, Timothy   II. Turner, R. Kerry
III. Series
711   HT166

ISBN 0-08-024669-9 (Hard cover)
ISBN 0-08-024668-0 (Flexicover)

Printed in Great Britain by A. Wheaton & Co. Ltd., Exeter

Preface

IT MAY appear inappropriate and untimely to prepare a reader on the general theme of man and the environment. Inappropriate because bookshops seem to be well stocked with edited volumes on environmental matters generally, and ill-timed because of the apparent general decline in the public interest in matters of an environmental nature. But we feel that there is still no comprehensive reader on this topic and certainly no title where readings are linked together through the medium of lengthy introductory essays which set the writings in perspective and provide the interested reader with further guidance.

So the aim of this volume is to reproduce and place in context important writings in the social science and humanistic aspects of the man–environment relationship. The themes that are covered encompass politics, sociology, anthropology, psychology, law and economics. This is a wide canvas, so we have tried to choose articles and commentaries which are illuminating in themselves but which collectively tackle important topics from a variety of standpoints and which are written in such a way as to be intelligible to the general reader.

Needless to say the literature is so vast that it is impossible to accommodate all the most valuable readings. So we have been forced to expand our introductory essays to incorporate themes that would not otherwise be available without fairly drastic editing. We also realise how interconnected the principal ideas are. Time and again we found ourselves cross-referencing to other sections to avoid repetition and we hope that this practice will not inconvenience the reader too much.

We are most grateful to Peggy Ducker at Pergamon for her patience and assistance throughout the preparation of this book and to Julie Fox and Katie Watt for deciphering our manuscripts so accurately and so cheerfully.

University of East Anglia   TIMOTHY O'RIORDAN
                                               R. KERRY TURNER

Contents

List of Figures

The Nature of the Environmental Idea

Many people find it difficult to define or even to comprehend the idea of environmentalism. It is easy to sympathise with their frustration because the movement itself has a built-in paradox and is composed of at least four quite divergent patterns of thought and action. The paradox lies in a powerful resistance to many kinds of change on the one hand yet a wish for quite radical reforms in the organisation and process of government and in the equality of human wellbeing on the other. The confusion is increased when the term "environmentalist" is uncritically applied to someone who is an ecologist, or who fights to protect an attractive landscape or endangered species, or who objects to a noisy, polluting or otherwise hazardous activity that is planned for his neighbourhood, or who dislikes complex, capital-intensive technology, or who prefers to keep pigs, brew home-made beer and live in a commune. Although environmentalists are not the only people who object to much of what they interpret as modern-day values, aspirations and ways of life, it is probably fair to say that one of the two themes which unite their disparate perceptions is a wish to alter many of the unjust and foolhardy features they associate with modern capitalism of both a state and private variety. The other common interest is a commitment to cut out waste and reduce profligacy by consuming resources more frugally. Environmentalists do not agree, however, about how either of these objectives should be attained, or what an "environmentally conscious" society would look like, and how the transition should be achieved. It is in these very critical areas that environmentalism is most frustratingly vague and indecisive.

In the first of this collection of readings Cotgrove seeks to explain the underlying motivations of the environmental movement. He recognises initially two major divisions: the "millenial utopian elements" who seek a total restructuring of modern society, its values, institutions and economics, and the "radical socialists" who hope to channel science and technology for socially useful purposes through more centrally directed planning, but who do not demand a wholesale revolution in current paradigms. This latter argument is developed by Burger. Cotgrove, however, prefers to dwell on the utopian component of environmentalism which he identifies as being opposed not merely to some of the manifestations of modern science and technology, but more so the underlying modes of thought, particularly a seemingly uncaring attitude toward nature and weaker human species, which such manifestations express.

The Historical Development of the Environmental Idea

What exactly is it that environmentalists are so disturbed about and how influential are they likely to be in the politics of the uncertain future? This introductory essay and the readings that follow seek to answer those questions.

Regarding the matter of what environmentalists dislike, one has to look at the movement in historical perspective. To do this we have to look back almost 150 years to consider the arguments of various people contemplating the beginning of the first industrial revolution. One group lived in the United States and were known as transcendentalists because of their belief that close communion with nature transcended the soul from the mundaneness of ordinary life and its many problems thus permitting man to explore his creative virtues. A number of well-known literary figures were associated with this movement including Henry Thoreau, Walt Whitman, Ralph Waldo Emerson and John Muir.[1] A flavour of their feelings about the importance of nature and solitude can be tasted by reading this extract from an essay by Emerson written in 1836[2]:

"In the woods we return to reason and faith. There I feel that nothing can befall me in life— no disgrace, no calamity . . . which nature cannot repair. I become a transparent eyeball; I am nothing; I see all; the currents of the Universal Being circulate through me; I am part or parcel of God. . . . In the tranquil landscape, and especially in the distant line of the horizon, man beholds somewhat as beautiful as his own nature."

The transcendentalists were alarmed at what they saw of the early American industrial economy. They disliked the emergence of the city with its "effete snobbery", its cruel class divisions and disparities of incomes, its symbolism of materialism and the importance attached to the making of money, all of which they believe led to the degradation of man. Burch[3] described their feelings thus:

"If anything there is an intense moral concern with the nature of human nature, social and individual elements. What is clearly attacked is American commercialism which drives man to destroy themselves and others by placing a price tag on everything, by desecrating natural beauty without ever discovering the simple resources of human existence."

In part, the misgivings of the transcendentalists (who preached and in many cases lived their message for over 50 years) was a concern that the fundamental rights of individual liberty and creativity were being lost in the new commercialism which was driving out a sense of personal responsibility for the present and future wellbeing of mankind in general. Despite the fact that they lived in a free, democratic and open society, the transcendentalists feared that the emerging institutions of what we now know as modern capitalism would destroy the spirit of communality and self-reliance and irreparably damage the vestiges of a love of things beautiful and inspirational. Nature became the appropriate metaphor because nature was seen as free, and as providing a working unity out of its component diversities.

An uncaring destruction of natural things they felt, would not only damage necessary life-support mechanisms but degrade man even further into a mechanistic robot. The transcendentalists thus preached the notion of a *bioethic*, a sense of responsibility for the earth and a plea for a basic ecological understanding before tampering with its resources. In the modern era this has emerged in a form of a powerful ecological agressiveness where some advocate that man's actions must be circumscribed by ecological realities. In other words, human morals should be based on ecological principles, not attuned to merely socially derived rights and wrongs[4,5]. A whiff of this argument can be smelt in Sections 4, 5 and 6 that follow, especially the reading by Pearce. Those wishing to see this philosophy carried to extremes should read an essay on ecological humanism by Skolimowsky[6]. Here is a short extract:

> "Ecological humanism marks the return of the unitary view in which the philosophy of man and the philosophy of nature are aspects of each other. Thus, the conjunction of ecology and humanism is not arbitrary, but the perception of the essential unity of the natural and human world. Ecological Humanism requires the broadening of the concept of ecology to encompass the balance of the human environment; the natural world then becomes vested with the same 'value' as the human world."

The other group of which can be described as the earliest environmentalism were the so-called "anarchists" of mid-nineteenth-century Europe of whom probably William Morris and Peter Kropotkin are best known as a result of their popularity in magazines such as *The Ecologist* and *Vole* in the UK, *Alternatives* in Canada, and their counterparts across the channel. These people were less interested in the wonders of nature as much as in channelling the undoubted benefits of technological and economic progress into more egalitarian and enjoyable social forms. They advocated the concept of the self-reliant community preferably part agricultural and part industrial where people shared jobs, enjoyed the companionship as much as the income that work provided, helped each other in work and play and generally avoided the alienation and sense of frustrated helplessness that they believed befall those who are the unfortunate victims of the machine age. Thus the utopia pictured by Kropotkin[7] consisted of a simple life based upon limited expectations where there was little demand (and little need) for constant material progress. But neither Kropotkin nor Morris were romantics harking after a nostalgic past: they were fully aware of the enormous potential of labour-saving technologies that released drudgery and freed both the mind and body for more creative endeavours. They would have embraced the microprocessor as much as they did the steam engine. What they were most concerned about was that inventions were designed for the good of the individual spirit and communal life rather than for economic progress as such. For them the pattern of living, the structure of settlements and the decentralisation of government into a workable federation were far more important than economic growth for its own sake. It is this reorientation of priorities that remains one of the most important features of their intellectual legacy. Cotgrove characterises this legacy as the traditional wing of environmental utopianism based upon the sociological notion of a *Gemeinschaft*-type society "in which the social bond is the traditional authority of a natural social order".[8]

Much of what is now regarded as mainstream environmental writings have picked up these twin themes of the bioethic and the self-reliant participatory community. They are popular today for similar reasons that caused them to emerge more than a century ago, namely an anxiety about where modern technology will take us, a fear that whatever constitutes "humanitarianism" will atrophy, a belief that as resources become more scarce nation states or larger politico-economic blocks will embark upon resource-grabbing wars probably with catastrophic consequences, and a deep sadness that various species of animal and plant life and the habitats upon which they depend are likely to be destroyed simply because people in authority do not seem to care. A sense of these feelings can be gained from reading the extract by Hall that follows, though one is advised to read the whole report which he edited.[9]

This brief historical exploration is revealing in that it indicates that there is nothing particularly new about environmentalism, for very few of the basic ideas are twentieth century in genesis. It is also sobering in that it indicates that mankind seems to learn little through advance warning. In the true Christian sense it appears that he must first suffer before experiencing salvation. The difference today compared with a century ago lies more in the scale of the problem than in its qualities. Western affluent society has just passed through 25 years of unprecedented economic growth where real incomes were rising at least 3 percent annually. This was partly the result of impressive developments in productivity which in turn caused real resource costs (especially energy costs) to fall, though this was also because the social and environmental costs of their extraction were not fully calculated. In short, pernicious damage to environmental quality subsidised low resource prices.

Nowadays much of that has changed. Energy prices are likely to rise (in an unpredictable manner) relative to the cost of living because they are no longer solely dictated by market economies or multinational oligopolies. Other resource prices will also probably rise if the Third World producers get their way because of new commodity trading agreements. However, this remains to be seen as the battle between them and the rich importing nations is not yet resolved. Affluence has brought its own crop of environmental problems. Rising consumer demand may have been good for economic growth but it depleted forests, created enormous demands on new energy sources, led to widespread pollution of both a toxic and non-toxic kind and congested formerly peaceful beauty spots and quiet beaches. As the environmental stress of affluent living became more noticeable so society began to realise that it had to start paying for the clean up. It also found that it had less room for manoeuvre than it had optimistically imagined, since it discovered that to do the job properly would either cost a lot of money during a period of falling productivity, or would mean a lot of heated but unresolved argument as various interest groups continued to object to all compromise solutions, no matter how costly.

The Collage of Environmentalist Beliefs

Environmentalism was reborn in the sixties. It was not, however, a unitary movement because there were so many different interpretations of what constituted the problem. Following up some of the points developed in the four readings that follow, particularly that by Burger, O'Riordan[10] put together a simplified representation of the principal themes that constitute modern environmentalism. This is reproduced, with variations, as Figures 1.1 and 1.2. A matter that gave some trouble in drawing up Figure 1.1 was how to depict, within the rubric of environmentalism, a set of ideas which most people who regard themselves as environmentalists believe are the opposite of their convictions. This is what O'Riordan called the "technocentric mode" of thought and action typified by a faith in the technological and organisational supremacy of man, a genuine belief that progress can only be achieved through expertise and professionalism and an acceptance that man and nature can live in *productive* harmony, in the sense that both human and non-human life can prosper and grow simultaneously so long as man designs his activities with due care. In drawing up Figure 1.1 he realised that environmentalism is really a dialectical phenomenon, which exists in the mutual opposition of two quite different modes of thought and action, namely technocentrism and ecocentrism. The ecocentric mode is

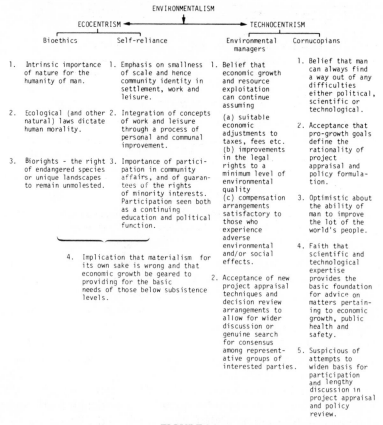

FIGURE 1.1

Patterns of environmentalist ideologies. This diagram is a modification of that produced by O'Riordan, T. (1977) Environmental Ideologies (*Environment and Planning*, Vol. 11, No. 1, p. 4). The modification is the incorporation of the environmental manager, the reform wing of the technocentrists, who we believe will play a prominent role in environmental affairs in the forseeable future.

characterised by the twin themes handed down from the last century, namely the bioethic and the participatory commune. Though in practice it is difficult to find examples of those who espouse either mode in purely distilled form, there are major differences in ideologies between the two patterns of thought which become most evident when challenged (see Figure 1.3). But it is fair to say that many technocentrists see themselves as environmentalists because they passionately believe that they can improve human wellbeing (and ecological welfare) with suitable modifications to technology and social institutions.

The technocentrist mode is thus characterised by a faith in the interventive power of man to make the world a better place for all its peoples

	Technocentrist	Ecocentrist
Conservative	The morality of growth → Technological optimists → Managerial optimists → Political optimists	The morality of limits → The "lifeboat" ethics of the commons → The no-growth school → Ecological planners → Amenity protectionists
Liberal	The cautious reformers → Social democrats → "Spaceship earth" economists → "Alternative" technologists	The radical ecological activists → Environmental / political educators → Environmental / political citizens → Research arms of environmental lobbies

FIGURE 1.2

Environmentalist options for the future. This diagram is based on that provided by Burger in the reading that follows. Each of the options is discussed in the accompanying text.

and to convert a hostile nature into benign productivity. Again there is a wealth of historical tradition here. For example, in his monumental history of man–nature attitudes, Glacken[11] described how many early philosophers believed in the notion of a "designed earth" where nature was regarded as raw material for man to manipulate and improve. Turning a marsh into dry farmland or a desert into irrigated agriculture would be quite as acceptable as would redesigning a wilderness into manicured parkland or beautiful gardens. Until relatively recently few worried about what would now be called the "environmental impacts" of such activities mainly because the concept of systematically recording and weighing quite different kinds of advantages and disadvantages was quite unknown and in any case few cared about possible damage to nature and to their weaker human brethren.

In the last few years, however, all this has changed and environmental impact assessment is very much in vogue. This is the result of four factors. First, better scientific knowledge and publicity which alerted the general public to some at least of the dangers associated with major resource-development schemes and proposed new technologies. Second, the activities of what are known as public interest environmental pressure groups such as the Sierra Club and the Natural Resources Defense Council in the US and the Council for the Protection of Rural England and Friends of the Earth in the UK.[12] The political effectiveness of these groups has been enhanced by the advances in scientific understanding and sympathetic media coverage already referred to, for they now undertake their own research starting from a different set of assumptions than is common in "establishment" thinking and actively encourage publicity so that they can take their case over the heads of the experts to the people. This is very evident in the efforts to stop the

	Dominant Social Paradigm	Alternative Environmental Paradigm
CORE VALUES	Material (economic growth)	Non-material (self-actualisation)
	Natural environment valued as resource	Natural environment intrinsically valued
	Domination over nature	Harmony with nature
ECONOMY	Market forces	Public interest
	Risk and reward	Safety
	Rewards for achievement	Incomes related to need
	Differentials	Egalitarian
	Individual self-help	Collective/social provision
POLITY	Authoritative structures: (experts influential)	Participative structures: (citizen/worker involvement)
	Hierarchical	Non-hierarchical
	Law and order	Liberation
SOCIETY	Centralised	Decentralised
	Large-scale	Small-scale
	Associational	Communal
	Ordered	Flexible
NATURE	Ample reserves	Earth's resources limited
	Nature hostile/neutral	Nature benign
	Environment controllable	Nature delicately balanced
KNOWLEDGE	Confidence in science and technology	Limits to science
	Rationality of means	Rationality of ends
	Separation of fact/value, thought/feeling	Integration of fact/value, thought/feeling

FIGURE 1.3

The structure of two dominant social paradigms. This diagram is drawn from Cotgrove, S. and Duff, A. (1980) Environmentalism, Middle Class Radicalism and Politics *The Sociological Review*, 28, 331–351. Cotgrove and Duff hypothesise that these two belief structures are internally consistent and strongly held so that conflict between advocates of each is inevitable. This is already in evidence in the nuclear debate and might well expand to engulf the wider questions of strategies to cope with widespread unemployment. As they put it: "The debate about environmental issues becomes a dialogue of the blind talking to the deaf. It is such experiences . . . which contribute to the decline in political legitimacy, a falling off in support for traditional political parties and processes, and an increase in direct action."

killing of whales and the development of new nuclear power stations.

A third factor is the sheer scale of resource-development projects, especially in the energy extraction, timber and mineral development fields the associated environmental repercussions of which when added together could have global repercussions. The present debate over the effect on global climate of widespread deforestation especially in tropical countries and of exponential increases in the burning of hydrocarbons is illustrative of this point.[13] One noted ecologist[14] believes that as many as one animal species per year and one insect species per day are being lost as a result of habitat changes caused by a combination of increased agricultural development, urbanisation and deforestation.

Fourth, all of these factors have made Western developed man more cautious. This means that he has provided more opportunity for debate and objection through public hearings and commissions of inquiry and that he has insisted that more money and time be devoted to the identification and analysis of the possible risks associated with any new proposal. By opening up avenues, policymakers have provided more room for argument and probably have reduced rather than improved the efficiency and authoritativeness of decision-taking. They have also made it much more difficult for the technocentrist to operate with impunity. This is particularly evident in the emerging field of risk assessment where a hazard not experienced is a hazard to be avoided almost at all costs. In the current nuclear debate, for instance, it is unlikely that protagonists will ever agree about the likelihood of a heretofore not experienced "maximum credible accident" simply because one man's fault-free computer printout is another man's point of departure. Biocides — viruses and bacteria that can kill insects—have been known for over 20 years but few are marketed and none is applied to food crops because of a fear of possible health effects. It seems that at least in the area of risk assessment much has to be learned from mistakes and accidents, the very phenomena that the whole technique tries to avoid.

The net outcome of this is that the unbridled technocentrist—the one who is interventionist, optimistic about man's capabilities, resistant to looking at different possibilities of reaching a given objective and irritated by what he regards as uninformed criticism—is a dying breed. Yet it was this kind of enterprising individual who, to a large extent, created the prosperity that many in industrialised nations currently enjoy. However, while the pure strain of technocentrist is dying, a new variety of environmental manager is emerging, one who seeks to compromise (not always a middle ground) between the demands of creating more wealth and the need to safeguard against risk, environmental damage, loss of scenic heritage and unacceptable disruption to the way of life of various subcultures. The modern specialist is steadily equipping himself with an interdisciplinary training to varying degrees. Within a decade most planners will have to be familiar with the intricacies of environmental impact appraisal, most nuclear physicists with the complexities of designing systems that are incapable of being usurped or copied by terrorists or malevolent nations, and most engineers with a basic understanding of ecology.

A broader and more detailed scientific understanding will, however, not be sufficient training for the technocentrist of tomorrow since with that understanding must come a sympathy with if not wholehearted support for the feelings of the groups identified as "ecocentrists". This will probably be the most difficult challenge for this means reforms in education at all levels, changes in the consultative devices for soliciting reactions to proposals (via public hearings, commissions of inquiry and legislative committees), improvements in techniques for identifying and comparing costs and benefits, and new ideas about the question of governmental authority and accountability. It is in these rather vague areas of analytical technique, political process, and ecocentric understanding that the real message of environmentalism lies and why this particular reader is structured as it is. For one can argue at least from one vantage point that the "enlightened technocentrist" of tomorrow ought to be the true environmentalist — the environmental manager who seeks to reduce the adverse consequences of economic development and social improvement to acceptable levels. This will undoubtedly cost more—most modern environmental impact analyses result in a 10–25 percent additional spending on environmental amelioration and "bribes" to disaffected groups living nearby—but in the longer term it may be more expeditious as protestors are better incorporated in the consultative processes in a sincere attempt to reach acceptable compromises.

We recognise that this view is based upon only a minor modification of "business as usual" with little concession to major reforms in governmental authority, the control of capital or the operations of science and technology. It is unlikely to satisfy either the socialist–marxist or the committed ecocentrist both of whom will accept nothing less than major political reforms and quite new patterns of thinking. But we feel that it is the most practical short-term outcome of present-day environmentalism, even though it may be quite an unsatisfactory approach for the longer term. People's minds, like agency ethos, cannot be transformed overnight: we believe that economic circumstances will have to change quite substantially and along with that severe ecosystem damage will have to become far more noticeable and alarming than it currently is before any of these more far-reaching transformations can take place.

The Future of Environmentalism

A number of political observers believe that environmentalism is fairly typical of other social movements, such as racial justice and women's rights, that will rise in protest at unjustness and fall as governments act and social attitudes become more responsive. The most prominent of these is Anthony Downs[15] who feels that the environmental movement would follow an "issue-attention cycle" where certain individual problems "leap into sudden prominence, remain there for a short time, and then gradually fade from public attention—though still largely unresolved". However, the commitment to environmental quality does not seem to be waning. According to a recent American survey[16] the environmental idea is still flourishing across a wide spectrum of American society despite fears over economic recession and inflation. People judge environmental problems to be serious, they express a willingness to increase government spending for their mitigation and when trade-offs between pro-environmental positions and jobs, taxes, etc., are faced, the pro-environmental arguments prevail. Also revealing is that the survey found that a majority feared that a deteriorated environmental quality would remain for many years to come and that environmental concern was equally felt across all classes, regardless of income and education. Public interest environmental groups may be filled with "middle-class" members, but they seem to represent the views of a widely based constituency.

This evidence tends to support the view that modern environmentalism has grown up out of an anxiety about rates of growth and consequences of rapid change. Its most intense concern is directed at the future of the globe. Its own future depends upon the relative influence of the four groups of environmentalists depicted in Figure 1.2 and on actual future events. In Figure 1.2 the technocentrist and ecocentrist modes are split into two components, representing those who see reform without any fundamental alteration of existing political and economic institutions (the conservatives) and those who regard an environmental future as requiring major changes in the whole approach to economic activity, social wellbeing and forms of government (the liberals). The conservative technocentrists are epitomised by futurists such as Herman Kahn and Norman McCrae[17] who are convinced that a much wealthier economy is possible given the right kinds of incentives for industry and business. In their analysis, it is only through economic growth that environmental improvement and greater economic and social equality can be attained. Needless to say, they cite the literature that is favourable to their argument (especially that which indicates that growth reduces income disparities) and choose to play down the warnings of ecologists and anthropologists about the effect of deforestation, increased agricultural activity and new energy developments on global climate and the traditional livelihood of native peoples. They admit that in the light of these scares "concern and prudence are indeed warranted", but believe that a sense of the "fragility" of the environment may be misleading because man has already survived many disasters and strains (though he had less to lose and there were fewer of him) and that both the environment and most ecological systems "must be tough and largely self-correcting or self healing; otherwise neither would have survived".[18] They also chastise the doom-mongers, saying that while

"much of the industrial imperative and its appurtenances will [eventually] erode or expire... to weaken it prematurely, *before it has run its natural course*, would be to impose unnecessary trauma and suffering and make even more difficult the full exploitation of the many opportunities now available"[19] (italics added).

From any vantage point other than theirs, it seems hard to believe that widespread economic growth is possible without unacceptable ecological and social damage. Certainly nothing has occurred in the years since the slump of 1974/5 to indicate that sustained economic growth is possible. Even the economists of the Organisation for Economic Cooperation and Development, representing the thirteen more economically advanced nations and not normally noted for their pessimism, see no hope of sustained economic recovery and declining unemployment in the foreseeable future.[20]

So we turn to the cautious reformers, those who advocate tinkering with economic incentives such as effluent fees, depletion taxes and multiple discount rates, and adjusting social institutions to include environmental impact assessment and public analysis of policy options. This is the group of "enlightened" technocentrists already referred to who are increasingly to be found among economists, engineers, planners and administrators. Some of their views will be discussed in Sections 3, 4, 5 and 7 but Brubaker and Ayres have written helpful books that are fairly representative of this thinking.[21] In addition, many of those who advocate the use of so-called appropriate technology fit into this category.[22] They also regard growth as a prerequisite for reform but recognise that growth must be contained by the practical needs of ecological sustainability and the ethical issues of safeguarding the ways of life of minority societies and future generations. This group is less optimistic about the future than the first but still cheerful. Because their analyses are backed up by indications of undesirable environmental damage and social distress their views are gradually being heard more and more by those who count. While we accept that there are many who do not subscribe to this perspective, we believe that over the next generation this kind of thinking will dominate the public scene simply because it is the least disruptive way of dealing with problems. In other words, it fits the incremental mould of political and administrative response to change without hurting unduly those who are most influential in making those changes. We believe that in the short term, given no major catastrophes or politically inspired resource scarcities, this is the only acceptable option for Western capitalist societies noted for their adaptability to meet new social demands yet given that their existing structure of power remains substantially unchanged. In this respect we do not entirely subscribe to the views of Burger that follow, though much of what he says makes a lot of sense.

But looking past the twentieth century the future becomes far more uncertain and the precise nature of environmentalism much more difficult to visualise. Obviously much depends on how successful the emerging corps of environmental managers will be in providing for improved economic wellbeing and income redistribution. In our view this is not going to be possible for long in a world threatened with continued population growth and depleting resources. We accept the conclusions reached by many authors[23] that real economic growth cannot continue into the next century without either serious ecological damage and/or serious impoverishment for many millions of people. Some of the ecological damage is already alarming. Fertile topsoil is now removed from over one-third of the world's agricultural areas. Nearly one-third of the tropical forests have already been cut down and it is likely that most of the rest will disappear in 60 years. The desert margins are now advancing by 50,000 km² per year so that one-third of present arable land is threatened. The stocks of many well-known edible fish species are now seriously depleted, and there are continued difficulties in finding new sources of reliable energy supplies without substantial demands on water supplies, landscape attractiveness and the good will of local people.

Unfortunately there is no comprehensive review of the precise nature and extent of all this damage and no one has attempted to place it all in perspective. Books by Wilson, Dorst, Nicholson, Ward and Dubos and Ward are helpful though rather depressing but they do not provide much sense of the cumulative effect or possible trends.[24] What is sobering, however, is the apparent inability of either national governments or international institutions substantially to get to grips with this damage. International aid can and does alleviate suffering in the worst crises as, for example, in the Sahelian drought of 1972/4, but it is a patch-up job that does not get to the root of the trouble. This is a function of population pressure, serious poverty and malnutrition, the dispossession of land and a lack of real effort to help the very poor who are thereby forced to destroy the environmental resource base upon which their livelihood depends. It would appear that some kind of structuralist solution as outlined by Stoneman would probably alleviate some of the disparity of misery in such countries, but the outlook is bleak.

Because the future ought to be something that mankind should create rather than be propelled into, one would like to see some shift in post-industrial societies toward some of the traditional liberal ecocentric ideals as outlined by Cotgrove and lucidly described by Hall in the extract that follows. But we suspect that there may be a decade or two of quite considerable difficulty ahead in which two classes of people emerge — those who have wealth and job security and environmental amenities (many of which they can buy) and those who have none of these. In the former group we list the conservative ecocentrists, many (but not all) of whom are comfortably off, usually enjoy or have recently retired from a reasonably well-paid occupation and who are anxious to protect their quality of life. These people supply the ranks of those who resist new noxious developments in their neighbourhood (with a considerable degree of effectiveness) and who are least willing to see any major redistribution either of economic or environmental wealth. At a larger global scale, but in a national context, they form the majority of those who support a protectionist economic stance in the form of import controls and other trade barriers in order to safeguard their jobs and the nation's economy from low-cost international competition. Whether jobs will be saved and the quality of goods improved remains a moot question.[25]

The other class of people would be those who do not experience at present many of the privileges and amenities enjoyed by the first group. In developing countries there are many millions who do not have enough to eat let alone adequate housing or health care. But even in the so-called affluent nations, up to 20 percent of the population survive only just above subsistence level, particularly among the elderly and racial minorities. We add to this group those who are or who will be structurally unemployable due to international competition and technological change, including the advent of the microprocessor, and to general economic recession. The most susceptable are those who are not unionised and who are peripheral to the labour force, especially women and school-leavers. Already there are some 25 million people unemployed in the OECD countries and it is difficult to see how this number will not double within 15 years with rates of up to 40 percent unemployed among the more vulnerable sections.[26]

It is almost impossible to predict with accuracy what will happen if society does not get to grips with this dilemma. Hall spells out a fairly realistic transition to a more do-it-yourself state based upon quite new attitudes to job sharing, communal activity and leisure time. A Study Group of the British Association for the Advancement of Science[27] reaches similar conclusions. We believe that as this basically economic transition takes place, so governments will be compelled to consider seriously how such a society as Hall described should emerge, otherwise we cannot see how various forms of civil strife can be avoided.

Nevertheless, the kind of picture that both Hall and Burger paint is probably not going to be a particularly enjoyable one for many people who are used to the comforts of affluence. Few get excited about the prospect of widespread do-it-yourself especially if it also means do-it-with-others. Even in communes where people try to get on with each other, social harmony is not by any means guaranteed and much time and effort are devoted to resolving disputes. Many, too, do not want to be bothered with any more democratic responsibilities, other than voting once in a while, despite the advent of new forms of electronic communication. A long period of extensive and varied education would not be justified, in the minds of many, if "payment" was only from a state or communal fund and where there were few opportunities for improving one's income. Even the Chinese and Israeli communes now recognise that income differentials must take the place of pure egalitarian idealism. The idea of some form of a socialist state dictating needs and activities, no matter how anarchistic, is regarded by many with a lot of misgiving. The only way in which this kind of picture might be palatable is where there seems no alternative and where new social institutions actually mould new attitudes. This of course is the nub of the argument but the transition will not be easy. Lerner,[28] who is studying how societies react under conditions of general crisis, suggests that there are two possible outcomes: either the weak will succumb violently so that terrorism through desperation will become rampant, or the weak will be exterminated (deliberately or inadvertently) so that only the strong control the machinery of government and the labour force. Death might then become a matter of political expediency and not a natural event.

So we return to the suffering analogy. We can only foresee that matters will have to get worse before people really get to grips with a different approach to growth and redistribution, though a great variety of stalling tactics which can only be short-term palliatives will be explored in the interim. If national economic protectionism becomes widespread, it is possible that behind the tariff walls the kind of society that Hall envisages could emerge. Eventually the established political parties will accept the reality that "business as usual" economics cannot work. Indeed the Labour Party in Britain has already begun the debate started a long time ago by the Liberal Party and spurred by the modest success of the Ecology Party in the May 1979 election.[29] While it is most unlikely that either British or any of the European green parties will ever gain power, it is possible that they will become more popular and hence politically more influential as they improve on the practicability of their manifestos and as people become more attracted by their message. It is also possible that some of the existing public interest environmental groups, such as Friends of the Earth, may channel part of their efforts into direct political action. This might take the form of a "green alliance" among similarly minded groups, although there may be problems over reconciling personality differences.[30] It is also likely that local branches of environmental organisations may take it upon themselves to help in the community directly by, for example, advising and assisting people to conserve energy in a variety of ways, form co-operatives for the production and distribution of food and clothing, and expand education and social welfare services to suit particular local needs. There are a number of practical difficulties here, not the least of which will be organisation and sustained motivation, not to say willing acquiescence on behalf of recipient groups, and there may be trouble with public sector unions and criticism by those who fear that voluntary community service might keep a capitalistic, public sector cost-cutting government in office. As

always much will depend upon how society responds to altered economic conditions, but it is possible that the kind of radical ecological activists
of which Burger talks could become instrumental in creating the very
social and political reforms they espouse.

Notes and References

1. For an excellent analysis of the intellectual importance of the transcendentalists, see Burch, W.
R., Jr. (1972) *Daydreams and Nightmares: A Sociological Essay on the Human Environment*,
Harper & Row, New York, especially pp. 89–108.
2. This extract is abridged from an anthology by Opie, J. (1971) *Americans and Environment: The
Controversy over Ecology*, D. C. Heath, Lexington, Mass., p. 3.
3. Burch (1972) *op.cit.*, p. 92.
4. The most comprehensive statement of this philosophy is provided by Stone, C. (1975) *Should
Trees Have Standing? Toward Legal Rights for Natural Objects*, Avon Books, New York. Stone
believes that natural objects should have legal standing in their own right and be asserted by a
guardian and that any damage to them should be ascertained as an independent factor in considering judgement.
5. For a good analysis of the Tellicoe Dam decision see Aushermann, C. (1978) Tennessee Valley
Authority v. Hill: Protection of Endangered Species Under Section 7 of the Endangered
Species Act of 1973, *Natural Resources Journal*, Vol. 18(4), pp. 913–934, and Godspodarek, M.
P. (1978) The Little Fish v The Big Dam — Background and Implications, *Environmental
Policy and Law*, Vol. 4(4), pp. 178–181.
6. See Skolimowsky, H. (1977) Ecological Humanism, *Tract* Nos. 19 and 20, Gryphon Press, 38
Prince Edwards Road, Lewes, Sussex. The quotation is from p. 37.
7. See Ward, C. (ed.) (1974) *Peter Kropotkin: Farms, Fields and Factories Tomorrow*, Allen &
Unwin, London.
8. In recent years there has been a tremendous amount of literature on this anarchistic theme. For
a representative selection see Roszak, T. (1973) *Where the Wasteland Ends: Politics and Transcendence in Post-Industrial Society*, Doubleday, Garden City, NY; Thompson, W. I. (1973)
Passages Around the Earth: An Exploration of the New Planetary Culture, Harper & Row, New
York; Theobald, R. (1976) *An Alternative Future for America's Third Century*, Swallow Press,
Chicago; Henderson, H. (1978) *Creating Alternative Futures: The End of Economics*, Bakeley
Publishing Corp., New York; Robertson, J. (1978) *The Sane Alternative: Signposts to a Self-
fulfilling Future*, James Robertson, 7 St. Anne's Villas, London.
9. Hall, P. (ed.) (1977) *Europe 2000*, Duckworth, London.
10. O'Riordan, T. (1977) Environmental Ideologies, *Environment and Behaviour*, Vol. 9(1), pp.
13–27.
11. Glacken, C. J. (1967) *Traces on the Rhodian Shore: Nature and Culture in Western Thought
From Ancient Times to the End of the Eighteenth Century*, University of California Press, Berkeley, California.
12. For a discussion on the organisational structure and political tactics of public interest environmental groups in Britain and the US, see Nicholson, M. (1972) *The Environmental Revolution:
A Guide for the New Masters of the Earth*, Penguin Books, Harmondsworth, Middlesex; Lowe,
P. (1976), The Environmental Lobby, *Built Environmental Quarterly*, June, pp. 73–76; September, pp. 158–161; December, pp. 235–238 and March 1977, pp. 79–82; Brooks, S. K. and
Richardson, J. T. (1975) The Environmental Lobby in Britain, *Parliamentary Affairs*, Vol. 28,
pp. 312–328; and O'Riordan, T. (1979) Public Interest Environmental Groups in the United
States and Britain, *Journal of American Studies*, Vol. 13(3), pp. 409–438.
13. For a recent, comprehensive summary see US, Council on Environmental Quality (1978) *Ninth
Annual Report on Environmental Quality*, Government Printing Office, Washington, pp.
450–493.
14. Myers, N. (1979) *The Sinking Ark*, Pergamon, Oxford.
15. Downs, A. (1972) Up and Down with Ecology: the Issue-Attention Cycle, *Public Interest*, Vol.
28, pp. 38–50.
16. Mitchell, R. C. (1979) Silent Spring/Silent Majorities, *Public Opinion*, August–September, pp.
16–20, 55.

17. Kahn has written a number of books most of which are variations on a similar theme. See Kahn, H., Brown, W. and Martel, L. (1976) *The Next Two Hundred Years: A Scenario for America and the World*, Morrow & Co., New York; and Kahn, H. (1979) *World Economic Development 1979 and Beyond*, Croom Helm, London. See also McCrae, N. (1976) The Coming Entrepreneural Revolution: A Survey, *The Economist*, 25 December, pp. 41–65.
18. Kahn H., Brown, W. and Martel, L. (1976) *op. cit.*, p. 180.
19. *Ibid.*, p. 211.
20. OECD, Interfutures Group (1979) *Facing the Future: Mastering the Probable and Managing the Unpredictable*, OECD, Paris.
21. Brubaker, S. (1972) *To Live on Earth: Man and Environment in Perspective*, Mentor Books, New York; Brubaker, S. (1975) *In Command of Tomorrow*, Johns Hopkins University Press, Baltimore; Ashby, E. (1979) *On Reconciling Man with his Environment*, Oxford University Press, London; Ayres, R. U. (1979) *Uncertain Futures: Challenges for Decision-Makers*, Wiley Interscience, New York.
22. Appropriate technology is a difficult term to define but basically it means technologies, the operation of which is understandable to the user, the materials of which it is made are local or readily available and which uses energy efficiently. In short, appropriate technology is technology appropriate to the particular local circumstances, including, where possible, locally available energy supplies.
23. For example, Heilbroner, R. L. (1974) *An Inquiry into the Human Prospect*, Harper & Row, New York; Pirages, D. C. (ed.) (1977) *The Sustainable Society*, Praeger, New York; Goldsmith (1978) *The Stable Society: Toward a Social Cybernetics*, Wadebridge Press, Cornwall; Ward, B. (1979) *Progress for a Small Planet*, Norton, New York.
24. Wilson, C. (ed.) (1972) *Study of Critical Environmental Problems*, MIT Press, Cambridge, Mass.; Dorst, J. (1972) *Before Nature Dies*, Penguin Books, Harmondsworth, Middlesex; Nicholson (1972) *op cit.*; Ward, B. and Dubos, R. (1972) *Only One Earth*, Penguin Books, Harmondsworth, Middlesex; Ward (1979) *op. cit.*
25. There is much discussion in Britain in favour of tough import controls so that British domestic industry can continue to flourish. But a recent report by the Consumer Association (1979) *The Price of Protectionism*, 14 Buckingham Street, London, WC2, indicates that in the case of the textile industry where import controls have been operating for a number of years, jobs have not been created, prices have not been lowered and the quality of the British product has not improved.
26. A recent survey by the Independent Treasury Economic Model Team: Reading, B., Morgan, W. and Cockle, P. (1979) Rush to Destruction, *The Guardian*, 2 July, p. 8, estimates that in the UK through to 1981, real GDP will fall 2.1 percent, total private investment will drop by 16 percent, capital expenditure in the public sector will be cut by 12 percent, unemployment will increase by 660,000 with 500,000 lost jobs in manufacturing and 50,000 redundancies in the public sector, to make total unemployment reach 2.1 million.
27. Study Group on the Quality of Life (1979) *The Quality of Life*, British Association, 23 Savile Row, London W1.
28. Lerner, S. C. (1979) Behaviour in the "Crunch", *Alternatives*, Vol. 8(2), pp. 5–13. The whole issue of this volume is devoted to an analysis of how society has behaved or might be expected to behave in a global crisis.
29. See Goyder, M. (1979) *Socialism Tomorrow: Fresh Thinking for the Labour Party*, Young Fabian Pamphlet 49, Fabian Society, 11 Dartmouth Street, London SW1H 9BN. As to the success or otherwise of the Ecology Party, see Thibaud, P. (1978) The Green Vote, *Mazingera*, No. 5, pp. 70–76. In the May 1979 general election in the UK, the Ecology Party ran a total of 53 candidates thereby getting it free radio and television time to publicise its manifesto. There was a tremendous response to that publicity for membership almost doubled (to about 3000) as a result. In the actual election, the Ecology Party candidates achieved a total of just over 40,000 votes, 1.6 percent of all the votes cast. Not very impressive, perhaps, but it was the top party of all the minor parties represented in the election. See *Econews* (1979) No. 2, 15 Lower North Street, Exeter.
30. There is in fact a green alliance of sorts in the UK today. This consists of leading members of a number of UK environmental organisations plus other prominent individuals on the political scene. The Alliance seeks to promote liberal ecocentric values into conventional British politics. Its coordinator is Tim Beaumont, Francis House, Francis Street, London SW1. For a statement of its aims, see *Vole* (March 1979) No. 2, pp. 3–4XI.

READINGS

ENVIRONMENTALISM AND UTOPIA*

Stephen Cotgrove

DESPITE the increasing public concern with environmental issues, there has been surprisingly little reaction by sociologists. Yet apart from the magnitude of the possible threats to human survival, even a cursory reading of the flood of books, articles, pamphlets, and conference reports opens up a rich store of challenging and stimulating analyses and prescriptions – including far-reaching blueprints for the future of human society. Indeed one of the most fascinating facets of this voluminous literature is the way in which environmental problems are so readily used as levers to promote particular recipes for social action.[1] Yet it is precisely at this point that the difficulties facing any attempt at generalisation emerge. If there is anything that can be described as an environmentalist movement, what unites it is an agreement that the environment is a problematic issue of major importance. Beyond this, consensus evaporates into a bewildering disagreement over what are the most pressing environmental dangers, what are their causes, and how they can best be tackled. And of central interest for this paper is the wide diversity of ideologies and utopias which can be detected just beneath the surface of arguments about pollution, limits to growth, or the population explosion, ranging from recipes for anarcho-socialist communes, or for proto-feudal communities, to technocratic solutions for world government.

Serious environmental problems are not new, some having reached alarming proportions in earlier stages of industrialisation. Yet the social response is episodic and specific.[2] Above all, the meaning of the environment varies widely —seen by some as a threat to be mastered and overcome, and by others as a natural habitat—a source of peace and fulfilment. Similarly, the perception of our present dangers spans the whole gamut from an optimistic confidence that rational policies and the vigorous application of science and technology will enable man to meet the challenge, to the deepest pessimism of impending doom. Why then should the environment erupt into consciousness at this time? And how do we explain the quite different meanings attached to the environment, especially those of the ecology movement? Why do some see the danger in pollution, others in the population explosion, some in energy-consuming and ecologically-damaging technologies, and others in economic growth and the exhaustion of resources?

Two main issues emerge for sociology. First, we need a more systematic understanding of the various blueprints for survival. Here it will be argued that alternative scenarios for future society maximise different and often incompatible values. Any thinking about the future, therefore, will need to face up to this central difficulty in utopian thought. Secondly, the widely differing perceptions of the environment and of the sources of pollution and danger raise questions for the sociology of knowledge. What specifically are the social mechanisms underlying the construction of the various sytems of belief about nature and the environment? More specifically, we may ask whether the use of environmental dangers as ideological levers is related in any systematic way to the construction

*Reprinted by permission of *Sociological Review*, Vol. 24, pp. 23–42, 1976.
(Professor Cotgrove is Professor of Sociology at the University of Bath. See also his *Catastrophe or Cornucopia*, Wiley, Chichester, 1982.)

of beliefs about the environment? It is on the first of these problems that this discussion will concentrate. But from this exploration, some clues emerge which provide tentative insights into the sources of differences in the perceptions of environmental dangers.

Environmentalism as a social movement

Whether environmentalism can be seen as a single social movement or as a series of related social movements is in part a question of definition. If by social movements we mean those forms of collective behaviour which are relatively unstructured, self-conscious attempts 'to introduce innnovations into a social system',[3] then certainly the changes advocated by the local conservation societies, Friends of the Earth, the Soil Association, and the eco-activists (to name but a few), are all very different. And not all would qualify as social movements by this definition.[4] A more unified category of environmental activists could be constructed by omitting those preservationist and conservationist groups whose policies constitute no kind of challenge to the dominant value system, and are in this sense basically conservative. By contrast, something more like a coherent movement emerges if we focus on those groups who openly challenge what is in many ways the central or master-value in industrial society —the primacy of economic goals—and set against these welfare-values which are incompatible with or in conflict with purely economic ends. We would of course need to exclude those who see the solution simply in terms of an extension of welfare economics to include 'externalities', but would include those who press the incompatiblity of maintaining both economic growth and the quality of the environment.[5] It is along these lines that Kruse distinguishes between two forms of environmentalism.[6] The first of these he identifies with the 'limits to growth' policy, which 'bows down before Nature and its systemic properties'. The second puts its faith in human ingenuity to solve the problems and seeks to integrate environmental values into existing culture. This second version is ideological, justifying the existing order, whereas the first is utopian (using Mannheim's distinction between these two concepts[7]). It is on the utopian expressions of environmentalism, which seek to use environmental dangers as levers to promote fundamental social change, that this paper will focus.

There is one further possible basis for differentiation. There is a strong millenial flavour to the rhetoric of many environmental activists, especially those who derive their message from ecology.[8] For them, no piece-meal tinkering is possible: the blue print for survival is holistic, requiring the total transformation of society. Such social millenarianism can be contrasted with revolutionary social movements whose capacity 'to learn from their mistakes and to try again with something different is what distinguishes them from millenarian prophets inspired by the belief in the omnipotence of desire'.[9] This analysis will focus particularly on the more millenial-utopian elements in the environmentalist movement who derive their inspiration from the holistic perspectives of ecology. By contrast, the Marxist and socialist critiques are limited in their prescription to changing the control and direction of science and technology, and do not offer the same radical rejection of the core values of industrial society with its faith in economic growth and political solutions.[10]

Alternative utopias

An adequate description of the various types of society prescribed as solutions to our environmental problems would have to rest on systematic and extensive analysis which has not yet been undertaken. But it is possible to attempt ideal-typical constructs on the basis of an analysis of the literature. At first sight there appears to be a considerable similarity across an extensive range of writings, from the pages of *The Ecologist* or *Undercurrents* to various expressions of what may be loosely described as the liberation movement. All condemn the economism of contemporary industrial society (by contrast with the simple pleasures of rural life), the impersonality of mass urban society, and the centralisation of authority with its threat to individuality. There is at best an ambivalence towards modern science and technology and even an outright opposition. The search is for alternative technologies [11] consistent with the operation of small-scale local communities, and which do less violence to the natural environment, and are less polluting and wasteful of irreplaceable resources.

But on closer examination, fundamental differences emerge which make it possible to construct two major variations of utopian environmentalism—a traditional and a liberal form. The traditional form, exemplified specifically by the *Blueprint* and by many articles in *The Ecologist*, sees the size, scale and mobility of industrial society as the major source of disorder and social pathology—the cause of marital instability, illegitimacy, infidelity, crime and delinquency, drug abuse, alcoholism, and the loss of identity. [12] What emerges is a picture of a *Gemeinschaft*-type society in which the social bond is the traditional authority of a natural social order—the expression of a common life and a common will. [13]

It is around this issue of order and freedom that the differences between the traditional and liberal forms of utopianism are most marked. Although, for example, the campus radicals condemn modern technology, mass society and the centralisation of impersonal bureaucratic authority, their interest in small-scale communities is as a means of liberation, spontaneity, and the conditions for intense mutual involvement. [14] It is the search for a Dionysian culture of ecstasy and unreason by contrast with the Appollonian culture of order and light. [15] It is a world apart from the traditional post-feudal community—it is the search for *communion*. [16] Both the traditional and liberal forms of environmental utopianism use ecological evidence and environmental dangers as levers to promote quite different utopias.

Alternative value orientations

It is the alternative values and goals which underlie the blueprints for social change which are central to any understanding of social movements. But these in turn are grounded in deeper-lying meaning systems embedded in the culture. Perhaps the most fundamental of all the changes to contemporary industrial culture is the emphasis of utopian environmentalism on the finiteness of the earth and its resources, and of man's potency to master nature—a view encapsulated in Boulding's telling metaphor: 'space-ship earth'. This is in sharp contrast to the Promethean image which modern man has of himself and which underlies his confidence in his economic systems and the science and technology

Figure I

Alternative Value Orientations

ORGANIC	MECHANISTIC
natural, integrated, holistic	artificial, atomistic
interdependent	independent
community (collective)	association (individual)
FEELING	THOUGHT
intuition, experience (mystical)	analysis, knowledge
inductive, divergent, lateral	deductive, convergent, linear,
holistic	reductionist
creativity,	construction
(fusion of means and ends)	(separation of means and ends)
belief	scepticism
subjective (fusion of thought and	objective (separation of thought
feeling	and feeling)
sacred (religion)	secular
MATERIAL	SPIRITUAL
economism	humanism/welfare
means, instrumental	ends, expressive
quantity	quality
ORDER	FREEDOM
authority (traditional,	anarchy
charismatic, etc.)	
ritual, rules (customary,	spontaneity
legal, moral)	
hierarchy	equality

on which they rest.[17] It is this essentially Baconian view of man's relations with 'nature' as one of mastery which is incisively challenged by utopian environmentalism.[18] The organic and systematic properties of nature are stressed, with the injunction that man must learn to work with nature and not against it. Underlying this view, there is an image of nature which is seen as benign rather than hostile[19] – in short, a 'romanticist' desire for one-ness with nature. The other side of this coin is an opposition to the mechanistic and the atomistic, exemplified by the frequent condemnations of mass society.

But despite their appeal to nature in order to justify small-scale, decentralised communities, nature is used by the traditional and liberal forms to legitimate quite different presciptions for order and freedom. The *Gemeinschaft*-type of social order of the traditional form has already been touched on briefly. This is a natural order in the sense that community antedates the individual. Traditional order derived from an *a priori* unity, based on the sentiments which grow out of the community, locality and shared physical life. Authority is derived from the general will of the community rather than imposed from outside. And it is a unity which generates a natural inequality.

'In so far as enjoyment and labour are differentiated according to the very nature and capabilities of individuals, especially in such a manner that one part is entitled to guidance, the other is bound to obedience, this constitutes a natural law as an order of group life, which assigns a sphere and function, incorporating duties and priviledges to every will.'[20]

Tönnies' description of the basis of order and the social bond in the traditional community is frequently reflected in the pages of *The Ecologist*, albeit in more contemporary language and style. Thus we are told,

> 'Undifferentiated individuals competing for the same ecological niche cannot co-operate in any way . . . It is only when as a result of competition, they have been found to specialise in such a way that each one learns to exploit a different sub-niche, that co-operation is possible . . .'
> 'Competition is a means whereby a hierarchy is set up. In the right conditions . . . the competing individuals eventually arrange themselves so as to constitute a hierarchy and learn to accept their respective positions within the hierarchy.'[21]

So aggression, hierarchy and ritual are all natural and therefore good.[22] Only in small decentralised communities can the conditions emerge to regulate and control aggression, and legitimate hierarchy and inequality.

The emphasis on order and traditional authority emerging from the will of the community is forcefully expressed in Garrett Hardin's much quoted paper 'The Tragedy of the Commons'.[23] Here he concludes that some freedoms, such as the freedom to breed, are intolerable. Far from being a dirty word, coercion is essential. But it is the coercion of the collective will.

> 'To many, the word coercion implies arbitrary decisions of distant and unresponsible bureaucrats: but this is not a necessary part of its meaning. The only kind of coercion I recommend is mutual coercion, mutually agreed upon by the majority of the people affected.'

Again in his writings we find reflected the justification of natural differences and inequalities. Thus he argues that because the natural wilderness would be destroyed if open to all, it must be restricted only to the most fit.

> 'The heritage of wilderness must be open only to those who can earn it again for themselves. The rest, since they cannot gain the genuine treasure by their own efforts, must relinquish the shadow of it.'[24]

By contrast, the 'eco-activists', 'eco-freaks', and other environmentally-oriented expressions of the counter-culture are opposed to almost everything that the traditional community stands for. Indeed many of its activities—the challenge to traditional sexual ethics, the use of drugs, the rejection of hierarchy and institutionalised rule-governed behaviour in the pursuit of liberation— are among the indicators of social pathology which the traditional environmentalists' reassertion of community seeks to cure.

> 'Ecology activists are not concerned with power: at least they are anarchists, like the underground people. They have no wish to take political or economic power from one section of society and give it to another section. They are not Marxist . . . . The revolution in this sense is much more akin to a religious conversion "a turning about at the seat of consciousness".'[25]

On a third value-polarity, feeling versus thought,[26] the two forms of utopian environmentalism have more in common with each other and stand in contrast to the dominant values of the contemporary scientific culture. Again we find an expression of essentially romanticist themes, with a condemnation of reductionist modes of thought because they cannot encompass the wholeness and one-ness of nature.[27] By contrast, ecology provides a more acceptable model with its holistic attempt to understand the inter-relations between the parts of complex natural systems. But, on this dimension, the counter-culture perspectives of the liberal utopian environmentalists go much further in the search for intuitive and mystical modes of thought.[28] In their search for meaning and experience they share the perspectives of the 'underground', influenced by the religious symbolism of Tolkien's magic world of supernatural powers.[29] For them reductionism (the attempt to explain nature in terms of its constituent particles, describable in mathematically law-like relationships) is the root source of man's ability to dominate nature. But such mechanistic science is also seen by many liberal utopians as a threat to human freedom and dignity.[30] Moreover, because values and ends cannot be analysed in objective terms, they are excluded from contemporary culture which becomes preoccupied with means not ends, dominated by technical-rationality to the exclusion of any consideration of value-rationality.[31] Here the attack on science and technology is part of the attack on the 'technological society'. The ecological evidence of man's threat to the environment is quoted as evidence of the inevitable outcome of a reductionist and mechanistic science which seeks to dominate nature. Domination is inherent in the project of modern science.[32]

In short, both the traditional and liberal forms of utopian environmentalism are opposed not only to some of the manifestations of modern science and technology, but more fundamentally, to the underlying modes of thought which they express. Both would agree that a reductionist and mechanistic science is at the root of our ecological problems. Both would use a similar vocabulary, preferring intuition to analysis, and questioning the separation of thought and feeling in modern science. Both would stress the limits to science and argue that the contemporary crisis cannot be solved by more science and the 'technological fix', but demands a fundamental change in values. But whereas the liberal form uses such arguments to promote the liberation of man, traditional utopianism is more likely to seek justification for forms of social control in the more mystical notion of Nature, 'blood and soil', and the group will.[33]

There is an exception: the alternative technology movement differs from other expressions of liberal environmentalism. Although it is basically anarchistic, and favours self-sufficient communes as a means of resisting the centralising bureaucratic trends in industrial society, it rejects neither science nor technology. It is not technology *per se* which is seen to be repressive, but only the forms which technology has taken — harnessed to the objectives of a repressive society. The search is for alternative technologies which facilitate independence from centrally-controlled services — small-scale systems for localised energy and communications, and self-sufficient living.[34]

Anti-industrialism

An understanding of the utopian forms of environmentalism can therefore be advanced considerably by locating them within the sociological debate around the concepts of *Gemeinschaft* and *Gesellschaft*. The nineteenth century reaction by sociologists such as Durkheim, Tönnies and Simmel to industrialisation reflected a profound anxiety about its impact on traditional society, its disruption of traditional social bonds and the resulting problem of order. Utopian environmentalism in its traditional form can be seen as an heir to this debate, seeking to re-establish the values of the small-scale traditional community, and finding itself in head-on collision with the norms and values of industrial society—the primacy of economic/technical rationality harnessed to the pursuit of economic growth as the master-value[35]—unquestioned by most until recent events began to shake the almost unbounded optimism of modern man about his material future. The nineteenth century reaction against economic individualism and utilitarian rationalism was essentially conservative—seeking to conserve what were seen to be important values, against the socially disruptive effects of unbridled economism and its consequences in the break-up of medieval communal securities rooted in church, family, and guilds.[36] And it was essentially illiberal in the sense that its concern was with the reassertion of traditional forms of order and hierarchy.[37] Indeed, far from being descriptive, the conceptualisation of community was heavily coloured by such values and ideological preferences.[38]

What most distinguishes the liberal forms of environmental utopianism from the traditional is their preoccupation with freedom and liberation. Here, much of the reaction against contemporary society resonates rather with Weber's profound anxiety about the thrust of industrialisation and rationality, and the threat to individuality and spontaneity from the routinisation and bureaucratisation of social life. In its more extreme forms, it is in the anarchist tradition of Kropotkin, Godwin and Thoreau.[39] But while some embrace the rejection of science and the anti-rationalism of the romantics, others look rather to a 'radical' science and technology as a basis for a smaller scale of human living, free from the centralisation and bureaucratisation of a mass society which they see as threatening to engulf individuality.

Utopianism and social change

Despite the agreement of the utopian environmentalists that all is not well with industrial society, the conclusion which emerges most strongly from this review is the total lack of consensus about the alternatives. On the desirability of *Gemeinschaft*-type organic societies, the preference for order or freedom, and the value of science and rationality—there is no consensus. They agree only in their rejection of the hegemony of economic values. Yet utopias are essentially blueprints for societies in which there *is* consensus on prevailing values and institutional arrangements, and an absence of conflict and change. What is generally missing is any account of how we get from here to there.[40]

In other words, the distinctive feature of utopias is order and control—even (paradoxically) if the value which is desired to maximise is freedom. The objective is to achieve an ordered, controlled, stable system, to achieve values such as peace, individuality, self-fulfilment, the assured enjoyment of an environment. And there are a limited number of strategies by which the transcendent condition can be achieved. The formalist system design (blueprintism) constructs rational models, exemplified by the Club of Rome's computer model for world survival.[41] It may fail, as did Owen's *New Harmony*, because any model rests on assumptions, and abstracts from the total reality only those variables that can be handled by the model. Heuristic programming provides general principles as guides to action—such as Proudhon's pursuit of justice, or some contemporary communes' dedication to liberation.[42] Thirdly, the 'operating unit' approach 'begins with people or machines carefully selected or tooled to possess certain performance characteristics'.[43] So Skinner's *Walden Two* was based on building reliability and conformity by behavioural conditioning and engineering.

Figure 2
Alternative Utopias

	Organic/ holistic	Intuition feeling	Spiritual welfare	Ordered
1. *Gemeinschaft*/traditional	+	+	+	+
2. Liberal/anarchist/romantic	+	+	+	−
3. Liberal/anarchist/rational	+	−	+	−
4. Technocratic	+	∓	∓	+

1. Typified particularly by the *Blueprint* and *The Ecologist*.
2. Eco-activists, counter-culture, liberatory communes.
3. Alternative technology.
4. Club of Rome, futures/systems analysts.

Now whatever the path to utopia, all preempt the debate about values. Each utopia is a blueprint to maximise some value—but the value is authoritatively stated and beyond dispute. The key question then is, how is society to reach consensus on the values it wishes to maximise? And this in turn prompts the more fundamental question of the sociological mechanisms underlying value preferences—why some prefer liberation to order and control,[44] or poetry to science, hierarchy to equality, or economic growth to quality of life.

The questions raised are both empirical and theoretical. We know little about the distribution of value preferences, or the kinds of clusterings which occur. On one aspect, at least, there is some evidence. The challenge to the value of economic goals and economic growth would not seem to have much support. All the evidence suggests that support for the environmentalist movement in general, and this aspect of its policies in particular, is essentially a middle-class radicalism, confined to a small section of the community.[45] A recent survey found little support for the values of a 'post-acquisitive' society. Indeed, the acquisitive or materialist 'bourgeois' values of high living standards and the maintenance of law and order are as firmly in the saddle as ever—with no difference between the 1930s and post-war generations. The survey concludes:

'I believe that there has been a change in the values of the British people. A larger proportion of us now place much greater emphasis on the terminal value of a comfortable life, and on the instrumental value of more money. Indeed, "more money" has for many become almost a terminal value...'[46]

In short, economism, the central value and dominant ideology of industrial society, seems firmly on course to becoming the central value of post-industrial society.

Notes

1. In her studies of tribal societies, Mary Douglas has observed how frequently:
    '...the laws of nature are dragged in to sanction the moral code: this kind of disease is caught by adultery, that by incest; this meteorological disaster is the effect of political disloyalty, that the

effect of impiety' (M. Douglas: *Purity and Danger*, Penguin, London, 1974, p. 13).

Or again, Enzensberger comments on the ecological literature:

'They often employ the most dramatic strokes to paint a future so black that after reading their works one wonders how people can persist in giving birth to children, or in drawing up pension schemes. Yet at the conclusion of their sermons, in which the inevitability of the End—of industrialisation, of civilisation, of man, of life on this planet—is convincingly described if not proved, another way forward is presented. It is impossible not to feel that those warnings and threats, which present us with the consequences of our actions, are intended precisely to soften us up for the conversion which the anxious preacher wishes to obtain from us in the end ...'

(H. M. Enzensberger: 'Political Ecology', *New Left Review*, No. 84, 1974, pp. 25–26).

See also G. Seddon: 'The Rhetoric and Ethics of the Environmental Protest Movement', *Meanjin Papers*, Vol. 31, 4 December 1972, pp. 427–438.

2. See, for example, T. C. Sinclair: 'Environmentalism: A la recherche du temps perdu—bien perdu?', in H. S. D. Cole *et al.: Thinking About the Future: A Critique of the Limits to Growth*, Chatto and Windus, London, 1973.

3. J. Banks: *The Sociology of Social Movements*, Macmillan, London, 1972, p. 17. *The Blueprint for Survival* claims to herald 'the formation of the MOVEMENT FOR SURVIVAL ... and, it is hoped, the dawn of a new age ...' (see note 12 below).

4. For an account of some of the variety of environmentalist movements, groups and associations, see M. Allaby: *The Eco-Activists*, Charles Knight, London, 1971. It might be possible to discover some order and pattern by attempting a taxonomy using Smelser's distinction between norm-oriented and value-oriented movements, or reformist and revolutionary movements. Any such attempt would require an identification of the norms and values explicit in the various expressions of environmentalism, and would present an empirical task of some magnitude, N. J. Smelser: *Theory of Collective Behaviour*, Routledge and Kegan Paul, London, 1962.

5. E. Mishan: *The Costs of Economic Growth*, Penguin, Harmondsworth, 1969; and E. F. Schumacher: *Small is Beautiful*, Sphere Books, London, 1974.

6. Hans Kruse: 'Development and Environment', *American Behavioral Science*, Vol. 17, No. 5, May/June 1974, pp. 676–689. I have not adopted Kruse's labels (eschatological and chiliastic) for these versions as they seem to me to be misleading.

7. K. Mannheim: *Ideology and Utopia*, Routledge, London, 1966, p. 173. This operational definition should not conceal the lack of consensus on the meaning of the concept. Many writers identify the terms with a particular set of values or ideals. So W. H. G. Armytage (*Heavens Below*, Routledge, London 1961, p. 463) considers the search for anti-bureaucratic anarchic communities to be the essence of utopian idealism. Mannheim distinguishes four forms of utopian mentality: orgiastic chiliasm, liberal humanitarianism, the conservative idea, and socialist-communist utopia, each relative to particular historical situations and expressing the discontents of identifiable groups in society (ibid., Ch. IV).

The analysis of utopian thought is now attracting some attention. For review articles on this extensive literature, see M. Q. Sibley: 'Utopian Thought and Technology', *American Journal of Policital Science*, Vol. 17, No. 2, May 1973, pp. 255–281; and E. I. Friedland: 'Utopia and the Science of the Possible', *Polity*, Vol. 7, No. 1, Fall 1974, pp. 105–119. A useful source book is P. E. Richter: *Utopias: Social Ideals and Communal Experiments*, Holbrook Press, Boston, 1971. See also C. Nordhoff: *The Communisitic Societies of the United States*, Dover Publications, NY, 1966; and W. H. G. Armytage: *Yesterday's Tomorrows,* University of Toronto Press, Toronto, 1968.

A particularly valuable analysis which relates types of utopianism to computer models is R. Boguslaw: *The New Utopians: A Study of System Design and Social Change*, Prentice Hall, NJ, 1965.

8. There is considerable evidence on the millenarian characteristics of the ecology movement. Following the interest generated by Sir Frank Fraser Darling's Reith lectures in 1969, Anne Chisholm interviewed a number of distinguished 'ecologists', both in the restricted and more general use of the word

'What interested me, first of all, was not the actual content of ecology but the ecological message. Here, it seemed, was a new morality and a strategy for human survival rolled into one ... During the autumn of 1969, ecology caught on like a new religion among the young on college campuses across the country . . . The ecologists could, it seemed, offer a general philosophy of life that explained man's dependence upon, and responsibility towards nature . . . In an increasingly directionless, secular world, the intricate patterns traced by the ecologists offered a potential source of comfort, a sense of the unity and beauty of life.' (A. Chisholm: *Philosophers of the Earth: Conversations with Ecologists*, Sidgwick and Jackson, London, 1972, pp. xi–xii.)

9. Banks: *op. cit.*, 1972, p. 54.
    It is a matter of definition whether social millenarianism is included or excluded from the category of social movements. In so far as it involves specific value-orientations it would seem reasonable to include it as a type of the more general phenomenon.
10. The Marxist critique is limited and recent. For examples see H. Rothman: *Murderous Providence*, Hart-Davis, London, 1972; Enzensberger: *op. cit.*
11. 'Alternative technology' (discussed later) is not to be confused with 'intermediate technology'.
12. E. Goldsmith and M. Allaby: *Blueprint for Survival*, Penguin, London, 1972, p. 62.
13. F. Tönnies: *Community and Society*, Harper & Row, NY, 1963.
    'The word (community) . . . encompasses all forms of relationship which are characterised by a high degree of personal intimacy, emotional depth, moral commitment, social cohesion . . . Community is founded on man in his wholeness rather than one or another of the rôles . . he may hold . . . It draws its . . . strength from levels of maturation deeper than mere volition or interest . . . is a fusion of feeling and thought . . .'
    (R. A. Nisbet: *The Sociological Tradition*, Heinemann, London, 1970, pp. 47–48.)
14. T. Roszak: *The Making of a Counter Culture: Reflections on the Technocratic Society and Its Youthful Opposition*, Faber, London, 1970; T. Roszak: *Where the Wasteland Ends: Politics and Transcendence in Post Industrial Society*, Faber, London, 1973; and A. Rigby: *Alternative Realities: A Study of Communes and Their Members*, Routledge, London, 1974.
15. This distinction was used by Ruth Benedict in her *Patterns of Culture* (Routledge, London, 1935) and has recently been revived in discussions of youth culture. See J. S. Curl: *European Cities and Society*, Leonard Hill Books, London, 1970, p. 178. Frank Musgrove has developed this distinction in his important exploration of the counter-culture—which came to hand after this piece was completed—(*Ectasy and Holiness*, Methuen, London, 1974, see especially in Ch. 5). Since we arrive at a broadly similar typology by a somewhat different route it may be as well to make a virtue of necessity and leave the reader to make the comparisons.
16. H. Schmalenbach: 'The Sociological Category of Communion', in T. Parsons *et al.*: *Theories of Society*, Free Press, NY, 1961, pp. 331–347. I am indebted to Colin Bell for drawing my attention to this paper and its crucial distinction. Tönnies distinguished between Fellowship and Authoritative type *Gemeinschaft* relationships — the father-child relationship being the prototype of the latter, while brotherly relations characterise the former (*op. cit.*, pp. 252–253).
17. Kruse: *op. cit.*, p. 685.
18. For an analysis of the emergence of this distinctive feature of industrial culture, see Lynn White, Jnr.: 'The Historical Roots of our Ecological Crisis', *Science*, No. 155, March 1967, pp. 1203–1207; and T. S. Derr: 'Man against Nature', *Cross Currents*, Vol. XX, No. 3, Summer 1970, pp. 2432–75.
19. On this variety of attitudes to nature see Raymond Williams: 'Ideas of Nature', in Benthall: *op cit.*, 1972.
20. Tönnies: *op cit.*, p. 47.
21. E. Goldsmith: 'The Ecology of War', *The Ecologist*, Vol. 4, No. 4, May 1974, p. 125. This is not meant to imply that *The Ecologist* reflects a homogeneous value orientation, either in its contents or readership. Indeed, its general support for small-scale decentralised communities results in sympathetic treatment of anarchist literature: e.g. G. Woodcock: 'Anarchism and Ecology', *The Ecologist*, March 1974, pp. 84–88.
22. This echoes Barry Commoner's ecological third law – 'Nature knows best'.
23. Garrett Hardin: 'The Tragedy of the Commons', *Science*, No. 162, December 1968, pp. 1243–1248.
24. G. Hardin: 'The Economics of Wilderness', *The Ecologist*, February 1974.
25. Allaby: *op cit.*, p. 76. See also M. Bookchin: *Post-Scarcity Anarchism*, Wildwood House, London, 1974. This is close to Mannheim's *orgiastic chiliasm*, with its ecstatic immediacy, and revolution as an experience of value in itself. Compare this with Musgrove's Godwin-Shelley Scale in *op. cit.*, pp. 91–92.

26. The dimension is difficult to capture precisely. We are seeking here to identify what Mannheim refers to as styles of thought. Perhaps the deepest and most sensitive exploration is Robert M. Pirsig: *Zen and the Art of Motorcycle Maintenance*, Bodley Head, London 1974. He labels them romantic and classical, but the elements come close to those distinguished here. Reason versus imagination, or intuition versus analysis are alternative possibilities. For a perceptive exploration of false antitheses between science and imagination, see P. Medawar: 'Science and Literature', in his *The Hope of Progress*, Methuen, London, 1972, pp. 18–38.

27. 'Essentially, all the brilliant triumphs of the physical sciences . . . are with *linear* problems, in which a very complicated whole can be . . . studied . . . simple piece by simple piece, and then the complex whole reassembled and understood as no more than the (linear) sum of its parts . . . While powerful and general mathematical methods can be used for linear problems, non-linear problems in the physical sciences (such as gas-liquid transitions or turbulent fluid flow) are notoriously intractable'.

(R. M. May: 'The Environmental Crisis: A survey', *Search*, Vol. 2, No. 4, 1971, p. 129.) For a critique of the limitations of reductionist perspectives in the life sciences, see A. Koestler and J. R. Smythies (eds.): *Beyond Reductionism*, Hutchinson, London, 1969.

28. See for example Roszak's discussion of mysticism (*op. cit.*, 1973, pp. 99–106 and 247–254).
'But what I have mentioned—the censoring of the dark mind, the sensory predominance of the anaesthetized eye and ear, the undoing of organic sensibility—seem to me the cruelist wounds of our personal alienation . . . the major contours of the psychic wasteland we carry within us as we make our way through the "real" world of the artificial environment' (p. 99).
Or again,
'If our powers of perception could recover a portion of their original brilliance—the "visionary gleam" . . . we should see that . . . all things are enveloped in magic . . . The well-focused eye may see sharply . . . but its studies a lesser reality than the enraptured gaze' (p. 254).
For a powerful rejection of intuition, mysticism, and 'word magic', see K. Popper: *The Open Society and Its Enemies*, Routledge, London, 1945, Vol. II, Ch. 24, 'The Revolt Against Reasons': '. . . he who teaches that not reason but love should rule, opens the way for those who rule by hate' (p. 236).

29. Allaby: *op. cit.* 'Perhaps too they find in the life of the hobbits their ideal—small, contented, smug creatures, who eat and drink well, love to sit outside their burrows on warm days, telling stories of adventures in which they hope never to be called on to take part!' (p. 108).

30. Frazier, the 'hero' of B. F. Skinner's utopia, *Walden Two* (Macmillan, NY, 1948) asserts 'I deny that freedom exists at all. I must deny it—or my program would be absurd. You can't have a science about a subject matter which hops capriciously about' (p. 214). In short, Skinner rejects freedom as incompatible with his methodological (and metaphysical) assumptions. See E. I. Friedlander: 'Utopia and the Science of the Possible', *Polity*, Vol. 7, No. 1, 1974, pp. 116–117.

31. For a more detailed discussion see S. Cotgrove: 'Technology, Rationality and Domination', *Social Studies of Science*, Vol. 5, No. 1, 1975. Compare this with Musgrove's Ruskin-Shelley Scale, which measures anti-technology, anti-bureaucracy values (*op. cit.*, pp. 90–91).

32. For an analysis and critique, see W. Leiss: *The Domination of Nature*, Braziller, NY, 1972.

33. J. Passmore ('Removing the Rubbish', *Encounter*, Vol. XLII, No. 4, 1974, pp. 11–24) comments on the views of F. Fraser Darling:
'His simultaneous appeal to immanence and aristocracy . . . is only too typical, in its intellectual incoherence, of the Western mystical tradition. And the aristocrat who is also a servant— whether of God, of the people, or of the planet—is just as characteristic of authoritarianism' (p. 11).

34. See especially, Peter Harper: 'What's Left of Alternative Technology', *Undercurrents*, Vol. 6, March/April 1974; and D. Dickson: *Alternative Technology*, Fontana, London, 1974.

35. Affective neutrality, universalism, achievement and specificity are not alternative value orientations, argues Habermas: they are demanded by systems of purposive-rational action. See J. Habermas: *Toward a Rational Society*, Heinemann, London, 1971, pp. 90–91.

36. R. A. Nisbet: *The Sociological Tradition*, Heinemann, London, 1970, Ch. 3. If Marx's socialism was capitalism without private property, so Comte's utopia was medievalism minus Christianity, argues Nisbet (p. 58).

37. Ralf Dahrendorf: *Society and Democracy in Germany*, Weidenfeld and Nicolson, London, 1968.

38. R. Plant: *Community and Ideology*, Routledge, London, 1974, pp. 15–36.

'The liberal critique has seen the decline of community as providing the conditions for the growth of individuality, while others have sought to construct a radical conception of community, stressing participation, fraternity and egalitarianism' (p. 27).

39. See Rigby: *op. cit.*, 1974, Ch. 4, for an exploration of the anarchistic elements in the counter-culture.

40. Ralf Dahrendorf: 'Out of Utopia: Toward a Reorientation of Sociological Analysis', *Am. J. Soc.*, Vol. 64, No. 2, September 1958, pp. 115-127. The authoritarian, totalitarian and essentially irrational character of utopianism is also argued by Popper: *op cit.*, 1945, Vol. 1, Ch. 9, 'Aestheticism, Perfectionism, and Utopianism'.

41. Boguslaw: *op. cit.*, 1965, pp. 61-62. This is essentially Engel's approach. In place of an idealist solution evolved out of the human brain in the pursuit of some absolute justice, reason, or truth, scientific socialism has discovered the laws governing the system. It is the 'real' basis which will replace 'the mishmash of utopian thought' (F. Engels: 'Socialism: Utopian and Scientific', in L. S. Feuer (ed.): *Marx and Engels*, Fontana, London, 1969). For a critique of the Club of Rome's model, see H. S. D. Cole *et al.*: *Thinking about the Future: A Critique of Limits to Growth*, Chatto and Windus, London, 1973.

42. Boguslaw: *op. cit.*, p. 16; and Rigby: *op. cit.*, pp. 102-115 and 181-200.

43. Bosuslaw: *op. cit.*, p. 17.

44. On the structural factors which lead to a preference for ritual and order, see Mary Douglas: *Natural Symbols*, Penguin, London, 1973.

45. This is explored more fully in S. Cotgrove: 'Ecology, Ideology and Utopia', unpublished discussion paper, Science Studies Centre, Univeristy of Bath, 1974.

46. Mark Abrams: 'Changing Values', *Encounter*, October 1974, pp. 29–38.

ECOLOGICAL VIABILITY: POLITICAL OPTIONS AND OBSTACLES*

W. Burger

I. Introduction

'If we plan remedial action with our eyes on political rather than ecological reality, then, very reasonably, very practically and very surely we will muddle our way to extinction', thus reads paragraph 162 of the 'Blueprint for Survival'.[1] But the opposite strategy may also produce unattractive results. If we attempt to plan remedial action while ignoring political reality, very surely we can only do so with the help of some absolute central power which may, very reasonably, transform our society into an ecological paradise with, very practically, a fair chance that it will have the social and cultural characteristics of a forced labour camp. No-one would like to opt for either of these two strategies. But what alternatives do we have?

L. J. MacFarlane, in a comment on the 'Blueprint' writes, 'the failure to give any thought to the vital political implications and aspects of the "Blueprint" seriously mars ... the chance of its being accepted or applied.'[2] To call this limitation a failure is not, in my opinion, quite justified. To develop ideas about future, more responsible, societies is as necessary as to explore the political possibilities for the realisation of any such better society within, or departing from, a particular socio-political and cultural reality. On the other hand, over the last few years much has been written about how bad the present situation is and how much better it could be in the future, but very little about the political

*Reprinted by permission from *Man and Environment Ltd.*, ed. H.G.T. van Raay and A.E. Lugo, 1974, Rotterdam University Press, pp. 237–256. (© The Institute for Social Studies, The Hague.) (Dr. Burger is a sociologist at the Institute for Social Studies.)

road that might lead to such a better future. It is high time to lessen this disproportion in order that many valuable ideas on the environmental issue may not be doomed to political sterility.

I shall attempt in this paper to explore some political aspects of the ecological problem and also its possible solution, taking the socio-political and cultural framework obtaining in the highly industrialised world as my frame of reference. The paper first charts the most common lines of thought on the ecological situation, distinguishing some implicit and explicit ideological elements. An estimate is then made of the political significance of these elements in terms of their potential to ward off or perhaps to hasten the physical collapse or socio-political bankruptcy of the industrialised world. The last section deals briefly with vital aspects of public opinion formation that may enable the political processes to meet the ecological challenge.

II.   Political judgement and ideological prejudice about environment problems

II.1   *A paradox: a long-term and yet urgent problem*

In *The Closing Circle*, Commoner refers to what he sees as 'an air of unreality about the environmental crises',[3] a perception which most people will experience regularly and which I consider of the greatest political significance. The air of unreality may alternate with a sense of urgency when we read about the disasters impending unless we act quickly. Objectively, the problem calls for immediate if not radical action, for determined efforts to introduce changes that will aim for, and in the long run will produce basic reforms.

That nevertheless the problem often has an air of unreality can be traced to the fact that we do not perceive the destruction of the environment as an immediate threat to our present wellbeing. Very few of us are so seriously affected in our daily lives that our usual, more direct problems in the spheres of personal relationships, work, career or family-life are pushed into the background.

Commoner places his main emphasis on the 'apparently hopeless inertia of the economic and political systems'.[4] We must indeed take very seriously the psychological tendency of people who are confronted by bigger problems than they feel able to handle, to show an escapist reaction and to leave the solutions to those whose job they feel it is to solve great problems.

The lack of reality about the ecological crisis thus seems to result from the disparity between its objective magnitude and the lack of felt urgency on the one hand, and on the other the discrepancy between what we objectively think should be done and what we feel is practically feasible. In accordance with a wellknown socio-psychological 'law', this ambiguity creates widely divergent opinions about policies to be followed, in which ideological prejudice and wishful thinking form major components. This being an important factor in political reality, it seems worthwhile to briefly inventorise the most common views regarding man and environment in the present phase of history.

II.2   *Two types of opponents to reform*

1.   A decreasing but still influential strain of thought actually denies the

need for any particular attention to the ecological issue. Its apologetic arsenal is basically that of liberal capitalism and classical economics. Although its adherents acknowledge the existence of some environmental problems, they consider that these should be handled as any other problem that accompanies social and economic progress. Temporary shortages of raw materials have so far been overcome by intensified exploration efforts and the introduction of substitutes. Science, technology and the market mechanism give modern society an enormous adaptive capacity which can be relied upon to keep pollution within socially acceptable limits. As long as we keep the basic structure of our developed societies intact, especially its main driving force of sufficient opportunity for free enterprise and healthy competition with government regulation to check temporary imbalances, nothing need be worried about. A no-growth policy is viewed as particularly dangerous since only growing economic surpluses can enable industrialised nations to make the necessary expenditures for pollution control and other 'social' expenses that may be deemed necessary.[5]

Many of these growth-optimists and defenders of the structural status-quo stigmatise the story of impending ecological catastrophe as being invented by the enemies of capitalism who want to undermine the belief that capitalism is a basically good system by which to organise production. To add to the confusion, however, there are also renowned social-democrats who ascribe the no-growth ideology to the middle and upperclass origins of its protagonists, who have everything they want and now tell others that further growth is no longer possible, thus 'kicking the ladder down behind them'.[6]

2.   Some opponents of liberal capitalism, especially orthodox Marxists, also show a belief in the blessings of industrialisation, technological progress and material growth, that has lost little of the strength it had in the 19th century. Quite logically perhaps, these people see the recent growth of official attention to environmental control as part of a conspiracy, in this case of monopoly-capital or the exploiting classes. As a consequence of its chaotic development the capitalist system now faces great problems; while avoiding a discussion of the real causes, capitalism seeks to postpone its own collapse by trying to ease the tensions created by its inner contradictions through slowing down economic expansion and technological progress. In vain, of course. The no-growth ideology should be strongly opposed, not only because it is immoral in view of the poverty prevailing in large parts of the world, but because it is a false solution to a problem which need not exist at all. Only after revolutionary transformation of our production relations will it be possible to successfully tackle the environment problem; until then we should not allow it to divert our attention.

Granting that we should not have any illusion that the environment issue will be taken advantage of by political interest groups if they see a chance to do so and whatever the merits of their views in other respects, the opponents to reform evidently bet heavily on future uncertainties. Can we really be sure that ecological disasters will be prevented either by timely discovery of new technological or economic devices, or by a timely collapse of capitalism? It seems rather a gamble to do little other than wait for history to follow its 'natural' or 'necessary' course and not show any inclination to allow, even temporarily, certain political changes of strategy or other purposive moves, if only for gaining time or as a safety measure.

II.3   *Four types of reformers*

Contrary to the optimistic opponents of reform, the 'reformers' though not necessarily pessimistic, have less confidence in the general validity of a particular political doctrine.

1.   An important category of reformers believes and expects that the ecological crisis which threatens all human beings irrespective of nationality, race, class or religion, will at last bring the longed-for harmony to our societies and to the world as a whole. The impending disaster will convert sworn enemies into allies, make rival groups join in making the sacrifices necessary to avert the catastrophe.

If this view were merely naïve, to be unmasked as soon as reality claims its rights, it might be discarded as politically unimportant and therefore irrelevant to our analysis. But political danger lies in the fact that the expectation of a public consensus often is a mere expression of the demand that consensus should actually come about. If, for instance, underprivileged groups and countries refuse to line up for national or international programmes to prevent ecological disaster under terms stipulated by the ruling powers, moral indignation about their irresponsibility may then all too easily prepare the ground for holy wars. New socio-economic regimes aiming at no growth, for instance, may be forcibly imposed on us with the argument that we should no longer waste our time and energy on political issues which have become inappropriate in this critical phase of human history. Contemporary holders of political and economic powers will take upon themselves the 'historical, though not always pleasant' role of saving mankind (or Europe, the United States or East Asia) from ecological holocaust.

It is unnecessary to argue, on the basis of recent historical experience, that if such views become widely shared fascism will lurk around the corner. Paradoxically, because this strain of thought does not recognise any political problem it is politically very dangerous.[8]

2.   In a similar rather a-political ideological frame is couched a more sympathetic, but I fear in its pure form rather ineffective line of thought often found among liberal reformers who also have an over-optimistic belief in the power of reason. But conscious of the danger of ready-made solutions imposed by power élites, they argue for societal reform mainly along educational lines: help the masses of the population to realise what we, as a collectivity, are doing, and each individual will regulate his private and public behaviour in an ecologically more responsible manner. The problem is thrown into the consumer's lap. Aren't we all consumers? If we change our demands, the producers will have to follow in order to meet them. If we limit our demands, economic growth and technological innovation will automatically slow down.

This argument reveals the inability of many well-meaning middle class citizens to see the rationale of large sections of the population who refuse to make sacrifices for the public benefit: not owing to 'labour class materialism' as is so often alleged, but because they feel they have been consistently denied a fair share of the national wealth for as long as they can remember. Consumers who wish major changes to be made in the range of goods offered to them will indeed face considerable short-term sacrifices. The production system will deliver new types of goods only after great delay and probably against higher prices.

Furthermore, a buyers' strike intended to force down levels of material consumption will not rally much support among people who already consume little beyond their basic necessities – in most societies the majority of the population.

This does not mean that activities to increase consumers' awareness about harmful consumption habits will not have results. But structural reforms are unlikely except perhaps indirectly, once it is realised how limited is the consumers' control of the socio-economic process.

The two types of reformers discussed so far, whom we might call 'corporatist-centralist' and 'liberal-educational' respectively, both have their leftist counterparts.

3.   Leftist centralist reformers are as convinced as those Marxists who would prefer to await a dialectical turn in the social history of the West, that an ecologically more favourable socio-economic system will never be established within the framework of industrial capitalism. But the strength of their conviction, combined with their sense of urgency regarding the environment problem, makes them ascribe similar views to large and rapidly growing numbers of people. These reformers predict that public debate about the ecological crisis will soon cause a major shift to the left among the majority of politicians in the Western capitalist welfare states, thus making these nations ripe for basic reform. The people who matter politically will gradually become convinced that nationalisation of the key industrial, financial and insurance sectors, curtailment of national and international economic competition, and a systematic policy for decreasing income differences, can no longer be avoided. This 'socialist revolution' will clear the way for an international policy on ecology that is centrally guided per country or world-region. Social unrest will be kept at a minimum as the price for the reforms in terms of reduced material wealth and consumption will primarily be paid by the higher and middle income strata.[9]

According to this model, political struggle that leads to important structural reforms is preconditional to an effective environment policy. However, its adherents often create the impression that this 'revolution' is at first confined to the political and cultural elites, who will then persuade the public at large to accept the new societal structures. It might be feared that in such a reform élitist and technocratic tendencies will be hard to control, so that conditions will be unfavourable for the long-term development of a more radical cultural and ideological reform movement that has its roots in the population as a whole. If this is a prerequisite to a democratic society of mature citizens, a 'revolution from above' may well defeat our ultimate social ideals: it may buy us a physically viable future but at the price of further postponing a really humanised society.[10]

4.   Leftist reformers who consider this price too high and who fear that even a post-revolutionary society, if it is élitist and centralist may tend to develop corporatist or even fascist tendencies, form a fourth group which might be designated as 'radical ecological activist'. Social and political action at the base of society occupies a central place in the strategy of these reformers. They try to prevent anti-social or ecologically harmful decisions being taken by local authorities, government departments or political parties by organising those population groups who are most seriously threatened. They also lobby for the acceptance of alternative plans and projects that are developed with the help of experts, technicians and scientists who join their ranks.

Perhaps it is reasonable to say that the activists are less naïve in their thinking on societal change than the three other reform groups. They have no illusions about the rationality or goodwill of political and economic power-holders or official experts and authorities, whether in a capitalist or a socialist society, unless these are constantly and forcefully reminded of the immediate needs of particular groups of people, communities, neighbourhoods and regions.

At the same time the activists expect that continuous confrontation and the resulting conflict will produce increasing awareness about how society operates, not only among the population at large but also among people in leading and executive positions, and far more quickly than through educational action of the liberal enlightenment type.

They acknowledge the importance of education but place strong emphasis on its philosophy and ideology which, in their view, should in the first place form people who know when, why, and how to be effectively disobedient. Such a philosophy should ultimately guarantee the effective exposure and counteraction of manipulative practices by persons in power positions who may pervert positive results obtained in the regular political process.

Diagram 1 summarises this classification of main trends of thought on the politics of environmental control and the necessity for societal reform.

Diagram 1

	'The problem will take care of itself'	'The problem is urgent and requires basic reforms'	
		Advocates of centralist reforms	Advocates of reform at the base of society
'rightists'	growth-optimists	the corporatist reformers	liberal educational mobilisers
'leftists'	revolutionary optimists	state-socialist reformers	radical ecological activists

III.   The battle is on

III.1 Political consensus decreases

A wide array of opinions on the environment issue does not necessarily produce a low degree of political consensus. If particular views should dominate among a large majority of people and their leaders, other opinions would be doomed to political insignificance. But the opposite is the case. Until recently few people of whatever political conviction ever questioned the positive value of rapidly developing industrial mass production to provide consumer goods and durables in ever greater varieties and quantities. The majority were willing to accept that governments and industrialists, helped by expert technicians and economists, should direct and accelerate that development. Now, however, there is a tendency in all ideological corners of our industrialised societies to take a critical view not only of the production system as such but also of the values underlying our societies. The increasing awareness of wrongdoing, requiring a basic review of much that has been taken for granted in the past, naturally assails the various established economic, social and political institutions – government departments, planning agencies, labour unions, political parties of all kinds. These are often forced onto the defensive and then show greater readiness to seriously consider the need for increasing control of free enterprise, higher taxation and greater expenditure on government measures and programmes for pollution control, research into new forms of energy, greater care in planning and expanding industrial regions, etc.

Perhaps rightly, many would interpret these tendencies as a general shift to the left of overall political opinion. In my view, however, it is not realistic to expect that large working majorities of leftist political groupings will soon be willing to radically attack the ecological problem.

For the time being this shift merely seems to sharpen conflict and to increase antagonism.[11] This is not so much due to diverging views regarding the many technical and economic questions that need to be solved, however important these may be. It is more because of the realisation that, however the ecological problem is to be tackled, considerable sacrifices will have to be made. In spite of growing perception of future disaster, most people think that there is still time in which to settle differences of opinion about who is to make these sacrifices in the first place. And this is, I think, the main reason why we should prepare for a prolonged political battle over a very long-standing political concern: how to share the burden of our collective survival.[12] This crucial point will be elaborated more fully in the following section.

III.2   *The bill will be high: who is to pay?*

An interesting estimate has recently been made of the enormous resources squandered in the United States for purposes of very doubtful or even negative social benefit under the present system of production and consumption.[13] However useful and necessary such estimates may be, in my opinion they are more pertinent to the question of which type of society (not necessarily less prosperous) we may conceive for the future, than that they provide much insight into the short and medium-term costs of establishing such a society. Indeed, the impression may be created that the costs of following the path to an ecologically more responsible society are negative. If we would stop being so wasteful we could increase our material prosperity and at the same time safeguard our ecological future. Although of course it is correct that we should try to finance environment control by reducing expenditure on things that are least useful or possibly even harmful, I tend to hold the view that, at least for the phase in which our societies are restructured on new production and consumption patterns, we should prepare ourselves for a drastic lowering of our material living standards. I cannot imagine such a restructuring without the following short and medium-term consequences:

- a politically-imposed decreasing profitability of that (large) part of existing 'conventional' capital which, in its utilisation, is wasteful of natural resources and detrimental to the environment;
- high investments to be made in new industrial equipment to enable ecologically more acceptable production processes;
- major expenditure for scientific research to develop alternative technologies;
- retraining and re-education of large sections of our labour force;

- unemployment problems through the contraction of certain economic sectors and branches of industry before sufficient new employment opportunities in others can be created.[14]

Countries embarking on such policies will need to face two serious secondary economic consequences:

- a dramatic shrinking of government budgets owing to decreasing tax income or, if this is not feasible, a sharp increase of taxation rates;
- a thorough revision of external economic relations by subsidising or terminating the export of non-competitive commodities and setting up import barriers to some goods while liberalising imports of others. For example, natural products may be imported to substitute those synthetics whose production can no longer be tolerated at home; natural products grown at home may be made competitive to imported synthetics.

Economic retaliation will only aggravate the problems of ecology-minded countries or world regions which are forced to steer a course of greater autarchy in a world which, as a whole, is not yet ready to make short-term sacrifices in order to prevent longer-term ecological calamities.

The political consequences of costly ecological reforms must be tremendous. Is it unrealistic or pessimistic to predict that, at the outset, the privileged socio-economic strata in those countries that are determined to attack the ecological crisis will at best only support a policy which spreads the economic burden over the different population groups proportionate to their present levels of income?

But this would imply that people in the lower income stratum would have to suffer indefinite prolongation of their present condition of relative or even absolute poverty. Absolute increases of material wealth can no longer mitigate the felt injustices or large income differences.

H. C. Wallich has written: 'growth is a substitute for equality of income. So long as there is growth there is hope, and that makes large income differentials tolerable.'[15] In other words, the rapid pace of economic growth in the industrialising and industrialised countries bought them their relative social and political peace; but as we have since realised, this was done at the expense of nature's future capacity to sustain the human race. Now, for the sake of our future survival, to return to nature what we owe her at the expense of our under-privileged groups not only appears ethically unjustifiable but politically not very promising.

The alternative – during the phase of transformation – can only be to maintain the present material living standards of the low income stratum, or to allow even slight improvement, while sharply diminishing the affluence of the higher income groups. There may be immediate improvements in the quality of life for large sections of the population, but no-one can fail to see the political obstacles to such policies. As Peter Bunyard has phrased it: 'One cannot help but ask, how in a capitalistic materialistically-oriented society like ours would the establishment sell . . . the idea of qualitative growth to its electorate.'[16]

III.3   *The dim prospect of political halfheartedness: the crisis is exported*

Given the state of affairs described above, there is a great probability that political struggle over the environment issue may be avoided as soon as it produces the first political defeats of sincere reformers. A political confrontation is necessary on such normative issues as western consumerism, mobilisation of labour and capital resources through the rat race called free enterprise and competition, and purposively maintained social and economic inequalities. If this does not earn the necessary support of the electorate, it must be feared that political leaders, whether leftist or rightist, will be tempted to transfer the aggravating ecological problem to the international political arena. Each country or each politico-economic bloc will desperately try to secure for itself a continued supply of natural resources and cheap raw materials from the Third World.[17] Major investments in the most severely polluting industrial sectors will be made in countries where widespread poverty and unemployment form a sufficient safeguard that the environment issue will not create much of a political problem.[18] The higher the investments, the stronger will be the pressures in the rich countries to maintain their control over the poor countries and keep them loyal to the interests of the investors. Little imagination is needed to foresee another round of imperialist military confrontations, not only between industrialised countries or their blocs but also with 'insubordinate' Third World countries. Such a course of events can only produce an absolute political, economic and moral impasse – even though the 'victory' of the rich industrialised nations over the rest of the world were not complete. For the world as a whole the ecological consequences will be disastrous whether or not large scale wars are the result. The anticipation of such wars would cause an accelerating arms race which by itself would be totally incompatible with economic and industrial reform policies and would frustrate any attempt to diminish the squandering of raw materials and energy.[19]

The political attitude which acknowledges that measures must be taken to avert an ecological crisis but simultaneously stresses that they should not be allowed to basically change our socio-political and economic systems, differs only a shade from the shortsighted opinion that the ecological problem will take care of itself, if not in theory then at least in practice. Too much concern that the precarious balance of our economic or socio-political situation does not allow for radical policies can only result in such a slow change of the status quo that, in the long run, serious disruption along the lines just sketched will be unavoidable.

III.4   *The choice: radical democratisation or totalitarianism*

If the struggle for our ecological future is not transferred to the international political arena, it would signify that the industrialised rich nations recognise that they should primarily solve the problem among and within themselves. From all sides appeals will be made for social and political solidarity in view of the emergency situation. Much moral weight will be added to this appeal by the fact that, under the assumed circumstances, the rich countries of the world do not want to make the poor countries pay the bill for the former's misbehaviour in the past.

But even after prolonged ideological debate will the leading elites and middle classes be convinced that solidarity should primarily mean solidarity with the underprivileged? Will they put their political weight behind a policy which over

10 or 15 years for instance, will drastically reduce income differences and other social injustices as a necessary precondition to popular response to a call for solidarity in undertaking ecological reform?[20]

The struggle over this issue will probably be long and exhausting: a highly critical period of social unrest, frequent political strikes, repeated electoral and parliamentary stalemates. The risk is that eventually these will not alternate with fruitful compromises and political breakthroughs in a direction that is socially and ecologically desirable but will cause a hardening of stands of the two major opposing parties and a complete political deadlock.

Conservatives who hysterically cry 'wolf' at the first signs of polarisation among the public, fearing that the forthcoming conflict might change the political status quo, should be strongly opposed. In the name of peace and harmony they will probably try to maintain their own social, economic or political privileges. On the other hand, leftist dogmatists who reject compromise even when conflict has sufficiently matured that their fruits may be reaped, may invite the rule of violence to take hold of the political scene.

The longer a political deadlock lasts, the louder will be the calls for strong leadership, if not for one strong leader, turning the chances in the favour of a reactionary takeover of power, very much as we have seen in critical phases of the history of Portugal, Spain, Italy and Germany between the two world wars, France during the Algerian crisis and, more recently, in many developing Third World countries which are unable to solve the problem of poverty.

Thus, not a victory of enlightened progressive thought in leading political and economic circles, as predicted by many of the more optimistic progressive reformers, but a victory of authoritarianism if not of brute violence, accompanied by the usual mystifying phraseology for popular consumption.[21]

III.5   *The method determines the outcome: fight for political consciousness*

What are the chances for a favourable outcome of the political struggle over the environmental issue? I have tried to show that the political and social conditions in our industrialised consumption societies tend to change many solutions to ecological problems that are advocated by different ideological circles into non-solutions, or to set in motion social processes that lead to what might be called 'political regression': the formation of some central power which justifies the political means it utilises by the goal of saving our societies from ecological disaster. The reason for the strength of this propensity may have to be sought in the weakness of our democracies – not as reactionaries often use this term but in the sense that, in spite of mass education and other democratic institutions, we have not succeeded in creating a high level of awareness among the people about the structure, operation, virtues and defects of our societies. Western culture, like others, has been as successful in 'brainwashing' as in enlightening people. Moreover, the mass character of most of our institutions, whether in the sphere of social services, material production or culture, has seriously alienated people from their existential basis, their 'human condition'. Therefore, if we wish our societies to take the tremendous political hurdle of radically reforming our production system while avoiding totalitarianism, we have to ensure that people realise their cultural and political situation so that, as a political force, they become sufficiently immune to those powerful weapons of the politicians: mystification and demagogy.

But we cannot wait for this cultural process to get under way before starting work on tangible measures with which to avert the more immediate ecological calamities. With few exceptions, the ecological measures that are now being planned or are already being undertaken in our industrialised countries under the pressure of established political forces can only be welcomed. But in view of the laggardness and conservatism of most bureaucracies, the numerous circumventions of laws and regulations, and the relative impotence of established political institutions in these and other respects, the political strategy which I term 'radical ecological activism' should have an important if not decisive role to play in averting major ecological disasters during the coming decennia. In several countries it has already produced substantial results, giving proof of great potential to heighten awareness among those directly involved in the actions and among the public at large about ecological problems and about ways in which official authorities and established politics tend to deal with them.

III.6   *Struggle for disorder, struggle for order*

From the previous section an important and for some of us perhaps consoling conclusion can be drawn: we must never rely on radical activism as the only strategy with which to safeguard our ecological, political and cultural future, just as it would be unwise to leave the urgent task of changing our political, cultural and economic aims and efforts to the established, regular political powers.

Radical activism alone would lead to chaos, unopposed ruling power would soon degenerate into absolute bureaucratic dirigisme, which would be hell. If radical activism does not want chaos and central planning and coordination does not wish to dehumanise society into a computerised robot, they need each other even though they are undoubtedly sworn enemies in daily political practice.

In other words, the best of all possibilities during the phase of transformation of our western societies is a process in which periods of sharp conflict alternate with periods of mutual accommodation in the relationships between different groups of the population, sectors of the economy or sections of the administration. Some of these will incline more to the side of the Establishment, others to the opposition. But their alliances should preferably shift rather than freeze, producing new power configurations which over a longer period of time, with or without political revolution, will allow for a process of social, cultural and economic development very different to that which the world has seen over the past few centuries.

Such a turbulent process, as I see it, is the sole guarantee that ecological goals will not be used to sanctify political means, i.e. that the physical survival of our societies will be bought at such a cultural and moral price that the whole effort may no longer be worthwhile.

IV.   **How to widen political 'tunnel-views'. A concluding note**

It will appeal to reason that if public debate on the environment issue and its social and cultural ramifications is to achieve its goal of widening and ultimately destroying the 'tunnel views' of the entrenched political, economic and bureaucratic interests, it cannot afford to become dogmatic.

Although full elaboration of this theme would require another essay, it seems relevant to briefly summarise it here. Public debate will be tremendously important if we are to survive the political crisis that is hopefully ahead of us: hope based on the insight that a period of crisis is unavoidable if the environment issue is to be taken seriously in our over-developed western world.

The problem will be to cultivate a particular critical attitude towards our cultural values, science and technology, economic power concentrations (monopoly capital, conglomerates, multinational corporations), bureaucracies, and other nuclei of societal organisation; namely, a critical attitude which feeds on radicalism but rejects dogmatism and fanaticism. In the short run, we cannot simply discard our institutional and cultural heritage, however much we realise that it has created the bad situation in which we find ourselves. We have no choice but to keep it in operation for some time while we work towards its change and ultimate replacement by something better. This requires that at least in one respect we allow little room for compromise: we, as citizens of rich industrialised countries, must bring our political, economic and cultural power concentrations under control and break their monopolies. Although this in itself is a structural change, it means that the outward shape of our institutional framework need not change very much for some time to come.

For example: as long as we need large economic and bureaucratic organisations to provide us with our prime necessities, it is better to curtail their power, to prevent them from blocking necessary change, and even to involve them in long-term transformation of the structure of which they form part. Given the great complexity of our densely populated industrial societies, utter chaos and great human suffering seem inevitable with, again, great probability that reactionary forces will fill the power vacuum if we allow premature and precipitate destruction of our political, administrative and economic institutions. To get our own structures under control in order to reform them through a carefully managed revolutionary process, policial debate must not only be intensified at all levels and in all corners of our societies, but a new conceptual arsenal must be developed by which ideological deadlocks may be prevented from blocking the political process. This is what I mean by 'avoiding dogmatism'. Although I would contend that compared to other policial strategies the activist approach perhaps less easily falls victim to dogmatism – inter alia because it generally concentrates on concrete, limited, though 'exemplary' issues, thus sowing the foment of disobedience – tendencies of leftist dogmatism can nevertheless be observed, especially when activist movements become too strongly dominated by an established political or ideological force.

A new conceptual arsenal can, in my opinion, only be created during a debate on issues of public concern. However, it should be based on a methodical refusal to accept terms, concepts and slogans at their face value, whether these are used by our opponents or by our comrades-in-arms. General statements on policy issues should be made down-to-earth, qualified as to place, time and circumstance, in order to make them operational or to expose them as unworkable; again, in particular socio-historical conditions and time perspectives.

Most topical controversies in the discussion on man and environment suffer seriously from lack of specificity and of space-time qualifications of the stands taken, and therefore tend to get bogged down in inconclusiveness. Examples are: the discussion of growth versus no growth, of the importance or unimportance of population control, of economic autarchy of countries or world regions versus international division of labour, of 'simple life' versus affluence as the prospect of people in ecological utopia, of industrial versus 'arcadic' economy, of pollution tax versus enforced pollution standards for production processes, etc., etc.

Slogans can fulfil a useful function in initiating the discussion of issues connected with the problem of man and environment, but the debate itself should aim at de-sloganising issues once they have reached the centre of public attention. In good Socratic tradition, we may thus help to prevent that mystification and false consciousness will once again predominate over real understanding. If in other respects we cannot be too optimistic about political consensus on how the ecological crisis should be handled, our politicians could perhaps reach agreement, at least on one general policy guideline: that in order to meet the political challenge ahead of us they should seek to ensure the highest possible political and social awareness of all people.[22]

How should this be done? By guaranteeing maximum openness in the process of economic, political and bureaucratic decision-making at all institutional levels of society; by developing sources of information about matters of great socio-economic relevance and facilitating public access to them by a liberal attitude towards extra-parliamentary political action; by demonopolising the mass media and liberating them from the grip of governmental and commercial interests; and finally and perhaps most important, by allowing scope for critical political education in schools – if only by reforming the teaching of history, geography, economics and civics, and by radically democratising schooling, in structural and pedagogical terms.

Many countries in recent years have shown promising achievements along some of these lines. However, anti-democratic forces with their wellknown phrases (that confusing the people would threaten our democratic institutions, that social and political stability is needed for development and that leadership and authority should not be further weakened) have managed to prevent or delay many new developments towards greater democratisation and political awareness.

Notes

1. 'Blueprint for Survival', *The Ecologist*, January 1972.
2. L.J. McFarlane, comment on the 'Blueprint', *The Ecologist*, January 1973, p. 39.
3. B. Commoner, *The Closing Circle*, New York, 1971, p. 293.
4. *Ibidem*, p. 294.
5. Edward Heath, speaking at Nottingham University on 27 March 1973, declared: 'Economic growth gives us more resources to use for improving the quality of our environment . . . The new resources and the new technology now at our disposal, as the result of past growth, mean that we can now do more to make Britain a better country to live in. But if we are to continue to reap the rewards of growth and prosperity we must be prepared to . . . take the risks that will be needed to maintain it.' (quoted from *News Service*, Conservative Central Office, 27 March 1973).

6. *The Ecologist*, February 1973, p. 61, quoting a Labour Member of Parliament. Professor W. Beckerman, (then) teacher of economics at the University of Southampton, declares that: 'I suspect that most of the people who are currently anti-growth are motivated by middle class judgements, and that if this were more apparent they would not receive such uncritical support.' *Ibidem*.
7. Professor W. F. Wertheim in 'Eclipse of the Elite' (valedictory lecture at Amsterdam University, March 1973) came very close to this line of thought when stating: 'Slowing down economic growth, slowing down population growth, a moratorium on technological development – these are the medicines since recently advocated by quacks not interested in fundamental change, in real cure'. [My translation, W. B.]
8. The conclusions to which centralist thinking can lead are demonstrated *inter alia* by Kenneth Boulding's ideas for keeping populations stable. Boulding proposes a system of licences for childbirth to be issued to each married couple. These licences may be bought and sold. Sanction against couples who have a child without a licence: a choice between a fine, a jail sentence or sterilisation. Boulding's proposal is sympathetically discussed by H. E. Daly on 'How to Stabilise the Economy', *The Ecologist*, March 1973.
9. A typical exponent of this strain of thought is Dr. Sicco Mansholt, former member of the European Commission. Also R. L. Heilbroner, 'Ecological Armageddon' in *Between Capitalism and Socialism*, New York, 1970, p. 283: 'Like the challenge posed by war, the ecological crisis affects all classes, and therefore may be sufficient to induce sociological changes that would be unthinkable in ordinary circumstances.'
10. On the need for extended public control of society and the 'different mold' in which capitalism 'will surely be cast' if it survives at all, see R. L. Heilbroner, 'Growth and Survival', *Foreign Affairs*, 51, 1, October 1972, p. 150 ff.
11. Cf. Commoner, *The Closing Circle*, p. 271, and R. England and B. Bluestone, 'Ecology and Class Conflict', *Review of Radical Political Economics*, Fall/Winter 1971.
12. This in contrast to what Malcolm Stresser has stated: 'the startlingly cruel awareness of our environmental limitations has put the skids under almost every assumption of political organisation', *The Politics of Government*, quoted in *The Ecologist*, February 1973.
13. J. Hardesty, N. C. Clement and C. E. Jencks, 'Political Economy and Environmental Destruction', *Review of Political Economics*, Fall/Winter 1971, pp. 81–102.
14. Cf. by D. L. Meadows *et al.*, *The Limits to Growth*, Report for the Club of Rome, Universe Books, New York, 1972, p. 175 ff; Commoner, *Closing Circle*, Chapter 10; H. E. Daly, 'The Stationary State Economy', *The Ecologist*, July 1972; England and Bluestone, 'Ecology and Class Conflict', and Colin Stoneman, 'The Unviability of Capitalism' in *Socialism and the Environment*, London, Spokesman Books, 1972.
15. H. C. Wallich, defending economic growth in *Newsweek*, January 1972; quoted by H. E. Daly, 'How to Stabilise the Economy', *The Ecologist*, March 1973.
16. Peter Bunyard, *The Ecologist*, March 1973, p. 112.
17. This would be nothing new insofar as the creation and maintenance of advantageous trade relations with the Third World has always been the essence of neo-colonialism. But the world market of raw materials which is rapidly turning into a sellers-market is already producing the first symptoms of an extraordinary and grave political concern in the rich industrialised part of the world. In 1972 Japan concluded an agreement with Iran for investments of around one billion dollars as development aid up to 1976; in 1973 the US concluded a new agreement with Iran for military aid and sales of arms for several billion dollars; early 1973 the US took the initiative for a conference of rich industrialised nations in an attempt to form a common front against oil-producing Third World countries; soon after the ceasefire in Indo-China in 1973 some big oil companies concluded an agreement with the Saigon government allowing them to drill for oil off the coast of South Vietnam; the role of the US in trying to maintain and strengthen 'cooperative' regimes in important raw material-producing countries is even more openly defended with the argument of 'US interests'.
18. England and Bluestone, 'Ecology', p. 38, illuminatingly elaborate this tendency, which is already observable.
19. Cf. Colin Stoneman, 'Unviability of Capitalism', p. 60.
20. Cf. England and Bluestone, 'Ecology', p. 45 and Commoner, *Closing Circle*, pp. 207–208.
21. Daly, 'How to Stabilise the Economy', states pessimistically: 'Distribution is the rock upon which most ships of state including the stationary state, are very likely to run aground' (p. 95).

22. In the Netherlands in 1971, a proposal to provide funds for investigating the country's economic and financial power structure was voted down in Parliament. Commercial advertising for radio and television was maintained though a majority of the people, in a public opinion poll, had declared for its abolishment. In 1972 a Dutch Cabinet Minister, in a public speech, gave as his opinion that radio and TV bothered the people too much with political issues instead of 'sticking to their function of providing entertainment'.

FROM IDEOLOGY TO UTOPIA: TOWARDS FEASIBLE SOLUTIONS FOR 2000*

Peter Hall

THE central problem of all forecasting and all planning, which has provided a central theme of this book, was pinpointed by Karl Mannheim in the 1930s: it is to try to bridge the gap between ideological and utopian thinking. Ideology, in the sense used by Mannheim, focuses on the here and now: it sees history as an unfolding of possibilities constrained by an established system of order; it views the world as a relatively fixed place, and the burden of the past hangs heavily. In practice it concludes that there exist only marginal possibilities at most for changing the *status quo*. Utopian thinking, by contrast, sees the world in terms of a preferred future: it creates a new reality that represents a sharp break with the past; and it can be used, and almost certainly will be used, by those who desire radical change. Utopians will accuse ideologists of being justifiers of the *status quo*; ideologists will accuse utopians of being historically unrealistic (Friedmann 1973, p. 27).

In fact, and as Mannheim recognised, neither of these modes of thought can by itself give us a total perception of how social change, even fundamental social change, can come about; yet we know that it does. Utopianism fails adequately to explain how social change arises out of the existing historical situation – it is insufficiently historicist in the sense in which we have used the word throughout this book. And neither mode of thinking can explain the central dilemma of planning: how to get from here to there, from the existing state of affairs to the desired state of affairs; nor does either provide an explanation of sudden reversals of trends or attitudes, the arrival of new questions on to the political or scientific agenda, the unexpected influence or power of new social groups.

Anyone concerned to influence the course of social change, therefore, must try to bridge this gulf. Marx did it with a theory of history resting on the metaphysical principle that any historical trend would produce its antithesis. Marxism, like any historicist theory, is confronted by the dilemma: if history unfolds according to its own rules, what influence on events can the individual have? Marx was the first to recognise the way out of this dilemma: the individual could influence events by being the first to understand the laws of social development, and thus equip himself to help the process. In Marx's words, the individual could not bring about the birth of a new social order, but he or she could shorten or lengthen the birth pangs (Marx 1867, 1961, I, p.10).

That dilemma has faced sociologists of planning ever since. Mannheim's answer is not very different from Marx's: it is to find what he calls the *principia*

*Reprinted with permission from *Europe 2000*, ed. P. Hall, Duckworth, London, 1977, pp. 239–263. © European Cultural Foundation. (Professor Hall is Professor of Geography at the University of Reading and Professor of Urban Planning at the University of California, Berkeley.)

media, the vital development processes that lead to structural change within society – or, as John Friedmann puts it in modern systems language, the strategic system parameters. They are the levers that effect social change; they cannot be reversed, but if the forecaster-planner can discover them early he can help in the process of guiding social change. This, for Mannheim, was the planner's critical task. It demanded that he made a bridge between the one and the other (Friedmann 1973, pp. 32-33).

We accept that argument. But it creates for the planner-forecaster a daunting task. He must possess in large measure what C. Wright Mills calls the 'sociological imagination'. He must analyse economic, social and cultural history to try to isolate the mainsprings of social change. Above all, he must have the quality which Max Weber called substantial or value-orientated rationality (*Wertrationalität*): he must have intelligent insight into complex social systems, including their final ends. If we accept the argument of the previous chapter, contemporary European society is itself moving haltingly towards this higher kind of rationality. Dominated since World War Two by economic and political forms of rationality – themselves classic forms of the more limited functional or goal-orientated rationality (*Zweckrationalität*) concerned only with the relating of means to given ends – society is now showing the first signs of accepting a wider cultural rationality. At present these signs are few, but they are particularly associated with key groups of society who could be expected to spearhead social change. If this analysis is plausible – and we shall develop it further in this chapter – then the forecaster-planner must himself attain such rationality in order to guide society in that direction.

Since World War Two, the argument in previous chapters has run, the dominant thought mode in Western society has been ideological in a very special sense. We can distinguish it by the label *scientism*. It is superficially rational, but it is not historicist, since it assumes that historical trends do not offer any fundamental constraints to human action. Rather, it asserts that once the planner has discovered how society or the economy works now, then he can mediate or regulate it in any desired way. Thus, if there is a problem of unemployment, it can be dealt with by classical Keynesian regulators; if there is a problem of alienation on the shopfloor, it can be resolved by more effective participation; if there is a problem of student revolt, it can be met by curriculum reform or membership of Senate. Our argument in this book is that measures will be completely misleading and unreliable for long-term planning: it ignores just those deeper forces of social change which can cause sudden reversals – in mass values, in the direction of scientific research, in the political agenda – that in a wider historical context can be seen as the most important.

Historicism, we argue, provides the route out of scientism. But we are not therefore committed to one theory of historicism, nor are we asserting that complete knowledge of historical forces will ever be possible. As far as the individual or groups of individuals are concerned, historical reality will always contain a great deal that is incomprehensible and unpredictable.

Along that road we come to the notion of contradiction. The word is almost automatically associated with Marx: but it has a long history going back to Plato and Aristotle. In the course of history, it is only natural that any trend – whether in the facts of economic and social development or in the history of ideas – should in time produce a challenge, a counter-principle. Firms, political parties, individual politicians, classes in society, encourage rival groups to compete for resources or power. Left-wing ideologies will stimulate the emergence of right-wing ideologies, and vice-versa. Suburban neighbourhoods produced campus revolutionaries and campus revolutions may in turn produce a reaction in favour of the values of suburbia.

Contradiction is particularly important for planner-forecasters, for it is just what conventional planning modes, tied to the notion of trend extrapolation, tend to ignore. If one really wishes to move the levers of social change, as Mannheim advocated, one should look first at the developing counter-eddy under the apparently smooth wave of history: the disaffected group, the radical ideology (whether of right or left), the rival product or firm or nation. And that is what we have tried to do in these pages: to follow present trends just so far as to illuminate the contradictions, the conflicts, the possible counter-reactions, that may result from them. It is time now to try to bring these into some broad general structure of social change.

Key trends

First, we have to return to the central dilemma that has recurred throughout this book. In seeking to develop an historicist view of the future, do we start with the material facts of the evolution of economy and society, or with the evolution of ideas? Our answer has been that history is a seamless web: facts create values but these in turn help shape facts. Nevertheless, since we believe that values essentially arise in response to facts, there is a strong case for starting with economic and social evolution.

We believe that we can isolate six broad trends which will pose acute problems – perhaps even apparently insoluble problems – for European society of the 1980s and 1990s.

First and foremost among these is a deepening *international economic crisis.* The European economy has been developed to a unique degree on the basis of mass-produced industrial goods, a large proportion of which are sold internally within the frontiers of western Europe, but which also have to provide the payments which are needed for imports of vital food and raw materials. Increasingly, the production of these goods has come under the control of multinational corporations. Aided by modern well-equipped factories and by pliant workers recently recruited from agriculture, European producers of consumer durables have achieved high productivity levels and an enviable standard of quality control, enabling them to compete vigorously in world markets. But more recently, our analysis has suggested, European competitive power has been threatened. On the one hand, as the oil crisis shows, European producers are dangerously dependent on imported raw materials from countries that may decide to develop their own manufacturing outlets – as is already occurring, for instance, with the car industry in Iran. On the other hand, recently industrialising nations (such as Iran, Korea and Brazil) have in even greater measure all the advantages that Europe possessed a quarter-century ago: modern factories equipped with automatic machinery, plus a highly-disciplined and weakly-unionised workforce. At the same time, mounting evidence demonstrates that in the advanced industrial countries themselves – not merely in Europe but also in North America – young industrial workers are becoming growingly disenchanted with the monotonous, soulless character of assembly-line production. Thus the advanced industrial nations are finding it increasingly difficult to compete with their new competitors. For them, it seems, the post-industrial age is truly arriving. But the question remains: how do they now make a living?

The signs of this crisis, it must be admitted, are as yet partial and faint. Profitability in European industry is everywhere declining; that can be interpreted as a mere cyclical phenomenon of the mid-1970s, not as a deeper structural phenomenon. Our argument is that it is in fact structural, that this can already be seen in weaker economies such as those of Italy and Britain, and that within quite a short time it will also affect the stronger European economies. Shortages of raw materials are not yet acute: again, our argument is that these shortages will begin to bite only later, sometime in the 1980s and 1990s, as the newly-industrialising countries begin to demand materials and energy on an exponentially-rising curve. In any event, as observers like Robert Heilbroner have eloquently argued, such an increasing rate of resource consumption would inevitably lead to ecological breakdown sometime in the next century (Heilbroner, 1975, pp. 47-55). So in one way or another, world industrialisation must lead to world conflict – not only in the economic sphere, but also, as critical supplies of materials and energy become more and more scarce, in the political and military spheres.

This, then, is the second problem area: *world conflict concerning resource use*. We have suggested that it will not take the form of a world conflagration: the prospect is rather one of limited wars associated with guerilla armies – on the model of the Viet Cong or and Angolan MPLA – in areas of the world, such as the Middle East or the Zambian copperbelt, that contain critical concentrations of industrially-vital raw materials. The pattern of such conflicts will be by no means simple, since nationalist movements will often be at war with each other in the same country (as in Lebanon or Angola), and world power blocks will be found to give moral or even material support to one or the other. There seems a strong likelihood, though, that all such movements will be tempted to put pressure on the nations of the advanced world by acts of terrorism and sabotage. The prospect, then, for the countries of Europe is one of increasing personal insecurity (Heilbroner 1975, p. 43).

The third problem has already been mentioned in the discussion of industrial prospects; but its ramifications extend far outside the industrial domain. It is the apparently *increasing alienation** of many people, especially young people, from the whole system. Essentially, they are rejecting the scheme of values that sustained their parents and grandparents. They are no longer willing to sell themselves to an organisational machine – whether to stand on an assembly line making industrial goods, or to sit in a typing pool producing standardised letters – in order simply to make money to pursue the goals of an acquisitive society. Rather, they are saying that their central objective is to live a satisfying life – which includes satisfying work. Again, the signs here are partial and vague: they include the behaviour of younger workers in countries such as Sweden, and

---

* Here 'alienation' is used in its general sense.

the evidence from the United States that the values of college youth are now diffused far into the young blue-collar working population. We would argue that they are the auguries of a possible mass movement.

The fourth problem is almost the antithesis of the third. It is *the decline and even the collapse of the older agrarian society of Europe*, when its stress on the mutual aid which members of the same extended family provided for each other, and on the security and trust that was only feasible through the face-to-face acquaintance of all in a village. The result of that collapse is that vital functions, once performed naturally by family members or fellow villagers for each other, now come to be identified as problems to be resolved only through professional bureaucracies. Education and preparation for life become the province of the nursery school, the school system, the college or university plus their supporting bureaucracies. Health becomes the specialised province of doctors, nurses, hospitals and again their supporting bureaucracies. Production of food and other necessities becomes the monopoly of agricultural or manufacturing industries and their supporting distributive networks. Increasingly, stages in the life cycle come to be defined as problems – the child development problem, the problem of the young mother, the geriatric problem – each requiring a professional bureaucracy to cope with it. The family, now redefined as the nuclear family of husband, wife and children, ceases to exist as its members find more and more of their satisfactions outside the home (Commission of the European Communities 1977). Old people are isolated in senior citizens' colonies or institutions, young people in campus towns. As women assert their right to liberation, career and family maintenance come ever more into conflict.

Related closely to these problems is another: that of *access to information*. There is widespread dissatisfaction with the traditional structure of education, which was inherited from an elitist society and which seems ill-adapted to a rapidly changing world. At the same time, the quantity of information received by the ordinary citizen appears almost out of control; but he has little chance of regulating it or using it for his own advantage. Whether he considers his own newspaper or television set or his child's education, this typical citizen may well think that the control of information is again in the hands of a professional bureaucracy responsible to almost no-one.

Lastly, there is perhaps a growing threat of *polarisation of the entire society*. Though all to some extent feel alienated from real contact with their fellows and from society, some groups – the immigrant workers, the unemployed school-leavers, the low-skill workers who cannot find jobs, the old – may come to feel permanently and irretrievably excluded. As we have emphasised, it is hardly in the nature of such groups to unite in some kind of revolutionary movement. But if their discontent continues to simmer beneath the surface, we should expect it to erupt from time to time in demonstrations, revolts, occupations and general petty disorder. In this way, as in others, the immediate future is hardly likely to prove serene.

Formative ideas

These are some of the key problems of the coming decades as we see them. The list, it may well be said, is hardly an original one. With that we could only agree.

The more one explores the literature of future speculation, the more one is struck by the remarkable similarity of the analyses contained there. That might indicate simply a tired and conventional quality of thinking – though that is a charge hard to prove against writers such as Illich, Mumford, Schumacher, Heilbroner, and Friedmann. We would prefer to argue that it shows how clear the broad underlying trends are.

It is the same with the answers. Again and again, one is struck by the similarity of the basic ideas for the transformation of society to meet the challenges ahead. The precise terminology may differ from author to author, but the essential concepts are the same. We find ourselves in substantial agreement with them.

Many of these ideas could be attacked, and have been attacked, as utopian in the pejorative sense. They seem to suppose a reconstruction of society that is too radical to be realistic. In terms of the analysis earlier in this chapter, they do not show how it would be possible to get from the here and now to the desired future. We are by no means convinced of that argument, for two reasons. First, we think that it ignores the vital principle of contradiction, or reaction. As John Friedmann tellingly suggests, anyone in 1960 who would have forecast that by the mid-1970s California would have seriously considered legislation to ban the private car would have been regarded as eccentric if not a lunatic (Friedmann 1973, p. 130). Yet such a thing happened. Secondly, we are not asserting that such changes, or any changes, could come overnight. What we are talking about is a process of diffusion of ideas from thought-leaders to followers and then to general public, whereby – as we argued earlier in this book – ideas emerge into Good Currency. Therefore, we think that these ideas – unconventional though they may be – need to be taken seriously.

The first is that society, above all in the advanced industrial world, will need to become much more *resource-conserving*, particularly in relation to energy supplies. We do not know, nor do we believe anyone now knows, what such an energy-conserving society would be like. But we can develop some partial notions first from the few studies that exist of energy consumption patterns in different urban societies, and secondly from speculations by some of the more utopian writers in this field. We know, for instance, that different cities now have very different energy consumption levels, ranging from 25 Megajoules per head per year in Singapore or 34 in Hong Kong to 328 in Cincinnati, 331 in Los Angeles or a record 740 in Fairbanks, Alaska (Kalma and Byrne 1976, p. 5). These differences at national level seem to be related clearly to Gross National Product per head and to population density, though the relation is less good for cities in the same country. Tropical cities seem to have lower consumption levels, per head, than temperate cities, though different per capita incomes confuse the comparison; island economies seem to have low consumption levels (compare West Berlin with 67, against Nordrhein-Westfalen with 287).

Some tentative conclusions can be drawn. The first objective should be to increase thermal efficiency: to get greater energy expenditure out of a given, input. At present, an official American study suggests that overall three-quarters of all energy inputs are wasted, and in domestic heating this may be as much as 99 per cent and more. Home heating and transportation should be the main targets here. Secondly, energy consumption can be drastically reduced by cutting down the amount of transportation of both people and goods, and by transferring to modes that use few energy resources – especially bicycles, which according to Illich will triple the mobility of the unaided human being while posing no threat to the mobility of others (Illich 1974, pp. 29-30, 74). This last point is particularly important; for above a certain critical average speed, which Illich claims to be 15 miles per hour (24 km/hr), greater mobility to some will mean reduced mobility to the rest. Thirdly, as a corollary, the aim should be to optimise the size and distribution of facilities in terms of the social objectives they are designed to serve. It does suggest that in most circumstances, small units well-distributed among the population are preferable to large units requiring long journeys to reach them. Offices, shops and factories should all be planned so as to be readily reachable on foot or by bicycle; the era of the giant factory, the huge office, even the great urban complex is perhaps over (Heilbroner 1975, p. 139). This, as Kalma and Byrne recognise, may involve a clash with existing patterns of human behaviour; but that behaviour has been grounded in a period of apparently unlimited cheap energy, so that here as elsewhere a major psychological adaptation may be needed (Kalma and Byrne 1976, p. 14).

Lastly, the strong suggestion is that, as far as possible, low-energy communication needs to be substituted for high-energy transportation. Clearly, this can be true only of the transportation of information, not of the movement of goods. But, given the stress on service activities that automatically follows from a resource-scarce economy, this becomes an important consideration. It underlines a point made by Illich and others: that the aim of a new resource-conscious technology is not to return to some medieval or rural arcadia where the innovations of the last two centuries are eliminated, but rather to use those pieces of technology appropriate to the new situation. That could include the conscious development and encouragement of new communications devices to substitute for bodily movement and face-to-face communication across long distances, such as the conference telephone, the videotape and closed-circuit television, and the home computer. But these devices have other roles than the saving of energy, and we shall need to return to them.

The resource-saving society, therefore, is likely to be a great deal more efficient than now. Thus it can be fully competitive with other economies still based on economic rationality, even though its decision-makers have regard for social and ecological factors. It will use some resources more generously (building materials) in order to use other resources a great deal more frugally (energy for home heating). It will substitute energy-saving for energy-consuming machinery (small cars with less performance but more economy). It will stress less transportation, above all less long-distance transportation. It will plan cities so that many more activities can be combined within walking or bicycling distances. It will develop communications devices to the same end. And almost certainly, it will make a massive shift away from the production of things to the production of services, ideas and entertainment, in activities like justice, health, education and the arts (Heilbroner 1975, p. 87). In a literal sense, it will be a post-industrial economy. But notice here that services, too, can lay massive claims on resources: consider the education programme. What is needful, first of all, is the calculation of economic input-output tables that show the energy and resource needs of each economic sector. For this is an essential prelude to development of cheaper ways of doing the same thing.

A second major feature of the future society, to borrow Illich's phrase, is that it will be *tool-using* rather than *machine-used*. Or, in Schumacher's equally celebrated words, it will use *intermediate technology*: a set of instruments vastly superior to the primitive technology of the past but much simpler, cheaper and freer than the present technology of the affluent world. Schumacher also calls it self-help technology or people's technology, since it can be readily accessible to all; and for him its first use must be in the countries of the Third World (Schumacher 1973a, p. 154). This also is very much Illich's notion; but for both authors, the idea goes further, to affect the quality of work everywhere. For Illich, the essential feature of tools is that they allow what he terms convivial work:

> ... autonomous and creative intercourse among persons, and the intercourse of persons with their environment; and this in contrast to the conditioned response of persons to the demands made upon them by others, and by a man-made environment (Illich 1973, p. 11).

Tools, in other words, liberate the individual and allow him better to work to shape his own environment, in contrast to machines which enslave the individual to labour for money. They did this once before, in what Mumford calls the polytechnic craft society of the Middle Ages, in which:

> ... Playful relaxation, sexual delight, domestic tenderness, esthetic stimulation, were not spatially or mentally separated completely from the work in hand (Mumford 1971, p. 137).

All that was destroyed in the course of the Industrial Revolution, when a vast cultural resource of craft skills was wiped out. But there was no need for this; and, as Illich argues, the time is now ripe for its return. The point is that quite recently new technologies have arrived which again give the individual autonomy. Tools can now be given to laymen to allow them to cure sickness that formerly needed the expertise of professionals and their attendant bureaucracies. Simple public trucks, or bicycles, can give everyone mobility. Self-built do-it-yourself housing can allow everyone to be reasonably housed at a minimum cost. Voluntary learning, or access to information, allows everyone to acquire appropriate skills without elaborate formal education and the attendant ritual of certificates and qualifications. Many quite new tools – the typewriter, the copying machine, the camera, the tape recorder – are essentially convivial, in Illich's meaning, though they may often have been used for non-convivial (or anti-convivial) labour up to now (Illich 1973, pp. 33-40, 64).

The idea of a resource-conserving society based on parsimony (Heilbroner 1975, p. 139), and the idea of a tool-using society seeking autonomy for the human being, come together in yet a third key concept: *Quality*:

> ... If you want to build a factory, or fix a motorcycle, or set a nation right without getting stuck, then classical, structured, dualistic subject-object knowledge, although necessary, isn't enough. You have to have some feel for the quality of the work. You have to have a sense of what's good. *That* is what carries you forward. This sense isn't something you're born with, although you *are* born with it. It's not just 'intuition', not just unexplainable 'skill' or 'talent'. It's the direct result of contact with basic *reality*. Quality, which dualistic reason has in the past tended to conceal (Pirsig 1974, p. 284).

This notion of quality comes from within, and the quality of society can be made right only if individual values are first of all right:

... if we are going to reform the world, and make it a better place to live in, the way to do it is not to talk about relationships of a political nature, which are inevitably dualistic, full of subjects and objects and their relationship to one another; or with programmes full of things for other people to do ... The social values are right only if the individual values are right. The place to improve the world is first in one's own heart and head and hands, and then work outward from there. Other people can talk about how to expand the destiny of mankind. I just want to talk about how to fix a motorcycle. I think that what I have to say has more lasting value (Pirsig 1974, p. 297).

For Pirsig, quality has disappeared from the 'primary America' which is the modern industrial nation of 'freeways and jet flights and TV and movie spectaculars' because there people have become objects, isolated in lonely attitudes of objectivity. It is only in the older America that people still relate to their environment. Yet – here Pirsig makes a point similar to Illich's – technology can actually be used to attack the problem:

... technology could be used to destroy the evil. A person who knows how to fix motorcycles – with Quality – is less likely to run short of friends than one who doesn't. And they aren't going to see him as some kind of object either (Pirsig 1974, p. 357).

'Quality', for Pirsig, is thus a philosophical concept, and those who connect with it have what the Greeks called *enthousiasmos*, filled with *theos* or God or quality. It is almost the same as Illich's *conviviality*. It has to do with people's relation to their work and with their simultaneous relation to other people. It is close to what Schumacher identifies as the first two principles of Buddhist economics: to give a person the chance to use and develop his faculties, and to join others in a common task (Schumacher 1973a, Ch. 4). Thus, coming from very different starting points, three people – a British economist working for the National Coal Board, a Viennese-born priest working in Mexico and an American philosopher-novelist – have arrived at almost identical notions about the essential principles of social reconstruction.

These notions, again, connect with another: the idea of *social and economic life reorganised in small-scale units*. Partly this follows naturally from earlier considerations. A resource-conserving society, since it must minimise movement of people and goods, will naturally be small and as far as possible – in a modern world – self-sufficient. A tool-using society will allow the dismemberment of large bureaucratic structures, and so will allow production to occur in small units again. If people are to discover the principle of Quality for themselves, they are more likely to do so in small groups. But above and beyond this, small-scale organisation is needed to reduce alienation and to allow people to come autonomously to grips with rapid change.

Thus, in the proposal of the psychiatrist Ivor Browne, the only way of restructuring society to allow adequate personal development of the individual is to find some scale of organisation between the isolated individual and the mass collective society. This could be a group of adults and children of all ages, not necessarily blood-related: people or whole families might move freely from one living group to another, so long as this conformed to a basic cellular network. (The *kibbutzim* of Israel, as well as traditional bodies like colleges and less traditional grouping like modern communes, offer possible examples.) Such a society could evolve logically and naturally out of the women's liberation movement, Browne argues, because that movement must cause the traditional nuclear family to disappear. Within such a small-unit society – echoing Illich – the techniques and skills for living would no longer be monopolised by professional or technical bureaucracies, but would be freely and flexibly available to groups of people. Many jobs now done by specialists, ranging from garbage collection to social work, could be done by ordinary people perhaps on a part-time basis: the notion of a job as a separate full-time activity would disappear from many walks of life (Browne 1975).

Such a basic unit for a reorganised society would, in Browne's view, be one small enough to allow people to relate to each other as individuals, but big enough to perform essential functions such as education, housing, welfare and employment. It might contain between 30,000 and 50,000 people – the size recommended by Ebenezer Howard as long ago as 1898 for his proposed garden cities, which were realized many years later in the British new towns programme (Howard 1946). It should be divided up (again as Howard proposed) into units or cells that provided for direct face-to-face contact. And it should have some definable barrier or membrane – not merely physical but also socio-psychological – differentiating it from the outside world, a function Howard supplied by a wide green belt. A concept like this might be thought utopian, and indeed that charge was brought against Howard. But his concept has proved anything but utopian: in practice, as Howard always argued they would, the British new towns have proved exceptionally good social investments.

The idea of small-scale organisation can, however, be taken further into the whole structure of decision-making. For John Friedmann this is the essence of what he calls Transactive Planning: a style based on translating knowledge to action through an unbroken series of interpersonal relations. It demands the capacity for dialogue, of a kind now only generally found among members of the same family or close friends. Transactive Planning, for Friedmann, would be organised through a cellular structure of working groups consisting at most of twelve people and connected through flexible channels of communication (Friedmann 1973, pp. 171-97). Such groups would be temporary, self-appointed or representative in character, self-guiding, and responsible for a certain sphere of action. They would be readily permeated by new members, but once they become too big they would automatically subdivide. They would be based on effective, continuous learning, which constantly confronted theory with the reality of experience – within which the professional planner would merely be a kind of gentle educator basing his style on that of the Tao: bend (not destroy) social rules, appear to do nothing (but learn), do not compel learning, lead but do not be master. It requires an extraordinary leap of the imagination to see such a self-guiding society in practice. And the details – especially of conflict resolution where parts related to wider wholes – are as yet unclear. Indeed, one of the critical unanswered questions about all such utopias is that of hierarchical organisation and the transmission of decisions up and down. True, in a low-energy low-movement society, some of these kinds of conflict might have lessened or even disappeared – but surely not altogether.

Such a society would depend very greatly on the communications linkages between the many small units. They alone could provide a way of aggregating or disaggregating the many decisions or suggestions that must be passed up and down the hierarchy. Here we return to a central notion of Illich: that many recent technological developments, now used as machines, could become flexible tools giving people greater control over their environments. Television, now organised on a one-to-many basis, could be reorganised on a many-to-many basis by the development of video-recording machines and cable television. Thus many different small groups could present their views and argue their points, and the responses of whole societies could be fed in via telephone responses – or, eventually, through two-way cable television. Home computers, drastically reduced in price by the late twentieth century and communicating over ordinary telephone lines, could achieve an even more sophisticated many-to-many set of communications channels. In this way, small groups of people could, for instance, begin to design their own built environment:

> ... The reason why film and traditional television have been unsuccessful as design tools is that they operate one-way, and in the case of television (with the exception of closed-circuit educational systems and amateur television clubs) the public is prohibited from access. In the UK and in other countries operating 'public TV', the medium is not public but private. As a creative medium it resembles the state of the printed word in England in 1643 when the public was compelled by law to obtain a license for the printing and sale of books (Nicholson and Schreiner 1973, p. 44).

Active community decision-making, as Nicholson stresses, is possible only where communities have access to, and locally originate, live programming. A two-way communications system is for him one in which there is a dialogue where all parties have equal access to the medium and where the user can assemble his or her message out of loose parts (such as words or visual images). We are a long way from that ideal in contemporary European society.

Correspondingly, we are a long way from decentralised community control – whether in the city, the factory or the school. Indeed, in the last few decades European society seems to have been moving in the opposite direction. So it is not very easy to know what it would be like to live in a society where power over the human environment was given back to small groups:

> ... We can answer this by looking at the societies and communities where this is so, such as the many historic societies, and some modern tribal societies, and the communes and the *barriadas* to which we have referred, but it is more difficult to imagine the adaptive changes that would be needed in a contemporary city which is largely fixed (Nicholson and Schreiner 1973, p. 22).

As witness of that fact, notice that most descriptions of a decentralised society are either placeless, in that they seem to exist in a locational vacuum, or follow the traditional utopian pattern in being new communities. As with a resource-conserving society, so with a decentralised decision-making society, *we cannot easily imagine what it would be like.*

Indeed, perhaps there is an impossible contradiction: perhaps the whole notion is after all utopian in the perjorative sense. Robert Heilbroner has argued that, in a society of resource crisis, the most obvious response would be not a freely and locally democratic society, but a highly centralised and autocratic one appealing to a childlike belief in leadership and perhaps based on the nation-state as a psychologically-valid surrogate for the family (Heilbroner 1975, pp. 106-109). But he offers one intriguing possibility: that such a society could, as in China today, be highly egalitarian-structured in small groups while still being intensely conformist. Indeed, the dream of the democrats – that their local groups could somehow achieve harmony by a process of rational discussion – seems to ignore the fact that, in an era of scarcity, the rich would be defending the *status quo* while the less rich would still be committed to getting more of the material good things. To overcome this would seem to need some mass psychological transformation in a very short time – a transformation that is not easy to conceive of without a very highly centralised control over communications. So we come back to our starting dilemma: the missing connection between the here-and-now and the imagined future.

That connection could come only through a change in consciousness resulting from crisis. A society based on the principle of parsimony would necessarily be somewhat puritanical, though not in a joyless sense: it might resemble some experimental communes of the present time. It would rely heavily on inner discipline and harmony among its members. The right parallel perhaps is seventeenth century New England, though without the bigotry and intolerance which marked that society at its worst. Europe 2000 may be some way on the road towards such a society.

Could such an economy compete with other parts of the world still based on economic rationality? The argument is that it could, because in a wide sense it is more efficient in use of resources. By this time, indeed, the more recently industrialised countries may be paying a fearful price – and may in consequence be willing to follow the lead set by Europe. But first a change in values, expressed through political action, would have had to occur. We cannot posit how that would happen because we do not know, nor does anyone. One of the objects of this book is simply to put the possibility on to the political agenda.

Towards 2000

We now have to make the effort to think the unthinkable. It may be easier if we stress that the Europe of the year 2000 promises to be a *transitional* society between the one we know and a quite different one—at least as different, perhaps, as ours is from the society of the middle ages. The reaction against our present organisational forms and our present social priorities will have gone a good deal further, but it will by no means be complete: too many people gained too much from that older society, too many more people still wanted to join in the gains, to give it up without a struggle. And nostalgia may be a very prevalent emotion in Europe 2000. Just as to the bourgeoisie of Europe the years immediately before 1914 seemed a golden age, so the wide strata of society may come to regard the 1960s as the apogee of a certain kind of civilisation. But events will surely have exerted their own logic.

The first change is that, whether through the operation of market forces, governmental intervention or a combination of both, many of the basic resources of life promise to be more expensive, more hard to obtain, in 2000 than now. That particularly applies to energy and to other non-renewable resources. So new homes everywhere will be designed to produce their own energy, and to conserve what they produce or bring in, to a much greater degree than now. Similarly, transportation will be reduced in amount and changed in character.

People will live more of their lives in small place-bounded societies. When they do travel it will be by economic modes, such as small cars or airships. They will communicate more by electronics and less by face-to-face contact.

The second is that within these societies they will tend to work in rather small units, such as workshops or small offices of a few people. A number of such units will be found within a local community, offering the possibility of a wide range of work without moving them far from home. Indeed, partly for energy-conserving purposes, homes and workplaces will probably tend to be combined under one roof (or one set of roofs) rather as the different functions of the traditional farmstead were combined in contiguous buildings. The group of people living together and manning these various workplaces could be described as an extended, non-blood-related family or a commune group. It will contain a nucleus of nuclear families which dissolve and combine for different purposes, plus a number of more transient members.

The third is that these groups will necessarily use a rather different technology from that which we recognise today. Though many of the basic elements will be identical – machine tools, presses, lathes, typewriters, copying machines, tape recorders – they will be used as ancillary aids to work rather than substitutes for labour. And many people will do more than one job, combining intellectual work with craft skills and with work of general social value (such as looking after children). This general sharing of work will serve to break down the present barriers of class and sex. But, in any event, the end products of such work will be quite different from those today. A much smaller part of total human activity will be applied to making mass-produced consumer goods, which will be scarcer and made to last. Conversely, more people will be involved in craft industry using minimal materials and maximum labour; in the arts and entertainment; and in education. These will be the basic skills which the advanced nations of Europe sell to the rest of the world, since by then their capacity to compete in mass-production industry will be minimal.

The fourth is that the nature of both rural and urban life will change. Though a large part of European agriculture will continue to follow the path of mechanisation and higher productivity in order to meet the challenge of world hunger, there will be a powerful movement in the opposite direction. Greater understanding of and sensitivity towards ecological damage by pesticides and other chemical aids will lead to a new concern for natural regeneration of the land – and thus to a return to mixed farming, with a greater demand for labour. This will be especially the case on the medium-grade lands less suitable for mechanised farming in the upland areas of Europe. Here there may well be a large-scale return to the land by people who combine part-time farming with a range of other activities, including crafts and services. The new communications technologies, with their opportunity to perform a wide range of jobs away from the cities, should be a powerful stimulus here.

The cities will continue to decentralise as they have for the past two centuries. But there will be both a quantitative and a qualitative change in that growth. A stable population, plus a concern for qualitative economic growth, will lead to a lessening of the demand for land, and the new emphasis on ecological considerations will lead to a much more cautious policy on the release of land for urban development. It is more likely that many urbanites will migrate some distance from the city, where the new technologies will allow them to work in close contact with it. Within the city, there will be a much greater emphasis on rehabilitation and regeneration of the existing stock of buildings. The pace of physical change in European cities will therefore be much slower than in the quarter-century after World War Two.

The fifth change is that the nature of industry will subtly alter. Qualitative growth will mean an actual speeding-up of the process whereby European industry specialises in the lines of production, and in the productive methods, which it is best suited to supply. That means a greater emphasis on service industry, which is a generous employer of labour and an economical user of material resources; on science-based industry, which employs a great deal of skilled labour to work on rather valuable semi-processed materials and components; on research and development of all kinds, but especially focussed on the new resource-conserving 'soft technologies'; and on craft industry. A central feature of all these kinds of industry is that they can be decentralised – and indeed may best function when decentralised – into rather small units having a great deal of autonomy over such matters as productive emphasis, production methods and charging. These units may or may not remain members of larger productive organisations; whatever the case, such large organisations will almost certainly tend to be reorganised on a federal basis by the year 2000. Within each small productive unit, all members will have their say in the management of the enterprise, and may indeed have a great deal of responsibility for keeping it viable. But, at the same time, the present narrow emphasis on economic rationality will have been replaced by a wider social responsibility enforced through regulation or changing systems; and some at least of the entrepreneurs within each organisation and unit will need to have special regard for these wider matters.

The sixth is that this will be rather a serious, concerned society. It will be very concerned with its own survival in the face of unprecedented challenges. Though there will still be joy, there will be little frivolity. Though it may be quite highly decentralised in its decision-making structures, there will be a considerable degree of inner conformity. Above all, the society will be puritanical in being intensely concerned with the pursuit of individual quality in man's relations with his work, his environment and his fellows.

One day in Europe 2000

We have said that we cannot imagine exactly what it would be like. But nevertheless we should try.

There will be no typical European family of the year 2000, because the European economy and European society will be in a state of transition. Many Europeans in the year 2000 will lead lives very like the lives of 1976: one has only to compare the life styles of 1952 with those of 1976 to see that. The chief difference between those two dates, twenty-four years apart, has been one of material affluence. A few more or less new technologies have appeared – the computer for instance. But most of the story is the diffusion of material goods, already invented and available by 1952, from the richest members of society to the less rich. Accompanying that diffusion has been a spread of mass education and a marked increase in expectations. Everywhere, the net result has been a more egalitarian society based on mass consumerism. But for most people the change has been fairly imperceptible.

We expect the same to be true of the twenty-four years from 1976 to 2000. No cataclysm will occur. Many people will find their lives changed subtly and imperceptibly. Having already identified the key changes, we should now stress change in what follows. But in doing this, we should again repeat that for many the transition will bring more of what has already been occurring to them in 1976.

One typical European family of the year 2000 – we can call them the Dumills or the Deuxmilles or the Zweitausends – live in a converted eighteenth-century farmhouse on the edge of a hill area between 70 and 150 kilometers from a major city: we can imagine them in the Peak District or the Pentlands, or the Ardennes or the Eifel or the Monts de Morvan or the Sierra de Guadaramma. Built in an energy-conscious age, this farmhouse has properties of insulation which make it very apposite to a new age of conservation. But, with the aid of a government grant under the EEC Energy Conservation Act 1982, our family have converted it into a Low Energy Living Unit (LELU). They have further insulated it to reduce heat loss. They have installed a windmill for electric power, though they can still draw from the electric grid. They recycle farm refuse for fuel. And in summer they can draw on solar energy.

The farm is one of a group forming a small rural hamlet. It is occupied by a number of families that moved into them and reoccupied them after they were abandoned in the late 1950s, during the great age of European agricultural depopulation. Lower down the valley are other such family groups, forming a loose cluster of about fifty nuclear families or about two hundred people. Together with other such clusters and the nearest village they form a sufficiently large group to support a village primary school and community centre.

To speak of families, though, gives a wrong impression. Many of the children have broken away during adolescence and have joined other groupings, sometimes with other adults, sometimes with each other. The main point is that each person has a number of primary affinities: with a blood-related group, with a work-group, with one or more groups of like-minded people. He or she may shift groups from time to time, depending on individual needs and on personal development.

During the day almost every member of every living group is involved in some kind of work: this applies to the youngest and to the oldest in the community. The young may be involved in a preschool group in the care of an adult, who may perform that role only one or two days a week. The old may be indeed performing that very role, or doing ancillary work in shops or offices. Some very old people are still employed in positions of responsibility, as are some surprisingly young people – for age has less significance in this society, where retirement has been abolished. The critical point about these groups, and about the whole society, is the extreme flexibility of the roles. People do not follow lifetime careers. Very few do just one job from nine to five. Instead, people mix different roles. They may be postmen or milkmen in the mornings, students in the afternoon and entertainers in the evening. Similarly, they may be managers at 25, students again at 35, and craftsmen at 45.

Consequently, this is even less of a stratified society than was the European society of 1976. Not only have traditional barriers like middle-class/working-class or white-collar/blue-collar been broken down; traditional skill categories have gone too, because the emphasis is on adaptability and free entry. Anyone who chooses, provided he or she has the talent, can aspire at any time to become a craftsman or a master chef, a professor or a long-distance truck driver. And, consequently, not only the prestige but also the differential payments for different jobs have been largely eroded. The differentials are related only to the disagreeability of the job on the one hand, the length of training required on the other. So, over a lifetime, given that everyone shares the more and the less agreeable jobs, earnings are roughly equalised. So are prestige and interest; and in this way, alienation is sharply diminished.

Most of these jobs can be done locally. There are a couple of distinguished restaurants which employ a score of chefs; there is a research institute serving as an input channel to the Open University of Europe; there are a great variety of small craft workshops which work up wool, leather, locally-smelted metals and a variety of other indigenous materials. But one critical point is that most activities are now freed from locational constraints. The two restaurants serve some diners directly; they serve many more by exporting their deep-frozen gourmet meals, which are famous across Europe and beyond. And their boast is that they largely depend on locally-produced farm materials. The university teachers write course material in their own homes; they broadcast from the local television studio; and they conduct seminars and tutorials by conference phone and videophone. All of them can communicate directly from home with the Eurodata network, which can supply them with microfiche facsimiles of any book or paper within seconds. Similarly, the craftsmen get technical information from the same source, and can communicate with the National Crafts Centre when they want advice. The master chefs write textbooks in their spare time, and similarly broadcast cookery lessons both to the general public and to apprentice chefs in schools all over Europe. And all this without leaving the local community.

This is thus a more service-oriented economy than the Europe of 1976. But it still contains a considerable volume of manufacturing. However, much of this work is carried out in a radically different way. Because of increasing discontent in big urban factories in the 1970s and early 1980s, expressing itself in strikes and disruptions and poor quality, the big multinational companies have decentralised many of their operations to small workshop units consisting of between ten to fifty people, which are given a great deal of autonomy; in many ways they represent a return to the domestic system of industry characteristic of the age before the Industrial Revolution. Many of these workshops are in the new rural communes, where they employ a variety of people – students taking time out, women with small children seeking part-time employment, older people, people who want a holiday from urban life and who are combining farming and factory life. Many of the workshops are indeed parts of farm communities. Most of them produce goods of high quality and great durability which indeed is a requirement for European industry under the EEC Industrial Quality Law of 1992. They have varying degrees of freedom to buy their own materials from sources outside the organisation. Some, indeed, have been given virtual independence, and produce their goods simply to the specifications of the manufacturers – specifications which come from Eurodata via the microfiche system – selling them to the main manufacturers in competition with many other small rural works. Most of the components for the car industry, for instance, are now made in this way. And in this particular commune there are assembly plants which produce Fords and Volkswagens by craft methods. The final products, known as Craft Cars, cost more than the factory-made product but are preferred by many customers on the grounds of their reliability. Because they have exceptionally long life, these cars are given preferential tax concessions under the Materials Conservation Act 1988.

Most members of the community do some work on the farms, especially at peak periods such as harvest, when there is a general custom that other work stops. Farming in an area like this is necessarily mixed farming and it is quite labour-intensive, so that overall more people work on farms in the year 2000 than in 1976. Further, as with industry, farmers must now have regard to the wider consequences of their work. The use of pesticides and other chemical aids is carefully regulated, and there are incentives for farming methods that maintain or restore the ecological balance. Under these regulations there has been a strong emphasis on natural farming methods and on reafforestation, for instance. And these farmers meet more of their own needs and those of their neighbours than did the farmers of the area in 1976.

Such a dispersed rural pattern of life, it might be thought, must place big demands on resources for transportation. But those demands have been limited in a number of ways. First, because of the varied character of the rural population it is able to satisfy so many more of its social and cultural needs locally. Secondly, the development of information technology has been so rapid that many needs are met in this way without having to travel at all. (And because the new technology is two-way, the people have much greater control over the information they receive than the less information-rich society of the 1970s.) Thirdly, because the age of expensive energy has created its own response in the form of more energy-conserving vehicles and organisational arrangements. To move about locally, most villagers use small mopeds in which the motor is used only as a supplementary device. To move longer distances, they rely on a system of shared rides whereby anyone leaving the village is under an obligation to offer seats in his car, truck or van. In return, he receives tickets for a national lottery – a system developed in Poland as long ago as in the 1970s. In this way, *Europe 2000* actually manages to generate rather more person-kilometers of travel than the Europe of 1976 with fewer energy demands.

Perhaps the most striking change about this society is that it marks a partial return to the extended family, or caring group, of earlier ages. It is in a real sense a community. Within it, very many more tasks are performed by people simply as members of the community, often on a part-time basis, without the need for an exclusive professionalism. There are many more people in this society who can be a teacher, a nurse, a policeman if the need arises. Roles are less well-defined; people are again generalists rather than specialists. And nowhere is this more important than in the division of responsibilities between the sexes. Women and men share the task of child-rearing to a much greater degree than today – and this involves not merely the immediate parents, but a great variety of other helpers of all ages. Indeed, this becomes a most important responsibility for the older members of the community.

Half an hour or an hour's drive away by shared taxi or truck, life in the city continues on a more traditional track. But here, too, the tendency is to stress much more the local neighbourhood and the group. The urban economy, too, has been deeply infused with the idea of small, autonomous, self-directing production units. People are organising their urban lives round the local ward or commune. Physically, the city has seen much less change in the last quarter of the twentieth century than in the period 1950-1975. The slower population growth, the emphasis on qualitative growth of the economy, the new concern for ecological impact and for conservation of the urban fabric have all tended to restrict the amount of urban destruction and reconstruction. That means that the city feels an older place than in the 1960s and 1970s. It could in consequence be a drabber and a more dilapidated place – unless positive attempts were made to restore its fabric.

Many trends, in fact, have worked to the city's disadvantage in the last quarter century. Transportation costs, especially by public transport, have risen. Housing costs and pressures have not greatly diminished, due to the tendency of the population to split into smaller households. Above all, terrorism and guerilla warfare have caused gradual demoralisation causing many people and businesses to flee the city. Among those who remain, there is a disproportionate concentration of dysfunctional groups, some of whom present acute social problems in the form of unemployment and crime. So many have left the city, taking their work with them. The difference is that they have no longer gone to nearby suburbs of the city; they have fled into the countryside. Some, as we just saw, have gone right outside the city's sphere of influence. Even headquarters' offices have begun to decentralise to small country towns within easy reach of the white-collar workers who prefer to live in such places. Others have migrated shorter distances, to smaller towns still within the city's sphere of influence. There they live in what are, in effect, polynuclear urban clusters of towns, very much on the model that Ebenezer Howard suggested in his pioneer book on Garden Cities (Howard 1946, 1898). So, within every European country – the south following a trend set earlier by the north – large cities have lost people and jobs relative to medium sized and small towns.

These people live in European nation-states that are for the most part recognisable from the Europe of the 1970s. But there may well be some significant changes in the political map, formed by newly-independent states in the peripheral frontier zones of Europe. An independent Scotland or Pays Basque or Corsica is by no means an impossibility. Each will be led by a highly nationalistic government representing a former set of freedom fighters; and some at least are likely to be strongly left-wing in composition. The same applies to several of the countries of southern Europe. These countries are by no means automatically likely to line up with the eastern bloc – which by then is likely to be considerably more fragmented. Rather, they may well be neutral in the strategic sense, aligned with a wider EEC in an economic sense. For almost certainly, all European countries – both old and new – will find it necessary, in order to preserve their competitive stance in a difficult world, to surrender even more of their power to supranational institutions. So it is by no means inconceivable that by the year 2000 we could find a neutralist left-wing Scottish government next door to an English government still aligned to NATO; or a Communist Italian government as a member of the EEC.

This picture, we stress, is a caricature that stresses change; it underplays the elements of continuity. Not everyone will live like that; this is a society only some way along a certain path. There will still be industrial mass-production, mechanised agriculture, streams of traffic on multi-lane highways, big cities, elements of the candyfloss society. Indeed, some of the quantitative indicators by the year 2000 may well be higher than those of 1975 – though we would expect many to be already lower. Change in society, even fundamental change, is always a matter of degree.

The cultural rationality which we have posited as a desirable response to the needs of our society may, almost certainly will, experience difficulty in asserting itself. Internal politics – a majority may not want it – and external opposition from nations still adhering to economic rationality which may therefore be more efficient will ensure that. The political dimension could be decisive: organised working class governments – the Labour Party in Britain, the Communist Party in Italy – may very well be insensitive to the demands of cultural rationality and in fact resist them.

But, just as there was no one day when feudal society gave way to capitalist or when an aristocratic order gave way to a liberal-democratic, so there will be no one red-letter day marking the end of the era we live in and the start of another.

Yet since millennia are always intrinsically memorable, the year 2000 may well prove to be the historian's closest approximation to it.

Last words

This is the end of *Europe 2000*. But it should be the start of cooperative research into Europe's future.

The countries of Europe devote countless resources to grappling with the problems of the present – problems that sometimes appear to be overwhelming them. They devote miniscule amounts, in comparison, to trying to anticipate problems before they arrive. That perhaps is why they seem to be overwhelmed. Their approach resembles a medical system that pours money into building hospitals and dispensing drugs, but spends nothing on preventive medicine. In government as in health, that is bad practice. For it needlessly wastes scarce resources – including the most precious resource of all, human creative ability.

If, hopefully, this book has shown something, it is that speculative anticipation of future problems is both possible and useful. To pursue that activity further in depth, Europe should now have an International Institute of the Future.

References

Browne, I. (1975) *The Family in Modern Society* (mimeo). Dublin.
Commission of the European Communities (1977) *A Project for Europe*. Brussels: The Commission.
Friedmann, J. (1973) *Retracking America*. Garden City: Anchor Press/Doubleday.
Heilbroner, R. L. (1975) *An Inquiry into the Human Prospect*. London: Calder and Boyars.
Illich, I. (1973) *Tools for Conviviality*. London: Calder and Boyars.

Kalma, J. D. and Byrne, G. F. (1976) Energy use and the Urban Environment: some implications for planning. In: *Proceedings of the World Meteorological Association Symposium on Meteorology as Related to Urban and Regional Land-Use Planning*, Asheville, N. C., November 1975. Geneva: WMO.

Marx, K. (1867, 1961) *Capital*. London: Lawrence and Wishart.

Mumford, L. (1971) *The Myth of the Machine: The Pentagon of Power*. London: Secker and Warburg.

Nicholson, S. and Schreiner, B. K. (1973) *Community Participation in City Decision Making*. Milton Keynes: Open University Press.

Pirsig, R. M. (1974) *Zen and the Art of Motorcycle Maintenance*. London: The Bodley Head.

Schumacher, E. F. (1973) *Small is Beautiful: Economics as if People Mattered*. New York: Harper and Row.

Environmental Economics: Some Theoretical Perspectives

INTRODUCTION

Environmental economics is a recently established sub-discipline of the more general social science of economics. Its development (particularly in the USA has been stimulated, since the early 1960s, by the intensification, spread and perception of "environmental" problems such as, for example, pollution in its various forms and resource depletion that now face mankind;[1] and by the recognition of the importance and complexity of the interrelationships (as yet ill-understood) between mankind, the global resource base and the encompassing environment. The Ehrlichs[2] state that: "As the number of people grows and the amounts of goods and services provided per person increase, the associated demands on resources, technology, social organisation, and environmental processes become more intense and more complicated, and the interactions among these factors become increasingly consequential." Thus the relations between an economic system (a man-made institution created in order to facilitate the allocation of scarce resources with the ultimate aim of satisfying as far as possible human wants and needs) and an ecosystem (a system of relationships among organisms and between organisms and their physical environment) are of paramount importance in the understanding of environmental problems and their possible mitigation. A growing number of economists have begun to stress that analytical efforts should be concentrated on how the economy and environment interact and on how economic rules and institutions impinge upon these interactions.[3] In the past the two systems had been studied separately by two sets of scientists, economists and ecologists. This separation, many would argue, has now become obsolete and a positive hindrance to the development of research programmes at the economics/ecology interface. Such research, the argument continues, offers the best hope for the mitigation of the general problem of environmental quality deterioration. ·

Economics and Ecology

While it is true that both sciences have developed similar approaches in the sense of studying the system's stocks, flows and exchanges, of food, materials, energy and waste products; the establishment and maintenance of equilibrium states and the phenomenon of growth and succession; there are nevertheless important differences and points of emphasis. The economist focuses on the flows of goods and services within human society. The economic activities of production and consumption create interdependencies and exchange relationships between the different agents both producers and consumers (households, firms and the government) in the economic system. The economist is primarily concerned with the study and evaluation of human choice, with the allocation of scarce resources (land, labour and capital) in as efficient a manner as possible.

The ecological view, however, focuses on the dependence of human society on the physical and biological systems of the total environment. It places greater emphasis on such issues as species diversity and ecosystem stability and the long-term survival of all species including mankind. Man requires a range of inputs from the natural environment and relies on the natural assimilative capacity of the environment to handle a great deal of his waste products (residuals). Environments and their natural assimilative capacities are, ecologists would argue, much more complicated and vulnerable than economists in general seem to realise. Nevertheless, over-concentration, in isolation, on either the economic or the ecological aspects of an environmental problem is likely to produce an incomplete analysis which neglects vital elements and therefore produces only a partially useful management programme.

A Systems Approach to Human Society and Nature

Given the complex interrelationships which seem to characterise the so-called "environmental crisis", analysis of the problems would seem to be best undertaken utilising a systems approach. Drawing from general systems theory James *et al.*[4] define some system S as composed of some set A of interrelated objects plus the interrelationships themselves. Now the environment of such a system S would be a set E of objects that do not belong to A but affect other objects that do belong to A. The biosphere, i.e. that part of earth where life exists, can be described as a system – an organised whole of interrelated parts – which can be simulated in a mathematical form. Within the biospherical system a set of sub-systems, ecosystems, can be distinguished. A bio-ecosystem includes all organisms (in groups), their relations with each other and their relations with the abiotic environment. A human ecosystem represents a society of human beings and their relations with each other plus their relations with their environment. Both types of sub-systems function on an input–output basis. The two categories of inputs are energy inputs and materials inputs which flow through the sub-system. Energy, unlike materials, however, cannot be re-used (recycled). In bio-ecosystems natural materials recycling processes take place while in economic systems much thought has been given recently to the possibilities for and limitations of waste materials (secondary materials) recycling programmes.[5]

In many cases the analyst is unable to observe directly the likely important interrelationships within a system. Thus the scientist (whether ecologist or economist) assembles what direct data he does have and uses it to aid him in constructing a theory – i.e. a model or a paradigm in the sense of the L set of factors which form the whole underlying structure of the scientific process – of the systems functioning. The test of a good model is not so much how simple or complicated its structure is but rather how closely it mirrors reality. Unfortunately, there is always the risk of over-simplifying these complex systems when one attempts to gain a better understanding of the systems through model-building techniques. An ambitious computerised systems model utilising the principle of systems dynamics, the Limits to Growth Model,[6] was constructed in the early 1970s in an attempt to model and forecast future industrialisation, pollution, resource depletion, population growth and food-supply problems on a global scale. The model and its doomsday scenarios have, however, been severely criticised on technical and other grounds, particularly by economists.[7] We examine the so-called Limits To Growth debate in detail in Section 7 below.

We mentioned earlier that despite similarities the approaches taken by economists and ecologists are currently less than totally compatible. Probably the major difference concerns the rather anthropocentric approach which economists, in general, adopt in their analytical work. Their analysis is restricted to human systems and their environment. Pollution is defined and recognised only in terms of negative effects on human utility (well-being or welfare) functions. Immediately, this approach will be found wanting if human perception of pollution damage is less than perfect; which it is especially when the so-called stock or long-lived pollutants (DDT, cadmium, mercury, radioactive substances, etc.) are involved. Stock pollutants tend to accumulate, after discharge, somewhere in the biosphere often over a long period of time until they reach some "threshold" level when damages manifest themselves. Perception of the problem and initiation of some corrective procedure only when the threshold is breached is akin to "shutting the stable door after the horse has bolted". It is quite simply too late to avoid damage. Depending on the time scale involved the environmental-damage impact inflicted by the actions of the current generation may have been postponed only to re-surface in an intractable form in a future time period imposing a heavy cost burden on future generations. Ecologists and some economists have pointed out forcefully that this anthropocentric view neglects the physical dimension of pollution. The fact is that pollution could ultimately alter the species composition in ecosystems and could reduce system maturity in terms of species diversity thereby hindering the ability of the system to withstand further pollution shocks. In Section 5 below we examine in more detail the attempts that have been made by some economists to incorporate an environmental dimension into their models. The debate over whether these attempts are adequate or whether a more radical "paradigm shift" is required in the science of economics is also presented and examined. Finally, some of the readings in Section 3 address the problem of intergenerational equity and the implication that future generations' preferences concerning the environment and possible inherited damage cost burdens be included in the environmental policies of the current generation.

The Conventional Neoclassical Economic Paradigm

Scarcity and environmental goods and services

The economist sees the environment as consisting of a collection of goods and services. The environment supplies us with so-called "natural goods", including a variety of landscape forms and scenery from which we derive aesthetic pleasure. It also provides us with a natural resource base, the materials and energy which the economic system transforms into economic goods. This transformation process results in the discharge of a range of residuals which find their way back into the environmental media. Fortunately for us the environment has a certain natural residuals assimilative capacity but this disposal capacity is being put under an increasing strain by industrialised economies. Perhaps most importantly the environment supplies an integrated and highly sensitive life-support system.

The technological advances made by the rapidly industrialising economies in the nineteenth and twentieth centuries have made available a vast range of economic goods and services. Barkley and Seckler[8] conclude that for the average and upper-income groups of such societies the marginal utility (satisfaction derived from additional units of the goods or service in question) of such goods and services has begun to fall. In contrast, the opposite trend seems to have affected environmental goods and services. The progressively more widespread impacts of industrialisation have begun to bring home to mankind the message that the environment's resources are scarce and exhaustible. The marginal utilities of such goods and services must therefore be increasing as the residuals disposal services are put under severe pressure; natural resource bases are depleted and we become increasingly dependent on inferior reserve deposits; natural goods are despoiled by industrial development or tourist overcrowding and even the life-support system itself is perhaps being threatened by, for example, the build up of carbon dioxide in the upper atmosphere, due mainly to the burning of fossil fuels and deforestation, with possible consequent global temperature build up and climatic change.

Resource allocation: market versus central planning

In the face of scarcity choices have to be made in order to allocate all resources among competing uses. Now the neoclassical economic doctrine is dominated by the concept of market processes. Such processes represent decentralised, deconcentrated decisionmaking systems for resource allocation. In a decentralised system it is the preferences of individual consumers that in principle dominate the allocation of resources; if the system is also deconcentrated then all decisions concerning the price of goods and services and the output of goods and services are made autonomously by (individual) producers.[9] The term "market process" as used by economists refers both to the actual functioning of economic activities in some societies and also to a theoretical structure or model which explains and evaluates the market process under ideal conditions. The ideal market model functions with a large number of individuals who enter the market either as members of consuming households or as producers owning firms. The behaviour of the households and the firms is hypothesised to be dominated by, for the former group, the rational pursuit of satisfaction (utility) and for the latter group, profit maximisation. Thus consumers aim to maximise their utility by allocating their time either to work or leisure pursuits. The factor rewards they receive from work activities are spent on goods and services; total expenditure being constrained by income levels, prices and the total time available for work or leisure. Productive firms, on the other side of the market process, are guided by the aim of profit maximisation. In order to achieve this goal firms must strive to produce their outputs as efficiently as possible by finding the lowest cost factor input combination available to produce a given output. Having achieved this optimum factor combination firms strive to sell their output at the highest possible price. The total amount of profits earned will be constrained by, among other factors, the price and availability of factors of production (land, labour and capital); by technological limits on the firm's production possibilities; and by the degree of competition in the industry.

Figure 2.1 below illustrates in a simplified way the place of the market in an economic system which for simplicity's sake is assumed to be closed to any foreign trade and in which all incomes are spent and not saved.

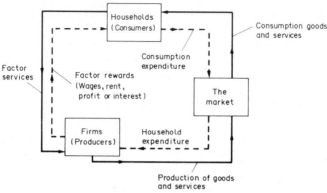

FIGURE 2.1

A simple model of an economic system.

Thus in this model system the economy's national product (output of goods and services) = its national income = its national expenditure (value of total output). Similar figures can be found in any introductory economics textbook[10] with extensions to include the effects of foreign trade and savings and investment flows, but typically there is no analysis of the interrelationships between the economic system and its surrounding environment.

Householders on one side of a market (defined as any situation in which buyers and sellers come into close contact) demand (wish to purchase) goods and services on the final goods market and supply (offer for sale) factor services to firms in the factor market. Firms, on the other side of a market, produce and supply goods and services for sale on the final goods market and demand factor inputs such as labour in the factor market. Now the activities of production, consumption, financing, buying and selling appear to be to some extent unplanned and uncoordinated involving as they do millions of firms and consumers and vast numbers of goods and services. However, the end result of the market process is a set of ordered results, a general equilibrium situation, which has simultaneously satisfied both the consumers and the producers of goods and services. What we seem to have is a self-regulating economic system guided only by what has been called the "invisible hand of the market". In the face of scarcity the market process has produced answers to the "what", "how" and "who" choice questions: what goods and services are to be produced: how are these goods and services to be produced: who will receive the goods and services.

Demand, supply and market equilibrium

The economist uses the term "demand" to indicate the whole set of factors determining purchases of goods and services. Economists have derived functional relationships between the quantities of a given good that a consumer would buy (dependent variable) and independent or predictor variables such as, the price of the good in question, the prices of all other goods, the consumer's income, etc. Thus an individual demand function may take the following general form:

$$QD_z = f(P_z;\ P_a \ldots P_y;\ Y;\ T;\ U)$$

where QD_z = quantity demanded of some good z,

P_z = price of good z,

$P_a \ldots P_y$ = prices of other goods,

Y = income,

T = tastes,

U = all unknown variables.

Typically a demand curve describes how quantity purchased per period of time varies due to changes in price. Under certain conditions (all other independent variables except price held constant) it can be shown that, in general, when the price of a good or service goes up the quantity demanded by individual consumers decreases and vice versa for a price fall (see Figure 2.2). Changes in any other of the predictor variables except price will lead to changes in the shape and position of the demand curve.[11]

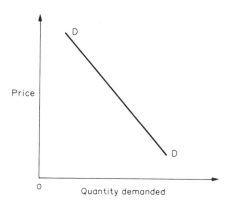

FIGURE 2.2

A demand schedule.

Horizontal summation of all individual demand functions for a particular good yields a *market* demand curve for that good. Thus, for example, the residential market demand for electric power is thought to take the following form:

$$D_E = f(\text{POP};\ Y;\ P_E;\ \text{AP}_E;\ P_G)$$

where D_E = residential demand for electricity,

POP = population,

Y = income per capita,

P_E = price of electricity,

AP_E = stock of electrical appliances in households (complementary goods),

P_G = price of gas (a substitute good).

Utilising similar analysis it is possible to derive supply functions for individual firms or the totality of firms (industry) producing a given good. In general as the price of a good increases the quantity offered for sale increases, other factors held constant. A supply curve is illustrated in Figure 2.3 below. An individual supply function may take the following general form:

$$S_z = f(P_z;\ P_a \ldots P_y;\ P_f;\ O;\ T;\ U)$$

where S_z = amounts of good z offered for sale,

P_z = price of z,

$P_a \ldots P_y$ = prices of all other goods,

P_f = prices of the factors of production required to produce good z,

O = objectives of the producer,

T = current state of technology,

U = unknown variables.

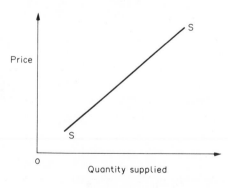

FIGURE 2.3

A supply schedule.

Prices have a central role to play in any market process acting as information signals and incentive forces. They are a cost element to consumers of goods and services and a revenue element to producers of goods and services. The market process eventually reaches an equilibrium position and a *market* price is determined for the good in question. At this market price both the buyers and sellers of the good in question are satisfied. In terms of our simple market model and assuming that price is the dominant independent variable (all other independent variables held constant) we can derive the following set of equations:

$$D_z = f(P_z),$$
$$S_z = (P_z),$$
$$S_z = D_z \text{ in equilibrium.}$$

In graphical terms we can derive Figure 2.4, where D_z is the market demand function and S_z is the supply function for some good z. Market

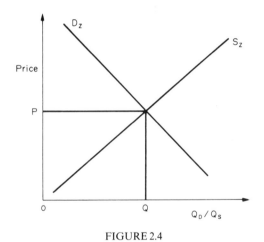

FIGURE 2.4

Market equilibrium model.

equilibrium is attained when the price charged for good z is at the level OP. At this price OP the quantities of good z demanded and supplied are equal and the market "clears". Neither the producers nor consumers have an incentive to change the quantity bought or sold.

Efficiency and the allocation of resources

The demand curve D_z in Figure 2.4 indicates how much of good z individuals would be willing to buy at different prices. Economists argue that the curve also indicates the *value* buyers place on a unit of, in this case, good z at the margin. This is the so-called marginal willingness to pay for the good. We will return to this concept later in the essay in Section 3 when we examine valuation procedures in more detail. The supply curve S_z in Figure 2.4 indicates, as we have seen, the amount suppliers are willing to sell at different prices. If the market is competitive (no single large firm dominating the market and thereby influencing market price) the S_z curve can also be interpreted as a marginal cost of production curve (including normal profits) at each output level. Marginal cost is merely the addition to total costs of production induced by an extra unit of output. A firm will go on increasing output until the marginal cost of each additional unit of output is equal to the price at which the output is sold. At the equilibrium price OP in Figure 2.4 the individual consumer's marginal willingness to pay just equals the marginal cost of production; this is in fact the condition for an economically efficient allocation of resources.[12] Thus in an efficiently functioning market process we have consumers maximising their utilities and signalling their preferences to producers in a competitive market. The producers guided by the profit maximisation rule produce goods and services consumers wish to purchase and do so at least cost. Finally, resource owners (suppliers of factors of production) sell their services to firms for the highest price possible.

Certain structural characteristics are necessary, however, for the market process to not only yield an equilibrium solution to the resource allocation problem but also guarantee that the solution is an economically efficient one. To meet the efficiency criterion all goods must be produced at lowest possible cost and the composition of the total output of goods must be such that consumer satisfaction cannot be improved by any alteration in the output mix. This means that no alternative allocation of resources would make one person better off without simultaneously making someone else worse off. The efficient market solution is defined as a so-called Pareto optimal position; we will return to the concept of Pareto optimality in the essay in Section 3. For now we merely note that at this optimum position all possible gains from voluntary exchange between buyers and sellers have been exhausted. When no additional exchanges can be made no one individual can make himself better off without making someone else worse off. The characteristics necessary for efficiency are as follows:

(a) All markets must be competitive; large numbers of buyers and sellers must exist so that no one single individual is able to influence market prices by altering his demand for or supply of goods and services.

(b) Producers cannot be experiencing increasing returns to scale; returns are the physical amounts of the goods produced by a firm utilising some set of factor inputs; the greater the physical output produced by a given quantity of factor inputs the more efficient production is deemed to be. If as output is increased the return to each unit of the factors (marginal products) increases then economists say that increasing returns are present. In other words, it must not be the case that ever larger firms can produce the same product at a lower per unit cost than can relatively smaller firms.

(c) There must be adequate market information; all participants in the market must know the quantitative and qualitative characteristics of the goods and services available and the terms of exchange.

(d) All firms must follow a profit-maximising strategy and all consumers must seek to maximise their utility.

(e) All resources and goods can be individually owned and all the costs of production and consumption must be fully reflected in market prices.

We should remember at this stage that what we have been discussing is a theoretical model operating under, as we have just seen, a set of very idealistic conditions.* Real world markets do not duplicate the theoretical model. Many of the assumptions do not hold when empirical economic systems are examined. The existence of monopoly elements in the economy and the pervasive influence of commercial advertising are two reasons, for example, why in the real world governments have intervened in the economic process. The industrialised economies of North America and Western Europe are in fact "mixed" economies in which the market process is constrained by government intervention and which contain some wholly state directed (nationalised industries) sectors. Further, we have not proved that the market process is the most desirable mechanism for resource allocation, only that in principle, given the right conditions, it can produce an efficient allocation of resources. To argue that the market process is desirable one would have to accept a basic value judgement. Nath[13] distinguishes two ethical postulates that have to be accepted:

(a) Individualism is a "good thing", i.e. that it is correct that the personal wants of individuals should guide the use of society's resources; this postulate, therefore, ignores the existence of a concept we might label the "common good" except insofar as this concept refers to a weighted sum of individual utilities. We should also note that it is by and large the preference of the present generation of individuals that dominates over the possible preference pattern any future generation might exhibit.

---

* The neoclassical assumptions about rational economic man are neglected, for example, by members of the humanistic school of thought. See Lutz, M. A. and Lux, K. (1979) *The Challenge of Humanistic Economics*, Benjamin/Cummings. Even some conventional economists have questioned the underlying psychology in economic theory. See Scitowsky T. (1977) *The Joyless Economy*, Oxford University Press, and Collard, D. (1978) *Altruism and Economy*, Martin Robertson.

(b) The prevailing distribution of income and property in society is "just"; since each individual can only satisfy his personal wants to the extent that his income allows.

Central Plan Economic System

The market process is not the only mechanism that can theoretically establish equilibrium between production and consumption activities. Planning is an alternative mechanism which, in contrast to the market process, involves the centralisation and concentration of resource-allocation decisions. The key feature of this type of model economy is that the means of production are owned by society. The central authority (government) working through a central planning agency allocates all the resources in the economy by issuing plans and directives. The system can be said to be centralised in the sense that the central authorities' preferences dominate the allocation of resources. The system is also fully concentrated with the central authority taking charge of all detailed decisions on price and output policies. Turner and Collis[14] present an outline taxonomy of the different types of planning systems both theoretical and empirical. No taxonomy yet developed, however, is without drawbacks as a description of actual central plan economies. Two polar cases can possibly be identified, the "Soviet type" developed under Stalin since 1928 and the "French type", the indicative planning system. In terms of practical approximation the former has come as close as feasible to a fully state-administered, centrally directed socialist economy; the latter to a state guided, market directed and largely private-enterprise economy. For an introduction to the comparative economic systems literature see Dalton[15] and Eidem and Viotti.[16]

Market Failures

Public goods, property rights and externalities

We have already hinted that a number of the conditions necessary for the market model to produce an efficient allocation of resources are absent or modified in the real world. Now when it comes to the allocation of environmental goods and services the market process faces especially difficult problems. Environmental resources are typically not privately owned and hence tend to be over-exploited because they lack the protection that private property ownership often provides. Such resources often carry no market price tag at all and are therefore treated as "free" goods. No economic incentives exist in these cases to ration the use of these increasingly scarce resources. Hardin[17] focused on this "commons" problem in a now famous article and forecasted continued and increasing abuse, as well as congestion and quality deterioration problems for environmental resources. We examine this "commons" concept and the work of Hardin in detail in Section 4. The efficiency of the market process also depends on the identity of so-called private and social costs and that the market price charged for a good or service reflects the full social costs of its production and consumption. Standard economic theory assumes that decisions are made by a process of comparing the positive aspects (benefits) and negative aspects (costs) to the decision maker. But if the full social costs of production and consumption are not reflected in market prices then the market system will systematically produce too much of some goods and too little of others (on the basis of social efficiency); because relative prices of these goods and services are incomplete indicators of total benefits and costs. A major cause of market failure is the existence of external costs and benefits (externalities) which drive a wedge between private and social costs and benefits but which are overlooked by the market.

Environmental resources as public goods

The collection of environmental goods and services are mostly types of what economists have labelled public or common property goods and services; or at least have elements of "publicness" about them because of the lack of a well-defined and enforceable system of property rights. We may define a pure public good as a good which is capable of being consumed by one individual without any consequent reduction in any other individual's consumption of that good (known technically as the non-rivalness in consumption condition). Thus a public good if it is supplied to one individual in society is automatically supplied to others. Good examples of this polarised definition are not easy to find; perhaps the best are national defence services, lighthouse services and television programmes. The important point is that the market would fail adequately to provide such goods because consumers bid for a good (thus revealing its worth to them) only if those who do not pay are excluded. But exclusion is inefficient if consumption is non-rival. If consumers do not competitively bid for a good the producer does not pick up the market signal and will not supply such goods. Provision of such public goods on an adequate scale has become a task for governmental rather than market processes.

Environmental resources while not being pure public goods in the strictest sense do have elements of "publicness" about them. They are often characterised by the condition of non-excludability, which may coincide with a condition of non-rival consumption, or pose technically difficult or costly exclusion problems even though consumption is rival. Thus in the former case the benefits of clean air and water if made available to one consumer in an airshed or waterbasin would automatically become available for all consumers. In the latter case very attractive beaches or scenic landscapes often become over-crowded because such resources are used simultaneously (economies of joint consumption) by large numbers of people. Eventually as the numbers increase each individual user will interfere with other users' enjoyment of the resource thereby reducing the quality of the resource to them. Exclusion here while not impossible may well prove very expensive to administer or be socially unacceptable. Thus Musgrave[18] concludes that "public provision is needed where the exclusion mechanism of the market is inapplicable, be it (i) because the use of exclusion, while readily possible, would be inefficient since consumption is non-rival; or (ii) because the use of exclusion is impossible or too costly".

Economists have derived some general principles for the management of public goods.[19] We mentioned earlier that an individual demand curve illustrates a consumer's willingness to pay for a particular good and that the estimation of society's (total) willingness to pay for the good is found by *horizontally* adding the demand curves of all the relevant individuals to arrive at the *market* demand curve. This analysis is only applicable to private goods, that is goods which when consumed by one person or a family cannot be consumed by other individuals. Environmental goods and services typically retain public good characteristics and often can be consumed equally by everyone in a region, i.e. air quality in a given airshed. Now the total willingness to pay for public goods can, in principle, be found through a *vertical* summation of the demand curves of individuals. The economically efficient level of provision for a public good is then derived in the conventional way by finding the point where the total willingness to pay curve for the good crosses the marginal cost curve (supply curve) for the good. Dorfman[20] provides an illustrative example dealing with the provision of a smoke-precipitator for a local power plant which would reduce smoke emissions in the local airshed and hence improve air quality for all the local population (see Figure 2.5). A precipitator which removes OA percent smoke emissions is the economically efficient size (scale of provision) because at this point Z in the diagram the cost of removing an additional percentage point of smoke is just equal to the amount that all consumers in aggregate terms would be willing to pay for it.

Property rights and externalities

The lack of a system of property rights covering many environmental resources means that their usage results in spillover effects or externalities (uncompensated benefits or costs). Nath[21] defines an externality as "a favourable or unfavourable effect of one economic agent (individual or firm) on the production, income, leisure, wealth or welfare of another economic agent—the effect is such that the present techniques, customs or laws do not permit the payment or receipt of a price for the benefit or the harm that comes about through that effect". The presence of an externality (either beneficial—a positive externality or external

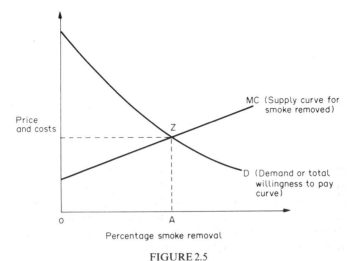

FIGURE 2.5

Efficient provision of public goods. (*Source*: adapted from Dorfman (1977) p. 5.)

benefit—or harmful, a negative externality or external cost) due to a particular production or consumption activity, means that the market price being charged has failed to encompass the full social costs (benefits) arising from that economic activity. Thus the full social costs of a particular production activity, say the production of pulp for paper and packaging products in an integrated pulp and paper mill, will include both the private costs of production, raw material costs, labour costs, etc., and any external costs if they are present. Pulp production in fact typically results in the discharge of a considerable amount of residuals, usually in solution, to the nearest watercourse. Now this residuals discharge may well lower the water quality in the river or stream concerned. Downstream users of water, whether they are other producers requiring intake water or recreationalists using the river for fishing, boating or aesthetic pleasure, will have external costs imposed on them. The plant requiring intake water may well have to install better water-purification plant and the recreationalists will also suffer a loss even though it may be less tangible. Of course if the water quality deteriorated significantly even the recreational losses would become much more apparent. Sport fishing and swimming activities, for example, may have to cease altogether. If these losses, both industrial and recreational, are borne without any compensation then the pulp and paper plant's costs of production are below the true social costs of production. In effect consumers of the output of the pulp and paper mill are being subsidised since the price they pay for the goods is less than the true social costs of production. The production of the mill is above the socially optimal level and should be contracted until the marginal social costs of production are equal to the marginal social value of the output.

In diagrammatic terms Figure 2.6 summarises this cost externality situation.

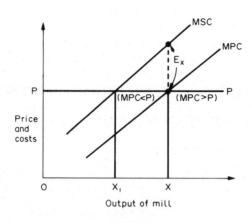

FIGURE 2.6

A negative externality situation.

Before we explain the figure in detail it is necessary to point out two simplifying assumptions that have been made. We assumed our mill is operating in a perfectly competitive market and hence is a price-taker. The mill's output is too small a percentage of the industry's output to have any effect on the market price (OP) charged for its products. Secondly, the marginal private cost curve (MPC) and marginal social cost curve (MSC) have been drawn as straight lines. In reality it is unlikely that marginal external costs would be constant per unit of output (which is what the straight line curve implies). More realistically increasing output would probably result in increased residuals discharge, increased water-quality deterioration and increasing external costs to downstream users of water. Pollution-damage cost functions are often very complicated in real world situations and detailed knowledge of such functions is currently not available for many pollutants or for the synergistic effects of a number of pollutants combined together in some environmental media. We will return to these informational-deficiency problems below.

In Figure 2.6 the private cost equilibrium position for our mill is at the output level OX where marginal private costs of production (MPC) are equal to market price (which indicates the consumer's marginal valuation of the good). The production of output level OX, however, also involves pollution damage costs (external costs) which we assume have been quantified at Ex per unit of output. Thus the true marginal social costs of production (MSC) lie above the MPC schedule. Production in the mill ought to be contracted to a level OX_1 where marginal social costs are equal to price (marginal social value). Our example has concentrated on two types of cost externality: (a) production on production effects, where a downstream plant's production was affected by the upstream mill's discharge of residuals; (b) production on consumption effects, where downstream recreationists were affected by the upstream discharge of mill effluent. Two other cost externality types can be identified, consumption on consumption effects and consumption on production effects.[22] We should also not forget that externality effects can be beneficial,[23] for example, in certain circumstances thermal discharges to watercourses can provide more favourable conditions for fish.

Informational Deficiencies and the "Economic" Optimum Level of Pollution

The discharge of a wide range of production residuals in industrialised economies has created a number of different forms of environmental pollution and associated damage costs. Human health, property, aesthetic and recreational services, and agricultural and industrial output have all been damaged in certain circumstances over time. The conventional economic approach to the problem of pollution seeks to define and estimate the negative aspects of the problem (pollution damage costs) and compare them with the positive aspects (the benefits of a cleaner environment). At the individual firm level it seems possible, in principle, to estimate the cost of measures for controlling residuals discharge and hence pollution, e.g. in-plant recycling systems, filters in chimney stacks to reduce air pollution, etc. These costs are defined as abatement or pollution-control costs and can be compared with the damage costs being inflicted by the residuals discharge in the absence of abatement (see Figure 2.7).

Total pollution-damage costs (TDC) increase progressively after an amount of pollution OP has been attained and the assimilative capacity of the environmental media concerned has been breached. Note again, however, that this level OP ($>$zero pollution) is defined in economic terms with regard to human preferences and perceptions of pollution damage. In Section 5 we will look at some criticisms of this "homogeneous pollution" model which question the model's static nature and point out the need to include dynamic ecological stability constraints, particularly if stock pollutants are present.[24] Total abatement costs (TAC) increase progressively as the required reduction in pollution increases; what empirical evidence has been collected seems to support this general argument.[25] Figure 2.8 illustrates selected abatement function drawn up in the GDR for various industries. In a survey

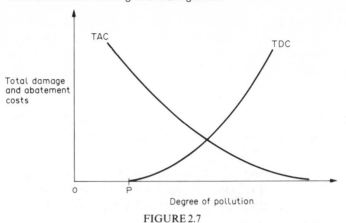

FIGURE 2.7

Total pollution damage and abatement cost curves.

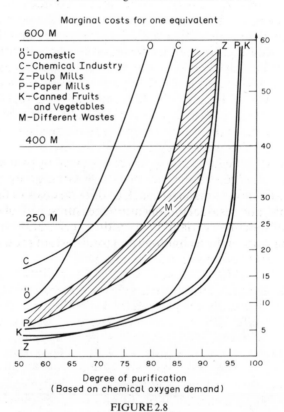

FIGURE 2.8

Selected marginal costs of abatement curves.

* Reproduced from Rinke, G. (1978) The German Federal Law on Wastewater Charges, in *Progress in Water Technology*, Vol. 10 (3/4), p. 99.

of water-pollution-abatement costs Hanke and Gutmanis[26] argue that the proper conceptual framework for studying residuals management, when there are no legal constraints on pollution discharge, can be expressed in the following terms:

$$R_{git} = f(RM, PP, PO),$$

where R_{git} = quantity of residual, i, generated, g, per unit time, t;

   RM = type of, and hence characteristics of, raw material inputs;

   PP = technology of production process, including technology of materials and energy recovery and technology of by-product production; and

   PO = product output specification.

The actual discharge of residuals into the environmental media will be a function of the variables identified above plus the pollution-control strategy actually being implemented by government and the currently available technological options for residuals modification. Such a modelling approach does, however, require an enormous amount of detailed data and while the approach has been used to some extent in studies in the USA[27] (though even here simulation has replaced unavailable empirical data at various points in the studies) empirical pollution-abatement studies in the UK and elsewhere have been limited in number and in scope.[28] Hanke and Gutmanis[29] themselves stress that their recommended modelling approach is constrained by problems of "lack of data on residual generation; lack of data describing the physical transformation and flow of materials; lack of data on costs of factor inputs, process units, and residual modification measures; lack of cost data on the effects of short-run variability in residuals generation; and difficulty in obtaining data on the technology and total costs of producing a given product without pollution control regulations".

The objective of the "economic" approach to pollution and pollution control is to determine an optimum weighting of abatement and damage costs (and consequently an optimum level of pollution). At the optimum position the total combined costs of pollution (abatement plus damage costs) will be minimised.[30] The total cost schedule is minimised at the point where the marginal damage costs (MDC) are equal to the marginal abatement costs (MAC) per unit of pollution (see Figure 2.9). In the figure the non-zero economic optimum level of pollution is P*.

Putting on one side the difficulties of empirically estimating pollution-abatement costs in various industries and the limitations of this static homogeneous pollution model in the face of dynamic ecological changes, there are still further constraints on the usefulness of this approach. The model implies a one-to-one correspondence between

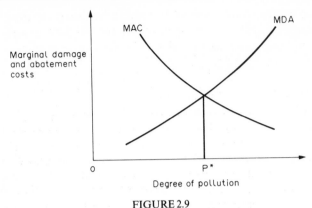

FIGURE 2.9

The economic optimum level of pollution

residuals discharge and environmental damage. This is in fact a gross simplification as the damage costs eventually suffered will be dependent on a range of variables including: the types of pollutants involved and possible synergistic effects; the timing of discharges; the spatial location of discharges and the influence of a number of random climatic variables. Baumol and Oates[31] recognise that damage functions are multivariate relationships, functions of a vector of variables, and stress that many of the variables are outside the control of the policymaker.

The simplified flow diagram (Figure 2.10) illustrates the conceptual stages necessary to translate discharges of residuals into the economist's monetary estimates of the damage involved. Scientists have modelled the process by which various pollutants are dispersed, absorbed, degraded and combined with other chemicals. The end result, the concentration of pollutants at various places and times, determines the so-called ambient environmental quality. While knowledge of transfer functions is being progressively increased it seems fair to conclude that a great deal remains to be discovered about the effects of a large number of pollutants and in particular the synergistic effects of a combination of

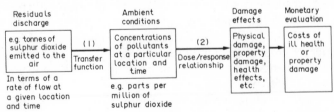

FIGURE 2.10

The procedure for the monetary evaluation of pollution damage costs. (*Source*: adapted from Fisher and Peterson (1967).)

pollutants in any given location.[32] The establishment of dose–response relationships for different pollutants presents an even more formidable problem and the currently available information is correspondingly less than that accumulated about transfer functions. Concentrating for a moment on water-pollution damage costs[33] we find that quantification is complex because of the multidimensional nature of water usages, qualities and receptors. The different water uses and benefit or cost recipients may compete with, or complement, one another. Moreover, each recipient may well be uniquely sensitive to different components of water quality. The US National Commission on Water Quality used five variables: dissolved oxygen (DO) and DO depletion; nutrients (nitrate and phosphorus); turbidity and suspended solids; total dissolved solids; and coliform bacteria; in its assessment of water quality. This list, however, is not fully comprehensive and was drawn up on the basis of current data availability. It seems to be generally agreed, given limited empirical evidence, that recreation and aesthetic damages are largest when water-quality levels fall. Nevertheless other damage costs — domestic water supply damages, irrigation water and industrial intake water damages and commercial fishing losses — are often significant.

We will consider the final step in Figure 2.10, the monetary valuation of the damage function, in the next section when the technique of cost benefit analysis (CBA) will be examined in detail. Where market prices are available fairly reasonable estimates are possible for the value of the social costs of pollution but imputing shadow or surrogate prices, in the absence of markets for the environmental resources concerned, is currently a very imperfect art.

Central Planning and the Environment

In the previous sections we have surveyed some of the reasons for the market system's failure adequately to safeguard our environmental resources. We should be careful, however, not to give the impression that only decentralised, deconcentrated "private enterprise" economic systems suffer from environmental disruption. Goldman[34] has argued that the Soviet economy has environmental problems as extensive and severe as any found in the Western economies; though some writers,[35] while not questioning Goldman's main thesis, have argued that he perhaps over-states some of the specific pollution problems created in the USSR, for example, the pollution threat to Lake Baikal.

In principle, in a centralised system where the centre's (planners') preferences are dominant it should be easier to enact or to implement antipollution legislation. The Soviet Union has indeed passed a series of environmentally-related laws in the 1950s and 1960s. But as Goldman,[36] Bush[37] and Shever Taga[38] have pointed out the ideology and formal legislation have to a significant extent been offset by other built-in economic, political and technical forces present in the Soviet economic system. Ideologically, all resources in the socialist economy belong to the state as a whole and there has therefore been a tendency, by state enterprises in the USSR, to regard such resources as "free" goods. The continued absence of a charge (price), or inadequate charges (prices that fail to reflect scarcity values), for natural resources has led the Soviet economy to over-deplete resource stocks and to waste resources. The protection of the environment itself has, these writers argue, been accorded a fairly low rank on the centre's scale of priority goals. The maximisation of economic growth has historically always been the dominant goal of the leadership. Because of this dominant objective the centre engaged in what has been labelled the practice of "taut" planning. The economy would be deliberately pressurised by the central planning agency setting and striving for very ambitious yearly output plan targets. To try and ensure the fulfilment of plans a complex system of performance criteria or "success indicators" for production enterprises was developed. The prime criterion and the main yardstick for awarding plant manager bonuses was the fulfilment or overfulfilment of the gross output plan. Pollution-abatement measures or resource-conservation practices if they conflicted with plan output fulfilment would be neglected or ignored completely at the enterprise level.

McIntyre and Thornton,[39] however, argue that the observation that the Soviet Union suffers from some serious environmental problems should not lead one to the, as yet unsubstantiated, conclusion that a socialist economic system is as operationally unable to deal with environmental externalities as a capitalist system. The writers make the point that it is important to distinguish between the actual amount of environmental pollution produced by an economic system and the theoretical environmental efficiency of an economic system. Evidence of the former does not necessarily prove that both capitalist and socialist economic systems are likely to be uniformly susceptible to pollution even if the USA and the USSR can be taken as archetypal representatives of capitalism and socialism, which is itself a gross simplification of reality. As far as air pollution is concerned McIntyre and Thornton[40] put forward a number of reasons why the USSR is likely to suffer from more severe problems. They argue that at "any given level of national commitment to air purity, the colder climate, dirtier fuels, and more frequent inversions require the Soviet Union to allocate more resources than the US to the reduction of emitted pollutants". They also point to the differences in the sectoral composition of GNP in the USSR and the USA and the Soviet practice of locating important centres of industrial production within major cities. But, overall, the lower level of *per capita* GNP itself (and they argue consequently lower levels of environmental disruption) and the fact that lower *per capita* GNP raises the opportunity cost of reducing pollution damage further, tend to offset the disadvantageous factors cited above. On the basis of what limited empirical evidence there is available the McIntyre and Thornton analysis tentatively concludes that "the extent, coherence, and apparent seriousness of Soviet air quality efforts, especially in the major population centres, are surprising and suggest either a relatively high degree of environmental efficiency for Soviet-type economic systems, as the economic theory of socialism would predict, or a particular emphasis on pollution avoidance in the 'planners' or political leaders' preference functions". Clearly, much detailed research on a number of fronts remains to be done before any firm conclusions can be drawn either on the general question of which if any economic system is more environmentally efficient or on the comparative magnitude of environmental disruption in socialist economic systems.

Notes and References

1. See Fisher, A. C. and Peterson, F. M. (1976) The Environment in Economics: A Survey, *Journal of Economic Literature*, vol. 14 (1).
2. Ehrlich, P. R., Ehrlich, A. H. and Holdren, J. P. (1977) *Ecoscience: Population, Resources, Environment*, W. H. Freeman.
3. See, for example, Edel, M. (1973) *Economics and the Environment*, Prentice Hall;
   Pearce, D. W. (1976) *Environmental Economics*, Longmans;
   Victor, P. A. (1972) *Pollution: Economy and Environment*, George Allen & Unwin;
   and Kneese, A. V. (1977) *Economics and the Environment*, Penguin.
4. James, D. E., Jansen, H. M. A. and Opschoor, J. B. (1978) *Economic Approaches to Environmental Problems*, Elsevier Scientific Publishing.
5. See Pearce, D. W. and Walter, I. (Eds.) (1977) *Resource Conservation: The Social and Economic Dimensions of Recycling*, New York University Press and Longmans.
6. Meadows, D. H., Meadows, D. L. *et. al.* (1972) *The Limits To Growth*, Earth Island.
7. See, for example, Nordhaus, W. D. (1973) World Dynamics – Measurement Without Data, *Economic Journal*, vol. 83 (332);
   Solow, R. M. (1974) The Economics of Resources or the Resource of Economics, *American Economic Review*, vol. 64 (2);
   and Cole, H. S. D. *et al.* (1973) *Thinking About the Future: A Critique of "The Limits to Growth"*, Chatto & Windus.
8. Barkely, P. W. and Seckler, D. W. (1972) *Economic Growth and Environmental Decay*, Harcourt Brace Jovanovich.
9. See Turner, R. K. and Collis, C. (1977) *The Economics of Planning*, Macmillan.
10. See, for example, Dorfman, R. (1978) *Prices and Markets*, Prentice Hall; or McCormick, B. J. *et al.* (1976) *Introducing Economics*, Penguin; or Lancaster, K. (1974) *Introduction to Modern Microeconomics*, Rand McNally.
11. See Dorfman, R. (1978), Lancaster, K. (1974) or McCormick, B. J. (1976) *op. cit.*
12. For a more comprehensive treatment of these efficiency conditions see Bohm, P. (1974) *Social Efficiency: A Concise Introduction to Welfare Economics*, Macmillan;
    and Seneca, J. J. and Taussig, M. K. (1974) *Environmental Economics*, Prentice Hall.
13. Nath, S. K. (1973) A Perspective of Welfare Economics, Macmillan.
14. Turner, R. K. and Collis, S. (1977) *op. cit.*
15. Dalton, G. (1974) *Economic Systems and Society*, Penguin.
16. Eidem, R. and Viotti, S. (1978) *Economic Systems: How Resources Are Allocated*, Martin Robertson.

17. Hardin, G. (1968) The Tragedy of the Commons, *Science*, vol. 162.
18. Musgrave, R. A. (1974) On Social Goods and Social Bads, in Marris, R. (ed.) *The Corporate Society*, Macmillan.
19. See Musgrave, R. A. (1959) *The Theory of Public Finance*, McGraw Hill.
20. Dorfman, R. and Dorfman, N. (1977) *Economics of the Environment: Selected Readings*, Norton.
21. Nath, S. K. (1973) *op. cit.*
22. See Nath, S. K. (1973) *op. cit.*
23. For a survey of the externality concept see Lancaster, K. L. and Dulaney, R. A. (1979) *Modern Economics: Principles and Policy*, Rand McNally;
    Mishan, E. J. (1971) The Postwar Literature on Externalities; An Interpretative Essay, *Journal of Economic Literature*, vol. 9 (1); and Freeman, A. M., Haveman, R. H. and Kneese, A. V. (1973) *The Economics of Environmental Policy*, Wiley.
24. See James, D. E. *et al.* (1978) *op. cit.*
25. Hanke, S. H. and Gutmanis, I. (1975) Estimates of Industrial Waterborne Residuals Control Costs: A Review of Concepts, Methodology and Empirical Evidence, in Peskin, H. M. and Seskin, E. P. (eds.) *Cost Benefit Analysis and Water Pollution Policy*, The Urban Institute.
26. Hanke, S. H. and Gutmanis, I. (1975) *op. cit.*
27. See, for example, Russell, C. S. (1973) *Residuals Management In Industry: A Case Study of Petroleum Refining*, Johns Hopkins Press; and Russell, C. S. and Vaughan, W. J. (1976) *Steel Production: Processes, Products and Residuals*, Johns Hopkins University Press; and Bower, B. T. (1975), Studies in Residuals Management in Industry, in Mills, E. S. (ed.) *Economic Analysis of Environmental Problems*, Columbia University Press.
28. For some pioneering attempts in the UK see Atkins, M. H. and Lowe, J. F. (1977) *Pollution Control Costs in Industry – An Economic Study*, Pergamon Press; Atkins, M. H. and Lowe, J. F. (1978) *The Economics of Pollution Control in Non-Ferrous Metallurgy*, Pergamon Press; and Atkins, M. H. and Lowe, J. F. (1979) *Case Studies in Pollution Control Measures in the Textile Dyeing and Finishing Industries*, Pergamon Press.
29. Hanke, S. H. and Gutmanis, I. (1975) *op. cit.*
30. See Freeman, A. M. *et al.* (1973) *op. cit.* and Pearce, D. W. (1976) *op. cit.*
31. Baumol, W. and Oates, W. (1975) The Instruments for Environmental Policy, in Mills, E. S. (ed.) *Economic Analysis of Environmental Problems*, Columbia University Press.
32. See Peskin, H. M. and Seskin, E. P. (eds.) (1975) *op. cit.*
33. See Pearce, D. W. (1978) *The Valuation of Social Cost*, George Allen & Unwin.
34. Goldman, M. I. (1972) *The Spoils of Progress: Environmental Pollution in the Soviet Union*, MIT Press.
35. See the contributions in Volgyes, I. (ed.) (1974) *Environmental Deterioration in the Soviet Union and Eastern Europe*, Praeger.
36. Goldman, M. I. (1972) *op. cit.*
37. Bush, K. (1974) The Soviet Response to Environmental Disruption, in Volgyes, I. (ed.) *Environmental Deterioration in the Soviet Union and Eastern Europe*, Praeger.
38. Shever Taga, L. (1976) Externalities in a Command Economy, in Singleton, F. (ed.) *Environmental Misuse in the Soviet Union*, Praeger.
39. McIntyre, R. J. and Thornton, J. R. (1974) Environmental Divergence: Air Pollution in the USSR, *Journal of Environmental Economics and Management*, vol. 1 (2).
40. McIntyre, R. J. and Thornton, J. R. (1974) *op. cit.*

SECTION 3

Traditional Cost–Benefit Analysis and its Critique

INTRODUCTORY ESSAY

The formal CBA technique

CBA can be defined as a formal procedure for resource allocation in which all the relevant costs and benefits of a public investment decision or course of action are analysed. In practice the technique has been used to enumerate and evaluate a wide range of projects such as river-management schemes, motorway and airport construction, health and education services and many others. Prest and Turvey[1] have defined CBA as "a practical way of assessing the desirability of projects, where it is important to take a long view (in the sense of looking at repercussions in the further as well as the nearer future) and a wide view (in the sense of allowing for side effects of many kinds on many persons, industries, regions, etc.), i.e. it implies the enumeration and evaluation of all the relevant costs and benefits".

Freeman[2] notes that a single government expenditure objective, the improvement of human welfare, would probably be dominant in an open and rational democratic society. However, since we have no direct measure of welfare this ultimate goal can give little practical guidance to policymakers. Steiner[3] argues that policymakers have multiple planning objectives and individual projects are bound to affect more than one dimension and the objectives themselves will often conflict. The central problems of multiple objective planning became how to define an appropriate measure for each objective and how to resolve the problem of conflicting objectives. In formal CBA desirability is, however, based on the cost benefit (economic efficiency) criterion. A given project or course of action should be undertaken when the additional benefits to be derived from the action or project exceed the corresponding additional costs. If the criterion is met then the action or project has contributed to an increase in the economic efficiency of the system. An improvement in efficiency is attainable if it is possible to increase the value of the economic system's output for any given amount of resource input (i.e. a net increase in national income).

It is recognised that policymakers can and do evaluate actions and projects in terms of other criteria apart from efficiency, e.g. distributional equity, political feasibility, environmental quality or national security. However, these other objectives are ignored or given only secondary attention in formal CBA depending on how strictly the analyst adheres to neoclassical economic principles.[4] Formal CBA attempts to mimic the decisions that a perfectly competitive (Pareto efficient) market mechanism would have arrived at and apply them in the public sector. According to the Pareto definition of efficiency, a change in the state of affairs (due to some policy or project) increases the common good (i.e. is welfare increasing) if the change permits improving the position of someone without hurting that of someone else. But a Pareto optimum is the highest welfare position for the society only in relation to the given distribution of income and resources. It is neutral in terms of the "justice" or "fairness" of the distribution of income and resources and provides no help to a policymaker who has to choose between two courses of action, both of which are Pareto efficient but which involve different distributions of costs and benefits. Further this efficiency criterion is highly restrictive because real projects and courses of action nearly always involve losses to some individuals and benefits to others and thus do not fit the Pareto rule. A more general criterion, the Hicks–Kaldor compensation criterion (termed a "potential Pareto improvement criterion" by Mishan[5]) was developed in order to try and overcome the disadvantages of the Pareto rule.

Collard,[6] in principle, divides the basic procedure of CBA into five steps:

1. Draw up a list of alternative projects.
2. List all the social (private + external) costs and benefits associated with each project.
3. Quantify, in technical terms, the costs and benefits associated with each project; for example, in the case of a project to increase water quality in a river, benefits may accrue in terms of increased fish yields from sport or commercial fisheries, increased recreational opportunities or aesthetic pleasures and reduced costs for industrial intake water users.
4. Calculate a money valuation of the costs and benefits — individual benefits will usually have their values reflected in market prices but collective benefits derived from quasi-public goods such as the aesthetic enjoyment of an unpolluted watercourse which are not marketed will have no market prices and shadow prices will need to be imputed; project costs refer to the value foregone

(opportunity costs) by using a resource in one activity (the project) rather than in its next best alternative use.

5. Submit the final valuations.

If the costs and benefits of a particular project are measured respectively in terms of compensation for foregone benefits (opportunity costs) and willingness to pay, the Hicks–Kaldor compensation principle lays down that any project which yields sufficient benefits to some individuals (in terms of willingness to pay) such that these gainers could *hypothetically* compensate the losers from the project and still remain better off themselves is desirable in efficiency terms. It is still possible, however, that due to the effects (cost and benefits) of a project or course of action the poor sections of a community can be made relatively poorer and the rich relatively richer for the compensation criterion does not seek to incorporate distributional impacts. Where the analyst is faced with the problems of choosing a few projects from a large number of independent projects, and capital expenditure is constrained, the CBA ultimately reduces to a ratio in which the numerator expresses the so-called total present value of all discounted benefits (ΣDB) (these terms will be defined more fully below) and the denominator measures the total present value of all discounted costs (ΣDC). If the ratio turns out to be

$$\frac{\Sigma\,DB}{\Sigma\,DC} > 1$$

the project passes the efficiency test in that it has the potential to make a net contribution to society's economic welfare (ΣDB$\rangle$$\Sigma$DC). The projects can then be ranked according to their cost–benefit ratios and the capital constraint applied to find a "cut-off" point. The analysis becomes more complicated if the projects to be considered are interdependent. If the analyst is faced with the choice of a few interdependent projects from many candidates under a capital expenditure constraint then the correct procedure, in efficiency terms, would be to determine the economically feasible set of projects and apply a maximum net present value criterion (NPV).[7]

Present value and the discounting technique

Many public sector projects are designed to operate over a long period of time (dams, airports, roads, etc.) and therefore they will yield costs and benefits streams over a number of years. Often the costs of major projects are distributed over time such that after initially large construction costs are incurred relatively low annual recurring maintenance costs are generated and stretch out over the rest of the project life. Benefits, on the other hand, tend to be distributed more evenly. For the policymaker the problem is that he requires information now (in the current time period) about what the future stream of costs and benefits mean in terms of value today in order to make a rational decision. This is the discounting technique that CB analysts utilise in order to calculate the present-day values of future benefits and costs. The discounting procedure is based on the assumption that people in general exhibit *positive rates of time preference*, i.e. they prefer to receive a given sum of money sooner rather than later. Thus the pound one expects to receive in the future is less valuable than a pound one receives today. The discount rate measures how much less valuable the future pound is and will give less and less weight to returns the further into the future they are expected to be realised. Now we know that a sum of money invested today in, for example, a bank deposit account or in a building society will be worth more in a year's time; exactly how much more is dependent on the rate of interest being offered by the bank or society. Reversing the logic of this example, if the rate of interest (i) is given, we can compute the present value of a known future return (benefit) by calculating the sum of money required to be lent out now (with the given interest rate (i)) in order to generate the future sum at a known date. Thus in general the present value (PV) of future dated benefits (B_t) is calculated in the following way:

$$PV = \frac{B_t}{(1 + i)^t}.$$

The present value of a series of benefits (PVB) accruing over a number of years is calculated by the formula:

$$PVB = \sum_{t=1}^{T} \frac{B_t}{(1 + i)^t}$$

where total project lifetime $= T$ years.

On the costs side, project construction costs (Co) are all incurred in the current time period and are therefore not discounted but the recurring maintenance costs (RC_t) do need to be discounted. The present value cost (PVC) formula takes the following general form:

$$PVC = Co + \sum_{t=1}^{T} \frac{RC_t}{(1 + i)^t}.$$

The full CB ratio can now be computed.[8]

$$\frac{PVB}{PVC} = \frac{\sum_{t=1}^{T} \frac{B_t}{(1 + i)^t}}{Co + \sum_{t=1}^{T} \frac{RC_t}{(1 + i)^t}}.$$

Turning now to the choice problem involving the selection of a few interdependent projects from a number of alternatives the analyst needs to apply the net present value (NPV) criterion. The NPV formula takes the following form:

$$NPV = \frac{B_0 - C_0}{(1 + i)^0} + \frac{B_1 - C_1}{(1 + i)^1} + \ldots + \frac{B_n - C_n}{(1 + i)^n}.$$

The combination of economically feasible projects with the greatest NPV should then be selected for implementation.

The choice of a discount rate

The computed cost–benefit result is very sensitive to the choice of interest rate used to discount the costs and benefits stream and therefore the choice of the appropriate social discount rate is very important. There is considerable disagreement among economists over the proper derivation of a social discount rate (SDR). Pearce[9] identifies three schools of thought. *The Social Time Preference Rate School* basically argues that present society has a collective responsibility for future generations and that the positive time preferences of individuals of the current generation should not dominate the selection of the social discount rate. The government, on behalf of society, should select the appropriate rate which will presumably be less than the rate indicated by individual time preferences. Because the present value of a given stream of future costs and benefits is less the greater the rate of discount projects (especially long-life projects) will, in general, look more favourable at the lower rate of discount. *The Social Opportunity Cost Rate School* suggests that the SDR for use in public projects ought to reflect the fact that private markets represent an alternative use of resources required by the public projects. Therefore, the return that resources could accumulate in private investment projects is the social opportunity cost (the rate of return foregone) of utilising resources for public projects. The private rate of return must then be the true opportunity cost of public investment and therefore the appropriate SDR. Finally it is argued that some *synthetic* SDR would combine influences from both the previous schools of thought. Nevertheless, all three lines of thought face difficulties when it comes to the actual choice of a specific rate. In practice in the UK public sector discount rates are determined by the government and at least partly reflect the relative scarcity of central government funds. Since 1967 this so-called test rate of discount has been 8 percent, 10 percent and now 5 percent. Hanke and Walker[10] provide an interesting example, the Nebraska Mid-State Irrigation Project, of how sensitive the ultimate cost–benefit ratio is to different discount rates suggesting the use of sensitivity analysis. Other economists have suggested the use of multiple discount rates in the context of multiple objective planning.

The Limitations of Formal CBA

Despite an earlier intellectual heritage the widespread application of CBA is usually dated from the implementation of the US water-project-planning programmes in the 1930s. Over the years, with increasing government involvement in the "mixed" economies of Europe and North America among others, CBA has been applied to an ever wider spectrum of projects. In its early applications the technique was used to evaluate projects which basically produced intermediate outputs—the classic examples being irrigation projects designed to stimulate farm productivity. The essential point to note is that such projects yielded outputs which were generally amenable to evaluation via market prices. As the project spectrum has widened to cover the fields of education, transport, health, recreation and other environmental services provision, however, CBA has increasingly appeared to many critics to be less useful than at first thought. For some critics the technique's early promise has flattered only to deceive in the face of projects, for example, producing outputs of an intangible or regionally localised nature. Difficult problems of evaluation in the absence of adequate market prices (shadow pricing) and of distributional equity have been recognised and have served to increase the growing doubts voiced by some commentators concerning the precise value of CBA as a decision-making tool.[11] Herfindahl and Kneese[12] note that governments have increasingly sought evaluation of projects involving small initial investments but requiring operation, maintenance and replacement cost streams stretching out into the distant future; while other projects have required "implicit" rather than direct investment. Thus the preservation of the UK's Vale of Belvoir or a North American "wilderness area" in their "natural" states involves the loss of the explicit benefit streams that would be produced by mining or forestry operations. On the other hand, such projects if given the go ahead would in many cases involve *irreversible* effects and the possible consequent foreclosing of options, not to mention the thorny problems of *intergenerational equity* and decision-making with *uncertain* costs and benefits.[13]

Over time the projects that CBA could have been confronted with have been increasing both in size and complexity. Rational decisions have been required, for example, with regard to nuclear power-generation programmes and waste recycling plants; large resource extraction programmes such as the proposed Vale of Belvoir and Selby Coalfield developments; North Sea oil-developments and flood-protection schemes such as the Thames Barrage and the proposed Yare barrier in Norfolk. Inevitably such schemes produce complex environmental and distributional effects (both intragenerational and intergenerational), and a number stimulate difficult "social disruption" effects because of their rural location and consequent disruption to small, often fragile local economies and communities.[14] A growing general awareness of the need for some measure of environmental protection and consideration of environmental values has led to the construction of so-called environmental impact assessments (EIAs) at some stage in the planning process for a number of projects in the USA and a call for similar, though not identical, analysis to be implemented in the UK.* Section 4 in this volume covers the EIA technique and the general field of environmental planning.

Distributional Equity as an Underlying Principle of CBA

The terms benefits and costs can only be defined precisely with reference to a particular decision criterion and underlying objective. Nash *et al.*[15] argue further that any decision criterion must reflect some set of value judgements which determine what effects should be regarded as benefits and costs; so that there can be no uniquely "proper" way to do CBA. As we have seen formal CBA is based on an economic efficiency criterion. Mishan[16] has argued that cost–benefit analysts should confine themselves to procedures that do in fact produce a potential Pareto improvement in welfare. Both the Pareto criterion and the compensation criterion entail the acceptance of the value judgements that individual preferences should count and that these preferences are weighted by market power. Hypothetical compensation could well involve inequitable redistributions of income in society. Little[17] reformulated the basic compensation principle suggesting that a project be accepted if the sum of its discounted net benefits is positive and if it does not cause a deterioration in the prevailing distribution of income. This statement, however, only serves to highlight the practical operational problems of how a distributional weighting system for costs and benefits is to be constructed and trade-off ratios between efficiency and equity established.

Some analysts seem to argue that the economist's role should be to advise government on efficiency matters alone and to let the government decide, through direct instruments the question of distributional equity.[18] Steiner[19] is doubtful, however, about complete reliance on direct methods to correct for overall maldistributions of income. He argues that social change is such that this would in practice overweight the current distribution of income and would constrain any redistribution. A number of approaches seeking to integrate efficiency and equity effects can be identified in the economics literature. One such approach involves the application of weights to different arguments in

---

* Some would like to see EIA supersede CBA as the principal advisory tool for decision makers but there are many reasons why the two techniques should be regarded as complementary. For an introductory survey see Turner, R. K. and O'Riordan, T. (1982) Project Evaluation, in Haynes, R. (ed.) *Environmental and Science Methods*, Chapman and Hall, pp. 372–398.

the objective function in order to derive a single-valued measure of benefits. Within this general approach there are two viewpoints concerning the weighting procedure. One view seeks to establish weights prior to the taking of any decisions either by direct consultation with decisionmakers or by detailed analysis of previous government decisions on resource allocation and taxation.[20] Other researchers take the view that weights can only be established by an iterative political decision making process working on a case by case basis.[21] Reliance is therefore placed on the choices actually made by policymakers. Discovering what any government's preferences really are is a formidable task and none of the suggested weighting systems is without limitations. Nash *et al.*[22] conclude that advocates of what they term this "Management Science" approach will need to use sensitivity analysis. A series of welfare-weighted calculations using alternative weighting functions should be presented to the policymaker.

An alternative approach to the problem of objective integration rejects the notion of a single-valued measure of benefits because of the severe difficulties of ensuring that a range of public policy objectives can be made commensurable. Steiner[23] believes that the single number measure of benefits approach in practice submerges real issues behind a facade of faulty measurements. Williams[24] also sees little scope for systematic incorporation of redistributive effects in CBA but stresses the need for incidence effects to be included as separate exhibits in the analysis presentation. Lichfield[25] too stresses the importance of presenting CBA in a disaggregated fashion. The final judgement on conflicting objectives is left to the policymaker and no attempt is made to articulate how this judgement should be made. Other economists[26] appear to support much of Steiner's argument but see the calculation of distributional effects as essentially supplementary to the dominant efficiency calculations.

The Valuation of Costs and Benefits

Physical (technical) quantification of the impacts of alternative projects alone, although providing important and necessary information, often presents the policymaker with a difficult choice if the projects concerned generate different types of effects, e.g. one project may stimulate agricultural productivity while another increases recreational possibilities. Pearce[27] argues that without *monetary measurement* the policymaker will have little idea of how much of a good to provide or how much of a bad to remove. However, if it is possible to measure all project effects in a common unit, money, then we can adopt the simple cost–benefit rule of maximising net benefits. A number of benefits and costs are amenable to monetary evaluation. Maler and Wyzga[28] divide aggregate project or policy effects in financial effects and amenity effects; the former can generally be expressed in monetary terms while the latter, with the possible exception of recreational benefits and losses, present difficult evaluation problems because of their intangible nature.

The more tangible benefits and costs such as, for example, the increased agricultural output stimulated by an irrigation project, the reduced and measurable capital asset and resource damages afforded by a flood-control project, or the remedial health care costs induced by a power-plant project which increases air-pollution damages often share the common characteristics of being intermediate goods and/or private goods which allows the market process to value them fairly efficiently. Market price is, however, only a *minimum* measure of value if, say, the social (private plus external) benefits of a particular project are very large. Thus, for example, if the increased output stimulated by a large irrigation project proved to be a non-marginal impact on the existing market for the good then the market price itself would change (fall). This situation can be analysed theoretically in terms of the so-called *consumers' surplus* concept. This concept refers to the difference between what all purchasers would be willing to pay for a particular quantity of the good rather than go without it and the amount they actually have to pay on the market (market price). In terms of Figure 3.1 let ST represent

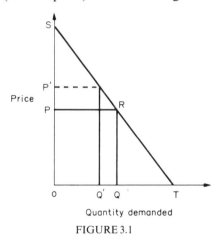

Quantity demanded

FIGURE 3.1

The consumers' surplus measure.

the market demand curve for the good concerned (technically this should be an income-compensated demand curve, see Mishan[29]) and OP represent the market price. Now if the amount of the good offered for sale fell to OQ, then some people would be willing to pay a price OP' rather than do without the good. In fact they only pay OP and gain a bonus (consumer surplus). Total consumer surplus would be represented by the triangle PRS. If the irrigation project increases farm output such that the market price for the good falls the gross benefits are the amount paid for the new production (at the new market price) plus the increase in consumer surplus for new and existing consumers. Market prices will also not yield an accurate reflection of willingness to pay in situations where prices are controlled or goods rationed; or where goods are subject to subsidy or are sold on the international market.

The value of the total social (private plus external) costs of a project is taken to be the minimum amount required by the affected parties (households and producer firms) to compensate them for the imposition of the cost. In general, external costs imposed on households are more difficult to estimate than those experienced by producers. It is usually assumed in project-appraisal studies and the academic economics literature that household-compensation values for assets in current use will only differ significantly from willingness to pay values if the external cost involved is a large fraction of the household's income, and that therefore willingness to pay values represents suitable approximations. If the external costs represent major losses (significant wealth (income) effects) then compensation values may be estimated—we examine estimation techniques that have been developed so far below. Gordon and Knetsch,[30] however, point out that currently available observations of individual willingness to maintain rights or access to a resource, facility or asset, and of the compensation value for denial, are probably not quantitatively or qualitatively satisfactory. But the available evidence, such as it is, suggests large differences in the two measures of value, too large possibly to be accounted for just in terms of income effects.

Secondary Benefits

Projects often produce so-called *secondary benefits*. These usually involve changes in some people's wellbeing at the expense of other individuals' welfare. In other words, they are redistributive effects rather than efficiency increasing effects. If the strict efficiency approach to CBA is adhered to such secondary benefits—e.g. if because of a particular project the water quality of a stretch of river was significantly improved and sport fishing activities increased dramatically the profits accruing to local fishing equipment shops might well be increased as might extra tourist facilities in the local area—should not be included in the CBA unless the economy is suffering from less than full employment conditions. Under conditions of less than full employment the extra tourist traffic and sales revenue in the local area would create new employment for previously unemployed resources and would thus contribute to the overall efficiency of the economy.

We noted earlier that CBA has been applied to an ever wider range of projects and that both the scale and complexity of many of these projects have increased dramatically. Complex problems have therefore been set for the analyst attempting to attach money prices to costs and benefits in order to reflect society's valuations of the goods and resources involved. Despite the optimism of some economists the practical difficulties presented by many environmental costs and benefits are immense and the current state of the art cannot be said to represent anything like an adequate solution to the social cost–benefit valuation problem.[31] McKean[32] is not optimistic that shadow prices will ever be accurately constructed for a range of intangible effects and stresses the high informational costs involved in even a small increase in accuracy. Williams[33] shares in this fairly pessimistic view but is prepared to accept that there is a role in CBA for the "postulated" price. He defends its use on the grounds that it at least provides a focus for discussion by others who might disagree with the policymaker's judgement.

A number of ingenious valuation techniques have been developed in order to produce proxy or surrogate values for the unknown true shadow prices. These proxy values, however, can at best be regarded only as lower limits to the "true" values of various environmental costs and benefits. The techniques themselves include survey or questionnaire methods to gauge willingness to pay or compensation. There are two basic obstacles to the successful implementation of such methods: the problem of interviewee perception (individuals often find it difficult to perceive the personal implications of hypothetical changes in environmental quality); and the problem of incentive and response distortion where individuals may not reveal their true preferences if, for instance, the question of taxation is involved. Other techniques operate on the principle that it may be possible to deduce surrogate monetary amenity losses or benefits from observation of consumer behaviour.* Thus the Clawson–Knetsch method attempts to estimate recreational benefits through observation of recreationists and the amount of money they are willing to spend on travel costs to a site.[34] This method has been heavily criticised over the years in the literature.[35] Methods utilising the so-called "hedonic" pricing approach assume that changes in and patterns of property and land values will reflect external amenity or disamenity again allowing a proxy measure of the shadow price to be derived. Studies using this approach have also been severely criticised.[36]

Bradford and Feiveson[37] argue that the inability of analysts to construct monetary surrogates for important intangible values has had little perceptible effect on the degree to which they will be regarded or disregarded by policymakers. The authors are generalising on US

* Opinions differ over the magnitude and significance of the potential sources of bias in actual valuation studies but Schulze, W. D. *et al.* (1981) Valuing Environmental Commodities: Some Recent Experiments, *Land Economics*, vol. 57, concluded that biases do not appear to be an overriding problem. Bishop, R. C. and Heberlein, T. A. (1979) Measuring Values of Extra Market Goods: Are Indirect Measures Biased?, *American Journal of Agricultural Economics*, vol. 61, however, came to much more pessimistic conclusions.

experience and they do insert the caveat that often efforts were made to inform the policymakers about the intangible effects by detailed presentations of physical data. Other factors which will also determine whether intangible factors get incorporated into the decision making process will include the political importance of the issues, the degree to which certain values have general rather than minority support and the preferences and values of the policymakers themselves. Clearly it is difficult to generalise internationally but it is not difficult to think of British cases where intangible effects have appeared to get very little consideration.

We will now examine briefly one illustrative example, that will be analysed further in the following section, namely the proposed Yare barrier flood-protection scheme in Norfolk.* The official CBA report[38] had in its terms of reference "the need for the preservation of the existing character of Broadland and the conservation of the area's unique ecological habitats". Despite this the report devotes just a couple of pages to the possible ecological effects (judging them to be insignificant) and neglects completely any amenity issues. If constructed, however, the barrier is expected to stimulate a tenfold increase in arable farming acreage. Indeed the project meets the criterion of positive discounted net benefits largely due to the estimated agricultural benefits stimulated by an expansion in wheat cropping. This change in farming practice will mean the complete disappearance of portions of the characteristic Broadland valley grazing marsh landscape. Some of this area could reasonably be described as of critical landscape significance and includes marsh dykes which are still rich in flora. There will be keenly felt amenity and aesthetic losses for some groups, though perhaps not for all groups (it is claimed that for some water recreationists it does not really matter whether they pass by marshland or arable fields) as well as ecological losses. The extent of such losses must nevertheless be qualified by the fact that agricultural practice has changed in the past and will continue to change in the future whether the barrier is built or not. Paradoxically though, the greater the rate of this "ongoing" change the more difficult it will be to gauge the estimated agricultural benefits supposedly dependent on barrier construction. Both the sample size and questionnaire methods used in the CBA to determine rates of arablisation with and without the barrier are open to criticism.

Andrews and Waits[39] take the view that the whole debate over whether or not environmental values can or should be quantified is not a meaningful one. They argue all such values can be quantified either ordinally or numerically or monetarily. The important question for

---

* See O'Riordan, T. (1980) A Case Study in the Politics of Land Drainage, *Disasters* vol. 4 and Turner, R. K. *et al.* (1982) Valuation of the Environmental Impact of Wetland Flood Protection and Drainage Schemes, *Environment & Planning*, vol. 13, for more detail.

them is what indicators provide appropriate representations of environmental values, and how precise they are. They call for a further comprehensive research effort to answer this question. Brooks[40] believes that it is possible to formulate fairly precisely, if not quantitatively, some implicit criteria for the valuation of nature. He lists the concepts of uniqueness, reversibility or resilience, aesthetic beauty, human life-support capacity and naturalness. Brooks agrees that there is no independent, rational basis for assigning a price to such criteria in a CBA, but argues that criteria definition is an important first step that aids analysis by permitting testing of the impact of various assigned prices.

Conservation, Irreversibility and Intergenerational Equity

The problems of quantifying intangible effects can lead one to the question of what role the human species ought to play in the natural order of things. Leaving on one side the possible ethical-religious criticisms of man-centred CBA a more moderate"environmentalist" position would be that society should utilise CBA as a decision making tool subject to the constraint "that a broad range of animal and plant life exists in a substantial geographic range under conditions these life forms find congenial" (ecological diversity).[41] Given limited funds a trade-off must somehow be struck between preservation and the satisfaction of more pressing human wants. It would seem reasonable to first try and protect all of the most "valuable" of the landscapes and ecologically important or fragile areas, assuming that such areas can be identified using perhaps the Brooks criteria. Krutilla and Fisher[42] remind us that the natural biota represent our reservoir of genetic information, which has economic value. Advances in agriculture in terms of improved crop varieties can depend on genetic information found in the diversified natural biota. The same biota has in the past also provided the basis for a wide range of medicinal drugs and only a small portion of the potential medicinal value of biological specimens has yet been tapped.

In circumstances where environmental effects are uncertain and irreversible, as is the case for many of the larger projects, the quantification and valuation problems become exceedingly complex. Following Hirschleifer and Shapiro[43] the terms "risk" and "uncertainty" express a situation in which analysis requires us to take into account the possibility of a number of alternative outcomes or consequences of actions. Risk aversion is then interpreted to mean that the very existence of uncertainty is regarded by individuals as a cost. On the basis of the so-called Arrow–Lind Theorem,[44] however, it has been argued that there are circumstances when individuals may be risk averse but society as a whole may be risk neutral, and that, therefore, uncertainty can be neglected in social evaluations. The underlying idea here rests upon the law of large numbers in statistical theory. A number of writers[45] have suggested, nevertheless, that environmental damages, especially irreversible damages, are probably sufficiently different to prevent them being subject to the above theorem. Irreversible environmental damages are significant effects which permanently, or for a very long period of time, reduce the variety of future choices. Thus projects such as large-scale strip mining, wetland drainage and arablisation or dam construction with its consequent valley flooding all come under the umbrella of irreversibility; as does pollution from stock pollutants such as mercury, cadmium or radioactive waste.

Irreversible damage effects may serve to reduce individuals' options to experience the environmental good or service in question, i.e. hike or picnic in the previously dry valley behind the dam or on the hilltops levelled by mining activities. An individual's option value can be defined as a benefit accruing to an individual as a result of his retaining an option to consume the good at some time in the future.* In effect it is a premium for risk avoidance, an additional willingness to pay to insure oneself against the irretrievable loss of some environmental good.[46] Irreversibility is not, however, an easy concept to pin down and a moment's thought leads one onto questions of absolute irreversibility or long-term irreversibility with the possibility of eventual retrieval (this latter possibility being dependent on costs and technological advance). Further, there is the debate over the "authenticity" of the restoration process; clearly the outdoor-recreation market is in reality a complicated structure of numerous submarkets (we touched upon this question earlier when discussing the boating recreationalists' preferences for different kinds of agricultural landscapes on the Norfolk Broads).

The difficulties inherent in dealing with the issues of risk, uncertainty and irreversibility are very great and the current state of the art in economics is a long way from providing full solutions. Practical CBA typically employs the assumption of a certain world or incorporates some rather imprecise (but perhaps not dangerously incorrect) adjustments to take account of uncertainty. Haveman[47] in the reading below suggests, as far as uncertainty in the costs stream is concerned, the following adjustments:

(a) increase the stream of costs according to the degree of risk aversion which the policy maker feels is present;
(b) lengthen the time horizon over which the damages are expected;
(c) reduce the discount rate used in the present value calculations.

Krutilla and Fisher[48] conclude that a conservative decision taking policy is required with respect to irreversible environmental effects.

---

* It may also relate to disutility suffered by consumers who value an environment regardless of the fact that they feel certain they will never demand *in situ* the services it provides (existence value). Some individuals may also possess bequest motivations. See Bishop, R. C. (1982) Option Value: An Exposition and Extension, *Land Economics*, vol. 58.

They argue that if the costs and benefits of alternative uses of the environment are not known with any certainty then for a risk-averse society there will be a value in retaining an option to use the environment in a way that could otherwise be foreclosed. It is necessary to bear in mind, however (as the authors do), that this path-breaking work has not yet faced squarely the important question of whether or not any particular real course of action is in fact irreversible (the analysis assumes irreversibility to be a fact). Thus we have not yet reached the level of generality in this complex area necessary for real world decision making. Suffice it to note at this stage that a policy of non-foreclosure of options may in practice turn out to be very restrictive. The problem of irreversibility is intimately bound up with the problems of intergenerational social choice criteria and the concept of intergenerational equity. The introductory reading by Pearce[49] below introduces the intergenerational equity concept. Page[50] in his reading below demonstrates that questions of resource depletion and stock pollutants are fundamentally questions of equitable distribution of burdens across generations. For Page the equity question is, what is a fair distribution of risk to impose upon the future? He concludes that there is no easy way to add up the costs and risks along with the benefits and no way to guarantee that future generations will enjoy a higher level of welfare than the present. The discounting method used as an intergenerational social decision rule can ensure intergenerational efficiency but in terms of equity it only serves to bias choice in favour of the present generation. When the losers from a project cannot vote as is the case for future generations, the hypothetical Pareto improvement criterion breaks down. Freeman[51] suggests that compensation to future generations (the losers) actually be paid by setting aside a sum of money now which when cumulated forwards at the discount rate (now a familiar rate of interest) would provide monetary compensation for future losers. Page[52] adopts a Rawlsian standpoint[53] on the question of intergenerational equity. This view carries with it the presumption of equal distribution with a bias towards the least well-off. For Page the least well-off are likely to be future generations whose welfare the current generation is reducing by policies which over-exploit resources, lead to accumulations of stock pollutants in the biosphere and destroy unique landscapes and ecosystems. Mishan[54] offers a dissenting view to those described above and concludes that the economist has really nothing of substance to contribute to the debate on the "ideal" intergenerational time path.

The Role of CBA

Rowen[55] has identified two different points of view towards CBA. One, which he argues has often been expressed in the economic literature on CBA, sees the objective of CBA to make a choice. A decision rule is constructed which allows efficient choices to be made. To what extent this view is still generally held by economists is, however, open to debate, a number of writers being difficult to pin down on this score. There is less doubt that the economists' work has been used by others either to justify past choice or as a delaying tactic. Dorfman[56] notes that CBA has suffered from being an economic approach to a political problem. The results of CBA were wrongly presumed to be determinative and the technique was unrealistically expected to fulfil a role it was not capable of discharging. Rowen argues that the decision-rule role of CBA is of limited utility because over a range of policy areas and decisions, individuals (including decision makers) do not have preferences among broad goals, nor, in general, among overlapping policy objectives.

The second view of CBA identified is one which sees the technique as a means of assisting choice. It is recognised that CBA does not eliminate the need for the political resolution of conflicting objectives but that it can assist in the process of objective formulation and choice. The real debate here is how far CBA can go in assisting choice. Mishan[57] cautions economists undertaking CBA to utilise the potential Pareto improvement criterion and no other. This would seem to many to be an overly restrictive role for CBA to play. Nevertheless, precise information on the efficiency aspects of various projects does represent a very important source of data for decision making. Henderson[58] notes the criticisms that have been made of the CBA technique but argues that there may be some public expenditure projects (he examines the Concorde and Advanced Gas Cooled Nuclear Reactor programmes) for which CBA might provide early danger signals in terms of prospective losses. Henderson uses CBA to review past policy decisions in order to learn from past events and possible mistakes. He goes on to call for some kind of neutral review body separate from the government to analyse UK public expenditure programmes. But to play a broader role traditional (Paretian) CBA must be extended to encompass not just efficiency but many other objectives as well. We have seen that some analysts see multiple objective planning as the search for a single-valued benefit measure while others reject this approach on practical grounds and leave the final judgement to the policymaker.

CBA interpreted in a broader context (policy analysis) can be of great utility to the policymakers identified by Rowen as lacking clearly articulated or well-defined preferences. In his reading below Rowen argues that policy analysis can make an essentially heuristic contribution in this situation providing a conceptual framework for relating resources to objectives, an ordering device for information and exposing the individuals to a range of objectives. Many commentators have stressed the need for CBA or policy analysis, if it is to be a genuine component of democratic policymaking, to be presented in a disaggregated format. The aim must be to encourage a wider public participation in decision making and this can only be achieved by presenting information in a more accessible and understandable manner. Tribe[59] argues that the process by which a decision is arrived at is often at least as important as the result itself. There is a danger, nevertheless, that participatory decision making may involve such time delays that projects (even desirable and much needed ones) will be effectively hamstrung. For Brooks[60] the ultimate difficulty with participatory decision processes is the lack of assurance that all the relevant interests and perspectives will be represented in a balanced way.

Perhaps a new synthesis of the participatory and the old technocratic style of decision making is required. Dorfman[61] argues that a number of what he terms adversary analyses ought to be presented in any major project decision problem; and the funding of such analyses should be controlled by some quasi-judicial body. Brooks[62] would add a second component, a technical–analytical court, that is capable of reviewing the various analyses presented and which would present an understandable overview of the choices for public and policymaker consumption. The final judgement would still, however, rest with the policymakers. Nevertheless, the establishment of such a "neutral" court would seem to be an enormously difficult problem.

There are two issues here. First, there is the matter of how far should complex technical issues that have enormous ramifications for society be taken out of accountable political control. The challenge surely is to reform political institutions and encourage elected representatives themselves to become more expert rather than to establish another tier of elitest committees. Second, there is the problem of representativeness. No matter how sincere are the efforts to involve a cross-section of interested parties in such a court there will always be some interests which will be ill-represented — if for no other reason than not all interests are recognisable until the work of the court is completed. We raise this matter again in the section that follows when discussing the advantages of local steering groups to guide environmental impact assessments. There is no simple solution to these problems: whichever way one turns there are potential pitfalls that could seriously damage good intentions depending on the management issue under consideration, the operating ethos of the agencies involved and the vision or narrow mindedness of the principal participants.

Notes and References

1. Prest, A. R. and Turvey, R. (1965) Cost Benefit Analysis: A Survey, *Economic Journal*, vol. 75.
2. Freeman, A. M. (1977) Project Design and Evaluation with Multiple Objectives, in Haveman, R. and Margolis, J. (eds.) *Public Expenditure and Policy*, Rand McNally.
3. Steiner, P. (1977) The Public Sector and Public Interest, in Haveman, R. and Margolis, J. (eds.) *Public Expenditure and Policy*, Rand McNally.

4. Mishan, E. J. (1975) *Cost Benefit Analysis*, Allen & Unwin.
5. Mishan, E. J. (1975) *op. cit.*
6. Collard, D. (1972) *Prices Markets and Welfare*, Faber & Faber.
7. See Mishan, E. J. (1975) *op. cit.;* Pearce, D. W. (1971) *Cost Benefit Analysis*, Macmillan; Layard, R. (ed.) (1976) *Cost Benefit Analysis*, Penguin; Sassone, P. G. and Schaffer, W. A. (1978) *Cost-Benefit Analysis: A Handbook*, Academic Press.
8. For other formulations of the CB ratio see:
   Seneca, J. J. and Taussig, M. K. (1974) *Environmental Economics*, Prentice Hall; Peskin, H. and Seskin, E. (eds.) (1975) *Cost Benefit Analysis and Water Pollution*, The Urban Institute;
   Anderson, L. G. and Settle, R. F. (1977) *Benefit-Cost Analysis: A Practical Guide*, D. C. Heath; Abelson, P. (1979) *Cost Benefit Analysis and Environmental Problems*, Saxon House; and Pearce, D. W. and Dasgupta, P. (1972) *Cost Benefit Analysis*, Macmillan.
9. Pearce, D. W. (1971) *op. cit.*
10. Hanke, S. H. and Walker, R. A. (1974) Benefit–Cost Analysis Reconsidered: An Evaluation of the Mid-State Project, *Water Resources Research*, vol. 10 (5).
11. See Ackerman, B. *et al.* (1974) *The Uncertain Search for Environmental Quality*, The Free Press; Self, P. (1975) *Econocrats and the Policy Process*, Macmillan; Bradford, D. and Feiveson, H. (1976), Benefits and Costs, Winners and Losers, in Feiveson, H. *et al.* (eds.) *Boundaries of Analysis: An Inquiry into the Tocks Island Dam Controversy*, Ballinger.
12. Herfindahl, O. and Kneese, A. (1973) *Economic Theory of Natural Resources*, Charles E. Merrill.
13. These issues are outlined in the introductory essay and covered in more detail in the following references:
   Page, T. (1977) *Conservation and Efficiency*, Johns Hopkins University Press; Krutilla, J. and Fisher, A. (1975) *The Economics of Natural Environments*, Johns Hopkins University Press;
   and Haveman, R. (1977) The Economic Evaluation of Long-Run Uncertainties, *Futures*, vol. 9 (5).
14. Broady, M. (1978) Method and Methodology in Social Impact Analysis. Paper Presented to the Institution of Water Engineers and Scientists Symposium on *Engineering and the Environment: Harmony or Conflict?*;
   and McEvoy, J. and Dietz, T. (1977) *Handbook for Environmental Planning*, John Wiley.
15. Nash, C. *et al.* (1975) An Evaluation of Cost–Benefit Analysis Criteria, *Scottish Journal of Political Economy*, vol. 22 (1).
16. Mishan, E. J. (1975) *op. cit.*
17. Little, I. (1957) *A Critique of Welfare Economics*, Oxford University Press.
18. See Musgrave, R. (1969) Cost Benefit Analysis and the Theory of Public Finance, *Journal of Economic Literature*, vol. 7 (3).
19. Steiner, P. (1977) *op. cit.*
20. See Eckstein, O. (1961) *A Survey of the Theory of Public Expenditure Criteria in Public Finances: Needs, Sources and Utilisation*, Princeton University Press;
   Weisbrod, B. (1968) Income Redistribution Effects and Benefit–Cost Analysis, in Chase, S. (ed.) *Problems in Public Expenditure Analysis*, Brookings Institution;
   and Haveman, R. and Weisbrod, B. (1977) Defining Benefits of Public Programmes: Some Guidance for Policy Analysts, in Chase, S. (ed.) *op. cit.*
21. See Mass, A. (1966) Benefit–Cost Analysis: Its Relevancy to Public Investment Decisions, *Quarterly Journal of Economics*, vol. 76 (2);
   and McKean, R. (1958), *Efficiency in Government Through Systems Analysis*, John Wiley.
22. Nash, C. *et al.* (1975) *op. cit.*
23. Steiner, P. (1977) *op. cit.*
24. Williams, A. (1972) Cost–Benefit Analysis: Bastard Science? and/or Insidious Poison in the Body Politick?, *Journal of Public Economics*, vol. 1 (2).
25. Lichfield, N. (1968) Economics in Town Planning, *Town Planning Review*, vol. 39 (1).
26. See Herfindahl, O. and Kneese, A. (1973) *op. cit.*
   and Anderson, L. and Settle, R. (1977) *op. cit.*
27. Pearce, D. W. (ed.) (1978) *Valuation of Social Cost*, Allen & Unwin.
28. Maler, G. and Wyzga, R. (1976) *Economic Management of Environmental Damage*, OECD.
29. Mishan, E. J. (1975) *op. cit.*

30. Gordon, I. M. and Knetsch, J. L. (1979) Consumer's Surplus Measures and the Evaluation of Resources, *Land Economics*, vol. 55 (1).
31. See Pearce, D. W. (ed.) (1978) *op. cit.*
32. McKean, R. (1968) The Use of Shadow Prices, in Chase, S. (ed.) *Problems in Public Expenditure Analysis*, Brookings Institution.
33. Williams, A. (1972) *op. cit.*
34. Knetsch, J. (1974) *Outdoor Recreation and Water Resources Planning*, American Geophysical Union.
35. For a survey see:
    Flegg, A. (1976) Methodological Problems in Estimating Recreational Demand Functions and Evaluating Recreational Benefits, *Journal of Regional Studies*, vol. 10 (3).
36. Pearce, D. W. and Edwards, R. (1979) The Monetary Evaluation of Noise Nuisance, in O'Riordan, T. and D'Arge, R. (eds.) *Progress in Environmental Planning and Resource Management*, vol. 1, John Wiley. This debate is continued by Nelson, J. and Pearce, D. W. and Harris, A. in O'Riordan, T. and Turner, R. K. (eds.) *Progress in Environmental Planning and Resource Management*, vol. 4, (1983), John Wiley.
37. Bradford, D. and Feiveson, H. (eds.) (1976) *op. cit.*
38. Rendell, Palmer and Tritton (1978) *The Yare Basin Flood Control Study*, Vols. 1–3.
39. Andrews, R. and Waits, M. (1978) *Environmental Values in Public Decision*, University of Michigan.
40. Brooks, H. (1976) Environmental Decision Making: Analysis and Values, in Tribe, L. (ed.) *When Values Conflict*, Ballinger.
41. Ackerman, B. *et al.* (1974) *op. cit.*
42. Krutilla, J. and Fisher, A. (1975) *op. cit.*
43. Hirschleifer, J. and Shapiro, L. (1977) The Treatment of Risk and Uncertainty, in Haveman, R. and Margolis, J. (eds.) *Public Expenditure and Policy Analysis*, Rand McNally.
44. Arrow, K. and Lind, R. (1970) Uncertainty and the Evaluation of Public Investment Decisions, *American Economic Review*, vol. 66 (3).
45. See readings in this section by Haveman.
46. Olsen, G. (1975) Option Value, *Australian Journal of Agricultural Economics*, vol. 19 (3).
47. See reading in this section.
48. See Fisher, A. C. and Krutilla, J. V. (1975) Valuing Long-Run Ecological Consequences and Irreversibilities, in Peskin, H. and Seskin, E. (eds.) (1975) *op. cit.*
49. See reading in this section.
50. See reading in this section.
51. Freeman, M. (1977) Equity, Efficiency, and Discounting, *Futures*, vol. 9 (5).
52. See reading in this section.
53. Rawls, J. (1974) *A Theory of Justice*, Oxford University Press.
54. Mishan, E. J. (1977) Economic Criteria for Intergenerational Comparisons, *Futures*, vol. 9 (5).
55. Rowen, H. (1975) The Role of Cost–Benefit Analysis in Policy Making, in Peskin, H. and Seskin, E. (eds.) *Cost–Benefit Analysis and Water Pollution*, The Urban Institute.
56. Dorfman, R. (1976) An Afterword: Human Values and Environmental Decisions, in Tribe, L. (ed.), *When Values Conflict*, Ballinger.
57. Mishan, E. J. (1975) *op. cit.*
58. Henderson, P. D. (1978) Two British Errors: Their Possible Size and Some Possible Lessons, *Oxford Economic Papers*, vol. 29.
59. Tribe, L. (ed.) (1976) *op. cit.*
60. Brooks, H. (1976) *op. cit.*
61. Dorfman, R. (1976) *op. cit.*
62. Brooks, H. (1976) *op. cit.*

READINGS

POLICY ANALYSIS AS HEURISTIC AID: THE DESIGN OF MEANS, ENDS, AND INSTITUTIONS*

Henry S. Rowen

"POLICY ANALYSIS" refers to a set of procedures for inventing, exploring, and comparing the alternatives available for achieving certain social ends — and

*© 1976 The American Academy of Arts and Sciences. Reprinted with permission from *When Values Conflict*, ed. L. Tribe, Ballinger, Cambridge, Mass., pp. 137–152. (Professor Rowen is Professor of Public Management, Graduate School of Business, Stanford University.)

for inventing, exploring, and comparing the alternative ends themselves—in a world limited in knowledge, in resources and in rationality. Policy analysts use scientific data and theories as inputs, employ the method of science in many of their procedures, and sometimes stimulate the creation of new fundamental knowledge, but theirs is not a science. Rather it is a profession—possibly a bit beyond the state of medicine early in this century, when Lawrence J. Henderson asserted that the average patient who came into contact with the average physician stood an even chance of benefiting from the encounter.

I

Policy analysis can be put to many uses. It can be used to help make routine decisions (e.g. the optimization of a system for responding to fire alarms) and to help make decisions on nonroutine events (e.g. the structuring of the main features of a national health insurance system). It can be used to raise questions about, and explore the consistency among, objectives of the same or different government programs (e.g. programs to increase irrigated agricultural land versus programs that remove land from cultivation). It can be employed in advocacy against competition (e.g. by the Air Force and Navy on the merits of their respective strategic nuclear forces). It can provide nonmembers of powerful bureaucracies (e.g. political appointees) with arguments against some of these bureaucracies' programs at the same time that it helps the bureaucracies to fight back. And it can point to directions for seeking new knowledge that might eventually contribute to solving policy problems (e.g. the effect of environmental stimulation on early childhood development). Policy analysis can be used in all of these many ways, and, in its now quite substantial history, it has been so used.

Policy analysts therefore play many roles. They are staff advisors to decision makers, or may even be decision makers themselves with their thinking caps on. They are members of career services. They can also be found in firms which sell analytic services. Important concentrations of them are to be found in research institutions and universities. Theirs is a peripatetic community. The diffusion of ideas and methods is greatly promoted by the movement of analysts from place to place. They bring or develop subject area expertise, institutional knowledge, quantitative analytic skills, problem solving skills, and occasionally skills in communicating the nature and validity of their findings to decision makers and wider audiences.

In some of these roles, analysts are overtly partisan; in others less so. (Wherever they are located, many analysts have some values that do not correspond in any obvious way to those of the institutional setting in which they work.) But it is not required that analysts be completely nonpartisan, assuming that we could identify zero on a scale of partisanship. Analysts need be no more neutral in their fields nor saintly in their character than are contributors to pure science. But whatever the appearance or reality of partisanship, what matters is the work done and the applicable standard of evaluation is that of the scientific method: careful use of data, explicitness in stating assumptions and the production of replicable calculations. Moreover, partisanship has social value because it can be a motivator of discoveries that affect policy choices. "Blowing the opposition out of the water" may not be the most noble of motives but it may have useful social consequences.

With so varied a set of purposes and players, what, if anything, can be said about the characteristics of good analysis? In my view, good analysis does the following:

1. Uses methods tailored to the character of the problem and the nature of the data; treats data skeptically.
2. Explores, reformulates, and invents objectives; recognizes the multiplicity of the objectives that are held; recognizes hierarchies of objectives and the fact that one is always working on intermediate objectives.
3. Uses criteria of choice sensitively and with caution, giving weight to qualitative as well as quantitative factors.
4. Emphasizes the design and invention of alternatives; tries to avoid concentration on too narrow a set of alternatives.
5. Handles uncertainty explicitly.
6. Evidences that the analyst understands the central technical facts of the problem.
7. Uses simple models to illuminate important aspects of the problem and avoids large models that purport to represent much of reality but that conceal the basic structure of the problem and uncertainties among parameters.
8. Displays truth in labeling of assumptions, values, uncertainties, hypotheses, and conjectures.
9. Shows understanding that the task is usually not to optimize but only to find better alternatives.
10. Shows that an effort has been made to understand decision makers' problems and constraints especially if the analyst proposes a radical reformulation of the problem.
11. Tries to take into account the organizational factions that shape the alternatives generated and influence the outcomes of decisions.
12. Exhibits awareness of the usefulness of partial analysis and of the limits of analysis generally.

This may seem counsel of perfection. If institutional arrangements invariably provided for review, criticism and counteranalysis of analytic work, these characteristics would be more in evidence than they are. Indeed, it might be argued that although no single analysis is likely to exhibit all of the desirable properties listed above, the corpus of analytic work done on a problem over time may approximate this ideal. This may leave uncomfortable those who, although rejecting the model of decision makers as philosopher-kings, conceive of policy analysts as philosopher advisors to kings. I am inclined to see analysts in a more modest role, equipped with certain tools, and subject, intermittently and imperfectly, to certain standards of performance, and therefore to place more reliance on a competitive analytic process.

Points 2 and 3 from this list, concerning objectives, criteria and the handling of qualitative factors, have been central to our project and deserve particular attention. These are not just matters of analytic technique; they are intimately connected to ways we form preferences and to the role of performance indicators in our institutional structures. I will return to this topic later.

II

Robert Dorfman's essay in this volume* traces the historical evolution of policy analysis from maximization under constraint, through recognition of the importance of choosing the objective function, to a greater concern about values. Clearly there has been an evolution along these lines, but this characterization gives insufficient emphasis to what I believe have been two principal contributions of this line of work: clarification of issues, and the design and invention of objectives and alternatives. This view is in marked contrast to the emphasis placed on optimization and evaluation in the literature on this subject. It is not that the latter are not useful, indeed often necessary, activities, but that the payoffs from the former are so much greater. As Edward Quade has put it, "A good new idea is worth a thousand evaluations." (But a good evaluation may be a condition for getting a good idea.) More fundamentally, this view is based on the observation that those responsible for policy choices often do not have a clear concept of what needs to be done, are not in possession of the relevant facts, do not know the alternatives available and do not know, even approximately, the consequences of choosing particular courses of action. Let us refer to someone in this state of mind as being in Position A.[1]

The salient facts about Position A are these:

First, often those responsible for making public policy decisions do not have clearly articulated or well defined preferences among broad goals nor preferences among specific policy objectives. One reason is that the policy issues involved often concern public goods—goods not sold on markets. The value placed on these goods by members of the community is largely unknown because they have few occasions to obtain information on what these goods are worth to them or what they cost. This is also true in the related phenomenon of spillovers from private actions, if the effects are diffused among large numbers of people, few of whom are affected strongly enough to voice concern.[2] In these and other circumstances, decision makers are unlikely to possess strong personal preferences nor are they likely to receive strong signals from the environment. The existence of wide agreement on broad social goals such as economic growth, wilderness preservation, or improvement in the situation of the poor, does not help much in dealing with specific problems as they arise. Therefore, especially for choices which involve unfamiliar factors and thus are of a nonroutine sort, considered preferences will be confined to choices that bear on subordinate issues rather than on the larger ones.

Second, the nature of the problem may be obscure. The occasion for believing that "something should be done" may be the emergence of a symptom (e.g., an unexpected increase in a price index), an event (e.g., the failure of New York City to sell a bond issue), a new technological possibility (e.g., a report that asserts that supersonic transportation is technically feasible), a proposal (e.g., for building a dam on the Delaware River). The event that brings the problem to the top of the action agenda focuses attention but does not define it well enough for sensible decision. Instead, events generate a search for information about the problem and possible alternative courses of action and objectives. The ends to be sought and the means that might be employed are a joint product of the inquiry undertaken.

*The reference is to the volume L. Tribe *et al.* (eds.) *When Values Conflict*, Chap. 7, Ballinger.

Third, available "solutions" are unpersuasive. They do not seem to deal with the problem, however it is perceived; they seem infeasible, or at least too costly. And even if some appear at first glance to be adequate, there may be large uncertainties about how well they would really work.

Fourth, policy decisions are, in general, not made by single individuals acting over time. Nor are they usually made by a group of people acting jointly in committee. They are usually shaped instead by the interaction over time and space of individuals with different attitudes, skills, information, and influence. Most of the participants operate in organizations with missions that inevitably filter data and shape the policy alternatives generated. Organizational biases often interfere with the process of consensus building. But agreement on the consequences of choices and values is not needed for action and therefore normally does not occur. All that is essential is agreement on the next step.

In Position A, therefore, a decision maker must develop or construct his preferences and the alternatives for meeting them. He does this by using methods that have worked in the past for himself or for others in similar situations; or he defines away the problem by declaring that it falls within existing policy; or he uses intuition; or he calls on expert advice; or he fools around with data in different ways and tries out different objectives and alternatives. To those in Position A, *the contribution of policy analysis is essentially heuristic: to provide a conceptual framework (or several) for relating means to ends, for thinking about ends, for identifying the existing technical alternatives, and for inventing new ones.*

The analysis of Tocks* provides examples of a heuristic process at work. Although most of the participants may have begun with a notion—indeed, a conviction—about what was the "right" thing to do, the process of investigation did turn up some new things: alternative means of providing various degrees of flood control, clarification about the different kinds of recreation that would be provided by dam and no-dam alternatives, ideas about other sources of water for New Jersey. Quite a few forecasts were made, about water quality and population growth for instance. I do not know what the total effect of these estimates and alternatives was on the analyst participants or on the governors who have recently made some decisions on Tocks, but it seems to me more plausible to conjecture that many of the participants went through a learning process than that they merely generated—or received—inputs for some predetermined objective functions.

In short, for many participants the analytic process will contribute to beliefs about facts and relationships and will help in the construction of value preferences. The phrase "construction of value preferences" is deliberately chosen. This reflects the view that preferences are generally built through experience and through learning about facts, about relationships, and about consequences. It is not that values are latent and only need to be "discovered" or "revealed". There is a potentially infinite number of values; they are not equally useful or valid, and part of the task of analysis is to develop ones that seem especially "right" and useful and that might become widely shared. Because value

*The Tocks Island Dam Project on the Delaware river in the USA aroused much controversy which is analysed in two volumes: Feiveson, H. A. *et al.* (eds) (1976) *Boundaries of Analysis: An Inquiry into the Tocks Island Dam Controversy*, Ballinger, and Tribe, L. *et al.* (eds) (1976) *When Values Conflict*, Ballinger.

preferences are formed through a process of choice in specific cultural and institutional settings, and because, as Laurence Tribe observes, avoidance of dissonance causes us to prefer what we have chosen, the factors that influence our choices get imbedded in our values. Those that are fuzzy, fragile, not immediately useful, are likely to be excluded and therefore are not built into the value system that we are constantly constructing and reconstructing.

III

Another decision maker is in a different position (let us call it Position B)—a position he perceives as less ambiguous than Position A because he has well defined objectives. (Other people may believe that his goals *should* be different ones.) He is looking for better alternatives, perhaps even for an optimum. He may engage in a vigorous search for alternatives. He will probably look for it by searching in the neighborhood of other alternatives that have worked well for him in the past or seem to have worked well for others in similar situations.[3] If this isn't sufficient, he may have to do more serious searching over a wider domain. He may put his analytic staff to work inventing broadly different alternatives. Here also is to be found the policy maker who has a "solution" and is looking for a problem (e.g., a bureau head looking for business for his agency). He may put his analytic staff to work identifying unmet or inventing hitherto unknown needs of whose importance other decision makers might be persuaded, along with the desirability of his solution.

Recently, a search process was engaged in by the National Aeronautics and Space Administration as it neared the end of the Apollo Program. The "solution" was employment for the existing manned space program. An extensive search was undertaken for jobs to be done through that program within budgets that might be available. During the course of these analyses, a good deal of work and a certain amount of ingenuity was applied to the problem of defining tasks that could be done by men in space and in arguing that the benefits would exceed the costs. The Corps of Engineers' advocacy of the Tocks Island Dam on the Delaware River looks like a similar case. Much of the behavior of government agencies is similarly motivated. Agencies have product lines or specialized services that they promote in the political marketplace, and they sometimes use the tools of analysis both to help improve their products and to help sell them.

Often, nongovernmental (although not necessarily nonpartisan) analysts are also to be found in Position B. The analyst who "knows" it is a terrible mistake to build a large dam at Tock *has* his values. What analysis can do for him is to marshall the evidence on the costs and benefits of proceeding with this project, to spell out consequences that may have been overlooked, and—most important—to provide a framework for proposing alternatives (e.g., different ways of providing flood control on the Delaware flood plain).

A person in Position B is more likely than one in A to perceive analysis as useful, not only heuristically, but also in providing what might be called a "decision rule" for choosing a preferred alternative. However, the decision rule use of analysis requires that outputs be well defined, quantifiable, and preferably reducible to the same currency as costs, or at least that enough of them can be so expressed to make it a useful exercise. This is unlikely to be possible in the case of larger and more complex policy issues that arise and more likely to work on repetitive and narrower questions. In both, however, there is a significant role for design and invention. Indeed, it is in circumstances in which commitments to policies and programs are strongest, where conflicts with other explicit public purposes or with poorly represented values are greatest, that inventive ingenuity is most valuable. The invention of new possibilities may help shift policy choices away from perhaps intractable zero-sum choices to nonzero-sum choices — from choices where what some people gain others lose to those where there are gains for all.

Policy analysis, as described so far, would seem to be an unalloyed good. This is not universally believed to be so. Practical men sometimes say that it is too complicated to be useful, that analysts are more interested in exercising their analytical skills or merely adding to the sum of human knowledge than in helping to solve policy problems. These practical men are not always wrong. Other, more fundamental, criticisms of policy analysis, expressed most eloquently by Laurence Tribe,[4] are that policy analysis: (1) concentrates on tangible, quantifiable factors and ignores or depreciates the importance of intangible, unquantifiable ones; (2) leaves out of consideration altogether certain "fragile" values —e.g., ecological or esthetic concerns; (3) focuses on results and, in its search for common measures, ignores both the processes by which preferences and decisions are formed and significant qualitative differences among outcomes; (4) tends to operate within limits set by the interests and values of the clients; (5) in the effort to be objective, employs deceptively neutral and detached language in dealing with intensely moral issues; (6) artificially separates facts from values; and (7) tends to overlook distributional objectives in favor of efficiency objectives.

These criticisms clearly apply to bad analysis—i.e., to analysis that fails to possess the characteristics listed earlier. And much analysis is bad. But they excessively depreciate the value of analysis that is incomplete or partisan. For example, as Allen Carlin and Alain Enthoven have argued in our discussions, even a narrow analysis can sometimes make a powerful case that an unwise proposal is in fact a bad one (e.g., that a supersonic transport will not be economically viable). Such analyses are useful. The criticisms listed above do have validity, but they are most appropriately cited against the claim that analysis provides a rule for choice. Their relevance to the heuristic function, which I argue is the principal one for analysis, is less clear.

There does not seem to be serious disagreement about some of the characteristics of the kind of analysis that is needed. Proper analysis as proposed by Laurence Tribe, for example, would point

... in the general direction of a subtler, more holistic, and more complex style of problem solving, undoubtedly involving several iterations between problem formulation and problem solution and relying at each stage on the careful articulation of a wide range of interrelated values and constraints through the development of several distinct "perspectives" on a given problem, each couched in an idiom true to its internal structure rather than translated into some "common denominator."[5]

I would add: "and which seeks to develop new action possibilities and new objectives that might be sought." But I think it should be recognized that a pluralistic political system in which the participants use the techniques of policy analysis – narrow and partisan though they may be—can approximate the holistic style Tribe advocates, although I would not claim that the observation of such an analytic marketplace at work is an everyday experience.

This view of analysis is, I believe, a helpful one in relation to our central concern—namely, the neglect of fragile, fuzzy, currently nonoperational values. It has often been observed that we have invented institutional means for the protection or representation of values that are systematically neglected. We have done this by passing laws to protect the rights of minorities or to require an environmental impact statement for projects; we have done it by setting up government agencies to promote arms control and disarmament or environmental protection or the interests of the poor. But the threshold for the passage of laws and the creation of new agencies is not low. It is fair to ask what analysis can do to help to improve on this situation.

One way is to study complex environmental phenomena and to try to identify unexpected consequences of private or public actions. Another is to explore some of the long-run consequences of the neglect of certain values, and to stimulate the collection of illustrative data. Many people who do not think much from day to day about the decline in the number of whales or black-footed ferrets, when presented with data and analyses that record their decline and predict their extinction, may come to feel that this is a problem about which something must be done. And because the political process sometimes leads politicians to search actively for causes that have not been preempted by others, it is sometimes possible to connect neglected interests with those looking for issues to promote. This is a kind of lottery and it is also a kind of market test; those values that cannot command the votes or capture the imagination of politicians or are not protected by constitutional guarantee will not do well. It is a challenge to analysts not only to do the kind of substantive analysis they have traditionally done, but also to devise ways of describing fuzzy or neglected phenomena and to invent ways of injecting them into decision processes.

IV

One of the most urgent needs, in my view, is achieving much deeper knowledge of the nature of governmental processes than the conventional learning provides. Policy outcomes are strongly influenced by the missions and structure of Executive branch agencies and congressional committees. Initially structured by law, they have evolved through time and experience, and have been constrained by technology and influenced by interest groups. It is not much of an oversimplification to assert that each major bureaucratic entity—bureau, agency, department—comes to have a special character which dominates its behavior. For example, the Corps of Engineers and the Bureau of Reclamation do not have as objectives the avoidance of flood damage, improvements in the efficiency of transportation, or increases in electric power production, but rather the carrying out of large-scale construction projects which contribute to these ends. An alternative, such as use of the price mechanism to help achieve those goals, is not generally within the policy space available to these agencies.

This kind of constraint on instrumentalities might be thought to be less in the case of departments with broader missions, such as Justice, Defense, or State. To some extent this is so, but these departments consist of aggregations of organizational entities, each with its own limited perspective, and the behavior of the collective largely reflects the behavior of the constituent parts. Congress usually proceeds in a similarly constrained manner through the action of committees that occupy well marked out turfs. And members of these committees are often moved by concerns even more parochial than those of the agencies they oversee. How a problem is treated is therefore largely determined by which agency gets the action. How differently might the Tocks problem have been viewed if it had been initially defined principally as a recreation problem and preempted by the National Park Service as a Delaware Water Gap National Recreation Area project?

Both the definition of the problem and the range of admissible solutions differs according to which agency comes to have principal responsibility. Moreover, the probability is low in most arenas that the dominant problem definition will be seriously challenged by other bureaucratic interests. The boundaries of territorial rights are well known and usually observed. Struggles do occur from time to time, but they are costly; and a taste for the quiet life leads agency heads usually to prefer private horse trades to public fights. Nongovernmental interests are much more likely to mount overt challenges, but they are usually less well entrenched legally, they are less well armed with analytic resources, and they often have less staying power.

Organizational behavior can also plausibly be associated with many of the observed shortcomings in analysis discussed earlier. Does the frequently observed failure of analyses to use choice criteria sensitively or to give adequate weight to qualitative factors reflect only or mainly the limitations of analytic techniques or of the analyst's values or training? I think not. One must also look to the organizational setting in which analysis is done. If the performance of bureaucrats and analysts is judged on the basis of certain numbers (and it often is), then these performance measures have a powerful incentive on behavior. It should not be surprising that importance is attached in analyses to dollar measures such as sales of timber from national forests or physical measures such as recreation-days if these criteria are of great importance within the organizations that dominate many environmental decisions.

Observing the powerful role of organizational interests suggests an area of inquiry that is almost totally neglected by policy analysts, whose work has been largely focused on improvements in the tools of analysis or on applying these tools to substantive problems. This is the systematic study of the behavior of the principal institutions that shape public choices, their perception of their central purposes, the rules by which they operate, their internal systems of incentives and controls, and the means by which they seek to influence their external environment. The resulting hypotheses about their behavior could then be used to predict the alternatives that might be suggested when policy issues arise and to predict outcomes of policy decisions.

Perhaps the greatest current need, a need that organization theorists and students of bureaucratic functioning have only begun to meet, is the systematic study of policy implementation. We often refer to a "a policy decision" as the end point of the analytic process. But more often than not "a policy decision" is but one move in a continuing decision process. An authoritative decision or cluster of decisions (e.g., the passage of a law and the appropriation of funds) may be necessary for *something* to happen, but it is usually not enough to determine *what* will happen. The realm of administrative discretion is usually large. This is as it should be, for the alternative of trying to legislate ever more detailed means as well as broader purposes would be worse.

Many important choices are made during implementation; but neither the choices made by people at a low level in the organizational hierarchy nor the consequences of their actions may be obvious to what is somewhat inaccurately called the "policy levels". And sometimes the "policy levels" have little incentive to find out what is actually going on. In short, analysts who do not understand the salient characteristics of the bureaucratic system responsible for carrying out any given policy alternative cannot predict with much confidence what actually would happen if that alternative were adopted. With the kind of organizational knowledge that only a few now possess and that none possesses as fully or deeply as desirable, analysts could help to design alternatives which would have a higher probability of achieving the predicted or desired results. They would also be in a position to propose organizational changes that would alter the incentives and therefore the behavior of the dominant institutions.

In sum, the study of implementation behavior in organizations is the study of instrumentalities for achieving social purposes. And those who believe that important social values are neglected need to exercise ingenuity in devising mechanisms for the representation of these values. If the Sierra Club, the Friends of the Earth, and the Environmental Protection Agency did not exist they would probably be invented. But many more inventions are still needed to promote values of the sort these groups embody. The encouragement and support of the type of policy analysis they perform—perhaps it should be called meta-policy analysis—should be high on the agenda of any national environmental research program.

V

It is important to consider what components a fully developed system of analytic organizations that was equipped to carry out a broad spectrum of policy-related studies on environmental questions would include. The following array would represent a well-developed capacity for handling the analytic aspects of environmental problems:

1. In-house government staffs to do staff analyses, to make use of the policy analysis of external researchers, and to stimulate and sponsor new outside research.
2. Laboratories — governmental and nongovernmental — working in a wide range of technical areas.
3. A for-profit analytical services industry.
4. Manufacturing industry that produces prototypes and production items.
5. Academic research on a wide range of basic and applied areas.
6. Broad, interdisciplinary, long term research programs carried out in one or more large nongovernmental research institutions.
7. Small special purpose research institutes that concentrate on specific problem areas such as wildlife preservation.
8. State or regional analytic organizations to do project analyses in depth.

9. An environmental research agency responsible for identifying and funding important gaps in the research and analysis carried out by the mission agencies.
10. A set of membership organizations, trade associations, and consumer oriented groups that engage in advocacy analysis.
11. One or more journals that regularly review major policy analysis on environmental questions.

Parts of this environmental-industrial-governmental complex already exist, and the supply of trained analysts is increasing. A recent development of potential importance is a Ford Foundation grant to Resources For the Future for a broader program of work that could permit RFF to become a major contributor to policy-related analysis in the environmental field. If so, it would fill one of the more obvious institutional gaps—the absence of a broad environmental research institute of the type proposed a few years ago. The concept then was to create a private organization that contracted with government agencies to do both policy-oriented research and related background studies. It was also to have had a significant amount of relatively unconstrained nongovernmental funding. Much of its work was to have been organized on a long term programmatic basis; but some would have been on near-term policy issues. The institute's program would have included systematic analysis of the generalized waste products problem, the theory of exploitation of depletable resources, land use problems, the technologies of pollution control, the use of market vs. nonmarket instruments, the study of behavior of organizations which affect the environment, and—not least—mechanisms by which environmental values might be effectively incorporated into public sector decision processes. This model is close to that of Rand; the major difference is that the proposed institute would have had a greater proportion of nongovernmental foundation funding. The central feature of this model is that both work on policy issues *and* broad system studies would be carried out within one organization. Perhaps now RFF will become that organization.

The proposal for a gap-filling environmental research agency is based on the observation that the bureaucratic constraints of operational mission agencies inevitably cause important research and analytic questions to be overlooked. This institution's tasks would, therefore, be to sponsor work on important neglected topics. Its work would be done largely on contract with outside organizations because the areas of need would shift substantially over time. The institutional model here is ARPA, the Advanced Research Projects Agency of the Defense Department.

Small special purpose research organizations would have the advantages of the concentration, technical competency, and dedication that can be achieved through a focused effort in a specific area. Some possible missions for such special purpose institutes might be wildlife preservation, development of recreational opportunities, studies of land use (e.g., a Land Use Center has been established recently by the Urban Institute), wetlands preservation, and energy and materials conservation. These organizations could serve as sources of information by providing inputs to other project analyses, but most important, they would generate ideas to further their own missions.

State and regional analytic organizations could provide resources for project analyses and act as a counterbalance to the federal agencies which dominate project analyses now. These regional institutes might be financed by both federal and state funds.

There is, in addition, the important task of developing and maintaining professional standards, exposing shoddy work, and arranging to have analyses done from different perspectives meet head-on. The academic journals do this in scholarly fields. But this mechanism has not worked well in the field of policy analysis because the range of substantive areas covered is large, publication channels are varied, and the standards of performance are ill-defined. Disciplined, thorough review of major pieces of policy analysis is rare. A recent effort to review standards in one area suggests a reason why: the inquiry undertaken several years ago by the Operations Research Society of America (ORSA) into the analytic aspects of testimony on antiballistic missiles led to a useful review of some of the calculations that were used to support widely varying policy positions taken on the ABM.[6] But it also raised controversial questions about the proper role of professional organizations in purporting to "police" the analytic and advisory activities of their own, and related, professionals. Therefore, groups like ORSA are unlikely to make this kind of inquiry a regular activity, and other means for carrying out careful review of major analytic and advisory products are needed. Fortunately, a new journal being started at the University of California (Berkeley) Graduate School of Public Policy has this as one of its stated purposes.

VI

Finally, it can hardly be doubted that environmental problems are among those most in need of, and ultimately susceptible to, systematic analysis. Many of them are enormously complex — so much so that counterintuitive consequences are often to be expected. After all, one of the basic concepts in ecology is the notion of the "system", with its complex interrelations and with the possibility of remote repercussions from current decisions. This is a field of endeavour that requires an enormously wide range of research: basic scientific investigation, methodological innovations, the forecasting of trends, specific policy studies, the investigation of decision processes, and devising means for bringing together the knowledge and skills of experts from many fields in close and continuing working arrangements. If this can be done, it is likely to have a very high payoff indeed.

But in the end, the work of the analyst must be supplemented by that of the artist, poet, and novelist. Policy analysis has its virtues, but the large changes in society are brought about through processes of which it now knows little — processes about which it can hope to learn a little more.

Notes

1. For a similar view of preference formation and the role of analysis see James G. March, "The Technology of Foolishness," in *Civiløkonomen*, Copenhagen, Vol. 18, May 1971, pp. 4–12. For an earlier statement see Albert Wohlstetter, "Analysis and Design Conflict Systems," in *Analysis for Military Decision*, ed. by E.S. Quade (Santa Monica, Calif.: Rand Corp., 1964). This essay was based on lectures given at Rand in 1954–55.
2. See the article by Mancur Olson in *Evaluation*, Vol. 1, no. 2, 1973.

3. John D. Steinbruner, *The Cybernetic Theory of Decision — New Dimensions of Political Analysis* (Princeton, NJ: Princeton University Press, 1974).
4. See Laurence Tribe, "Policy Science: Analysis or Ideology?" *Philosophy and Public Affairs* (Fall 1972); pp. 66–110.
5. *Ibid.*, p. 107.
6. "Guidelines for the Practice of Operations Research," *Operations Research* 19 (5) (September 1971); pp. 1123–1258.

ACCOUNTING FOR THE FUTURE*

David Pearce

MANKIND has already entered into a "Faustian bargain" with Nature, trading evident and desirable increases in material standards of living for unknown and unforeseen costs. That life itself is a risky event no one would question. Why then should there be any special concern *now* about the nature of this bargain?

The discovery of long-term and harmful effects from DDT or mercury or cadmium has resulted in varying reactions. In some cases, outright bans of their use in specific areas or for specific products have resulted. The gains from such apparently socially considerate acts tend to be invisible and long-term. The losses, perhaps in increased malarial fever or simply in more costly products, are more evident. Any act implies a judgement of costs and benefits. Put in this framework it is possible to adduce several reasons why in the last quarter of the 20th century there must be more, and not less, "accounting for the future".

First, the accidents have already happened. While there may be debate about the damage from DDT, there can be no doubt about the ingestion of mercury and cadmium,[1] or dioxin at Seveso. Too many chemicals and drugs enter the natural or social environment without knowledge of their consequences: thalidomide provides evidence of this.

Second, the errors of the past fade into insignificance when we consider the negative pay-offs from the technologies that are now being contemplated. The most obvious concern applies to those nuclear technologies which produce plutonium. For not only is the scale of the possible damage orders of magnitude higher than that for past technologies, the scale of the technologies themselves could be vast. One or two nuclear plants may be an "acceptable" risk: 100 may well not be.

Third, while man's capability for understanding the future effects of his actions grows, there must be a considerable doubt as to whether his capability for controlling the technologies that may generate those effects will grow at the same pace, and whether institutions will exist to deal with the problems.[2] The impact of CO_2 on the global environment is debated; if the pessimists are correct however, we must ask whether an integrated global CO_2 control programme could ever come about without centralised world government.

Fourth, there are indications, no more than that, that an ethical shift is taking place. The new ethic commands us to consider the fact that trade-offs are all too easy to make when the gain is ours and the cost is someone else's. For the current generation, a situation where A gains and B loses at least implies a potential for A and B to negotiate or to establish protective laws. But the nature of the bargain

*© 1977 IPC Business Press. Reprinted with permission from *Futures*, Vol. 9, 1977, pp. 365–374. (Professor Pearce is Professor of Political Economy, University of Aberdeen.)

is now one where the losers are future generations who, by definition, have no voice and hence no chance to alter the behaviour of current generations. In short, without an ethic of concern for the future, future generations near and distant may have to bear a disproportionate share of the costs of actions taken now.

Future environments

It is significant that the debate about the new technologies and their future costs has largely taken place within the context of the natural environment. Nowhere has this been more evident than in the concern for the supply of natural resources and for the nature of the research and development that should now be taking place to conserve nonrenewable resource stocks. Arguments to the effect that "technology" will solve the resource problem are naive in that they fail to comprehend the fact that technological change is not itself costless. Breeder reactors and ultimately nuclear fusion may indeed "solve" the future energy supply problem, but not without a cost—in the form of potential pollution and, perhaps more disturbing, nuclear proliferation. At the other extreme, renewable resources such as tidal, wind, and solar power may well provide the basis for a safer energy future, but again at a cost in terms of the resources necessary to introduce them. Only now are we beginning to research the actual costs involved in such "soft technology" futures.

The essential point remains that, for the immediate future, reliance on depletable resources will be high. Even without soft energy technologies and without advanced-technology reactors, there is still the immediate issue of rationing resources through time. In other fields the same issue arises with perhaps more force, since the scope for substituting renewable resources for nonrenewable ones appears more limited outside the energy sector. Recycling and extending product life to reduce the throughput of virgin materials have their roles to play; but close familiarity with case studies reveals the severe limitations on major increases in rates of change in these areas, while simple reflection will show how easily even a major change can be swamped by an exponential growth in national production.

There can be no avoiding the intergenerational rationing problem. Even allowing for all the potential for substitution, technological change, and recycling, there remains the issue of how the "resource base" is to be distributed between generations. Closely linked with this question is the issue of whether economic growth is desirable. For if resources are allocated, let us say, equally between generations up to a certain date—after which a renewable-technology world is foreseen—then this will have implications for economic growth. If some technological change takes place, a distribution policy of equality of resources will permit future generations to secure higher real incomes than the current generations. There may therefore be an argument for biasing resource allocation to the present, although whether that bias should be the same as that which results from the use of positive real discount rates (of about 10% in advanced economies), is very questionable.

If we adopt a Rawlsian standpoint[3] and argue that there should be a presumption of equal distribution with a bias towards the least well-off, we may find a resource allocation which favours current generations slightly, depending on the rate of technological change. But the requirement to consider the least well-off could be ambiguous. The neoclassical tradition in economics has always *presumed* that future generations would be better off in the light of the larger capital stock they inherit from the previous generation. This has been a reasonable assumption to date, given the historically exponential nature of economic growth, but it may no longer be correct, as Page notes,[4] if social costs are shifted forwards in time, reducing the real welfare of future generations. So, concern for the least well-off *could* bias resource allocation to the future.

Unless a future-orientated ethic is rejected (we argue shortly that it cannot be) and unless the supply of resources for future generations can be quickly converted to a renewable-resource base, the issue of resource rationing between generations is inescapable.

Economics and ethics

There is, of course, nothing which precludes noneconomists from seeking prescriptive rules for the allocation of resources through time. Equally, however, it is wrong to suppose that economics is fundamentally inconsistent with the prescription of rules for behaviour. Traditionally, economists have engaged in both the positive and the normative aspects of their science, although all too often they have pretended, more out of ignorance than intended deceit, that economics is in some sense "value free". Some have gone further and espoused the logical positivism of the 1920s, and have declared that economists *qua* economists can only pronounce upon causative, descriptive, or predictive issues of the type, "if you do this, such and such will happen".

This philosophy, apart from being dated in terms of current thinking on the difference in meaning between "is" and "ought" statements, has perhaps created more danger for economics than anything else. For the very verb "to economise" implies making the *best* use of resources, and *best* can have no meaning without a normative aim. The normative content of economics tends to confine itself to prescribing outcomes which are "socially preferred". The concept of social preference is replete with difficulties, but the basic idea is that it represents no more than the aggregation of individual preferences.

If, as will necessarily be the case, some gain and some lose from any policy, welfare economics is reduced to simply asking whether the gainers could compensate the losers (e.g. by giving them a sum of money) so that the losers are no worse off than they were before. If such compensation payments can be made and the gainers would still have something left over, then the policy is declared "socially preferred".[5]

Intergenerational compensation

Clearly, when the losers cannot vote, as is the case for future generations, this principle breaks down and we are forced to seek some other ethical base for deciding on the allocation of resources betwen generations. In this issue,*

---

*See Freeman, M. (1977) Equity, Efficiency, and Discounting, *Futures* Vol 9 (5) [eds].

Myrick Freeman raises the interesting possibility of resuscitating the compensation principle by setting aside now a sum of money which, when cumulated forwards at the discount rate (it then becomes an interest rate in the familiar sense), would provide cash compensation for future generations.

Apart from all the practical difficulties of deciding the value of future damages (will future generations have the same tastes?), such a procedure conflicts with the ethic proposed above. That is, the sums to be set aside would in most cases be trivial simply because of the existence of a market rate of interest. As such, the compensation fund is unlikely to figure prominently in any single project's budget, making concern for the future a relatively unimportant aspect of decision making. At the other extreme, if future costs are infinite in the sense that social collapse or nuclear holocaust ensues, the rule would at least serve the function of precluding projects which are thought even likely to generate such an outcome.

For the moment, we need only note that *some* moral standpoint is necessarily implied by whatever rule is chosen for the intergenerational allocation of resources. There can be no separation of an economic standpoint from that of the moralist—any rule is a moral rule. Accordingly, economists either imply or explicitly state such rules when discussing intertemporal equity. No judgement can be made as to the relative moral value of the different rules: all that can be done is to offer the rules for their moral appeal. However, it is certainly not valid to suggest that the standard cost–benefit framework incorporating a discount rate is *the* appropriate rule. The stand taken here is to suggest a Rawlsian objective of a probably equal allocation. Once the period of reliance on nonrenewable resources is ended, whether by deliberate policy or by simple exhaustion, then the rule must be formulated in terms of each generation extracting only the sustainable yields of renewable resources.[6]

Options and irreversibilities

So far we have suggested that feasible futures will involve a resource rationing problem and a problem of valuing costs imposed by earlier generations on later ones. Moreover, it has been argued that there is no escape from moral values in the resolution of either problem. The idea that economics is a science unrelated to moral science is false—as is the idea that simply because economists have studied the subject most, their rules are morally superior to any other rule.

As a final illustration of the problems of dealing with the intergenerational question let us consider irreversibility. Increasingly, the decisions that will have to be made in the next two or three decades will have as a cost the loss of some unique asset. In his article in this volume,* Haveman has drawn attention to the various ways in which the recent economic literature has looked at the problem. But we might extend the idea of *option value* a little to see if this suggests any behavioural rules.

The fundamental problem is that we cannot know now what future generations will think, although the fact that values are passed from one generation to another should lead us to think that future values will be fairly closely related to

*Included as a reading in this volume [eds.].

prevailing values.[7] Where costs and benefits are reversible, little problem arises. If we believe that future generations will value motorways, then their future valuation is properly included in any present assessment of motorways (which immediately raises questions about the efficacy of discounting). Moreover, such an inclusion is legitimate if we judge that, with existing technology, future generations can reverse the investment if they do *not* like motorways—i.e. if we make a mistake in judging their views. To be cautious, we need make no assumptions about future technology: we can judge technical reversibility on the basis of whether current technology can or cannot reverse any effects of the decision or investment.

Now, if we judge that future generations will *not* like high probabilities of radiation pollution, then again, their valuations are relevant. Again, discounting is suspect since it would have the effect of downgrading these valuations. As long as the pollution is reversible, no major change is required in our assessment procedure save that of introducing valuations based on what we think now that future generations will want. If we make a mistake, and future generations *like* radiation then we have erred on the side of caution which, given the likely magnitude of the future pay-offs we have discussed, seems correct.

But if the cost is *irreversible* then we have to ask what the appropriate valuation is since we have now precluded future generations from exercising an option. We have not only imposed a cost but we have also prevented anyone from investing in the removal of the cost. In this respect such a "double cost" should surely attract an extra penalty. How great that penalty is, is something that the present state of the art of futures thinking seems unable to answer. One approach might be to seek the current generation's value and cumulate that value forwards to some time horizon. Of course, if the time horizon is unlimited, then the value is finite (however small) and discounting is judged illicit because it removes votes from future generations; the effect of this procedure would be to attach an infinite cost to any nonreversible effect, and no project containing such effects would be undertaken.

Such a policy, of always holding options open, could easily become heavily restrictive. But this may indeed be the logical outcome of the adoption — which is itself a moral and logical necessity — of a future-oriented ethic. Precise answers, precise outcomes are as yet beyond the capability of this field of study; and the limited scope of the present, introductory article permits no more than a suggestion of guidelines for possible developments in the field. The following articles in this issue do, however, elaborate the implications of particular aspects of "accounting for the future".*

Notes and References

1. See H. A. Schroeder, *The Poisons Around Us* (Bloomington, Indiana, Indiana University Press, 1974).
2. For examples, see A. Scott, "Transfrontier pollution: are new institutions necessary?", in Organisation for Economic Co-operation and Development, *Economics of Transfrontier Pollution* (Paris, OECD, 1976).
3. J. Rawls, *A Theory of Justice* (London, Oxford University Press, 1974).

*October Issue of the Journal, *Futures*, Vol. 9 (5) [eds.].

4. Page, "Intertemporal and international aspects of virgin materials taxes", in D. W. Pearce and I. Walter, (eds) *Resource Conservation: The Social and Economic Dimension of Recycling* (New York, New York University Press, 1977).
5. This is the so-called "Kaldor-Hicks compensation test".
6. For an extensive discussion, see T. Page, *Conservation and Efficiency* (Baltimore, Johns Hopkins Press, 1977).
7. Values in futures research are discussed in Jib Fowles, "Values in futures research", *Futures*, August 1977, 9 (4), pages 303–314; Gordon Rattray Taylor, "Prediction and social change", *Futures*, October 1977, 9 (5), this issue.

THE ECONOMIC EVALUATION OF LONG-RUN UNCERTAINTIES*

Robert H. Haveman

WITH economic change increasingly dominated by technological developments, the decisions of both private-sector households and firms and the public sector have consequences which extend into the distant future. Given imperfect foresight, knowledge of these consequences will be partial and hence uncertain. Moreover, many of these consequences are "public" in nature, in the sense that they are not confined solely to those responsible for the decision. If such decisions are to be purposive, that is designed to achieve some defined goal or set of objectives, evaluation of their impact must be based on a firm theoretical underpinning.

At the present time, there are two fundamental issues which dominate discussions of the proper evaluation of long-term and uncertain events. These two issues are:

● Assuming no change in tastes from one generation to the next, how should one evaluate uncertainty regarding future effects when framing a social decision?

● How should the evaluation be done if the tastes of the current generation are not likely to persist into the future?

A good deal of work on the first of these questions has been done in recent years, primarily because of concern with the long-term and persistent effects associated with environmental decisions. Perhaps more than any other policy area, environmental policy is confronted with the problems of uncertainty and risk, and the role of future generations and their tastes.

This article describes the evolution of the economics literature concerned with the evaluation of uncertain, long-term environmental damages, summarises its current status, and examines the implications of the currently accepted analysis of that evaluation problem.

While the issue of uncertainty also relates to the matter of intergenerational preferences in evaluating impacts which extend over several decades, this problem will only be explicitly considered in one brief section—dealing with intergenerational taste changes. The justification for this neglect of the question of future generations' preferences is that the issue is far from resolved in the economics literature. The bulk of the discussion in *this* article will assume that future generations have tastes which are similar to those of people living today. In the discussion, it will also be assumed that the standard economic treatment

*© 1977 IPC Science and Technology Press, Guildford. Reprinted with permission from *Futures*, Vol. 9, 1977, pp. 365–374. (Professor Haveman is Professor of Economics at the University of Wisconsin-Madison.)

of time is appropriate for effects expected to extend for hundreds of years, as well as for those which will occur within a single generation.

Uncertain long-term effects and private risk aversion

To provide the discussion with an empirical focus, I will cast the problem of the evaluation of long-term and uncertain effects as one of evaluating decisions creating persistent and adverse impacts on the environment. This is convenient, given that most of the literature on this problem has been related to the environmental issue.

In order to isolate the issue of uncertainty and long-term effects, it is helpful to lay down a few general ground rules to guide the discussion:

● Any action taken, whether accidental or deliberate, which leads to the emission of residuals into the environment or to the destruction of some environmental amenity will create environmental costs, and these costs may or may not be accompanied by benefits associated with the action.
● Costs and benefits of an activity are to be calculated according to standard economic efficiency criteria. Individual tastes and preferences, as reflected in the willingness to pay for goods and services obtained and foregone, are the basis for such a calculation. The distribution of benefits and costs is ignored.
● As far as possible, the expression of benefits and costs is to be in terms of a monetary unit.
● Although they are technically distinguishable, the terms risk and uncertainty will be used interchangeably in this discussion.[1] Both will be taken to refer to the existence of a distribution of alternative outcomes for any particular action.
● The attitudes toward risk and uncertainty are crucial to the treatment of those factors. Two attitudes are often considered in discussions of risk and uncertainty: *risk neutrality* in which uncertainty attached to an event does not affect how an individual appraises the event—he will simply accept its mathematical expectation as its value) and *risk aversion* (in which uncertainty attached to an event leads an individual to appraise its worth at less than its mathematical expectation. The value attached to the event by such an individual is known as the *certainty equivalent* of the event.) Allusions to both attitudes will be made in this discussion.

Let us presume that such activity leads to environmental damages which persist for each of a known number of years into the future; that the value of these damages (the willingness to pay to forego them) is known with certainty for each year in which damages will occur; and that individuals have a preference for present rather than future consumption, which preference is called their *time preference*. If there exists smoothly functioning capital markets, the decisions taken by consumers in allocating their consumption over time, and the decisions taken by producers in undertaking investment activities, will lead to the establishment of a *market rate of interest* which reflects this time preference.

If this time preference interest rate is known, along with the time stream of certain environmental damages, the present value of these damages can be calculated by a procedure known as *discounting*. Stated symbolically, the present value of these damages (P) is:

$$P = \frac{D_i}{(1 + r)^i}$$

in which

D_i is the certain damages expected in year i, and
r is the time preference interest rate.

This present value of damages must be compared with the present value of the benefits of an activity to determine if the implementation of the activity increases the economic welfare of the community.

The approach to risk

If the environmental damages of an activity are uncertain in their value, the calculation of the present value of damages becomes more difficult. Assuming that people are *risk neutral*, the uncertain nature of damages in any given year could be transformed into its mathematical expectation, and then a present value could be calculated, as above. If probabilities can be attached to the range of possible values in any year, the mathematical expectation is easily calculated. Indeed, even if only *subjective probabilities* can be attached to these possible events, a mathematical expectation can be determined, and the present value calculated.

On the other hand, if people are *risk averse* rather than risk neutral, the simple calculation of the mathematical expectation will be inadequate. Risk aversion implies that the value of an uncertain phenomenon will differ from its mathematical expectation because the very existence of uncertainty is a cost. Suppose one is risk averse and one's $20000 home is on fire. If $10000 of damages could be averted if a fire truck comes within five minutes, and no damages would be averted if it doesn't, and if there is a 0·5 probability that a truck will come, the mathematical expectation of the value of the fire truck's appearance would be $5000. However, if one is risk averse, one would be willing to trade this possible appearance of a fire truck with the certain appearance of a torrential rain shower that would avert, say, only $4000 of damages. The $4000, then, is the certainty equivalent of the mathematical expectation of $5000, and the existence of uncertainty has created a cost of $1000.[2]

Because it is generally accepted that risk or uncertainty aversion exists, people require a premium on purchases which have uncertain values. Thus, a risky bond will have to offer a higher interest rate than a risk-free bond. There is a structure of interest rates, with higher rates associated with instruments having high variability in outcome, and lower rates associated with low variability instruments.

If we presume the existence of risk or uncertainty aversion, the question arises: "How is risk or uncertainty to be accounted for in evaluating decisions with enduring and uncertain consequences?" This question has occupied economists for some time, and a number of rules of thumb have been suggested for adjusting the benefits of such decisions to reflect the cost of uncertainty. The primary suggestions are:[3]

● Observe every year's expected value (mathematical expectation) of benefits, and make a judgement on the degree of uncertainty which surrounds this value; then on the basis of the degree of risk aversion which is felt, substitute a lower certain equivalent value for the expected but uncertain value.

● Place a limit on the length of time over which the benefits are expected to occur which is shorter than the expected length. This technique ignores uncertainty in early years, and uncertainty in years beyond the limit is implied to have a cost at least as great as the expected value of benefits in those years.

● Add a premium to the interest rate used for discounting benefits, with the size of this added premium reflecting a judgement of the cost of the uncertainty involved in the benefit stream. If a single premium is added to the discount rate used for discounting all future years' consequences, the effect is to reduce benefits in distant years by more than benefits in proximate years. This is a reasonable approach if the degree of uncertainty is positively related to the delay in the experiencing of benefits.

If risk aversion is relevant, each of these procedures will lead to a reduction in the present value of benefits attributable to an activity. The gap between the present value without the adjustment and that with the adjustment reflect the cost of uncertainty.

These procedures are also relevant for evaluating the adverse and uncertain consequences stemming from any decision. In this case, however, it must be emphasised that the stream of effects which is being evaluated is a cost stream rather than a benefit stream. Hence, the cost of bearing uncertainty must be added to the stream of effects and must result in a *higher* present value, if risk or uncertainty aversion is relevant. Thus, the three rules of thumb mentioned earlier must be altered in evaluating a stream of adverse consequences. In particular, the mathematical sign of the adjustment must be reversed:

● A *higher* certainty equivalent value can be substituted for the expected but uncertain value.

● The length of time over which the damages are expected to accrue can be *lengthened*.

● A discount can be *subtracted* from the interest rate used to calculate the present value.

This alteration, it must be noted, is fundamental and yet it is often not recognised in the literature. Because nearly all analysis has presumed the existence of positive net benefits, limits on length of life, reductions of expected value, and risk premiums have almost exclusively been considered. All of these adjustments are in precisely the wrong direction for evaluating an uncertain stream of costs or damages.[4]

The social evaluation of long-term uncertain effects

Few would deny that individual decision makers are averse to risk and uncertainty and should therefore apply adjustments of the sort discussed in the previous section to uncertain events;[5] but from the point of society as a whole it is not clear that an activity's uncertain future effects convey the same sort of cost. While private risk aversion exists, social risk aversion may not.

In the economics literature, two reasons for neglecting uncertainty in social evaluations have been suggested. They are the pooling argument, and the Arrow–Lind theorem.

The pooling argument

According to this argument,[6] individuals experience a cost associated with uncertain returns because they have limited resources and, hence, are unable to pool their risky events. For society as a whole, however, the uncertainty attached to the effects of one activity is pooled with the uncertainty attached to the effects of numerous other activities. If these activities are independent (i.e. uncorrelated), the pooled effect of the individual uncertainties has zero impact on the total uncertainty of real national income and, hence, can be ignored (see Arrow[7]).

Even the proponents of this position, however, recognise that pooling only has this effect if there is no relationship between the variability (uncertainty) in the outcome of a particular activity and the variability in the performance of the economy as a whole. If there is such a relationship, the pooling argument breaks down.

The Arrow–Lind theorem

In a recent paper, Arrow and Lind have demonstrated that as the effects (costs or benefits) of an activity are shared by an increasing number of individuals, the cost of uncertainty to any one representative individual decreases until, at the limit, this cost vanishes.[8] If the number of individuals sharing the effects is large enough, then only the expected value of the effects should be taken into account, even though each of the individuals is risk averse.

In addition, Arrow and Lind have demonstrated that the aggregate costs of this uncertainty—added up over all individuals—also approaches zero. The implication of this in the evaluation of costs and benefits (including environmental damages) is that, from the social point of view, risk neutrality is the correct position.

However, it should be noted that the Arrow–Lind theorem requires that the effects (benefits and costs) be spread over a very large number of individuals —indeed, an infinite number—if social risk neutrality is to be presumed. In a comment on the Arrow–Lind paper, McKean and Moore suggest that not even a total of 80 million US taxpayers is a sufficiently large number to permit uncertainty to be neglected.[9] In those cases in which effects or costs are distributed among a limited number of individuals, risk aversion is still to be presumed and a cost for uncertain effects is to be subtracted from expected benefit estimates and added to expected cost estimates.

And a further reservation to the Arrow–Lind theorem has been expressed. It has been pointed out that Arrow and Lind have implicitly assumed that the effects of private and public activities are uncorrelated. However, if for any particular effect generated by a public activity (and spread over a large number of individuals), there is an equivalent and correlated effect in the private sector, the risk aversion of the small number of individuals affected by that influence from the private sector should be applied in evaluating the former. Therefore, individual risk aversion should be a guide for social evaluation.[10]

In the literature, then, the existence of social risk aversion is an unsettled matter. Under certain conditions, the Arrow–Lind risk neutrality appears to hold; under others, social risk aversion exists and should be accounted for in evaluating the consequences of activities, whether private or public. In spite of the Arrow–Lind theorem, numerous economists consider that social risk aversion is relevant in evaluating uncertain activities.[11]

Evaluating uncertainty in special cases

Even if it is presumed that the conditions required for the Arrow–Lind theorem do prevail, it may be the case that some kinds of effects have characteristics such that social evaluation should presume risk aversion. Within the last few years, several papers have appeared which indicate that such characteristics do exist.

Long-term, uncertain, "public good" effects

Fisher[12] considers the example of an activity which generates a stream of benefits or damages which are spread across risk-averse individuals in such a way that what is incurred by one does not diminish what is received by others. Such effects are public goods (or, perhaps, public "bads"). Employing a model similar to the Arrow–Lind model, Fisher demonstrates that, in addition to the expected value of the benefit or cost stream, the evaluation must also consider "the amount that would be required to compensate those who bear the risk" or uncertainty associated with the future uncertain stream. That is, an "adjustment for risk should be made".

For this reintroduction of social risk aversion to hold, Fisher notes that the benefit or cost must represent a non-negligible fraction of the real income of those affected, and that the risk or uncertainty is not (or cannot be) costlessly transferred from the effected individuals to the larger community.

Long-term, uncertain, irreversible effects

Many activities are accompanied by environmental damages which significantly and permanently—or merely for a long period—reduce the variety of future choices. An example of such irreversible damage would be the destruction, by the erection of a hydro-electricity dam, of a natural gorge.

Recent literature, concentrating on environmental damages, has demonstrated that when individuals are uncertain about their future use of a facility (or when the supply of the facility is uncertain), if an adverse impact on the facility is irreversible, and if the individuals are risk averse, an extra cost—called *option value*—must be added to the expected value of future damages.[13].

The existence of this option value—a sort of risk or uncertainty cost—is now accepted in the literature — although it may be that, applying the Arrow–Lind theorem, the cost is irrelevant from the social point of view. However, in a very recent paper, Arrow and Fisher have argued that if such effects (for example, environmental damages) are irreversible, *and* if information about these effects results in a *change* in their expected value in a later period, an addition to the expected value of damages—similar to an uncertainty adjustment—must be made.[14] Hence, even though risk neutrality is assumed for the social evaluation of uncertain future effects, if the impact is irreversible and if further information is expected, there exists "a quasi-option value having an effect in the same direction as risk aversion". The value of irreversible expected damages should be adjusted upward to reflect the resulting loss of options, and, similarly, the value of irreversible expected benefits should be adjusted downward. This same result, it should be pointed out, was obtained by Henry, employing a quite different approach.[15] Simulating the extent of the required adjustment for uncertainty using reasonable values for the discount rate and levels of uncertainty, he concludes that "13 percent seems to give a good idea of the degree of magnitude of the irreversibility effect".

Long-term uncertain effects with shifting evaluations

Finally, a recent contribution to the question of evaluating uncertain future effects has considered the issue of intertemporal taste instability. This contribution by Fisher and Krutilla[16] was the first to allow the tastes of future generations for environmental services and for risk and uncertainty to deviate from those of the present generation. The issue raised in their paper concerned the evaluation of environmental damages when tastes toward the environment may be shifting over time. Where there is such uncertainty regarding future tastes, Fisher and Krutilla argue that an additional cost must be added to the expected value of damages. If, for example, it is possible that future generations will place a higher value on environmental damages than present citizens, and if an activity is generating irreversible (or at least long-term) environmental damages, *ex post facto* evaluation of the damages would exceed the current evaluation. To reflect these changing tastes—and to avoid the approval of activities generating environmental damages which, from "tomorrow's" perspective, should have been disapproved—an additional cost should be added to the expected level of the damages. This is true even when uncertainty is irrelevant, from a social point of view, according to the Lind–Arrow theorem.[17]

Summary

The literature reviewed in this article indicates that there are numerous cases in which the presence of uncertainty requires an adjustment to the expected value of anticipated future costs or benefits. In spite of the Arrow–Lind theorem —implying that *social* risk aversion is irrelevant—numerous circumstances exist which require that a premium be added to the expected value of future damages (and a discount subtracted from the expected value of future benefits) in calculating the social value of proposed activities. The circumstances which are relevant in determining the need for and extent of such an uncertainty adjustment are:

● the presence and degree of *risk aversion* among the population affected by a proposed activity;

● the extent to which the effects of the activity are *irreversible*, in which case an *option value* is created;
● the economic attributes of the expected effects, in terms of their public- or private-good character and, in the latter case, the number of people affected;
● the extent to which the expected effects are *correlated* with other economic activities;
● the extent to which information on the effect of activities is expected to improve over time because of *learning from experience*; and
● the extent to which it is anticipated that *tastes* with regard to environmental questions will be altered over time.

In Table 1, combinations of these characteristics are shown and the need for uncertainty adjustment in each combination is indicated. Where more than one

Table 1

Evaluations of Benefits or Costs Requiring Uncertainty Adjustments

	Individuals assumed to be risk neutral		Individuals assumed to be risk averse	
	effect irreversible	effect reversible	effect irreversible	effect reversible
The effect is correlated with other economic activities			×	×
Economic characteristic of effect:				
public good			×	×
private good affecting few individuals			×	×
private good affecting many individuals			×	×
Change in tastes with regard to effects	×		×	
Improvement in information expected	×		×	

source of adjustment is indicated in a column, the aggregate adjustment required is the cumulative effect of all of the sources. All of these adjustments can be translated into a reduction (or increase) in the discount rate used to estimate the present value of future damages (benefits) and, hence, an increase (decrease) in the social valuation of these effects from that indicated by their expected value.

Looking at the table, it is apparent that many prominent issues awaiting public resolution fall into categories which require an aggregate adjustment for uncertainty, reflecting several sources. Many of the major technological developments—for example, nuclear power—appear to carry with them irreversible negative effects, often having the character of a public good. Assuming that individuals are risk averse, evaluation of those activities would be guided by column three of the table. The cumulated adjustment for uncertainty in these cases implies a need for substantial caution in appraising requests for the commitment of additional social resources to these activities.

Notes and references

1. The distinction between them is set out most clearly in F. H. Knight, *Risk, Uncertainty and Profit* (New York, Harper and Row, 1965).
2. This statement overstates the simplicity of evaluating many decisions creating long-term uncertain consequences. As Conrad has pointed out, in evaluating the damages of acts which disturb the environment (such as oil spills): "the number of extenuating factors is so complex that no true or ideal set of states which exhaustively describes the future could be constructed. In this case the uncertainty prevailing in the mind of the decision maker would not appear to be capable of being synthesised or reduced to the single elementary level required for formulation in the standard decision making problem under uncertainty.

   The dilemma is particularly real for most of the contemporary environmental problems ... because (1) ... the combination of circumstances may be so unique as to preclude formation of frequency estimates based on past (objective) observations; that is, only subjective probability statements can be made and (2) many of these ... consequences [are produced] only after sufficient lags or cumulation of past discharges so that ... knowing what state of nature has occurred or obtained is not a trivial exercise". Jon Conrad, *Uncertain Externality: The Case of Oil Pollution*, unpublished PhD dissertation, University of Wisconsin-Madison, 1973.
3. For a more detailed discussion of these techniques and their implications, see R. Dorfman, "Basic economic and technologic concepts: a general statement" in A. Maass, M. Hufschmidt, R. Dorfman, H. A. Thomas Jr, S. A. Marglin, and G. M. Fair, *Design of Water Resource Systems* (Cambridge, Mass, Harvard University Press, 1962).
4. See R. Haveman, *Water Resource Investment and the Public Interest* (Nashville, Vanderbilt University Press, 1965) for a discussion of this. See also J. Hirshleifer and D. Shapiro, "The treatment of risk and uncertainty", in R. Haveman and J. Margolis, *Public Expenditure and Policy Analysis*, second edition (Skokie, Illinois, Rand-McNally, 1977).
5. See J. Hirshleifer and D. Shapiro, *op cit* (reference 3).
6. This position is defended in W. Vickrey, "Principles of efficiency—discussion", *American Economic Review*, 54 (Papers and Proceedings), May 1964.
7. K. J. Arrow, "Discounting and public investment criteria", in A. V. Kneese and S. C. Smith, eds, *Water Resources Research* (Baltimore, Johns Hopkins Press, 1966).
8. K. J. Arrow and R. C. Lind, "Uncertainty and the evaluation of public investment decisions", *American Economic Review, 40*, June 1970.
9. R. N. McKean and J. H. More, "Uncertainty and the evaluation of public investment decisions: comment", *American Economic Review, 42*, January 1972.
10. See A. Sandmo, "Discount rates for public investment under uncertainty", *International Economic Review*, June 1972.
11. See O. Eckstein, *Water Resource Development* (Cambridge, Mass, Harvard University Press, 1958); J. Hirshleifer, "Investment decision under uncertainty: applications of the State-preference approach", *Quarterly Journal of Economics, 80*, May 1966; J. Hirshleifer, "Préférence sociale à l'égard du temps", *Recherches Economiques de Louvain, 34*, 1968; J. Hirshleifer, J. C. de Haven, and J. W. Milliman, *Water Supply: Economics, Technology, and Policy* (Chicago, University of Chicago Press, 1960); and J. S. Bain, R. E. Caves, and J. Margolis, *Northern California's Water Industry* (Baltimore, Johns Hopkins Press, 1966).
12. A. C. Fisher, "Environmental externalities and the Arrow–Lind public investment theorem", *American Economic Review*, 1974.
13. See C. Cicchetti and A. M. Freeman, "Option demand and consumer surplus: further comments", *Quarterly Journal of Economics, 85*, October 1971.
14. K. J. Arrow and A. C. Fisher, "Environmental preservation, uncertainty, and irreversibility", *Quarterly Journal of Economics*, May 1974.
15. C. Henry, "Irreversible decisions under uncertainty", *American Economic Review, 64*, December 1974.
16. A. C. Fisher and J. V. Krutilla, "Valuing long-run ecological consequences and irreversibilities", in H. Peskin and E. Seskin, *Cost Benefit Analysis and Water Pollution Policy* (Washington DC, The Urban Institute, 1975).
17. An example of the evaluation of uncertain environmental damages of this sort is found in A. C. Fisher, J. V. Krutilla, and C. J. Cicchetti, "The economics of environmental preservation: a theoretical and empirical analysis", *American Economic Review, 57*, September 1972. For additional discussions regarding the role of future generations in appraising uncertain events,

see S. A. Marglin, "The social rate of discount and the optimal rate of investment", *Quarterly Journal of Economics, 78*, May 1964. The current status of this intergenerational issue was described by US National Academy of Sciences, *Decision Making for Regulating Chemicals in the Environment* (Washington DC, 1976) as follows: "There is as yet no generally accepted method for weighing the intergenerational incidence of benefits and costs".

SHARING RESOURCES WITH THE FUTURE*

Talbot Page

FOR many years there have been two approaches to the formulation of materials policy, one associated with the traditional thinking of resource economists and the other with that of conservationists. An important purpose of this book is to develop a unifying conceptual structure to join together these two approaches.

In the past, national policy has followed the assumption that the more we extract and use our natural resources, the faster we build up the economy. The larger the volume of materials we process, so the idea has gone, the richer and more secure we become. Instead of letting our mineral resources lie fallow in the ground, they should be turned into productive assets, benefiting future generations as well as our own. For example, for two centuries the United States favored mineral extraction on its national lands, codifying the practice in the 1872 mining law. The extraction of minerals, including energy minerals, was encouraged by depletion allowances and other tax preferences; energy consumption was encouraged by a promotional price system that gave volume discounts for larger consumption. The ostensible cost of energy and materials was reduced by ignoring the environmental costs associated with extracting and processing them.

By materials we mean here the basic raw materials of the economy — minerals, metals, and nonfood fibers. In 1972 the United States consumed 290 million tons of forest products, 140 million tons of metals (mostly iron), 1.9 billion tons of fuel minerals, and 2.1 billion tons of nonmetallic, nonfuel materials (mostly stone, sand, and gravel).

The consumption of materials has doubled every thirty-five years since 1870. This is bound to change, for we cannot go through many more doubling periods. Much of the growth in materials consumption is driven by population growth, and historically the growth in consumption of materials has been about 0.3 percent greater than the growth in population. Thus, some of the increase in materials consumption is likely to melt away automatically and painlessly as population levels off. And some of the growth will be attenuated, however painfully, if we move into an era of sharply higher costs for both energy and materials. Whatever changes take place, our historical experience remains built into our economic structure, and our economy still favors extraction and use over conservation. Perhaps the most basic question of materials policy formulation is this: After two centuries of favoring materials extraction, should we now take active steps toward a more conservative materials policy, and if so, how?

By what standards do we judge the best, or optimal, balance between depletion and conservation of materials, between disposal and recycling, durability and original cost, maintenance and new production? These questions

* Reprinted with permission from *Resources*, No. 56, 1977, pp. 1–3.

lead directly to another: How should we account for the very long-run costs which may be associated with materials depletion and waste generation?

Efficiency criterion. The market itself provides a standard of sorts in that it defines a balance between depletion and conservation, recycling and disposal, and durability and initial cost. Market forces lead to a certain flow of material through the economy, extending from extraction to discharge into the environment (or material throughput). In the exploitative view, the extraction of virgin materials is an engine of economic growth and development, so that extraction should be encouraged beyond what the market would do by itself. Opposing this view is the belief that markets do not provide adequately for the future, so that provision for the future, in the form of conservation, should be encouraged beyond what the market would do by itself. It is interesting that both the exploitative and conservationist views are largely justified in terms of benefit to the future, yet they recommend opposite materials policies.

Generally, economists have taken a more neutral view. The market is indeed flawed, they agree, but if the flaws were corrected, there would be no need for a national materials policy; the market would provide the right balance between depletion and conservation, disposal and durability, and so forth. In this view, recycling is neither good nor bad in itself; it is the correction of market failures that is important. If the market failures cannot be corrected, or if upon examination they turn out not to be failures at all but "distortions" to bend market allocations toward worthy and intended policy goals, then the market can still be used as a standard to measure by. By this view, we estimate what the market would do in the absence of distortions, calculate the gaps by examining what the market is actually doing, and choose materials policy goals on the basis of closing these gaps. To follow this prescription is to act under the *efficiency criterion.* This criterion, which can be used as a basis for materials policy, says that material flows *should* be arranged as if they were operating in a perfect market.

There are four causes of market inefficiencies that are important for our purposes and that manifest themselves in imbalance between prices and marginal costs. These are (1) monopoly pricing power; (2) the market system's inability to include environmental and disposal costs in product prices; (3) distortions in the federal tax system; and (4) price systems, such as freight pricing, which discriminate among products on the basis of what the traffic will bear.

Correction of the last three market inefficiencies would lead to more recycling and less material throughput. Is this enough? Is the efficiency criterion sufficient as a basis for a materials policy? Would even perfect markets provide adequately for the future?

Intertemporal fairness. Markets can be expected to allocate resources more or less efficiently relative to a given distribution of wealth or market power (a hypothetical ideal market would actually achieve efficiency). But markets cannot be expected to solve the problem of what is a fair or equitable distribution of wealth, either among different people at a point in time (intratemporally) or among different generations (intertemporally). The questions of depletion and generation of long-lived wastes are fundamentally questions of equitable distribution of burdens across generations. The problem of a fair intertemporal distribution arises because the material resource base is potentially long-lived, as are some wastes (the plutonium waste generated by reactors has a half-life of 24,500 years). Thus the same materials must be shared among many generations.

It is sometimes assumed that future generations will be better off than the present one, even taking into account future burdens from long-lived wastes and depleted resource stocks. The assumption is usually derived from extrapolations of past trends in capital formation and other economic aggregates. In the past it was often assumed that increases in knowledge were always net benefits and that capital accumulation was always a homogeneous good thing. Under such assumptions, with knowledge and capital growing, the only intertemporal welfare problem is how much saving the present generation should do and how fast the future should be made better off. Under the assumption that the future is going to be better off no matter what, the question of intertemporal equity is not a pressing matter.

However, the costs of long-lived material wastes or material resource depletion are not certainties or even mathematical expectations. The burdens associated with resource use that we are placing upon the future are largely risk burdens. With respect to both material wastes and depletion, the equity question is: What is a fair distribution of risk to impose upon the future? For many long-lived wastes, we have exceedingly little idea of the intertemporal distribution of risk. And in order to judge the distribution of a depletion burden, we would first have to forecast the strengths of each of the price determinants of the major material resources. Clearly this is a very difficult thing to do and involves a great deal of uncertainty in the assessment of risk.

While technology is ultimately the only way of renewing "nonrenewable" material resources, it adds to the legacy of risk to be bequeathed to the next generation. Technological solutions are not inevitable. As the flows of nonrenewable resources become larger for the United States and increasingly so for other countries, our dependence on technological fixes becomes greater. The power of technology itself becomes greater, with uncalculated and perhaps unmanageable side effects. Thus, the burden as we use up oil is the risk burden that we will not come up with a substitute technology in time. Alvin Weinberg has called one alternative, nuclear power, a Faustian bargain. More generally, the present is in the process of imposing many Faustian lotteries upon the future. Our legacy to the future is not homogeneous and is not composed entirely of benefits. Intertemporal equity emerges as an important problem because there is no easy way to add up the costs and risks along with the benefits and no way to guarantee that the future is going to be better off than the present.

Two means of achieving direct price effects are of considerable importance. The first is the severance tax; this is simply a tax on virgin material extracted from the ground or environment. It may be based either upon the dollar value of the material extracted (ad valorem) or upon the weight or quantity of the material extracted (specific). Severance taxes increase the nominal scarcity of virgin materials, from the point of view of users and consumers. Severance taxes also slow down the rate of extraction, buying time to develop substitutes and increasing their payoff. In the past the severance tax has been levied principally at the state level, but here the tax is considered at the national level as an instrument of intertemporal fairness.

The second means of achieving direct price effects, other than resource reservations, is the percentage depletion allowance. As will be seen later, this provision is almost a mirror image of a severance tax and is nearly equivalent to a subsidy per unit of material extracted. Not only is it the best known provision favoring mineral industries and a direct price effect, but in addition its close relationship with the severance tax makes it instructive for our purposes. Percentage depletion allowances began in 1926 and have grown over the years largely in ignorance of their long-run effects. It appears, but it is by no means clear, that the short-run effects of percentage depletion allowances are not highly disruptive but the long-run effects may be substantial; the same may be true of the severance tax. In the long run, measures such as percentage depletion allowances and severance taxes affect the renewability of the resource base, especially when we think of technological change as a method of renewing nonrenewable resources.

Keeping the resource base intact. The problem of intertemporal fairness becomes greatly simplified when the resource base is kept essentially intact over time. Suppose, for example, that as we are forced to use less rich ores, say $\frac{1}{2}$ instead of 1 percent copper ore, technology progresses, allowing the cost of copper per unit extracted (including the environmental costs) to remain constant. Then it is a matter of indifference which generation one is born into, at least with respect to the copper resource. Copper is being managed on a "sustainable yield" basis. In such a case, at least with respect to the materials base, there would be a world of equals between generations. It might be an attractive goal, as a matter of intertemporal fairness, to keep the resource base essentially intact, but it is not a goal that markets can be expected to achieve automatically, even if they were perfected.

Conservationists have long held it an important goal to keep the resource base essentially intact from generation to generation. And when the resource base appears threatened, as it now does with respect to fossil fuels, preservation of this base becomes an important goal for society as a whole. Economists will recognize this goal as a macroeconomic one, and the severance tax, in this context, as a macroeconomic policy instrument. Economists often recommend macroeconomic policies on employment, inflation, interest rates, and the balance of payments. These policies are designed to establish a context within which market forces can interact on their own to the advantage of society at large.

In the past, economists have not included preservation of the resource base in their list of macroeconomic goals needing explicit policy measures. They have relied on the invisible hand of the market to match new technology against depletion, much as, before the Depression, they counted on the invisible hand to eliminate unemployment. But now, as material flows are becoming enormously larger, lead times shorter, and the environmental and technological effects more pervasive, it is time to make preservation of the resource base an explicit policy issue.

Planning and Environmental Protection

INTRODUCTORY ESSAY

"Let us abandon the self mutilation which has been our way and give expression to the potential harmony of man–nature. The world is abundant, we require only a deference born of understanding to fulfil man's promise. Man is that uniquely conscious creature who can perceive and express. He must become the steward of the biosphere. To do this he must design with nature."

These words, written by the Scottish-American planner Ian McHarg,[1] express the essence of the thinking of the technocentrist environmental manager introduced in Section 1. This particular section is largely devoted to the views and practices of this group of people and to the manner in which they are changing, and are being forced to change, techniques of project appraisal and procedures for reassessing environmental management policies. McHarg himself was the most prominent of the new breed of ecological planners who emerged during the heyday of the new public interest in ecology around the turn of the decade of the seventies. Over a surprisingly short period the science of ecology moved out of the academic shadows into the glaring spotlights of politics and public administration. People known formerly only to a few colleagues gradually became almost household names, for example Rachel Carson,[2] Paul Ehrlich,[3] Barry Commoner[4] and Garrett Hardin,[5] Max Nicholson[6] and Frank Fraser-Darling,[7] Raymond Dasmann,[8] Jean Dorst[9] and Nicholas Polunin.[10]

Slowly but surely ecology and other environmental sciences are becoming an integral part of modern-day planning. And planning is beginning to lose its fascination with settlement patterns, building design and grand regional development strategies, to consider more carefully how man can design with nature. Progress is slow and it will be a little while yet before environmental planning is fully embraced by the profession but at least the wheels have been set in motion. An important factor here is the introduction of environmental impact assessment (EIA) as part of the kitbag of project assessment techniques in Europe having proven its value in North America for nearly a decade.[11] This will require that planners become more familiar with the environmental sciences and that their proposals from the very earliest design stage take into account potentially irreversible environmental consequences. But more of this below. We must set the stage by asking why EIA has come of age and thus why planning and the environmental sciences are intermixing. There are three basic reasons.

First of all ecologists began to do their sums: they collected admittedly patchy but nevertheless alarming evidence of what an ignorant and uncaring society was doing to its natural heritage. A number of national reports showed how habitats were being destroyed and various plant and animal species lost, partly as a result of particular development schemes but largely due to the cumulative effect of apparently inconsequential planning decisions. For example, the US Council on Environmental Quality (CEQ)[12] reports that since the sixteenth century in America alone the species extinction rate has jumped to 150 species each century, with 85 species or subspecies of vertebrate animals alone known to have been destroyed since 1900. The CEQ also concludes that the rate of species loss is accelerating due primarily to ill-considered planning and thoughtless agricultural development. The Annual Reports of the United Nations Environment Programme produce equally disturbing reading. Even though there needs to be a great improvement in the coordination and comparability of the monitoring of ecological change, the conclusions of the current crop of surveys are extremely worrying. Reference to the extent of global ecological damage has already been made in Section 1.*

In Britain one of the chief causes of anxiety is the loss of important habitats due to farming practices which are not normally subject to planning controls. A recent report from the Nature Conservancy Council[13] indicates that there has been a progressive loss of woodland, moorland and marsh habitats since the war and that the accelerating rate of these losses is now alarming. The Council guesses that there may have been as much as a 30 percent loss of the rarer British plants between 1930 and 1960 judging from their surveys of a representative sample of agricultural landscapes but among the rarest species the loss has been much greater. The present danger lies most in the largely unprotected (from a planning perspective) English lowlands where as much as one-tenth of all British flora are to be found. Yet clearly the Council does not yet feel that the message has sufficiently been driven home.

"The danger of underestimating the extent and rate of declines in habitats and populations of flora and fauna is a very real one, because it encourages people to think that all is well and that there is no urgent need to take effective action. All the factual evidence suggests that Britain faces a serious reduction in wildlife if present trends continue. This is as far as science can take us."[14]

*See also Holdgate, M., Kassas, M. and White, G. F. (eds) 1982. *The World Environment 1972–1982.* Tycooly International Publishing Ltd., Dublin. [eds].

A second reason why environmental sciences are intruding into planning is that ecologists in particular have begun to show that habitat loss and species decline is not merely a moral matter (a line of reasoning which, unfortunately, does not always stir the hearts of man) but an economic one, since poor management can easily turn a healthy renewable resource either into a dead wasteland or, more likely, into a problem area where remedies are costly and often ineffective. McHarg illustrates the point by showing that the building of holiday homes on the vulnerable sand dunes of the New Jersey coast not only destroys the dune but exposes the homes (and the area behind them) to the ferocity of hurricane-driven storms which undermine foundations and cause unnecessary millions of dollars' worth of damage.[15] Figure 4.1 illustrates his points diagrammatically. In the developing world soil erosion caused by excessive grazing on the desert margins (often encouraged by the well-meant but ill-thought placing of water wells in such areas) or by deforestation of hills, strip the fertility of these regions and create damaging duststorms and excessive siltation of rivers and lakes.

The use of chemical pesticides to kill unwanted insect species is a further example of where thoughtless intervention can create not only serious ecological damage but unnecessary economic costs. Before 1940 crop rotations, pest-resistant crop varieties, cultivation and natural predation dealt with agricultural and public health pests in a reasonably satisfactory way. Nowadays with enormous pressures to increase agricultural productivity, changing public attitudes to blemishes on crops and the growing need to control public health pests, these measures were judged to be ineffective and insufficient. So the chemical pesticide industry was born, designed initially to provide cheap biocides that were effective across a wide range of species. The results are now well known; first of all, all kinds of benevolent species died directly or indirectly through concentration of poisons through the food chains. Secondly, the most annoying of insects developed genetic strains that were resistant to one or more of the chemicals. At present there are 364 species of insects, mites and ticks which are known to be pesticide-resistant. Nineteen species of disease-carrying mosquito and 121 species of housefly have developed almost complete immunity.[16] Consequently more and more expensive efforts are being made to produce target-specific biocides which do not have unacceptable environmental repercussions while nearly a third in value of all agricultural production in the US is lost due to agricultural pests of one kind or another.[17]

There is no doubt that adverse consequences of ecological mischief has done much to drive McHarg's philosophy home and to make EIA a regular feature of project appraisal, though one should never forget the persistent, niggling role of environmental pressure groups. But a third and related factor is that ecologists, and to a lesser extent other

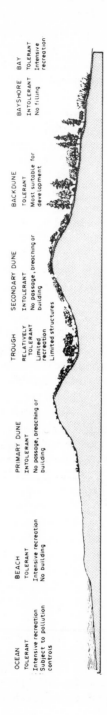

FIGURE 4.1

Coastal planning and dune protection in an ecological context. This schematic diagram is drawn from McHarg, I. (1965) *Design with Nature* (Doubleday, New York, pp. 14–17). In McHarg's view, the dune ecology sets its own rules for planners, providing zones for development and conservation. Failure to obey these rules could result in catastrophe.

environmental scientists, have actually begun to penetrate the planning profession. This is now widely the case in the US where EIAs are now well established. But even in Britain, a recent survey by Elkington and Roberts[18] showed that there was a "population explosion" of ecologists in planning departments (a total of thirty-three official ecologists were employed by local planning authorities in 1978) and evidently a widespread recognition on the part of chief planning officers that their presence was vital. Despite this, it seems that ecologists are not always accepted as full professional colleagues by many planners and hence their credibility and promotional prospects are not as good as they ought to be, so the ecologist/environmental scientist needs to be a little more pushy and a little more patient before his influence is properly felt.

Environmental Planning and Political Decisions

The general discussion takes us to the more delicate question of what precisely should be the relationship between the environmental scientist, the planner, the elected member (politician) and the public. The matter is delicate because there are many differing interpretations of professional ethos involved. First we should ask ourselves why environmental scientists have taken so long to be listened to by planners. One answer, in the British context, is that ecological research has traditionally been conducted by specialist scientific research institutes or research units within government departments or through university departments funded by contracts awarded by the major national research councils. Generally speaking, all of these organisations were primarily conducting research that had no specific relevance to particular planning matters. When planning departments wanted ecological advice, for example, they asked bodies such as the Nature Conservancy Council, the Institute for Terrestrial Ecology (and possibly the local County Naturalists' Trust — a voluntary body) for advice on a consultative basis. The Elkinton–Roberts survey[19] found that almost all local authority ecologists contacted one or other of these bodies at least once per year for particular pieces of information. The trouble here is that these organisations are not well equipped to undertake this role in a big way, and though the Nature Conservancy Council is regarded as the statutory body responsible for giving advice on conservation and ecological matters, its views are often treated as part of the consultative procedure that follows a crucial decision to proceed in principle rather than a central component of the preliminary discussions that take place before a proposal is fully formulated.

So a second reason why environmental science input into planning has still to come of age in the UK is the difference in professional approach and especially timing between environmental scientists and planners.[20]

Very often planners have to make quick decisions, quick that is in terms of the necessary ecological research, and their political masters normally look for unambiguous advice as to how to proceed. Elected members are normally most unhappy if presented with qualifications and uncertainties—especially if these are quantified. In the case of major proposals, such as energy-related schemes or mining developments, neither planners nor politicians nor the proponents of the proposal are usually prepared to await the results of a thoroughly detailed environmental appraisal, evidence of which ought to be incorporated into the final project design. (Some would argue this information should be known before the scheme is even contemplated.) Basic ecological research can easily take 3–5 years, and in areas of climate stress sometimes 10–20 years. In any case, really sound ecological analyses requires a fair amount of baseline information about species mix and rates of change. This kind of information is very costly to produce because it requires continuous monitoring and skilled manpower. In truth, succeeding British governments have never given the research institutes sufficient funds to undertake this kind of work, so when major proposals are contemplated (e.g. tungsten mining on the edge of Dartmoor National Park, reservoir expansion in the Lake District, coal development in the Vale of Belvoir in Leicestershire, land drainage in the Norfolk Broads) the vital baseline data are not available and crude, rule-of-thumb substitutes have to be superimposed. Admittedly it would be economically unwise to invest in a major programme of baseline data collection, for much of the material probably would never be used, but a case can be made for strategic ecological monitoring of critical landscape areas and natural habitats that are representative of a variety of threatened areas across the nation. From a conservation viewpoint it is a tragedy that this kind of approach has not yet been recognised in political circles as being so vital.

All this means that in terms of professional practice, environmental scientists have sometimes to provide advice on the basis of flimsy research or by means of intuition or experience. And try as they will to persuade planners that their advice may be speculative or based on qualifications, limitations which are disliked by serious-minded scientists, their advice is often acted upon by planners as if it was gospel—or it may be mistreated by vested interests who see political advantage in recalculating or undermining the credibility of environmental appraisal. In short, environmental advice is usually embodied within the rubric of planning and political ideologies and accommodated to fit. An interesting report which devotes much time to the relationship between the environmental sciences and planning puts it this way.[21]

"In planning, a limitation to the practical use of most information produced by environmental scientists is that it includes only what is observed. *Human values, ethics, and morals, are considered by scientists as factors which should not be included* within the realms of science because they cannot be assessed objectively. Environmental scientists may form their own conclusions on those matters, but the scientific ethic dictates that they should not allow such considerations to interfere with the objective and impersonal nature of the research. In practice this is extremely difficult and it can be argued to be impossible, which accounts for some of the variation in and different interpretations of, particular environmental phenomena." (Italics in original.)

In practice, scientists are loathe to become directly involved in political disputes. The traditional ethos is that the scientist provides research evidence, say as to the ecological consequences of a particular course of action, and to leave the evaluation of that evidence to the political process. Unfortunately this approach begs the question that any kind of environmental impact appraisal no matter how "objectively" measured embodies latent values. The loss of a rare species or an interesting ecological habitat is an emotive matter that even the most objective ecologist will find hard to disguise. If the ecologist does not become an advocate for his advice (or prompts pressure groups to speak for him) he is in danger of seeing his evidence distorted to suit particular political interests. In modern planning where environmental consequences are so much a matter of powerful minority concern, it is unlikely that ecologists or other environmental scientists can remain free of the almost inevitable political turmoil that is commonly associated with environmentally sensitive planning decisions. Frankly, they are in a dilemma if they do stand aside, they are in danger of being misinterpreted or ignored; yet if they enter the fray they may undermine their own professional ethos and credibility. But they cannot always leave it to the mobilisation of environmental interests to ventriloquise for them, for they too have an unfortunate tendency towards wishful reinterpretation.

An interesting example of this dilemma is currently taking place in Britain over the proposal by the UK Atomic Authority to drill holes into various kinds of rock to see whether these are suitable repositories for spent nuclear fuel. The Radioactive Wastes Management Advisory Committee, acting to some extent on the prompting of the Institute of Geological Sciences, has written to the Environment Secretary and the Scottish and Welsh Secretaries to emphasise that without this crucial experimental evidence scientists cannot ascertain whether nuclear waste can safely be disposed of. So they have in effect asked the Secretaries to overturn some if not all the objections for all but one of the local planning authorities which have refused to give planning permission to allow the drilling to proceed. Any decision is bound to be politically controversial, for though in the minds of UKAEA and establishment geologists there may be all the difference in the world between drilling experiments and final disposal sites, this is not the way either the local population or their elected representatives interpret the request. So the geologists are in effect becoming politically active simply in making the recommendation (which they regard as a perfectly respectable one in scientific terms) that the test drilling proceeds.*

Also at issue here is the thorny question, to which we shall return below, of how to balance national need against local environmental interests. The Town and Country Planning Association[22] have entered this argument by suggesting that instead of conducting a whole series of local planning inquiries where the terms of reference may well be limited, a single comprehensive inquiry be held at which important arguments regarding need, safety and adequate public health safeguards would all be brought together and discussed by representatives of all major parties, following which local decisions can be made on their merits. The TCPA brief takes us into yet another realm of the environmental planning debate, namely the relationship between local planning inquiries and national policy issues such as public safety and suitable energy mix. We discuss all this later on. We only need make the remark here that had the TCPA suggestion been heeded it would have made even more pertinent the points already raised about the relationship between scientist, planner, elected member and the public.

Planning and Environmental Amelioration

McHarg did the planning profession some service in drawing out the relationship between environmental processes and planning. His objective was unashamedly to mould planning to suit the dictates of nature, or as he put it, physiographic determinism. In his book *Design With Nature* he developed the first examples of the technique now known as environmental impact assessment, ironically at a time when the famous piece of enabling legislation, the US National Environmental Policy Act, was being discussed and passed by Congress (see below and the reading by Garner). McHarg's principal contribution was to devise a set of indicators that related seemingly disparate environmental processes (soil drainage, compactability and erodability, aspect, groundwater flows, etc.) first of all into a set of criteria based on environmental intolerance (areas or processes under stress and hence to be avoided) or opportunity (areas of tolerance which could take roads, housing, sewage works, etc.). He believed that planners could draw up maps of zones of opportunity and resistance which would subsequently guide regional plans.

The trouble with the McHarg approach, at least as it was first proposed, was that it ran contrary to established thinking about the role of economics in relation to environmental protection (see next section), it failed to understand the powerful political component (in terms of the disposition of power) that permeates most planning decisions, and it did not take into account the fact that people rarely see the whole, only their part of it (see Section 6). In a helpful critique, Gold[23] made the point that

*In the event the British Government has abandoned the test drilling programme [eds].

environmental determinism tends to lay stress on absolute limits while man is a creature who seeks many different kinds of benefit from a given area or resource and hence likes to make choice based on comparative advantage. In his own words:

> "The economists' [*sic*] reference point is the individual and the society composed of individuals. All allocations are made with respect to human values, not to natural values—whatever they may be.... The McHarg scheme fails to recognize that it is intrinsic suitability in conjunction with the values people place on intrinsically suitable land that should determine the correct allocation [of resources]."

For an example in which human perceptions distort natural values, let us look at the story of the excellent ecological plan which McHarg and his associates devised for the Bandywine Creek in Maryland. His aim was to concentrate settlement and roads on the tolerant plateau tops, with dispersed housing on the upper valley sides set amongst carefully cleared woodland, leaving the flood plain vulnerable to flash floods and unsuitable because of poor drainage, free for recreation, nature conservation and relatively low output agriculture (for a general picture, see Figure 4.2). Unfortunately neither the real-estate developers nor the landowners saw the region's future in these terms. Even though McHarg showed how his proposal would produce more money in development value than an uncontrolled planning alternative (with all kinds of environmental damage), and even though he proposed the innovation of a real-estate syndicate which would buy up all the development rights for the whole area in order that the profits from all development would be shared by those whose land was not to be developed, the scheme still fell foul of the local landowners, each of whom saw potentially more profit

FIGURE 4.2

The Brandywine Valley plan. This sketch is drawn from McHarg (1969, *op cit.*, p. 87). Again the physical setting provides a guide for the developer pointing out zones for development and protection. The principal problem lies in persuading landowners to accept a plan that emphasises collective advantage over private gain.

by "going it alone" than by acting collectively and purposefully.[24] One of McHarg's associates described the reaction.

> "Those outraged by the plan used such expressions as 'conservation not confiscation, land is manhood, the plan is castration', and 'stop the land grab—keep out Big Daddy government'.... Essentially many landowners wanted to be free to sell out whatever the market warranted, free to get maximum return for their land regardless of the impact of development on nearby land. They preferred to lodge all land use control at the municipal level because they knew municipal elected officials to be subject to pressure."[25]

This kind of reaction is fairly typical of what is known as "commons myopia" and is discussed in more detail in Section 6.

The reaction to McHarg's proposal provides us with two important lessons concerning environmental planning. The more obvious point is that ecological determinism is based on a set of values that rarely coincide with the dominant thought patterns in Western capitalistic society even though McHarg and his followers are by no means no-growth advocates. Indeed, by planning for greater overall densities than would occur in an uncontrolled growth pattern, McHarg's plan provided for $7million worth of greater land-value profits over the "free enterprise" model. As the point is developed in Section 6, suffice to say here that neither the nature of conventional economics nor the exercise of power by the most influential in Western industrialised societies encourages a responsiveness to a genuine sense of sharing, let alone primacy of ecological processes. In our view this will only be changed when widespread ecological damage results in serious economic consequences and the loss of a sufficient number of plant and animal species for the implications to sink into the public consciousness. Neither the prevailing economic principles involved in project appraisal nor the pattern of existing legal rights to the protection of public amenities allow for ecological determinism, nor, for that matter, do normal planning approaches as we have already shown. Total integration of ecological values within the rubric of conventional economic values is still some distance off, though some optimists see some signs of a purposeful transition (see Section 5).

The other lesson from the Brandywine experience poses a dilemma which will take longer to solve. This is the matter of adequately compensating those, who, in the interests of environmental preservation, and hence the "public good", must forego real income or potential profit. Examples abound. In the Yorkshire Dales National Park, farmers have to roof their old buildings with traditional slate in order to protect a particular landscape quality. They are not fully compensated for the £2000–3000 additional costs involved in slating rather than tiling. In some areas of Exmoor National Park, farmers are not able to obtain grants from the Ministry of Agriculture Fisheries and Food to enable them to plough up part of the Moorland and convert it into higher-quality grazing land, though under certain circumstances they may get some compensation —for example if their land lies in an area designated as one of high amenity value.[27] In fact there was a Bill before the British Parliament that would make parts of Exmoor inalienable from ploughing even by farmers who have sufficient capital to finance conversion on their own, though this proposal was not acceptable to the present Conservative administration.[28]

These two examples refer to agricultural dwellings and land which are normally exempt from the kinds of planning control found in built-up areas which specifically take into account the interests of neighbours and the public at large. This point will be returned to in the case study that follows. But while in Britain the presumption lies against self-interest in development control, in the US the presumption lies in favour of self-interest. The Fifth Amendment to the US Constitution states that "private property shall not be taken for public use without just compensation". The critical word here is "taken" for the kind of loss which is common in Britain, namely the loss of maximising income due to a wider environmental interest, is interpreted by some to mean a "taking" and hence requires compensation. After a lot of legal argument, many US Courts are accepting that where there is a significant environmental interest, for example the preservation of a wetland vital to feeding and breeding habits of wading birds, or where there is a state or regional environmental plan of the kind McHarg was trying to develop which incorporates environmental protection within the context of growth, that the matter of "taking" does not arise and thus no compensation need be paid.[29] The important point here is that environmental protection must be deemed to be justified on a number of grounds of which moral responsibility to living species is but one, before a "taking" can be justified without full compensation.

In another context, but equally relevant to the argument, we can include the "subsidy" that certain people provide for the nation as a whole by being prepared to live (or having no choice to move away from) nuisance-creating activities such as motorways, airports, chemical complexes and nuclear power stations. By tolerating an additional nuisance or risk for which they are never adequately compensated they are absorbing a cost, the benefits from which are spread across the nation at large. Good environmental planning should seek to minimise this form of subsidy, either by upgrading safety standards, improving aesthetic design or by providing money and/or facilities for disadvantaged groups so that their social welfare is not unduly diminished. In short, modern planning has to get to grips with the problem of environmental impact amelioration.

Since this is not an easy concept to grasp in the abstract let us take a specific case example already mentioned briefly — the proposal to control the saltwater flooding of the lower Yare basin in eastern Norfolk and Suffolk by means of a surge-protecting barrier that would hold out high tides from the southern North Sea (see Figures 4.3 and 4.4). The farmlands of the lower Yare basin lie below the river levels so a total of 20,000 hectares constantly has to be pumped to maintain water tables below root level. All the river banks are backed by floodwalls, many of which are constructed in soft, unconsolidated peats, parts of which are leaking, and all of which require repair from time to time. (The annual repair bill is approximately £350,000.) The serious flood problem is the surge tide coming in from the North Sea when high tides are pushed

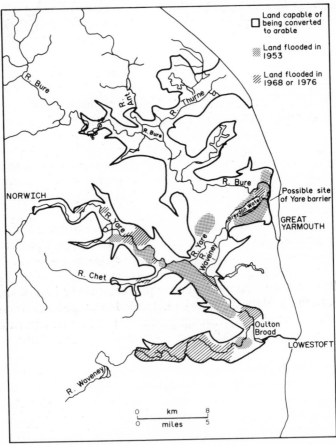

FIGURE 4.3

The Yare barrier site and the farmland it would protect. The proposed Yare barrier would be situated in the River Yare immediately downstream of the confluence with the River Bure. This would protect all the river valleys from exceptionally high tides and consequent salt water flooding in the lower reaches. All the farmlands within the heavy lines are protected by river bank floodwalls and are constantly drained. The shaded areas indicate flooded zones since the major disaster of February 1953 when much of the northern area was inundated by salt water following the big North Sea surge that is calculated to recur statistically once in 100–175 years.

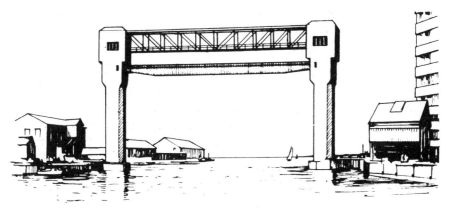

FIGURE 4.4

The proposed Yare barrier. This is a schematic representation of the proposed Yare barrier. Basically it is designed like a garage door which will lift up and lie horizontally when not in use and thus will permit unimpeded navigation. It is designed to be lowered when high tide levels reach 1.8 m but there are fears that it could be used as a river regulating device to control leakage through crumbling floodwalls and thus be lowered during high tides of 1.7 or 1.6 m.

south by strong north-westerly winds. This surge tide can rise to as much as 2 m above ordinary high tides and can breach or overtop the floodwalls causing saltwater flooding that in turn can damage soils for up to three years.

The surge-protecting barrier is a simple engineering solution to the problem of flood protection, but if it is constructed, it will encourage a number of farmers in the lower Yare valley to convert from the present permanent grazing to a more productive arable cropping. This would result in two environmental consequences, (a) the loss of some of the scenic heritage of the region which is noted for its peaceful vistas of grazing animals, small copses, hedgerows and traditional cattle gates, and (b) the removal of many of the shallow drainage dykes (ditches) which presently pepper the grazing marshes, and which harbour much of the remaining vestiges of the once rich floral and faunal ecology of the area known as the Norfolk Broads. It is perhaps worth stressing here that the wildlife of the Broads is already seriously impoverished due to pollution and an increasingly popular hire cruiser industry so the marsh dykes really represent the last refuge.[30] While there would be better safeguards for farmers, who claim they cannot convert to higher productive crops without the insurance of the proposed barrier, there would be ecological and aesthetic consequences which many believe would be serious and irreversible to a region whose ecosystem is unique to the nation.

This is a controversial issue which need not detain us in all its detail. The aspect that is relevant to our discussion here is how to ensure that some of the characteristic landscape and critical areas of the drainage dykes can be kept as they are now (this means continual management through clearance and deepening for the dykes become ecologically valueless if they are left alone) without either seriously undermining the very purpose of flood protection, namely agricultural improvement, or failing to ensure that a viable ecosystem for certain vulnerable plants and insects is maintained. For simply by isolating certain sections of marsh, one cannot be sure that the present ecosystem will remain viable in ecological terms: the habitats have to be linked so that birds and insects can interchange between them. The problem from an environmental planning viewpoint is that in Britain at present there are no legally or politically sanctioned measures available to safeguard areas of land or water for ecological or aesthetic purposes.* In fact the very opposite is the case: farmers are eligible for grants both from the Exchequer (via the Ministry of Agriculture, Fisheries and Food) and the EEC (via the Common Agriculture Policy)[31] which encourage them to drain wetlands and plough moorlands and no compensatory schemes are available to help them protect critical environmental areas. It is true that the Nature Conservancy Council and the Countryside Commission can enter into management agreements[32] with landowners, but this is a purely voluntary arrangement that cannot guarantee ecological or aesthetic safeguards in perpetuity. A number of reports[33] have recently been published all of which argue for a specific compensation principle to be applied to environmental protection in rural areas (via tax concessions, incentive payments or actual cash grants), but the fact remains that in lowland Britain there are virtually no planning safeguards for the protection of critical areas of landscape and ecology where a wider public interest is at stake.

By highlighting this point, the Yare barrier controversy may well lead to a re-thinking of the compensation principle in environmental planning. We have already noted that this may occur in certain moorland areas of high amenity: it needs to be extended throughout the country to include the needs of nature conservation. At the very least, conventional cost–benefit analysis should have added to it an analysis of the costs of protection and/or amelioration with suitably lower discount rates (see the previous Section). Much more necessary is the preparation of an environmental strategy for each region of the nation but set in a national context, which would ensure that critical zones of landscape value and ecological heritage are identified before new developments are proposed. It is only on this basis that a properly thought-out scheme of compensation can be put into practice. It will be evident that this work should be undertaken by environmental scientists and conservationists working closely with planners.

*Under the 1981 Wildlife and Countryside Act about 10 percent of the British countryside is given some degree of protection against land use alterations caused by agriculture and forestry [eds].

Other aspects of environmental amelioration are a little easier to deal with. Clearly it is vital to ensure that environmental protection is built into a planning application for say a mining development, or that adequate pollution control and other hazard-reducing safeguards are incorporated into planning consents for energy-generating schemes and new factories.[34] In the case of mining, some elements of this are now occurring. For example, an American mining company, Dresser Industries, is about to create legal history in Britain by guaranteeing a bond of £175,000 via the Sun Alliance Insurance Company to ensure that adequate land restoration is undertaken once it has completed its mining of fluorspar in the Peak District National Park where there has already been much controversy over mining.[35] On the basis of this bond, the Park Authority has given permission on the assumption that an agreed plan of restoration will be followed even if the firm goes bankrupt. But critics see this as a means of placing the corporate foot in the door: the company would like to dig out 400,000 tonnes of fluorspar which would mean one new mining site per year for up to 20 years. They doubt that all the apparent good intentions are really genuine and, because few planners really know how to judge the viability of a restoration programme, they feel that the company may pull the wool over their eyes.

When it comes to compensating for involuntary acceptance of risk, we are no longer talking of environmental amelioration through the cosmetics of landscape architecture. This is a much more profound matter that requires new approaches to project assessment other than that of the public planning inquiry, changes in procedure which have yet to be adequately thought through. We believe that fairly revolutionary changes will take place, spurred on by the experience of conducting and evaluating environmental impact assessments which are increasingly becoming a necessary part of the planning consent process. However, we also see the onset of EIA as an intermediate stage in this revolution which will ultimately involve sophisticated devices for reviewing policy options, determining acceptable risk levels and providing novel forms of compensation for those who must still absorb certain potentially dangerous impacts in the wider public interest. The intermediate stage of environmental impact assessment is now upon us, but it is only a step in a longer process of reform.

Environmental Impact Assessment

Environmental Impact Assessment (EIA) was formally introduced to the Western world with the passage of the US National Environmental Policy Act (NEPA). The history of this legislation and its effect on agency thinking in the US is described in part by Garner in the reading that follows. While NEPA is well known for its EIA requirements contained in section 102(2)(c), in fact it is a profound statement of liberal technocentricism, namely that by good management, the principle of man–environmental harmony can be infused within a paradigm of growth. For in passing the legislation, the US Congress was indicating that it believed that economic activity and social welfare improvement could continue along with better environmental quality: Congress believed that these things were compatible given sound policies, clearly defined priorities, a good research base, plenty of open public discussion and properly conducted democratic procedures for seeking acceptable decisions.

In short, EIA involves (a) the search for all relevant effects, which in turn requires discussion with all relevant interested parties and some agreement on the boundaries of analysis, (b) the analysis of the inter-relationships of all these effects as they impinge on ecosystems and social processes, and (c) the balancing or the setting in proportion of all the likely residual consequences (once amelioration procedures and/or compensation arrangements have been agreed upon) in the context of the benefits of a proposal (see Figure 4.5). EIAs do not stop developments they merely make more precise (and, hopefully, more public) the likely outcomes of proceeding. Thus they make final decisionmaking more political in the sense of placing more squarely on the shoulders of elected representatives the responsibility of determining the true public interest. This is one of the two major challenges of EIA — namely its demands upon the political process, its demands upon planners and other technical experts to make sure that their analyses are full and

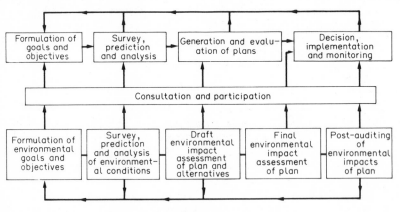

FIGURE 4.5

Integration of the physical planning process and the EIA system. This diagram is reproduced, with permission, from Lee, W. and Wood, C. (1978) EIA – A European Perspective (*Built Environment* Vol. 4, No. 2, p. 106). It indicates an idealised relationship between conventional planning procedures and the introduction and operation of environmental impact assessment. In practice the pattern may not be so clearly defined, nor the relationship so close.

acceptable, and its demands upon the traditional practices of consultation through expertise and confidentiality that plague the British administrative processes. The other challenge—that of bringing into the open better procedures for considering various policy mixes—will be discussed below.

It is not too surprising to learn that EIA has not been embraced so heartily in Europe as it has in North America, especially the US. In the US, the administrative process is geared to the likes of EIA because it is open, adversary, allows great opportunities for legal intervention and encourages the participation by various kinds of citizens' environmental action groups. In most European countries, with the possible exception of Sweden, convention has it that most government departments do not have to account publicly for the manner in which a policy is prepared or a particular decision taken. The guiding legislation is often permissive but not mandatory. For example, Section 11 of the Countryside Act, 1968 for England and Wales requires that all public bodies "have regard to the desirability for conserving the natural beauty and amenity of the countryside" when proposing schemes such as reservoirs, flood protection, transmission lines or power stations. Similar wording appears in Section 22 of the Water Act, 1973 also for England and Wales but again there is nothing in the law that requires that any balancing process is made public. Indeed there is much resistance within the British governing establishment to any demands for greater openness and accountability in this most important area. This can be seen in the attempt by UK environmental groups to insert a general declamatory amendment to the Protection of the Environment Bill (the forerunner of the Control of Pollution Act, 1974) during committee stage in the House of Lords.[36] Baroness White (Labour) moved the amendment:

"it shall be the duty of all public authorities, in reaching decisions affecting the use of land, water and air, to have regard to possible pollution, including noise, arising therefrom, and to take all practical steps towards the avoidance or mitigation of such pollutant effects; in particular, it shall be the duty of a planning authority to obtain all possible information on the likely pollutant effect of any proposed development, and, where necessary, to attach appropriate conditions to any consent which may be given."

In reply, on behalf of the government, Baroness Young (Conservative) noted that while the government would, in general, want public authorities to consider the environmental consequences of any particular development,

"it would be very difficult for an authority to prove that it had taken every practical step towards the avoidance or mitigation of pollution . . . it would be open to objectors to frustrate and delay decisions to a substantial extent. . . ."

This is the crux of the suspicion over the introduction of EIA among European governing circles. The prevailing view is that existing procedures for environmental review are adequate, that normal consultation arrangements among interested parties allow for the wider implications of major developments to be discussed, that, where relevant, public planning inquiries provide an opportunity for objectors to state their case and hence to point out undesirable effects, and that any legal requirements for EIA would mean more delay, greater likelihood of protest, and considerable additions to manpower and budgets of local planning departments at a time when public expenditure is to be reduced.

However, British planners and environmental pressure groups were not really prepared to accept this line of defence. Thirlwall, who was one of two consultants asked by the Department of the Environment to look into the matter,[37] explains why. For a long time there continued to be resistance from senior officials and ministers, partly on the grounds that EIAs would mean more planners or at least higher budgets for planning departments at a time when public expenditure cuts were under review. Nevertheless, in September 1978 the (then Labour) Environment Secretary did give a commitment to the principle of EIA, but not to any particular form and certainly not to any legislation.[38] In hinting that industrial development was too important to be delayed by excessive discussion, he indicated that if EIA was to be deployed at all, it would only take place for major schemes, at most about ten per year throughout the country. This is very much in line with the feeling in British industry, that EIAs, even if undertaken by the developer, would be costly, cumbersome, encourage more objection (because the more that is published the more there is to argue about) and result in greater uncertainties about long-term planning guarantees. This last point is worth emphasising. Many promoting bodies do not believe that most local authority planning departments have sufficient expertise even to review an impact report, let alone conduct it. They see great dangers in the delays and difficulties that would inevitably ensue as planning departments passed through a transition into EIA competence.

These arguments by governing interests and development groups have relevance, but they beg the question that public suspicion of the environmental aspects of large development schemes is growing, that the conventional planning inquiry is quite unsuited to coping with the discussion of such studies unless they are properly analysed beforehand, and that existing consultative procedures are simply not adequate to ensure that all the relevant effects and the views of affected parties are known, taken into account and explictly dealt with in the final project design. Ideally what is needed at a minimum, is for an independent advisory group to be established whenever any major scheme is contemplated, and for this group to steer the EIA process through from its inception to completion. The membership of this group would obviously have to include key interested parties (developers, conservationists, academics, planners, citizens groups), though admittedly the matter of its representativeness would be a problem. Despite this difficulty we remain convinced that some independent regional body, armed with reviewing and coordinating powers and responsible for ensuring that adequate publicity is provided and opportunities for consultation are available, must have a key role in EIA preparation in the future. The steering group would therefore act as a general overseer and should provide a valuable forum for discussion which hopefully should result in acceptable plans that minimise environmental and social disruption and provide for compensation where necessary. A prototype version of this scheme can be found in the Aberdeen area where much oil-related development is taking place, but the arrangement is not yet very satisfactory because the steering group is too *ad hoc* and it has no effective powers of review and appraisal.

Environmental Impact Assessment in Practice

There are many books and reports on EIA in practice, so we will concentrate our attention on events occurring in Great Britain.[39] Nor do we have space to cover much detailed discussion of EIA techniques. We include the original essay by Bissett to give some indication of the methodologies that can be employed. Though British planning legislation provides a fair amount of scope for planners to request "other material considerations" when considering the merits of an application, the fact remains, the present arrangements are too *ad hoc*. The authors of a special report into EIA in Britain comment as follows:[40]

"It is not . . . necessary to think in terms of a special system for particular kinds of development which would be outside the planning system. It is rather a question of how the operation of the planning system can be geared to deal with the big development in the right degree of depth so that decisions can be made in the light of better knowledge of what the environmental consequences are likely to be and the public are not dismayed by results which were not foreseen when permission was given. Since the future of the environment has become so much a matter of concern to the public, the public should be able to know more about the issues that have to be examined on the way to a decision and how they are examined".

Despite continued official resistance to EIA in Britain,* the idea is catching on, ironically because promoting bodies see it as a means of obtaining planning consents more quickly. For example, the British Gas Corporation, sensitive to the fact that coastal sites for terminals are prized areas, and smarting over the roasting it received over its (finally successful) application to place a terminal at Bacton in North Norfolk,[41] set up an environmental department in 1966 partly so that it could help the recipient planning department by providing all the

*For a good statement of the official position, see evidence taken before the Lords' Select Committee on the European Communities, 1980–81, *The Environmental Assessment of Projects*. H.L. Paper 69, HMSO, London [eds].

necessary specialised information required, and partly to help the Corporation prepare a report looking at both the need for the scheme, the various alternatives to be considered, the likely environmental effects and any proposals for amelioration. The Corporation claims that before a particular site is chosen, answers to the last two factors have to be obtained and discussed with the planning department and its chief environmental adviser is quite honest in admitting that the Corporation regards this as a necessary means of expediting planning permission.[42]

Similarly, the English Central Electricity Generating Board, recognising that it is running out of the "easy" sites, has embarked on a major programme of environmentally-related research (worth some £4 million annually) so that it can reduce the environmental hazards associated with major power developments. The CEGB now reckon that it takes between 10 and 15 years to plan a big scheme and that the full EIA procedure (to which they now reluctantly subscribe) will add another 2–3 years. It plans to double the staff of its environmental studies section (at present eight full-time employees) to cope.[43]

Probably the most impressive example of an EIA in Britain is that undertaken by the National Coal Board in relation to its proposed development of a major coalfield at Belvoir in north-east Leicestershire.[44] The site is estimated to contain 510 million tonnes of recoverable reserves and is regarded by the NCB as vital to its long-term strategy of coal development. Opposition to the scheme has come from all the local planning authorities, largely on the grounds of amenity and social impact, and from national environmental groups on the basis of need. The Board is extremely sensitive to the fact that it would face a lot of opposition at the local planning inquiry that was convened in October 1979, so it conducted a very elaborate EIA, estimated to have cost £5 million, to devise the most economical yet environmentally acceptable scheme. The EIA was based on visual impact of tips and mine shafts, noise, effect on agriculture, load capacity and traffic intrusion, and was undertaken both by the Board itself and a number of consultants. Parallel with this investigation the Commission on Energy and the Environment, set up after the controversy over the uranium oxide-processing plant at Windscale, is undertaking a wider investigation of the environmental impacts of coal development. What effect its observations will have on the Belvoir decision remains to be seen.

The water industry in Britain is also becoming more environmentally minded if for no other reason because it has to in order to obtain planning permission and placate objectors at public inquiries, and meet its statutory duties "to have regard to the desirability of preserving natural beauty, of conserving flora, fauna and geographical and physiographical features of special interest ... and of taking into account any effects which its proposals would have on the beauty of, or amenity of, any rural or urban area or on any flora, fauna, features, buildings or objects" (Section 22 of the Water Act, 1973). For example, the North West Water Authority recently commissioned a study of the environmental implications of four reservoir sites—enlargement of Haweswater, new reservoirs at Borrow Beck and Hellifield and estuarial storage at Morecambe Bay — which was conducted in consultation with its engineering department and the structure planning authorities. The actual EIA was based on the following six procedures.[45]

 (i)   examining existing planning policies relevant to the proposal;
 (ii) surveying the environmental characteristics of the areas potentially affected by each scheme variant;
 (iii) analysing the characteristics of the engineering proposals;
 (iv) defining the probable interactions between the engineering proposals and the environmental character of the existing area (ecology, landscape, agriculture, recreation, transport, local economy, community, historical and cultural aspects) and assessing the relative significance of particular impacts;
 (v)   examining the scope for reducing or modifying the effects of adverse environmental impacts by altering the engineering proposals;
 (vi) making a final assessment of those environmental impacts which were inherent and unavoidable.

Even though the Consultants tackled the study with enthusiasm and commitment, their task was a daunting one for they had to look at the implications for eight quite disparate factors, for four quite different schemes and a total of sixteen variants. At the end of the day all they could do was indicate whether an impact was, in their view, reversible or not, regional or local, long term or short term, adverse or beneficial or simply uncertain. The task is by no means complete: one can sense the sheer scale of the consultation effort yet to come by the penultimate chapter of their report.[46]

"It is clear ... that the interpretations based upon these facts may vary between different groups of people with different aims in mind. For this reason, it has always been foreseen that a wider range of informed public opinion would need to be sounded, and it is understood that this will occur during the consultation phase ... at the end of which a comprehensive understanding of technical and economic data will have been assembled, together with the findings of the present Environmental Impact Study, and a wide range of comment and informed observations as the basis upon which the North West Water Authority can found its future policy decisions on water resource developments for the region."

It is this "consultation phase" which is such a drain on managerial and professional effort. The more detailed and wide ranging the EIA the longer and potentially more tendentious the discussions. Objectors normally see their role as one of protest: they are not required (nor usually do they have the resources to do so) to produce alternative proposals, let alone design them. Those who advocate full-blooded EIAs tend to discount the demand on administrative time that the whole process requires, no matter how politically and environmentally necessary it may be. This is particularly the case when the remit of the proposing organisation and hence its whole operating ethos is to develop a resource not to protect the environment. It is not at all easy to produce good environmentally–sensitive proposals which are satisfactory to all reasonably minded people, let alone to placate the objections of the less reasonably minded.

This tends to reinforce the point made earlier that some kind of local independent steering group should be on hand to guide the EIA throughout the whole cycle of project development. In the reading that follows, Garner would go much further for he advocates legislation backed up by an Environmental Council with strong scrutinising powers. This is a very ambitious proposal and not one that is likely to get much support from a British government at present, but some version of this idea could materialise if the Commission of the European Communities has its way. For both the EEC and the OECD[47] are encouraging their member states to adopt EIA on a comparable systematic basis as part of their planning procedures for major development proposals. The EEC has actually prepared a draft directive to this effect, though it is likely to be watered down before it finally becomes law. This is because of member government hostility to "harmonising" administrative activities and their conviction that their planning arrangements work best when tailored to the idiosyncracies of their respective political cultures. In any case, the EEC directive does nothing to advance the claims for more openness in government nor does it provide any solace for environmentalists who are seeking the right of legal review of administrative actions and the opportunities to discuss formally the assumptions underlying the policies that promote large-scale energy transportation, water and mining schemes. So while Garner may be right in intent, his proposals are too radical to be acceptable to establishment interests in practice. Administrative reform in Britain oozes slowly, it does not catapult forward in leaps and bounds. In any case the British pride themselves on decentralisation in planning practice as well as the flexibility of administrative discretion. Local authority planning committees would not welcome any move towards excessive central government control over the quality of EIAs.

It is worth emphasising the difference between EIAs and CBAs at this juncture. Detailed EIAs can produce a comprehensive statement of the wider ramifications of a project, but even if EIAs are undertaken for a number of schemes (a formidable task) they do not help the decision maker to choose the best among the alternatives: they merely produce an enormous mass of information. The use of more adventurous cost–benefit analysis with separate displays for the distributional implications and alternative objectives (regional development, social equity, environmental protection) is capable of yielding an ordered display of cost and benefit streams that are more readily comparable. There is clearly scope for the two approaches to converge. CBA can be made to encompass the wider aspects of a project, whereas EIA could be deployed to search for acceptable management compromises including improvements in project design, safety measures, risk-reducing devices and compensatory arrangements, all of which are capable of being costed for useful analytical comparison.

Project Assessment and the Role of the Public Inquiry

In one respect, however, Garner's arguments may well be influential, namely the matter of analysing major development proposals which have a national as well as a local interest. Under the Town and Country Planning Acts, a local planning inquiry is held when planning permission is either refused, and there is an appeal by the proposer to the relevant minister; or where the minister feels that there are so many objections of such substance that the national as well as local interest would be served if an inquiry was held. Normally the minister appoints an Inspector to review the evidence which, in the bigger cases, is presented through lawyers in a quasi-judicial fashion complete with cross-questioning of witnesses.[48] The point of the inquiry is to "inform the minister's mind" on the relevant aspects of the case, to hear the views of both opponents and proponents, and for an independent "judge" (or tribunal where expert assessors are involved) to reach a recommendation upon which the minister will base his final decision. Hundreds of local planning inquiries are held every year in Britain, and for the most part they work well, for they are usually competently handled, objectors are given much scope to express their views and there is a fair degree of flexibility as to what evidence should be presented and how it is put across.

But in recent years there has been growing discontent over the planning inquiry arrangement. This is partly due to the nature of some of the "big" schemes that nowadays are promoted in the area of energy, transportation, hazardous industrial processes and mining. In some cases these proposals involve very complicated, inherently dangerous technologies that create risks which are not readily calculated: consequently many people are suspicious of their merits and anxious that public safety may be endangered by too much reliance on mathematical modelling and engineering equations. Also, many critics realise that most of the big proposals are advanced either by government itself, or by state-run corporations, or by the private sector whose economic power is important to the ruling party. These bodies can afford to spend enormous sums on the preparation of evidence for a major inquiry while objectors depend almost entirely upon voluntary donations for their funding. For example, British Nuclear Fuels Ltd are thought to have spent at least £500,000 on their submission to the Windscale thermal oxide-reprocessing plant inquiry, while the "opposition" combined could only muster £150,000.[49]

Consequently many environmental groups are concerned that the conventional planning inquiry is no longer suitable to handle the "big" proposal. Apart from the whole question of whether an EIA is undertaken and how well it is done, there is a much more fundamental issue —that of reviewing the whole policy context in which the proposal is advanced. Traditionally, it has been British practice to confine policy review to parliament and hence to forbid the discussion of the merits of a scheme in a public inquiry. Here is a typical example of the establishment view on this matter.[50]

> "Once Parliament has determined as a matter of high policy that a series of schemes should be carried into execution for the benefit of the nation . . . vested interests, whether of property owners or the various unofficial organisations . . . should no longer be permitted to oppose the policy thus determined upon, or delay or add to the expense of its execution."

However, many informed people, including a fair number of back-benchers, no longer accept that parliament can undertake this role of policy review: it does not have the time or the energy to do this, MPs are not fully informed as to what policy options are available and how they compare, the special select committees of inquiry which report on policy issues from time to time are rarely taken seriously by parliament or by Whitehall and the government, and actual debates on policy issues are few and far between.[51]

Simmering discontent with the undemocratic nature of policy formulation in Britain broke to the surface over the apparent inability of planning inquiries to cope with the EIAs of major motorway proposals (which are statutorily required[52]), the controversy over traffic demand forecasts (which are vital in influencing whether the scheme is required at all[53]) or with wider matters of transport policy within which motorways play a part. For a while, Inspectors were instructed not to allow these matters to be discussed at inquiries, but this action proved to be counterproductive because protestors became so angry that they simply refused to allow the proceedings to take place. Subsequently a vital judgment by Lord Denning, Master of the Rolls, has supported their actions, for Denning has ruled that both forecasting methods and evidence on the need for a road should be admissible as being relevant to an inquiry. This particular dispute has still to be resolved in the House of Lords but whatever the outcome, Lord Denning's ruling will encourage those who want to reform the planning inquiry when "big" schemes are to be considered.*

What are the options for reform of the planning inquiry? One possibility is the Planning Inquiry Commission (PIC) which is available under sections 47 to 49 of the Town and Country Planning Act of 1971. The PIC differs from a planning inquiry in that it consists of a number of knowledgeable people presumably reflecting different views and interests, who would not only have all the powers available to an Inspector and his assessors, but would be able to call for evidence and request that research be undertaken if it was not satisfied that the necessary research would be undertaken. However, the PIC is similar to the inquiry in that it can only be invoked when there is an appeal or when a project is "called in" by the relevant minister or where the proposal comes from a public sector organisation: in short, it can only take place when a proposal has reached a fairly advanced stage (and one that is too late for many critics) and is of a certain character. [54] Nevertheless, the PIC has never formally been put into operation in Britain. Why? Some people believe that it could be too "nosey", many feel that the major development interests fear the length of time and potential cost of an investigation of this nature, and some cynics argue that a properly conducted PIC could put really controversial decisions such as the commercial fast-breeder nuclear reactor) into mothballs for at least a decade while all the uncertainties were resolved.

Another suggestion is that reported by the Outer Circle Policy Unit, again in a reading that follows, namely that there be a twin inquiry arrangement, the first dealing with substantive matters of policy, safety, risk acceptability, economics and generic environmental and social implications, plus all feasible alternatives, that would fit between any parliamentary disussion and a specific local planning inquiry. This is called a project inquiry, the primary objective of which would be "to ensure that all assumptions, material facts, issues and arguments are brought out, tested, and fully and fairly discussed". The report of the project inquiry would be subject to wide public discussion and parliamentary debate. Wynne discusses some of the difficulties involved in this approach, particularly its inadequacies regarding the complex relationship between the presentation of scientific facts and their interpretation as political values.

Though Wynne's comments are fair and should be heeded, the project inquiry idea for particular kinds of developments is a good one. It remains to be seen how the British government will act,† but at least it is beginning to recognise that some changes are due. In April 1979 the

---

*The House of Lords ruled that Lord Denning was wrong and that official traffic forecasts were not matters for cross-examination by objectors. This ruling caused a storm of protest but it is likely that official "demand" forecasts will be cross-examinable in future enquiries [eds].

†The two stage inquiry proposal is officially discredited [eds].

Environment Secretary appointed an Inspector to convene a "preliminary meeting" into the Belvoir coalfield proposal, so that he could identify the major issues on which he considered an inquiry proper should concentrate and indicate what documentation would be required. This meeting, which included a discussion on the need for the coalfield, was regarded by most participants as both helpful and illuminating. Though this meeting did not go nearly as far as the project inquiry idea, at least it should assist the Inspector and all participants to marshal their arguments in a fairly constructive way, and for evidence on various thematic aspects of the proposal to be presented *en bloc* rather than be scattered, with tedious repetition, across submission after submission.

The project inquiry idea is still not enough, for what is ultimately required is a link between parliament, the civil service, all relevant interested parties, independent research organisations and possibly some kind of standing royal commission. Unfortunately there is a "chicken and egg" argument here because improved policy review, which is really the crucial stage of the proceedings, means a reformed parliament, and a reformed parliament means better paid, more specialised, and more committed legislators armed with adequate investigatory powers and backed by a research secretariat. As John Tyme remarks:[55]

> "It may, of course, be doubted whether our democratic and representative system has ever 'worked' in the full or ideal sense, but this in no way invalidates the need to identify what is wrong now and to do our best to put it right. There is an important reason why this is so. In the past we could perhaps afford all sorts of inefficiencies and imperfections; *it can justifiably be argued that we can do so no longer, in that the scale of our great technocracies and the effects of decisions made are now so great that, more than any other time in our history, there is a need to operate effective checks and balances within our decision making and our system of government."*
> (Italics in original)

Tyme proposes a cyclical process of parliamentary review, policy output and suitably tailored public inquiries for a national transport policy and programme (Figure 4.6). Note the key role of an upgraded parliamentary select committee, its links to the civil service and particular interests and relatively minor role played by statutory local planning inquiries. These would only deal with the particular environmental and social impact studies relevant to the locality and would thus concentrate on the ameliorative and compensatory aspects of project design to which we have already referred. Figure 4.7 presents a similar kind of arrangement with a number of minor modifications, for dealing with energy policy. Again, note the relatively specific role of the local planning inquiry, which is really the third stage in a lengthy process of policy review and project appraisal.

The Town and Country Planning Association have proposed a similar arrangement to that depicted in Figure 4.7, though it placed much emphasis on a Standing Royal Commission on Energy.[56] This

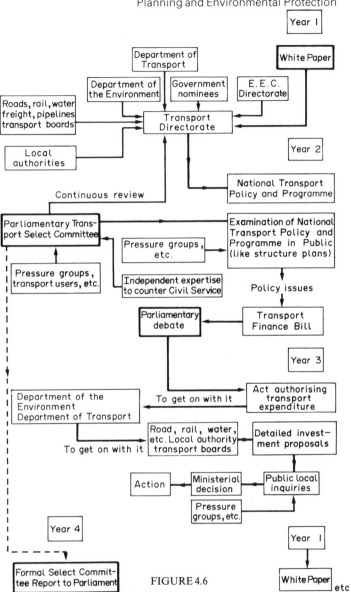

FIGURE 4.6

The link between policy review procedures and the local planning inquiry for major motorway schemes. This diagram is reproduced, with permission, from Tyme, J. (1978) *Motorways versus Democracy* (Macmillan, London, p. 103). Tyme envisages a new consultative organisation (Transport Directorate) which would feed technical advice into an annual National Transport Policy and Programme and which in turn would be monitored by a Parliamentary Select Committee on Transport. This committee would review major policy issues and would help steer parliamentary debates and determine budgetary priorities among competing transport options. Public local inquiries would only be invoked once general matters of need, traffic forecasts, social protection and budgetary allocation had all been determined and hence would be free to concentrate on the choice of the least damaging alignment and design.

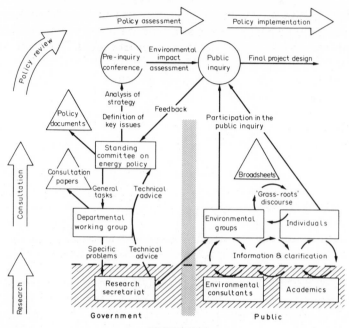

FIGURE 4.7

The link between policy review procedures and the local planning inquiry for major energy schemes. Although this diagram looks fairly complicated it is based on similar principles to those presented in Figure 4.6. Basically there are three stages to a major energy decision. First, there is the policy framework which determines matters such as need, levels of safety and environmental protection and mechanisms for public participation. This would be shaped by a parliamentary standing committee on energy policy backed by a research secretariat and aided by civil service committees and consultation with interested parties. Second, there would be an inquiry conference, possibly convened by a project inquiry commission, that would look at these general issues in the context of a particular proposal (say the fast breeder reactor) and in the light of the possible environmental effects of realistic alternatives. Third, there would be the planning inquiry proper which would largely be concerned with the EIA of a proposal already accepted in principle and which would be devoted to ensuring that there would be minimum disruption to the community and the environment.

would have broad and flexible terms of reference to advise on national, European and wider international matters concerning energy demand and supply, energy conservation and the adequacy of research into these matters with particular reference to the development of alternative energy sources. The Commission would also be responsible for advising the government on a range of feasible alternative energy strategies and for recommending a particular mix of options for the next two decades. Needless to say, its reports would be discussed widely both inside and outside parliament.

It is unlikely that in the immediate future any of these proposals will receive official blessing. It is not yet the custom of British governments to open up their policy formulating procedures to any kind of responsible public discussion: advice and consultation in a fairly *ad hoc* manner, perhaps, but genuine participation in the preparation of policy strategies, certainly not. While governments in other European countries are considering new arangements for relating scientific and technical argument to political judgement, the British are only inching forwards in a most tentative manner. For example, in reply to the TCPA brief regarding a single project inquiry for nuclear waste disposal a junior Energy Minister has rejected the suggestion for the test sites, but he did leave the door open for a wider ranging inquiry later on when specific decisions regarding radioactive waste disposal are made.[57] Let us look at five rays of hope.

First, parliament has agreed to streamline its select committee structure and has appointed twelve new committees each dealing with a particular governmental department.[58] These have greater investigatory powers than their predecessors, but because neither ministers nor senior civil servants are required to attend and answer questions, one remains suspicious of how much more effective in scrutinising policy these new bodies will be.* The fact remains that neither governmental ministers nor their civil servants are anxious to give too much power to backbench investigatory bodies. Nevertheless, the new committees will have research staff and will be able to look more closely at thematic policy issues: how far they will be able to follow certain lines of inquiry into other governmental departments remains to be seen. This is not an unimportant matter, for many environmentally-related policy areas (e.g. energy conservation, agriculture and amenity) cut across departmental boundaries.

Second, the Windscale inquiry, for all its faults, did at least make the point that wider issues should be set in context. The Belvoir preliminary meeting is a step further in the right direction but again it remains to be seen whether the kind of points Wynne raises will be heeded before the government embarks upon any inquiry into the commercial fast-breeder nuclear development.†

Third, EIAs are now very much part of the scene. Admittedly they are patchily done and their conclusions are not always made public or properly heeded, nor do they emerge before vital commitments are made, but they are now part of the UK planning input and doubtless will become more sophisticated and more open over time. In addition, as EIAs improve so the social ramifications of big schemes should also be subject to fuller analysis and more explicit balancing: already social impact assessment techniques are being improved though much needs to be done in this most difficult area.[59] This should make decision-making more properly political in the sense that the balancing of

*In practice ministers and civil servants appear regularly before the new committees [eds].
†Pre-inquiry meetings for major inquiries are now accepted practice. For a major inquiry into the first British pressurised water nuclear reactor, three pre-inquiry meetings have been arranged [eds].

incommensurate interests will increasingly become a responsibility of elected representatives acting more in the open and on the basis of evidence that has been publicly debated, but that is right and proper in an elected democracy.

Fourth, planning departments and developers are improving their communications; they are agreeing on what topics should be raised as part of an EIA and, with the help of steering committees, managing to agree over the potentally troublesome issue regarding the boundaries for analysis (including the number of options reviewed). This is important, for acceptable confinement of EIAs is vital if the technique is to have any meaning and be reasonably helpful. In Canada and the Netherlands this "scoping" issue is treated very seriously indeed. Formal meetings are held between planners and developers and certain interested parties to determine just what should be included in an EIA and how far down the chain of reactions an investigation should be undertaken.

Fifth, there are signs of official sympathy to the idea that objectors appearing at "big" inquiries (and presumably at preliminary meetings or their equivalent) should be helped either financially or in terms of research advice. This is a thorny topic, for governments are wary about giving public money to groups who aim to delay and possibly to thwart a major development proposal. Nevertheless there is an important issue of principle at stake. Why should objectors operate on a shoestring to such an extent that they cannot prepare an adequate case, when the development interests which they are opposing are backed by major reserves of private or state capital? Lawyers cost a lot of money and expert witnesses cannot give up too much of their time voluntarily or at low retainer fees. A point in favour of the project inquiry idea is that the expense of legal intermediaries should be saved since much of the argument can be handled directly by the objectors themselves. In any case the project inquiry commission should have a certain amount of funds at its disposal to grant aid to objectors where they can show that, without funding, they would not be able to play a full part in the proceedings and where the project inquiry commission is satisfied that it is in the national interest that they should.

The Town and Country Planning Association[60] have looked at various possibilities for financing a fund for public interest objectors and conclude that as an independent trust would not be sufficiently accountable, the only practicable solution is for an independent commission to be appointed by government, analogous to the science research councils, and composed of members with a wide range of scientific and technical expertise and experience of environmental planning and social issues. The TCPA recommend that the commission would administer a public fund for an experimental period of 3 years and that the Exchequer should make available a minimum of £50,000 for each of, say, ten big inquiries over that period, the inquiries being selected to be representative of a cross-section of major development schemes such as motorways, airports, liquid gas terminals, nuclear power stations, mining in national parks and other key amenity areas, reservoirs and a major urban development.

The TCPA are conscious of the problems of determining who should get aid and how much of it. This is a particularly difficult matter for almost any allocation (or refusal) will lead to the accusation that the content of the argument affects the funds available to promote it. The TCPA do not resolve this dilemma, but merely suggest that each party make an application for funding, setting out a summary of their case and a justification of the costs requested. The TCPA also recommended that the process be open-ended in that additional money should be made available, subject to the discretion of the funding commission, which would have to be accountable for its actions. The practical problems of implementing this ambitious proposal are clearly formidable.

The whole idea of "public interest attorneys" — groups acting on behalf of under-represented interests against big bureaucracy and the promoters of complex technology—is now building up a tremendous head of steam. For, throughout the Western world, governments are scratching their heads over how to permit reasonable discussion over controversial developments without either becoming bogged down in protracted discussons or failing to innovate at all. This is a very serious problem and one where there are no ideal solutions. The main reason for this difficulty is that the ideologies that clash over major development schemes are essentially irreconcilable, but one can add the remark that policy-formulating devices are not yet suited to the changes in public thinking about the wider and longer-term repercussions of major developments. Webb makes the point that is also endorsed by the Outer Circle Policy Unit: "policy is secreted through the interstices of individual decisions, and evolves over time as a consequence of the decisions that are already taken and carried out. Too often this happens without consideration of all the implications. . . ."[61]

The proposals now emerging fly in the face of the many conventions that are dear to civil servants and politicians. They demand much more openness of government, a greater attention to policy options well before final commitments are made, a substantially closer relationship between parliament, independent commissions and various public interests, and an improved right of access to judicial review over administrative actions. To liberalise all these areas would require a heroic transformation in political practice, so one should not be too optimistic: but those interested in the "state of play" should keep an eye on official responses to public interest group financing and the multistage process of policy review and project appraisal. We suspect that various pressures resulting from both the economic and environmental front will bring about reform, and that the EEC will play a fairly important role, but we fear that the necessary changes will be delayed too long to avoid a lot of frustration and confrontation.

Notes and References

1. McHarg, I. (1969) *Design With Nature*, Natural History Press, New York, p. 5.
2. Carson, R.L. (1968) *Silent Spring*, Houghton Mifflin, Boston.
3. Ehrlich, P.R. and Ehrlich, A.H. (1972) *Population, Resources, Environment: Issues in Human Ecology*, Freeman & Co., San Francisco (various editions now published).
4. Commoner, B. (1972) *The Closing Circle: Man Nature and Technology*, Knopf, New York. Commoner, B. (1976) *The Poverty of Power: Energy and the Economic Crisis*, Jonathan Cape, London.
5. Hardin, G. (1977) *The Limits of Altruism*, Indiana University Press, Bloomington, Indiana.
6. Nicholson, M. (1972) *The Environmental Revolution: A Guide to the New Masters of the Earth*, Penguin Books, Harmondsworth, Middlesex.
7. Fraser-Darling, F. (1971) *Wilderness and Plenty*, Ballantine Books, New York.
8. Dasmann, R.F. (1972) *Planet in Peril: Man and the Biosphere Today*, Penguin Books, Harmondsworth, Middlesex.
9. Dorst, J. (1970) *Before Nature Dies*, William Collins, London.
10. Nicholas Polunin is a leading figure in the International Union for the Conservation of Nature and editor of the journals *Resource Conservaton* and *Biological Conservation*.
11. The whole topic of environmental impact assessment will be discussed in some detail below. For a good review of the technique, see Munn R.E. (ed.) (1977) *Environmental Impact Assessment* (SCOPE 5), John Wiley, Chichester, Sussex. For an analysis of the state of EIA in Europe, see Wandesforde–Smith, G. (1979) *Environmental Impact Assessment in the European Community*, International Institute for Environment and Society, Potsdamerstrasse 58, Berlin.
12. US Council on Environmental Quality (1978) *The Ninth Annual Report on Environmental Quality*, Government Printing Office, Washington DC, pp.310–341.
13. Nature Conservancy Council (1977) *Nature Conservation and Agriculture*, Belgrave Square, London W1, pp. 6–23.
14. *Ibid.*, p. 23.
15. McHarg (1969) *op. cit.*, pp. 7–17.
16. Third Annual Report of the UN Environment Programme (1979) Nairobi, Kenya.
17. It is now estimated by the pesticide manufacturing companies that some £2 million of a total of £10 million research and development costs are required simply to be sure that there are no unacceptable toxic effects to wildlife or humans. In the past this kind of effort is the result of the environmental conscience, but largely it is due to the requirements of the regulatory agencies which will not allow a product to be used until they are satisfied that it is environmentally safe. For an economic analysis of the problems of pesticide usage see Gartak and Turner (1978) Some Aspects of the Economics of Pesticide Use and Economic Policy on LDCs, *Food Policy*, vol. 3(2), pp. 136–146, who have utilised CBA to the problems of pesticide usage in less-developed economics and simultaneously exposed the limitations of the CBA technique.
18. Elkington, J. and Roberts, J. (1977) Who Needs Ecologists?, *New Scientist*, 27 October, pp. 210–212; Is There an Ecologist in the House?, *Ibid.* November, pp. 276–278; The Ecology of Tomorrow's World, *Ibid.*, 17 November pp. 411–413. See also the proceedings of the Conference on Ecology and Planning held by the Royal Town Planning Institute in February 1979.
19. Elkington and Roberts (1977) *op. cit.*, p. 210.
20. For a discussion, see O'Riordan, T. (1979) Ecological Research and Political Decisions, *Environment and Planning*, vol. 11 (7), pp. 805–813, and Tips, W. and Salleh, W. (1979) The Sociology of Ecologists in Planning: A Viewpoint, *International Journal of Environmental Studies*, vol. 14, pp. 61–64.
21. Institute for Operational Research (1976) *The Environmental Sciences in Regional and Structure Planning* Volume II: *A Guide for Planners and Scientists*, Station Square, Coventry, p. 25.
22. This evidence is contained in a letter to the Environment Secretary dated 12 August 1979. See Morris, M. (1979) Planners Urge Inquiry into Nuclear Dumps Search, *The Guardian*, 13 August, p. 2.
23. Gold, A.J. (1974) Design With Nature: A Critique, *Journal of the American Institute of Planners*, vol. 40, pp. 284–286. The quotes are from pp. 284 and 286.

24. The McHarg proposal forms a chapter in his *Design With Nature* (McHarg, 1969, *op. cit.*, pp. 79–93.
25. Strong, A.L. (1975) Regional Land Use Planning: The Conflict Between National Objectives and Local Autonomy, *Environmental Policy and Law*, vol. 1 (2), pp. 82–86. See also Strong, A.L. (1975) *Private Property and the Public Interest: The Brandywine Experience*, Johns Hopkins University Press, Baltimore.
26. Elkington and Roberts (1977) *op. cit.*
27. This point is dicussed in some detail by Lord Porchester (1977) *Study of Exmoor*, HMSO, London.
28. Clause 3 of the 1978 Countryside Bill empowered the county planning authority and the responsible ministers to make moorland conservation orders prohibiting the carrying out of certain agricultural operations on specified land in a designated area where it appears to the authority making the order that the area would be likely to be adversely affected by the carrying out of the operations. See Countryside Commission (1979) Countryside Bill, 1978. Comments by the Countryside Commission, John Dower House, Crescent Place, Cheltenham. The Government announced in October 1979 that it would not seek compulsory powers to safeguard critical amenity areas. Instead it supported the present arrangement of management agreements.
29. For a detailed discussion, see O'Riordan, T. (1976) *Environmentalism*, Pion, London, pp. 144–150.
30. For a general summary of the Broads' ecological problems, see Moss, B. (1979) An Ecosystem out of Phase, *Geographical Magazine* (October), pp. 47–50, and George, M. (1977) The Decline in Broadland's Aquatic Flora and Fauna: A Review of the Present Position, *Transactions of the Norfolk and Norwich Naturalists' Society*, vol. 24, pp. 42–53.
31. The Ministry of Agriculture, Fisheries and Food grants are the Farm and Horticulture Development Scheme and the Farm Capital Grant Scheme both of which provide for up to 50 percent financing.
32. For an excellent review of the advantages and failings of compensaton agreements see Fiest, M. (1978) *A Survey of Management Agreements*, Countryside Commission, Cheltenham.
33. Nature Conservancy Council (1977) *op. cit.*; Advisory Committee for Agriculture and Horticulture for England and Wales (1978) *Agriculture and the Countryside*, HMSO, London; and Countryside Review Committee (1978) *Food Pollution and the Countryside*, HMSO, London. Fiest (1978) *op. cit* also makes a number of similar rcommendations.
34. The whole matter of pollution control and planning is currently being studied by the Pollution Unit, Department of Town and Country Planning, University of Manchester. See Wood, C. (1977) *Town Planning and Pollution Control*, Manchester University Press, and Wood, C. (1979) Land Use Planning and Pollution Control, in O'Riordan, T. and d'Arge, R.C. (eds.) *Progress in Resource Planning and Environmental Management*, John Wiley, Chichester, pp. 281–315.
35. Pithers, M. (1978) Parks Face Mining Influx, *The Guardian*, 25 September, p. 3.
36. *Lords Hansard*, vol. 347 (13 December 1973), cols. 1304–1352. The two quotes come on cols. 1304 and 1309.
37. Catlow, J. and Thirlwall, C.G. (1977) *Environmental Impact Analysis*, DoE Research Report No. 11, Department of the Environment, Marsham Street, London.
38. Mr. Peter Shore, Environment Secretary in the 1974–1979 Labour Government, in a speech on 13 September. Department of the Environment (1978) Press Release No. 488, Marsham Street, London. The present Conservative administration will not pursue this policy in view of their even greater determination to reduce public expenditure.
39. For a review of EIA in a comparative context, see O'Riordan, T. and Sewell, W.R.D. (eds.) (1982) *Project Assessment and Policy Review*, John Wiley, Chichester. For an American perspective, see Munn (1978) *op. cit.* and Jain, R.K. and Hutchings, B.L. (1978) *Environmental Impact Analysis: Emerging Issues in Planning*, University of Illinois Press, Urbana, Illinois. Wandesforde-Smith (1979) *op. cit.* covers the European scene.
40. Catlow and Thirlwall (1977) *op. cit.*, p. 8.
41. The Bacton case was written up by Gregory, R. (1971) *The Price of Amenity*, Macmillan, London.
42. British Gas Corporation: EIA is "Good Business", *Environmental Data Services Ltd.*, No. 9 (September 1978) pp. 5–9.
43. The Central Electricity Generating Board: "Clean Power and the Environment", Environmental Data Services Ltd., No. 21 (September 1978) pp. 6–10.

44. For details of the Belvoir proposal, see National Coal Board (1977) *North East Leicestershire Prospect*, Eastwood Hall, Eastwood, Nottingham. For a discussion of the EIA in relation to the planning process, see Williams, K., Hill, P. and Cope, D. (1978) EIA and the Vale of Belvoir Coalfield, *Built Environment*, vol. 4 (2), pp. 142–151.
45. Land Use Consultants Ltd (1978) *Environmental Appraisal: Haweswater, Borrow Beck, Morecambe Bay, Hellifield*, 137 Fulham Road, London SW6.
46. *Ibid.*, p. 180.
47. OECD (1979) *Environmental Impact Assessment: Analysis of the Consequences of Significant Public and Private Projects*, Report by the Urban Planning Group, OECD, Paris.
48. For an excellent review of the public inquiry mechanism in Britain, Wraith, R.E. and Lamb, G.B. (1971) *Public Inquiries as an Instrument of Government*, George Allen & Unwin, London.
49. For a good discussion of the Windscale case, see Breach, I. (1978) *Windscale Fallout*, Penguin Books, Harmondsworth.
50. Lord Cooper (1952) *Report of the Committee on Hydro Electric Development in Scotland*, Cmnd.640, HMSO, London, paragraphs 71–72.
51. For a good discussion of the failure of parliament to discuss policy options in the transportation sector, see Tyme, J. (1977) *Motorways versus Democracy*, Macmillan, London.
52. The First Schedule, part I, paragraph I of the Highways Act, requires that a notice be published "stating the general effect of the proposed order" which has been interpreted to mean a *de facto* EIA of the motorway proposal, though there is still some dispute about this. See Tyme, J. (1975) Motorway Inquiries: A Corruption of Government?, *New Scientist*, 6 November, pp. 321–323.
53. For an excellent critique of traffic-demand forecasting see National Motorways Action Committee (1976) *A Case Against the M16 Motorway*, 9 St. Catherines Place, London SW1.
54. For example, the Germans tried a version of PIC in a proposed nuclear reprocessing plant at Gorleben in Lower Saxony. Eventually the project was stalled until better safeguards and improved waste-disposal arrangements were developed.
55. Tyme (1977) *op. cit.*, p. 92.
56. Town and Country Planning Association (1979) Energy Policy and Public Inquiries, *Town and Country Planning* (March) pp. 3–7.
57. Replies to the TCPA from Mr. Tom King, Minister of Local Government and Environmental Services (7 September 1979) and Mr. George Younger, Secretary of State for Scotland (11 September 1979).
58. See First Report of the Select Committee on Procedure, Session 1977/8, H.C. Paper, 588–1, HMSO, London.
59. For a discussion of social impact assessment techniques see McEvoy, J. III and Deitz, R. (eds.) (1977) *Handbook for Environmental Planning: The Social Consequences of Environmental Change*, John Wiley, New York.
60. Town and Country Planning Association (1979) *Financial Assistance for Objectors at Major Public Inquiries*, 17 Carleton Terrace, London SW1.
61. Outer Circle Policy Unit (1979) *op. cit.*, p. 31.

READINGS

A CRITICAL SURVEY OF METHODS FOR ENVIRONMENTAL
IMPACT ASSESSMENT*

Ronald Bisset

Introduction

Since the National Environmental Policy Act (NEPA) became law in the US, in 1970, environmental impact assessment (EIA) has spread to many countries. Eire, Australia and France also possess laws requiring that certain major developments be assessed for environmental impacts. Other countries such as

*Specially commissioned for this volume. (Mr. Bisset is associated with the Geography Department at the University of Aberdeen.)

the Netherlands are considering the introduction of EIA legislation.* Generally, EIA procedures are not legally instituted, instead developments are assessed on a discretionary basis depending on the type of project, the identity of the proponent and/or the authorizing body. This situation characterizes EIA procedures in the UK, West Germany and Belgium. These procedures may change soon because of an initiative being taken by the Commission of the European Communities. The Commission wishes to introduce a directive requiring the compulsory preparation of Enviromental Impact Statements (EISs) for a wide range of private and public sector developments in the nine Member states of the EEC.

The introduction of EIA procedures does not imply necessarily the successful preparation of EISs. For EISs to be comprehenive in coverage, acceptable to both the scientific community and lay people and be reasonably accurate in their predictions requires considerable attention to methods for EIS preparation. It is surprising, therefore, that concern for EIA procedures in Europe is not paralleled by interest in methods. On the surface, this appears strange as faulty, incomplete, substandard and incompetent EISs would negate the very reasons for requiring their production. A possible explanation for the lack of attention to methods for preparing EISs will be provided after an examination of the various types of methods which have been developed.

As a comparatively recent activity, EIA has not yet developed a body of agreed terms. The literature abounds with references to methods, methodologies, technologies and techniques. This chapter will deal with methods, sometimes referred to as methodologies. Conceptually, methods can be distinguished from techniques. *Methods* are concerned with various aspects of assessment such as the identification or description of likely impacts. Methods may also incorporate means whereby impacts can be scaled, weighted and compared for relative importance. Methods aid the collection and classification of impact data while *techniques* provide the data which are organized in accord with the operational principles of particular methods. For example, the prediction of noise contours or the likelihood of a major hazardous event can be carried out by using specific techniques. Information from utilization of such techniques may be organized, presented and evaluated according to method guidelines. Many methods are variations on a limited number of organizing principles and in this chapter only those which exemplify these princples will be discussed. Some judgements on the relative merits of the methods will be made. Methods to be discussed are matrices, networks/systems diagrams, quantitative/index methods, manuals and models.

Matrices

The most commonly used EIA method is the matrix, appearing in a number of guises. The best known, devised by Leopold and his colleagues, is based on a horizontal list of development actions and a vertical list of environmental characteristics (Leopold *et al.*, 1971). Impacts are identified by relating systematically each development action with all the specified environmental

---

*EIA is now enshrined in Dutch legislation. See Kennedy, W. V. (1982) The Directive on Environmental Impact Assessment, *Environmental Policy and Law*, 8 (3), 84–95.

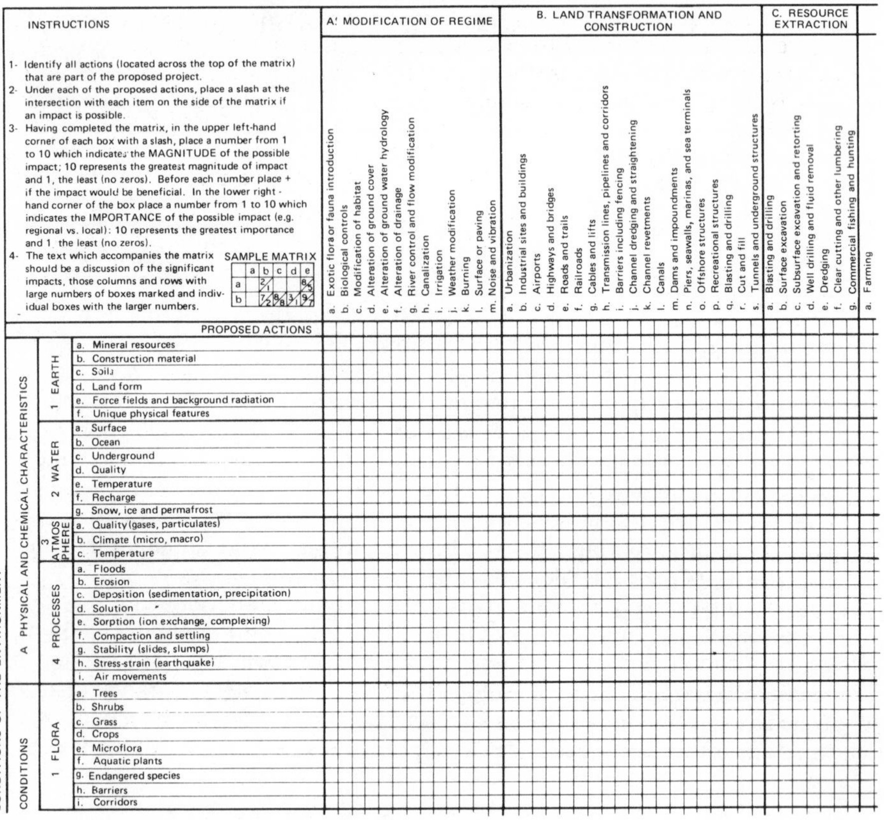

INSTRUCTIONS	A. MODIFICATION OF REGIME	B. LAND TRANSFORMATION AND CONSTRUCTION	C. RESOURCE EXTRACTION

1. Identify all actions (located across the top of the matrix) that are part of the proposed project.
2. Under each of the proposed actions, place a slash at the intersection with each item on the side of the matrix if an impact is possible.
3. Having completed the matrix, in the upper left-hand corner of each box with a slash, place a number from 1 to 10 which indicates the MAGNITUDE of the possible impact; 10 represents the greatest magnitude of impact and 1, the least (no zeros). Before each number place + if the impact would be beneficial. In the lower right-hand corner of the box place a number from 1 to 10 which indicates the IMPORTANCE of the possible impact (e.g. regional vs. local): 10 represents the greatest importance and 1 the least (no zeros).
4. The text which accompanies the matrix should be a discussion of the significant impacts, those columns and rows with large numbers of boxes marked and individual boxes with the larger numbers.

SAMPLE MATRIX

	a	b	c	d	e
a		2			
b	7/8	3	5	2	

Column headings (A. Modification of Regime): a. Exotic flora or fauna introduction; b. Biological controls; c. Modification of habitat; d. Alteration of ground cover; e. Alteration of ground water hydrology; f. Alteration of drainage; g. River control and flow modification; h. Canalization; i. Irrigation; j. Weather modification; k. Burning; l. Surface or paving; m. Noise and vibration

Column headings (B. Land Transformation and Construction): a. Urbanization; b. Industrial sites and buildings; c. Airports; d. Highways and bridges; e. Roads and trails; f. Railroads; g. Cables and lifts; h. Transmission lines, pipelines and corridors; i. Barriers including fencing; j. Channel dredging and straightening; k. Channel revetments; l. Canals; m. Dams and impoundments; n. Piers, seawalls, marinas, and sea terminals; o. Recreational structures; p. Offshore structures; q. Cut and fill; r. Tunnels and underground structures

Column headings (C. Resource Extraction): a. Blasting and drilling; b. Surface excavation; c. Subsurface excavation and retorting; d. Well drilling and fluid removal; e. Dredging; f. Clear cutting and other lumbering; g. Commercial fishing and hunting; a. Farming

PROPOSED ACTIONS

CONDITIONS OF THE ENVIRONMENT — A. PHYSICAL AND CHEMICAL CHARACTERISTICS

1. EARTH
- a. Mineral resources
- b. Construction material
- c. Soils
- d. Land form
- e. Force fields and background radiation
- f. Unique physical features

2. WATER
- a. Surface
- b. Ocean
- c. Underground
- d. Quality
- e. Temperature
- f. Recharge
- g. Snow, ice and permafrost

3. ATMOSPHERE
- a. Quality (gases, particulates)
- b. Climate (micro, macro)
- c. Temperature

4. PROCESSES
- a. Floods
- b. Erosion
- c. Deposition (sedimentation, precipitation)
- d. Solution
- e. Sorption (ion exchange, complexing)
- f. Compaction and settling
- g. Stability (slides, slumps)
- h. Stress-strain (earthquake)
- i. Air movements

CONDITIONS — B. FLORA

1. FLORA
- a. Trees
- b. Shrubs
- c. Grass
- d. Crops
- e. Microflora
- f. Aquatic plants
- g. Endangered species
- h. Barriers
- i. Corridors

FIGURE 1

A section of the Leopold *et al.* matrix (courtesy of the US Geological Survey).

characteristics. When an impact between a project activity and an environmental component is likely the appropriate cell is marked (see Figure 1). Although the Leopold matrix has the potential for identifying 8800 impacts, Leopold and his colleagues have estimated that individual projects are likely to result in only 25–50 impacts.

Apart from being used to identify impacts, Leopold and his colleagues devised a scheme to provide an indication of the magnitude and importance of identified impacts. Magnitude refers to the scale of an impact while importance refers to its significance. It is suggested that both these characteristics be represented by a score on a scale of 1–10 indicating increasing magnitude or importance. For example, a proposed project may reduce the water table over a wide area by a few centimetres. The magnitude score might be 8, but the importance scale might only be 2. Leopold *et al.* suggest that impact cells be bisected and that magnitude scores be placed in the top left-hand corner and importance scores be placed in the opposite corner (see Figure 1). When completed, the Leopold matrix provides a useful visual summary of some of the characteristics of impacts.

This matrix relies on the subjective views of experts for assigning impact scores. It cannot be used to evaluate beneficial or harmful impacts *in toto* or alternative projects because there is no standardized way of assigning the scores nor is there a means of assigning weights to different impacts to determine relative importance (Clark *et al.*, 1978). It has been criticized for not coping with indirect impacts, the likelihood that an impact on one environmental factor might lead to effects on others (Andrews, 1973; Environment Canada, 1974). This inability results from the matrix compartmentalizing the environment into discrete entities. In reality, environmental systems are integrated units in which components are interlinked by complex processes of interactions. Finally, the matrix is unable to deal with impacts changing over time.

A recent, interesting use of a Leopold-type matrix in assessing drilling sites for geological research in Antarctica is described by Parker and Howard (1977). Initially, the Leopold matrix was used, but this was modified by collapsing the magnitude and importance scales from 1–10 into a composite scale of 0–4. It was felt that magnitude would not vary greatly, but that importance would change significantly depending on the local ecology. Scores on this scale reflected subjective estimates of drilling impacts on the existing environment and the future scientific value of the sites (see Figure 2). In all, twenty matrices were prepared to evaluate sites. To ensure the inclusion of the time component the sequence of five numbers for each impact represents the time scale of impacts. For example, in the case of the impact of drainage alteration on soils, immediate effects (given a score of 1) are not serious. However, the effects increase in importance as time passes. The last digit (4) represents a severe long-term impact (see Figure 2).

The account by Parker and Howard deserves close attention. In the EIA literature, most methods are tested on "real-life" projects by those who have developed them. Parker and Howard have shown that an innovative adaption

	Modification of habitat	Modification of surface or paving	Alteration of drainage	Well drilling and fluid removal	Emplacement of tailings and overburden	Drilling fluid discharge
Soils	11111	11111	12344	11000	33333	32110
Surface, including streams	11111	11111	11111	33211	11110	33211
Stability (slides & slumps)	12321	11111	11110	.....	11000	11000
Microorganisms	44432	21111	33211	11111	33211	44432
Benthic organisms	.....	.....	.....	.....	.....	.....

FIGURE 2

A section of the Impact Matrix for Ross Island Drill Site, 1973–74 (modified after Parker and Howard, 1977).

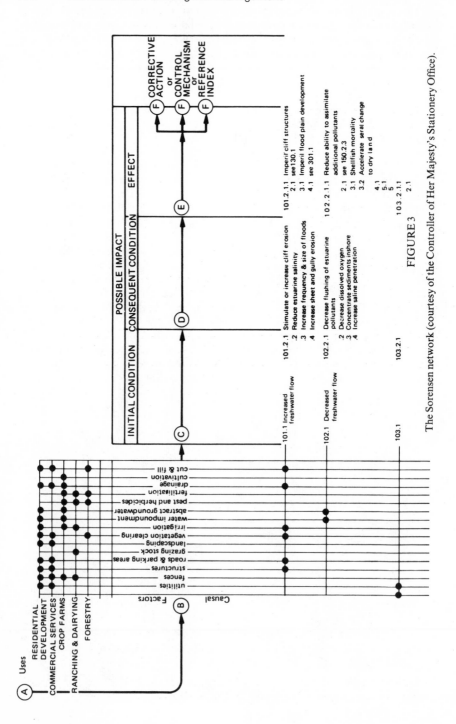

FIGURE 3

The Sorensen network (courtesy of the Controller of Her Majesty's Stationery Office).

of the Leopold matrix helped to achieve their assessment objectives. They monitored drilling impacts and used the results to check and improve the predictive accuracy of the matrix. This experience shows the utility of matrices and that, despite certain practical and theoretical limitations, matrices can be useful methods in EIA.

Networks/Systems Diagrams

These methods explicitly recognize that environmental systems consist of a complex web of relationships between particular components. Thus, they can trace indirect impacts and overcome one of the limitations of a Leopold-type matrix. Sorensen (1971) developed a network of environmental impacts arising from a variety of land uses, such as crop farming and residential development, in the coastal zone of California by obtaining information on their environmental effects (see Figure 3). Sorensen stopped when an initial impact on an environmental feature had been traced through a subsequent condition change to a final effect. This was due to time and other resource constraints. Once constructed, this network could be used to test both the environmental effects of a new land use and its compatibility with existing uses. Sorensen points out that

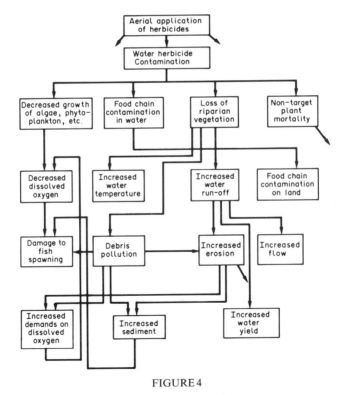

FIGURE 4

A section of the IMPACT network (courtesy of Dr. E. Thor).

networks are laborious to construct and time-consuming to use manually for impact identification.

Work on computerizing networks has been undertaken at the Pacific Southwest Forest and Range Experiment Station of the US Forest Service at Berkeley, California (Thor *et al.*, 1978; Thor, 1978). A computerized network known as IMPACT has been devised for developments in forest and rangeland areas (see Figure 4). IMPACT has an extensive information base consisting of "... a single, massive, unstructured cause-and-effect network of the social, economic and natural environmental effects of man's activities in forest and rangeland settings" (Thor, 1978). The network was developed by experts after examination of scientific and technical literature. To use IMPACT it is only necessary to have some knowledge of the characteristics of a proposed development. The computer supplies information on the chain of effects likely to arise if a particular activity were undertaken.

Networks do not provide information on impact characteristics such as probability, importance and magnitude. There would not appear to be inherent reasons to prevent such information being provided in manual or computerized networks. However, networks tend to be used to make sure that all possible direct and indirect impacts are investigated. This ability distinguishes networks from nearly all other methods. The exception being a specialized Component Interaction Matrix developed by Environment Canada and discussed by Clark *et al.* (1978) and Bisset (1980). Networks can be used easily for a particular type of environment, but a great deal of information collection is required.

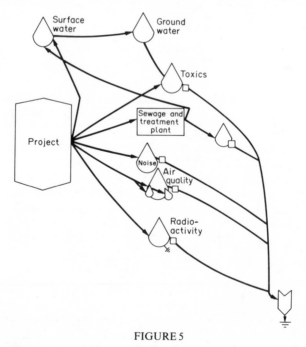

FIGURE 5

A section of a systems diagram (courtesy of the Journal of Environmental Management).

Systems diagrams have been developed from the work in ecological energetics by Odum (1971). A diagram of energy flows between environmental components is constructed by linking components with solid lines showing the direction and magnitude of energy flows. Most of these flows are described in kilocalories, but when appropriate other units such as decibels and curies can be used. Gilliland and Risser (1977) describe the use of a systems diagram in the assessment of a missile range in New Mexico. The diagram contains sixty-one links beween environmental components (Figure 5 shows a representative section). Activities associated with the development are included in the diagram and impacts traced through it. Impacts are expressed in terms of their effects on gross primary production. Examination of the effects of particular impacts on energy flows gives an indication of the relative magnitude of impacts and allows impacts to be aggregated to give a composite score in kilocalories (for example, missile impact and recovery operations are estimated to decrease gross primary production by 0.48×10^{11} kcal/year). This allows the effects of a proposal to be compared directly with the pre-development situation and a judgement made on the overall effects of a project. The use of kilocalories provides a common measurement unit which enables comparison of impacts in terms of magnitude and distinguishes systems diagrams from networks and matrices.

The utility of systems diagrams is restricted to certain ecological impacts. They do not cater for ecological relations which are not dependent on energy flows. For example, the dependence of a rare bird species on a particular plant for shelter, food and nesting sites cannot be included in a systems diagram. Because social and economic impacts cannot be reduced to kilocalories, networks would have to be used in the case of non-ecological impacts. Systems diagrams involve a considerable amount of time and resources in their construction especially in the determination of energy-flow figures. Consequently, they are only justified in situations where ecological impacts are of paramount importance.

Quantitative/Index Methods

There have been repeated attempts to devise methods capable of comparing the relative importance of all impacts. This is accomplished by weighting, standardizing and aggregating impacts to produce a composite index for either beneficial or harmful impacts or for alternative project designs. Once this has been completed, it is a simple matter to reach a decision on a project or to select the "best" option from alternatives. These methods go further than the ability of systems diagrams to compare impacts in terms of their consequences for energy flow. Systems diagrams can only compare ecological impacts, but other impacts involving energy flow not measurable in kilocalories cannot be compared with each other or with those measured in kilocalories.

The best known quantitative/index method is the Environmental Evaluation System (EES) devised at the Battelle Laboratories of Columbus, Ohio, for the US Bureau of Land Reclamation (Whitman et al., 1971; Dee et al., 1973). EES was devised for assessing water-resource developments. It consists of a checklist of seventy-four environmental, social and economic parameters which may be affected by a proposal. It is assumed that these parameters can be expressed numerically and be related to the quality of the environment. For example,

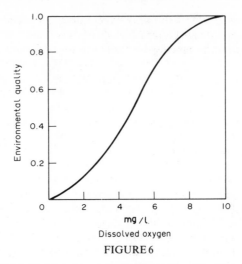

FIGURE 6

Value function for dissolved oxygen (courtesy of the Controller of Her Majesty's Stationery Office).

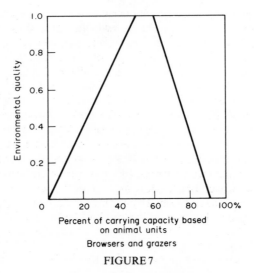

FIGURE 7

Value function for browsers and grazers in the western USA (courtesy of the Controller of Her Majesty's Stationery Office).

dissolved oxygen is a parameter and can be expressed numerically in mg/1. The particular concentration of dissolved oxygen can vary from place to place and the "quality" of an aquatic environment can be determined from knowledge of the concentration of dissolved oxygen. It is assumed for all the other parameters that similar relationships between the condition of a parameter and environmental quality can be made. Environmental quality for each parameter is subsumed in an arbitrary scale of 0–1 where 0 is a degraded environment and 1 is a high-quality environment. To show the relationship between parameter states (for example low and/or high concentrations of dissolved oxygen and environmental quality) experts designed value functions for each parameter. Figures 6 and 7 show the value functions for dissolved oxygen and browsers and grazers respectively. Using value functions the current or expected state of one of the seventy-four parameters can be normalized to a notional idea of environmental quality.

Impacts are measured in terms of likely changes in environmental quality for each parameter. This is done for impacts on each of the seventy-four parameters. For example, consider the possible effects of a dam and reservoir on a population of deer. Figure 7 shows that environmental quality in the western USA is highest, in terms of the relationships between rangeland and deer, when approximately 50 to 60 per cent of the net annual above-ground production of plants is consumed. When this percentage is exceeded, the stability of the system is disturbed (overgrazing), when it is not reached, the full potential of the system for grazing is not used. In this example it can be seen that if only 40 percent were consumed, the environmental quality score would be 0.8. Should a project be likely to halve the deer population then the resulting environmental quality score would be 0.4.

To enable impacts to be compared directly each parameter is weighted by distributing 1000 points amongst the parameters. This is done by experts using the Delphi technique. Once weights have been distributed and impact scores normalized on the 0–1 quality scale it is possible to compare and aggregate impacts. This is done by ascertaining two environmental quality scores for each parameter. These relate to the current state of the environment and the predicted state once the project is operational. The two scores are multiplied by the appropriate weights. For example, if browsers and grazers were allocated 14 points then both the environmental quality scores of 0.8 and 0.4 would be multiplied by 14. In this case the post-development score would be less than the pre-development situation and the impact a negative one. Should the score be positive then the impact would be beneficial. A composite score either for beneficial and adverse impacts of a single project or for the net impact of a number of alternative projects can be obtained by adding up individual impact scores.

While EES was developed a similar method known as Optimum Pathway Matrix Analysis was devised at the Institute of Ecology at the University of Georgia (Institute of Ecology, 1971). It was developed to help assess alternative highway proposals by examining impacts on fifty-six environmental, social and economic parameters. Impacts were described numerically and these scores later normalized by characterizing all impacts of each alternative on a particular factor as a decimal fraction of the highest impact score on that factor. Weights were developed for factors and combined with individual impact scores. Subsequently, these scores were aggregated to provide a composite index for each alternative route. Unlike EES, this method caters directly for the time factor in impact duration. Long-term irreversible impacts were considered to be more important than short-term reversible impacts and were given a weight 10 times greater than that awarded to short-term impacts. In addition, a sensitivity analysis was undertaken to determine whether errors in impact estimation and weight assignment would have a significant effect on the ranking of alternative highway routes provided by the method. Conceptually similar methods have been advanced by Wenger and Rhyner (1972) and the School of Civil Engineering and Environmental Science and Oklahoma Biological Survey (1974).

In the US, the Army Corps of Engineers is responsible for many major water-resource projects for which EISs are required. Consequently, considerable work has been undertaken to develop an appropriate assessment method. After examination of fifty-four methods it was concluded that no method fulfilled all the needs of the Corps (Solomon *et al.*, 1977). However, it was felt that methods such as EES had most potential. Therefore, the organizing principles and rationale of EES were influential in forming the Water Resources Assessment Methodology (WRAM) finally developed by the Corps.

Impacts arising from projects are assigned to four Accounts (Environmental Quality, Regional Development, National Economic Development and Social Well-Being). Factors in each Account are weighted using a pairwise comparison technique and expressed in common terms by use of functional curves (similar to the value functions used in EES) and aggregate impact scores for each Account obtained. Account scores are not aggregated since it is felt that separate scores allow the identification of trade-offs in decisionmaking. A composite score over all Accounts would tend to hide the particular effect of a project on separate Accounts.

A quantitative/index method, having the same objectives as EES, Optimum Pathway Matrix Analysis and WRAM, but exhibiting different organizing procedures has been advocated by Sondheim (1978). This method requires use of two specially constituted groups of people called panels. One of these, a rating panel of experts, assesses the effects of alternative projects on environmental or social factors. Individual specialists assess all alternatives on a single factor— for example, geomorphological features — and each expert produces an individual preference rating scheme for all alternatives for the factor which s/he assessed. Rating schemes are normalized and standardized so that comparisons between schemes can be made.

Weights to indicate relative importance are assigned to each factor by the second panel, termed the weighting panel. This body consists of representatives of government, industry, community organizations, interest groups and other parties. Each member of the panel produces individual weighting schemes assigning importance scores to each factor. These schemes and the normalized ranking scores are manipulated using matrix multiplication techniques and an aggregate score representing the total impact of each alternative is obtained.

Quantitative/index methods have a number of failings as well as considerable advantages. They treat the environment as if it were made of discrete units. Impacts are only related to particular factors. These methods are unable to provide the insight into impacts which can be obtained by the use of networks/systems diagrams. A great deal of information on impacts is lost in the reduction of impacts to numbers. These methods are difficult for lay people to understand and their acceptability depends on the assumptions, especially the weighting schemes, built into them. The value judgements which may be hidden in the technical sophistication may enable those carrying out assessments to manipulate results by changing the assumptions contained in the method (Bisset, 1978).

The attraction of these methods lies in their ability to provide "proof", in terms of numbers, that a particular course of action is better than others. This may save considerable work and interpretation on the part of decisionmakers when faced with a great deal of descriptive information on many impacts. It is an open question whether this is desirable or not. Such methods effectively take decisions away from decisionmakers. The latter are provided with decisions determined by the method used and by those who have devised or operated it. Some commentators consider this "professional theft of evaluation" to be a harmful, non-democratic tendency (Van Norman, 1975; Skutsch and Flowerdew, 1976). On the other hand, by having rigid logico-mathematical rules governing use of a method, consistency in assessment and results can be obtained. More subjective, less structured methods cannot guarantee this.

Evidence for the practical utility of these methods is not easy to come by. WRAM has been used on a flood-control project and further tests are underway (Richardson et al., 1978). Smith (1974) tested EES on a proposed rapid-transit rail line and found it useful, but necessitating a great deal of work. The recent comments of some of the workers who helped develop EES are illuminating. In the context of outlining a new method, they state that EES and methods based on scaling, weighting and aggregation into a composite index were not, and might never be, accepted by decisionmakers, politicians and environmentalists in the US (Duke et al., 1977). Like cost/benefit analysis, quantification in EIA generates controversy on similar issues. It is just as likely that controversy will act as a spur to the development of quantitative methods as it is likely to result in their demise. Political acceptability may be the determining feature for the future of these methods.

Manuals

Most accounts of EIA methods contain discussions of a few main types such as matrices, networks and EES (Andrews, 1973; Warner and Preston, 1974; Skutsch and Flowerdew, 1976 and Clark et al., 1978). This focus has been criticized by Coleman (1977) as being restrictive. In his view, ". . . the standard definition of the range of assessment methodologies is too narrow". It is argued that EIA is comprehensive and lengthy and goes beyond the simple environment. Most methods have been devised to aid some of the tasks involved in EIA (such as identification of impacts and presentation of results) or to help in the assessment of particular categories of impacts, for example, ecological impacts. Only a few methods can be used for all EIA activities and such methods (EES, etc.) have not met with unanimous approval. To help overcome some of the deficiencies, omissions and shortcomings of particular methods, considerable work has been carried out to develop comprehensive, structured approaches to EIA which act as handbooks for assessing specific developments.

These handbooks have been produced in large numbers in the US and to a lesser extent in other countries. Often, they are termed "Manuals" and are produced, mostly, for the assessment of particular types of project. For example, the US Environmental Protection Agency (1973) has produced a Manual for waste-water treatment plants and the US Department of Transportation (1978) has produced a guidebook for the assessment of airports. A Manual has also been produced to help local governments in the US to assess a variety of projects (Schaenman, 1976). The utility of Manuals has been recognized outside the US. A Manual has been prepared for the assessment of major developments in the UK (Clark *et al.*, 1976) and for certain linear developments in British Columbia (Environment and Land Use Committee, 1977). Such Manuals contain comprehensive guidance on how to assess particular projects and on the type of data which should be included in EISs. Often, the format and means of presenting information in EISs is suggested. In addition, Manuals may contain a particular type of method, such as a simple interaction matrix, to help the implementation of assessment. However, the scope of Manuals is broader than most methods. They are concerned with more than the ability of particular

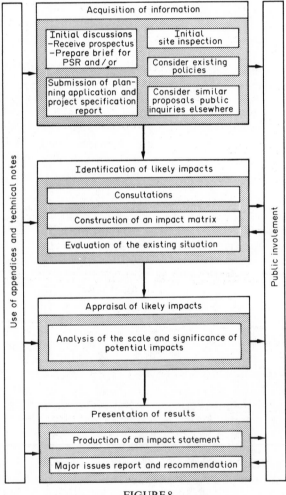

FIGURE 8

Linked activities in the appraisal method of the Clark *et al.* Manual.

methods to carry out some EIA activities such as the ability of networks to identify impacts. Instead, they are concerned with a broader perspective and unlike methods they may contain techniques for prediction of impacts. Manuals have received little attention in the EIA literature because there are large numbers in existence and many are project specific. In contrast matrices, networks and other methods can be applied to a wide variety of projects in differing environmental settings.

A Manual for the assessment of industrial development in the UK (Clark *et al.*, 1976) has been revised and reissued. It contains a comprehensive set of linked assessment procedures (see Figure 8) which includes an impact matrix to aid impact identification (Figure 8). The Manual contains technical notes giving information on the prediction of a wide variety of impacts, such as determination of noise impacts and the effects of a project on landscape. Guidance is also given on the presentation of impact data to decisionmakers.

Evidence for the utility of this Manual has been accumulating. For example, a major study of the environmental impacts of four alternative water-storage schemes in north-west England was initiated in 1976. Following a review of the available EIA methods, it was decided by those undertaking the assessment to use a modified version of the Manual. The final report containing the findings of the impact study has now been published (Land Use Consultants, 1978). Reaction to the report from a range of sources has been favourable. The report is considered to be a comprehensive and thorough account of probable environmental impacts.

Environmental factors

Data required	Information sources / predictive techniques
Air quality **Health** Change in air pollution concentrations by frequency of occurrence and number of people at risk.	Current ambient concentrations, current and expected emissions, dispersion models, population maps.
Nuisance Change in occurrence of visual (smoke, haze) or olfactory (odor) air quality nuisances, and number of people affected.	Baseline citizen survey, expected industrial processes, traffic volumes.
Water quality Changes in permissible or tolerable water uses and number of people affected—for each relevant body of water.	Current and expected effluents, current ambient concentrations, water quality model.
Change in noise levels and frequency of occurrence, and number of people bothered.	Changes in nearby traffic or other noise sources, and in noise barriers; noise propagation model or nomographs relating noise levels to traffic, barriers, etc.; baseline citizen survey of current satisfaction with noise levels.

FIGURE 9

A section of the Schaenman checklist (modified after Schaenman).

In 1976, a Manual was published by the Urban Institute of Washington, DC., which covers environmental, social and economic impacts and contains a descriptive checklist of forty-seven factors to be considered in EIA (Schaenman, 1976). For each factor information is provided on appropriate measurements and predictive techniques (see Figure 9). A particular feature of this Manual is the emphasis on relating impacts on the forty-seven factors to people affected. In addition, it is advocated that impacts should be considered in terms of their differential distribution between social groups. Like the Manual developed by Clark and his colleagues the Schaenman Manual contains advice warning against the dangers of weighting and aggregating impacts. Both Manuals consider weighting and aggregation to hide more impact information than is revealed.

Models

Models have been used as predictive techniques in EIA for a number of years although some commentators have been sceptical of their success (Carpenter, 1976). Models for predicting animal population responses and pollution concentrations have been the most commonly used. Recently, there has been considerable work in the development of models, which may be used to predict a variety of environmental, social and even economic impacts (Suzuki *et al.*, 1977; Holling, 1978). Suzuki *et al.* developed a model to aid regional planning in Japan. The model enables decisionmakers to determine the effects of various management strategies on regional levels of air pollution, water pollution and solid-waste generation.

Models are advocated by Holling because of a perceived failing of the EIA process as practised generally since 1970. "Traditional" EIA is considered to be static in its orientation. It only operates when a proposed action materializes and finishes when an EIS is prepared. Often, a quick survey of existing environmental conditions is made onto which are superimposed the effects of a proposal. Once the EIS has been prepared and a decision on a proposal made EIA has little role to play. This approach to EIA is thought to ignore the dynamic nature of environmental systems. Such systems are changing constantly and impacts on a dynamic system will alter the existing processes of change. These changes will alter the system(s) and the continuation of impacts will cause further change in the altered systems. Models, which take account of the major determining features of environmental systems, are thought to be the best means of investigating impacts.

EIA, therefore, is not primarily for assessing proposals, instead it is a strategy for aiding environmental management through continuous use and validation of the model not only during assessment, but also once a proposal is operational. This provides the opportunity for changes to be made should a proposal be seen to be having serious adverse effects. Dynamic models are thought to be the best means of ensuring that EIA recognizes a dynamic perspective.

Holling (1978) describes the use of dynamic ecosystem models in a number of contexts. Most are resource-management problems involving only one or, at most, a few environmental objectives, for example, proposals to control the pest known as spruce budworm in New Brunswick forests. Evidence on the utility of these models is scarce. In June 1979, a seminar to discuss the use of models was organized by the International Institute of Applied Systems Analysis in Laxenburg, Austria. Two papers reported only limited success in using models. Hirsch *et al.* (1979) of the US Fish and Wildlife Service concluded that, ". . . only a modest measure of success" was achieved in solving problems, ". . . of significant management concern to the agency". Baskerville (1979) states that models had been successfully used by his organization to discover and evaluate a ". . . range of possible policies" for a forest management problem, but he notes that success in achieving "on-the-ground" changes was, ". . . limited to the initiation of the learning process in a small cadre of people" in management. A lack of practical application of model results need not be seen necessarily as a fault of a model, blame may lie in the institutional framework. As Atkins (1979) points out a final judgement of the modelling approach advocated by Holling is still awaited.

Possible problem areas in the use of these models may be identified at present. It remains to be seen whether they can be applied to developments having a large variety of environmental impacts. If it were shown to be applicable to all types of proposals, ranging from industrial installations to environmental management plans, this method might have to be adapted to achieve general political acceptability. At present, the models described by Holling are constructed by environmental and modelling experts, and it is their assumptions that will determine the results. Holling and his colleagues advocate that periodic workshops consisting of scientists, administrators, decisionmakers and developers should meet to aid model formulation and implementation. At present, the public is excluded from the assessment process. The lack of public influence on assumptions built into quantitative/index methods has been one of the main criticisms of such methods (Bisset, 1978; Bisset, 1981). Consequently, models may be subject to similar criticisms unless provision is made for the achievement of a wider basis of political acceptability.

Conclusions

Methods have been devised continually since 1970 and this process is likely to continue. Some lessons are becoming apparent as a result of 12 years' experience. Matrices and networks still find favour. Quantitative/index methods are still developed, but as Duke *et al.* (1977) have admitted, such methods do not appear to have achieved general acceptance in the US. Manuals and models will continue to be developed. The future of models is likely to be more uncertain than Manuals, however, because of inherent difficulties of constructing a meaningful model which is sufficiently comprehensive in its impact coverage.

The choice of a particular method for a specific project assessment depends on the political and administrative context. Should a public authority or developer wish to carry out assessments internally then a quantitative/index method may be suitable because of its ability to provide "answers". Those carrying out assessments and making initial decisions among a number of competing sites or project designs may be identical. Outside interests would not be involved and might not be concerned until project and/or site planning is well advanced. However, should an assessment be carried out in a public, political arena then such methods may be unsatisfactory because of their operational complexity and hidden value assumptions.

It is difficult to predict likely trends in method development. In the years immediately after the implementation of NEPA, EIA was considered as a bureaucratic, technical exercise. One of the most important indirect effects of NEPA has been an increase in public input to environmental decisionmaking. One of the consequences of this trend could be a move away from complex quantitative index methods to those which present disaggregated, qualitative information. Should public participation play a significant role in EIA procedures likely to be introduced in Europe then a similar trend may be expected. The development of methods during the 1980s in Europe will be a useful barometer in assessing the characteristics of EIA procedures. It may show whether emphasis is placed on EIA as scientific/technical input to bureaucratic decisionmaking or as a means of informing public debate before the finalization of project decisions.

At present, in many countries, EIA is an unstructured adjunct to project authorization procedures. In only a few countries is it a legally-sanctioned process. However, a number of European countries are considering the issues involved in introducing formal EIA procedures. This orientation explains, in part, the relative lack of emphasis on methods in recent debates on EIA. Methods only become important once the system in which they may operate is established. Other features of EIA may also help explain lack of concern for method development. Methods are concerned with ensuring that impact predictions in EIS are comprehensive and scientifically acceptable. These EISs are produced within a political context which focuses on the benefits and disadvantages of proposals. Once a decision has been made political interests wane and local coalitions often break up. There is little interest in the post-development situation should a proposal proceed. Political pressure for EIA tends to focus on the need for some form of public assessment procedure and this provides the focus for government responses. The actual utility of EIA procedures in terms of accurate prediction for particular projects is a secondary consideration. Therefore, the utility of various methods receives little attention in the current debate on EIA in the US and elsewhere in Europe. Once EIA procedures are established this may change, but as public concern concentrates on the pre-decision period, it is unlikely that methods will be treated in a serious manner until the lack of post-development data on method performance is made good by the introduction of monitoring programmes for major projects.

Acknowledgement

I am extremely grateful to Ms Pearl Allan for typing the manuscript.

References

Andrews, R. N. L. (1973) Approaches to Impact Assessment: Comparison and Critique. Paper presented to Short Course on Impact Assessment in Water Resource Planning, Ann Arbor, Michigan, 9 June.
Atkins, R. (1979) Usefulness of Environmental Impact Analysis in Small Scale Planning and Development Control Decisions, Evaluated by Means of a Case Study. Unpublished MSc thesis. London: Imperial College of Science and Technology, Centre for Environmental Technology.

Baskerville, G. (1979) Implementation of Adaptive Approaches in Provincial and Federal Forestry Agencies. Paper presented to seminar on environmental policy, Laxenburg, Austria, June.

Bisset, R. (1978) Quantification, decision-making and environmental impact assessment in the United Kingdom. *Journal of Environmental Management*, 7 (1), pp. 43–58.

Bisset, R. (1980) Methods for environmental impact analysis: recent trends and future prospects. *Journal of Environmental Management*, vol. 11(1), pp.27–43.

Canter, L. W. (1979) *Water Resources Assessment: Methodology and Technology Sourcebook*. Ann Arbor: Ann Arbor Science.

Carpenter, R. (1976) The scientific basis of NEPA—is it adequate? *Environmental Law Reporter*, 6, pp. 50014–9.

Clark, B. D., Chapman, K., Bisset, R. and Wathern, P. (1976) *The Assessment of Major Industrial Applications: A Manual*, Research Report 13. London: Department of the Environment.

Clark, B. D., Chapman, K., Bisset, R. and Wathern, P. (1978) *US Environmental Impact Assessment: A Critical Review*, Research Report 26. London: Departments of the Environment and Transport.

Clark, B. D., Bisset, R. and Wathern, P. (1980) *Environmental Impact Assessment: A Bibliography with Abstracts*. London: Mansell.

Clark, B. D., Chapman, K., Bisset, R., Wathern, P. and Barrett, M. (1981). *A Manual for the Assessment of Major Development Proposals*. London: HMSO.

Coleman, D. J. (1977) Environmental impact assessment methodologies: a critical review, in Plewes, M. and Whitney, J. B. R. (eds.) *Environmental Impact Assessment in Canada: Processes and Approaches*. Toronto: University of Toronto, Institute for Environmental Studies, pp. 35–59.

Dee, N., Baker, J. K., Drobny, N. L., Duke, K. M., Whitman, I. and Fahringer, D. C. (1973) An environmental evaluation system for water resources planning. *Water Resources Research*, (3), pp. 523–35.

Duke, K. M., Dee, N., Fahringer, D. C, Maiden, B. G., Moody, C. W., Pomeroy, S. E. and Watkins, G. A. (1977) *Environmental Quality Assessment in Multiobjective Planning*. Columbus, Ohio: Battelle Columbus Laboratories.

Environmental Canada (1974) *An Environmental Assessment of Nanaimo Port Alternatives*. Ottawa: Environment Canada.

Environment and Land Use Committee (1977) *Guidelines for Linear Development*. Victoria, British Columbia: Environment and Land Use Committee.

Gilliland, M. W. and Risser, P. G. (1977) The use of systems diagrams for environmental impact assessment: procedures and an application. *Ecological Modelling*, 3 (3), pp. 188–209.

Hirsch, A., Andrews, A. K. and Roelle, J. E. (1979) Implementing Adaptive Environmental Assessment in an Operating Agency. Paper Presented to Seminar on Environmental Policy, Laxenburg, Austria, June.

Holling, C. S. (ed.) (1978) *Adaptive Environmental Assessment and Management*. Chichester: John Wiley.

Institute of Ecology (1971) *Optimum Pathway Matrix Analysis Approach to Environmental Decision-Making*. Athens, Georgia: University of Georgia, Institute of Ecology.

Land Use Consultants (1978) *Environmental Appraisal of Four Alternative Water Resource Schemes*. London: Land Use Consultants.

Leopold, L. B., Clarke, F. E., Hanshaw, B. B. and Balsley, J. R. (1971) *A Procedure for Evaluating Environmental Impact*, United States Geological Survey Circular 645. Washington, DC: US Geological Survey.

Odum, H. T. (1971) *Environment, Power and Society*. New York: Wiley Interscience.

Parker, B. C. and Howard, R. V. (1977) The first environmental monitoring and assessment in Antarctica: the Dry Valley Drilling Project. *Biological Conservation*, 12 (2), pp. 163–77.

Richardson, S. E., Hansen, W. J., Solomon, R. C. and Jones, J. C. (1978) *Preliminary Field Test of the Water Resources Assessment Methodology (WRAM); Tensas River, Louisiana*, Miscellaneous Paper No. Y–78–1. Vicksburg, Mississippi: US Army Corps of Engineers.

Schaenman, P. S. (1976) *Using an Impact Measurement System to Evaluate Land Development*. Washington, DC: The Urban Institute.

School of Civil Engineering and Environmental Science and Oklahoma Biological Survey (1974) *Mid-Arkansas River Basin Study—Effects Assessment of Alternative Navigation Routes from Tulsa, Oklahoma to Vicinity of Wichita, Kansas*. Tulsa: US Army Corps of Engineers.

Skutsch, M. McC. and Flowerdew, R. T. N. (1976) Measurement techniques in environmental impact assessment. *Environmental Conservation*, 3 (3), pp. 209–17.

Smith, M. A. (1974) *Field Test of an Environmental Assessment Methodology.* Georgia: Georgia Institute of Technology, Environmental Resources Center.

Solomon, R. C., Colbert, B. K., Hansen, W. J., Richardson, S. E., Canter, L. and Vlachos, E. C. (1977) *Water Resources Assessment (WRAM)—Impact Assessment and Alternative Evaluation,* Technical Report No. Y–77–1. Vicksburg, Mississippi: US Amy Corps of Engineers.

Sondheim, M. W. (1978) A comprehensive methodology for assessing environmental impact. *Journal of Environmental Management,* 6 (1), pp. 27–42.

Sorensen, J. C. (1971) *A Framework for Identification and Control of Resource Degradation and Conflict in the Multiple Use of the Coastal Zone.* Berkeley, California: University of California at Berkeley, Department of Landscape Architecture.

Suzuki, Y., Ito, K. and Ono, T. (1977) A simulation model for regional environmental impact analysis—a case study of the Kinki region. *International Journal of Environmental Studies,* 10 (2), pp. 91–99.

Thor, E. C. (1978) IMPACT—A new Approach to Environmental Impact Assessment. Paper presented to Society of American Foresters National Workshop, Lexington, Kentucky, 10 August.

Thor, E. C., Elsner, G. H., Travis, M. R. and O'Loughlin, K. M. (1978) Forest Environmental Impact Analysis—a new approach. *Journal of Forestry* 76, pp. 723–25.

US Environmental Protection Agency (1973) *Manual for Preparation of Environmental Impact Statements for Wastewater Treatment Works, Facilities, Plans and 208 Areawide Waste Treatment Management Plans.* Washington, DC: US Environmental Protection Agency.

US Department of Transportation (1978) *Airport Planning and Environmental Assessment,* 4 vols. Washington, DC: US Department of Transportation.

Van Norman, M. (1975) The professional theft of evaluation. *DMG–DRS Journal,* 9, p. 57–66.

Warner, M. L. and Preston, E. H. (1974) *Review of Environmental Impact Assessment Methodologies.* Washington, DC: United States Environmental Protection Agency.

Wenger, R. B. and Rhyner, C. R. (1972) Evaluation of alternatives for solid waste systems. *Journal of Environmental Systems,* 2 (2), pp. 89–108.

Whitman, I. L., Dee, N., McGinnis J. T., Fahringer, D. C. and Baker, J. K. (1971) *Design of an Environmental Evaluation System.* Columbus, Ohio: Battelle Columbus Laboratories.

ENVIRONMENTAL IMPACT STATEMENTS IN THE UNITED STATES AND IN BRITAIN*

J. F. GARNER

WHAT is an Environmental Impact Statement and what is meant by environmental impact analysis? As the subject is much discussed in planning circles at the present time, it was thought desirable to attempt an understanding of the practice in the land of its birth, the United States of America, with a view to its possible application in Great Britain.

The American system

The idea of an Environmental Impact Statement (E.I.S.) first appeared in a legal context when the National Environmental Policy Act was passed by the Federal Congress and signed into law by President Nixon with much éclat in 1969. Section 102(2) of this Act provides as follows:

"All agencies of the Federal Government shall—

(A) Utilize a systematic, interdisciplinary approach which will insure the integrated use of the natural and social sciences and environmental design arts in planning and in decision-making which may have an impact on man's environment;

*Reprinted by permission of the Department of Land Economy, Cambridge, 1979. (Professor Garner is Emeritus Professor of Law at the University of Nottingham.)

(B) identify and develop methods and procedures, in consultation with the Council on Environmental Quality established by title II of this Act, which will insure that presently unquantified environmental amenities and values may be given appropriate consideration in decision-making along with economic and technical considerations;

(C) include in every recommendation or report on proposals for legislation and other major Federal actions significantly affecting the quality of the human environment, a detailed statement by the responsible official on

(i) the environmental impact of the proposed action,

(ii) any adverse environmental effects which cannot be avoided should the proposal be implemented,

(iii) alternatives to the proposed action,

(iv) the relationship between local short-term uses of man's environment and the maintenance and enhancement of long-term productivity, and

(v) any irreversible and irretrievable commitments of resources which would be involved in the proposed action should it be implemented.''

This interesting and novel provision may be described as the "bedrock" of federal environmental legislation, although the subject matter has been considerably augmented since 1969.[1] The requirement to provide an E.I.S. applies to all federal projects and to all private projects sponsored by federal funds. Section 102 of the National Environmental Policy Act 1969 now also applies to federally aided local projects under the Housing and Community Development Act, 1974. The provision is reinforced procedurally by requirements to the following effect:

(a) The statement should first be prepared in draft by the sponsoring agency, and that draft must be sent to the Council on Environmental Quality[2] and also to all concerned federal, state and local agencies. Any observations made by any of these bodies must then be included with the final definitive statement; and also

(b) A final statement, prepared after the draft has been revised and after consideration of any observations received, must be sent to the President of the United States and to the Council on Environmental Quality, and be made generally public.

This procedure, supplemented by Guidelines (which do not have the force of law) for the preparation of an E.I.S. issued by the Council on Environmental Quality on 23rd April 1971 has proved elaborate, time-consuming and expensive, but effective (as will appear below).

However, the procedure does mean that there should be ample opportunity for public awareness of what is proposed. Since 1969, the process has become standardised and reasonably well known; increasingly so since some 18 of the States, California and North Carolina in particular,[3] have introduced similar legislative requirements applying to State or local government projects. One U.S. writer[4] has said, "seldom has a new law generated as widespread and immediate action through government agencies"; by the middle of 1974 no less than 5,430 draft or final statements has been filed.*

---

* Between 1970–1980 more than 12,500 E.I.S.s have been filed by 70 agencies: during the same period 1191 lawsuits were instigated [eds].

An E.I.S. is subjected to at least two independent forms of scrutiny:
(i) In the first place, at both the draft and the final stages, each statement is received by a Clearinghouse (or similar body, whatever may be its title) established by each of the relevant State governments. In some States the Clearinghouse is little more than a depository, but in most States, statements are there examined for local relevance and are forwarded either to all State and local agencies in that State, or to a select group of such agencies. In some States the Clearinghouse then collates observations received from agencies and formulates a State view to be returned to the federal agency concerned; in yet other States the Clearinghouse may even operate as an environmental agency itself, employing its own experts, and formulating, on behalf of the State, recommendations for action.[5] It is in those States that the fullest analysis is likely to be required, and where citizen opinion is most likely to be expressed. Even where a standard procedure has been established, however, the State agency does not always make any comments, nor are adverse comments always processed further, partly because of the sheer numbers of federal projects involved.

(ii) The Council on Environmental Quality advises federal agencies generally on environmental matters, but it has no enforcement powers. Nearly a year after the passing of the National Environmental Policy Act the President set up a new federal agency, the Environmental Protection Agency which was primarily made responsible for setting standards for water and air pollution. Unlike the advisory Council on Environmental Quality, this Agency is primarily an executive body, and has wide powers to carry out research on environmental issues. The Environmental Protection Agency works closely with the Council and comments from time to time on draft Environmental Impact Statements. The Agency, like the Council, has issued guidelines for the preparation of certain types of E.I.S., but the executive activities of the Agency themselves on occasion involve the preparation of an E.I.S.. Questions as to whether an E.I.S. is legally necessary for a particular project, and if so, whether the statement prepared complies with the provisions of the National Environmental Policy Act, have to be referred for a decision to the Federal Courts. Questions of this kind may be raised by the Council on Environmental Quality or, more commonly, by some environmental or other pressure group, perhaps one formed locally to oppose a specific project, or one having regional or even national interests, such as the very influential Sierra Club. These bodies are generally allowed standing to sue in such matters before the Federal Courts. The basic test of adequate standing seems to be that the organisation should be able to establish that its members are "users" of the affected area and might therefore be injured in fact by the proposed agency action.[6]

General purpose

Environmental impact analysis, it has been said in an authoritative U.S. publication,[7] "involves the prediction, evaluation and public discussion of the direct and indirect effect that policies, programs, and investment have on the social and natural environment. The goal of impact assessment is to come as close as possible to making decisions which minimise harm to biological and human communities yet maximise the fulfilment of the wide range of needs of various public and private interest groups". The preparation of an E.I.S. is thus something more than a required procedural step; the statement must be taken fully into account and be considered in the process of making a decision as to whether the proposed project should go forward. It is one of the most important factors to be taken into account in applying the principle of proportionality,[8] that should be the foundation of every important administrative decision—Is the harm that will be caused to the environment if the project goes forward, outweighed by the advantages to public and private interests that would result in that event? Or is the anticipated harm so great that the project ought not to be undertaken at all, or only in modified form?

Should the requirement to prepare an E.I.S. be introduced into the English (and Scottish) development control system? Environmental impact assessment, although not recognised to be such, has of course been undertaken in relation to at least two recent large scale projects in Britain; in the case, for instance, of the Third London Airport[9] and the Windscale proposals[10], but in both those cases the investigation and assessment was carried out in the course of a lengthy public inquiry. Section 11 of the Countryside Act 1968, which requires public bodies to have regard to the "desirability of conserving the natural beauty and amenity of the countryside", when observed, also goes some way towards demanding environmental impact analysis.[11]

Practical problems

In considering whether the E.I.S. procedure should be introduced, we must first consider the problems that would have to be resolved, profiting from the American experience.

1. Any legislation introduced must make it clear as to *when* an E.I.S. is required. The expression used in The National Environmental Policy Act is "*major* Federal action *significantly* affecting the quality of the environment" (author's italics). The courts had little difficulty in recognising "major Federal action" in such projects as "a continuous barge motorway joining the Upper Mississippi and the Ohio valleys so as to provide a through route to Mobile, Alabama on the Gulf of Mexico",[12] and "the channelising of sixty-six miles of river in North Carolina".[13] Difficulties have arisen, however, if projects are splintered or fragmented; can the administration avoid preparing an E.I.S. for a complete new highway if they plan for a series of short stretches, one at a time, and prepare statements for each separate stretch? This problem was raised in the recent case of *Kleppe v. Sierra Club*,[14] where the complaint was that the Federal Departments of Agriculture and the Interior were planning development of the coal resources in the northern great plains (crossing several States), without preparing an E.I.S. for the entire project. The court agreed that "broad regional development programs" were involved, which amounted to major federal action, and granted an injunction, although the government agencies were intending to carry out the actual work piecemeal. On the other hand it was also held that the National Environmental Policy Act does not require the preparation of an E.I.S. before the action is proposed; if the government departments

merely carry out studies, this does not necessarily amount to a *proposal* for action for which an E.I.S. is required. This causes a real practical problem. When does a research study, for example, become a proposal for action? Only when it is accepted by the executive of the sponsoring body? It may then be difficult, politically speaking, to stop it going forward.

2. *Who* should be required to prepare an E.I.S.? In the United States the expression "agency of the Federal government" is used, and this is obviously wide enough to include government departments, and also the more independent Agencies, such as the Federal Aviation Authority,[15] but it does not include development carried out by the private sector, unless it is federally assisted. Clearly in any application to Britain the legislation would have to apply not only to government departments *stricto sensu*, and local authorities, but also to the public corporations such as the National Coal Board (relevant for Selby and Belvoir), the Atomic Energy Authority, the gas and electricity boards and British Rail. The requirement should also apply to developments in the private sector. Should this be confined to the major industries, such as the Windscale scheme, operated by British Nuclear Fuels Ltd? Pipelines, oil refineries and many other major developments are in the private sector of industry in legal theory only, especially where, in cases such as British Leyland Ltd. or Rolls Royce Ltd., large proportions of the share capital are owned by the central government or the National Enterprise Board.

3. *What* must the E.I.S. contain? Here s.102 of National Environmental Policy Act appears reasonably clear, but because the statement is required to consider possible alternatives and what would result if the project were not carried out, this has meant in practice that many statements have become very lengthy. Much time and resources are expended in exploring all possible side issues, with the result that many an E.I.S. is so complicated that few people have the time or energy to consider it carefully. Statements can sometimes run to thousands of pages and cost many thousands of dollars to prepare, although this may not always be strictly necessary. The very object of the whole exercise can thus be destroyed. The Act has been described as "an environmental full disclosure law". Whereas it has been said that adequate detail must be given and all possible alternatives discussed,[16] it has also been pointed out that there must be some limitations.

"Nothing would be more paralysing to an administrator than to take seriously the prescription . . . that he make no decision until he canvas all possible alternative ways of reaching well-formulated goals making sure that he has investigated every possible major consequence of each possible alternative".[17] English legislation could perhaps avoid this danger in some measure by an express requirement of concise drafting.*

4. There must be *publicity* for the E.I.S., so that some degree of public participation in the decision-making process is possible. This is assured in the United States by the requirements prescribed by the National Environmental Policy Act. The Council on Environmental Quality and the Environmental Protection Agency hold watching briefs and the State Clearinghouses should

---

* In 1979 the C.E.Q. issued new regulations requiring E.I.S.s to be shorter, more readable and more directly relevant to other decision making criteria. See O'Riordan, T. (1982) US Experience in E.I.A.—Lessons for Britain, *ECOS*, vol. 3(3), pp. 6–11 [eds].

make aware all concerned State and local agencies. But there must be an alert public, informed and ready to take notice of an E.I.S. when it is published, and also a public prepared to oppose or support and to criticise the project in a responsible manner as they may consider desirable. This role is filled in the United States in most instances by such bodies as the Sierra Club and the Environmental Defense Fund Inc., and also by many locally-based pressure groups.

5. *Who* is entitled to challenge formally the need for an E.I.S. in a particular case, or the contents of an E.I.S. when it has been prepared? Clearly in the United States the challenge is made (in the case of federal matters) before the federal courts; they have no competitor, as the Council of Environmental Quality and the Environmental Protection Agency have no judicial or enforcement role. Who then can take such a case before the courts? The generous rules as to standing have already been referred to and there seem to be many zealous bodies ready to litigate these matters.[18]

Application to Britain

Being so warned of the principal problems that may arise if there is to be a statutory requirement in this country, it is perhaps now appropriate to attempt an answer to the question—do we want an E.I.S. requirement introduced into our planning law and, if so, how should it be drafted?

Adoption of the E.I.S. idea is essential in many cases. A Department of the Environment research team concluded in 1976 that "there is need to employ a system of environmental impact analysis for some kinds of development in Great Britain", and they also formed the opinion that the process should "be integrated into the existing planning system".[19] The American experience shows that the need to prepare an E.I.S. has focussed attention on environmental issues, it has provided new knowledge, particularly about relationships between different ecological issues, and in a number of instances there have been major changes made in the draft projects proposed. It is clear, agreeing with the Department of the Environment team, that any requirement to prepare an E.I.S. introduced into English law should be linked with the existing planning control system. The Secretary of State has recently stated publicly[20] that he intends to require some form of environmental analysis to be carried out for the proposed Vale of Belvoir coal field, as part of his special treatment of a major planning inquiry. This is welcome, but it is to be hoped that the procedure will be fully structured and formulated in regulations prepared after consultation with the Council on Tribunals. It is also not sufficient that environmental analysis should be undertaken only for projects of national importance. There are many other projects, that have significant effects on the local physical and social environment, that should similarly be thoroughly assessed before planning permission is given.

A local planning authority, therefore, should be required to defer any relevant application for planning permission until an adequate E.I.S. has been prepared. In the public sector, in cases where express planning permission may not be required, the sponsoring agency should be required to file an E.I.S. with the appropriate government department, and any necessary approval (for instance, loan consent) should be withheld until this has been done. Monitoring of this process is discussed in more detail below.

Critical considerations

1. *Which projects should need an E.I.S.?* Definition could in theory be by size; all projects affecting an area in excess of x acres, for example; but some projects which could have a highly significant effect on the environment may occupy only a small area of land, such as certain industrial plants. "Projects likely to have a significant effect on the environment" would probably be a satisfactory formula to be written into the legislation: the California phrase is simply "significant effect on the environment".[21] The Department of the Environment research team recommended that the circumstances in which an E.I.S. is to be required should be identified by the local planning authority or, in the case of development in the public sector, by a central government department. Would it not be preferable to leave the issue (of whether the statutory requirement applies) to the courts?

However, the legislation would have to cover the American case law showing that fragmentation of a project may enable a developer to avoid the substantive requirement. This perhaps could be achieved by providing that an E.I.S. must be prepared for any significant project, whether or not forming part of a larger project, and also that due account must be taken of a fragment of the project when preparing the E.I.S. for any project of which the fragment forms part.

The whole process should, as already stated, be integrated with existing development control, and so it should be made clear that, in the private sector, the E.I.S. should be presented as part of the application for planning permission. In the public sector, it would similarly form part of such an application or of an application for the approval of a supervising central government department. If the project is undertaken by a government department itself, then an E.I.S. should be prepared and made public an appreciable time before the final decision to go ahead is taken. This is not to exclude the probability of the developer (private or public) discussing the E.I.S. in draft with the planning authority before any application for permission is formally made.

2. *Who is to be required to prepare the E.I.S.?* This responsibility, it is submitted, should be placed on the developer. He knows most about his project, and if he wants to obtain planning permission, that is, a licence which may add considerably to the value of his property, he should bear the necessary cost and trouble of obtaining that licence. In the public sector, it would similarly be the responsibility of the public agency or department sponsoring the project to prepare the E.I.S. The local planning authority, who will eventually have to scrutinise the E.I.S. when it has been prepared, should be ready and willing to assist and give advice in the course of the preparation.

3. *What should an E.I.S. contain?* Any legislation should, it is suggested, prescribe the required contents of an E.I.S. in some detail, partly so that the courts, in case of dispute, will have a standard by which to assess a particular E.I.S., and also so that there may be some limitation on the size and complexity of the E.I.S., thereby avoiding the abuses of the American experience.

An E.I.S. should be prepared as a means of arriving at the optimum planning decision on a particular proposal, not as a justification for a decision already taken. It should examine not only ecological and amenity matters but also all relevant sociological factors. Taking these into account, the statement should amount to a carefully compiled cost/benefit analysis. The legislation should therefore require the following matters to be included in any E.I.S:

(a) the impact the project would have on the physical environment;
(b) any possible pollution of the soil, of waters of all kinds (surface, underground, estuarine and coastal), and of the atmosphere;
(c) the impact of the project on wild life, the natural habitat and all other ecological factors;
(d) the project's likely influence on the qualities of life of the local population;
(e) any influence the project may have on existing industry and employment;
(f) any need that may result for new or improved infrastructure (utilities, transport, housing, schools, recreational amenities, etc.); and
(g) any incidental advantages (for example recreational facilities as a consequence of constructing a new reservoir) that may result.

In order to prepare such a statement, full use must be made of the latest scientific knowledge, including the environmental data banks being prepared by the European Communities' Joint Research Centre at Ispra in Italy.

It is thought to be unnecessary to require an evaluation of all possible alternatives. It is this requirement in particular in the National Environmental Policy Act that has caused so many American statements to become unnecessarily voluminous and expensive.

4. *Administrative action to be taken*. An E.I.S. should first be prepared in draft, and sent to the planning authority or appropriate Minister, who should then be empowered to require any additional information that may be considered necessary. When finalised, a copy of the E.I.S. should be sent to the Environment Council (to be discussed below) and made available for public inspection. The authority or Minister should at that stage be required to take into account the E.I.S. (with all other material considerations[22]) and any observations made by the Environment Council or members of the public before granting planning permission or giving any necessary approval.

5. *Monitoring and enforcement*. There should be an Environment Council, established as a public corporation with functions similar to those of the Council on Environmental Quality, but without the executive functions of the Environmental Protection Agency in the United States, and possessing in addition, powers of enforcement. This body would have the primary duty of advising Government Departments, local authorities and other public bodies, such as the Countryside Commission, on ecological and environmental matters, and it would act much as an American State Clearinghouse. In addition it would be required to scrutinise each E.I.S. and satisfy itself that the statement complied with the requirements of the legislation as to form and content. The Council should be further empowered to institute proceedings in the High Court (by way of an application for judicial review[23]) for an injunction to prevent a project from proceeding if

(a) no E.I.S. had been prepared in a case where under the legislation one ought to have been required; *or* where
(b) the E.I.S. prepared did not satisfy the statutory requirements; *and*
(c) at a later stage if the project departs from the E.I.S in any material respect.[24]

The defendant in any such proceedings would be the developer, or the agency in the public sector, with (in an appropriate case) the local planning authority or government department as co-defendant. The injunction, if granted by the court, would operate to suspend any progress with the project until such time as an E.I.S. complying with the legislation had been filed or the project had been modified to meet the description in the E.I.S. A period (say, 3 months) would also be required within which the E.I.S. could be studied by all concerned, including members of the public.

It would also be desirable for the legislation to provide that accredited environmental societies and similar pressure groups, and also individual property owners whose legitimate interests would be affected by the project, would have sufficient *locus standi* to institute similar proceedings for an injunction. By "accredited" groups is meant those societies which had registered previously with the Environmental Council as being responsible bodies, much in the same way as bodies attain charitable status with the approval of the Charity Commissioners.[25]

The Environment Council would be a public corporation established by Royal Charter and its 12 to 16 or so members would be appointed by the Secretary of State for the Environment; some would be nominated by such bodies as the National Trust, the Council for the Protection of Rural England, Friends of the Earth, the Conservation Society and the Royal Society for the Protection of Birds, other members would be chosen from scientists and experts known for their work in ecological and environmental matters. The Council should be based in London but have regional offices.

Conclusion

Such a procedure would obviously cause delay in dealing with planning applications and, as suggested by the Department of the Environment Research Report, it would be necessary to amend the existing law so as to allow for a considerable lapse of time, perhaps 12 months, after the filing of an application for planning permission, in cases where an E.I.S. is required, before the planning authority would be required to give their decision. It is not thought that it would prove necessary for planning authorities to employ more staff — after all, impact analysis is already carried out on a small scale by some planning authorities, and most of the work under this new procedure would be carried out by private developers and the sponsoring public authorities. The Environment Council would need a staff of experts to advise them, but this is the only new expense that would fall on public funds if these proposals were implemented. As to the delay, it is only right and proper that there should be the fullest possible consideration and opportunity for proper public participation before further irreparable harm is caused to our already hard pressed natural environment. The American experience shows that the E.I.S., properly used, is an effective instrument to assist in this desirable objective. Opposition is alerted and there is time for responsible political pressures to operate in proper cases. A number of federal projects have been withdrawn as a consequence of public opposition once the E.I.S. has been filed.

At least one country, with a very different legal tradition from that of the United States or of England, has passed legislation requiring the carrying out of environmental analysis. A French statute of 10 July 1976 requires "études d'impact" to be undertaken, which would examine the effect of proposed public works; the resultant documentation must show the effects on the environment that would result from the project, and also outline the remedial action that will be taken to alleviate any harmful results. Very recently a draft Directive was prepared by the European Commission making the preparation of an E.I.S. compulsory for most major forms of development in the public or private sector in all the countries of the EEC, but our own Department of the Environment has refused so far to agree.

A proposal to introduce these requirements into English Law would of course need legislation; perhaps the electorate might be more willing to accept this than politicians and civil servants seem to suppose. Examples of projects where an E.I.S. should be essential, apart from projects of national importance such as the Vale of Belvoir and the proposed fast breeder nuclear reactor, are the construction of a motorway or reservoir, the building of an oil refinery or a power station, or any industrial process which may amount to a scheduled process under the Alkali Acts, or require a licence from the water authority for the discharge of any substantial quantity of effluent to a public sewer or to inland waterways, or the carrying out of open cast mining. But this is merely a descriptive, not an exclusive list, and final definition of the expression "projects likely to have significant effect on the environment" must be left to the courts. It is not sufficient to leave the decision whether to carry out environmental assessment to the discretion of central or local authorities; although perhaps we are past the pre-Windscale era, when it was only after very considerable public pressure, including the intervention of the Archbishop of York, that the Secretary of State agreed even to the holding of a public inquiry. Even now his acceptance of analysis for Belvoir is limited to this and cases of similar national importance.

The price of a good environment in the future is, like that of liberty, the eternal vigilance of an informed public; the E.I.S. would at least enable the public to be better informed.

Notes and References

1. See, in particular, the Endangered Species Act of 1974, which in the interests of preserving a hitherto unknown species of fish, the snail darter or *Percuna Imostoria tanasi*, prevented the further construction of the Telicoe Dam on the Little Tennessee River; to this effect the opponents of this major federal project had first obtained a provisional injunction from a local federal court holding up the project until an adequate E.I.S. had been prepared: *Environmental Defense Fund v. T.V.A.* 371 Fed. Supp. 1004 (1973). The injunction was discharged when an E.I.S. had been prepared, but this did not prevent the Supreme Court from granting a further injunction when it was found by a biologist that the habitat of this rare species of fish would be endangered if the construction of the dam (by then almost completed) were proceeded with, although this fact had not been disclosed in the E.I.S. — *T.V.A. v. Hill* 90 S.C. 2279 (1978).
2. Established by the Act of 1969 to advise the President on environmental matters.
3. And at least one city — Bowrie, Maryland, which also has a Commission for Environmental Quality: see 6 *Urban Lawyer* 95, 1974. The California Environmental Quality Act, 1970 requires an environmental impact report to be prepared for any State project which will have "a significant effect on the environment".
4. J. L. Rodgers in *Environmental Impact Analysis, Growth, Management and the Comprehensive Plan*, p.32.
5. The Clearinghouses have been carefully analysed by The Institute on Man and Science (Rennsselaerville NY) in their publication *Beyond NEPA Revisited*, March 1978.
6. *U.S. v. SCRAP* 412 U.S. 669 (1973); *Sierra Club v. Morton* 405 U.S. 727 (1972); *Kleppe v. Sierra Club* 427 U.S. 390 (1976).

7. *Environmental Impact Assessment Review* (1980) No. 1, M.I.T., p. 3.
8. A doctrine that has been worked out most fully in continental jurisprudence, especially in French planning law. Vestiges of the doctrine are to be seen in our own case law, and it also appears in Mr. Justice Holmes' famous dictum in *Pennsylvania Coal Co. v. Mahon* 260 U.S. 393 (1922): "The general rule at least is that while property may be regulated to a certain extent, if regulation goes too far it will be recognised as a taking". In other words, there must be a balancing between the police power and constitutional due process.
9. *Commission on the Third London Airport*, Department of Trade & Industry, H.M.S.O., 1969–70.
10. Windscale Inquiry Report (3 vols.), Department of the Environment, H.M.S.O., 1978.
11. In practice very few authorities pay more than lip service to this section, and there is no enforceable sanction against any defaulting authority. British Gas are however a notable exception; they often prepare quite an elaborate environmental statement when preparing a major project.
12. *Environmental Defense Fund v. Corps of Engineers of the U.S. Army* 331 Fed. Supp. 95 (1971).
13. *National Resources Defense Council v. Grant* 341 Fed. Supp. 356 (1972). This case and the one referred to in the previous note are cited in "The E.I.S., a small step instead of a Great Leap", by D.T. Greis in 5 *Urban lawyer* 1973, p. 275.
14. 427 U.S. 390 (1976).
15. So held in *City of Boston v. Coleman* 397 Fed. Supp. 698 (1975).
16. *Environmental Defense Fund v. Corps of Engineers of the United States Army* Fed. Supp. 916 (1972).
17. Cited by D.T. Greis (*supra*, note 13) from an article by Granton and Berg, "Enforcing NEPA in Federal Agencies", 18 *Prac. Law*, 1972, vol. 5, p. 91.
18. The plaintiffs in the Mississippi bargeway case (*supra*, note 12), for example, were (in addition to the nominate plaintiff) the Committee for Leaving the Environment of America Natural, and also a resident of the State of Mississippi who desired "to continue to derive benefits from the Tonibigbee River as it exists in its natural state".
19. *Environmental Impact Analysis*, A study prepared by J. Catlow and C. G. Thirlwall, Department of the Environment, 1976, paras. 7.1 and 7.5.
20. *Journal of Planning and Environmental Law*, November 1978, p.731.
21. Rodgers, *op. cit.*, p.143/4.
22. Section 29 of the Town and Country Planning Act 1971 would need to be amended accordingly.
23. Under the new (1978) Order 53 RSC procedure.
24. In the United States there is no guarantee that a private developer will not decide to forego federal aid and then proceed with his project in some respect that ignores the provisions of the E.I.S.
25. This system of accreditation of environmental societies by the Environmental Council could be extended so that such societies would be entitled to claim government financial assistance to oppose environmentally harmful projects at planning and other inquiries.

OUR PROPOSALS: A 'PROJECT INQUIRY'
THE OUTER CIRCLE POLICY UNIT*

FROM what we have said so far, one conclusion stands out: neither the conventional, statutory local planning inquiry (SLPI), nor (it seems) a Planning Inquiry Commission (PIC), is a suitable forum for investigating the many-sided national, let alone international, implications of some very large projects—especially if they involve new or complex technology, and more especially still if they are promoted by some agency that is close to Government. Some other forum must therefore be found. That conclusion is not new: what the then Secretary of State for the Environment, Mr. Peter Shore, said in Manchester on 13 September 1978 makes it clear that both he and his Department have been thinking on similar lines;[1] and the Conservative Party's 1979 Election Manifesto, in the context of the important environmental issues raised by energy developments, has also promised "the fullest possible participation in major new decisions".

*Reprinted with permission from *The Big Public Inquiry*, pp. 30–44 and 60–68, 1979.

As a quite separate issue, there are today also mounting calls for more open government. These include proposals for some new procedures for submitting *central policy-making*, in general, to more profound, critical and expert scrutiny than is provided by existing arrangements — such as, for example, more powerful, and better supported, Select Committees of both Houses of Parliament, or the setting up of more permanent Standing Commissions, on the model of the new Standing Commission on Energy and the Environment.*

There is a strong case for proposals of that kind—not only in the field of energy, but perhaps in some others also, as for example transport. But, quite apart from the difficulties of ensuring adequate public participation in such procedures, they could not resolve the quite different problem with which we are concerned here. In Great Britain, "policy" is not made at a kind of intellectual drawing-board, where designers map out a complete and detailed scheme and then pass it on to others to put into practice. Instead, policy is secreted in the interstices of individual decisions, and evolves over time as a consequence of the decisions that are taken and carried out. Too often, this happens without full consideration of all the implications, and that is how our particular problem comes about.

Our concern is therefore not with central policy in the abstract, but rather with the procedures which precede those individual and concrete decisions. They are the points where broad questions of policy focus on to the traditionally conceived questions of "land use planning". By the time that such a focal point has sharpened into a specific planning application (whether in outline or in detail), a good deal of money and other resources have been invested in the project, and a good many people have become committed to it. As a result, the project will have gathered a great deal of momentum—and it is this realisation, perhaps more than anything, which leaves objectors at such SLPIs with their present sense of helplessness.

What is wanted, therefore, is a thorough and public investigation of projects of this kind *before* they have reached that stage, in the form of an *ad hoc* public inquiry which can fill the empty space between a Standing Commission or Parliamentary Select Committee scrutinising general policy, and an SLPI scrutinising a specific planning application. For want of a better word, we shall call such an inquiry a "Project Inquiry" (PI).

The principal purpose of a PI should be to investigate, impartially, thoroughly and in public, the need for the project, the benefits which are claimed for it, and the costs and risks of all kinds which it will or may entail—in short, all the foreseeable economic, social and environmental implications and repercussions of the project, which may go far beyond its direct impact. In doing that, the PI should consider all feasible alternatives, and should give people who are not themselves involved in the decisionmaking process a wide range of opportunities for contributing relevant material to it, and at the same time help to inform them about the project and its implications. The primary objective should be to ensure that all the assumptions, material facts, issues and arguments are brought out, tested, and fully and fairly discussed.

At the end of that procedure, the PI should submit a report, which should set out the investigations it has carried out; the facts it has discovered; the

* This body was disbanded by the Conservative Government in 1982 [eds].

arguments it has heard; the policy options about the project which are open in the light of all that; and the benefits, costs and risks of those options.

That report should be published, and would doubtless be widely debated in the Press and elsewhere. But above all, it should be debated in Parliament, where there should be a vote on whether the project should, in principle, be further pursued.

A PI would therefore be quite separate, and serve quite different purposes, from an SLPI. Indeed, if a project which had been investigated by a PI received Parliamentary support, and later became the subject-matter of an application for planning permission at a specific site, an SLPI would still need to be held—but it should then take a great deal less time.

In what cases should PIs be held?

The occasions which will call for a PI are likely to be infrequent. Such a procedure will only be needed in special and exceptional cases. To justify one, the following criteria will need to be satisfied:

1. The project must have substantial national or international implications, and not merely local ones with which an SLPI can competently deal.
2. Those implications must be complex, and not obviously foreseeable.
3. The project must be so controversial that a decision about it either way without a thorough, impartial and public investigation would not be readily acceptable.

The case for holding a PI will be particularly strong where the proponent of the project is a UK public authority with close links to central government. Although large corporations in the private sector also make it their business to have such links, they will often have the option—which a public authority has not—of carrying out their project abroad, especially if the corporation is multi-national, operating in several countries. To impose a PI in such cases, in addition to a later SLPI, might therefore risk driving major private projects, with their attendant economic benefits, away from the UK. That might be a reason for saying that PIs should only be held where the potential investor's capital is "captive" rather than "mobile".

We see the strength of that argument, but we do not regard it as conclusive. We can imagine cases where the social and environmental costs and risks of a very large private project could appear, on first inspection, to be potentially so large as to be comparable with the economic loss to the nation if the investment were not made here at all. In such cases, we think it would be irresponsible not to hold a PI if the criteria for such an inquiry were otherwise satisfied ...

... Unless and until there is a statute—or a future EEC Directive, of the kind now under discussion,[3] takes effect—the ultimate criterion for establishing a PI will therefore be a "political" one. We do not mean this in any derogatory sense. But a Government may find it difficult to make a decision in a highly controversial field until the facts and issues have been much more fully investigated; and until the public has been much better informed, has had wider opportunities for participating in the debate, and is therefore more likely to understand and support the reasons for the decision.

At any given time, a small number of major projects is known to be in contemplation which might provide suitable candidates for a PI. As time goes on, new ones are likely to appear over the horizon. Today, the clearest case would be a proposal for the construction of a Commercial Demonstration Fast Reactor (CDFR), either by the UK Atomic Energy Authority or by one of the Generating Boards. Such a proposal has all the features which call for a PI—and indeed Mr. Shore, in the speech to which we have already referred,[1] announced that the Government intends to follow a special procedure for investigating the implications of that project.

He said little about what that procedure should be. But such procedures can be very important: the better the procedure, the better (and more confidence-inspiring) is the likely outcome. In the rest of this paper, we shall therefore take CDFR as a paradigm case, and as our model for describing how a PI could work. But a few other possible candidates are also visible, and it may be that PIs on similar lines might be suitable for them also, though necessarily with modifications to suit the particular case. Among those we have in mind are any proposals which may be made for a Severn Barrage, a Channel Tunnel, and perhaps a Third London Airport. Major mineral workings might also make good candidates, though it now seems too late to use our proposed PI procedure for the Vale of Belvoir coalfield.

At what point of time should a PI be appointed?

For PIs, as for any other kind of inquiry, it is important to get the timing right. There is no point in holding them too early, when the project is no more than a gleam in a potential developer's eye. At that stage, no one—not even the developer himself—will have enough information for a PI to be able to draw any useful conclusions, and changes of circumstances might later cause the project to be abandoned anyway. But if a PI is not held until the project has gathered substantial momentum, that too can present problems: a good deal of investment and commitment would need to be dismantled, and the cost of delay to the project might by that time be substantial.

Wherever possible, a PI should not be held until the project is far enough advanced for there to be a high probability that it will result in a formal application for planning permission in the foreseeable future. At the same time it should be held before the investments in resources, and the commitments in policy terms, are so substantial as to make it difficult to retract from the project. That "best" time will vary from case to case: typically, it might be around two years before planning permission would normally be applied for.

In practice, such proposals should by then be known to government, at all events if the proponent is a UK public authority, especially one that is using public money allocated to it for evolving the project. But even where that is not the case, it would not be difficult for government to ensure that it received appropriately early warnings of projects which might be suitable candidates for PIs. Developers would, for example, have a strong incentive to give early notice of their intentions if the Secretary of State made it known that, as a matter of policy, he would call in all planning applications which fell within the PI criteria, appoint a PI for them, and would not hold an SLPI until the PI procedure had run its full course.

Under what legal powers should PIs be appointed?

By our own definition, PIs should be held only in those cases where neither an SLPI, nor a PIC, would be a suitable forum for investigating the wider implications of the project. Fortunately as we have seen, there are wide powers to appoint commissions or committees of inquiry without the need for any statutory authority. This gives the advantage of great flexibility, not being tied to any detailed legal procedures, and allows useful scope for experiment, for *ad hoc* changes from case to case, and for learning from experience. If, in the light of such experience, it is ultimately thought desirable that legislation should be introduced to put such inquiries on a statutory footing, that can be done later. Until then, we recommend that PIs should be appointed extra-statutorily.

Who should decide whether to appoint a PI?

For obvious reasons, the decision whether or not to appoint a PI should not rest with the Minister whose Department would be the natural "sponsor" of the project—e.g. in the case of CDFR, the Department of Energy. Instead, that should be the task of a Minister whose Department is responsible for planning procedures (and their improvement), and has a direct concern for the expectations and rights of objectors in this field, which are of a kind that do not exist in other policy areas. In any future statute, the power (and duty) to decide whether or not to appoint a PI should therefore be specifically given [generally to the Cabinet but specifically] to the Secretary of State for the Environment.

Who should choose the members of a PI, and how?

If a PI is to serve its purpose, it is of the first importance that it should be conducted by people (whom, for want of a better name, we shall call "Commissioners") who command the widest possible respect. Their choice is therefore one of the most critical steps in the entire procedure—if it is seriously flawed, it will invalidate most of the rest.

The first question here is whether a PI should be constituted so as to reflect a "representative balance"—of the kind, for instance, which ordinarily includes a trade unionist, an employer, a Scot, and at least one "statutory woman". We certainly hope that some or all of these will be found on a PI, but not because they are thought to "represent" some sections of the community. If representation were a relevant criterion, the first to insist on it would be the proponent of the project and the principal objectors—a course of action which would only ensure that the Commissioners would advocate cases rather than investigate questions, doubtless carrying their advocacy into persuasive (but mutually contradictory) minority reports at the end of the day. That is not at all the purpose which we envisage for a PI.

Instead, we believe that the Commissioners should be selected by reference to two other criteria: a sufficient degree of expertise, and the maximum degree of impartiality. We are, of course, well aware that there are no absolutes in either of these things. In particular, everyone's perceptions are coloured in some degree by their established views and attitudes. But, on any given issue or group of issues (such as, for example, those that surround CDFR), some people will already have formed clear views and others will not. Again, some people are decidedly more open-minded, and more willing to learn, to be persuaded by evidence and rational argument and, if necessary, to change their positions, than others are. It is in that sense, and not in any absolute one, that we use the concept of "impartiality".

There is, of course, a tension between our two criteria of expertise and impartiality. Ideally, the Commissioners should dispose between them of enough expert knowledge in the fields with which the PI will be concerned to be able to understand and evaluate the material which is put before them without first having to go through a major educational process. As much of that material will necessarily be technical—and probably from several different areas of technology at that—there is a case for appointing some outstanding experts in these areas as Commissioners. But that raises more than one difficulty. If a Commissioner is a distinguished expert in a certain field, he or she will probably long since have formed a view on the controversial questions which will arise, and will have aligned with one or other of the contending schools of thought. Moreover, there is every likelihood that prospective Commissioners will have made their views known, perhaps even in public. If that is so, either the proponent or one or other of the objectors will regard one or more of the Commissioners as partisan, or will suspect them of hostility, or at least will assume that their evaluation of the material will be coloured by their previous judgements. And there is also the risk that some Commissioners might defer too readily to the authority of one of their number — against, perhaps, the opinions of expert witnesses in the same field.

This problem is particularly acute where the project comes from an industry which has a virtual monopoly of expertise in its field.[4] Nuclear power, and therefore CDFR, is a classical example: it would be difficult to find a nuclear engineer to serve as a Commissioner whose practical experience had not been gained within the nuclear industry, and who would not therefore be regarded with at least some suspicion by most of the objectors to CDFR.

We are satisfied that it would be far wiser to resolve this dilemma on the side of impartiality rather than of expertise. Expertise can always be supplemented by the material which is submitted to the PI and, if necessary, by the appointment of expert consultants by the Commissioners themselves. But impartiality cannot be supplemented if it is not there in sufficient measure in the first place. We therefore recommend that demonstrable impartiality, in the sense of a genuinely open mind about the issues surrounding the project under investigation, should be the primary criterion for the choice of Commissioners. The acceptability and credibility of any PI, of its report, and of any decision about the project which is ultimately made, will depend in large measure on the degree to which that criterion has been, and is seen to have been, satisfied.

We see no reason why the choice of Commissioners should not remain the responsibility of the Secretary of State, as it is now in comparable cases, but we believe that, in the case of PIs, he or she should consult very widely before deciding on the appointments, and let it be known that he is doing so. It is already the practice, in appointing Royal Commissions and other bodies, to invite some selected non-governmental organisations to put forward names —though of course without any commitment that any of them will necessarily be chosen.

That is a sound practice, and should be followed in the case of PIs. But we hope to see it extended considerably, to organisations which may not yet be on any official departmental consultation list, but which have expressed more than a passing interest in the national issues which the project raises. In the case of CDFR, for example, we would expect those objectors who presented substantial cases at the Windscale Inquiry to be invited to put forward names for consideration as Commissioners —not, of course, from among their known supporters, but from people in whose impartiality they would have confidence.

In emphasising the importance of impartiality as against expertise, we do not wish to be taken as saying that expertise should have no part to play. On the contrary, it is very important: for example, a PI on CDFR should include among its Commissioners people familiar with the theories and practices of engineering, physics, public health, economics, the social sciences, and the problems of environmental planning. But it would be preferable if none of these people had previously specialised in the field of nuclear energy, which might imperil the criterion of their visible impartiality. Neither nuclear physics and engineering, nor the health risks of ionising radiation, are subjects so arcane that only *nuclear* experts can understand, assess and evaluate the problems they present.

Each of those "experts" would, of course, be able to play a "lay" role outside his particular expertise. But there is also a case for adding two or three people from the category which has become known as "intelligent lay-people", who would test what at first sight might seem to be purely technical questions from the point of view of the ordinary citizen of common sense, and could take a broad and rounded view of the problems with which the PI was presented.

In order to emphasise impartiality, it might be tempting to choose a member of the judiciary as chairperson of a PI. There are two recent precedents in the case of the Third London Airport inquiry, which was chaired by Mr. Justice Roskill, and the Windscale Inquiry, where Mr. Justice Parker sat as the Inspector, with two expert assessors. But we believe that it would be wise to resist that temptation, for two reasons which will become clearer as we develop our proposals for the working procedures of a PI. As will be seen below, we envisage a degree of informality, as well as a many-sided inquiry concerned not to answer "yes" or "no" to a single question, or even to several questions, but rather to investigate the scope, importance and degrees of uncertainty of many questions, and to clarify the policy options which remain available at the end of such an investigation. Neither the special techniques of the law, nor the skills which lawyers have developed for handling them, are particularly well suited for a process of that kind. While a lawyer of independent mind could doubtless make a substantial and useful contribution as a Commissioner, we do not think that the specific need is for a chairperson drawn from the judiciary.

We envisage the total number of Commissioners for a PI at around seven, with a maximum of perhaps nine or ten, rather than the much larger number which is now customary for Royal Commissions.

Terms of reference

It goes without saying that, the more narrowly a PI's terms of reference are drawn, the less public confidence there will be in its work. The exclusion of any discussion about "need" from motorway inquiries for so many years still rankles with many, and it proved to be a fatal defect for the Roskill Commission. A PI's terms of reference must therefore expressly direct it to investigate the need for the project, now or at some future time, in the light of all the feasible alternatives. They must also be so drawn as to enable the PI, within reason, to investigate all the possible implications of the project — environmental and social as well as economic and technical.

There is sometimes thought to be a risk that, if terms of reference are drawn too widely, a Commission will lose its way and spend a great deal of valuable time in the fringes of its subject, or chasing down blind alleys. But we do not believe that, with a sensible set of Commissioners, this is a real hazard, and we think it more important that too narrow a set of terms of reference should not preclude them from going down an alley which they, as well as the parties, regard as important—even if, at the end, it should prove to be blind . . ..

Procedures after the PI's Report

Formally, the PI's Report will be submitted to the Secretary of State who has appointed it. When it is received, it should be published. It will necessarily be long, and few people will have the chance to read it in full. There should therefore be a summary, prepared by the Commission itself. That document should be written in the simplest possible language, and be available either free or at a price so moderate that virtually everyone can afford it.

The PI's Report will doubtless attract wide public attention, and comment in the press and the media. It will be studied and discussed, formally and informally, in many places up and down the country.

When there has been enough opportunity for study and discussion, the PI's Report should be fully debated by both Houses of Parliament. We regard that stage as crucial, and we think it equally important that the debate should end with a vote, on a motion which would reflect the views in principle of Parliament on whether the project should be further pursued.

At some appropriate stage, the Government too will need to make up its mind on that issue, in the light of the PI's Report. Here, there are two options: the Secretary of State could announce a decision first, and leave Parliament to approve or disapprove it, or could wait until after the "temperature" of Parliament has been taken.

The first of these courses has the demerit that, once committed in principle to a decision, the Secretary of State might feel that he or she would lose face if Parliament overruled the decision and might therefore be tempted to apply the pressures available—including the party whip—to ensure that Parliament will provide a majority.

The second course has the demerit that Parliament, on such an occasion, might expect a lead from Government, and might feel itself floundering if it does not get one.

Which of these courses will be followed in a particular instance must be decided *ad hoc*. It will depend on several factors, including the nature and importance of the project, and on political considerations at the time. However, a Parliamentary decision will clearly command greater public confidence if

Government has not tried to influence it by announcing its decision first, and then seeking support for it. In the case of Windscale, that sequence was necessary on legal grounds; in the case of a PI, it will not be. Nor will there be any need at this stage to resort to the device of a Special Development Order.

Whatever the sequence, the PI proceedings will effectively end with a decision in principle, by Government and Parliament, for or against the project. If the decision is favourable, the proponent will have to decide whether or not to take the project to the next—and final—stage, by applying formally for planning permission to construct it at some specific site.

A subsequent SLPI

If and when that happens, there will in practice always need to be an SLPI —either because the local planning authority refuses the application, or because the Secretary of State will necessarily have to call it in. That inquiry will proceed under the normal statutory rules, but it will be affected in several ways by the fact that the project has already been the subject of a PI.

Firstly, it will be a great deal shorter than if—as in the case of Windscale—it had to investigate all the questions which formed the subject-matter of the PI's work. Once Government and Parliament have decided, on full information and after a full public debate, that the project should in principle proceed, that question (which has so often bedevilled motorway inquiries) can be properly treated as the starting point for the SLPI, which can then apply itself to the site-specific questions in the light of the PI's Report. Local objectors would, of course, be in no way precluded from discussing that Report at the SLPI.

Secondly, the SLPI can—and in our view should—be held by an Inspector who was not one of the PI's Commissioners, so avoiding the principal objection which has been raised against PICs.

Lastly, the report of the SLPI too could be made the subject of a subsequent parliamentary debate, by using at that stage—as in the case of Windscale — the device of a Special Development Order.

Staff and money for a PI

To function successfully, a PI—like any Commission of Inquiry—will need a competent secretariat. Since it will be an *ad hoc* body, and not a permanent one, it is unlikely to be able to recruit its own staff, and will need to take people on secondment, from the civil service and elsewhere. We foresee no difficulty about this—if Government decides to appoint a PI, it will also be willing to provide the means to enable it to do its work.

Apart from staff and premises, the Commission will probably also need money to carry out some investigations for itself, and perhaps to fund some objectors (see below). But the amounts concerned will be comparatively small.

Who should fund the objectors?

One of the principal complaints of objectors at SLPIs is that the developer commands substantial financial resources, while they do not, and that this severely distorts the desirable end of equality of arms.

In the procedure which we recommend for PIs, that inequality will be far less extreme. At SLPIs, the principal costs for objectors lie in the expense of hiring lawyers and expert witnesses. Both these should cost a great deal less at a PI.

Lawyers will, in most cases, not be needed at all until the stage of argument, which should be comparatively short—certainly very much shorter than if the subject-matter for a PI were to be debated by the procedures of an SLPI, as was the case at Windscale. Many objectors may not even think it necessary to employ lawyers at the stage of argument of a PI, by which time they will have had ample opportunity to absorb and master the material which will have emerged from the stage of investigation. If the Commission employs its own counsel at the stage of argument, that too may reduce the need for objectors to employ their own.

As for expert witnesses, many of the major objectors to projects of the kind which we are considering already dispose of a respectable amount of scientific and technical expertise of their own, made available to them either voluntarily or on the basis of a standing consultancy. These experts will doubtless prepare much of the material which the objectors will submit to a PI during the stage of investigation, at no—or not much—extra expense.

However, it may happen that an objector wishes to have a particular line of investigation pursued — e.g. to check some information submitted by the proponent, or to have some calculations re-worked on different assumptions or by a different method, or to conduct an original investigation, and that may involve extra expense.

In such a case, the first step in the system we envisage would be for the objector concerned to persuade the Commission that the work needs to be done. Assuming the objector succeeds in this—and if the work is important enough, that should present no difficulty—several possibilities are open.

Firstly, the Commission could call on proponents to do the work, at their own expense.

Secondly, the Commission might decide to do the work itself, or to have it done by some outside consultant, or university department or laboratory, at the expense of the Commission.

Thirdly, the objector could nominate someone independent who would be willing and able to do the work, again at the Commission's expense. If the Commission were satisfied of that person's competence and integrity, it could ask that person to do it and be paid for it.

Lastly, the objector might offer to do the work. In such a case, the Commission would treat the objector as it would anyone else: if that party could show that it was well placed to do the work and could demonstrate the necessary competence and integrity, the Commission could accept its offer and pay it for doing the work.

In all these cases, it would, of course, be an essential condition that whoever carried out the work disclosed the assumptions and methods used, and the results obtained, not only to the Commission, but also to the other parties, in sufficient detail to enable them to be checked.

In the result, therefore, we think it unlikely that, in the case of a PI, any objectors would find themselves severely handicapped through lack of funds. But if they were, and if they could make a credible case to the Commission that this was so, we think it highly desirable that some way should be found to mitigate that handicap.

There has been a great debate about the merits and demerits of funding objectors at public inquiries, and we need not rehearse the arguments here. However, PIs will be both exceptional and of great national importance. Whatever the demerits, therefore, we think that a PI should have a fund out of which it is able to give financial aid to objectors, in those cases where the objectors can show that, without such aid, they would not be able to take a full part either in the stage of investigation or in the stage of argument, and the Commission is satisfied that it is in the public interest that they should.

The time-scale

Clearly, a PI will take some time to do its job. While it does, the project is delayed, and that may give rise to problems. Some see delay in investment as a major disadvantage, since it holds off the economic benefits expected to flow from the investment, and may frighten the investor off altogether, especially if his capital is "mobile" rather than "captive". Others would welcome delays over investment decisions as controversial as those which would be suitable candidates for a PI, on the ground that, by definition, these are investments which should not be made in a free democracy until they have been thoroughly, publicly and above all impartially investigated—and if they are turned away for fear of such an investigation that is probably all to the good. They would argue that the delay introduced by the Roskill Commission saved the country a vastly expensive airport which it did not in fact need at that time, and that it would have been just as beneficial to save the enormous sums which were in the event wasted on Concorde.

But how great would the delay of a PI, in practice, really be? In the case of Roskill, the total time from the announcement of the Commission to the decision to build the TLA at Foulness was 35 months. In the case of Windscale, the time taken from the date of BNFL's first application for planning permission to the parliamentary approval of the Special Development Order was a total of 23 months.

The timescale for a PI is difficult to determine in advance, since none has yet been held. Much would, of course, depend on the project, and the kinds of question it would raise. But, taking CDFR as an example, we could guess (very roughly, and doubtless with wide margins of error) at a timescale something like this:

	Months
From decision to appoint a PI, through consultation about its membership, approaches to possible members, drafting of terms of reference, to appointment and announcement of members	3
Thence to first public meeting	2
Thence to conclusion of stage of investigation, and final public meeting	18
Thence to opening of stage of argument	1
Stage of argument	1
Thence to submission of report	3
Thence to publication of report	1
Thence to parliamentary debate and vote	1
	$\overline{\underline{30}}$

As against that, any SLPI which will need to be held in a case where a PI has already taken place will be a great deal shorter, and would take weeks rather than months—with a saving, in the case of CDFR, for example, of perhaps as much as 6 months.

Very roughly, therefore, we think that the extra "inquiry time" entailed in appointing a PI as well as an SLPI (if Government and Parliament decide that the project can proceed, and the proponent applies for planning permission) would be of the order of 2 years.

But that does not mean that the "delay to investment" will necessarily be as long as this, since a PI, unlike an SLPI, can—and in our view should —be appointed *before* there is a formal application for planning permission. If, for example, a PI were to be appointed 2 years before such an application would normally be made—and this would seem to be a suitable time in many cases—there might well be no real delay at all.

But even if there is some delay, that may be no bad thing. Any project which warrants the appointment of a PI will have important long-term implications. Time spent on getting it right cannot be time wasted.

Notes

1. Department of the Environment Press Notice No. 488.
2. Page 17.
3. Preliminary Draft Directive concerning the assessment of the effect on the environment of public and private development projects (EIE/OU/1O).
4. See *Superstar Technologies*, Council for Science and Society, 1976.

Editorial Note The Council of Science and Society followed up many of these points in a subsequent publication *Deciding about Energy Policy* (1977) but their ideas have apparently had little impact. In a symposium on *Communal Nuclear Power—Legal and Constitutional Issues* (ed. R. McRory) (Imperial College, London 1982) a number of distinguished lawyers involved at the Windscale Inquiry dismissed much of the arguments raised in this article.

THE BIG INQUIRY*

Brian Wynne

How should the government organise public inquiries into the big technological decisions whose outcome could dominate our lives for many years to come? The Windscale Inquiry was the first real attempt—albeit *ad hoc* —to answer this question. Although an advance on the conventional planning inquiry, Mr Justice Parker's investigation was far from perfect. Soon, the government will have to decide how—or even whether—to organise an inquiry into the first commercial fast breeder reactor.

Thus the report *The Big Public Inquiry* from the Council for Science and Society and the Outer Circle Policy Unit is timely indeed. The working party that wrote the report consisted of Windscale veterans, experienced lawyers, academics, and others with practical and analytical experience of the politics of technology and planning. As a member of the working party, I believe its report makes several sensible advances on the Windscale model. But the working party deliberately restricted its field of vision and left key ambiguities in its proposals.

*Reprinted with permission from *New Scientist*, Vol. 82, 28 June 1979, pp. 1078–1079. (Dr Wynne is at the School of Independent Studies, University of Lancaster.)

One of the strengths of *The Big Public Inquiry* is the accumulated force of several proposals pushing in the direction of natural justice—a fair fight—in such inquiries. It proposes much stronger rights, at least for a certain class of objectors, in return for greater mutual organisation and discipline. Even if the government accepted these proposals, they would be only a small step down the road to natural justice, but they could change the whole climate of decisions about big technology. Some of the proposals echo others' recommendations: more time and powers for extracting (and analysing) strategic information; resources for objectors' research; and, crucially, a clear acknowledgement of the social perspectives that often underly different technical standpoints in the energy debate.

But there are problems with the project inquiry idea. No government would set up such an elaborate and expensive process in the abstract—there has to be something concrete at stake. And there is no single ripe time to make a decision about complex technology. Conceivably a project inquiry for the fast breeder reactor could have decided in favour in 1974 only for us to regret that inquiry as a disastrous waste of money, say in 1980. Just as there was great pressure on Mr Justice Parker not to issue a supposedly watery "not yet" verdict on Windscale, so there would be even more pressure on a commission holding a project inquiry to arrive at a clear-cut decision. A commission would risk being lampooned for wasting public money on a "non-decision", and the industry would inevitably demand to see its future laid out in black or white—even if, on the evidence, procrastination would be the best policy.

In theory, the two-year notice period proposed by the CSS/OCPU report would accommodate the project inquiry and so cancel out any delay. But in practice a rigorous project inquiry could last longer than two years. Against the timescale of potential consequences, even an inquiry lasting five years would not be unjustified. To its credit, the CSS/OCPU working party did not flinch from this observation. But an even greater problem is that things change: a good decision one year may be a bad one 10 years later, after billions of pounds have been wasted, or serious energy shortages invited. A decision as important as that on the fast breeder reactor will *make* the future because it will foreclose some options and open up others. The bigger and more pervasive the technology, the more these options include broad social effects, and the more irrevocable they are. The bigger the technological commitment in a decision, the more we apparently gain control.

Too big to handle

But this control may be illusory because the bigger the decision to be made, the more ignorant we are of its implications and of the social and other changes we set in train. It may be that grandstand decisions on big technologies like the fast breeder reactor are intrinsically too big for our democracy to handle—a point against the development for that reason alone. This logic redefines the problem in terms of the political economy of technology—its scale, centralism, inflexibility, and so on—and not in the relatively superficial terms of formal procedure. Our society may well have been better equipped to face the awesome decision to enter into (or refuse) the "commercial" stage of fast reactors, if it were used to routine openness and debate about the safety, economics and technology of the fast reactor instead of occasional ritual ordeals.

One of the key ambiguities in the CSS/OCPU report concerns the role of the commission that would conduct the project inquiry. Although, in theory, the project inquiry would be a public process, it could easily be dominated by a series of separate written exchanges between the commission and different parties. After an initial hearing to define the issues, requests for documents, information and research funds would be in writing. Only the commission would have its finger on the pulse of the inquiry. Further, it would have immense power to rule whether documents should be released, whether an apparently dead issue should be pursued, resources given to a party, when to call a halt to proliferating argument, and so on. Such powers place extraordinary importance on the membership of the commission, which, the report recommends, should be appointed by the Minister after consultation with objectors—among others. Even with a durable, patient, and broadminded commission, project inquiries could become so private as to be virtually invisible to the outside world beyond the elite of professional objectors, and incoherent and fragmented even to them.

After much internal debate, the CSS/OCPU was undecided about how much cross-examination should take place at a project inquiry. Some members felt that written commission proceedings would focus attention on a few questions where credibility was at stake. In particular they felt that a project inquiry should not subject technical experts to the supposed indignity of cross-examination. If the report's advice were accepted, adversary hearings would therefore be very limited.

But credibility is always at stake in judgements between different schools of thought, social or scientific. Bare evidence alone decides nothing. Furthermore, written exchanges would be woefully inefficient, because it is so easy to misread a request and provide the wrong or partial replies. It is only possible to pose alternatives clearly and starkly through cross-examination. Adversary proceedings, including the cross-examination of government witnesses, should be a major part of the project inquiry, a point whose rather furtive acceptance at Windscale does not yet render the principle secure. Cross-examination not only resolves factual questions but also (and more importantly) exposes the social premises and uncertainties underlying different technical points of view. Perhaps the view that the scientist's constitution is too delicate for the public rough house of adversary proceedings was a reflection of the presence of eminent scientists from the CSS on the working party. Yet adversary proceedings expose valuable truths, at times, even if the truth is that no one knows. Further, public legitimation requires a public ordeal for the experts, whatever they think they might achieve in semi-sheltered correspondence with the project inquiry commission.

The debate on the CSS/OCPU working party on cross-examination signals a basic failing in its report. A project inquiry with limited public hearings and debate would be almost inscrutable to outsiders. Yet the report makes no mention of the need to stimulate the interest and intelligence of a wider public and to assess its views. Not that the man or woman on the proverbial Clapham omnibus would have very much to say about the fast breeder reactor. But the fact that he or she has nothing to say may be the most important limitation to the practicability of inquiries like that on the fast breeder reactor (which the new government may not hold after all).

It would be ironic if the report's recommendations on the shape of the fast breeder inquiry helped the hard core of professional objectors (who need little help)—only to make participation all the more daunting for interested but less experienced, less organised groups or individuals. Representation becomes less and less meaningful the more inquiries are highly elite, professionalised, and semi-private exchanges between strongly committed adversary parties. More elaborate inquiries may buy more natural justice for professional objectors only at the expense of even more alienation of the wider public. Such procedures only widen the cultural gap between decision-making elites (including objectors) and the public.

The CSS/OCPU report is a constructive contribution to the debate about big technology inquiries. But it fails to understand the deeper currents in the economic and political structure of technology which so influence the consequences—intended and unintended—of whatever formal procedures we evolve. Such currents may well be the undermining harvest of too much adaptation of "democratic" procedures to the exigencies of "the technological society". Perhaps the adaptation should be in the reverese sense. Otherwise we might be like the man walking up a landslip—if he keeps his eyes on his feet, he can pretend he is making progress.

Economics and Ecology: Towards A New Paradigm?

INTRODUCTORY ESSAY

In this section we first review some of the models that have been constructed by economists in order to try and incorporate some of the important interrelationships between the economic and ecological systems. We begin by briefly reviewing the so-called materials balance principle and some methodologies which attempt to take this basic conservation principle into account.[1] We then address the issue of whether these economic models go far enough in their incorporation of ecological impacts. The question becomes: is a more radical paradigm shift required in the science of economics to fully incorporate the environmental dimension?[2]

The materials balance principle

The neoclassical economic doctrine[3] has been based implicitly on the assumption that the economy is an open system not apparently constrained by any environmental limits in terms of finite resource bases or limited residuals disposal capacities. This "open" economic system is determined by positive feedback effects controlled by the going rate of investment in the economy. Economists within the neoclassical tradition concentrated their attention on market processes, as we stressed in the essay in Section 2, and tended to regard the consumption of goods and services as somehow the final act of the economic system. Resources (whether matter or energy) apparently disappeared with the act of consumption and the economic system as a whole was geared to the fulfilment of one ultimate goal, the maximisation of "welfare" or "utility", which could only be derived from the consumption act. In reality, of course, an economic system is a "closed system" encompassed by the natural environment from which it draws a range of inputs and into which it discharges a variety of residuals. Boulding[4] was probably the first economist to point out the deficiencies of the open system or "cowboy economy" view of the economic system. He called for the development of a methodology which explicitly recognised the closed-system nature of the economic processes (constrained by negative feed-back effects) and stressed that all processes must comply with the physical laws of conservation—the first and second laws of thermodynamics. The first law states that matter–energy in all its forms cannot be destroyed; physical processes may alter the distribution of matter–energy but never its total sum. Thus the economic process does not eliminate the throughput of matter–energy it merely alters its form. The second law indicates that energy and matter flow more or less irreversibly through the economic process to re-enter the biosphere as dissipated heat and waste. In thermodynamic terms matter–energy enters the economic process in a state of low entropy and comes out of it in a state of high entropy. Thus the concentrations of high-availability materials and energy (valuable natural resources) enter the economic process and are eventually emitted as low-availability material residuals and dissipated energy at low temperature both of which are much less useful.[5] Boulding[6] called for a reversal of the thinking of the "cowboy economy" in which welfare is linked to the rate of material throughput and its substitution by a "spaceship" mentality which sees throughput as something which should be minimised not maximised. The ultimate aim of the economic system should be the maintenance of desirable states or conditions. To this end the acts of production and consumption should be used to maintain the system's "capital stock" (which includes the state of human bodies and minds).

Implicit in Boulding's path-breaking essay was what has become known as the materials balance view of economic–ecologic interaction. The practical implications of this view were first explicitly exposed in the work of Ayres and Kneese.[7] The economic heritage of these models can be traced back to the general equilibrium analysis of Walras, first published in 1874. Walras noted that the working of the economic system in terms of the quantities and types of goods and services produced resulted in a general equilibrium solution relating to all goods and services simultaneously. So Walras constructed a theoretical model based on a series of simultaneous equations, each of which represented a good or service.

From a systems modelling point of view the economic process can be divided into four interrelated sets of activities: the natural resource extraction process; the production of goods and services process (including processing and conversion activities); the distribution and consumption process; and the waste-disposal process. Figure 5.1 illustrates in simplistic and partial fashion a materials–balance model in which materials and energy inputs (economic throughput) flow from the extraction stage through to the final disposal stage.

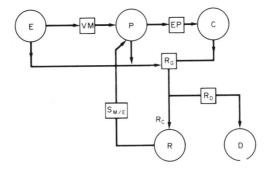

Key

E = Extraction of natural resources

P = Production activities-taken to include, processing, fabrication and distribution activities

C = Consumption activities and prior distribution activities

R = Recycling activities-both in-plant and via the secondary materials industry (taken to include storage, collection, processing and transport)

D = Residuals disposal activities to air, land and water

VM = Virgin raw materials inputs

EP = End-product output

R_G = Residuals generated by the various activities

R_D = Residuals discharged to the environment

R_C = Non-production outputs diverted to recycling system

$S_{M/E}$ = Secondary material and energy inputs

FIGURE 5.1

A partial and simplified materials balance model.

According to a number of economists and engineers, wastes should more properly be re-termed residuals and placed in an economic context.[8] Since no productive activity transforms all of its inputs into useful products the left-over materials and/or energy have been termed non-production outputs (NPOs). If the NPOs do not have a ready market available or their value is less than the collection and processing costs that the secondary materials recovery firms would have to incur in order to recover the NPOs, then they are termed residuals. As far as the residuals generating plant is concerned the aim is to dispose of these residuals at minimum cost. Overall the materials balance teaches us that when the economic system absorbs resource inputs from the environment, it must discharge over time an equal mass of materials to the environment as residuals.

Victor[9] and Pearce[10] have argued that although the pioneering work of Ayres, and Kneese and D'Arge is to be commended their models contain some important weaknesses. The models really only dealt with materials and energy flows up to the point of entry into the environmental media (land, air and water) and impact on the assimilative services of these media. Pearce[11] presents his own flow diagram (see Figure 5.2) which seeks to include the environmental assimilative capacity impact of the residuals streams.

Many of the residuals discharged by an industrialised economic system can be degraded and "neutralised" by the natural degrader populations that exist in ecosystems and which recycle "waste" products into nutrients as part of the general ecosystem functioning. The problem has increasingly been, however, that with industrialisation has come an ever wider spectrum of technologies and as a consequence a wider range of residual types requiring disposal facilities. As the natural assimilative capacities of the environmental media are limited they cannot degrade all and any residuals. At certain times and in certain locations both the quantity and types of residuals being discharged have often been sufficient to overload the assimilative capacity. If, in the diagram, the residuals loading (R) exceeds the assimilative capacity (A), it could

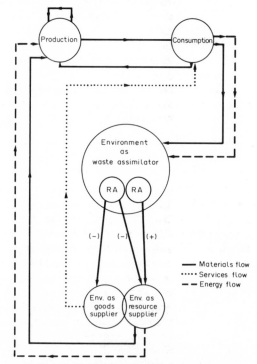

Source: Pearce, D. W. (1976), Environmental Economics, Ch. 3.

FIGURE 5.2

Pearce's modified materials balance model.

remain as a potentially noxious stock and could affect the stability of the degrader populations over time. Thus, for example, the bacteria in water systems which are capable of dealing efficiently with a certain quantity of sewerage discharges can become overloaded. There are many examples in the industrialised economies where stretches of rivers flowing through major conurbations or heavily industrialised areas are effectively dead. A graph of one of the indicators of water quality, the level of dissolved oxygen in the water, would show a pronounced dip in these heavily polluted regions, the so-called DO "sag".[12] Pearce [13] takes the analysis a stage further by developing a taxonomy of pollution based on the concept of the assimilative capacity of the environment. The analysis suggests that conventional economics is not particularly helpful to policymakers trying to set ambient environmental quality standards when so-called persistent stock pollutants (which have no counterpart degrader populations) are involved. Nobbs and Pearce[14] have taken the example of cadmium to argue that as the pollutant cannot be measured in flow terms and the existing stock in the ambient environment is non-reducible, the conventional economic marginal abatement and damage-cost analysis cannot be utilised in order to determine an economically optimal level of cadmium pollution.

Pearce's analysis[15] seeks to demonstrate the possibility of a basic incompatibility between the conventionally determined economic optimum level of pollution and an ecologically "sound" optimum level. The implication of the analysis is that although over time an economic system may well be achieving what the conventional economic paradigm considers to be an optimum (or close to optimum) level of pollution the human population of the system will suffer a continuing decline in ambient environmental quality. In the reading below Pearce surveys the paradigm shift debate and includes in diagrammatic form some of the analysis reviewed above. Neglect of the effects of economic activity on the common property services of the environment is a theme we will return to in the context of neoclassical economic growth and resource depletion models in Section 7.

Input–output models

Within the established body of economic theory the input–output tool invented by Leontief in the 1930s has been modified by a number of economists in order to incorporate an environmental sector. The pattern and level of industrial production present in an economic system depends upon the range of goods and services that are demanded in the system. Input–output analysis (again based on the Walrasian general equilibrium concept of economic interdepedence, but now placed in an empirical context) was developed precisely to relate individual industry input demands to other individual industry outputs. Thus input requirements per unit of output for each industry could then be established and produced in matrix form. Industry outputs were also related to final demands for end-products by consumers. It is this "final demand" which is the driving force of an input–output model. The technique is used to estimate the pattern and type of industrial production required to meet a specified demand for end-product commodities. In the past the conventional approach to input–output analysis utilised only industry-to-industry models. More recently work has focussed on the development of commodity-by-industry models in which it is assumed that each industry produces and uses several commodities and that any commodity may be produced by several industries.

It is possible to incorporate the environmental impacts of industry, for example, the effect of the establishment of a pollution-abatement industrial sector on the general industrial structure of the economy, or the effects of changes in consumer end-product expenditure patterns on residuals generation and on the demands by industry for resource inputs, into the input–output framework. The first attempt to incorporate economic–ecologic interrelationships in the input–output format was included in Cumberland's discussion[16] of a regional interindustry model. Cumberland's suggestion was to add an extra row —representing the costs of environmental damage to each sector of the regions economy—and an extra column—representing the costs of mitigating this damage — to the conventional interindustry input–output table for a region. The original 1966 version and other later versions of the model were not, however, fully operational. More detailed attempts to take into account the overall materials balance in input–output terms have followed the Cumberland model.[17] The detailed models incorporate four "quadrants" to account for residuals flows from the economy to the environmental media; the raw materials input flows from the environment into the economic system; interindustry flows of inputs and outputs; and finally ecological flows of matter and energy found within ecosystems.[18]

It is important to bear in mind, however, that the input–output technique is not without some fairly serious drawbacks. The data requirements are very substantial and inevitably the limited data that can currently be used in the model will be several years out of date. None of the more comprehensive economic–ecologic input–output models has as yet reached a truly operational state. Secondly, many input–output models utilise fixed or static coefficients relating inputs to outputs and this fact obviously casts some doubt on the usefulness of model predictions about future patterns of final demand. Dynamic input–output models become very complicated to handle and the massive data-collection requirements (in time and manpower terms) translate into rapidly escalating costs. On top of these problems any input–output model which includes an environmental sector will be faced with the difficult valuation problems we highlighted in Section 3. We concluded there that the state-of-the-art in the economic evaluation of environmental damage and abatement costs was rather rudimentary.

Regional environmental quality models (REQMs)

Victor[19] points out that a suitable methodology for the analysis of economic and ecological interrelationships must do more than merely comply with the laws of thermodynamics. Ideally, it must take into account all forms of resource use and analyse all forms of residuals disposal via air, water and land media simultaneously. A number of researchers in the USA, building on the earlier materials-balance work, have attempted to develop integrated residuals management models.[20] These researchers argue that there are a number of intermediate linkages which suggest that all residuals streams should be analysed and managed simultaneously through a regional residuals management model. Thus, for example, the process of incinerating municipal solid-waste residuals often results in the creation of secondary residuals, in this case gases and other airborne pollutants which are discharged from the incinerator chimneys. Despite the formidable data requirements attempts have been made to put such a regional model on a partly operational basis. The concept of an REQM is illustrated in Figure 5.3. Within any given region (an urban area, river basin, airshed, economic region, etc.) at a given

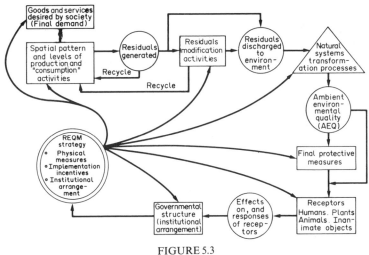

FIGURE 5.3

Residuals–Environmental Quality Management (REQM) System

Reprinted from Basta, D. J. *et al.* (1978) *Analysis for Residuals — Environmental Quality Management*, Johns Hopkins University Press, Baltimore.

point in time, there is a spatial distribution of economic activities which generate different sets of types and quantities of residuals; and also associated methods and processes used to handle the residuals flows. The released residuals are linked to different patterns of ambient environmental quality (AEQ) by a multitude of often complex transfer functions. Dose-response relationships then link human, plant, animal and material receptors to the prevailing AEQ. Finally, the effects on, and responses of receptors provide the stimulus for management action (in this case a selected REQM strategy). REQM formally consists of the following functions:

> "Analysis to develop REQM strategies; planning; legislation; translation of legislation into guidelines and procedures; implementation of guidelines and procedures via incentives imposed on residuals generating activities to induce those activities to install and operate physical measures for reducing the discharge of residuals into the environment and/or for modifying or making better use of the available assimilative capacity; design/construction/operation of facilities; monitoring and enforcement of performance by activities; monitoring of AEQ; and feedback of information from monitoring into the continuous planning and decision making functions. It is this total set of functions which yields the desired product of improved AEQ."

An REQM strategy would consist of three interrelated components: the physical measures for improving AEQ, i.e. product redesign with recycling in mind, process changes, raw material input mix changes, increased materials recycling, various methods for making better use of existing assimilative capacity or even increasing assimilative capacity; policy-control instruments, regulations, effluent taxes, effluent rights, etc., to induce the residuals generators to reduce or alter discharge volumes and/ or quality (reviewed in detail in Section 9 of this volume); and the institutional arrangements necessary for operational management.

The analysis function of REQM results in the generation of information on the costs and consequences of alternative strategies. The information is produced by combining "activity models" (for predicting residuals generation and modification) and "natural systems models" (which predict ecosystem changes) and relating the data produced to an explicit objective function, which encompasses the evaluation criteria necessary to compare alternative strategies and choose the best solution. Once the objective function has been specified the analyst is free to utilise either mathematical programming or manual methods in order to determine optimal solutions. As far as the UK is concerned it has yet to be established just how important and general transmedia pollution is although particular instances of such transfer problems can be readily identified. The fifth report of the UK Royal Commission on the Environment[21] did in fact contain a suggestion for the creation of a unified pollution inspectorate to oversee the management of the UK environment. It was intended that this new inspectorate would coordinate work previously undertaken by separate control agencies such as the

Alkali Inspectorate and local authorities for air pollution, regional water authorities for water pollution, etc. The idea does not, however, appear to have been taken up officially although there seems to be a clear need for a more unified and cooperative approach to pollution control in the UK (we examine this and other control issues in Section 9). Much more could be done to develop some coordination of effort or even better communications both between the various pollution control agencies in the UK and between the agencies and the public.

Towards a New Paradigm?

We now turn to the question of whether the ruling paradigm in the science of economics, basically "neoclassical economic theory", is capable of meeting the challenges of, among others, the problems of pollution and resource depletion. As Dopfer[22] puts it: "Is the current paradigm a basis which calls for the right kind of questions, allows for the formulation of relevant theories, suggests an appropriate degree of empirical testing, and, ultimately, proposes meaningful solutions to the most pressing problems of the future?" We have tried to illustrate in Sections 2 and 3 of this volume some of the weaknesses of the ruling paradigm that have been exposed by various writers at least as far as "environmental" problems are concerned. Given the alleged limitations of traditional economic analysis the next question we will try to examine is whether the economic–ecologic modelling attempts that we have already surveyed represent a significant change in the science of economics, a change radical enough to be labelled a paradigm shift.

Before reviewing the readings below which address the paradigm shift debate we first need to present a more comprehensive definition of the term "paradigm shift". According to Pearce[23] "A paradigm shift occurs when an existing tenet of faith that underlies the internally coherent structure of science is jettisoned in favour of a new paradigm which in turn tends to be generated by some anomaly thrown up by the first paradigm". Dopfer[24] stresses that a paradigm shift is much more fundamental a change than that represented by the process of hypothesis testing and rejection. It refers more to the whole underlying framework of the scientific process; "the kind of questions considered to be relevant for a science, the qualifications to its answers, the body of methods and techniques for testing of theories; the commonly consented degree of rigour required when accepting or rejecting theories, the institutional setting in which the researchers operate . . . "

The "Institutional" Economics School of Thought

The writings of K. W. Kapp[25] have been chosen as typical of the "institutional" line of reasoning. Kapp argues that the interdependencies between economic and ecological systems imply widespread redistributive (equity) effects, often intergenerational, which are not reflected in market prices. The latter cannot, therefore, be used to evaluate these changes (both costs and benefits). As we saw in Section 3 a number of equity weighting proposals have been put forward by economists to overcome the neglect of intragenerational distributional impacts in traditional cost–benefit analysis. But purists such as Mishan[26] have continued to argue that such analysis is not admissible in a neoclassical framework and the recent work of Page[27] serves to remind us that the market efficiency criterion neglects the issue of intergenerational equity.

Kapp[28] is also pessimistic about the adequacy of the methods based on revealed preferences, and willingness to pay or compensate, so far developed by economists in order to evaluate environmental costs and benefits. Again as we have tried to show in Section 3 such pessimism seems currently well founded especially in the context of uncertain, irreversible and long-run environmental costs and benefits. Kapp's criticisms of the traditional economic approach lead him to highlight the need to take a holistic approach (in his terms "system-wide" approach) to environmental problems. Because of the inherent complexity of the environment it is argued all phenomena have to be analysed within the context of this environment. The holistic approach requires interdisciplinary research and as we pointed out in the introductory essay in Section 2 systems analysis has been put forward as an appropriate methodology. In the reading below Kapp uses the modern agricultural system (with its mechanisation, reliance on chemicals and on generally energy-intensive methods and practices) to illustrate what he terms the "open-system" character of the economy. Kapp's use of the term "open-system" in this context is analogous to the term "closed-system" which we have been using in the introductory essays in this volume and which is commonly used in the environmental economics literature. Currently there would appear to be formidable constraints to the development of the necessary interdisciplinary research required by the holistic methodology. These constraints include both the massive data-requirements problem (stressed in Sections 2 and 3) and the communications problem between researchers from different disciplines.

Norton and Parlour[29] reinforce the arguments for an holistic approach in which the analyst is required to take a long-run view of the systems being studied. They argue that the "technical view of the environment" represented by the materials-balance model does not go far enough in recognising ecological chain reactions. The inevitable interactions of natural and social systems should be stabilised at some volume of production and consumption predetermined by ecological constraints. Both Kapp and Norton and Parlour conclude by calling for the development of a new social philosophy containing social goals and objectives which recognise the necessary and sufficient conditions that ensure the survival of society. As Dopfer[30] puts it a new valuation procedure is required which reflects the relative values of the entire set of utility variables according to a holistic (rather than just "economic") interpretation of welfare. Common and Pearce's[31] call for a strategy which minimises "survival risk" is another argument essentially along the same lines as those outlined above. This holistic, long-run survival line of reasoning has not so far been accepted or even recognised by the majority of the economics profession. Counter-arguments abound and a "middle of the road position" has been neatly summarised by Lecomber[32] commenting on the minimisation of "survival" risk argument:

> "this assumes either that 'survival' risk can be minimised without sacrifice of other objectives, for example current consumption, or that 'survival' is of overriding importance. Both assumptions seem questionable. Minimising 'survival' risk could involve a very sharp cut-back in all kinds of activities, including, for example, the use of D.D.T. to control malaria in underdeveloped countries, and the consequences would probably include a marked rise in the current death rate. Their statement [Common and Pearce] certainly seems too strong, and Meade's[33] vaguer claim is probably more acceptable: 'The disutility of Doom to future generations would be so great that, even if we gave it a low probability and even if we discount future utilities at a high rate . . . we would be wise to be prudent in our present action'."

The Steady-State Economy (SSE) Model

Some analysts have construed Boulding's[34] arguments as a recommendation for "zero growth" in national output. Daly[35] calls for the establishment of what he terms a "steady-state economy" (SSE).* He analyses the economic system in terms of two physical populations — people and artifacts — both of which are encompassed by a larger natural system; and three basic magnitudes: stock = total production of goods (producer and consumer) and human bodies: service = satisfaction expressed when wants are satisfied: and finally throughput = physical flow of matter–energy through the economic system. Now these physical populations have two important aspects: (a) they yield services and (b) the populations require maintenance and replacement. In the steady-state model the economic system is composed of constant stocks of people and artifacts, maintained at some desired sufficient levels by low rates of maintenance throughput (i.e. by the lowest feasible flows of matter and energy). According to Daly the SSE paradigm requires a "satisfying" approach to the level of stocks rather than a maximising approach. Not a great deal of guidance is

---

* Daly's writings can be categorised as belonging to the humanistic economics school of thought. See also Schumacher, E. F. (1973) *Small Is Beautiful*, Blond & Briggs.

given, however, about what the exact optimum value of this stock should be. The rather vague statement "some level of stock that is sufficient for a good life and sustainable for a long future" is all that is offered to guide us to the correct level and distribution of income and wealth in an "ecologically-sound" society. Service is to be maximised subject to the maintenance of constant stocks. Throughput is to be minimised but again at what level, how low is "as low as possible"?

The SSE model also requires some moral or ethical assumptions with regard to the principles that should guide man's behaviour in the "new" society. Mankind should assimilate or reassimilate the principles of "enoughness, stewardship, humility and holism". The lack of such qualities generally in the current industrialised societies of the world force Daly to turn to various forms of centrally-directed regulations. The following are suggested: maximum- and minimum-income limits; resource-depletion quotas; and birth licences or some other form of population-control mechanism; as necessary in order to achieve the paramount policy objective of stationarity.[36]

Entropy and the Economic Systems

Georgescu-Roegen[37] views the economic process not as a mechanical analogue, but as an entropic, unidirectional transformation. Valuable energy and matter (in a state of low entropy) are constantly being turned into valueless residuals (in a state of high entropy). The economic process is not a self-sustaining process, it only functions with a continuous exchange between itself and the environment.

The so-called "Entropy Law" is, according to the author, the "taproot of economic scarcity". In the context of entropy every action of man, other organisms or processes in nature must result in a deficit for the entire system. Georgescu-Roegen is at pains to stress that the "steady-state" or zero-growth economic system is in his view a myth. In the face of the "Entropy Law" a growing state, zero-growth state and even a declining state cannot exist forever in a finite environment. One doubts, however, if even Daly would argue that his SSE model was designed to function on an infinite timescale. Georgescu-Roegen has also put forward what he terms a minimal bioeconomic programme which he believes will significantly extend mankind's survival time. This radical programme is based on a population size constrained by the productive limits of an organic agricultural sector. Energy demands would have to be drastically curtailed and efforts made to develop solar or fusion power. Product durability and repairability would become important and advertising and fashion or style-dominated consumption habits abandoned.

Notes and References

1. The original materials-balance model can be found in Kneese, A. V., Ayres, R. U. and D'Arge, R. C. (1970) *Economics and the Environment*, Johns Hopkins University Press; and a modified version of the principle can be found in Pearce, D. W. (1976) *Environmental Economics*, Longmans.

2. The reading by Kapp (1976) presents the so-called institutional critique of the conventional economics paradigm; the Daly (1976) reading is a review of the steady-state economy model. Georgescu-Roegen (1976) emphasises the importance of the entropy concept and provides a critique of the steady-state approach. Norton and Parlour's (1972) article (see reference 29) stresses the failure of the conventional economics paradigm to take into account a long enough time perspective or to take a sufficiently holistic approach to the economic–ecological inter-relationships. Finally, Pearce (1976) in his reading offers a preliminary analysis of the economic and ecological optima in an integrated framework and makes some conclusions on the efforts made so far in terms of a possible paradigm shift.

3. For an analysis of the historical development of the neoclassical doctrine and other economic doctrines see Blaug, M. (1970) *Economic Theory in Retrospect*, Heinemann.

4. Boulding, K. E. (1966) The Economics of the Coming Spaceship Earth, in Jarrett, H. (ed.) *Environmental Quality in a Growing Economy*, Johns Hopkins University Press.

5. See Boulding, K. E. (1966) *op. cit.* and Georgescu-Roegen, N. (1976) *Energy and Economic Myths*, Pergamon Press.

6. Boulding, K. E. (1966) *op. cit.*

7. Kneese, A. V. *et al.* (1970) *op. cit.*

8. See Russell, C. S. (1973) *Residuals Management in Industry: A Case Study of Petroleum Refining*, Johns Hopkins University Press; Bower, B. (1977) Economic Dimensions of Waste Recycling and Re-use: Some Definitions, Facts and Issues, in Pearce, D. W. and Walter, I. *Resource Conservation: Social and Economic Dimensions of Recycling*, New York University Press and Longmans; and Basta, D. J. *et al.* (1978) *Analysis For Residuals—Environmental Quality Management*, Resources For The Future, Washington.

9. Victor, P. A. (1972) *Pollution: Economy and Environment*, Allen & Unwin.

10. Pearce, D. W. (1976) *Environmental Economics*, Longmans.

11. Pearce, D. W. (1976) *op. cit.*

12. See Ackerman, B. *et al.* (1974) *The Uncertain Search for Environmental Quality*, The Free Press.

13. Pearce, D. W. (1976) The Limits of Cost–Benefit Analysis as a Guide to Environmental Policy, *Kyklos*, vol. 29, Fasch 1.

14. Nobbs, C. and Pearce, D. W. (1976) The Economics of Stock Pollutants: The Example of Cadmium, *International Journal of Environmental Studies*, vol. 8 (1).

15. Pearce, D. W. (1976) in *Kyklos*, *op. cit.*

16. Cumberland, J. H. (1966) A Regional Interindustry Model for Analysis of Development Objectives, *The Regional Science Association Papers*, vol. 17; and Cumberland, J. H. and Korbach, R. J. (1973) A Regional Interindustry Environmental Model, *The Regional Science Association Papers*, vol. 30.

17. See Daly, H. E. (1968) On Economics as a Life Science, *Journal of Political Economy*, vol. 76 (3); Isard, W. (1969) *Some Notes on the Linkages of the Ecologic and Economic Systems*, mimeo; and Victor, P. A. (1972) *op. cit.*

18. Victor, P. A. (1972) *Economics of Pollution*, Macmillan, provides an introduction to input–output analysis and also reviews some of the attempts that have been made to incorporate the environment into such analysis.
Hite, J. C. and Laurent, E. A. (1972) *Environmental Planning: An Economic Analysis*, Praeger, present a modified version of the Isard model and suggest a possible operational role for such a model in planning.

19. Victor, P. A. (1972) *Pollution: Economy and Environment*, Allen & Unwin.

20. See Bower, B. (1978) *Regional Residuals: Environmental Quality Management Modelling*, Johns Hopkins University Press; and Basta, D. J. *et al.* (1978) *op. cit.*

21. UK Royal Commission on Environmental Pollution (1976) Fifth Report, *Air Pollution—An Integrated Approach*, HMSO.

22. Dopfer, K. (ed.) (1976) *Economics in the Future*, Macmillan.

23. Pearce, D. W. (1975) Are Environmental Problems a Challenge to Economic Science?, *Ethics and Medicine*, vol. 2 (1).

24. Dopfer, K. (ed.) (1976) *op. cit.*
25. Kapp, K. W. (1976) The Open-system Character of the Economy and its Implications, in Dopfer, K. (ed.) *Economics In The Future*, Macmillan.
    Kapp, K. W. (1970) Environmental Disruption and Social Costs: A Challenge to Economists, *Kyklos*, vol. 23, Fasch 4.
26. Mishan, E. J. (1975) *Cost Benefit Analysis*, Allen & Unwin.
27. Page, R. (1977) *Conservation and Economic Efficiency*, Johns Hopkins University Press.
28. Kapp, K. W. (1976) *op. cit.*
29. Norton, G. A. and Parlour, J. W. (1972) The Economic Philosophy of Pollution: A Critique, *Environment and Planning*, vol. 4.
30. Dopfer, K. (ed.) (1976) *op. cit.*
31. Common, M. S. and Pearce, D. W. (1973) Adaptive Mechanisms Growth and the Environment: The Case of Natural Resources, *Canadian Journal of Economics*, vol. 6 (3).
32. Lecomber, R. (1979) *The Economics of Natural Resources*, Macmillan.
33. Meade, J. E. (1973) Economic Policy and the Threat of Doom, in Benjamin, B. *et al.*, *Resources and Population*, Academic Press.
34. Boulding, K. E. (1966) *op. cit.*
35. Daly, H. E. (1977) *Steady-State Economics*, W. H. Freeman.
36. In the reading below Daly, H. E. (1976) The Steady-state Economy, in Wilson, K. D. (ed.) *Prospects For Growth*, Praeger summarises the main features of the SSE model.
37. Georgescu-Roegen, N. (1976) *op. cit.*

READINGS

THE OPEN-SYSTEM CHARACTER OF THE ECONOMY AND ITS
IMPLICATIONS*

K. William Kapp

I. Introduction

THE mainstream of economic theory did not foresee the global environmental crisis just as it did not, in the course of its history, anticipate other important problems which proved to be of major significance. The long-standing neglect of social costs is not the first, and the current food and energy scarcity will not be the last demonstration of the fact that economic theory and practice tend to take account of important problems only under the pressure of public opinion and the urgent necessity of coming to terms with far-reaching negative effects caused by specific emergencies.

Environmental disruption and the growing scarcity of resources have finally made us aware of the fact that production, allocation and the choice of inputs and location are taking place not in closed or semi-closed systems which economic science has traditionally used as theoretical models for the explication of economic processes but in basically open systems. Increasing awareness of the open-system character of production and consumption is, of course, no guarantee that its full methodological and practical consequences are fully comprehended. Have we really understood the full implications of the fact that serious incompatibilities may develop between economic and ecological (as well as social) systems, which threaten the economic process, its social reproduction, and hence the continued guarantee of human well-being and survival?

*Reprinted with permission from *Economics in the Future*, ed. K. Dopfer, 1976, Macmillan, London, pp. 90–105.

II.   Economic systems as open systems

The Physiocrats were the first to perceive the economy as a closed system of interdependent variables. They were led to this realisation partly by the prevailing notions of natural order, the moral philosophy of utilitarianism and the transfer of the equilibrium concept from mechanics to political and economic analysis and partly by their anti-mercantilist policy suggestions which they advanced as practical remedies to cope with the threatening economic and political crisis prior to the French and American Revolutions. The perception of production and reproduction as processes occurring in essentially closed and more or less self-regulatory systems served their pre-analytical notions and supported their normative policy judgements.

Hence the development of closed or semi-closed theoretical models which have survived in the predominant schools of economics both in its neoclassical and its Keynesian versions and have continued to shape the scope of conventional analysis, the formulation of basic concepts and, last but not least, the delimitation of the scope of its subject-matter. Institutional and, to a lesser extent, Marxist economists have always criticised this narrow scope of conventional economic theory and have insisted that economic systems are parts of a much broader political and institutional system from which they receive important impulses and which they, in turn, are capable of influencing and even changing in a variety of ways.

The degradation of the physical and social environment and the exhaustion of important non-renewable (capital) resources have merely added a new and decisive illustration of the fact that economic systems are intimately and reciprocally related to other systems and are in this sense fundamentally open systems. To view the economy as a closed system may be methodologically convenient and enable economic theory to formulate its concepts and theories in accordance with the canons of formal mathematical logic, but this tends to perpetuate a wrong perception of reality which narrows our theoretical horizon. In fact, the resulting perspective and the criteria of evaluation are those in terms of which the system of business enterprise tends to evaluate its performance. While this may be an explanation it is no justification for the continued adherence to the traditional closed-system approach of economic science which, as an empirical system of knowledge, must follow the lead of its subject-matter if its conclusions are not to become misleading and irrelevant.

The current discussion of environmental disruption has used air and water pollution caused by the emission of waste residuals by producers and consumers as typical illustrations of the impact of production and consumption on the environment. We are far from denying the importance and the typical character of the social costs represented by air and water pollution. In fact, they are the classical cases which have led to the growing awareness of the interdependence of economic and ecological systems. However, we have chosen modern agriculture in order to illustrate the essentially global and open-system character of economic processes and to show the full range of global consequences which production and specific techniques, that is economic choices guided by market costs and returns, may have upon ecological balance, society and social reproduction.

III.   Modern agriculture as an illustration of the global and open-system character of the economy

Agriculture, both in developed and less-developed countries, employs new techniques and new capital inputs with far-reaching ecological and socio-economic consequences. In fact, modern farming has become a highly capital-intensive mechanised industrial activity. High-yielding varieties have changed the character of agricultural production. The increased yields of these new varieties are due to their specific effective and 'aggressive' feeding characteristics which speed up the depletion of the soil. This, in turn, requires the application of considerable amounts of chemical fertilisers in addition to other complementary inputs as, for instance, water and pesticides as well as additional capital inputs such as farm machinery, tractors, harvesters, spraying equipment, aeroplanes, and so forth. It is these inputs that account for the higher yield per acre or per farm worker. As a result of these technological changes fields have become larger and the average size of farm has increased; plowing, sowing, the application of fertilisers, spraying of insecticides, harvesting, poultry raising, cattle breeding, feeding, milking, and so on – all have become mechanised operations resembling the assembly line in other industries. Millions of farms have disappeared; the rural population has declined and moved to cities thus adding to urban congestion and overcrowding.

The ecological consequences of these technical and structural changes may be summarised briefly and succinctly. Technology and mechanisation have taken command by imposing their imperatives upon farming as an industry. What used to be a highly diversified (biological) system of growing food and primary materials has been transformed into large-scale and highly specialised monocultures. Moreover, modern farming has become a major user of capital goods produced by farm-supporting industries employing an increasing number of industrial labourers and making heavy and increasing demands on scarce resources, particularly electricity and petroleum. Thus agriculture is now a major consumer of scarce energy and, viewed as a whole, uses perhaps more petroleum than any other single industry. In fact, farming has become a way of turning petroleum into food. Our harvests of food and primary materials may indeed be said to be 'harvests of oil'.[1] Despite the fact that farming could be a net energy-producing sector of the economy – by capturing the energy of the sun – and despite the growing energy crisis, we continue to measure efficiency in farming in terms of output per hour of labour or per acre instead of measuring it, for example, in terms of output per unit of energy.[2] This dependence of modern agriculture on petroleum is particularly dangerous for those countries which, like India, have opted for a 'Green Revolution' and the use of high-yielding varieties, and are now experiencing the first signs of a stagnation of their output.[3]

Nor is this all; the application of chemical fertilisers and the utilisation of pesticides (insecticides, herbicides, fungicides) are subject to diminishing returns. Hence, increasing doses of chemicals need to be applied to secure additional returns per unit of input. Not all of these chemicals can be assimilated by plants; they find their way into rivers and lakes. Growing specialisation with its emphasis on monocultures has made crops more susceptible to sudden massive losses due to pest invasions. The new varieties are themselves more resistant than non-hybrid varieties. Moreover, pesticides may kill not only the pests but their enemies as well; in addition, the resistance and immunity of certain pests are known to increase by natural selection. Hence increasing doses of pesticides are necessary in order to compensate for the loss of their effectiveness. Furthermore, modern farming tends to use pesticides quite mechanically according to generalised spraying time schedules provided by the manufacturers. This has led to indiscriminate operations of 'over-kill' which continue as long as additional applications of pesticides are, or are believed to be, profitable; in other words, returns are calculated without considering the system-wide social losses or the inflated price rises and other 'imperfections' of the market for farm products. It is true, costs may also be inflated due to 'administered' and inflated oligopolistic prices of farm inputs but the fact remains that the guiding commercial cost–benefit calculations according to which pesticides (and fertilisers) are being applied, do not take into account their ecologically-negative consequences.[4] The neglect of the social costs resulting from ecological hazards to flora, fauna and human beings, as well as the substantial energy requirements for the production of chemical inputs, is only one aspect of the situation; the other is the failure to take account of potential benefits of alternative techniques of production.

Finally, the new crops seem to be characterised by relatively low protein contents, that is a lower capacity (for example of hybrid corn) to feed and raise animals. This, in turn, has called for more imports of fish protein in the form of fish meal to supplement animal diets. As a result of these undoubtedly profitable imports – profitable both for the Peruvian fishing and export industries and the U.S. and European importers of protein-rich fish meal – we are confronted with the ecologically and, if properly calculated, also economically absurd situation that a continent with protein-poor diets (South America) supports today the relatively protein-rich diets of highly developed countries.[5] Monetary or market criteria of efficiency and of economic rationality and the resulting export–import pattern tend to give rise to a global allocation of inputs and a distribution of outputs which may be far from desirable either ecologically or in the light of a concept of substantive rationality which would take account of actual human requirements in different parts of the world. (We are not suggesting that Peru should stop all exports of fish protein to countries with protein-rich diets and should instead cover the protein deficiencies of South America. Export of fish meal will have to remain an important source of foreign exchange to pay for Peru's imports of capital goods. However, the existence of this protein-rich supply of fish and the widespread deficiency of the diet of Peru's poor population, as indeed of the population of the rest of South America, provides at least a basis for a realistic search for alternative solutions and new patterns of foreign trade. The problem under discussion is the neglect of basic nutritional needs in the process of planning and development.)

As a preliminary conclusion we may say that the organising principles of economic systems guided by exchange values are incompatible with the requirements of ecological systems and the satisfaction of basic human needs. Our traditional criteria of technical efficiency, of cost–benefit calculations and of economic rationality are the crucial points under discussion. Their limitations become manifest as soon as we view the dynamic interaction of open social and economic systems with specific ecological systems.

It is hardly necessary to add that, if we accept this point of view, as we believe we must, new criteria of rational action and planning are called for. Above all, alternative solutions different from those which we have pursued in the light of the narrow economic calculus in terms of market criteria impose themselves. In the concrete case of modern agriculture it may perhaps be useful to be more explicit in order to counteract any possible misinterpretation of our position. We are not suggesting a return to traditional agriculture or a ban on fertilisers, pesticides and modern technology; rather, the practical and theoretical implications of our position are to abandon our traditional notions of efficiency and rationality and to redefine them in the light of the 'new' realities of the inter-dependency of systems. In view of the system-wide repercussions of agricultural production, and indeed of production in general, it must be clear that neither technical feasibility nor technological imperatives nor micro-economic rationality, in terms of net private returns and entrepreneurial costs can provide adequate answers to the question of what are desirable aims and policies. Criteria of economic performance can neither be derived from technical feasibility nor from economic efficiency in the narrow sense, but must be for-mulated in the light of a system-wide appraisal of ecological, social and econom-ic advantages and disadvantages. As far as modern agriculture and the need for high levels of output and productivity are concerned, it will be necessary to en-visage and appraise a whole bundle of complementary aims and alternative strategies, such as a greater diversification of crops, the planting of specific crops in geographic regions less affected by pests, a return to appropriate crop rotation, the development of pest-resistant varieties which have the desirable yield and quality characteristics, the systematic implementation of bio-environmental controls,[6] and greater reliance on monitoring pest populations with a shift from methods of 'over-kill' or even '100 per cent pest elimination' to 'treatment when necessary' and the application of pesticides as stop-gap emer-gency measures. In countries like the United States, the return to cultivation of some of the nearly 60 million acres taken out of production at a cost of three to four billion dollars annually could compensate for the possible increase of crop losses due to a reduction of the present over-intensive application of pesticides with its disruptive effects on the environment.[7]

IV. The open-system approach

Of course, it is insufficient to say that the use of destructive technologies and techniques applied in accordance with the principle of maximising net returns has 'external' effects on regional, national and international scales. Nor will it be sufficient to call for more information and more interdisciplinary research. All this is true enough. As our discussion of modern agriculture has shown, the appropriate unit of analysis is neither the individual farm, nor the national farm economy, nor a particular ecological system. The relevant unit of analysis is much larger and the time span that counts is much longer than those in terms of which business enterprise and economic science have traditionally perceived and defined the notions of efficiency, rationality and optimality.

Thus the environmental crisis forces economists to acknowledge the limita-tions of their methodological and cognitive approaches and to reconsider the scope of their science. The classical economists – Adam Smith and his successors – could still claim with some justification that economic systems could be understood as semi-closed systems because, in their time, air, water, and so forth were, in a sense, 'free' goods and because they were convinced – wrongly – that rational action – under competitive conditions – had only positive social effects. This belief has turned out to be an illusion. To hold on to it in the face of the environmental crisis can only be regarded as a self-deception and a deception to others. Contemporary economists who continue to discuss economic and environmental problems in closed systems have much less of an excuse for this practice than the classical economists. Human action and economic decisions relating to production are not taking place in closed or even semi-closed systems but within a network of relationships and dynamic structures in continuous open interaction with one another. In short, we need a new approach which makes it possible to deal with the dynamic interrelations between economic systems and the whole network of physical and social systems and, indeed, the entire composite system of structural relationships. It would be an illusion to believe that such a system view of the economy can or will emerge from the traditional modes of analytical thinking; nor would it be realistic to expect systems thinking 'to spring into existence in a mature state ... it must evolve out of proposals, discussions, reformulations and experience'.[8] Systems thinking is inevitably complex inasmuch as it is concerned with discontinuous non-linear 'feedback' effects which characterise the dynamic interdependencies between the different systems as well as of each subsystem with the composite whole. In this sense, it is indeed a 'step away from traditional science'.[9] It is, by its very nature, multi-dimensional, multi-disciplinary and integrative. Thinking in terms of inter-dependent systems is an innovation and presupposes a new outlook which calls for an abandonment of old knowledge 'before the new can be created'.[10] Such innovation is, as a rule, experienced as a source of annoyance, a destroyer of routine, an underminer of complacency.[11] Innovations of this kind can hardly be expected to come from scholars with a conventional outlook but call for a wider range of reference than the representatives of 'normal' science bring to bear upon their subject-matter.[12]

While ecologists and natural scientists, as a rule, have a better understanding of complex interdependencies they too will have to widen their perspective in dealing with environmental and other global problems. Few ecologists seem to have dealt with the impact of economic decision-making and technological factors upon ecological systems; nor have they sufficiently come to terms with human values and problems of costs. 'Ecology works very well for families of plants and groups of animals, but up to now there does not exist an individual human ecology.'[13] We are only at the beginning of thinking in terms of inter-dependent systems and considerable research will be required to close the gaps in our knowledge as to the structure and interaction of a multitude of systems and their 'performance'. Nevertheless, it would be a mistake to believe that we have to start from zero. Systems analysis has a long history in other disciplines such as biology, particularly micro-biology, genetics, chemistry, nuclear physics and, last but not least, cultural anthropology.[14]

Of course, it will not suffice to aim at a merely formal representation of the open-system character of the economy in its interaction with something called environment. What is required is to overcome the essentially dualistic conceptualisation of economy and environment in order to give our analysis the necessary empirical content. Determination of basic needs and requirements of health and survival, of environmental norms and maximum tolerable levels of contamination; environmental-impact studies of alternative technologies in specific localities rather than linear physical flow models are some of the empirical and quantitative problems that call for exploration and analysis; social science will have to come to terms with the key problem of the open-system character of the economy – the fact, namely, that production derives material inputs from the physical and decisive impulses from the social system which, in turn, may be disrupted and disorganised by the emission of residual wastes up to a point where social reproduction itself may be threatened.

Systems thinking will have to avoid a number of pitfalls, some of which may be listed briefly within the context of the present discussion; the tendency of concentrating attention on aggregates and their historical correlation without a causal analysis of the effects of specific technologies, production, consumption and income patterns; the use of constant coefficients of correlation and the neglect of circular cumulative interdependencies; the failure to consider the influence of institutional factors including the role of vested and conflicting interest groups; the insistence upon determinate and precise solutions of formal problems instead of a search for practical and useful answers to urgent practical problems; and the neglect of a careful appraisal of alternative goals and technologies as well as of their opportunity costs and potential social impacts.

V. Economics as a normative science

The methodological and cognitive implications of the fact that economic systems are not closed but are fundamentally open systems would be far-reaching. Above all, it would be necessary to take account of the complex interaction and circular interdependencies between different systems. Production and consumption put in motion complex processes which have serious and determinable negative consequences on the physical and social environment with an inevitable impact on distribution; these interdependencies imply a forced transfer of 'unpaid' social costs, which constitute a secondary redistribution of real income primarily (but not exclusively) to economically-weaker members of society as well as to future generations. Moreover, individuals and groups whose income and health are adversely affected by destructive technologies under specific institutional arrangements are victims of a process of production over which they have no control, and against which they have no adequate legal redress. These inter-system relations with redistributive effects are not exchange or market relations. They represent extra-market physical flows from corporate production units and individual households to the environment and back from the latter to the former. The character of these flows needs to be understood and subjected to empirical and theoretical analysis and appraisal.[15] These non-market physical flows raise important problems of circular cumulative causation which must be recognised as typical characteristics of economic processes.[16] They have a direct bearing on actual costs and benefits: they are neither 'external' nor are they voluntary or contractual. In short, they are extra-market phenomena and market prices do not provide adequate (if indeed any) criteria for their evaluation.

The actual costs may be regional or system-wide in character because pollution affects not only single individuals in specific localities but entire groups of people and regions, extending frequently beyond national boundaries. Its effects, moreover, will be unequally distributed. The same applies to practically all other negative effects of environmental degradation. Noise, urban and traffic congestion, industrial accidents, occupational and civilisational diseases, fatigue, frustration – are only some of the symptoms of serious social dislocation experienced by individuals but system-wide in their repercussions and significance. Their impact will be felt in the form of a deterioration and dehumanisation of the quality of the living and working conditions of millions of people both today and in the future. These phenomena raise complex problems of measuring and evaluating environmental costs (and benefits) which are not solved by such conceptual tools as revealed preferences, willingness to pay or to compensate, Pareto optimality and so on, for these concepts are derived from our traditional approach based upon a 'methodological subjectivism'. The validity of this has never been generally accepted even in those fields of analysis for which they were originally developed. Instead of attempting to calculate benefit and cost in terms of subjective preferences and exchange values it would be necessary to assess the environmental and social impact of these physical flows socially and hence politically and to translate 'physical and social impacts into politically understandable and relevant trade-offs'.[17] Only in this way can we hope to arrive at reasoned choices between conflicting interests and objectives in the light of explicit political and, hence, moral judgements rather than in terms of calculated 'shadow' prices and costs derived from market values, which, upon closer analysis, can be shown to reflect either the subjective preferences and valuations of the experts and/or of powerful vested interests.[18]

The degradation of the physical and social environment and the recognition of economic systems as open systems would make it necessary to define socially desirable macroeconomic goals (or norms) of the economy. These social goals include a number of conflicting general objectives such as greater equality or justice in distribution, economic stability, full employment, efficiency in the utilisation of scarce resources, participation in decision-making, and so forth. At the same time, they will have to include the maintenance of dynamic states of ecological and economic balance as one of the fundamental prerequisites of socio-economic reproduction and growth. The definition and concrete determination of such macroeconomic goals is not an easy matter partly because they require a considerable amount of knowledge regarding the effects of alternative levels of output on the environment; of the consequences of alternative inputs, technologies and locations which, in the light of the carrying capacity of the environment, can be tolerated.

The determination of such macroeconomic goals requires an interdisciplinary-research effort which exceeds the competence of economists but which cannot be conducted without them. However, we do not believe that the price mechanism and the monetary calculus can be relied upon for the evaluation and determination of the relative importance of different goods and services including the choice of inputs, techniques and location, and this for several reasons. In the first place, the price mechanism and an evaluation in monetary terms reflect the willingness to pay of individuals and groups and hence also the inequality in the distribution of income and market power. The supply and demand mechanism is, in this sense, essentially a non-egalitarian and elitist mechanism of evaluating goods, services and environmental damages. Furthermore, the market and monetary calculus is not adapted to the social evaluation either of environmental damages or the type of public goods and services required for the maintenance of dynamic states of ecological and economic balance. We are not arguing that it is impossible to place a monetary value upon environmental damages or for that matter on the public goods and services. After all it is always possible to evaluate them at their monetary costs. However, it can be shown that monetary evaluation, in this sense, fails to ascertain and express their relative social importance in the sense of value to society (and individuals) both in the short and in the long run. Human life and human health may be evaluated in monetary terms (for example in terms of the accumulated income earned or lost over time at compound interest), but is such a procedure cognitively warranted? For several reasons we hold that such a procedure is not justifiable because monetary values are not an adequate criteria in terms of which the qualities under consideration can be expressed and measured.[19]

The fact that we deal with collective (public) goods and services and with dynamic states of balance including the use and exhaustion of non-renewable (capital) resources which will have negative effects on future generations complicates matters and make all monetary evaluations problematical if not indeed unacceptable and cognitively irrelevant. In short, as soon as the open character of economic systems is fully realised the formulation of social goals and objectives and the problem of collective choices can no longer be avoided. Such objectives and choices with respect to the maintenance of dynamic states of ecological and economic balance essential for the maintenance and improvement of the conditions of social and individual existence (quality of life) must become the point of departure for a normative science of economics. The elaboration of a quantitative framework for these social objectives is currently under way in the form of the development of work on social and environmental indicators. Such indicators provide at least the first step and the basis upon which social and environmental normative judgements and collective (political) decisions and priorities could be formulated. Here is the open frontier and the unexplored territory for normative economics.[20]

The next step would be the elaboration of the necessary strategies or alternative courses of action designed to guarantee the attainment of social goals decided upon. This is essentially a task of choosing alternative instruments of control (and economic policies) with a view to assuring that the desired social goals are indeed reached. These measures of control will have to go beyond the scope of traditional economic policies, for they will be concerned with the assessment and choice of technologies, of the quality and quantity of specific inputs and location, and with the change of behavioural and motivational patterns of producers and consumers. An equally if not more important task would be the systematic search for new inputs, alternative technologies, new patterns of location as well as new patterns of consumption or styles of life. In other words, the fact that economic systems are not closed but open systems which depend for their reproduction upon inputs drawn from the physical environment into which they emit pollutants and destructive residuals makes it necessary to consider most of the factors which economic theory has so far regarded as constant or given data as the very problem which needs to be solved or, methodologically speaking, as dependent variables. They are neither constant nor given. The socially warranted technologies, the required inputs (including the location of production) are not known beforehand; on the contrary, they need to be explored and determined. Which technologies, which input pattern, which locations are to be chosen and, ultimately, which output and which institutional behaviour patterns are required and socially warranted are in fact the very problems which call for a solution and which a normative science of economics would have to elucidate and help to explore in the light of the desirable social goals and objectives and the system-wide consequences and actual costs of alternative courses of action. In short, a normative science of economics taking account of the open-system character of the economy would imply a complete reversal of the analytical procedures of the discipline as hitherto practised and applied. Instead of postulating a given state of technology, given behaviour patterns and given individual preferences and aiming at the explication of the allocation mechanism of a hypothetically-closed system under autonomous and self-regulating market forces and on the assumption of rational optimising action of individual producers and consumers, the new task of economics would be to elucidate the manner in which collectively determined social goals and objectives could be attained in the most effective and socially least-costly manner.[21]

Two final observations may be useful with respect to both the concept of economic efficiency and also the educational requirements which the open system and normative approach to economics calls for. If economic systems are fundamentally open systems, and if, as we have implied throughout our discussion, uncontrolled economic decisions based upon the calculation of entrepreneurial costs and returns are basically incompatible with the maintenance of dynamic states of ecological and economic balance,[22] not only the concepts of costs and returns but, above all, those of economic efficiency and optimality need to be redefined and reformulated. They have to be broadened to take account of the fact that what may be efficient and optimal in a closed system of production and distribution may be inefficient and anything but optimal in the long run and may be destructive from a social and global viewpoint due to the neglected cumulative effect of the inter-system interactions between open systems.

The educational implications of the open-system character of the economy are equally far-reaching. Instead of introducing students in economics, especially freshmen, to the highly esoteric formal apparatus which fills the conventional textbooks it seems to me indispensable that they must first be introduced to the open character of economic systems. Systems thinking while undoubtedly complex offers no unsurmountable difficulties for the beginner. Problems of entropy (that is the tendency of increasing disorganisation), of feedback effects (that is the fact that part of the output is fed back and affects succeeding inputs and outputs), material balances, maximum limits of contamination, cumulative causation, need to become part of the teaching of economics in order to prepare economists of the future for the tasks with which they will be increasingly concerned.

VI.   'Conceptual freeze' or intellectual reconstruction

It was not our purpose to predict the future of economics but to show a possible and, in our estimation, necessary direction of its change and reconstruction. Of course, having come this far we face the question as to whether the notion of a normative science of economics is not a vision of an alternative which has no possibility of being realised in the calculable future. Is it not more likely that economists will continue to view economic systems as essentially closed sytems and to hold on to the established procedures and methods? There is indeed considerable evidence for an affirmative answer to this question. Neoclassical economic theory, just as the market economy, have shown a remarkable capacity to assimilate new problems and new developments. In this context we are thinking, for example, of such proposals as the establishment of private or public property rights with respect to rivers and lakes or the suggestion that rights to pollute (pollution permits) be sold and bought at auctions and/or be made the subject of bilateral negotiations between polluters and those who are damaged by pollution. What these proposals amount to is, in fact, a return to the conventional wisdom of relying on property rights and market costs and returns instead of preserving the principle of maintaining communal rights to nature and treating them as social use-values serving fundamental human requirements. We are also thinking of the current tendency of assimilating social costs into conventional economics by means of the empty-box concept of 'externalities' or of proposals for the 'internalisation' of social costs through fiscal policies, subsidies, and so on. I feel that neither the concept of externalities nor the introduction of social-cost curves into formal theory nor current proposals of 'deducting' social costs from gross or net national production measurements will get us very far. For these attempts to incorporate new facts 'painlessly' into conventional theory[23] follow the classical pattern which Veblen once described as the typical response of traditional economics to new 'facts'. In an age of business enterprise, Veblen wrote, new facts and ideas will impose themselves upon the imagination of a wider audience of economists and practical men of affairs only if they are expressed in terms of business finance and the market test. Veblen felt that ingrained habits of thought, reflecting the predominant climate of opinion characteristic of a system of business enterprise, had a tendency of being transmitted from one generation of economists to the next as they were prone to do in the past, that is via 'institutions of higher learning'. For this reason, Veblen, in his time, regarded the prospects for a reconstruction of economics as dim.[24] Of course, Veblen knew what he was talking about; he knew from his own experience as an analyst and as a critic of the system of business enterprise that established theories resist any change and do not simply fade away because they are in conflict with empirical evidence.

However, since Veblen published his essay on economics in 'the calculable future' some fifty years ago, economic conditions have changed and the gap between theory and reality has widened. The deterioration of the environment constitutes a more fundamental challenge to the scope and method of traditional economics than anything that has happened before. In addition, practically all the great current problems (such as inflation, the increase of oil prices, unemployment, monetary disequilibria and balance-of-payments deficits, the population explosion and the scarcity of food as well as famines) are not only world-wide phenomena but call for new global approaches and solutions. Moreover, these problems call for the formulation of specific goals and objectives and the selection and mobilisation of the necessary means (technologies, inputs, controls). It is true, unemployment may be 'remedied' by military and other expenditures even though the current inability to curb the inflationary impact of continuous public domestic and international deficits and the creation of new international 'liquidities' including the recycling of petro-dollars still present open and unsolved if not unsolvable problems within the framework of a 'market economy'. While unemployment may be reduced by an expansion of production, the degradation of the environment will increase with greater output unless alternative criteria of determining inputs and outputs as well as the choice of technology and of location are developed. For these reasons, the need for a reconstruction of economics under the impact of the current global crisis will increase and so will the pressure for a theoretical and methodological innovation of contemporary theories. While it is possible that the desire to retain the traditional doctrine may make the latter more and more dogmatic and give rise to a 'conceptual freeze',[25] it is not unlikely that this freeze will be broken in the calculable future under the impact of new facts, new evidence of environmental disruption, new catastrophes and an increasing public opposition to the deterioration of the physical and social environment.

Notes and References

1. Michael J. Perelman, 'Farming with Petroleum', *Environment*, vol. 14(8) pp. 8–13 (Oct 1972).
2. It has been estimated that the Chinese wet-rice farmer gets for each unit of energy expended more than 50 units of energy in returns; 'for each unit of fossil unit of energy we expend in the US we get about one fifth in return. On the basis of these two ratios, Chinese wet-rice agriculture is far more "efficient" than our own system'; ibid. p. 12.
3. Luc Bigler, 'Zur Stagnation der "Grünen Revolution" – Sozioökonomische Hemmungsfaktoren in der Diffusion neuer Technolgien in Entwicklungsländern dargestellt am Beispiel der Verwendung von High Yielding Varieites in der indischen Landwirtschaft', Basler dissertation, unpublished (1974).
4. Additional dollar returns from additional applications of pesticides are estimated to vary from $2.82 to $4–5 per dollar spent on pesticides: David Pimentel, 'Realities of a Pesticide Ban', *Environment*, vol. 15 (2) (Mar. 1978) p. 25.
5. Perelman, 'Farming with Petroleum', p. 13.
6. Such as the use of parasites, pathogens, predators, chemical and physical attractants, sterile males and genetic manipulations. On this subject and some notable failures of pesticides to eradicate pests, including those causing malaria, see the work of the Commonwealth Institute of Biological Control with headquarters in Trinidad and various stations throughout the British Commonwealth plus a European station in Delémont (Switzerland) as well as the following publications: Hubert Pschorn-Walcher, 'Probleme der biologischen Bekämpfung eingeschleppter Pflanzenschädlinge', *Biologie in unserer Zeit*, 2 (June 1972) pp. 67–75; Richard Garcia, 'The Control of Malaria', *Environment*, 14, no. 5 (June 1972) pp. 2–9: Göran Lofroth, 'Who cares about DDT', *Ecologist*, 1, no. 17 (Nov. 1971) pp. 8–9.
7. On the whole subject see Pimental, 'Realities of a Pesticide Ban', pp. 28–9.
8. R. L. Ackoff, 'Systems, Organizations and Interdisciplinary Research', *General Systems Yearbook*, vol. 5 (1960) p. 1.

9. Ibid. p. 1.
10. C. D. Darlington, *The Conflict of Society and Science* (London: Watts, 1948) quoted from John Dewey, *Reconstruction of Philosophy* (New York: Mentor, 1948) p. 14.
11. Ibid. p. 14.
12. As Darlington pointed out with references to new developments in the natural sciences, 'it is no accident that bacteria were first understood by a canal engineer, that oxygen was isolated by a Unitarian minister, that the theory of infection was established by a chemist, the theory of heredity by a monastic school teacher, and the theory of evolution by a man who was unfitted to be a university instructor in either botany or zoology', and, Darlington added, the great innovators 'are the first to fear and doubt their discoveries'; ibid. pp. 14–15.
13. René Dubos, 'Review of Barry Commoner, The Closing Circle', *Environment*, vol. 14, no. 1 (Jan–Feb 1972) p. 48.
14. In lieu of a detailed bibliography we must confine ourselves to listing a few key names: A. N. Whitehead, John Dewey, Joseph Needham, Thorstein Veblen, L. A. Kroeber, Gunnar Myrdal, L. von Bertalanffy. For further details cf. K. William Kapp, *Towards a Science of Man in Society* (The Hague: Nizlioff, 1961).
15. Cf. Alan Coddington, 'The Economics of Ecology', *New Society* (Apr 1970) pp. 595–7.
16. So far very little attention has been paid to these cumulative causal processes; the great exceptions are of course the institutionalists such as Veblen and Myrdal. For an analysis of their key concepts of circular interdependencies and cumulative causation within the context of economics as a subsystem of the socio-cultural institutional composite system, see K. William Kapp, 'In Defense of Institutionalism', *Swedish Journal of Economics*, vol. LXX, no. 1 (1968) pp. 1–18.
17. David W. Fischer, 'On the Problems of Measuring Environmental Benefits and Costs', *Social Science Information*, 13, 2 (1973) p. 104.
18. Ibid. p. 8. Cf. also H. H. Liebhafsky, *The Nature of Price Theory* (Homewood, Ill.: Dorsey, 1968) p. 266.
19. Cf. K. William Kapp, 'Social Costs, Neo-Classical Economists, Environmental Planning: A Reply', *Environmental Policies and Development Planning in Contemporary China and Other Essays* (Paris: Mouton, 1974) pp. 99ff.
20. For a distinction of social (including environmental) indicators and norms, see ibid. pp. 129–38.
21. This brings our notion of normative economics close to that of political economics: the theory of controlled economic systems as developed by Adolf Loewe, *Economic Knowledge* (New York: Harper & Row, 1965); Cf. also R. L. Heilbronner, 'On the Possibility of Political Economics', *Journal of Economic Issues*, IV, 4 (1970) and Francois Hetman, *Society and the Assessment of Technology* (Paris: O.E.C.D., 1973) pp. 379–90, esp. p. 389.
22. For a formal demonstration of this incompatibility, see David Pearce, 'An Incompatibility in Planning for a Steady State and Planning for Maximum Economic Welfare', *Environment and Planning*, vol. 5 (1973) pp. 267–71; and, by the same author, 'Economics and Ecology', *Survey Papers in Economics*, no. 10 (1974).
23. 'L'écologie est intégrée sans douleur par la théorie néo-classique et la Nature devient un secteur économique susceptible d'être comptabilisé dans les schémas rassurants de l'équilibre'. Jan Dessau, 'Modèles dualistes de l'Environnement et Choix de Techniques'; paper presented at Symposium International, Analyse socio-économique de l'Environnement, Problèmes de Méthodes, Grenoble Conférence, mimeo. (1972) p. 8.
24. 'Loosely speaking, no argument on economic matters will get a reasonably wide hearing until it is set out as a "business proposition" in terms drawn from the conduct of business administration, business finance, national trade, salesmanship and publicity', Thorstein Veblen, 'Economic Theory in the Calculable Future', *American Economic Review*, vol. XV, no. 1, supplement (Mar. 1925) p. 53.
25. J. J. Spengler, 'Economics: Its History, Themes, Approaches', *Journal of Economic Issues*, 2 (Mar. 1968) p. 21.

THE STEADY-STATE ECONOMY*

Herman E. Daly

"All the rivers run into the sea: yet the sea is not full."

Ecclesiastes 1:7

As readers of *Economic Growth in the Future*[1] will be aware, the growth debate involves two related questions: (1) Is there a feasible alternative economic strategy that is not based on an assumption of continual growth? and (2) Is continual growth itself a feasible economic strategy? The answer here given to question 1 is "yes". The alternative strategy is called a "steady-state economy" and is defined and elaborated in the first section of this chapter. The answer given to question 2 is "no." The reasons why continual growth is neither possible nor desirable are discussed in the second section. If these two answers prove convincing, then the obvious third question is: What policies will best allow us to make the transition from a growth economy to a steady-state economy? The third section offers some policy suggestions that, though they will appear radical to some, are nevertheless firmly rooted in our basic institutions of private property and the price system. The suggested policies seek to avoid the romantic fallacy of assuming a "clean slate," while not falling prey to the crackpot realism of "business-as-usual."

The concept of a steady-state economy

The steady-state economy (SSE) is defined by four characteristics:

- A constant population of human bodies,
- A constant population or stock of artifacts (exosomatic capital or extentions of human bodies),
- The levels at which the two populations are held constant are sufficient for a good life and sustainable for a long future,
- The rate of throughput of matter-energy by which the two stocks are maintained is reduced to the lowest feasible level. For the population this means that birth rates are equal to death rates at low levels so that life expectancy is high. For artifacts it means that production equals depreciation at low levels so that artifacts are long lasting, and depletion and pollution are kept low.

Only two things are held constant: the stock of human bodies and the total stock or inventory of artifacts. Technology, information, wisdom, goodness, genetic characteristics, distribution of wealth and income, product mix, and so on, are *not* held constant.

Three magnitudes are basic to the concept of an SSE:

Stock is the total inventory of producers' goods, consumers' goods, and human bodies. It corresponds to Irving Fisher's (1906)[2] definition of capital and may be thought of as the set of all physical things capable of satisfying human wants and subject to ownership.

---

*Reprinted with permission from *Prospects for Growth*, ed. K. D. Wilson, 1976, Praeger, New York, pp. 263–281. (Professor Daly is Professor of Economics at Louisiana State University.)

Service is the satisfaction experienced when wants are satisfied, or "psychic income" in Irving Fisher's sense. Service is yielded by the stock. The quantity and quality of the stock determine the intensity of service. There is no unit for measuring service, so it may be stretching words a bit to call it a "magnitude." Nevertheless we all experience service or satisfaction and recognize differing intensities of the experience. Service is yielded over a period of time and thus appears to be a flow magnitude. But unlike flows, service cannot be accumulated. It is probably more accurate to think of service as a "psychic flux."[3]

Throughput is the entropic physical flow of matter-energy from nature's sources, through the human economy, and back to nature's sinks, and it is necessary for maintenance and renewal of the constant stocks.[4]

The relationship among these three magnitudes can best be understood in terms of the following simple identity.

$$\frac{\text{Service}}{\text{Throughput}} = \frac{\text{Service}}{\text{Stock}} \times \frac{\text{Stock}}{\text{Throughput}}$$

The final benefit of all economic activity is service. The original useful stuff required for yielding service, and which cannot be produced by man, but only used up, is low-entropy matter-energy—that is, the throughput. But throughput is not itself capable of directly yielding service. It must first be accumulated into a stock of artifacts. It is the stock that directly yields service. We can ride to town only in a member of the existing stock of automobiles. We cannot ride to town on the annual flow of automotive maintenance expenditures, nor on the flow of newly mined iron ore destined to be embodied in a new chassis, nor on the flow of worn rusting hulks into junkyards and auto graveyards. Stocks may be thought of as throughput that has been accumulated and frozen in structured forms capable of satisfying human wants. Eventually the frozen structures are "melted" by entropy, and what flowed into the accumulated stocks from nature then flows back to nature in equal quantity, but in entropically degraded quality. Stocks are intermediate magnitudes that belong at the center of analysis and provide a clean separation between the cost flow and the benefit flux. On the one hand stocks yield service, on the other hand stocks require throughput for maintenance. Service yielded is benefit; throughput required is cost.

In the SSE a different behavior mode is adopted with respect to each of the three basic magnitudes. Stock is to be satisfied—that is, maintained at a level that is sufficient for an abundant life for the present generation and ecologically sustainable for a long future. Service is to be maximized, given the constant stock. Throughput is to be minimized, given the constant stock. In terms of the two ratios on the right-hand side of the identity this means that the ratio, Service/Stock is to be maximized by maximizing the numerator, with denominator constant, while the ratio Stock/Throughput is maximized by minimizing the denominator, with numerator constant. These two ratios measure two kinds of efficiency. Service efficiency (Service/Stock) depends on allocative efficiency (does the stock consist of artifacts that people most want, and are they allocated to the most important uses), and on distributive efficiency (is the distribution of the stock among alternative people such that the trivial wants of some people do not take precedence over the basic needs of others). Standard economics has much of value to say about allocative efficiency but treats distribution under the heading of social justice rather than efficiency, thus putting it on the sidelines of disciplinary concern. Maintenance efficiency (Stock/Throughput) depends on durability (how long an individual artifact lasts), and on replaceability (how easily the artifact can be replaced when it finally does wear out). Maintenance efficiency measures the number of units of time over which a population of artifacts yields its service, while efficiency measures the intensity of that service per unit of time. Maintenance efficiency is limited by the second law of thermodynamics (nothing lasts forever, everything wears out). Service efficiency may conceivably increase forever, since the growing "magnitude", service, is nonphysical. There may, however, be physical limits to the capacity of human beings to experience service. But the definition of the SSE is in terms of physical stocks and throughput and is not affected by whether or not service could increase indefinitely.

Conceptually it is easier to think of stock as the operational policy variable to be directly controlled. Practically, however, as will be seen in the third section, it would be easier to control or limit throughput directly and allow the stock to reach the maximum level sustainable by the fixed throughput. This presents no problems.

The above concepts allow us to make an important distinction between growth and development. Growth refers to an increase in service that results from an increase in stock and throughput, with the two efficiency ratios constant. Development refers to an increase in the efficiency ratios, with stock constant (or, alternatively, an increase in service with throughput constant). Using these definitions we may say that an SSE develops but does not grow, just as the planet earth, of which it is a subsystem, develops without growing.

How do these concepts relate to GNP, the most conventional index of "growth"? GNP makes no distinction among the three basic magnitudes. It simply adds up value estimates of some services (the service of those assets that are rented rather than purchased, including human bodies, and omitting the services of all owned assets not rented during the current year), plus the value of the throughput flow (maintenance and replacement expenditures required to maintain the total stock intact), plus the value of current additions to stock (net investment). What sense does it make to add up benefits, costs, and change in inventory? The concept of an SSE is independent of GNP, and what happens to GNP in the SSE simply does not matter. It could go up or down. The behavior modes of satisfying stock and minimizing throughput would tend to lower GNP, while maximizing service would tend to raise it. On balance GNP would probably fall. So what? The best thing to do with GNP is to forget it and replace it with two separate social accounts, one measuring the value of service (benefit) and the other measuring the value of throughput (cost). In this way costs and benefits could be compared, although this aggregate macro-level comparison is not at all essential, since regardless of how it turns out the behavior modes remain the same with respect to each of the three basic magnitudes. Aggregate economic indexes should be treated with caution, since there are always some kinds of stupid behavior that would raise the index and thus become "justified." The amount of waste that has been justified in the name of increasing GNP is surely astronomical. Maximizing a sum whose principal component (throughput) is a cost just cannot be good economics.

Neither the concept nor the reality of an SSE is new. John Stuart Mill (1881) discussed the concept in his famous chapter "on the stationary state."[5] Historically man has lived for 99 percent of his tenure on earth in conditions very closely approximating a steady state. Economic growth is essentially a phenomenon of the last 200 years, and only in the last 50 years has it become the dominant goal of nations. The SSE of the future can be much more comfortable than those of the past, thanks to development (but not to growth).

The necessity and desirability of the SSE

It is one thing to define a concept and something else to show that its realization is possible, necessary, and desirable. A good starting point for this effort is provided by the conventional textbook definition of economics as "the study of the allocation of scarce means among competing ends, where the object of the allocation is the maximization of the attainment of those ends." This rather ponderous definition at least has the virtue of emphasizing that economics' fundamental concern is with ends and means. GNP, prices, elasticities, and so on, are all secondary and instrumental to the basic task of using means to satisfy ends. The growth debate and arguments for the necessity and desirability of the SSE can be much illuminated by a consideration of the total ends-means hierarchy as shown in Figure 1.

At the top of the hierarchy is the ultimate end—that which is intrinsically good and does not derive its goodness from any instrumental relation to some higher good. At the bottom is ultimate means — the useful stuff of the universe, low-entropy matter-energy, which cannot be made by man, and hence cannot be the end of any human activity. Each intermediate category in the hierarchy is an end with respect to lower categories and a means with respect to higher categories. Below the ultimate end we have intermediate ends, which are in a sense means in the service of the ultimate end. Intermediate ends are ranked with reference to the ultimate end. The mere fact that we speak of priorities among our goals presumes a first place, an ordering principle, an ultimate end. We may not be able to define it very well, but logically we are forced to recognize its existence. Above ultimate means are intermediate means (essentially stocks), which can be viewed as ends directly served by the use of ultimate means (throughput of low-entropy matter-energy).

On the left of the line are listed the traditional disciplines of study that correspond to each segment of the hierarchy. The central, intermediate position of economics is highly significant. In looking only at the middle range, economics has naturally not dealt with ultimates or absolutes, found only at the extremes, and has falsely assumed that the middle-range pluralities, relativities, and substitutabilities among competing ends and scarce means were representative of the whole hierarchy. Absolute limits are absent from the economists' paradigm because absolutes are encountered only in confrontation with the ultimate poles of the hierarchy, which have been excluded from the focus of our attention. Even ethics and technics exist for the economist only at the very periphery of his awareness.

In terms of this diagram economic growth implies the creation of ever more

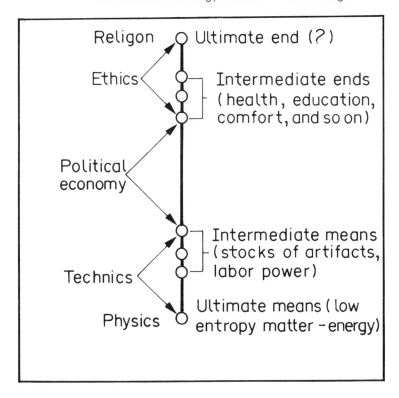

Figure 1. Ends—Means Hierarchy

intermediate means (stocks) for the purpose of satisfying ever more intermediate ends. Orthodox growth economics recognizes that particular resources might be limited, but does not recognize any general scarcity of all resources together.[6] The orthodox dogma is that technology can always substitute new resources for old, without limit. Growth economists also recognize that any single intermediate end or want can be satisfied for any given individual. But new wants keep emerging (and new people as well), so the aggregate of all intermediate ends is held to be insatiable, or infinite in number if not in intensity. The growth economist's vision is one of continuous growth in intermediate means (unconstrained by any scarcity of ultimate means)in order to satisfy ever more intermediate ends (unconstrained by any impositions from the ultimate end). Infinite means plus infinite ends equals growth forever.

A consideration of the ultimate poles of the spectrum, however, gives us a very different perspective. It forces us to raise two questions: (1) What, precisely, are our ultimate means, and are they limited in ways that cannot be overcome by technology? (2) What is the nature of the ultimate end, and is it such that, beyond a certain point, further accumulation of intermediate means (people and artifacts) not only fails to serve the ultimate end, but actually renders a disservice? It will be argued below that the answer to both sets of questions is yes.

The nature of the ultimate means limits the possibility of growth. The nature of the ultimate end limits the desirability of growth. Moreover, the interaction of desirability and possibility provides the economic limit to growth, which is the most stringent and should be the governing limit.

Paradoxically, growth economics has been both too materialistic and not materialistic enough. In ignoring the ultimate means and the laws of thermodynamics it has been insufficiently materialistic. In ignoring the ultimate end and ethics it has been too materialistic. Let us consider in more detail the implications of paying due attention to these ultimate poles. Since the subject of ultimate means is more concrete we will consider it first.

From a basic branch of physics, thermodynamics, we learn that for man's purposes the ultimate usable stuff of the universe is low-entropy matter-energy. To answer the question, "What is low entropy?" we can draw on the pioneering work of Nicholas Georgescu-Roegen.[7] In terms of materials, low entropy means structure, organization, concentration, order. Dispersed, randomly scattered molecules of any material are useless (high entropy). In terms of energy low entropy means capacity to do work, or concentrated, relatively high-temperature energy. Energy dispersed in equilibrium temperature with the general environment is useless (high entropy).

We have two sources of low entropy: terrestrial stocks of concentrated minerals, and the solar flow of radiant energy. The terrestrial source (minerals in the earth's crust) is obviously limited in total amount, though the rate at which we use it up is largely subject to our choice. The solar source is practically unlimited in total amount, but strictly limited in its rate of arrival to earth for use. Both sources of ultimate means are limited — one in total amount, the other in rate of use. Ultimate means are finite. Furthermore there is an enormous disproportion in the total amounts of the two sources: if all the world's fossil fuels could be burned up, they would provide the energy equivalent of only a few weeks of sunlight. The sun is expected to last for another 5 or 6 billion years.

This raises a cosmically embarrassing economic question: If the solar source is so vastly more abundant, why have we over the last 150 years shifted the physical base of our economy from overwhelming dependence on solar energy and renewable resources to overwhelming dependence on nonrenewable terrestrial minerals? An important part of the answer is that terrestrial stocks can, for a while at least, be used at a rate of man's own choosing—that is, rapidly. Solar energy and renewable resource usage is limited by the fixed solar flux and the natural rhythms of growth of plants and animals, which in turn provide a natural constraint on economic growth. But growth can be speeded beyond this income constraint, for a time at least, by consuming geological capital—by running down the reserves of terrestrial low entropy. If the object is high growth rates now, then it can be more easily attained by using up terrestrial sources rapidly. As growth results in population and per capita consumption levels that are beyond the capacity of renewable resources alone to support, then we face even greater pressure to continue consuming geological capital.

The difficulty is twofold. First, we will run out of terrestrial sources eventually. Second, even if we never ran out we would still face problems of ecological breakdown caused by a growing throughput of matter-energy. Even if technology were able to double the flow of solar energy (by far the cleanest source), the millions of years of past evolutionary adaptation to the usual rate would make a doubling of that rate totally catastrophic. The whole biosphere has evolved as a complex system around the fixed point of a given solar flux. Modern man is the only species that has broken the solar income budget. The fact that man has supplemented his fixed solar income by consuming terrestrial capital has thrown him out of balance with the rest of the biosphere. As stocks of artifacts and people have grown, the throughput necessary for their maintenance has had to grow also, implying more depletion and more pollution. Natural biogeochemical cycles become overloaded. Exotic substances are produced and thrown wholesale into the biosphere—substances with which the world has had no adaptive evolutionary experience, and which are consequently nearly always disruptive.

But are we not giving insufficient credit to technology in claiming that ultimate means are limited? Is not technology itself a limitless resource? No, it is not. All technologies, nature's as well as man's, run on an entropy gradient— that is, the total entropy of all outputs taken together is always greater than the total entropy of all inputs taken together. No organism can eat its own outputs and live, and no engine can run on its own exhaust. If the outputs of a process were of lower entropy than the inputs, once all inputs and outputs were accounted for, we would have a process that violates the second law of thermodynamics, and so far no such process has ever been observed. Technology itself depends on the ultimate means of low entropy. If low-entropy sources are not unlimited, then neither is technology.

It is especially ironic to be told by growth boosters that technology is freeing man from dependence on resources.[8] It has in fact done the opposite. Modern technology has made us *more* dependent on the *scarcer* of the two sources of ultimate means. In view of the popular belief in the omnipotence of technology, it is even more ironic to recall that the most basic laws of science are statements of impossibility: it is impossible to create or destroy matter-energy; it is impossible to have perpetual motion; it is impossible to exceed the speed of light; it is impossible to measure momentum and position simultaneously with greater accuracy; and so on. The remarkable success of physical science has been in no small measure due to its intelligent recognition of impossibilities and its refusal to attempt them. Paradoxically this success has, in the popular mind, been taken as "proof" that nothing is impossible.

The entropy law tells us that when technology increases order in one part of the universe it must produce an even greater amount of disorder somewhere else. If that "somewhere else" is the sun (as it is for nature's technology and for man's traditional preindustrial technology) then we need not worry. If "somewhere else" is here on earth, as it is for technologies based on terrestrial mineral deposits, then we had better pay close attention. The throughput flow maintains or increases the order within the human economy, but at the cost of creating greater disorder in the rest of the natural world, as a result of depletion and pollution. There is a limit to how much disorder can be produced in the rest of the biosphere and still allow it to function well enough to continue supporting the human subsystem. There is a limit to how much of the ecosphere can be converted into technosphere.

Although technology cannot overcome the limits here discussed, it could achieve a much better accommodation to them, and could work more in harmony with nature's technology than it has in the past. But an improved technological accommodation to limits, while certainly possible and desirable, is not likely to be forthcoming in a growth context, in an economy that would rather maximize throughput than reduce it. Such improvement is much more likely within the framework of an SSE, where profits would be made from development, not growth.

Let us now leave the issue of ultimate means and turn to a discussion of the ultimate end and the ways in which it limits the desirability of growth. The temper of the modern age resists any discussion of the ultimate end. Teleology and purpose, the dominant concepts of an earlier time, were banished from the mechanistic, reductionistic, positivistic mode of thought that came to be identified with the most recent phase of the evolution of science. Economics followed suit by reducing ethics to the level of personal tastes. Economics became the "mechanics of utility and self-interest," in Jevons' phrase. No questions are asked about whether individual priorities are right or wrong, or even about how they are formed. Whatever happens to interest the public is assumed to be in the public interest.

Our modern refusal to reason about the ultimate end merely assures the incoherence of our priorities, both individually and collectively. It leads to the tragedy of Herman Melville's Captain Ahab, whose means were all rational but whose purpose was insane. One cannot lend rationality to the reckless pursuit of a white whale by pointing to the sophisticated techniques of whaling that are being employed. To do more efficiently that which should not be done in the first place is a very perverse form of progress.

What is the ultimate end? The question is logically unavoidable. But only a minimum answer to such a maximum question is likely to command much consensus. As a minimum answer let me suggest that whatever the ultimate end is, it presupposes a respect for and continuation of creation and the evolutionary process through which god has bestowed upon us the gift of self-conscious life. Whatever values are put in first place, their further realization requires the continuation of life — the survival of biosphere and its evolutionary processes. This minimum answer begs many important questions: Survival and evolution in what direction? To what extent should evolution be influenced by man and to what extent should it be left spontaneous? For now, however, the only point is that survival must rank very high in the ends-means hierarchy, and consequently any type of growth that requires the creation of means that threaten survival should be forbidden. Nuclear power and the "plutonium economy" is a prime example of the kind of growth that must be halted.

But what about other kinds of growth? Are *all* kinds of physical growth subject to desirability limits? Is there such a thing as *enough* in the material realm, and is enough better than "more than enough"? Is "more than enough" inimical to survival? Certainly all organic needs can be satisfied and to go beyond enough is usually harmful. The only want that seems insatiable is the want for distinction, the desire to be in some way superior to one's neighbors. Even the want for distinction need not cause problems except when the main avenue of distinction in society is to have a larger income than the next fellow and to consume more.

The only way for everyone to earn more is to have aggregate growth. But that is precisely the rub. If everyone earns more, then where is the distinction? It is possible for everyone's *absolute* income to increase, but not for everyone's *relative* income to increase. To the extent that it is higher relative income that is important, growth becomes impotent. As British economist E. J. Mishan put it,

> In an affluent society, people's satisfactions, as Thorstein Veblen observed, depend not only on the innate or perceived utility of the goods they buy, but also on the status value of such goods. Thus to a person in a high income society, it is not only his absolute income that counts but also his relative income, his position in the structure of relative incomes. In its extreme form — and as affluence rises we draw closer to it — only relative income matters. A man would then prefer a 5 per cent reduction in his own income accompanied by a 10 per cent reduction in the incomes of others to a 25 per cent increase in both his income and the incomes of others.
>
> The more this attitude prevails — and the ethos of our society actively promote it — the more futile is the objective of economic growth for society as a whole. For it is obvious that over time everyone cannot become relatively better off.[9]

Aggregate growth can no more satisfy the relative wants of distinction than the arms race can increase security. The only way this self-cancelling effect and its resulting futility can be avoided is if growth is allowed to make the relatively well-off relatively better-off. But then the price of continuing growth would be ever-increasing inequality, and all the pious talk about "growth for the poor" would be seen as the evasion that it really is. When society has reached a level of affluence such that at the margin it is relative wants that are dominant, then aggregate growth becomes either futile or the source of increasing inequality. At some point growth becomes undesirable, even if still possible.

The effective limit to growth, however, is neither the desirability nor the possibility limit, but the interaction of desirability and possibility, that is, the *economic* limit. It is not necessary that the marginal benefits of growth should fall all the way to zero, nor that the marginal costs of growth should rise to infinity, but only that the two should become equal. As growth continues we know that marginal benefits fall and marginal costs rise and at some point they will become equal. We do not satisfy our ends in any random order, but strive always to satisfy our most pressing needs first. Likewise we do not use our low-entropy means in any order, but we exploit the highest-grade and most accessible resources first. This elementary rule of sensible behavior underlies both the law of diminishing marginal benefit and the law of increasing marginal costs, which are the very keystones of economic theory.

The possibility, desirability, and economic limits are depicted in Figure 2. As growth increases the total stock, total benefits rise at a diminishing rate, while total costs rise at an increasing rate. At point A the slope of the two curves are equal (marginal cost equals marginal benefit) and the vertical distance between the curves (net benefit) is a maximum. Point A is the economic limit and, though not easily recognized, is the relevant limit. If we overshoot point A we will meet either the possibility or desirability limit, though not necessarily in the order shown. (In fact, it is possible that marginal costs could discontinuously rise to infinity somewhere to the left of point A, and that the possibility limit would occur before the economic limit.) At point B the marginal benefit of

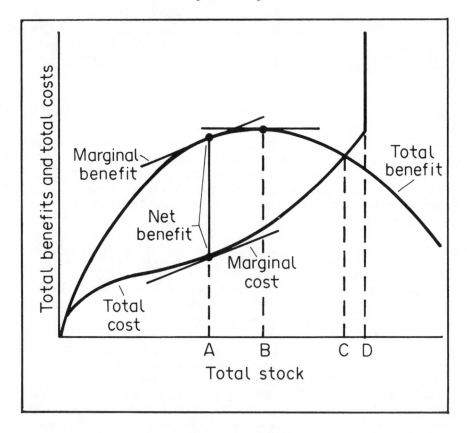

Figure 2. Economic Limits

growth (slope of total benefit curve) has fallen to zero (horizontal). Even if the costs of growth were zero we should not grow beyond B. At point D the marginal costs of growth become infinite (vertical slope) and growth would perforce end, regardles of benefits. Once we have passed point A, further growth makes us worse off, not better off. But it seems that the experience of reduced well-being is attributed to the heavy hand of commodity scarcity, and the call is for more growth, which makes us still worse off, leading to the call for still more growth, and so on. Like Alice on the other side of the looking glass, our image of reality becomes inverted and the faster we run the behinder we get. Our journalists and pundits defend growth by arguing that the total cumulative benefits of past growth still outweigh the total costs—"Thanks to growth the average man of today is better off than the average man of 300 years ago, therefore further growth must be good." They argue as if point C rather than point A were the economic limit and are guilty of confusing totals with marginals.

But the growth economist will rightly point out that our diagram is too static.

Technical progress and the emergence of new wants shift the cost curve down and the benefits curve up, and point A will move ever to the right, and growth in stocks will always be called for. There are two replies to this objection. First, even though the curves shift apart, point A need not move to the right. It could remain fixed or move to the left. It all depends on how the curves shift, because the location of point A is determined by the *slopes* of the two curves, not their positions. To assume that point A will always move to the right as the curves shift seems to overspecify the kind of dynamic change permitted. The second reply is that, even assuming the necessary rightward shift of point A, there are limits to how far apart the curves can be shifted. Our discussion of ultimate means and the second law assures us that there are limits to the efficiency increase represented by a downward shift of the total cost curve. Likewise our discussion of the ultimate end leads to the presumption that there is such a thing as enough in the material realm. Time sets a limit to how many artifacts can be serviceably used in a day. Perhaps the intensity of enjoyment of a given stock can increase forever (a doubtful proposition), but that would not contradict the SSE, which is defined in terms of constant stocks, not constant service. But in a growing economy service efficiency is likely to fall. As the growing throughput pushes against biophysical limits it provokes a decline in service efficiency. More of the stock must be devoted to the defensive use of repairing life-support systems that formerly provided their services gratis. Also, in our economy billions are spent to push up artificially the marginal benefits of growth by stimulating new wants through commercial propaganda. In a sense, these billions measure the degree to which our natural recognition of "enoughness" or sufficiency must be overcome by artful cajolery. Whether these expenditures really raise the benefit curve is debatable, since the stimulated wants are often meretricious. Likewise, billions are spent on research and development to lower the cost curve. The net result of these expenditures may be to raise the true cost curve as a result of irresponsible technical razzle-dazzle (for example, fission power and the supersonic transport), and the lavish use of resources induced by low prices that fail to reflect the full dimensions of scarcity.

But such diagrams, though of heuristic value, are not operational because we have no national accounts measuring either the costs or benefits of growth. We have only GNP, which is merely a measure of activity and lumps together costs, benefits, and changes in stock. As previously noted, an SSE would seek to measure the value of service (benefit) in one account and the value of throughput (cost) in a separate account. Only then would we have even a remote chance of getting an operational estimate of where point A lies.

But there are many sensible policies that can be taken in the absence of an operational estimate of the optimum level of stocks, which may in any case be a will-o'-the-wisp. Once the optimum level is reached it follows that the optimum growth rate is zero. But it is not necessary to know the optimum level in order to argue for a zero growth rate. Even if we have not yet reached the optimum we should still learn to live in an SSE so that we could remain at the optimum once we got there rather than grow through it. We can achieve an SSE at existing, historically given levels without being forever frozen there. If we later discover that a larger or smaller stock would be better, then we could always grow or decline to the preferred level, at which we would again be stable. Growth, or decline, would then be a temporary adjustment process, not a norm.

My own belief is that we have passed the optimum and in the future will have to reduce both population and per capita consumption. But the issue of the optimum level for a nation is enormously difficult because four related questions must be answered simultaneously: (1) What size population do we want, (2) living at what standard of stocks (and throughput) per capita, (3) for how long, (4) on the basis of what kinds of technology? The answer given to each of these questions affects the answers given to the others. Also, we should ask whether the level we choose for the United States can be generalized to the world as a whole. Currently, the 6 percent of the world's population in the United States consumes around 30 percent of the world's annual production of non-renewable resources. To generalize this standard to 100 percent of the world's people would require, at minimum, a sixfold increase in current resource flows. In addition, to supply the world with the "standing crop" of industrial metals embodied in the existing artifacts in the ten richest nations would require more than 60 years' world production of these metals at 1970 rates.[10] The ecological disruption caused by the next sixfold increase would be greater per unit of resource produced because of diminishing returns. If world energy use continues to grow at 5 percent annually, then in 200 years man would be producing as much energy as he receives from the sun. Before then global climatological limits will restrict energy use, and these limits may be felt within 30 to 50 years.[11] In fact, we may already be experiencing climatological changes provoked by man's energy use. In any event it is sobering to recognize that man's energy requirements are now as great as those of all other terrestrial organisms put together.

These considerations do not constitute proof, but they are sufficient to induce strong doubt that US levels are generalizable, either to the world as a whole or to very many future generations, much less to both. High and increasing levels of population and per capita consumption have been bought by sacrificing the possibility of extending such a condition either to the future or to poor nations of the present. Attempts to generalize the ungeneralizable are leading to technological adventurism of the most fanatical kind. Space, the green revolution, and atomic power are recent promises of a technical solution that have proven empty and are threatening much worse.

The SSE would stop mindless growth in stocks of artifacts and people and would allow a less driven and more judicious choice of technology, as well as the possibility of sparing more resources for use both by future generations and present people in poor countries. The SSE is not a panacea. Even an SSE will not last forever, nor will it overcome the entropy law and the law of diminishing returns. But it would permit our economy to die gracefully of old age rather than prematurely from the cancer of growth mania.

Policies for an SSE

How can we achieve an SSE without enormous disruption? The difficult part is mustering the moral resources and political will to do it. The technical problems are small by comparison. People often overestimate the technical problems because they mistakenly identify an SSE with a failed growth economy. A situation of nongrowth can come about in two ways: As the success of steady-stage policies or as the failure of growth policies. Nongrowth resulting from the failure of a growth economy to grow is chaotic beyond repair. But the fact that airplanes fall from the air if they try to stand still does not mean that a helicopter cannot stand still.

In an effort to stimulate discussion on policies for attaining an SSE, I have suggested three institutions that seem to me to provide the necessary social control with a minimum sacrifice of individual freedom. They build on the existing bases of private property and the price system and are thus fundamentally conservative, though they will appear radical to some. The kinds of institutions needed follow straight from the definition of an SSE: "constant stocks of people and artifacts maintained at chosen levels that are sufficient for a good life and sustainable for a long future, by the lowest feasible rate of throughput."

Let us leave population issues to one side. Of all the population control schemes suggested, I prefer the transferable birth license plan, first advocated by Kenneth Boulding,[12] then elaborated by Herman Daly[13] and by Heer.[14] For purposes of this discussion, however, I will invite the reader to substitute his own favorite population control scheme if he does not like that one.

A constant aggregate stock of artifacts will result from holding the throughput flow constant by means of a depletion quota auction, to be discussed below. Since aggregate growth can no longer be appealed to as the "solution" to poverty, we must face the distribution issue directly by setting up a distributist institution, which would limit the range of inequality to some justifiable and functional degree. This could be accomplished by setting minimum income and maximum income and wealth limits for individuals and families, and a maximum size for corporations. The maximum and minimum would define a range within which inequality is legitimate and beyond which it is not. The exact numbers are of secondary importance, but just suppose a minimum of $7,000 and a maximum of $70,000 on family income. The idea of a minimum income is familiar, but the notion of a maximum is not, because in the growth paradigm it is not necessary. But in the steady-state paradigm the total is constant and this implicitly sets a maximum on individual income. Some limits on inequality are essential, though we may debate just how much inequality is legitimate.

The key institution would be the depletion quota auction by which the annual amount extracted of each basic resource would be set and the quota rights auctioned by the government in conveniently divisible units. The resource market would become two-tiered. First, the government, as monopolist, would auction the limited quota rights to many resource buyers, who, having purchased their quota rights, would enter the second tier of the market where they would confront many resource sellers in a competitive market. Buyers would pay the resource producers the market price and surrender the requisite quota rights to the producer at the time of purchase. The firms in the extraction industry would be audited to make sure that production plus change in inventories balanced with quota certificates collected.

Figure 3 illustrates more clearly how things would work. DD′ is the market demand curve for the resource in question, and SS′ is the industry supply curve. A depletion quota in the aggregate amount Q is imposed, shown by the vertical line QQ′. The total price paid per unit of the resource (unit price paid to

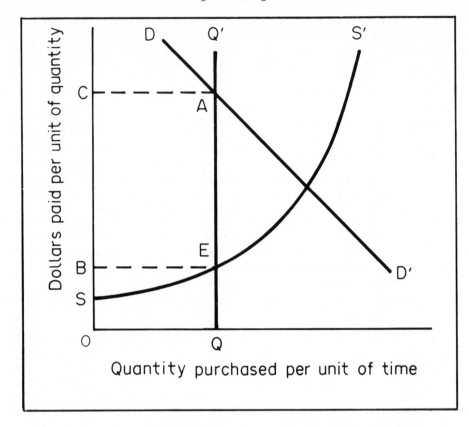

Figure 3. The Depletion Quota Auction System

resource producer plus unit price of the quota right paid to the government) is OC. Of the total price OC the amount OB is the price paid to resource producers, and BC is the price paid to the government for the quota right. Of the total amount paid, OQAC, the amount OSEQ is cost, reflecting necessary supply price (extraction costs), the remainder, SEAC is surplus, or rent. Rent is defined as payment in excess of supply price. Of the total rent area the amount BES is differential rent and accrues to the resource producers as profit. The remainder, the amount CAEB, is pure scarcity rent and accrues to the government. As a monopolist in the sale of quota rights the government is able to extract the full amount of pure scarcity rent that results from lower quantity and higher price.

Let us review what is achieved by the depletion quota auction. First, the throughput of basic resources is physically limited, and with it the rate of depletion and pollution associated with that resource. Allocation of the fixed resource aggregate among competing uses and firms is done by the market. The price of the resource increases; inducing greater efficiency of use, both in production and in consumption. Resource-saving technical improvement is induced, and so is recycling. The monopoly profits resulting from the higher prices are captured by the government, while resource producers earn normal competitive profits. The government revenues could be used to finance the minimum income part of the distributist institution. Efficiency is served by high resource prices, equity is served by redistributing the proceeds of the higher prices to the poor, and by a maximum limit on incomes of the rich.

What criteria are there for setting the "proper" aggregate quota amounts for each resource? For renewable resources there is the fairly objective criterion of maximum sustainable yield. For nonrenewables there is, of course, no sustainable yield. But economist John Ise suggested 50 years ago that nonrenewables should be priced equal to or more than their nearest renewable substitute.[15] Thus virgin timber should be priced at least as much per board foot as replanted timber; petroleum should be priced at its BTU equivalent in terms of sugar or wood alcohol, assuming that it is in fact the closest renewable substitute. For nonrenewables with no reasonably close renewable substitute, the matter is simply a question of how fast should we use it up, that is, an ethical weighing of present versus future wants. One further criterion might be added: Even if a resource is in no danger of depletion, its use may produce considerable pollution (for example, coal), and depletion quotas may be imposed with the objective of limiting pollution, the other end of the throughput pipeline.

The combination of these three institutions presents a nice reconciliation of equity and efficiency and provides the ecologically necessary macro control with the least sacrifice of micro freedom and variability. The market is relied upon to allocate resources and distribute incomes within imposed ecological and ethical boundaries. The market is not allowed to set its own boundaries but is free within the boundaries imposed. Setting the boundaries externally is necessary. It is absurd to expect that market equilibria will automatically coincide with ecological or demographic equilibria, or with a reasonably just distribution of wealth and income. The very notions of "equilibrium" in economics and ecology are antithetical. In macroeconomics equilibrium refers not to physical magnitudes at all, but to a balance of desires between savers and investers—equilibrium means full employment at a stable price level. This implies, under current institutions, a positive flow of net investment to offset positive savings. Net investment implies increasing stocks and a growing throughput, that is, a biophysical *dis*equilibrium. Physical boundaries guaranteeing reasonable ecological equilibrium must be imposed on the market in quantitative terms.

How do these proposals differ from the orthodox economists' prescription of "internalizing externalities via pollution taxes"? Pollution taxes are price controls on the output end of the throughput, while depletion quotas are quantitative controls on the input end. Depletion is spatially far more concentrated than pollution, and consequently much easier to monitor. Quantity should be the control variable rather than price because prices cannot limit aggregate throughput. Higher relative prices on resources would induce substitution and bring the resource content per unit of output down to some minimum. But prices cannot limit the number of units of output produced, and therefore cannot limit the total volume of resource throughput. For every increase in price there is an equal increase in someone's income, or in the government revenue. Aggregate income is always sufficient to purchase the growing aggregate supply, regardless of prices. In the famous words of Say's Law, "Supply creates its own demand." Taxes, by raising relative prices, could provide a one-shot reduction in aggregate throughput by reducing the throughput per dollar's worth of output down to some feasible minimum, but the number of units of output could keep growing, unless the government ran an ever-growing budget surplus. Finally, it is quantity that affects the biosphere, not price. It is safer to set ecological limits in terms of fixed quantities, and to let errors and unexpected changes work themselves out in price changes, than to set prices and let errors and omissions cause quantity changes.

The "internalization of externalities" is a good strategy for fine-tuning the allocation of resources by making relative prices better measures of relative marginal costs. But it does not enable the market to set its own absolute physical bounds. To give an analogy: proper allocation arranges the weight in a boat optimally, so as to maximize the load that can be carried. But there is still an absolute limit to how much weight a boat can carry, even if optimally arranged. The price system can spread the weight evenly, but unless supplemented by an external absolute limit it will just keep on spreading the increasing weight evenly until the evenly loaded boat sinks. No doubt the boat would sink evenly, ceteris paribus, but that is little comfort.

Two distinct questions must be asked about these proposed institutions for achieving an SSE. First, would they work if people accepted the need for an SSE and, say, voted these institutions into effect? Second, would people ever accept the goal of an SSE? In this last section I have argued that the answer to the first question is "yes." Although the answer to the second question would surely be "no" if a vote were held today; that is because the growth paradigm is still dominant. With time the concepts and arguments sketched out in the first two sections will look more and more appealing and will themselves be sharpened, as the real facts of life push the growth paradigm into ever greater anomalies, contradictions, and practical failures.

Notes

1. Edison Electric Institute, *Economic Growth in the Future: the Growth Debate in National and Global Perspective* (New York: McGraw-Hill, 1976).
2. Irving Fisher, *The Nature of Capital and Income* (London: Macmillan, 1906).
3. Nicholas Georgescu-Roegen, *The Entropy Law and the Economic Process* (Cambridge, Mass,: Harvard University Press, 1971).
4. Kenneth Boulding, "The Economics of the Coming Spaceship Earth," in *Environmental Quality in a Growing Economy*, ed. Henry Jarrett (Baltimore: Johns Hopkins University Press, 1966); and Georgescu-Roegen, *The Entropy Law*.
5. John Stuart Mill, *Principles of Political Economy* (New York: Appleton-Century-Crofts, 1881).
6. Harold Barnett and Chandler Morse, *Scarcity and Growth* (Baltimore: Johns Hopkins University Press for Resources for the Future, 1963), p. 11.
7. Georgescu-Roegen, *The Entropy Law*.
8. Barnett; *Scarcity and Growth*, p. 11.
9. E. J. Mishan, "Growth and Anti-Growth: What are the Issues?" *Challenge*, May/June 1973, p. 30.
10. Harrison Brown, "Human Materials Production as a Process in the Biosphere," *Scientific American*, September 1970, pp. 194–208.
11. Alvin Weinberg, Editorial, "Global Effects of Man's Production of Energy," *Science*, October 18, 1974, p. 205.
12. Kenneth Boulding, *The Meaning of the Twentieth Century* (New York: Harper and Row, 1964).

13. Herman Daly, *Toward a Steady-State Economy* (San Francisco: Freeman, 1973).
14. David Heer, "Marketable Licenses for Babies: Boulding's Proposal Revisited," *Social Biology*, Spring 1975, pp. 1–16.
15. John Ise, "The Theory of Value as Applied to Natural Resources," *American Economic Review*, June, 1925, pp. 284–91.

ARE ENVIRONMENTAL PROBLEMS A CHALLENGE TO
ECONOMIC SCIENCE?*

David Pearce

Introduction

In a characteristically stimulating introduction to a collection of essays on the "steady state" economy, Herman Daly likens the discovery of the social and economic implications of the earth's finite resources and finite capacity for coping with pollution to one of Thomas Kuhn's "paradigm shifts" in science.[1] A paradigm shift occurs when an existing tenet of faith that underlies the internally coherent structure of science is jettisoned in favour of a new paradigm which in turn tends to be generated by some anomaly thrown up by the first paradigm. Paradigm shifts have been common in economics where "schools of thought" seem not to prevail for much longer than half a century. Currently, the Keynesian paradigm is under serious attack from those who would seek to reintroduce variants of prior paradigms such as classicism and Marxism. Equally, the conventional paradigm in environmental economics is under attack from what we might best call the "ecological paradigm".

Basically, this paradigm seeks to produce an economic science that observes ecological limits to economic activity. Once these limits are introduced, it is argued, they imply the non-operability of the standard neoclassical welfare economics in which "optima" are identified according to the expressed valuations of goods and "disgoods" (e.g. pollution) made by individuals. Essentially, setting social standards and levels of activity according to these optimality rules cannot guarantee the longer-term survival of the human species or, at the very least, survival at some "reasonable" standard of civilised behaviour. The "optima" identified by neoclassical economics must therefore be illusory and the illusion must arise because of some failure on the part of the neoclassical paradigm to identify the essential features of a finite earth which is sustained by relations of ecological interdependence between species and between species and their environments. This may be contrasted with the "conventional" paradigm which sees environmental problems as instances of external effects and hence analysable in terms of market imperfections.

As Kuhn predicts, members of the opposing schools of thought find correspondence in their views difficult to achieve, and, indeed, communication itself becomes difficult, often degenerating into an *ad hominem* exchange of views. In the context of environmental economics, we have those who support the "ecological paradigm" referring to economics as being "obsessed with economic growth", "overly materialistic", ignorant of "physical and biological

*Reprinted with permission from *Ethics in Science & Medicine*, Vol. 2, 1977, pp. 79–88.
(Professor Pearce is in the Department of Political Economy, University of Aberdeen.)

processes", and so on. In terms of Kuhn's analysis, however, one oddity of this exchange of views is that the attack on conventional environmental economics has come, in the main, from non-economists. Paradigm shifts have invariably involved revolutions brought about from *within* the profession, and this is undoubtedly true of all paradigm shifts in economics to date. One is tempted to argue, then, that the ecological paradigm will not succeed unless it has adherents from within the profession. These exist. Indeed, the shift from conventional economics to ecological economics, if such it be, has already been marked by severe self-criticism in the economics profession. Kurt Kapp[2] has spoken of the need to "raise new questions about the adequacy and relevance of the old framework of analysis", and Alan Coddington has gone further in suggesting that "the greatest service economists can render to posterity is to remain silent".[3] On the other hand, it would be wrong to exaggerate the power of the ecological adherents within the profession, at least in terms of the vocal expression of their views. As such, whether a paradigm shift will finally occur is going to depend crucially on how well-informed the non-economist's criticism of economic approaches to the environment is.

The conventional paradigm

What the ecological paradigm seeks to replace is the systematic application of neoclassical welfare economics to environmental problems. It is instructive to consider how the neoclassical view has evolved.

Virtually any economic activity requiring social evaluation involves gains for some and losses for others. This fundamental fact of life immediately renders the application of the so-called Pareto principle — that a policy should be judged socially worthwhile only if at least some individuals prefer the new state of affairs and no-one prefers the old state — impotent for policy purposes. Hopes for developing a calculus that permitted the evaluation of states in which there are gainers and losers received a serious blow from Robbins in 1932 when he argued that we cannot compare preferences and dispreferences because of the impossibility of "interpersonal comparisons of utility".[4] The most we can say is that A prefers to move from social state X to social state Y, but that B prefers Y to X. We have no rules for aggregating the two preference orderings.

Whilst the success of Robbins' attack can be held to underlie the emergence of powerful positivist forces in economics, forces which to this day dominate the profession, it also generated fears that economics would end up "shirking live issues" so as to be "very conducive to the euthanasia of our science".[5] In the light of such worries, the so-called "compensation test" emerged, formulated in slightly different ways by Hicks and Kaldor in 1939. Essentially, the test sanctions a policy if and only if those who gain *could* use part of their gains to compensate those who lose. The compensation must be exact so that we can say of the losers that, after compensation, they are as content as they were before. Of course they will now hold a different "bundle" of commodities—they will have lost, say, some scenery but will have received instead some cash payment which they regard as equally valuable. Hence they can be held to be indifferent about the move to the new social state. The gainers, on the other hand, prefer the new state, even after compensation is paid out of their gains. We now have a situation which meets the Pareto rule: no one "disprefers" the new situation, and some prefer it.*

Although the compensation test has been subjected to numerous criticisms, many of them profoundly serious, it has survived in economics through its embodiment in cost–benefit analysis. For, to say that social benefits must exceed social costs for a project to be judged socially worthwhile is no more than to say that the beneficiaries must be *capable* of compensating the losers with some benefits left over. Indeed, one of the oddities of the recent history of the neoclassical paradigm is that the compensation rule grew in strength and influence through its subtle underpinning of a highly practical and practised evaluation technique, while at the same time being subjected to what many professional economists would have regarded as devastating methodological criticism in the theoretical literature.

Part of the attraction that the compensation test framework has had for normative economists comes from the fact that the value judgements underlying the framework are the same as those which underlie the operation of a free market system. That is, *laissez-faire* has an ethical attraction to those who think that social decision rules should universally reflect individuals' preferences, and that those preferences should be weighted according to the economic power of individuals—i.e. by income and wealth. Essentially, these two value judgements also define the ethical basis of neoclassical welfare economics, so that we can expect a perfectly functioning free market system to secure a welfare optimum in the Kaldor–Hicks sense. Indeed, a considerable economic literature has been devoted to theorems demonstrating exactly this. The emergence of external effects, such as pollution, has made the analysis more complex but the outcome requires only slight modification. For all that is necessary is that prices in the market system be adjusted through commodity taxes designed to reflect the external costs involved for the system to produce a welfare optimum. Of course, such a price system is no longer perfectly "free" in the original sense, but it continues to rely on purely behavioural response to market prices, albeit prices that now contain a pollution tax content.

The attractiveness of the neoclassical paradigm to economists thus rests on (a) its historical foundations, which are relatively long and deeply entrenched in economics, (b) its relationship to the supposedly optimal workings of free market systems, which themselves have always had a particular attraction to economists, and (c) the illusion that the compensation test in some way overcame the initial problem posed by Robbins, on interpersonal comparisons of utility, and, if not exactly value-free, at least had value judgements that commanded wide assent.†

---

*We shall not dwell on the real oddity of the Kaldor–Hicks rule, namely that it does not require compensation to be *actually* paid. But if it is not paid it is clear that losers really *are* in a dispreferred situation—i.e. are "worse" off—so that a distributional issue arises. Hence the need for a clear ethic on how welfare ought to be distributed. Equity issues are now much more in vogue than they were in the heyday of positivist economics, a few diehards apart.

†Some commentators take the view that the Kaldor–Hicks test was proposed *because* it obviated the need for value judgements. If this was the belief, it was clearly an erroneous one.[6]

While there probably is wide assent to the value judgement that social decision rules should reflect individual preferences, it is hard to imagine a consensus on letting those preferences be weighted by economic power. See Nash, Stanley and Pearce.[7,8]

In the context of environmental problems, the neoclassical paradigm argues for no special treatment. Pollution is a by-product of economic activity that generates gains to many, in the sense that it provides them with the goods they want, their wants in turn being expressed through the market mechanism. There are therefore gainers and losers. If the dispreferences about pollution exceed the preferences for the goods generating pollution, the cost–benefit rule says that the output of goods (and hence pollution) should be reduced, or that producers and consumers of the goods should pay higher prices for a given output in order to install pollution abatement equipment, thus reducing pollution. There must exist, then, some "optimal" level of pollution at which point the extra benefits from the goods produced just equal the extra costs in terms of pollution suffering. To reduce the level of pollution further is not justified on the neoclassical paradigm because the benefits from such a reduction (in terms of pollution reduced) are less than the costs (in terms of goods foregone).

It is important, then, to see that the argument for optimal levels of pollution greater than zero has a long heritage in economics. To secure a paradigm shift in environmental economics requires more than a critique of particular application of cost–benefit analysis. It requires either an actual overthrow of the neoclassical paradigm, itself, *or* a demonstration that the ecological constraints on economic systems dominate the search for neoclassical optima (or both).

The non-economists' critique

It was argued earlier that the success of a paradigm shift in conventional environmental economics requires valid criticism from outside the profession. Sadly, much of the criticism so far advanced is poorly based. Not a small part of it relies on some kind of emotive eloquence which, when subjected to closer examination, seems to reduce to nothing that can be said to constitute useful criticism. Thus, Ian McHarg has charged economists with seeing the "world as commodity", a view which "fails to evaluate and incorporate physical and biological processes".[9] In a revealing paragraph, he declares:

> "The economists, with a few exceptions, are the merchants' minions and together they ask with the most barefaced effrontery that we accommodate our value system to theirs. Neither love nor compassion, health nor beauty, dignity nor freedom, grace nor delight are important unless they can be priced. If they are non-price benefits or costs they are relegated to inconsequence. The economic model proceeds inexorably to its self-fulfillment of more and more despoilation, uglification and inhibition to life, all in the name of progress—yet paradoxically, the components which the model excludes are the most important human ambitions and accomplishments and the requirements for survival".

What the economist would like to know, however, is first, why the non-economist thinks concern about beauty, dignity and freedom will not be reflected in individuals' preferences, for if they are, then measuring preferences will automatically measure the degree of concern for these more grandiloquent variables in the system. Indeed, the economist would argue that these other variables are logically subsumed in preferences since it is difficult to see how else they would become translated into behaviour. Of course, the intensity with which such concerns are felt ought also to be reflected in any ultimate decision guiding calculus. Here again, the economist would argue that he can handle such a requirement within the bounds of cost–benefit analysis. Second, even if concern about beauty is in some way *extra* to the system of preferences we must ask the critic how he would then have *social* decisions made about activities that do involve trading off, say, beauty and something else. For the critic of economics it is clear that the trade-off is *personally* weighted heavily in favour of beauty, but, unless we are to have some elitist or dictatorial imposition of preferences, we must know how others express their trade-off between beauty and something else. For it is a fact of existence in a finite world that trade-offs must occur. In short, attacks on economics by the literary elite appear either to founder on lack of understanding of the role of preferences in normative economics, or on their own failure to offer any decision-guiding rules.

In a similar vein, Gordon Rattray Taylor speaks of the "bankruptcy of economics", arguing that economics works only for items which have market prices and not for items that lie outside the market system. Thus, economics "fails most seriously ... in preserving unique existing values, which nature provides free. However great the demand for fine scenery, no industry can manufacture it and sell it, just as no industry can manufacture and sell clean rivers or clean air. Moreover, since no price can be assigned to these assets, *when they come into competition with something on which a price can be set, they take second place*", (our italics).[10]

The argument that extra market phenomena have a lower importance rating in economics than market phenomena has a wide currency among critics of economic science. Unfortunately it too reflects a failure to understand the difference between what economists do and what decision makers do with the analyses produced by economists. There is nothing *in* economic science that declares non-market phenomena to be less important. If decision makers choose to attach lower weights to such things because of what has been called "misplaced correctness", this can scarcely be held to reflect some failing in economics. It would reflect a disagreement between the critic and the politician over the relevant weights. But this would seem to make the idea of placing monetary values on non-market phenomena *more* essential, not less. And yet those attempts that have been made by economists to put monetary values on non-market phenomena meet with still more vehement criticism. The economist is thus effectively precluded from public favour whatever his action—if he fails to value items the critic fears they will be downgraded, but if he offers a valuation he is accused of "measuring the immeasurable".

In fact, of course, what the economist is trying to do is to measure preferences for non-market phenomena. This aim at least is a laudable one unless, again, someone can show how else decision rules are to be formulated. The fact that the economist's measuring rod happens to be money is perhaps the real cause of the problem since it elicits almost theological objections about "materialism". But if instead of speaking of "money values" economists spoke of "preference measures" one wonders if the storm of controversy would be so great. And yet that is all that the money measure is, and it reflects the fact that the revelation of preferences is something that goes on repeatedly, day in, day out, through mar-ket *and non-market* behaviour. That economics began as a subject confined to market analysis in no way means that it is conceptually confined in this way.

It seems fair to argue, then, that the attempted "paradigm" shift towards an "ecological economics" cannot be justified in terms of finding criteria other than individual preferences by which to establish a normative framework. Nor does the market, non-market antipathy actually exist *within* economics. Those who seek to implement the paradigm shift must search elsewhere. There are however at least two important qualifications to a preference-oriented normative framework for environmental economics, one of which reflects deficiencies in information flows to individuals and the other of which concerns the problem of defining the population that is permitted to express preferences. Arguably, these modifications alter the framework of environmental economics, but not, one suspects, sufficiently to constitute a "revolution" such as we would expect from a Kuhnian paradigm shift. These important qualifications are discussed in the final sections of this paper. For the moment, however, we turn to the other main strand in the attack on conventional environmental economics.

Spaceship earth

The second strand of the "ecological" attack on economics does in fact have all the hallmarks of a Kuhnian paradigm shift in that the criticism appears fundamental *and* originates from within the profession. The criticism originates with Boulding's celebrated 'spaceship earth' essay.[11]

Essentially, Boulding draws attention to the finiteness of natural resources and to the finiteness of the environment's capacity for absorbing and degrading waste. In such a context, he argues, we cannot continue to seek maximisation of the *throughput* of the system (the *flow* of materials and energy, which is very roughly approximated by GNP) but must instead seek maintenance of the stock and preferably, an increasing ratio of stock to throughput with the stock held constant. If we are to measure the stock in economic terms it must be as some value of existing capital—man-made and "natural"—so that increasing the ratio of stock to flow can only occur by reducing the flow.

Boulding's highly general formulation of the aim of such a spaceship economy has usually been construed as a recommendation of "zero growth" in national output. Certainly, if national output constitutes the throughput of the system (the "gross national cost") it cannot, on Boulding's prescription, be permitted to rise. According to Boulding's actual words, however, it can fall as long as the stock measure remains constant, permitting efficiency in the use of throughput to be gained. The crucial issue, then, must be the size of the stock. But here, oddly, Boulding is of little help, as are his followers. For we have no guidance on the vital issues of (a) how to *value* the stock, and (b) how to determine the *optimum* value. On valuation, Boulding says that "the essential measure of the success of the economy is not production and consumption at all, but the *nature*, extent, *quality* and *complexity* of the total capital stock, *including in this the state of the human bodies and minds included in the system*".[11] [our italics] But this is scarcely helpful in thinking about how a social objective is to be framed. Elsewhere, Boulding has drawn attention to the fact that ecology lacks the kinds of single-valued aggregates (such as GNP) that economists use, but it is clear that his own comments imply some multi-valued entity the precise nature of which is difficult to pin down.[12]

Boulding's followers have narrowed the stock-flow problem down to conventionally measured income and wealth and to population. If we consider income and wealth alone, it is immediately clear that we require some rule for determining *both* (a) the level of wealth in an "ecologically-minded" society *and* (b) the level of income.

The level of wealth is not determinate in any of the "steady-state" models advanced in the literature. Rather it is (presumably) historically determined, being set at whatever level happens to pertain when the steady-state economy is implemented. But there can be no normative rationale for this: there may be good reasons for reducing the stock via the destruction of capital, or by letting depreciation of the stock exceed the throughput devoted to replacement. One "ecological" reason for such a move would be to reduce the rate of resource use and the pollution impact brought about by the level of real investment necessary to maintain a large stock. In short, the concept of spaceship earth tells us little or nothing about how the *size* of the stock in such an economy is to be determined.

The determination of the rate of throughput is similarly indeterminate. As Daly and others correctly note, a given stock can be sustained with a high level of throughput if the level of consumption out of income is set high, or with a low level of throughput if consumption levels are set low. The most that can be said for determinacy in such a system is that, once the stock level is established, the investment component of throughput is determined by the rate of depreciation of the stock since only replacement investment is permitted. But the consumption component is indeterminate. Daly's answer is that it should be set "as low as possible"[1] [p. 14] but we are offered no guidance as to how this should be determined. Of course, *any* positive rate of throughput is detrimental in terms of resource use and pollution impact unless (a) resource use is met from recycling of past wastes, and (b) residuals disposal is held below the environment's assimilative capacity. But the "total recycling society" is a myth if by it is meant that 100 percent of current consumption is met from past wastes. First, energy inputs are not recyclable, and, second, the restructuring of final demand necessary to produce products that can technically be recycled in such a way would be overwhelmingly complex. This does not mean that more recycling is not worthwhile. It may well be. But the ideal that all consumption demands can be met in this way is a fabrication of the more extreme environmentalist lobby.

If, then, we set resource use at the level necessary to maximise the system's life expectancy we must end up setting it at that level which, when added to recycled inputs, gives a bare subsistence level. Equally, we would wish to consider how pollution impacts are relevant and here we could establish that maximisation of system life expectancy requires that residuals disposal (= residuals from non-recyclable wastes + residuals from recycling processes) should not exceed the environment's capacity to assimilate those wastes. Whether the residuals disposal constraint will occur before or after the resource use constraint is difficult to say. It is not inconsistent for it to occur *before* if (a) the environment's assimilative capacity is already low (perhaps because of past pollution), and (b) global population already exceeds the level necessary to meet the pollution constraint. That is, establishing the pollution constraint as the determinant of throughput could involve a population *reduction* programme.

However throughput levels are to be determined, it is clear that a trade-off continues to exist in that throughput minimisation entails losses in welfare to current generations for the sake of welfare increases for future generations, or for the sake of permitting them to exist.

The essential point here is that the "spaceship economy" literature has not, as yet, provided us with sufficient rigour to constitute a shift from the conventional to the ecological paradigm. We turn now to the rudiments of a possible synthesis of the ecological paradigm by considering the anomalies that the conventional paradigm gives rise to when ecological constraints are introduced into it. In this way, it is possible that we shall have the beginnings of a more rigorous "ecological paradigm".

Ecological constraints in a conventional economic paradigm

It will be recalled that the "spaceship earth" literature fails, in our judgement, to constitute the ecological paradigm because it does not establish determinate rules for the level of throughput and stock. We propose here a rule for determining the throughput variable with respect to ecological limits set by pollution. In doing so we have to admit that no rules are given for determining the stock in the ecological paradigm. Nor do we consider the minimum resource use problem. Our defence is that what follows is intended as a preliminary venture in a longer programme of work.

Pollution is a by-product of economic activity. The economic activity—say, the output of a commodity—itself requires inputs and the good produces benefits. The standard rule of cost–benefit analysis (i.e. the conventional neoclassical paradigm) is that the level of output should be set at the point where total benefits *minus* total costs (including pollution costs) are maximised. This is the "social optimum". As we have seen, the force of the ecological paradigm is that such an optimum need in no way correspond to an ecologically stable situation: the optimum must therefore be illusory. We can investigate this further by considering Figure 1 which is a modification of a similar approach given in Pearce.[13-15]

In the upper half of the diagram we introduce the ecological data in a simplistic way. The amount of waste (W) is seen to rise with the output of commodity X. The assimilative capacity of the environment is fixed initially at A_0. Once output X_0 is exceeded, then, W exceeds A and the environment fails to degrade the waste. Pollution consequently occurs.* Now, if no-one cares about pollution it cannot have an economic magnitude in the neoclassical paradigm which, as we saw, always relates outcomes to preferences. To be generous to the neoclassical paradigm, however, we shall assume that pollution after output X_0 calls forth an immediate reaction of distaste (a negative preference). In this way we can relate the ecological data to the economic data shown in the lower half of the diagram. The curve TB–TIC shows the (money) value of the total benefits derived by consumers and producers from good X minus the non-pollution costs associated with its production (i.e. the value of inputs etc.). The curve TPC_0 shows the value of pollution costs, assumed here to have a known money value. Notice that TPC_0 can only start at X_0 although, if no-one cares

---

*Technically, pollution can, and does, occur during the assimilative process. Allowing for this does not however, significantly alter the conclusions of the analysis. See Pearce.[15]

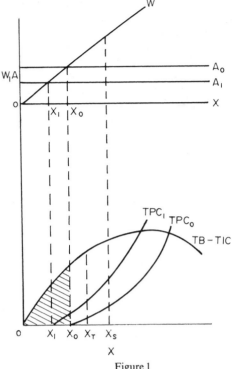

Figure 1

about pollution at output X_0 TPC will not begin to rise until some point further to the right of X_0. The neoclassical paradigm dictates that we establish output at X_S where total benefits minus total costs are maximised. We can now demonstrate an incompatibility between the conventional and ecological paradigms. For at X_S, W still exceeds A, as can be seen by referring to the upper half of the diagram again. But the crucial feature of such a situation is that the degrader populations in ecosystems, responsible for assimilating waste, are themselves reduced in number. This is the essential characteristic of the impact of pollution on ecosystems, namely, that pollution renders the system less and less capable of sustaining *further* pollution.[16] In other words, maintaining output at X_S must shift A_0 downwards to, say, A_1. Now, if we again assume immediate preference response, TPC_0 will move to TPC_1—i.e. people will *perceive* pollution occurring at levels of output beyond X_1 rather than beyond X_0. We have a new "optimum" on the neoclassical paradigm, this time at X_T. But inspection of the diagram shows that this too is unstable since $W > A$, and A_1 must therefore move downwards. The process recommences and, technically, does not cease until zero output occurs. This is indeed an "ecological doomsday" conclusion.

Is the neoclassical paradigm irrelevant? It is evident from Figure 1 that if it had dictated output X_0 as the optimum at the start, the dynamic process brought about by ecological instability would not have occurred. Further, *long-run* net benefits would have been maximised (the shaded area shown). Nor would there be *any* pollution, a result completely at odds with the neoclassical paradigm. But maximising long run benefits is not inimitable to neoclassicism. Indeed, if we had presented the problem as one of maximising benefits *over all time periods* we would have secured X_0 at the outset. In defence of the neoclassical view this much has to be admitted. On the other hand, X_0 could have been identified from purely *physical* information alone. Quite simply, $W = A$ defines the *maximum* output ("throughput" in the spaceship economy language) compatible with ecological stability. To find this output we therefore need only the dimensions of W and A. We need know nothing about preferences, the basic requirement of the neoclassical paradigm. In this way it seems fair to say that the ecological paradigm does contain the elements we require for it to constitute a "shift" in the Kuhnian sense.

Economics and ecological morality

In suggesting that the ecological paradigm is best developed along the lines of incorporating physical and ecological constraints into economic models and the testing for the validity of economic optima, we can further argue that some of the ethical features of the ecological paradigm are accounted for. That is, we may not need to return to square one and begin thinking out a new economics based on ethical premises different to those underlying the neoclassical paradigm. Instead, the introduction of constraints will itself generate a set of rules which limit social behavior without necessarily requiring human motivation to change. Obviously, there is one defect in such an approach, a defect that is not present if only morality could be changed so as to lead automatically to observation of the "ecological rules of the game". This is that human motivation based on wants and desires will remain in conflict with the requirements of ecological stability. Such a conflict may then contain the seeds of its own undoing. But altering wants and desires is open to an even more serious problem, namely, how it is to come about. Unless we have some Marxian ethic in which existing conflicts generate the changes in desires as part of some relentless historical process—and such a view cannot be dismissed lightly—or unless there is to be some theological revolution, it is difficult to see how placing reliance on such a change is much more than an act of faith. Instead, our suggestion is that "mutual coercion, mutually agreed upon" is more likely, not least because it is the principle that underlies the formulation of practical political constitutions. In other words, the kinds of political and moral ethic needed to observe the kinds of constraints that are necessary for the ecological paradigm to hold, are the kinds of ethic already prevalent in practical policy-making.

Attempts to trace the origins of the man–environment conflict, to ascribe "blame", and to elicit policy conclusions[17] are therefore interesting but not, it is argued here, germane to the problem of social policy. It is undoubtedly true that economics in the form of the neoclassical paradigm is as much to blame as anything else for the deterioration of the environment. Essentially, the only moral rights that enter into neoclassicism are property rights. Whoever owns them exacts the right to compensation if they are infringed, or the right to appropriate if others seek the product of that property. Where no property rights exist—as is the case with most environmental products—we know that over-use will result, a theorem generated by economists long before non-economists wrote of the "tragedy of the commons".[18] The neoclassical solution is then to bring the environment within the bounds of property rights, or, at least, to prescribe policy on the basis of seeing what is required *if* property rights existed in environment. As we have argued above, however, this can at best result in the securing of neo-Paretian style "optima" and these are not consistent with ecological stability.

Once again, what we can say is that those who urge the ecological paradigm on economics do not offer rules by which to determine policy. To say that resources held in common property are over-used is not telling the economist something he does not know. What is needed is a set of rules for determining the optimal level of use. The suggestion here is that the optimum, as derived from a reconsidered ecological paradigm, is likely to be different to that produced by the neoclassical paradigm.

Conclusion

The early part of this paper argued that neither the criticism of non-economists, nor the "spaceship earth" literature, generated from within the profession, has been sufficiently rigorously based for these criticisms to constitute a paradigm shift in environmental economics. It was then suggested that, nonetheless, the emphasis of ecologists and the spaceship earth economists on "ecological limits" permits the beginnings of a more rigorous analysis of an ecological paradigm.

It was further suggested that the ethical base necessary for the paradigm shift is already present, at least in democratic societies, and that, while a complete moral change perhaps based on social or religious revolution, will achieve the same end, the requirements for the shift are more efficiently and more certainly provided from within the existing ethical framework of economic and political systems.

References

1. H. Daly *Toward a Steady-State Economy*, W. H. Freeman, San Francisco, 1973.
2. K. Kapp Environmental disruption and social costs: a challenge to economics, in *Political Economy of Environment*, Mouton, The Hague, 1972.
3. A. Coddington Ecology and economics, *New Society*, 1970.
4. L. Robbins *The Nature and Significance of Economic Science*, Macmillan, London, 1932.
5. J. R. Hicks The foundations of welfare economics, *Econ. J.* December, 1939.
6. J. S. Chipman and J. D. Moore The End of the New Welfare Economics, Stanford University, Institute for Mathematical Studies in the Social Sciences, Technical Report No. 102, July, 1973.
7. C. A. Nash, J. Stanley and D. W. Pearce An evaluation of cost–benefit analysis criteria, *Scott. J. polit. Econ.* June, 1975.
8. C. A. Nash, J. Stanley and D. W. Pearce Evaluating project evaluation criteria, *J. Am. Inst. Planners*, May, 1975.
9. I. McHarg *Design with Nature*, Natural History Press, New York, 1969.
10. G. R. Taylor *The Doomsday Book*, Panther, London, 1972.
11. K. Boulding The economics of the coming spaceship earth, in *Environmental Quality in a Growing Economy*, (edited by H. Jarrett) Johns Hopkins University Press, Baltimore, 1966.
12. K. Boulding Economics and ecology, in *Future Environments of North America*, (edited by F. Fraser Darling and J. Milton) Natural History Press, New York, 1966.

13. D. W. Pearce Economic and ecological approaches to the optimal level of pollution, *Int. J. Soc. Econ.* **1**. No. 2, 1974.
14. D. W. Pearce Economics and ecology, *Survey Papers in Economics*, No. 10, June 1974.
15. D. W. Pearce The limits of cost–benefit analysis as a guide to environmental policy, *Kyklos*, 1976, vol. 29, Fasch 1.
16. G. M. Woodwell Effects of pollution on the structure and physiology of ecosystems, *Science* April 24, 1970.
17. L. White The historical roots of our ecologic crisis, *Science*, March 10, 1967.
18. G. Hardin The tragedy of the commons, *Science*, December 13, 1968. Reprinted in Daly[1].

The Commons Theme

INTRODUCTORY ESSAY

"The fact that people voluntarily do something or acquiesce in the consequences, does not mean they like the results. Often the individual is not free to change the result; he can change only his own position within it, and that does him no good . . . We might also conclude that some severe problems result not from the evil of people but from their helplessness as individuals. This is not to say that there aren't callous, even malicious, noise and waste and vandalism . . . But some is unwitting; some offers little choice; and some results from the magnification of small incentives into massive results."

This quote from Schelling[1] touches on some of the deeper issues associated with managing the commons. There is little doubt that the notion of the commons is central to environmental studies because it embraces so many aspects of economics, anthropology, sociology, morals, politics and the law. While we spend some time on the theme in this essay, elements of the commons idea will appear throughout the text. Many of the principles of environmental economics, for example, are based on variations of the commons theme. The term "commons" originally referred to resources, in the form of grazing areas, woodlots, fish ponds and turbaries which were collectively owned and used by communities of peasants in Saxon England.[2] There was a social and legal dimension as well as an economic function, for in those days the concept of individual ownership of land barely existed, so resources were commonly shared by a recognised community of farmers. Legal rights of access and use were territorially and socially defined by the size of the village and the social relations and customs that were associated with each settlement. Peasants could not afford to abuse their privileges of use because of their responsibilities to fellow villagers. And because rights of access were normally granted, by custom, only to those living in the village, even these early commons were not true common property resources as the phrase is understood today, but a form of collectively owned quasi-private resource. It is interesting to note in this connection that the physical and legal entity of the commons began to disappear as population increased and there were pressures to improve the productivity of the best land (i.e. that which was the earliest drained and cleared and to which the original commons concept applied). With improved ploughing technologies which were not suitable for preparing and harvesting scattered parcels of land, plus the rise of the feudal landlord and his successor, the capitalist landowner, both of whom were anxious to create surpluses and thereby make a profit, the legal and social restrictions associated with the early commons became increasingly irrelevant and tiresome. In modern England vestiges of the commons remain mainly in an anomalous legal state, used by farmers mainly in upland areas for cattle and sheep grazing but sought after by hikers and other recreationists anxious to obtain access to the countryside. Contrary to what is implied by their name, the modern common in Britain is not publicly owned but the property of "some legal person", usually a prominent local landowner: the public do not yet have automatic rights of access, though many amenity organisations feel that this should be rectified.[3]

While the original idea of the commons was a fairly circumscribed one, the modern concept is far more wide ranging. The principal distinguishing characteristics are the absence of specific proprietary ownership and consequent freedom of access to all. In one sense it is the ecosystem of the globe—its air, waters and living things—which is not legally owned by any single individual or nation state. Thus what is often known as the "assimilative capacity" of the environment — the ability of waters to purify polluting discharges and the air to disperse emissions —is a commons as are whales, cormorants and swallow-tail butterflies when they do not dwell on land or water owned by a legally designated proprietor. In another sense the concept of commons applies to any good or service which anyone can use but which when consumed by many people loses its intrinsic appeal. Most people know of a favourite beach or picnicing place that was once enjoyable precisely because they were the only ones there: its value lay in its sheer exclusiveness that was all the more pleasurable because no payment was required. But when many people come to the place (because its popularity gets widely known or because more people have cars and an interest in outdoor recreation) the privilege of exclusivity is lost and everyone who comes has to share a steadily depreciating asset. Eventually there is no one left to envy the few who formerly enjoyed seclusion.

The modern notion of the commons,* therefore, while focusing on goods and services that are freely accessible, encompasses many quite subtle issues that lie at the heart of environmental management. These involve questions relating to the rights of individuals and their duty to their fellows, to how far any single person can understand then comprehend what effects his actions have on the wellbeing of the ecosystem and the enjoyment of others, what the cumulative consequences are

---

* For a typology of common resources see Godwin, R. K. and Shepard, W. B. (1979) The use of the commons dilemma in examining the allocation of common resources. Resources for the Future Reprint No. 179.

when many abuse the commons each in small ways, and how should society regulate individual use so that freedom of access is not unfairly restricted yet the commons remain viable. The person who first really focused on these issues was Garrett Hardin, hence the reason why his essay is reproduced here.

The Hardin Essay

One should read Hardin's essay with some care for he really deals with two quite different topics which are not entirely related. On the one hand he was worried about the burden that each additional child would make upon global resources and used the commons analogy of the grazing cattle to illustrate the point that parents appear to have no moral or intellectual responsibility for the wellbeing of the globe when they add one more baby to the world's population. In Hardin's view conceiving and giving birth to a baby is "free" in the sense that the activity is not legally restricted or licensed by economic payment or official dictat. Superficially, there appears to be very little difference between the case of parents and the cattleman who wants to add an extra cow to the commons.

In point of fact, however, the commons analogy is rather a false one because not any cattleman could add his cow to the early commons, and a fairly powerful sense of community obligation would cause the village cattleman to talk with his fellow graziers before adding an extra cow. Also false in the Hardin analogy is the implication that an extra child creates a relatively small additional cost to the parent: what Hardin really means is that any damage or burden that a child might inflict on the global commons (for example by eating food, consuming energy and material goods and visiting formerly peaceful recreation sites) is a small if not infinitesimal cost to the child's parents relative to the economic and emotional advantages that they almost exclusively enjoy as a result of the child's existence.

Hardin was writing in the late sixties when there was much concern over world population growth, especially in developing countries, and when Paul Ehrlich[4] was getting a lot of publicity over his demands for compulsory birth control. This was the age of the resurrection of the views of Malthus when many began to become alarmed at the spectre of widespread famine or desperate wars of resource grabbing among the developing world.[5] Consequently, Hardin's conclusions that "mutual coercion, mutually agreed upon", particularly the emphasis on coercion, should be applied to population control struck a sympathetic chord. In fact the essay became so popular that Hardin decided to extend the thesis in a variety of imaginative ways.[6] In every case he pounds the theme that the spirit of communal responsibility (or altruism) is disappearing or has gone and hence that humanitarian assistance to those who are not prepared to shoulder responsibility for the causes of the plight in which they find themselves is not only senseless but counterproductive. One of his favourite themes is the gradual erosion of altruistic conscience.* Doing good simply produces what he called a "perjorstic" result[7]—a series of outcomes that worsen the original situation thereby weakening the resolve of those who are sincerely trying to help. In his own words,[8] "The more members of another species saved, in an act of pure altruism, the less space there is in a finite world for the saviour and his relatives". Hardin thus gives the impression of being the "hard man" of development assistance: help those only who are prepared to put their house in order and consume resources more frugally. Otherwise the very act of aid will be collectively destructive.

When Hardin's essay first appeared it produced a whelter of comment, for there is no doubt that it is one of the most thought-provoking articles that has been written for a long time. In this collection of essays we reproduce only two of these responses both of which are fairly critical of Hardin's use of the grazing analogy.

Fife makes the valid point that not everyone suffers when common amenities are damaged or depleted.[9] Once the individuals most responsible for the damage, namely the capitalistic entrepreneurs who exploit the commons and edge out competitors, realise that the resource base upon which their profitability depends is being eroded, they move on to new commons armed with sufficient capital to continue profit-making. In other words, the tragedy of the commons is not always the result of careless or ignorant people making micro-decisions that produce adverse macro-outcomes: in some cases it may be deliberately created by the mode of economic production and the attitudes of the owners of capital. Most whaling magnates, for instance, have long since left whaling because, as more whales are killed there is not enough profit for them all: but so long as there are a few whales left, and a market for their product, even one whaler can earn a living so whales will continue to be killed. Until the market for whale products disappears, either because substitutes become available, or sanctions on imports are imposed or through a new moral awareness on the part of consumers, the tragedy of the whaling commons will continue to occur. The same motives are found among those who traffic the hides and skins of endangered species or who climb trees to snatch the eggs of rare birds of prey. As long as there are those who are prepared to buy scarce objects regardless of the ethical implications of that purchase, they will encourage some to expropriate for illegal private ends a valued common resource.

Stillman's argument is self-explanatory. He correctly diagnoses that Hardin creates a set of conditions which make it inevitable that destruc-

*Many economists adopt a similar position, but some economists argue for a new approach see Collard, D. (1978) *Altruism and Economy*, Martin Robertson.

tion of the commons will occur, and emphasises the point that social institutions are adaptable and will change as the crisis of depletion looms. The implication of this argument is that mutual coercion and severe limitations on individual freedom need not be the only solution to the problem of managing a commons so long as people are made more aware of the consequences of their acts, they become more morally concerned about the effects of these consequences on others and on future generations, and they accept and respect the fact that some kind of governmentally imposed regulation of use is necessary in the public interest. We return to this point in Section 8.

Some Wider Issues

It appears then for the commons to become totally destroyed a number of quite specific conditions have to apply:
1. That there is free access available to anyone.
2. That the assimilative capacity of the commons to absorb increased use is not infinite.
3. That individuals entering the commons or making additional demands on commons resources are acting in isolation from their neighbours. Thus there is no sense of communal spirit.
4. That such individuals are not aware of the incremental effects that their additional use of the commons will have both on the commons itself and upon others using that resource, and moreover do not seem to care that they may be creating an environmentally and socially undesirable outcome, no matter how small.
5. Furthermore, the "atomic" individual cannot know, and hence cannot care about, the aggregate effects of similar apparently innocuous acts by myriads of others.
6. That no governmental or otherwise politically acceptable regulatory institution is developed in order to manage the use of the commons.

In reality none of these conditions hold absolutely even though elements of all of them are undoubtedly evident. Let us look briefly at how society manages to cope with each of the six conditions to ameliorate destruction of the commons.

Free access

There are many circumstances where free access is technically possible. Polluting the air from a car exhaust, turning on a radio in an open space, visiting a wilderness area as one of a large party are all examples. But as the cumulative effects of commons use become more noticeable and disliked some form of regulation is increasingly imposed. This may take the form of by-laws which in effect limit access (for example, separating non-smokers from smokers, prohibitions on the playing of transistor radios) or the specific piece of legislation, as for instance occurs with car exhausts under the US Clean Air Acts of 1970 and 1977 (see Figure 6.1). Generally speaking this kind of action takes place once the nuisance becomes unacceptable, at least to a politically prominent component of society. There remains the questions of whether such regulations are either enforceable or sufficient but we shall return to these matters below.

Another method of restricting access is to follow the example of the early Saxon peasants—namely make the commons quasi-private. In other words, restrict entry to a class of people who by virtue of their family or social connections, money or political influence become entitled

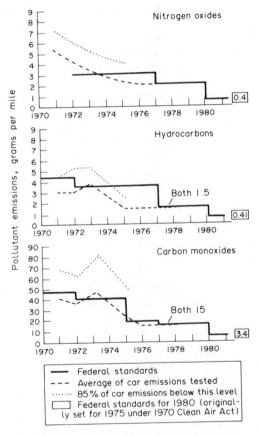

FIGURE 6.1

Statutory controls on US auto emissions and actual emissions as calculated by the big car manufacturers. This diagram is reproduced, with permission, from the *Seventh Annual Report of the US Council on Environmental Quality* (1976) (Government Printing Office, Washington, D.C., p. 7). It indicates that tough and specific legislation can bring about environmental improvements even though the process is expensive, time consuming and often engenders much ill-will.

to share the resource in a relatively exclusive manner. The licensing of taxi-drivers and ice-cream vendors is one example on the small scale, as is the nationalising of offshore resources in so-called "exclusive economic zones" on the larger scale. In the latter case, the long-drawn-out UN Conference on the Law of the Sea (UNCLOS) has finally accepted the principle that coastal states can control both access and use of the formerly common property resources of fish, minerals and hydrocarbon deposits in a zone up to 200 miles off their shores, so long as certain rules are followed.[10] Furthermore, these states can declare conservation areas within their EEZs where no exploitation is permitted so that the living species therein can be left unmolested. This is an inevitable outcome of a problem of resource management that could never be solved by mutual agreement. So long as offshore resources were commons and so long as international law failed to find a satisfactory method of controlling access, some means of nationalising the commons had to come. In fact it occurred through a series of technically illegal unilateral declarations by a number of countries (the US claimed a sovereign interest in the mineral and hydrocarbon resources of its continental shelf in 1948[11] and Canada proclaimed national jurisdiction over the Arctic waters in 1970[12]) aimed in part at the conservation of otherwise vulnerable assets.

In this connection it is worth recording that at the time of writing UNCLOS has not agreed about the proper management of one of the last true remaining unregulated commons on the globe, namely the open seas (i.e. those waters outside of the EEZs). While there is a presumption that these waters and the valuable mineral nodules on the deep ocean floor are part of the "common heritage of mankind" and therefore are owned by all nation-states, in fact the rich and poor countries continue to bicker over rights of access. The likely outcome is a carving up of the oceans between rich countries and an "international seabed authority" which will obtain funds from the sale of licences for exploration of the rich mineral resources under its jurisdiction. This money will be used partly to allow it to explore for the minerals and partly to help the economies of the developing world who will, in effect, be collective owners of the authority.[13] The details are still to be agreed upon as many related issues are at stake, but the final solution will undoubtedly mean the establishment of a group of "quasi-private" commons where formerly a true commons existed. Certainly, the "common heritage" concept will have to be modified in practice.*

*While the UN has now accepted the Law of the Sea convention and that the International Seabed Authority should have the power to licence (quota) exploration of deep sea nodules, the US has not yet done so, claiming that private commercial interests should have some degree of unregulated access. See *Environmental Policy and Law* 8 (1982) pp. 127–128. The UK, other western European countries and the Comecon Block abstained.

A third approach is to go the whole way and make the commons private so that access is absolutely controlled by law. One can include here the private country club and the usurpation of an attractive lake by a small number of landowners who collectively purchase the whole shoreline. As more and more people seek pleasure in natural surroundings and fresh air, so it is becoming necessary to purchase private rights to these commodities simply to keep others out. This is such an important issue both to land use planning and, ultimately, to economic growth itself, that we give it special treatment below.

Absorptive capacity of the commons

In Section 5 we observed that conventional economic paradigms about cost–benefit analysis and resource allocation do not adequately take into account the "environmental rent" that is placed on the commons when the ecological or social ramifications are not properly taken into account and when the absorptive capacity of the commons is depleted. We argue there that a new paradigm is necessary. We also pointed out in Sections 1 and 4 that environmental amelioration of the worst of environmental impacts associated with major resource-extraction schemes are bound to become a crucial feature of project design in the future. We took as examples payments to disadvantaged groups living in the locality so that they can develop socially and culturally with (hopefully) minimum interference and the use of landscaping and the designation of protected zones of critical ecological and landscape importance in order to safeguard natural heritage and scenic beauty. The point here is that these developments in enviromental design are just beginning, and as they become more common practice, hopefully the loss of some of the more precious assets of the heritage "commons" will be curtailed. This should at least slow down the reduction in the absorptive capacity of certain kinds of commons when major development proposals are planned. But we are aware that there are economic consequences associated with environmental design that may mean that some developments are commercially "uneconomic" and which therefore may cause those in power to reappraise the value of the design activity. We are also aware that most economic activity, no matter how well planned does absorb some of the capacity of the environmental commons as a source of beauty and a harbour of interesting flora and fauna. The "design palliative" cannot be treated as the ultimate solution so long as economic development tries to accelerate and socially created wants continue to escalate.

The atomistic individual

In the Hardin formulation the cattleman adds the extra cow because he acts independently of his neighbours. Moreover, he does not care if they lose a little as a result of his selfishness because he knows that they would do the same to him. What Hardin is implying is that there is no sense of community so no feeling for the wellbeing of others. Again a quote from Schelling[14] is apposite:

> "What we need . . . is an enforceable social contract. I'll cooperate if you and everyone else will: I'm better off if we all cooperate than if we all go our separate ways. In matters of great virtue and symbolism, especially in emergencies, we may all become imbued with a sense of solidarity, and abide by a golden rule. We identify with the group and we act as we believe or hope or wish to be the way that everybody acts. We enjoy rising to the occasion, rewarded by a sense of virtue and community . . . indeed a good deal of social ethics is concerned with rules of behaviour that are collectively rewarding if collectively obeyed (even though the individual may not benefit from his own participation).
>   But if there is nothing heroic in the occasion; if what is required is a protracted nuisance; if one feels no particular community with great numbers of people who have nothing in common; . . . and especially if one suspects that large numbers of people just are not playing the game —most people may cooperate only halfheartedly, and many not at all."

One can argue that in capitalistic societies where individualism is encouraged, where people see exploitation taking place all around them and where the scale in both work and urban living is so large as to kill a sense of community identity, the conditions creating the atomistic individual are rife. Certainly, it now appears that with modern communications and increased housing mobility, and the notion of community as physical place is giving way to community as social network: people relate to each other through common interests which do not necessarily relate to the local neighbourhood. Indeed, the cynic might observe that place-based community feeling only occurs when a new development is proposed and amenities and property values are threatened. Otherwise, community spirit as fondly imagined, does not exist[15]. In part this is the alienation argument raised by Hall in his reading in Section 1, and elaborated on by Schumacher and Robertson.[16]

Yet what is impressive is that despite the pervasiveness of forces which appear to encourage egotism, a sense of public spiritedness still to some extent prevails. Many people do sense a feeling of "belonging" to a locality, and those who do not often feel uncomfortable. Various kinds of social groupings form in places of work and play as people seek to maintain an identity and comradeship. Many individuals will risk their lives to help those in distress; community consciousness is especially evident during times of disaster: most people obey pleas not to pick wild flowers in nature conservation areas and some would admonish anyone caught in the act. Nevertheless this sense of community is not universal and is probably being eroded (though we have seen no systematic analysis of this) so Schelling's plea for a new kind of social contract is apposite. What we are touching on here is the difficult question of man–land ethic that also embraces a man–society morality, a matter that has exercised the minds of sociologists and political scientists for many years. The main problem is that social customs and institutions have an important influence on such an ethic and the forces that discourage its development in the individual, especially when he is acting unobserved, are still fairly powerful.

Consider, for example, the tanker master who has discharged his cargo but has a small amount of oil on the top of his ballast. He could travel to a waste oil-disposal facility and discharge it safely, but it would cost a fee and would take time. Indeed, the more the other tanker masters followed similar socially responsible behaviour, the longer the queue of tankers seeking to discharge their residual oil. But to tie up a vessel for 48 hours could cost the owners as much as £5000 even in these days of difficult oil market conditions. The powerful temptation therefore is to discharge the waste oil illegally at sea both to save time and the disposal fee, and one can see that the tanker owners would covertly encourage such behaviour by giving bonuses for rapid turnaround. Out on his own and approaching a refinery, the master with a conscience is in a dilemma: unless there are really foolproof means of detection backed up by severe penalties, and unless there are strong financial incentives for him to obey the law, he will be strongly tempted to offload into the commons thereby adding to the many thousands of tons of oil that are similarly discharged and which take such a toll of birdlife (see Figure 6.2 and Table 6.1).

If one follows Hardin's thesis the tanker master with a conscience will always be the loser *so long as other tanker masters discharge illegally with impunity*. For the master with a conscience will watch his fellows receive their turnaround bonuses while he waits to offload his ballast. So most masters discharge their oily ballasts, hence the statistics in Figure 6.2 and Table 6.1, largely because the incentives and the institutions that create these incentives operate to the detriment of both conscience and commons. For though the oil-tanker companies have agreed to a joint liability agreement whereby they pay for oil-pollution damage to the commons (in the form of after-the-event clean-up costs) but mainly to private property owners, this money is not available when the culprit is not caught. In any case seabirds do not live on money.

However, modern technology is coming to the rescue of both the environmentalist and the seabirds, for the Swedes have discovered that by adding a package of trace metals in a specific combination to the oil cargo of every tanker, they can "fingerprint" all transported oil and thus trace any culprit even when the tanker has left the scene of the crime[17]. If this new technique works, and it has yet to be proven, then there would be a powerful incentive for heavy penalties to be levied against polluters. Already the Shetland Island Council have threatened to refuse to supply oil for any tanker caught discharging oil illegally off the Sullom Voe terminal, so incensed are they over the harrowing increase in dead birds (and sheep which eat oil-infested seaweed) since the new terminal was

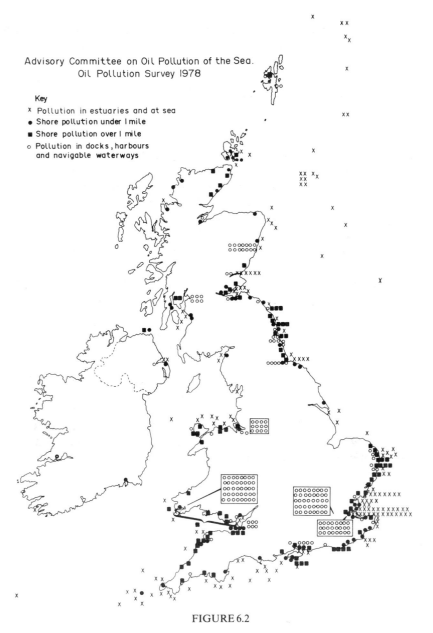

FIGURE 6.2

Oil spills off the coast of the United Kingdom. This diagram is based on material provided in the 1978 Annual Report of the Advisory Committee on Oil Pollution of the Sea (10 Percy Street, London). Of some 500 reported spills (probably far short of the real number of spills) only half could be traced to the type of oil and hence possible source and so no action was taken against an offender. In only 37 cases was prosecution brought of which 29 were completed in 1979 amounting in total to fines of £31,738.

TABLE 6.1

Effort and Expenditure Involved in Oil-spill Clean-up during 1978. Remember that only half the causes of oil spills are identified and that less than 1 in 15 actually result in prosecution. The total of fines levied amount to £31,738 compared with £996,263 spent on clean-up by local authorities. Much of these costs are not insurable though some can be reclaimed from central government.

Division of coast	Approx man-hours spent	Direct/Identifiable costs of:				Indirect additional costs	Overall costs incurred by authorities reporting
		Clean-up	Rehabil'n	Materials	Other		
		£	£	£	£	£	£
01 North-east England	2,907	6,038	0	5,938	330	738	10,166
02 Eastern England	3,753	438,697	0	0	0	32,000	804,560
03 Essex and Kent	9,273	55,503	215	7,376	10,495	7,114	45,548
04 Sussex	1,100	4,194	0	280	0	545	5,019
05 Southern England	2,453	11,184	0	200	110	635	12,129
06 Devon	0	415	0	0	1,194	454	2,063
07 Cornwall	436	2,619	0	26	0	396	2,462
08 Scilly Isles	0	0	0	0	0	0	0
09 Bristol Channel and South Wales	15,161	29,276	0	7,842	24,023	7,919	70,161
10 Lancashire and Western Wales	73	2,197	0	810	0	168	2,707
11 Cumbria	0	0	0	0	0	0	0
12 Western Scotland	537	4,184	0	69	0	702	2,815
13 Orkney and Shetland	330	1,662	0	162	500	890	3,218
14 Offshore North Sea	3	0	0	0	0	0	0
15 Eastern Scotland	852	3,755	0	186	320	1,153	5,445
Totals	36,878	559,724	215	22,889	36,972	52,714	966,293

opened in January 1979.[18] To return emptyhanded would be a severe penalty for an oil company and a tanker master since big oil cargoes today are worth at least £14 million. But equally important is the need for international law to catch up with this development so that culprit vessels once in another port can directly be apprehended and fined without recourse to cumbersome and often unsuccessful legal application either to the port, state or state owning the flag of registration. So the new fingerprinting technology may not only have repercussions on inappropriate economic incentives and legal institutions, it may also tip the balance in favour of an environmental conscience, because the tanker master out on his own could be freed from the strictures of "the double bind".

An environmental ethos

But do we always have to improve our crime-discovering technologies for an environmental ethos to prevail? Is environmental destructiveness an inevitable characteristic of mankind? We add one more reading by Burch to encourage the reader to explore the issue. Burch suggests that environmental destructiveness is not innate but a product of the nature of an economy and the pattern of social relations coupled with stresses created either by changing man–resource relationships (due to alterations in climate, or to population pressures meaning depletion of existing resources) or because of the interaction of new cultural ideas, for example, when a society comes into contact with a new culture. Wilkinson[19] looked at the economic history of western civilisations and observed that the innovation of technologies, most of which have turned out to be environmentally damaging, seems to occur when population–resource balance is under stress:

> "Development is needed when a society outgrows its resource base and productive system. As the established economic system is proved inadequate and subsistence problems become more severe, societies are driven to change their methods. Development comes out of poverty not out of plenty, as many economic theories would lead one to suppose. Poverty stimulates the search for additional sources of income and makes people willing to do things they may previously have avoided. It is the population's increasingly exploitable situation which provides the basis for the growth of capitalist institutions.[20]

This point was also taken up in a widely quoted essay by Lynn White, Jr.[21] in which he asserted that the combination of new technology backed up by enormous advances in scientific understanding coupled with a Christian commandment to "be fruitful and multiply and replenish the earth and subdue it", and followed by a growing secularisation of social institutions that originally promoted a sense of care or stewardship all led to an alienation of man from the land and hence to the demise of an environmental ethos. Black[22] also supports this thesis by noting that the loss of the sense of stewardship came with the growth of private property with all its associations of legal exclusivity and economic profit-taking. The ever-present dilemma between the preference for immediate profit and the recognition of the need to protect long term sustainability held crass exploitation in check for a while (though less so in the ecological tension-zones such as the desert margin) but as social controls over private actions weakened (with the rise of capitalism, inequalities and surpluses) so the ethos of stewardship also began to fail.

This point is further developed by Marxist writers who envisage the total secularisation of modern society and the control of individual minds and behaviour by mammoth impersonal institutions which cause man to lose any sense of caring about the life-support systems upon which his well-being ultimately depends and thus either to abuse natural processes or simply to be unaware of the damage his day-to-day requirements create on ecosystems. William Liess[23] develops this theme in connection with the frustration many Southern Canadians felt when told that their oil and gas will cost more because of the need to safeguard the caribou herds of the Arctic tundra below which the oil and gas fields are located:

"The chief paradox is the pervasive insecurity of a society whose economy's material output is so abundant. The larger this output becomes the more carefully it must be watched, and governments today have little time for anything except nursing the Gross National Product. Our insecurity stems mainly from the curious impermanence of what we want and how we produce it. Very little in our system is self-renewing, save the wants that drive it on, and thus we must search in ever more remote places, with escalating costs and more esoteric technologies, for materials and energy to feed it. . . . Thus the Porcupine caribou herd appears to threaten our wellbeing."

The herd no longer is deemed to have any biorights. It is simply an obstacle to prosperity. Those who vouchsafe that oil and gas resources not be exploited for the sake of marginal increments of energy in an energy-wasteful society are regarded at best as ecofreaks and at worst as traitors. The ethos of leaving the herd alone is lost.

The arguments of Marxist-orientated writers are reinforced in their analyses of the overlapping corporate relationships which pervade modern government and capital intensive technology. In order to protect their own existence and profitability, these powerful empires guide the development of environmentally damaging and otherwise hazardous technologies which in turn make themselves so indispensable to economic growth that they cannot effectively be controlled by governments. Studies of the nuclear industry[24] and the pesticide-manufacturing companies[25] illustrate this point. To a considerable extent, man becomes the passive victim of the capitalist state he has created and is consequently no longer able individually to extricate himself from a way of life that is inherently environmentally damaging without undertaking a fairly heroic programme of self-denial. It is very difficult, for example, to buy a household detergent that does not contain phosphates or nitrates or an applicator that does not use fluorocarbon gases except in places where these products have been specifically banned. So even the more environmentally conscious person will pollute largely because he is locked into a consuming pattern that is all-encompassing. Even when he does use soap or a polishing cloth instead of detergents and spray-on polish, in the words of Schelling that introduce this section, he "is not free to change the result; he can change only his own position within it and that does him no good". Only when there is universal regulation of all environmentally harmful products (a bureaucratic impossibility), or preferably, as the socialists believe, where an economic arrangement is devised whereby "socially responsible" co-operatives produce "socially needed" products can this loss of environmentally responsible ethos be checked.[26] Figure 6.3 illustrates in simplified diagrammatic form many of the issues raised in the preceding four paragraphs.

Burch's other point is that environmental ethos becomes eroded when different cultures interact. This is often illustrated when pre-industrial societies come into contact with Western values, and exhibit a disorientation of norms and loss of social control. Many continue to believe that so-called primitive societies lived in harmony with nature and that the stability of their existence was based on a man–land ethos that really worked.[27] There are, however, many serious criticisms of this view. Tuan[28] believes that most societies profess an "I–thou" relationship with nature but act in an "I–it" manner. "A culture's published

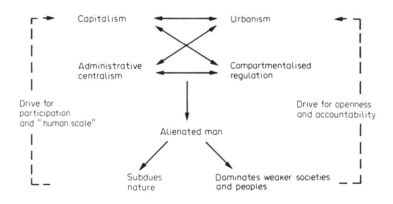

FIGURE 6.3

The relationship between man and nature in modern industrial societies. Man is visualised here as being alienated from both his object of work and object of consumption. He is the product of forces that help to shape his behaviour and cause him to damage his environment and exploit weaker members of the global community. Much of this is inadvertent and much cannot readily be changed by the individual acting unconsciously within "the system".

ethos about its environment," he observed, "seldom covers more than a fraction of the total range of its attributes and practices pertaining to that environment. In the play of forces that govern the world, aesthetic and religious ideas rarely have a major role." This inconsistency of word and deed seems to be universal and may serve to reduce the tension that occurs when the myth is contradicted in practice.

So here again we come to the problem of the commons: most people profess that it is "wrong" to damage the environment but do it anyway for the reasons outlined by Schelling in the introductory quote. To place a "primitive" society in contact with an exploitist culture almost certainly relaxes the all-important restraints that it may have developed to control for this inconsistency between ethos and action. Thus "westernised" Eskimo, once believing that all bears have souls "which do not perish with the body and which must therefore be propitiated lest they should avenge themselves on them for taking away their bodies",[30] now hunt bear with powerful rifles from snowmobiles or helicopters, strip the fur for its commercial value and leave the meat slowly to rot. The fear of revenge seems largely to have disappeared.

Managing the Commons

Sooner or later misuse of the commons requires some form of governmental intervention in its management, because almost by definition, individuals using the commons cannot comprehend the adverse nature of the sum total of their usage. In small, politically decentralised societies regulation is supposed to be achieved through custom and social controls, though in practice some kind of authoritarianism is often present. But in modern centralised capitalist society social and economic relations are too complex and specialised to be self-regulating so some form of governmentally imposed controls have to be established. We have already referred to the development of these in our discussion of the access question, and we will refer again to the problem when we look at pollution-control policies in Section 9. In practice, the threat to the commons is so widespread that a very complex arrangement of regulation is *now* required, ranging from safety standards and consumer protection laws through the whole paraphernalia of planning controls to restrictions on public access in national parks—ironically designated in part to encourage public access.

In one sense any form of governmental intervention requires the exercise of Hardin's dictum of "mutual coercion" mutually agreed upon, because without public acceptance of authority regulation cannot be enforced. In other words, the commons users have first to be persuaded that there is a need for regulation, i.e. that there is a potential tragedy, then they have to accept that the authority thereby established is both trustworthy and competent to do the job, and finally they have to submit themselves to its edicts even though their day-to-day activities are not being monitored all the time. This is a tall order in many countries where government generally is eyed with suspicion, regulatory officials are prone to bribery and corruption and their technical competence is questioned. So managing the commons is by no means an easy task even within the confines of nation states where at least the law is based upon a unitary code.

Where the commons is international, the matter of regulation is much more difficult because differing nation states do not always agree on the same basic principles of good conduct let alone share similar legal codes of practice. This is particularly evident in such matters as agreeing to a pollution control management plan for a bi- or multi-national water resource such as the Great Lakes, the Baltic or the Mediterranean. One defaulter can upset the whole scheme for usually there are few legal sanctions that can be brought to bear. The only hope is for combined political and moral persuasion to be successful, backed up, *in extremis*, by the threat of economic ostracism. Eventually, after almost endless talking and legal argument agreements of a sort are reached to manage various aspects of the international commons. Examples include the seven inconclusive sessions of the UN Law of the Sea Conference III and IV which have dealt not just with the matter of allocating resources of the high seas already referred to but the dumping of pollution, the establishment of conservation zones and the rights of innocent passage through international straits. So far the Conference has failed to produce a draft treaty acceptable to all parties: it has merely agreed to receive a series of negotiating texts each one supposedly an improvement on its predecessor, but none totally satisfactory to all parties. A sense of the difficulties of management of the international commons can be gained from reading the following extracts from informed commentaries on UN environmental protection efforts.

"The major gap in the new Law of the Sea draft, from the conservation point of view, is certainly the almost complete absence of any provision relating to the preservation of marine ecosystems. . . . There has been no attempt to bring all high seas fishing under the aegis of one single body and there is no global organization in charge of setting standards or issuing guidelines with regard to fisheries in water under national jurisdiction.[31]

Delegates representing 17 of the 18 Mediterranean nations at the intergovernmental meeting held in Monaco, January 1978, failed to reach agreement to combat land based pollution, the main source of pollution in the Mediterranean region. Since February 1978 only three out of a series of agreements for the protection of the Mediterranean Sea have come into force. . . . None of these agreements contains mandatory procedures for dealing with breaches of the convention and the protocols . . . The right to use environmental media for waste disposal is an economically valuable asset for any country. The negotiation of environmental controls can, therefore, be regarded as a process of conferring and limiting this right. Consequently, changes in the distribution of wealth and welfare are central to the international negotiations. The failure of the Monaco meeting in January 1978 seems to support the fact that in absence of an effective system of compensatory payments among countries for afflicted pollution damages, the prospects are undermined for achieving adequate international anti-pollution safeguards. ..."[32]

International law still has a long way to go before it gets to grips with managing the international commons. Though the fundamental principle that environmental damage inflicted on one state by the misdeeds of another requires compensation by the culprit has now been accepted by the international community,[33] this only deals with bilateral damage. There are still few safeguards for the wellbeing of living organisms in international commons, virtually no monitoring of the damage being caused and no adequate mechanism for compensating any organisation prepared to mitigate damage once caused.[34] The power of national sovereign rights still holds sway with only minimum concessions to weaken it. What is required is an international management agency armed with powers and backed by a prestigious and authoritative arbitration mechanism to sort out disputes and ensure that binding agreements are enforced. But since national governments do not enter international gatherings with anything like the same sense of accountability to their electorates that they at least nominally recognise when dealing with national policy issues, it is highly unlikely that any really effective device for managing the international commons will come about in the foreseeable future—until, that is, the commons become so abused that some form of action must be taken merely to protect the remains.*

At the national level, the problem lies with the authority and accountability of regulatory authorities responsible for managing commons problems. This is the age-old problem of *quis custodiet ipsos custodes*? —who oversees the regulators? Much depends upon the traditions and styles of regulatory practice. In the UK, for example, there has always been a tradition of pride among officials in their professional competence and in the freedom which they are allowed by law and custom both to consult with regulated parties and to make judgements free from the investigating eyes of various interested parties. In the US, on the other hand, the rule is one of openness and explicit accountability: regulators must justify precisely what they are doing and may be taken to court if interested parties are not satisfied either with their procedures or with their actual decisions. Curiously, even though the two styles are so different in both countries the representativeness and independence of the regulatory official is now being questioned for precisely the same reasons — namely that without independently produced research evidence and substantially improved methods of genuine consultation among the relevant interested parties (including those claiming to represent the public interest) regulations for, say, consumer safety, the

---

*A classic example is the failure to control acid rain, one of the major environmental issues of the early eighties. See *Environmental Policy and Law* vol. 7(4) (1981), pp. 155–161.

control of hazardous processes (including the nuclear fuel cycle) and the adequate assessment of environmental impacts cannot necessarily be accepted, and hence better monitoring and tougher enforcement will be essential. The case of oil pollution off the Shetland Isles illustrated this general point which is developed further in both Sections 4 and 9.

However, one related issue does deserve attention here, namely the question of private legal rights to a certain level of environmental quality. Just as commons problems stem in part because conventional welfare economic theory does not deal fully with the allocation of nuisances or bads, so also they occur because there is no legal right to peace and quiet, health or clear views in property which is commonly owned. When it comes to private property there is no problem: pollute my house or garden or create a nuisance near my residence and I can take you to court. But when plaintiff and defendant are in neutral territory neither has any rights over the other unless a by-law or other piece of legislation exists. In the absence of such safeguards the person creating the nuisance usually prevails because the sufferer either leaves or his protests are only heard when his wellbeing is seriously affected. So the regulator enters to establish a code of practice that in effect determines the quality of our lives. The point of all this is to emphasise that unless the regulatory process is fully accountable and open, then, in the absence of specific legal rights, the quality of the environment is determined by bureaucrats, administrators and scientist-experts who may not necessarily be sensitive to specific human requirements in particular circumstances. True, in the UK all administrative and regulatory actions are ultimately accountable to a Minister or local government committee and through them to Parliament or the relevant local government body, but in practice only the very worst cases of bureaucratic mischief are brought to the attention of elected members. The current controversy over the control of lead in petrol indicates all too clearly how circumscribed the choices of politicians can be even in the face of a serious public health hazard.[35] This is why American lawyers like Joseph Sax decries the meddling of what he terms "bureaucractic middlemen" and championed the doctrine of citizens' environmental rights.[36]

"The administrative voice tends to produce not the voice of the people but the voice of the bureaucrat—the administrative perspective posing as the public interest. Simply put, the fact is that the citizen does not need a bureaucratic middleman to identify, prosecute and vindicate his interest in environmental quality. He is perfectly capable of fighting his own battles—if only he is given the tools with which to do the job.... Litigation is thus a means of access for the ordinary citizen to the process of governmental decisionmaking."[37]

Despite his success in promoting the Michigan Environmental Protection Act, which enshrines the right of individuals to sue regulatory agencies, the doctrine of citizens' environmental rights has not been extended in the US and is far from being contemplated in the UK[38] (see also the concept of an amenity charter in Section 9).

Managing the commons by formal governmental authority is but one aspect of control. Many commons problems, such as picking wild flowers in remote nature reserves or walking off a beaten path in alpine areas where the vegetation cannot withstand any trampling, simply are not suitable for this kind of approach. Here the matter of control is a question of personal ethics and environmental values. It involves the development of an environmental conscience that operates when one is alone. We have more to say about this important matter in Section 8.

Social Limits to Growth

We noted at the outset that there were two widely differing notions of commons. So far we have concentrated on the matter of environmental damage resulting from misuse of common property resources which results in adverse effects not only to the commons itself but to other users of the resource. The other dimension is far more abstract but is one that is equally germane to this volume—hence the inclusion of the reading by Hirsch. Hirsch looks at the problem of people seeking to consume goods and services which are wanted since they command prestige largely because they are not available to all, but which when accessible to many lose their intrinsic appeal. He cites as examples utilities of a non-material kind such as privacy, quietness, space, unspoilt countryside, and creative and satisfying work. He contends that there is a social dimension to most private consumption in these areas in the sense that in their acquisition the owner enjoys status or position because his possession is envied by those who also want these assets but yet are not able to own them either because they are unavailable or too costly to purchase. As a society becomes more affluent, so the position attached to ownership is demeaned as more and more people are able to purchase similar goods. The exception lies with those who got there first (namely the wealthiest, those with special influence, or those with precious legacies and heirlooms) for they will always be at the front of the rush simply because they have the best (scarcest, choicest) assets, assuming they can protect their privilege of exclusivity.

This particular aspect has important planning implications and it is the driving force behind the very powerful amenity lobby, especially in the UK. The two major public interest amenity groups, the Council for the Protection of Rural England and the Civic Trust, are composed of many local branches most of which are organised by dedicated people with sufficient expertise and commitment to use the right of appeal and objection to fight planning proposals that may damage their aesthetic positional resources. Indeed a Civic Trust survey[39] discovered that four-fifths of their local groups regularly looked at the register of planning applications and that most have excellent relations with the planners, many of whom are sympathetic to their cause, and with the local press. One should never underestimate the potential power of the local amenity lobby: although one could argue that its activities are not always altruistic, it has done much to enhance the environmental sensitivities of the planning profession and keep the townscapes and countryside of Britain attractive and enjoyable to be in.[40]

Hirsch believes that by opening up more common access to positional goods and services, economic growth creates its own tensions and leads to an enormous amount of waste of effort, as people struggle harder to purchase positional resources that are becoming more widely available. In some respects Hirsch reaches the same doleful conclusions regarding the future of individual freedom as does Hardin:

"Excess competition in the positional sector has been seen to involve important external costs. If these costs are allowed to become large, a point will come when the damage to society appears too great to justify the individual freedom of action that results in such damage. The individual freedom will then be seen to be socially disruptive and ultimately self-destructive, and pressure to restrict such freedom will become irresistible."[41]

He advocates a deliberate effort to reduce social envy by trying to give everyone the basic necessities of life and by attempting to reduce the financial rewards attached to socially prestigious occupations. In this way he hopes that people will not try to become better educated for jobs that either do not require so much training or which are unobtainable. His solutions are, however, mild and essentially ineffective given the power of his arguments.* Nevertheless Hirsch does at least try to look for a social democratic solution based on a sense of fairness and community spirit. Other writers are not so optimistic and can only see a rise in some form of authoritarianism as the struggle for positional goods (including what is conventionally known as a job at present) becomes more fierce. Ophuls is probably the most articulate of this breed.

"... if under conditions of ecological scarcity individuals rationally pursue their material self interest unrestrained by a common authority that upholds the common interest, the eventual result is bound to be common environmental ruin. In that case we must have political institutions that preserve the ecological common good from destruction.... The only solution is a sufficient measure of coercion ... which if we face up to it, full political awareness will dispel its seeming nastiness ... a certain minimum level of ecological order or peace must be established ... a certain minimum level of ecological virtue must be imposed by our political institutions."[42]

The principle difficulty as so often is the case is to overcome the transition in a reasonable peaceable manner. It is difficult to be cheerful about this prospect because neither Western political leaders nor the

*A critique of the Hirsch thesis, highlighting the lack of any workable policy recommendations can be found in Reisman, D. (1981) Social Limits to Tolerable Survival, in Gaskin, M. (ed.) *The Political Economy of Tolerable Survival*, Croom Helm. Reisman sees the real social limit as a moral one, progress may well be limited because of the ethical vacuum that now exists in modern societies.

power blocks of commerce, industry and trade unionism are particularly responsive to the demands that are required of them. Indeed, the commons may have the last laugh, for it is the very dilemmas it produces which makes each of these leader groups impotent in the face of much needed reform.

Notes and References

1. Schelling, T. C. (1972) On the Ecology of Micromotives, *The Public Interest*, vol. 25, pp. 61–98. Schelling's article is well worth reading, not merely for its many incisive arguments but also for its amusing anecdotal style. One of his main conclusions is that people, making what they regard as "sensible" decisions as individuals, collectively produce perverse results that no one wants. For a wider analysis of the same theme see Schelling, T. C. (1978) *Micromotives and Macrobehaviour*, Norton & Co., New York, especially pp. 36–43, 110–115.
2. For a fine exposition of early commons law, see Jurgensmeyer, J. C. and Wadley, J. B. (1974) The Common Lands Concept: A "Commons" Solution to a Common Environmental Problem, *Natural Resources Journal*, vol. 14, pp. 361–381.
3. For a comprehensive statement of the law relating to the commons, see Campbell, I. (1976) A Guide to the Law of the Commons, Footpaths and Open Spaces Preservation Society, 166 Shaftsbury Ave., London WC2.
4. Ehrlich's most famous book is *The Population Bomb*, Ballantine Books, New York (1970). For an excellent critique of Ehrlich's views, see Neuhaus, R. (1971) *In Defense of People: Ecology and the Seduction of Radicalism*, Macmillan, New York.
5. For a typical example, see Ehrlich, P. R. (1970) Ecocatastrophe! in Ramparts, Editors, *Ecocatastrophe*, Cranfield Press, San Francisco, pp. 1–14.
6. Hardin, G. (1972) *Exploring New Ethics for Survival; The Voyage of the Spaceship Beagle*, Viking Books, New York; Hardin, G. and Baden, J. (1977) *Managing the Commons*, Freeman Books, San Francisco; Hardin, G. (1978) *The Limits of Altruism*, University of Indiana Press, Bloomington. Of these the reader by Hardin and Baden is by far the most comprehensive statement.
7. Hardin has some trouble in defining perjoristic thinking. In his essay Living on a Lifeboat (in Hardin and Baden, *op. cit.*, pp. 209–271), he applies the word to those systems which, by their very nature, can be relied upon to make matters worse. A world food bank coupled with sovereign state irresponsibility in reproduction is an example of a perjoristic system (*ibid.*, p. 270). But in another essay in the same volume entitled Rewards of Perjoristic Thinking (pp. 126–134) he describes a perjorist as someone who tries to make perjoristic systems better, i.e. someone who is trying to save the destruction of a commons. Hardin believes that because that kind of help is altruistic, it is simple-minded and naïve, hence it often produces perverse consequences.
8. Hardin, G. (1978) *The Limits to Altruism, op. cit.*, p. 12.
9. In the Hardin–Baden reader Fife makes the point that "ruining the commons does not bring ruin to the entrepreneurs". At this point Hardin and Baden add in parenthesis "The line in Hardin's essay that reads 'Freedom in a commons brings ruin to all', should read 'Freedom in a commons brings death to the commons'. Yet on p. 265 of the same reader Hardin repeats his earlier view, "In a crowded world of less than perfect human beings—and we will never know any other—mutual ruin is inevitable in the commons. This is the core of the tragedy of the commons." It seems that Hardin was a little peeved by Fife's analysis which implies that in a capitalistic economic system, the tragedy of the commons results in profit for a minority. See Fife, D. (1976) Killing the Goose, in Hardin and Baden, (*op. cit.*), pp. 76–81.
10. For a good review of the UNCLOS debates, see de Klemm, C. (1978) Conservation and the New Informal Composite Negotiating Text of the Law of the Sea Conference, *Environmental Policy and Law*, vol. 3, pp. 2–17 also vol. 7(2) (1981), pp. 66–71, vol 3(1) (1982) pp. 76–81.
11. Watt, D. C. (1979) First Steps in the Enclosure of the Oceans— The Origins of the Truman Proclamation on the Resources of the Continental Shelf, *Marine Policy*, vol. 8, pp. 211–224.
12. O'Riordan, T. (1976) The Role of Environmental Issues in Canadian-American Policy Making and Administration, in J. W. Watson and T. O'Riordan (eds.) *The American Environment: Perceptions and Policies*, John Wiley, Chichester, pp. 277–328.

13. For a simplified analysis of this very complex and delicate issue, see Fleischer, C. A. (1977) The 1977 Session of the United Nations Law of the Sea Conference, *Environmental Policy and Law*, vol. 3, pp. 100–108.
14. Schelling, *op. cit.*, pp. 69–70.
15. Michael Storm quotes the American sociologist Melvin Webber "the communities with which modern man associates are no longer the communities of place to which his ancestors were restricted. People are becoming more closely tied to various interest communities than to place communities, whether the interest is based on occupational activities, leisure pastimes, social relationships, intellectual pursuits or age groups." Storm rightly points out that changing community patterns, social and locational mobility and increased size of settlements all contribute to the demise of space-based communities. The notion of community, he argues, is something middle-class ideologies would like to think exists, but is largely a figment of wishful imagination. See M. Storm (1973) The Community and the Curriculum, *Bulletin of the General Studies Association*.
16. Schumacher, E. F. (1973) *Small is Beautiful: Economics as if People Really Mattered*, Harper Torchbooks, New York. Robertson, J. (1978) *The Sane Alternative: Signposts to a Self-Fulfilling Future*, 7 St. Anne's Villas, London.
17. See Catching the Culprits, *The Economist*, 11 August 1979, p. 101.
18. For a good account, see Sage, B. (1979) Disaster at Sullum Voe, *New Scientist*, 19 April, pp. 183–184, and Continuing Saga of Sullum Voe, *ibid.*, 26 April, pp. 260–261.
19. Wilkinson, R. G. (1973) *Poverty and Progress*, Methuen, London.
20. Wilkinson, *op. cit.*, p. 5.
21. White, L., Jr. (1967) The Historical Roots of Our Ecologic Crisis, *Science*, vol. 155, pp. 1203–1207.
22. Black, J. N. (1970) *The Dominion of Man: The Search for Ecological Responsibility*, John Black, Edinburgh.
23. Leiss, W. (1978) Political Aspects of Environmental Issues, *Alternatives*, vol. 7, pp. 23–32.
24. See the excellent account by Dave Elliott (1978) *The Politics of Nuclear Power*, Pluto Press, London.
25. For one example, see Castleman, B. (1979) Exporting Hazardous Industries, *New Ecologist*, vol. 3 (May–June), pp. 80–85.
26. For a comprehensive statement of this position read Coates, K. (ed.) (1978) *The Right to Useful Work*, Spokesman Books, Nottingham.
27. See, for example, the anthology of writings and sayings from the North American Indians, McLuhan, T. C. (1972) *Touch the Earth: A Self Portrait of Indian Existence*, Pocket Books, New York.
28. Tuan, Y. F. (1970) Our Treatment of the Environment in Ideal and Actuality, *American Scientist*, vol. 56, pp. 244–249.
29. Tuan, *op. cit.*, p. 244.
30. Quoted in Tuan, Y. F. (1971) *Man and Nature*, Resource Paper No. 10, Association of American Geographers, Washington, DC., p. 32.
31. de Klemm, *op. cit.*, p. 17.
32. Müller, F. G. (1979) Divide-up to Clean Up: A Geopolitical Solution to Mediterranean Pollution, *Environmental Policy and Law*, vol. 5, pp. 13–15.
33. This is embodied in Principle 21 of the UN Conference on the Human Environment held in Stockholm in June 1972.

   "States have ... the sovereign right to exploit their own resources pursuant to their own environmental policies, and the responsibility to ensure that activities within their jurisdiction or control do not cause damage to the environment of other states or of areas beyond the limits of national jurisdiction."
34. The United Nations Environment Programme was established in the aftermath of the Stockholm Conference with a remit to monitor environmental changes in the global commons. UNEP in turn set up the Global Environmental Monitoring System (GEMS) which is little more than a systematic compilation of existing national reports.
35. The lead-in-petrol-issue is best documented in the BBC TV film in the "Man-Alive" series, screened on 4 September 1979.
36. See Sax, J. (1970) *Defending the Environment* Knopf, New York. The topic is also covered in O'Riordan, T. (1976) *Environmentalism*, Pion, London, pp. 264–282.
37. Sax, *op. cit.*, p. 56.

. 38. The only attempt to discuss this concept in detail in the UK was by Lord Justice Scarman (1976) *English Law: The New Dimension*, Stevens, London. For a comprehensive review of the US scene, read Di Mento, J. (1977) Citizen Environmental Litigation and the Administrative Process: Empirical Findings, Remaining Issues and a Direction for Future Research, *Duke Law Journal*, vol. 1977 (2), pp. 409–452. For an economic viewpoint, see Mishan, E. J. (1974) On The Economics of Disamenity, in Marris, R. (ed.) *The Corporate Society*, Macmillan.
39. Civic Trust (1976) *The Local Amenity Movement*, Civic Trust, London.
40. There is a considerable literature in the British amenity lobby. For a comprehensive review, see Lowe, P. (1976) The Environmental Lobby, *Built Environment Quarterly*, pp. 73–76, 151–161, 235–238, and Brooks, S. K. and Richardson, J. J. (1975) The Environmental Lobby in Britain, *Parliamentary Affairs*, vol. 28, pp. 312–328, also Goyder, J. and Lowe, P. (1983) *Environmental Groups in British Politics*, George Allen and Unwin.
41. Hirsch, F. (1977) *Social Limits to Growth*, Routledge & Kegan Paul, London, p. 187.
42. Ophuls (1977) *Ecology and the Politics of Scarcity: Prologue to the Political Theory of the Steady State*, Freeman & Co., San Francisco. See also Ophuls, W. (1979) *Global Ecopolitics: The New Context for International Relations*, Freeman & Co., San Francisco.

READINGS

THE TRAGEDY OF THE COMMONS*

Garrett Hardin

AT THE end of a thoughtful article on the future of nuclear war, J.B. Weisner and H.F. York concluded that: "Both sides in the arms race are . . . confronted by the dilemma of steadily increasing military power and steadily decreasing national security. *It is our considered professional judgment that this dilemma has no technical solution.* If the great powers continue to look for solutions in the area of science and technology only, the result will be to worsen the situation."[1]

I would like to focus your attention not on the subject of the article (national security in a nuclear world) but on the kind of conclusion they reached, namely that there is no technical solution to the problem. An implicit and almost universal assumption of discussions published in professional and semipopular scientific journals is that the problem under discussion has a technical solution. A technical solution may be defined as one that requires a change only in the techniques of the natural sciences, demanding little or nothing in the way of change in human values or ideas of morality.

In our day (though not in earlier times) technical solutions are always welcome. Because of previous failures in prophecy, it takes courage to assert that a desired technical solution is not possible. Wiesner and York exhibited this courage; publishing in a science journal, they insisted that the solution to the problem was not to be found in the natural sciences. They cautiously qualified their statement with the phrase, "It is our considered professional judgment. . . ." Whether they were right or not is not the concern of the present article. Rather, the concern here is with the important concept of a class of human problems which can be called "no technical solution problems," and more specifically, with the identification and discussion of one of these.

It is easy to show that the class is not a null class. Recall the game of tick-tack-toe. Consider the problem, "How can I win the game of tick-tack-toe?" It is well known that I cannot, if I assume (in keeping with the conventions of game

*Reprinted with permission from *Science*, Vol. 162, 1968, pp. 1243–1248. (Professor Hardin is in the Department of Human Ecology, University of California, Santa Barbara.)

theory) that my opponent understands the game perfectly. Put another way, there is no "technical solution" to the problem. I can win only by giving a radical meaning to the word "win." I can hit my opponent over the head; or I can falsify the records. Every way in which I "win" involves, in some sense, an abandonment of the game, as we intuitively understand it. (I can also, of course, openly abandon the game—refuse to play it. This is what most adults do.)

The class of "no technical solution problems" has members. My thesis is that the "population problem," as conventionally conceived, is a member of this class. How it is conventionally conceived needs some comment. It is fair to say that most people who anguish over the population problem are trying to find a way to avoid the evils of overpopulation without relinquishing any of the privileges they now enjoy. They think that farming the seas or developing new strains of wheat will solve the problem—technologically. I try to show here that the solution they seek cannot be found. The population problem cannot be solved in a technical way, any more than can the problem of winning the game of tick-tack-toe.

What shall we maximize?

Population, as Malthus said, naturally tends to grow "geometrically," or, as we would now say, exponentially. In a finite world this means that the per-capita share of the world's goods must decrease. Is ours a finite world?

A fair defense can be put forward for the view that the world is infinite; or that we do not know that it is not. But, in terms of the practical problems that we must face in the next few generations with the foreseeable technology, it is clear that we will greatly increase human misery if we do not, during the immediate future, assume that the world available to the terrestrial human population is finite. "Space" is no escape.[2]

A finite world can support only a finite population; therefore, population growth must eventually equal zero. (The case of perpetual wide fluctuations above and below zero is a trivial variant that need not be discussed.) When this condition is met, what will be the situation of mankind? Specifically, can Bentham's goal of "the greatest good for the greatest number" be realized?

No—for two reasons, each sufficient by itself. The first is a theoretical one. It is not mathematically possible to maximize for two (or more) variables at the same time. This was clearly stated by von Neumann and Morgenstern,[3] but the principle is implicit in the theory of partial differential equations, dating back at least to D'Alembert (1717–1783).

The second reason springs directly from biological facts. To live, any organism must have a source of energy (for example, food). This energy is utilized for two purposes: mere maintenance and work. For man, maintenance of life requires about 1600 kilocalories a day ("maintenance calories"). Anything that he does over and above merely staying alive will be defined as work, and is supported by "work calories" which he takes in. Work calories are used not only for what we call work in common speech; they are also required for all forms of enjoyment, from swimming and automobile racing to playing music and writing poetry. If our goal is to maximize population it is obvious what we must do: We must make the work calories per person approach as close to zero as possible. No gourmet meals, no vacations, no sports, no music, no literature, no art. . . . I think that everyone will grant, without argument or proof, that maximizing population does not maximize goods. Bentham's goal is impossible.

In reaching this conclusion I have made the usual assumption that it is the acquisition of energy that is the problem. The appearance of atomic energy has led some to question this assumption. However, given an infinite source of energy, population growth still produces an inescapable problem. The problem of the acquisition of energy is replaced by the problem of its dissipation, as J. H. Fremlin has so wittily shown.[4] The arithmetic signs in the analysis are, as it were, reversed; but Bentham's goal is unobtainable.

The optimum population is, then, less than the maximum. The difficulty of defining the optimum is enormous; so far as I know, no one has seriously tackled this problem. Reaching an acceptable and stable solution will surely require more than one generation of hard analytical work—and much persuasion.

We want the maximum good per person; but what is good? To one person it is wilderness, to another it is ski lodges for thousands. To one it is estuaries to nourish ducks for hunters to shoot; to another it is factory land. Comparing one good with another is, we usually say, impossible because goods are incommensurable. Incommensurables cannot be compared.

Theoretically this may be true; but in real life incommensurables *are* commensurable. Only a criterion of judgment and a system of weighting are needed. In nature the criterion is survival. Is it better for a species to be small and hideable, or large and powerful? Natural selection commensurates the incommensurables. The compromise achieved depends on a natural weighting of the values of the variables.

Man must imitate this process. There is no doubt that in fact he already does, but unconsciously. It is when the hidden decisions are made explicit that the arguments begin. The problem for the years ahead is to work out an acceptable theory of weighting. Synergistic effects, nonlinear variation, and difficulties in discounting the future make the intellectual problem difficult, but not (in principle) insoluble.

Has any cultural group solved this practical problem at the present time, even on an intuitive level? One simple fact proves that none has: there is no prosperous population in the world today that has, and has had for some time, a growth rate of zero. Any people that intuitively identified its optimum point will soon reach it, after which its growth rate becomes and remains zero.

Of course, a positive growth rate might be taken as evidence that a population is below its optimum. However, by any reasonable standards, the most rapidly growing populations on earth today are (in general) the most miserable. This association (which need not be invariable) casts doubt on the optimistic assumption that the positive growth rate of a population is evidence that it has yet to reach its optimum.

We can make little progress in working toward optimum population size until we explicitly exorcise the spirit of Adam Smith in the field of practical demography. In economic affairs, *The Wealth of Nations* (1776) popularized the "invisible hand," the idea that an individual who "intends only his own gain," is, as it were, "led by an invisible hand to promote . . . the public interest."[5] Adam Smith did not assert that this was invariably true, and perhaps neither did any of his followers. But he contributed to a dominant tendency of thought that has ever since interfered with positive action based on rational analysis, namely, the tendency to assume that decisions reached individually will, in fact, be the best decisions for an entire society. If this assumption is correct it justifies the continuance of our present policy of *laissez faire* in reproduction. If it is correct we can assume that men will control their individual fecundity so as to produce the optimum population. If the assumption is not correct, we need to reexamine our individual freedoms to see which ones are defensible.

Tragedy of freedom in a commons

The rebuttal to the invisible hand in population control is to be found in a scenario first sketched in a little-known pamphlet in 1833 by a mathematical amateur named William Forster Lloyd (1794–1852).[6] We may well call it "the tragedy of the commons," using the word "tragedy" as the philosopher Whitehead used it[7]: "The essence of dramatic tragedy is not unhappiness. It resides in the solemnity of the remorseless working of things." He then goes on to say, "This inevitableness of destiny can only be illustrated in terms of human life by incidents which in fact involve unhappiness. For it is only by them that the futility of escape can be made evident in the drama."

The tragedy of the commons develops in this way. Picture a pasture open to all. It is to be expected that each herdsman will try to keep as many cattle as possible on the commons. Such an arrangement may work reasonably satisfactorily for centuries because tribal wars, poaching, and disease keep the numbers of both man and beast well below the carrying capacity of the land. Finally, however, comes the day of reckoning, that is, the day when the long-desired goal of social stability becomes a reality. At this point, the inherent logic of the commons remorselessly generates tragedy.

As a rational being, each herdsman seeks to maximize his gain. Explicitly or implicitly, more or less consciously, he asks, "What is the utility *to me* of adding one more animal to my herd?" This utility has one negative and one positive component.

1. The positive component is a function of the increment of one animal. Since the herdsman receives all the proceeds from the sale of the additional animal, the positive utility is nearly $+1$.
2. The negative component is a function of the additional overgrazing created by one more animal. Since, however, the effects of overgrazing are shared by all the herdsmen, the negative utility for any particular decision-making herdsman is only a fraction of -1.

Adding together the component partial utilities, the rational herdsman concludes that the only sensible course for him to pursue is to add another animal to his herd. And another. . . . But this is the conclusion reached by each and every rational herdsman sharing a commons. Therein is the tragedy. Each man is locked into a system that compels him to increase his herd without limit—in a world that is limited. Ruin is the destination toward which all men rush, each pursuing his own best interest in a society that believes in the freedom of the commons. Freedom in a commons brings ruin to all.

Some would say that this is a platitude. Would that it were! In a sense, it was learned thousands of years ago, but natural selection favors the forces of psychological denial.[8] The individual benefits as an individual from his ability to deny the truth even though society as a whole, of which he is a part, suffers. Education can counteract the natural tendency to do the wrong thing, but the inexorable succession of generations requires that the basis for this knowledge be constantly refreshed.

A simple incident that occurred a few years ago in Leominster, Massachusetts, shows how perishable the knowledge is. During the Christmas shopping season the parking meters downtown were covered with plastic bags that bore tags reading: "Do not open until after Christmas. Free parking courtesy of the mayor and city council." In other words, facing the prospect of an increased demand for already scarce space, the city fathers reinstituted the system of the commons. (Cynically, we suspect that they gained more votes than they lost by this retrogressive act.)

In an approximate way, the logic of the commons has been understood for a long time, perhaps since the discovery of agriculture or the invention of private property in real estate. But it is understood mostly only in special cases which are not sufficiently generalized. Even at this late date, cattlemen leasing national land on the Western ranges demonstrate no more than an ambivalent understanding, in constantly pressuring federal authorities to increase the head count to the point where overgrazing produces erosion and weed-dominance. Likewise, the oceans of the world continue to suffer from the survival of the philosophy of the commons. Maritime nations still respond automatically to the shibboleth of the "freedom of the seas." Professing to believe in the "inexhaustible resources of the oceans," they bring species after species of fish and whales closer to extinction.[9]

The National Parks present another instance of the working out of the tragedy of the commons. At present, they are open to all, without limit. The parks themselves are limited in extent—there is only one Yosemite Valley—whereas population seems to grow without limit. The values that visitors seek in the parks are steadily eroded. Plainly, we must soon cease to treat the parks as commons or they will be of no value to anyone.

What shall we do? We have several options. We might sell them off as private property. We might keep them as public property, but allocate the right to enter them. The allocation might be on the basis of wealth, by the use of an auction system. It might be on the basis of merit, as defined by some agreed-upon standards. It might be by lottery. Or it might be on a first-come, first-served basis, administered to long queues. These, I think, are all objectionable. But we must choose — or acquiesce in the destruction of the commons that we call our National Parks.

Pollution

In a reverse way, the tragedy of the commons reappears in problems of pollution. Here it is not a question of taking something out of the commons, but of putting something in—sewage, or chemical, radioactive, and heat wastes into water; noxious and dangerous fumes into the air; and distracting and unpleasant advertising signs into the line of sight. The calculations of utility are much the same as before. The rational man finds that his share of the cost of the wastes he discharges into the commons is less than the cost of purifying his wastes before releasing them. Since this is true for everyone, we are locked into a system of "fouling our own nest," so long as we behave only as independent, rational, free-enterprisers.

The tragedy of the commons as a food basket is averted by private property, or something formally like it. But the air and waters surrounding us cannot readily be fenced, and so the tragedy of the commons as a cesspool must be prevented by different means, by coercive laws or taxing devices that make it cheaper for the polluter to treat his pollutants than to discharge them untreated. We have not progressed as far with the solution of this problem as we have with the first. Indeed, our particular concept of private property, which deters us from exhausting the positive resources of the earth, favors pollution. The owner of a factory on the bank of a stream—whose property extends to the middle of the stream—often has difficulty seeing why it is not his natural right to muddy the waters flowing past his door. The law, always behind the times, requires elaborate stitching and fitting to adapt it to this newly perceived aspect of the commons.

The pollution problem is a consequence of population. It did not much matter how a lonely American frontiersman disposed of his waste. "Flowing water purifies itself every ten miles," my grandfather used to say, and the myth was near enough to the truth when he was a boy, for there were not too many people. But as population became denser, the natural chemical and biological recycling processes became overloaded, calling for a redefinition of property rights.

How to legislate temperance?

Analysis of the pollution problem as a function of population density uncovers a not generally recognized principle of morality, namely: *the morality of an act is a function of the state of the system at the time it is performed.*[10] Using the commons as a cesspool does not harm the general public under frontier conditions, because there is no public; the same behavior in a metropolis is unbearable. A hundred and fifty years ago a plainsman could kill an American bison, cut out only the tongue for his dinner, and discard the rest of the animal. He was not in any important sense being wasteful. Today, with only a few thousand bison left, we would be appalled at such behavior.

In passing, it is worth noting that the morality of an act cannot be determined from a photograph. One does not know whether a man killing an elephant or setting fire to the grassland is harming others until one knows the total system in which his act appears. "One picture is worth a thousand words," said an ancient Chinese; but it may take ten thousand words to validate it. It is as tempting to ecologists as it is to reformers in general to try to persuade others by way of the photographic shortcut. But the essence of an argument cannot be photographed: it must be presented rationally—in words.

That morality is system-sensitive escaped the attention of most codifiers of ethics in the past. "Thou shalt not . . ." is the form of traditional ethical directives which make no allowance for particular circumstances. The laws of our society follow the pattern of ancient ethics, and therefore are poorly suited to governing a complex, crowded, changeable world. Our epicyclic solution is to augment statutory law with administrative law. Since it is practically impossible to spell out all the conditions under which it is safe to burn trash in the back yard or to run an automobile without smog-control, by law we delegate the details to bureaus. The result is administrative law, which is rightly feared for an ancient reason—*Quis custodiet ipsos custodes?*–Who shall watch the watchers themselves? John Adams said that we must have a "government of laws and not men." Bureau administrators, trying to evaluate the morality of acts in the total system, are singularly liable to corruption, producing a government by men, not laws.

Prohibition is easy to legislate (though not necessarily to enforce); but how do we legislate temperance? Experience indicates that it can be accomplished best through the mediation of administrative law. We limit possibilities unnecessarily if we suppose that the sentiment of *Quis custodiet* denies us the use of administrative law. We should rather retain the phrase as a perpetual reminder of fearful dangers we cannot avoid. The great challenge facing us now is to invent the corrective feedbacks that are needed to keep custodians honest. We must find ways to legitimate the needed authority of both the custodians and the corrective feedbacks.

Freedom to breed is intolerable

The tragedy of the commons is involved in population problems in another way. In a world governed solely by the principle of "dog eat dog"—if indeed there ever was such a world—how many children a family had would not be a matter of public concern. Parents who bred too exuberantly would leave fewer descendants, not more, because they would be unable to care adequately for their children. David Lack and others have found that such a negative feedback demonstrably controls the fecundity of birds.[11] But men are not birds, and have not acted like them for millenniums, at least.

If each human family were dependent only on its own resources; *if* the children of improvident parents starved to death; *if*, thus, overbreeding brought its own "punishment" to the germ line—*then* there would be no public interest in controlling the breeding of families. But our society is deeply committed to the welfare state,[12] and hence is confronted with another aspect of the tragedy of the commons.

In a welfare state, how shall we deal with the family, the religion, the race, or the class (or indeed any distinguishable and cohesive group) that adopts overbreeding as a policy to secure its own aggrandizement?[13] To couple the concept of freedom to breed with the belief that everyone born has an equal right to the commons is to lock the world into a tragic course of action.

Unfortunately this is just the course of action that is being pursued by the United Nations. In late 1967, some thirty nations agreed to the following: "The Universal Declaration of Human Rights describes the family as the natural and fundamental unit of society. It follows that any choice and decision with regard to the size of the family must irrevocably rest with the family itself, and cannot be made by anyone else."[14]

It is painful to have to deny categorically the validity of this right; denying it, one feels as uncomfortable as a resident of Salem, Massachusetts, who denied the reality of witches in the seventeenth century. At the present time, in liberal quarters, something like a taboo acts to inhibit criticism of the United Nations. There is a feeling that the United Nations is "our last and best hope," that we shouldn't find fault with it; we shouldn't play into the hands of the archconservatives. However, let us not forget what Robert Louis Stevenson said: "The truth that is suppressed by friends is the readiest weapon of the enemy." If we love the truth we must openly deny the validity of the Universal Declaration of Human Rights, even though it is promoted by the United Nations. We should also join with Kingsley Davis[15] in attempting to get Planned Parenthood–World Population to see the error of its ways in embracing the same tragic ideal.

Conscience is self-eliminating

It is a mistake to think that we can control the breeding of mankind in the long run by an appeal to conscience. Charles Galton Darwin made this point when he spoke on the centennial of the publication of his grandfather's great book. The argument is straightforward and Darwinian.

People vary. Confronted with appeals to limit breeding, some people will undoubtedly respond to the plea more than others. Those who have more children will produce a larger fraction of the next generation than those with more susceptible consciences. The differences will be accentuated, generation by generation.

In C. G. Darwin's words: "It may well be that it would take hundreds of generations for the progenitive instinct to develop in this way, but if it should do so, nature would have taken her revenge, and the variety *Homo contracipiens* would become extinct and would be replaced by the variety *Homo progenitivus*."[16]

The argument assumes that conscience or the desire for children (no matter which) is hereditary—but hereditary only in the most general formal sense. The result will be the same whether the attitude is transmitted through germ cells, or exosomatically, to use A. J. Lotka's term. (If one denies the latter possibility as well as the former, then what's the point of education?) The argument has here been stated in the context of the population problem, but it applies equally well to any instance in which society appeals to an individual exploiting a commons to restrain himself for the general good—by means of his conscience. To make such an appeal is to set up a selective system that works toward the elimination of conscience from the race.

Pathogenic effects of conscience

The long-term disadvantage of an appeal to conscience should be enough to condemn it; but it has serious short-term disadvantages as well. If we ask a man who is exploiting a commons to desist "in the name of conscience," what are we saying to him? What does he hear?—not only at the moment but also in the wee small hours of the night when, half asleep, he remembers not merely the words we used but also the non-verbal communication cues we gave him unawares? Sooner or later, consciously or subconsciously, he senses that he has received two communications, and that they are contradictory: 1. (intended communication) "If you don't do as we ask, we will openly condemn you for not acting like a responsible citizen"; 2. (the unintended communication) "If you *do* behave as we ask, we will secretly condemn you for a simpleton who can be shamed into standing aside while the rest of us exploit the commons."

Everyman then is caught in what Bateson has called a "double bind." Bateson and his co-workers have made a plausible case for viewing the double bind as an important causative factor in the genesis of schizophrenia.[17] The double bind may not always be so damaging, but it always endangers the mental health of anyone to whom it is applied. "A bad conscience," said Nietzsche, "is a kind of illness."

To conjure up a conscience in others is tempting to anyone who wishes to extend his control beyond the legal limits. Leaders at the highest level succumb to this temptation. Has any president during the past generation failed to call on labor unions to moderate voluntarily their demands for higher wages, or to steel companies to honor voluntary guidelines on prices? I can recall none. The rhetoric used on such occasions is designed to produce feelings of guilt in non-cooperators.

For centuries it was assumed without proof that guilt was a valuable, perhaps even an indispensable, ingredient of the civilized life. Now, in this post-Freudian world, we doubt it.

Paul Goodman speaks from the modern point of view when he says: "No good has ever come from feeling guilty, neither intelligence, policy, nor compassion. The guilty do not pay attention to the object but only to themselves, and not even to their own interests, which might make sense, but to their anxieties."[18]

One does not have to be a professional psychiatrist to see the consequences of anxiety. We in the Western world are just emerging from a dreadful two centuries-long Dark Ages of Eros that was sustained partly by prohibition laws, but perhaps more effectively by the anxiety-generating mechanisms of education. Alex Comfort has told the story well in *The Anxiety Makers;*[19] it is not a pretty one.

Since proof is difficult, we may even concede that the results of anxiety may sometimes, from certain points of view, be desirable. The larger question we should ask is whether, as a matter of policy, we should ever encourage the use of a technique the tendency (if not the intention) of which is psychologically pathogenic. We hear much talk these days of responsible parenthood; the coupled words are incorporated into the titles of some organizations devoted to birth control. Some people have proposed massive propaganda campaigns to instill responsibility into the nation's (or the world's) breeders. But what is the meaning of the word conscience? When we use the word responsibility in the absence of substantial sanctions are we not trying to browbeat a free man in a commons into acting against his own interest? Responsibility is a verbal counterfeit for a substantial quid pro quo. It is an attempt to get something for nothing.

If the word responsibility is to be used at all, I suggest that it be in the sense Charles Frankel uses it.[20] "Responsibility," says this philosopher, "is the product of definite social arrangements." Notice that Frankel calls for social arrangements—not propaganda.

Mutual coercion mutually agreed upon

The social arrangements that produce responsibility are arrangements that create coercion, of some sort. Consider bank robbing. The man who takes money from a bank acts as if the bank were a commons. How do we prevent such action? Certainly not by trying to control his behavior solely by a verbal appeal to his sense of responsibility. Rather than rely on propaganda we follow Frankel's lead and insist that a bank is not a commons; we seek the definite social arrangements that will keep it from becoming a commons. That we thereby infringe on the freedom of would-be robbers we neither deny nor regret.

The morality of bank robbing is particularly easy to understand because we accept complete prohibition of this activity. We are willing to say "Thou shalt not rob banks," without providing for exceptions. But temperance also can be created by coercion. Taxing is a good coercive device. To keep downtown shoppers temperate in their use of parking space we introduce parking meters for short periods, and traffic fines for longer ones. We need not actually forbid a citizen to park as long as he wants to; we need merely make it increasingly expensive for him to do so. Not prohibition, but carefully biased options are what we offer him. A Madison Avenue man might call this persuasion; I prefer the greater candor of the word coercion.

Coercion is a dirty word to most liberals now, but it need not forever be so. As with the four-letter words, its dirtiness can be cleansed away by exposure to the light, by saying it over and over without apology or embarrassment. To many, the word coercion implies arbitrary decisions of distant and irresponsible bureaucrats; but this is not a necessary part of its meaning. The only kind of coercion I recommend is mutual coercion, mutually agreed upon by the majority of the people affected.

To say that we mutually agree to coercion is not to say that we are required to enjoy it, or even to pretend we enjoy it. Who enjoys taxes? We all grumble about them. But we accept compulsory taxes because we recognize that voluntary taxes would favor the conscienceless. We institute and (grumblingly) support taxes and other coercive devices to escape the horror of the commons.

An alternative to the commons need not be perfectly just to be preferable. With real estate and other material goods, the alternative we have chosen is the institution of private property coupled with legal inheritance. Is this system perfectly just? As a genetically trained biologist I deny that it is. It seems to me that, if there are to be differences in individual inheritance, legal possession should be perfectly correlated with biological inheritance—that those who are biologically more fit to be the custodians of property and power should legally inherit more. But genetic recombination continually makes a mockery of the doctrine of "like father, like son" implicit in our laws of legal inheritance. An idiot can inherit millions, and a trust fund can keep his estate intact. We must admit that our legal system of private property plus inheritance is unjust—but we put up with it because we are not convinced, at the moment, that anyone has invented a better system. The alternative of the commons is too horrifying to contemplate. Injustice is preferable to total ruin.

It is one of the peculiarities of the warfare between reform and the status quo that it is thoughtlessly governed by a double standard. Whenever a reform measure is proposed it is often defeated when its opponents triumphantly discover a flaw in it. As Kingsley Davis has pointed out,[21] worshippers of the status quo sometimes imply that no reform is possible without unanimous agreement, an implication contrary to historical fact. As nearly as I can make out, automatic rejection of proposed reforms is based on one of two unconscious assumptions: (1) that the status quo is perfect; or (2) that the choice we face is between reform and no action; if the proposed reform is imperfect, we presumably should take no action at all, while we wait for a perfect proposal.

But we can never do nothing. That which we have done for thousands of years is also action. It also produces evils. Once we are aware that the status quo is action, we can then compare its discoverable advantages and disadvantages with the predicted advantages and disadvantages of the proposed reform, discounting as best we can for our lack of experience. On the basis of such a comparison, we can make a rational decision which will not involve the unworkable assumption that only perfect systems are tolerable.

Recognition of necessity

Perhaps the simplest summary of this analysis of man's population problems is this: the commons, if justifiable at all, is justifiable only under conditions of low-population density. As the human population has increased, the commons has had to be abandoned in one aspect after another.

First we abandoned the commons in food gathering, enclosing farm land and restricting pastures and hunting and fishing areas. These restrictions are still not complete throughout the world.

Somewhat later we saw that the commons as a place for waste disposal would also have to be abandoned. Restrictions on the disposal of domestic sewage are widely accepted in the Western world; we are still struggling to close the commons to pollution by automobiles, factories, insecticide sprayers, fertilizing operations, and atomic energy installations.

In a still more embryonic state is our recognition of the evils of the commons in matters of pleasure. There is almost no restriction on the propagation of sound waves in the public medium. The shopping public is assaulted with mindless music, without its consent. Our government has paid out billions of dollars to create a supersonic transport which would disturb 50,000 people for every one person whisked from coast to coast 3 hours faster. Advertisers muddy the airwaves of radio and television and pollute the view of travelers. We are a long way from outlawing the commons in matters of pleasure. Is this because our Puritan inheritance makes us view pleasure as something of a sin, and pain (that is, the pollution of advertising) as the sign of virtue?

Every new enclosure of the commons involves the infringement of somebody's personal liberty. Infringements made in the distant past are accepted because no contemporary complains of a loss. It is the newly proposed infringements that we vigorously oppose; cries of "rights" and "freedom" fill the air. But what does "freedom" mean? When men mutually agreed to pass laws against robbing, mankind became more free, not less so. Individuals locked into the logic of the commons are free only to bring on universal ruin; once they see the necessity of mutual coercion, they become free to pursue other goals. I believe it was Hegel who said. "Freedom is the recognition of necessity."

The most important aspect of necessity that we must now recognize, is the necessity of abandoning the commons in breeding. No technical solution can rescue us from the misery of overpopulation. Freedom to breed will bring ruin to all. At the moment, to avoid hard decisions many of us are tempted to propagandize for conscience and responsible parenthood. The temptation must be resisted, because an appeal to independently acting consciences selects for the disappearance of all conscience in the long run, and an increase in anxiety in the short.

The only way we can preserve and nurture other and more precious freedoms is by relinquishing the freedom to breed, and that very soon. "Freedom is the recognition of necessity"–and it is the role of education to reveal to all the necessity of abandoning the freedom to breed. Only so, can we put an end to this aspect of the tragedy of the commons.

Notes

1. J. B. Wiesner and H. F. York, *Scientific American* **211** (No. 4), 27 (1964).
2. G. Hardin, *Journal of Heredity* **50**, 68 (1959); S. von Hoernor, *Science* **137**, 18, (1962).
3. J. von Neumann and O. Morgenstern, *Theory of Games and Economic Behavior* (Princeton University Press, Princeton, N.J., 1947), p. 11.
4. J. H. Fremlin, *New Scientist*, No. 415 (1964), p. 285.
5. A. Smith, *The Wealth of Nations* (Modern Library, New York, 1937), p. 423.
6. W. F. Lloyd, *Two Lectures on the Checks to Populations* (Oxford University Press, Oxford, England, 1833).
7. A. N. Whitehead, *Science and the Modern World* (Mentor, New York, 1948), p. 17.
8. G. Hardin, Ed., *Population, Evolution, and Birth Control* (Freeman, San Francisco, 1964), p. 56.
9. S. McVay, *Scientific American* **216** (No. 8), 13 (1966).
10. J. Fletcher, *Situation Ethics* (Westminster, Philadelphia, 1966).
11. D. Lack, *The Natural Regulation of Animal Numbers* (Clarendon Press, Oxford, England, 1954).
12. H. Girvetz, *From Wealth to Welfare* (Stanford University Press, Stanford, Calif., 1950).
13. G. Hardin, *Perspectives in Biology and Medicine* **6**, 366 (1963).
14. U. Thant, *International Planned Parenthood News*, No. 168 (February 1968), p. 3.
15. K. Davis, *Science* **158**, 730 (1967).
16. S. Tax, Ed., *Evolution After Darwin* (University of Chicago Press, Chicago, 1960), vol. 2, p. 469.
17. G. Bateson, D. D. Jackson, J. Haley, and J. Weakland, *Behavioral Science* **1**, 251 (1956).
18. P. Goodman, *New York Review of Books* **10** (8), 22 (23 May 1968).
19. A. Comfort, *The Anxiety Makers* (Nelson, London, 1967).
20. C. Frankel, *The Case for Modern Man* (Harper & Row, New York, 1955), p. 203.
21. J. D. Roslansky, *Genetics and the Future of Man* (Appleton-Century-Crofts, New York, 1966), p. 177.

THE TRAGEDY OF THE COMMONS: A RE-ANALYSIS*

Peter G. Stillman

THE "tragedy of the commons" has been a frequent and helpful tool for the analysis of ecological and other issues; it provides a neat and short-hand metaphor for a set of various and complex problems. But those who use the parable fail to see that the tragedy has no solution logically consistent with its

*Reprinted with permission from *Alternatives*, Vol. 4, pp. 12–15. (Dr. Stillman is a member of the Department of Political Science, Vassar College, Poughkeepsie, New York.)

premises; the failure to see that there are no logical solutions has hindered the search for solutions to problems of the type portrayed by the tragedy of the commons. The pervasive tragedy of the commons can be met only by recognizing that there is no logically consistent solution to the tragedy of the commons, and then by ascertaining how to avoid the tragedy . . .

Hardin's article quickly became well known and well respected, widely reprinted and widely used. It has provided the basis for much ecological theorizing: in addition to Hardin himself,[1] others—most notably Kenneth Boulding and William Ophuls—have drawn out the political and theoretical implications of the relentless ecological tragedy of the commons.[2] Similarly, the concept has spread to other areas of life, and has been used to analyze, for instance, international relations.[3]

No logically consistent solution

Unfortunately, Hardin and all those who have used Hardin's analysis of the "tragedy of the commons" together share a crucial misconception: that the tragedy of the commons can be "solved". For the parameters and assumptions of the parable make it unsolvable, in the sense that no solution can be found that is logically consistent with all these parameters and assumptions.

The parable contains three major parameters, One is that the commons is limited; obviously, if the commons were unlimited and infinite, it could not be overgrazed. The second is that the cow consumes more than it returns to the commons; obviously, if the cow returned more to the commons than it consumed, the cow would not ever overgraze. The third is that each herdsman, "as a rational being", has one particular type of rationality: the herdsman's rationality is short-term, self-interested rationality; the herdsman as rational thus tries to maximize his self-interest in the short term. If each of the herdsmen has a long-term perspective on his rational self-interest, none would overgraze the commons. Possibly, one herdsman's rationality might be aberrant, and he might be inclined to graze too many cows; but such a "free rider" could be easily dealt with, formally or informally, by the herdsman with long-term perspectives. In brief, a very short-term conception of rational self-interest is one parameter of the parable.

These parameters are such that there is no solution to the parable that is logically consistent with them. This lack of a logically consistent solution can easily be seen by examining closely some attempted solutions, and noting their fallacies. One common solution is a strong central government or a stronger ruler. But those who argue for a strong central government assume that the ruler will be a wise and ecologically-aware altruist; they conveniently overlook that their authoritarian ruler, if he is (like everyone in the society) "a rational, self-interested individual", will not act to solve ecological problems. He will not do so because he will perceive (or quickly learn) that ecologically-sound policies (like limiting the cows on the commons) go against the rational self-interest of each individual; and thus for the ruler to impose ecological solutions would be for him to act contrary to his own rational self-interest by increasing popular discontent, undermining consent, and reducing popular obligation. Just as economic calculations which assume rational, self-interested individuals produce continual economic optima at all points of growth until just before environmental costs become infinite and the system is on the verge of collapse,[4] so too the rational, self-interested ruler is always better off by allowing people to satisfy their self-interests and thus consent to his rule until just before environmental costs become infinite and the system is on the verge of collapse. Because of the difficulties and the costs of meeting ecological problems, a rational, self-interested ruler would avoid action as long as possible.

Hardin and some others emphasize not only a strong ruler but also mutual consent; the mutual coercion must be "mutually agreed upon". But, since the rational, self-interested individuals posited in the tragedy of the commons are individuals whose foresight is short, it is difficult to determine why Hardin assumes these individuals will ever get together to consent to mutual coercion in the first place, and how, having consented, they will then continue to consent, and obey the government. The only circumstance that could produce consent would be impending disaster. As soon, however, as the government solved the impending disaster, individuals with short-term rationality would withdraw their consent from the government whenever the government's policies went against their rational (short-term) self-interest. As more and more individuals withdrew consent, it would be more and more difficult for the government to enforce obedience through terror and threat of force. Finally, the government would weaken drastically; liberty to overgraze the commons would be restored; and the tragedy of the commons would be in motion again, to be halted only when the next disaster was obvious—or when it was too late to do anything about the next disaster. Coercion grounded in consent, then, is not a solution in any but a trivial sense: at best, mankind oscillates from impending disaster to strong government which solves the disaster and, doing so, loses consent, with the result that the commons is once more overgrazed, and disaster once again impends; at worst, mankind reacts too late to the disaster.

Neither the "solution" of an autocratic government nor the "solution" of coercion based on consent is logically consistent with the premises of the parable, since each "solution" relies on humans with characteristics different from the short-term rational self-interest that characterizes the herdsmen who precipitate the tragedy. Similarly, other popular "solutions" to the tragedy are logically inconsistent with the premises of the parable. The cultural or communitarian approach to the problem, which posits that the tragedy of the commons does not occur in a traditional society in which the behavior of the individual is subjected to and admits the constraints of that society's cultural pattern,[5] posits herdsmen whose rationality is not short-term nor self-interested, but rather long-term and community- or group-interested.

Furthermore, the dominant "solution" of the past few centuries has been a solution logically inconsistent with the parameters of the problem. John Locke and his successors[6] solved the tragedy of the commons in the seventeenth century, in a way satisfactory to generations of Britishers and Americans. Locke escaped the inexorable logic of the commons by changing one of the parameters. Locke argued that the commons was not in fact limited but could be made to be unlimited, for all practical purposes, by the application of human reason, industriousness, and labor. In a sense, the Lockean individual encroached upon the commons not by adding another cow, but (eventually) by building a factory.[7] As a result, the individual's utility was positive, and much more than merely plus one cow; and, argued Locke, the utilities of everyone else around the commons were also higher: they worked for wages, and no longer farmed for subsistence; and they now had new products they could consume as Locke noted, a common day laborer in England was better off than the richest Indian chief in America.[8]

The Gordian knot resolved

The most obvious conclusion of this essay is that there is no logically consistent solution to the tragedy of the commons. No attempt to resolve ecological issues can hope to do so in a way that maintains logical consistency with Hardin's paradigm.

Stemming from this seemingly pessimistic conclusion, however, is an optimistic conclusion. The search for a resolution, both to the tragedy of the commons and to our current ecological problems, must look at the parameters of the parable to see which must be changed, which may be changed, and which must remain unchanged.

Clearly, we cannot change the premise that Locke changed, the premise of the limitation of the commons. We know now that we do live on a spaceship earth. We can, however, try to change both the "cow" and the short-term rationality of the individual. We can apply technology to try to develop an improved cow. Like the traditional cow, but unlike the factory Locke substituted for the cow, the improved cow should be an integral and positive part of nature, returning to the ecosystem wastes that are valuable and that regenerate the system. Unlike the traditional cow, the improved cow should have a smaller appetite to conform to the limits on natural resources.

But, no matter how much we improve the cow, we must also change the individual herdsman; even with the best of cows, the logic of the tragedy will reassert itself if these cows are used by individuals acting from their short-term self-interest. All herdsmen must be changed to a degree that varies to some extent according to the technological improvements in the cow. At the least, all herdsmen must begin to act on longer- (rather than shorter-) term rational self-interest. If technology cannot improve the cow adequately, or if a margin for error and fate is desired, all herdsmen must act in part from altruism or from concern for the community or the group.

By realizing that these resolutions require breaking the premises of the tragedy, however, it is also easy to realize that it is not enough to call for a new Leviathan of vastly increased governmental power, or for "mutual coercion mutually consented to", or a neo-traditional society; none of these "solutions" will work, unless the individual herdsmen's attitudes are changed, i.e., unless one of the major premises of the parable is contravened. By realizing that a major premise must be broken, we can see the analytic and theoretical shortcomings of previous solutions, and we can focus precisely on where an effective contemporary resolution must come, namely, in the change of attitudes or definitions of rationality . . .

Notes

1. Hardin, G. *Exploring New Ethics for Survival* (New York; Viking, 1972).
2. Boulding, K. *The New Republic* **167**, 22(1972); Ophuls, W., in Daly, Herman E., ed., *Toward a Steady-State Economy* (San Francisco; W. H. Freeman, 1973). There have been two major reviews of the parable. One, by D. Fife (*Environment* **13**, no. 3, 20 [1971]), raises the important implication that the preservation and maintenance of a natural resource (like a commons or a goose) is not necessarily in the self-interest of the entrepreneur exploiting it: "the goose that lays the golden eggs is being killed for profit." But Fife's argument does not affect the basis of Hardin's parable, because the continuing destruction of specific commons—and the reinvestment of the proceeds from killing each specific goose—is a process that cannot be continued forever, since there are a limited number of commons (and thus of further investment opportunities) on spaceship earth. In other words, there is a limit to the number of geese that can be killed. As that limit is approached Hardin's original analysis and conclusions hold completely. The other, by B. Crowe (*Science* **166**, 1103 [1969]), argues empirically that there is no political solution to the tragedy in the modern United States; he also sketches an argument that modern institutions, with their emphasis on specialization and incremental rationality, can not respond to environmental problems, which demand generalized adaptability. Crowe concludes by suggesting that science can make some interim contributions to alleviate the tragedy, contributions based on the self-interests of the scientists. Except for Crowe's faith in science, his arguments are generally consistent with a thesis of this article; but this article goes beyond Crowe's by analyzing the theoretical reasons why the tragedy is insoluble within its own premises and by suggesting what must be changed in order to alleviate or resolve the tragedy of the commons.
3. Beres, L. R. *Western Political Quarterly* **26**, 649 (1974).
4. Pearce, D. *The Ecologist* **3**, 61 (1973).
5. *The Ecologist*, ed., *Blueprint for Survival* (Boston: Houghton Mifflin, 1972).
6. Locke, J. *Two Treatises for Government* (1690), esp. Second Treatise, Chap. V; A. Smith, *Wealth of Nations* (1776); and W. Ophuls, "Locke's Paradigm Lost," paper presented at the 1973 Annual Meeting of the American Political Science Association. While Locke, Smith, and others may not have had Hardin's parable explicitly in mind, they were dealing with the same type of problem that the parable raises.
7. Strictly speaking, the inequality of income and wealth (justified by Locke) lead to increases in commerce and investable capital, which then lead to the building of factories on the commons.
8. Locke, J. Second Treatise, paragraph 41.

TIME, HABITAT, AND SOCIAL STRUCTURE*

William R. Burch, Jr.

... Human populations have persisted and readapted even though centers of civilization have shifted. Therefore, no matter how instructive it may be to catalog the ecological failures of ancient civilizations, such lessons are societal specific not species specific. For a variety of internal and external reasons ancient Sumer was foolish with her water and turned a garden into a desert; consequently, a flourishing civilization is no longer with us. The fact remains, however, that mankind did not perish, merely one particular civilization. In other geographic centers other civilizations emerged, not in a linear pattern with Sumer but in quite different patterns, making use of resources, values, and goods not even imagined by the Sumerians. New civilizations organize on a quite different base, and if expansive enough, they may tinker with the odd

*Reprinted with permission from *Daydreams and Nightmares: A Sociological Essay on the American Environment* by W. R. Burch, Jr., pp. 30–50, 1972. Harper Row, New York. (Professor Birch is a Professor of Sociology in the School of Forestry and Environmental Studies at Yale University.)

monuments of lost civilizations for curiosity and perhaps for the sense of invidious comparison. They seldom re-create the old social patterns, values and resources. Even if they made a determined effort to do so, they could not; for it is, after all, a dynamic world and the conditions of existence for Sumer are not those for Rome and those for Rome are not those of modern Britain or the Soviet Union. If there is any borrowing, it is the desire to rummage through images of the past to find those which justify or curb present behavior.

Linked to the fact that nature and history play their own games of change, which compel adaptation by man, is the fact that man is not recently an ecological modifier. Recent data on Pleistocene man, though still the subject of theoretical controversy, suggest that severe ecological modifications by man are not confined to our era. In fact, early man may have exceeded us in his ability to exterminate other species of animals.

It may be expected that in the process of destroying these animals early man was unwittingly compelling a change in his social institutions as significant as the adaptations he had to make to the severe changes programmed by nature.[1] Thus, by using broad stretches of the time scale, we might see something like major cycles of natural change that compel significant alteration in the patterns of life by man. Within these cycles we might see man, through fires and other means, upsetting the food patterns he had established to such a significant degree that his social institutions were compelled to follow permutations not of his choosing. And so it might go throughout the range of time. Toulmin and Goodfield note:

> This discovery of time has had four aspects. To begin with, it has compelled men to recognize the sheer extent of the past—something which they might guess, but before the eighteenth century could never prove. Secondly, we can now establish the true antiquity of the world, just because we have also come to understand the general processes by which it has developed: the time-scale of these developmental processes provides our final measure of the past. Thirdly, these processes have, at every level, been of two kinds—some general and repetitive, others cumulative and progressive—and a central problem for any historical enquiry, whether about Man or Nature, is to distinguish universal factors, operative everywhere and at all times, from conditional ones, which arise out of earlier historical phases and so acquire significance only at a particular stage of temporal development. Finally, there is the question of motivation: in human history, at any rate, full understanding comes when we reconstruct for ourselves the reasons, fears, and ambitions of our fellow-humans caught up in historical events.[2]

When dealing with these ranges of time we are no longer interested in a specific society but are concerned with the species as a biological population. Nor need there be the intent to build a model of linear social evolution based upon scattered nonlinear groups. Rather we can begin to ask how specific populations have dealt with their environment. What is the relationship between habitat and social structure: Is overexploitation of the ecosystem a modern or a persisting characteristic of the species? If it is a persisting characteristic, what are the conditions under which it prevails or is suppressed? Do resource limits inhibit the development of more elaborate social forms? How is the nature of the social bond influenced by changes in habitat? Attempting to answer these questions may encourage us to follow the dictum of Toulmin and Goodfield.

> Historical understanding comes through exploiting continuities between the past and the present—matching the current patterns of relationships against what we know of earlier

events. So the idea of historical discontinuities is as unenlightening in the human realm as it is in natural science. The concept of "revolutions" has the same defects for the purposes of political history that the concept of "catastrophes" has always had for natural history. Only when we learn to relate the uniformities underlying political or geological change—however rapid—to processes or activities familiar to us in our own time, do we get a grip on the past.[3]

Habitat—stability and change

There seems little question that, like us, tribal societies must develop institutionalized means for dealing with death, birth, sexual relations, and other matters of survival and social consistency. We know that their myths, motives, and organizational patterns are quite different from a feudal or industrial order. Tribal groups contain mythologies and rituals which seem to ensure an ecological ethic. Certainly the majority of anthropological studies, either directly or indirectly, argue that tribal situations represent a natural and harmonious state of man—nature relations. For example, in discussing tribal attitudes toward nature Dorothy Lee provides an invidious contrast with the modern order:

> An old Wintu woman, speaking in prophetic vein, expressed this: "The White people never cared for land or deer or bear. When we Indians kill meat, we eat it all up. When we dig roots, we make little holes. When we build houses, we make little holes. When we burn grass for grasshoppers, we don't ruin things. We shakes down acorns and pinenuts. We don't chop down the trees. We only use dead wood. But the White people plow up the ground, pull up the trees, kill everything . . . How can the spirit of the earth like the White man? . . . Everywhere the White man has touched it, it is sore."[4]

The implicit anticivilization theme in Lee's data and discussion seems almost too familiar. In a study of the relation between soil and civilization Tom Dale and Vernon Carter, like those before them and those who will follow, see tribal hunter-gatherer groups as natural components of the ecosystem while civilizations erode themselves by depleting their soil.[5] In rather breathless fashion the authors manage to rotate through a vast number of civilizations demonstrating how the rise and fall of such organizational forms correlate with soil fertility. In addition to overextending the organic metaphor, such contrasts seem more than a little indulgence in romantic aspirations.

Can tribal structures be all that virtuous, either by accident or design? Does civilization really compel greater exercise in greed or higher magnitudes of error in exploitation? Or are we merely getting noble savage themes dressed up in scientific terminology? Data to examine these notions are scarce but highly suggestive. Perhaps the most detailed and most controversial is represented by Paul S. Martin's charge that Pleistocene man regularly engaged in severe depredations of fauna necessary for his survival. In tracing the movement of man from central Africa throughout the globe, Martin indicates that in each area shortly after the arrival of man several species become extinct. He succinctly concludes his argument by noting:

> To be sure there is much ignorance left to admit. We must beg the question of just how and why prehistoric man obliterated his prey. We may speculate but we cannot determine how moose, elk, and caribou managed to survive while horse, ground sloth, and mastadon did not. One must acknowledge that within historic time the Bushmen and other primitive hunters at a Paleolithic level of technology have not exterminated their game resources, certainly not in any

way comparable to the devastation of the late-Pleistocene. These and other valid objections to the hypothesis of overkill remain. But thus far the hypothesis has survived every critical chronological test. On a world scale the pattern of Pleistocene extinction makes no sense in terms of climatic or environmental change. During the Pleistocene, accelerated extinction occurs only on land and only after man invades or develops specialized big-game hunting weapons...

The thought that prehistoric hunters ten to fifteen thousand years ago (and in Africa over forty thousand years ago) exterminated far more large animals than has modern man with modern weapons and advanced technology is certainly provocative and perhaps even deeply disturbing. With a certain inadmissible pride we may prefer to regard ourselves, not our remote predecessors, as holding uncontested claim to being the arch destroyers of native fauna. But this seems not to be the case. Have we dismissed too casually the possibility of prehistoric over-kill? The late-Pleistocene extinction pattern leaves little room for any other explanation. [6]

Though Martin's argument may be a minority one, he and his colleagues still present enough evidence to raise questions as to whether a tribal system is a guarantee of continuing, long-run ecosystem stability. Harold J. Lutz in a painstaking examination of documentary sources suggests that the flora may also have suffered from tribal depredations. [7] Though his data are confined to Amerindians occupying the boreal forest, Lutz offers fairly clear evidence that early Americans, whether through carelessness, for pleasure, for game management, or for controlling mosquitoes, were responsible for vast areas of burned forests.

R. J. Cameron confounds a similar notion concerning the New Zealand Maori. He reports that contrary to conventional wisdom, the Maori rather severely destroyed many acres of indigenous bush. He argues:

The effect upon the forest of the itinerant form of agriculture that the Maori used to grow potatoes has been described by many of the early explorers and travellers. That a large area of forest was destroyed cannot be disputed; but just how large this area was will probably never be known. There is good reason for believing that during the first half of the nineteenth century the Maori potato growers cleared away forest at a rate not greatly inferior, if at all, to that at which the European settlers continued the despoliation in the years that followed ... It may be that forest ecologists will find in this a valid explanation for the many areas of secondary forest that have puzzled them for so long, and the soil scientists may see a reason for the periods of accelerated erosion that seem to have occurred in many districts during the early part of the nineteenth century. [8]

It should be noted that the Maori reached his height of timber destruction at a point when he still dominated his land and had the opportunity to maximize traditional values due to the new trading resource he found in the Europeans. Potatoes fit traditional Maori practices and values, and, thus, encouraged by his sense of dominance and an opportunity to expand trade, the Maori rapidly expanded the area of cultivation. The unintended effect was that under the new conditions traditional practices which formerly may have maintained some ecological balance now served to accelerate the level of exploitation.

Martin's puzzlement as to why some species survived while others were exterminated may reflect that these were totem creatures whose preservation would be gained at the expense of other animals. Some indication of a similar trained incapacity is provided by the woods-burning activities of Alaskan Indians described by Lutz. They were oriented to the resources of the sea and rivers and may have seen trees as sheltering their enemies and of little value for protecting the fisheries. They probably noted the regenerative capacity of the boreal forest and, not unlike some modern foresters, may have felt that destruction of old-growth timber was the means for establishing a vigorous, thrifty forest.

Martin, Lutz and others permit a break with the Arcadian romantic bathos which so often seems to surround discussions of interactions between tribal societies and nature. They illustrate that man must be a significant ecological factor and has been since the Pleistocene. They demonstrate that cultures are a functional part of their ecology and that *Homo sapien* has a persisting tendency to make nature into his own image. After all, man is basically a weak creature, and nature has played some frightful jokes on him. For most of his history he has been compelled to make rather direct accommodation to nonhuman conditions, though his symbolic tendencies have strained along opposite lines.

This does not mean that we need rest easy because environmental deterioration is "built into" the behavior of man. Rather, it means that by recognizing such a characteristic as persistent we no longer can retreat into ideological finger wagging. Instead we can begin to ask whether there are patterns of myth and social organization which are more likely to ensure and maintain man's survival base. How do those balancing mechanisms become upset? Certainly such considerations may compel us to stop treating modern man as morally reprehensible and to begin recognizing that he is but fulfilling a characteristic trait of survival — a capacity which may be directed in a fit or unfit manner, that is influenced by the nature of a given social order, its symbolic directives, and the limits of its habitat.

Social structure and habitat

A useful illustration of the influence of environment upon social structure is Lionel Tiger's discussion of the universality and persistence of the male bond.[9] Using data from ethology, paleontology, anthropology, and sociology, Tiger argues that the male–male bond is of the same biological order for defense, food gathering, and social-order maintenance as the male–female bond is for reproductive behavior. Interestingly, the key factor in making the male bond adaptively significant was the climatic change that compelled protohominids to move from trees to a savannah situation. Thus changes in the social structure — the elaborated dominance hierarchies and attendant political struggles — reflected the adaptive need for some centralized control if the horde were to survive under the new conditions of existence. Without necessarily accepting the full implication of his argument, we may tentatively suggest that habitat conditions have some influence upon whether or not a centralized authority pattern develops.

Anthony Leeds' study of the Yaruro Indians of Venezuela lends some support to this thesis.[10] He finds that the Yaruro chieftainship is characterized by its ineffectiveness, with the tribes operating on the basis of consensus rather than command. In spite of 250 years of diffusion and acculturation pressure from the Spanish to produce effective institutions of authority, such have not developed.

Leeds attributes the weakness of the chieftainship institutions to ecological factors. The tribal food resources require dispersed activities, and the lack of notable seasonality means gathering can be continuous. The fact of dispersal means that the absolute size of the work groups are limited, while the emphasis upon root crops requires no labor concentrative techniques. Such conditions require no technically determined positions of leadership and engender little demand for detailed organization; consequently, rank and superordinating prestige do not develop.

Leeds comments, "Thus, from the point of view of human organization, the technology, by itself, entails no managerial functions, no coordination of tasks which must be overseen by someone occupying an appropriately defined status."[11]

In an archaeological study Ralph Rowlett traces the response of two broad cultural aggregates to the combined processes of cultural diffusion and dramatic climate change. His location of interest is Europe north of the Alps. It is interesting to note that around 730 B.C. these peoples exhibited an egalitarian tribal structure similar to the Yaruro. "Social stratification was little developed, ... discrepancy in dwelling type and burial suggest that chiefs were here too merely 'first among equals."[12]

However, for the southern group this was changed with the diffusion of iron technology from the Mideast and the corresponding sub-Atlantic climatic phase, which extended forests eastward and inhibited the migration of groups from the eastern steppes. Under the joint impact of new technology and a protective barrier, the Hallstatt and La Tene cultural aggregates developed more elaborate technological and artistic works, trade relations, and greater social differentiation. Such a pattern persisted until the climate became similar to present patterns and the La Tene Phase III was incorporated into the Roman system.

Though the climatic change and the diffusion of new technology improved gains for the southern groups, for the northern lowland peoples the new technology and increase in humidity had almost an inverse influence. Rowlett says:

> Unlike the situation in the south, the coming of iron and the nearly simultaneous onset of the Sub-Atlantic climate had almost catastrophic consequences. During the previous Northern Bronze Age, an extremely effective economy (for the time and place) had been developed by importing foreign metal into Scandinavia in exchange for amber and perhaps other products, and often many of the handsomely finished bronze manufactures were exported south again, apparently being eagerly sought after in Central Europe and other places. This trading system, so beneficial for the north, collapsed once iron began in earnest to replace bronze for edge tools, thereby wiping out the mainstay of the northern economy. Coupled with this shock came the increasing precipitation and cool weather of the Sub-Atlantic climate, described as a "climatic deterioration" for the north, where naturally the effects of cooling were more severe. Its being a lowland as well meant even greater flooding and a more pronounced growth of swamps and bogs than in the south. Therefore, the beginning of the Iron Age sees a great, long economic depression hit the northern area. The first ethnohistoric sources from Classical Rome report the north when just barely emerging from this depression, a circumstance which influences our view of north European culture history to this very day.[13]

Rowlett's data suggest that climatic change has a significant impact on some cultures and engenders only slight alteration in the adaptive strategies of others. Such change would seem to have most impact when combined with another influential factor, such as a new technology and alteration in institutionalized practices, such as trading. With these changes the patterns of hierarchy move from a consensual and egalitarian pattern to more rigid and elaborately differentiated patterns of authority.

If data such as Rowlett's suggest something about the way things change, then what of those situations and social orders which remain relatively unchanging? Work among the Maring of New Guinea by Andrew Vadya, Roy Rappaport, and others may offer some clues.[14]

Rappaport studied the 200 members of the Tsembaga tribe to determine how ritual affects the relations between a group and its ecosystem. Ritual is viewed as the performance of conventional acts explicitly directed toward the involvement of nonempirical or supernatural agencies in the affairs of the participants. His interest in furthering a functional analysis makes ritual a class of communication events that convey certain information. Thus, ritual functions as a regulating mechanism which maintains the values of one or more variables within a range or ranges that permit continued existence of a system.

The Tsembaga, like other tribal groups, are basically egalitarian with only shifting authority. There are no hereditary or formal chiefs. Thus, social complexity is exhibited only in kinship ties and relations with other groups.

Rappaport treats the Tsembaga as one element in an ecosystem. Through measurements of caloric expenditures and gains, he is able to make some determination of the carrying capacity of the habitat. Thereby he is able to test his central notion that ritual has the latent function of maintaining the human population in balance with its habitat. He argues that there is a ritual cycle regulated by the demographic fortunes of the tribe's pig population. When the pig population becomes too large, there is the initiation of rituals where pigs are slaughtered to honor ancestors, repair alliances, establish marriages, and prepare for war. Therefore, though the people are acting to appease their ancestors and to fulfill social obligations, the unintended consequences are that (1) the frequency of warfare is limited, (2) the amount of calories expended in acquiring animal protein is limited, (3) gardens are protected from overforaging, and (4) the nutrient reservoir of the virgin forest is unharmed.

Rappaport suggests that the value of rituals is that they are sacred. Thus, the information has a certain reliability, and, without a strong authority structure, the sacred ritual specifies and coordinates collective action. In this sense it would seem that an egalitarian system is probably even more highly regulated than more differentiated social structures.

Finally, Rappaport suggests that a binary ritual system is functional only within a fairly steady system. Such a system would likely be inadequate where a complexity of variables had to be handled or were under conditions of dramatic change. Thus, under conditions of aggressive culture contact by a superordinate group or if extreme climatic change occurred, the very myths and rituals that ensured stability might become conditions of accelerated environmental deterioration. We might speculate that if the Australian authorities increase pressure for assimilation or began to establish a market for Tsembaga pigs, then like the potato for the Maori, there might ensue a fairly rapid period of habitat deterioration. Still Rappaport's study provides a useful clue as to the way large numbers of human groups have retained a relatively unchanging social structure.

In a remarkable synthesis of work on the Pleistocene period, Karl Butzer provides some substantive evidence and clues as to how stabilities in tribal organization would be pressed to develop new organizational strategies.[16] At the onset of the Holocene epoch and near the end of the Pleistocene, there was a period of significant ecologic change followed by a period of rapid cultural development in Europe. It was a period when, due to climatic change, the tundra was being succeeded by a boreal woodland complex. A consequence of this change was the replacement of the great herds of reindeer by more solitary game, such as elk, which compelled the prevailing human groups to face a change in their resource base. Gordon Childe has argued that this shift in the food resource required more arduous tactics and greater division of labor, and hence was the takeoff for cultural development. Butzer rejects this notion and convincingly argues that the biomass of the tundra is greater than the boreal forest; therefore, the specialized hunting of reindeer has permitted a high population density "such that no degree of skill short of agriculture could preserve mesolithic peoples from a drastic reduction of population density."[16]

Butzer explains that domestication occurred in Mesoamerica, the Near East, and Southeast Asia because these were areas where available wild plants and animals were suitable for domestication. Thus, he does not accept Arnold Toynbee's idea of dramatic challenge leading to the invention of agriculture. Rather, he contends, a bountiful natural environment having suitable domesticates made agriculture a logical possibility. Originating in the Levant around 7000 B.C., the new agricultural techniques began to be dispersed to other areas around 5000 B.C. Nomadic herdsmen emerged around 4000 B.C., perhaps in response to the thin rainfall of some areas. With the invention and dispersal of new resource techniques and the ecological change from tundra to boreal forest, the primitive European tribesmen would follow the unintended consequences so often characteristic of culture contact when the techniques of developed societies are dispersed to less developed social orders.

The adoption of agriculture provided a new fund of surplus energy at much lower cost. Butzer suggests this encouraged a population explosion, the physical transformation of the environment, and the creation of a cultural landscape. This is so because improved survival techniques permit higher densities. For example, unspecialized food gathering requires 100 square kilometers per person, while by the late Pleistocene five persons could be supported on the same area. With early agriculture the number maintained jumps to 1000, and with early urban development 2000 persons can be supported.

Butzer argues that urban patterns represented a culmination rather than a cause of the new organizational patterns that developed around 3000 B.C. The storage of food surpluses, trading, and the necessary centralization of authority, which emerged at certain key spots, required urban development. Although Butzer uses the terminology of social evolution, he is not proposing some grand linear pattern of development as may be observed only in organic beings. What he does note are the necessary preconditions for certain patterns of development, and these conditions were largely external to the groups so effected. Of course, the large bulk of mankind remained relatively unchanged in their organizational patterns.

Of importance to our interest is that habitat change provided the set for adopting new means to fulfill traditional practices. H. T. Waterbolk's study of northern Europe adds a slight variation to Butzer's contention about the influence of climatic change. Butzer suggests that population pressure and changes in the resource base were conditions for agricultural development.

Waterbolk adds the condition of sedentary social organization for the adoption of such techniques. He notes:

> As the Boreal-Atlantic Transition set in, people everywhere in western, northwestern, and northern Europe moved toward the coast and added coastal hunting, fishing, and collecting as means of subsistence to the traditional hunting of big game and inland collecting and fishing. The Atlantic forest as such was an unfavorable environment for man, and European man could best survive by adapting himself to the coast. In making this adaptation, however, there was an important consequence. The coastal resources allowed a considerably higher degree of sedentary occupation, freeing man of the necessity of continuous wandering. One precondition for the acceptance of farming—residential stability—was thus automatically fulfilled.[17]

Waterbolk's findings, as those of others, suggest that, although an ecosystem establishes certain limits upon the available resources, few human groups maximize their exploitation to the edge of these limits. The key factor seems to be some important conjuncture between the nature of the social structure and the nature of its habitat.

In this sense Betty Meggers is in error when she argues that the level to which a culture can develop is primarily dependent upon the agricultural potentiality of the new environment it occupies.[18] For her argument to hold we must assume that all groups limited by difficult conditions, such as the tropical forest, also invariably retain an egalitarian social structure. Such structures, though, seem less likely to persist under conditions of sedentary and fixed residence. D. E. Dumond, for example, convincingly argues that efficient swidden (or shifting cultivation) farming can produce a definite surplus.[19] Rappaport provides some evidence of this in his report that the ratio of caloric return to output was 16.1:1 for the taro yam garden, and 15.9:1 for the sugar sweet potato garden.[20]

Dumond argues that the Mexican tropics are capable of producing a maize surplus of from 20 to 110 percent of subsistence needs; therefore, a well-balanced system of shifting cultivation should be capable of supporting civilization. His focus of interest, the Mayapan in Yucatan, were supported for 250 years on swidden agriculture. Thus, he argues, sedentary conditions can be maintained with swidden agriculture if there is a centralized organizational structure. He cites, in addition to the Mayapan, the Azande of Sudan, the Land Dayak of Sarawak, and the African kingdoms of Dahomey, Benin, and Ashanti as cases where large urban, sedentary, centrally organized populations were supported by swidden agriculture.

Thus, for large numbers of cases, habitat and social structure may be reinforcing—dispersed subsistence and small population ensure perpetuation of an egalitarian structure, while situations which permit sedentary subsistence tend to develop more elaborate and centralized organizational forms. With these more elaborate and centralized patterns the available surplus energy can be better managed. As a consequence a greater number of social and ecological variables can be balanced than is the case where total reliance is upon ritual.

Chang's study of the rise of the Shang and Chou dynasties offers further evidence. He notes that climatic changes influenced a "horticultural revolution." Yet, "What marks off the civilized Shang culture from its barbarous antecedents are elements of an aristocratic complex that signifies the rise of a dynastic power, in contrast to the self-contained and more or less peaceful farming villages of the preceding Lung-Shan period."[21]

Jeffrey Parsons' study of the Teotihuacan Valley also assigns a 600 percent increase in population and 400 percent expansion in surface area to better organization of subsistence activities. He says:

> Early in the first century A.D. Teotihuacan made a critical breakthrough, a true organizational revolution whose principal archeological manifestation is the sudden appearance of a huge urban complex which continued to expand in size and population during the succeeding 500 years. The extent of population structuring and the low proportion of nonurban population in the Teotihuacan Valley during the Classic period clearly indicates the overwhelming local influence of the Teotihuacan urban center. A part of the basis for Teotihuacan's organizational breakthrough was almost certainly the productive capacity and coordinational requirements of full-scale canal irrigation in the rich alluvial plain below the city. Although direct evidence of Classic-period irrigation is lacking, the potential for such productive agriculture is the only obvious major element which sets Teotihuacan apart from several other large and elaborated Terminal Formative population centers in the eastern Valley of Mexico.[22]

It is interesting to note that Ronald Spores' study of the Mixtec attributes change to population pressure, but Parsons seems to use population size as some measure of organizational success.[23] Perhaps what is being observed is the persistence of mythological and organizational patterns which set up unintended problems that are met by the only means possible, traditional solutions. Thus, sedentary, centralized authority systems raise the amounts of surplus energy available, which, in turn, permit more people to survive. These events may encourage stepped-up colonization and pioneering efforts to replace or dominate tribal groups on the frontier, which encourages greater surpluses, further concentration, and further expansion until some ill-defined limits are reached. Spores concludes that technological innovation becomes one means of relieving population pressure.

> For the Mixtec the disastrous erosion so apparent in Nochixtlan Valley today was not simply the result of deforestation, intemperate grazing or agriculture that followed the Spanish conquest, but was intentionally induced and encouraged by pre-Hispanic Mixtec farmers who wanted to expand the terrace system.[24]

Perhaps such a pattern determines the symbolic and ecologic limits that are accelerated even more when dominance passes to an invading force, such as the Spanish in Mexico or the English in New Zealand after 1860.

A speculative summary

Although a variety of other studies might be, and probably should be, explored, this rather quick run through time and societies seems sufficient to illustrate the interchange between social structure and environment and to suggest some alternative approaches for further exploration. In order to survive, human societies must exploit their surrounding ecosystem. Under some conditions such exploitation becomes so extreme as to destroy the survival base of the society. Simple categories, such as modern versus early or civilized versus tribal, are of little help, for all such patterns are equally likely to present similar results. Nor are "pure" biological or sociological explanations likely to aid our understanding.

We need a better response than romanticizing prehistoric, tribal, or other Arcadian situations. We can find support for the notion that prehistoric man was a minor ecological influence, which is the position taken by Butzer, or we can follow Martin, Lutz, and others who suggest that in some areas he was a significant factor in many early environmental deteriorations. Perhaps in the Pleistocene epoch, as now, there was considerable variation between groups.

Might it be that extreme exploitation occurs when the social order is in a high state of flux — that is, when traditional frames of reference no longer seem operable? These might be frontier conditions such as the Maori found when he arrived in New Zealand and probably exterminated the moa, or when eighteenth-century Europeans began to remake their "new" world. Or it might be the introduction of a new food resource or technology which permits continuing traditional practices in new ways—such as the potato for the Irish or the New Zealand Maori, or the reintroduction of the horse to the plains Indians. Or it may reflect adaptation to significant climatic and ecological changes which demand new organizational forms if the group is to persist. It seems certain that for every group which made the correct adaptation there must have been several who perished.

Habitat-societal interactions do not fall into a neat deterministic pattern. There is sufficient evidence that ecologic changes, whether from the acts of men or gods, have a significant influence upon the social order. It does not seem that the touted cultural development of modern man makes him any less vulnerable.

Still, it is not strictly a one-way game with nature setting all the rules. The nature of a group's social order can have a significant influence upon the creation and expansion of resources. Some forms of social organization are better able to adapt to changed conditions than are others. In this case sedentary groups with centralized patterns of authority are more flexible than small, egalitarian groups, which are largely governed by ritual. Yet, as Rappaport demonstrates, under stable conditions the ritualistic enactment of myth, though intended to maintain social relations, may have the consequence of maintaining the group's habitat. Still, like other invisible hands, ritual may go astray when faced with quite altered conditions of existence. Perhaps this is not unlike the advertising rituals of the industrial order, which may go equally astray by encouraging an accelerating consumption pattern certain to destroy the resource base of the myths and the society that the rituals were intended to integrate and perpetuate.

We began with the problem of time and very quickly touched on some illustrations that, if followed more deeply, might help us to understand some issues often left untended between the bounded groves of biological and social science. This chapter has been basically concerned with how variations in habitat might influence the social order; the following chapters will explore the influence of symbolic variation.

References

1. Clark Wissler, "The Relation of Nature to Man as Illustrated by the North American Indian," *Ecology*, **5** (October 1924), 311–318.
2. Stephen Toulmin and June Goodfield, *The Discovery of Time* (New York: Harper & Row, 1965), p. 266.
3. *Ibid.*, p. 269.
4. Dorothy Lee, *Freedom and Culture* (Englewood Cliffs, N. J.: Prentice-Hall, 1959), p. 163.
5. Tom Dale and Vernon Gill Carter, *Topsoil and Civilization* (Norman: University of Oklahoma Press, 1955).

6. Paul S. Martin, "Prehistoric Overkill," in P. S. Martin and H. E. Wright, Jr. (eds)., *Pleistocene Extinctions, The Search for a Cause* (New Haven: Yale University Press, 1967), p. 115. Reprinted by permission of the publisher.

7. Harold J. Lutz, *Aboriginal Man and White Man as Historical Causes of Fires in the Boreal Forest, with Particular Reference to Alaska*, No. 65 (New Haven: Yale University, School of Forestry, 1959).

8. R. J. Cameron, "Destruction of the Indigenous Forests for Maori Agriculture During the Nineteenth Century," *New Zealand Journal of Forestry*, 9 (1964), 108. See also S. R. Eyre and G. R. Jones (eds.), *Geography as Human Ecology Methodology by Example* (New York: St. Martin's, 1966), especially Murray McCaskill, "Man and Landscape in North Westland, New Zealand," pp. 264–290.

9. Lionel Tiger, *Men in Groups* (New York: Harper & Row, 1965). See also C. D. Darlington, *The Evolution of Man and Society* (London: George Allen and Unwin, 1969).

10. Anthony Leeds, "Ecological Determinants of Chieftainship Among the Yaruro Indians of Venezuela," in Andrew P. Vadya (ed.), *Environment and Cultural Behavior*, Ecological Series in Cultural Anthropology (Garden City, N.Y.: Natural History Press, 1969), pp. 377–394. See also M. F. Thomas and G. W. Whittington (eds.), *Environment and Land Use in Africa* (London: Methuen, 1969).

11. Leeds, *op. cit.*, p. 383.

12. Ralph M. Rowlett, "The Iron Age North of the Alps," *Science*, 161 (July 12, 1968), 133. Reprinted by permission of the author and the American Association for the Advancement of Science.

13. *Ibid.*, p. 130.

14. Roy A. Rappaport, *Pigs for the Ancestors* (New Haven: Yale University Press, 1967). See also Karl J. Pelzer, *Pioneer Settlement in the Asiatic Tropics*, Studies in Land Utilization and Agricultural Colonization in Southeastern Asia (New York: American Geographical Society, 1948); and the classic study by C. Daryll Forde, *Habitat, Economy and Society* (New York: Dutton, 1963).

15. Karl W. Butzer, *Environment and Archaeology* (Chicago: Aldine, 1969).

16. *Ibid.*, p. 412.

17. H. T. Waterbolk, "Food Production in Prehistoric Europe," *Science*, 162 (December 6, 1968), 1096.

18. Betty J. Meggers, "Environmental Limitation on the Development of Culture." *American Anthropologist*, 56 (1954), 801–824. See also Joseph B. Birdsell, "Some Environmental and Cultural Factors Influencing the Structuring of Australian Aboriginal Populations," *American Naturalist*, 87 (1953), 171–207.

19. D. E. Dumond, "Swidden Agriculture and the Rise of Maya Civilization," in Vadya (ed.), *Environment and Cultural Behavior, op. cit.*, pp.333–349.

20. Rappaport, *op. cit.*, p. 52.

21. Kwang-Chih Chang, "Archaeology of Ancient China," *Science*, 162 (November 1, 1968), 524.

22. Jeffrey R. Parsons, "Teotihuacan, Mexico and its Impact on Regional Demography," *Science*, 162 (November 22, 1968), 875. Reprinted by permission of the American Association for the Advancement of Science.

23. Ronald Spores, "Settlement, Farming Technology, and Environment in the Nochixtlan Valley," *Science*, 166 (October 31, 1969), 557–569.

24. *Ibid.*, pp. 563–564.

INTRODUCTION: THE ARGUMENT IN BRIEF*

Fred Hirsch

THIS book tries to give an economist's answer to three questions.

(1) Why has economic advance become and remained so compelling a goal to all of us as individuals, even though it yields disappointing fruits when most, if not all of us, achieve it?

(2) Why has modern society become so concerned with distribution—with

*Reprinted with permission from *Social Limits to Growth* by F. Hirsch, Routledge and Kegan Paul, 1977, pp. 1–12.

the division of the pie—when it is clear that the great majority of people can raise their living standards only through production of a larger pie? (3) Why has the twentieth century seen a universal predominant trend toward collective provision and state regulation in economic areas at a time when individual freedom of action is especially extolled and is given unprecedented rein in noneconomic areas such as aesthetic and sexual standards?

Let us call these three issues (1) the paradox of affluence, (2) the distributional compulsion, and (3) the reluctant collectivism.

My major thesis is that these three issues are interrelated, and stem from a common source. This source is to be found in the nature of economic growth in advanced societies. The heart of the problem lies in the complexity and partial ambiguity of the concept of economic growth once the mass of the population has satisfied its main biological needs for life-sustaining food, shelter, and clothing. The traditional economic distinction between how much is produced, on what basis, and who gets it then becomes blurred. The issues of production, of individual versus collective provision, and of distribution then become intertwined.

This development marks a profound change. It is a change that economists in particular find difficult to accept because it has the appearance of scientific retrogression. Traditionally, the contribution of the economist to charting a way to economic progress has consisted largely of unscrambling the aspects of economic activity just mentioned—distinguishing between the share of the pie and its size, between the motivation of individual actions and their collective result. It was on these distinctions that the science of economics was launched by Adam Smith two centuries ago. Smith showed that pursuit by individuals in an uncoordinated way of their own interests could yet serve the interests of all and that the poor man in the rich community could live better than native kings.

The progress of economics has been devoted largely to developing and refining these insights, which has resulted in enormous advances in the quantification of economic phenomena. This quantification in turn supports not merely the claim of economics to primacy in the ranking of the social sciences but also its established primacy in the agenda of public policy. In the past generation, electoral politics throughout the industrial world, and beyond it, has been increasingly dominated by the big economic numbers—gross national product, personal disposable income, and the rate at which these indicators of material prosperity grow.

Yet in advanced societies, those in which the mass of the population has risen above merely life-sustaining consumption, the stage may now have been reached where the analytical framework that the economist has come to take for granted—but that the sociologist has long disputed—has become a hindrance in understanding some key contemporary problems. Confronting these problems in the framework of the traditional analytical separation leaves the answers in the air. The three broad questions listed at the outset—the paradox of affluence, the distributional compulsion, the reluctant collectivism—are puzzles or paradoxes when viewed in isolation. A clue to their resolution is to approach them as interconnected products of a neglected structural characteristic of modern economic growth. That is what this book tries to do.

I

The structural characteristic in question is that as the level of average consumption rises, an increasing portion of consumption takes on a social as well as an individual aspect. That is to say, the satisfaction that individuals derive from goods and services depends in increasing measure not only on their own consumption but on consumption by others as well.

To a hungry man, the satisfaction derived from a square meal is unaffected by the meals other people eat or, if he is hungry enough, by anything else they do. His meal is an entirely individual affair. In technical terms it is a pure private good. At the other extreme, the quality of the air that the modern citizen breathes in the center of a city depends almost entirely on what his fellow citizens contribute toward countering pollution, whether directly by public expenditure or indirectly through public regulation. Clean air in a metropolis is a social product. In technical terms, it is close to a pure public good.

These polar cases, however, are relatively few in number. It has recently become recognized by economists who specialize in these matters that the major part of consumption is neither purely private nor purely public. What is generally referred to as private or personal consumption is nonetheless affected in its essence—that is, in the satisfaction or utility it yields—by consumption of the same goods or services by others; and in that specific sense it can be said to contain a social element. Correspondingly, what is generally referred to as public consumption contains some of the characteristics of private goods, in the sense that its costs and benefits are or can be confined to a limited group.

The range of private consumption that contains a social element in the sense described is much wider than is generally recognized. In text-books on economics, public goods are discussed in the context of goods and facilities that can be provided only, or most economically, on a collective basis, open to all and financed by all. City parks and streets and national defense are prominent examples. In addition, elements of public goods are recognized in side effects of private transactions such as pollution and congestion occurring in particular identifiable situations. But a more general public goods element can be attributed to a wide range of private expenditures. Thus the utility of expenditure on a given level of education as a means of access to the most sought after jobs will decline as more people attain that level of education. The value to me of my education depends not only on how much I have but also on how much the man ahead of me in the job line has. The satisfaction derived from an auto or a country cottage depends on the conditions in which they can be used, which will be strongly influenced by how many other people are using them. This factor, which is social in origin, may be a more important influence on my satisfaction than the characteristics of these items as "private" goods (on the speed of the auto, the spaciousness of the cottage, and so forth). Beyond some point that has long been surpassed in crowded industrial societies, conditions of use tend to deteriorate as use becomes more widespread.

Congestion is most apparent in its physical manifestation, in traffic jams. But traffic congestion can be seen as only a special case of the wider phenomenon of social congestion, which in turn is a major facet of social scarcity. Social scarcity is a central concept in this analysis. It expresses the idea that the good things of life are restricted not only by physical limitations of producing more of them but also by absorptive limits on their use. Where the social environment has a restricted capacity for extending use without quality deterioration, it imposes social limits to consumption. More specifically, the limit is imposed on satisfactions that depend not on the product or facility in isolation but on the surrounding conditions of use.

What precisely is *new* about this situation? The limits have always been there at some point, but they have not until recent times become obtrusive. That is the product, essentially, of past achievements in material growth not subject to social limits. In this sense, the concern with the limits to growth that has been voiced by and through the Club of Rome[1] is strikingly misplaced. It focuses on distant and uncertain physical limits and overlooks the immediate if less apocalyptic presence of social limits to growth.

So long as material privation is widespread, conquest of material scarcity is the dominant concern. As demands for purely private goods are increasingly satisfied, demands for goods and facilities with a public (social) character become increasingly active. These public demands make themselves felt through individual demands on the political system or through the market mechanism in the same way as do the demands for purely private goods. Individuals acquire both sets of goods without distinction, except where public goods are provided by public or collective action; even there, individuals may seek to increase their own share by private purchases.

These demands in themselves appear both legitimate and attainable. Why should the individual not spend his money on additional education as a means to a higher placed job, or on a second home in the country, if he prefers these pleasures to spending on a mink coat or whiskey or to a life of greater leisure? That question was being loudly voiced in the mid-1970s as part of a middle-class backlash in both Britain and the United States. It can be answered satisfactorily only by reference to the public goods or social content of the expenditures involved.

Considered in isolation, the individual's demand for education as a job entree, for an auto, for a country cottage, can be taken as genuinely individual wants, stemming from the individual's own preferences in the situation that confronts him. Acting alone, each individual seeks to make the best of his or her position. But satisfaction of these individual preferences itself alters the situation that faces others seeking to satisfy similar wants. A round of transactions to act out personal wants of this kind therefore leaves each individual with a worse bargain than was reckoned with when the transaction was undertaken, because the sum of such acts does not correspondingly improve the position of all individuals taken together. There is an "adding-up" problem. Opportunities of economic advance, as they present themselves serially to one person after another, do not constitute equivalent opportunities for economic advance by all. What each of us can achieve, all cannot.

A break between individual and social opportunities may occur for a number of reasons; excessive pollution and congestion are the most commonly recognized results. A neglected general condition that produces this break is competition by people for place, rather than competition for performance. Advance in society is possible only by moving to a higher place among one's fellows, that is, by improving one's performance in relation to other people's performances. If everyone stands on tiptoe, no one sees better. Where social interaction of this kind is present, individual action is no longer a sure means of fulfilling individual choice: the preferred outcome may be attainable only through collective action. (We all agree explicitly or implicitly not to stand on tiptoe.) The familiar dichotomy between individual choice and collective provision or regulation then dissolves. Competition among isolated individuals in the free market entails hidden costs for others and ultimately for themselves. These costs are a deadweight cost for all and involve social waste, unless no preferable alternative method of allocation is available. But the same distortion may result from public provision where this responds to individual demands formulated without taking account of subsequent interactions . . .

. . . What is possible for the single individual is not possible for all individuals — and would not be possible even if they all possessed equal talent. Individuals, whether shopping for educational advance in the market place or pushing for educational advance through political demands, do not see the break between individual and social opportunity; that is, they do not see that opportunities open to each person separately are not open to all. It follows that response to individual demands of this kind, whether in market processes or in public provision, cannot deliver the order.

Consumers, taken together, get a product they did not order; collectively, this result involves potential social waste. Consumers individually find that their access to socially scarce goods and facilities, where these are attainable even in part through market processes, is determined in accord not with absolute but with relative real income. The determining factor is the individual's position in the distribution of purchasing power. Frustration of individual expectations that results from both these characteristics: from social waste, which cuts into the level of welfare available to all; and from an imposed hierarchy that confines socially scarce goods to those on the highest rungs of the distributional ladder, disappointing the expectations of those whose position is raised through a lift in the ladder as a whole.

So the distributional struggle returns, heightened rather than relieved by the dynamic process of growth. It is an exact reversal of what economists and present-day politicans have come to expect growth to deliver.

The compelling attraction of economic growth in its institutionalized modern form has been as a superior substitute for redistribution. Whereas the masses today could never get close to what the well-to-do have today, even by expropriating all of it, they can, in the conventional view, get most if not all the way there with patience in a not too distant tomorrow, through the magic of compound growth. But, as outlined above, once this growth brings mass consumption to the point where it causes problems of congestion in the widest sense — bluntly, where consumption or jobholding by others tends to crowd you out — then the key to personal welfare is again the ability to stay ahead of the crowd. Generalized growth then increases the crush.

Thus the frustration in affluence results from its very success in satisfying previously dominant material needs. This frustration is usually thought of as essentially a psychological phenomenon, a matter of our subjective internal assessment. What we previously had to struggle for now comes easily, so we appreciate it less. The analysis of this book fastens on a separate consequence of generalized material growth that is independent of any such psychological revaluation; it affects what individuals get as well as the satisfaction it brings them. What they get, in the growing sphere of social scarcity, depends to an increasing extent on their relative position in the economic hierarchy. Hence, the paradox of affluence. It embodies a distributional compulsion, which in turn leads to our reluctant collectivism.

These sources of frustration with the fruits of economic growth are concealed in the economist's standard categorization. Strictly speaking, our existing concept of economic output is appropriate only for truly private goods, having no element of interdependence between consumption by different individuals. The bedrock is valuation by individuals of goods and opportunities in the situation in which they find themselves. At any moment of time and for any one person, standing on tiptoe gives a better view, or at least prevents a worse one. Equally, getting ahead of the crowd is an effective and feasible means of improving one's welfare, a means available to any one individual. It yields a benefit, in this sense, and the measure of the benefit is what individuals pay to secure it. The individual benefit from the isolated action is clear-cut. The sum of benefits of all the actions taken together is nonetheless zero.

This reckoning, it should be emphasized, is still made on the measure of the individual's own valuation, the same valuation that imputes a positive benefit to the individual action. Since individual benefits of this kind simply do not add up, the connection between individual and aggregate advance is broken. Yet the modern concepts of economic output, and of growth in that output, are grounded on individual valuations and their addition. Individual preference is assumed to be revealed implicitly in market behavior—in the consumer's choice between products at their given market prices, in the worker's choice between jobs and between different opportunities of job training at the going rates of pay and conditions. If individual valuations do not add up, then the aggregated valuations based upon them become biased measures.

Unfortunately no better quantitative measure of economic output has yet been found. The need for a flanking set of social indicators is now widely accepted, at least in principle. The end product of such a system would be an integrated system of numbers comparable with the national income accounts. This objective is far from being realized. There is no social performance indicator that can be systematically calculated and easily understood...

...The ambiguity in the concept of economic output pointed out here is of secondary or even negligible significance in making use of the conventional measures of national accounts for the formulation of official policy designed to regulate or stabilize the short-term performance of the economy. For comparisons of welfare over extended periods of time, in estimates of long-term economic growth, and in league tables of living standards among countries in different situations at a given period of time, national accounting measures are notoriously less suitable.

What is stressed here is a different limitation, one almost wholly neglected by economists: the problem of translating individual economic improvement into overall improvement. In the standard model of thinking, if the fruits of aggregate advance appear inadequate or disappointing, the deficiency merely reflects inadequate economic effort or excessive demands by individuals, or poor organization or inadequate capital equipment currently available to them. Too much has been expected too soon. This conceptual framework adopted by economists concerned with policy has penetrated the thinking, expectations, and performance criteria of politicians and electorates of all western countries. As a consequence, conventional wisdom thinks in terms of "excessive expectations." The populace wants it now. It cannot have it now. It is too impatient. The implication is that the gathering of the fruit must await exercise of the necessary virtues—essentially, effort and restraint. Yet for those aspects of individual welfare where the connection between individual and aggregate advancement does not exist, or is broken under the stress of widening access to limited availabilities, the established conceptual framework is invalid. Its application to ultimate consumer satisfaction in this sector operates as a frustration machine.

Thus to see total economic advance as individual advance writ large is to set up expectations that cannot be fulfilled, ever. It is not just a matter of scaling down demand and expectations that cannot be fulfilled, ever. It is not just a matter of scaling down demand and expectations that are extravagant in relation to effort by workers or to the availability of technology or the use made of it. This view has become the conventional one on problems of excess demand and inflation. The appropriate solution to the problem so conceived is simple, at least in principle: to adjust expectations down and/or performance up. The necessary adjustment is purely quantitative. If all put a little more into the pool and take a little less out for a while, then present expectations can in time be fulfilled. So runs the predominant message of politico-economic managers in the postwar generation. Only hold back a little, and the good things you rightly crave will come to you or, at least, to your children. The inflationary explosion of the early 1970s and the severe world recession that followed attempts to contain it have been widely interpreted in this vein—as a painful interruption in a progressive improvement in living standards that could be restored and sustained once the public was prevailed upon to exercise the necessary restraint.

It follows from this line of thought that the chief culprits responsible for derailing the train of technological advance are those institutions that inflate economic demands beyond the steady but limited growth in capacity to fulfill them. Trade unions exercising the bargaining power of their collective strength stand out as such culprits. It is the collective element in their activities—the mobilization of economic strength greater than the sum of the individual parts —that is seen to intrude on the balance and viability of an individualistic economy. The unquestioned premise of this approach is that competitive individualistic advance can ultimately deliver the goods. If it cannot, which participants in collective activity may instinctively feel and as the present analysis explicitly argues, then defensive collective expedients must be looked at in a new light.

To the extent that the mismatch between current expectations and resources is qualitative rather than quantitative, the restraint necessary would be not patience but stoicism, acceptance, and social cooperation—qualities that are out of key with our culture of individualistic advance. Yet without such qualities, the traditional response by the public to the prospect of satisfaction as reward for extra effort or temporary abstinence will worsen the problem. For addition to the material goods that can be expanded for all will, in itself, increase the scramble for those goods and facilities that cannot be so expanded. Taking part in the scramble is fully rational for any individual in his own actions, since in these actions he never confronts the distinction between what is available as a result of getting ahead of others and what is available from a general advance shared by all. The individual who wants to see better has to stand on tiptoe. In the game of beggar your neighbor, that is what each individual must try to do, even though not all can. The only way of avoiding the competition in frustration is for the people concerned to coordinate their objectives in some explicit way, departing from the principle of isolated individual striving in this sphere. That is to say, only a collective approach to the problem can offer individuals the guidance necessary to achieve a solution they themselves would prefer. The principle is acknowledged in the standard liberal analysis, but confined to the exceptional case.

How a satisfactory collective view is to be arrived at, and then implemented, remains a large and mostly unresolved problem of its own. Collective action can involve familiar distortions and inefficiencies. The means to a collective solution may be inadequate. To the extent that this is so, the analysis put forward here carries no clear-cut implications for immediate policy. The distortions and frustrations entailed in uncoordinated individual actions may still appear as the lesser evil. However, a change in the nature of a problem is not undone by deficiencies in the tools available for tackling it. Correct diagnosis is likely to yield some implications for policy, if only to stop banging into the wall.

By collapsing individual and total opportunities for economic advance into a single process grounded on individual valuations, the standard view has obscured a significant change in the nature of the economic problem. It has thereby overstated the promise of economic growth. It has understated the limitations of consumer demand as a guide to an efficient pattern of economic activity. It has obscured the extent of the modern conflict between individualistic actions and satisfaction of individualistic preferences. Getting what one wants is increasingly divorced from doing as one likes . . .

Notes

1. The Club of Rome is an informal international association, styling itself as an invisible college, which is best known for its "world model" representing the interconnections of resources, population, and environment in the mode of systems dynamics. The message, which received worldwide popular acclaim and widespread professional criticism, was contained in Donella H. Meadows, Dennis L. Meadows, Jørgen Randers, and William W. Behrens III, *The Limits of Growth*, A Report for the Club of Rome's Project on the Predicament of Mankind (London: Earth Island Limited, 1972).

SECTION 7

Growth and Resource Depletion

INTRODUCTORY ESSAY

A Classification Scheme for Natural Resources

Two broad categories of resources can be distinguished based on the notion of a resource *stock*, i.e. a fixed initial availability.[1] Natural resources have one of two major distinguishing features: so-called *renewable* resources (e.g. fisheries and forests) are characterised by the fact that they are capable of regenerating themselves naturally, the available resource stock changing over time at a "natural" biological or biochemical rate; while *non-renewable* resources (e.g. fossil fuels, other minerals, natural landscapes) are not capable of self-regeneration to any significant extent, the available resource stock having been fixed at a predetermined level before the arrival of economic man. Artificial regeneration (recycling) of non-renewable resources is possible and most industrialised economies contain a highly developed system of secondary materials (recycled) industries and markets.[2] Nevertheless, the recycling rate is limited both by economic and physical constraints. In economic terms the relative prices of secondary and thus virgin material counterparts are important. Factors such as level of mass, homogenity (level of contamination) and location of residuals arising often mitigate against secondary materials (particularly post-consumer residuals generated by households and small-scale commercial organisations), by serving to increase collection and processing costs.[3] Further, there is no guarantee that recycling is always beneficial in terms of a reduction in the net pollution impact. Some recycling processes themselves involve difficult residuals handling and discharge problems.[4]

The entropy law reminds us that energy resources are not recyclable and often the uses that many materials are put to in a modern economy result in them being dissipated beyond use. Thus a 100 percent recycling society is a myth and even if technically possible a large-scale switch to renewable flow resources in society does not quite offer a panacea in the

322

very long run because of entropic degradation. It does, however, seem doubtful that the second law of thermodynamics should be considered critically important if it is accepted that policymakers are expected to plan over a time scale defined in terms of "the foreseeable future". On the other hand, the substitution possibilities between renewable and non-renewable resources are largely unknown and no major resource switch appears imminent. Given the above conditions the central resources-policy problem involves the determination of an intertemporal alloca-tion strategy in order to trade-off current resource usage and resource reservation *in situ* for future generations. We should also bear in mind that the complex relationship between man and his environment con-ditions man's appraisal of resources. Man does not come into contact with his environment directly but only through the medium of his culture (see Section 1). Thus anything that is sought from the environment is perceived or interpreted in cultural terms. A "functional" view of resources (i.e. objects to be used and exploited to satisfy man's needs and wants) is common to both Marxist and capitalistic ideologies. Only in a minor way do societies revere or sanctify resources.

Four resource sub-categories have been identified in the resource economics literature.[5] *Stock-energy resources* (e.g. coal, natural gas, oil and uranium used in nuclear fission reactors); *stock-material resources* (e.g. various non-fuel minerals, copper and lead). Both these first two sub-categories of resources are examples of non-renewable resources only the latter category being amenable to recycling. *Flow-energy resources* (e.g. solar, wind and wave power) and *stock-renewable resources* (e.g. forests and marine resources). The former sub-category is currently of limited potential in intertemporal terms because of tech-nological constraints but the latter sub-category can be "managed" with the intertemporal trade-off being determined by reproduction rates and initial population size.

For example, as we saw in Section 4 fisheries management should in-volve some attempt to determine the optimum rate of fish production over time and should include a regulatory policy to ensure that this optimum rate is achieved.[6] Needless to say management of the world's fisheries is an extremely complex business involving numerous economic, political and biological uncertainties.[7] But management is becoming in-creasingly important as fishing activities world-wide continue to expand and press against the biological limits set by the availability of fish stocks. Economic theory has demonstrated that competitive fishing is likely to be inefficient and may ultimately result in a serious depletion of fish stocks. Thus the argument runs that fisheries must be appropriated, preferably by governments, so that entry to the fisheries can be limited and exploita-tion maintained at the optimal level. Problems occur when the biological optimum level of fishery exploitation (the maximum sustainable level of catch) is exceeded by the economic optimum level of exploitation. The economic optimum in a private-ownership situation would occur at the point where the return (marginal revenue product of effort) from the last fishing unit employed on a fishery equalled the cost of its employment (marginal cost of the fishing effort). This profit maximising economic optimum will always be less than the biological optimum provided that the cost per unit of effort is positive. However, if we assume our fishery is a common property resource open to commercial exploitation by competing fishing units then the economic optimum occurs at the point where the return of the last fishing unit (now the average revenue product of effort) equals the average fishing effort cost for the fishing industry. Since all boats would be operating simultaneously on the fishery and catching roughly the same amount of fish it becomes impossible to differentiate between marginal and average returns per individual boats. Fishing units would continue to enter the fishery until the boats were just breaking even but with the very real likelihood of biological overfishing.

The Limits to Growth Debate

Before examining the problem of managing non-renewable resources in an intertemporal policy context we will first take a broader look at the so-called growth/no-growth debate and world futures forecasting in general. Freeman and Jahoda[8] point out that differences of opinion amongst futurologists in three key problem areas are fundamental to the debate. Opinion is divided in the areas of resources and technological progress; the desirable political framework for a future society; and the workings of the social/economic/political transformation mechanism. The current views of the future which we examine below, however, all have their origins in a much earlier set of writings by the so-called classical economists of the eighteenth and nineteenth centuries. These political economists were also concerned with the problems of growth and change in an industrializing society.

The 1950s and 1960s proved to be decades of rapid economic growth for many industrialised economies but this trend did not continue for long into the 1970s. In the pre-1970 era, economic policy in the industrialised world was formulated around the central goal of economic growth and seemed to require a fundamentally exploitative policy approach toward natural resource bases. The established thesis of growth is good *per se* was firmly entrenched. The basic assumption underlying the thesis was that the greater the economic throughput of the economy the higher the welfare levels that society could attain. On a global scale resources as opposed to reserves appeared on practical grounds limitless. Further, the inevitable generation of pollution and other environmental costs stimulated by the increasing levels of economic throughput were judged to be relatively localised and, therefore, manageable problems.

The established growth thesis came under sudden and severe attack, however, in the early 1970s. Wilson[9] divides the growth issue dialectic that developed into a number of phases. The first phase, in the early 1970s, contained strong attacks by a number of writers on the traditional values of growth and progress.[10] In particular, Mishan's[11] work emphasising the human costs of the growth-orientated society and the Limits to Growth publication[12] focused attention on the possible collapse of industrial society under the strain of exponentially increasing levels of population, resource consumption and pollution. A number of the above studies incorporated forecasts which are variations or extensions of the Malthusian thesis that population growth has an inevitable tendency to outstrip the growth of food supplies. The Club of Rome studies in 1972 and 1974[13] introduced a novel aspect to the world futures debate by applying large-scale computer models to the analysis of global trends. These studies essentially argued the case of imminent and stringent physical limits to global economic growth. The computer simulation models demonstrated that under certain conditions and making certain assumptions (not empirically validated) about technology, population, pollution and resource availability a continuation of current growth and consumption trends was not feasible. The main prediction of the models seemed to be that the global limits to growth would be reached in a matter of 100 years or so. The Ehrlichs[14] concentrate their attention on the possibilities of a world eco-catastrophe engineered by economic growth and industrialisation. They conclude that perhaps the "capacity of the planet to support human life has already been permanently impaired". Heilbroner[15] accepts most of the forecasts of the Limits to Growth model and believes the future problems of overpopulation and pollution will be so immense and inevitable that they will probably defy any solution except possibly far-reaching institutional changes that only a totalitarian government could bring about.

Other studies of possible future global scenarios take a much more optimistic view.[16] Typical of this line of thought are the reports written by Herman Kahn[17] and introduced in Section 1 in which technological advance is given a central role to play. Future technical innovations, it is argued, will be capable of mitigating environmental disruption albeit at some cost in terms of overcentralisation and loss of individual privacy in society. A second phase in the growth dialetic was ushered in with the publication of a series of responses to and criticisms of the Limits to Growth publication. A whole body of literature emerged devoted to the rebuttal of the doomsday scenarios and the development of more optimistic global resources and environmental quality scenarios following to some extent the Kahn tradition.[18] Much of the literature was written by economists who highlighted the technical deficiencies in the Limits models and the general lack of supporting empirical data for the crucial exponential growth equations put forward by the Limits team. It was also pointed out that no place was found in the analysis for the role of scarcity-induced adjustment mechanisms. These mechanisms had been analysed in an earlier work on resource scarcity by Barnett and Morse[19] which had made a considerable impact on academic economists and to a lesser extent US policymakers in the 1960s. The essential conclusion of this study had been that in terms of trends in "real unit costs" and relative prices over the period 1870–1957 no evidence indicating increasing resource scarcity could be found. The adjustment mechanisms argument pointed to the fact that the market mechanism through increasing price levels could stimulate a process of scarce resource substitution; recycling of previously uneconomic residuals; and increased levels of resource exploration and general technical research and development. All these trends would serve to postpone the day when the world must ultimately face the physical limits to growth. Thus there is unlikely to be any sudden and dramatic general global resource scarcity.

The Neo-classical Economic Model of Non-renewable Resource Depletion

This free enterprise line of reasoning defines optimality in terms of the rate of depletion that would occur in a perfectly competitive world. This rate is then taken to be Pareto optimal (economically efficient) in line with the standard theorems of welfare economics.[20] The basic line of reasoning is, therefore, that market forces should, in principle, be allowed to take care of the allocation of scarce resources both intratemporally and over time (intertemporally). Page[21] has argued forcibly that in fact markets cannot adequately solve the problems of either a "just" intratemporal or intertemporal allocation of resources and as we shall see later real world market failures also serve to inhibit the attainment of even efficient allocations. The economic optimisation problem is usually expressed in the following form.

Each resource owner will attempt to max the present value of profits (net price) v, where

$$v = (P_0 - C_0) + \frac{(P_1 - C_1)}{1 + r} + \frac{(P_2 - C_2)}{(1 + r)^2} + \frac{(P_T - C_T)}{(1 + r)\,T}$$

$$\max V = \int_0^T (P_t - C_t)e^{-rt}$$

where P = price of finished product (say a metal),

C = the marginal cost of processing and extracting the resource,

r = rate of interest (marginal rate of time preference),

T = the finite time horizon (at the end of which the resource is exhausted).

V is then the present value of the flow $P-C$, the net price of the resource *in situ* (under conditions of perfect competition market price—marginal extraction costs per tonne of ore).

A resource in the ground is seen as an investment, in that it involves current sacrifice of consumption with a view to a greater future consumption. According to the intertemporal economic efficiency criterion the own rate of return (net price or royalty) on any asset (including the resource in question) in the economy must be equal to that on any other asset. Now perfectly competitive markets in equilibrium under conditions of certainty ensure such a uniformity in asset rate of returns. A resource left in the ground now must always be worth in the future exactly what would be earned if it were extracted now and sold and the revenue received invested at the prevailing market rate of interest. In terms of economic efficiency, resource depletion is not a loss of wealth if the value of the resource is replaced, although the value need not be replaced in kind. The revenue received from currently profitable resource extraction and sale could be reinvested at interest and the value of the original resources would then be reflected in machines or other capital (which contributes to the future's stock of wealth).

If V is maximised, we obtain the requirement:

$$(P_0 - C_0) = \frac{(P_1 - C_1)}{1 + r} = \frac{P_2 - C_2}{(1 + r)^2} \ldots, \text{etc.,}$$

or more generally,

$$(Pt_j - Ct_j)e^{-rt}j = (Pt_j - Ct_j)e^{-rti},$$

i.e. that the present value of the net price (royalty, rate of return) must be equal in each period ($t-i$, $t-j$). If this equality does not hold it will pay the resource owner to shift resource production between periods.

The rate of return actually set is optimal (in terms of the economic efficiency criterion) if it is equal to the market rate of interest. Assume that individuals are choosing over time between holding rights to resources or holding other assets and that the present price at which rights to extract resources (e.g. mineral leases) are exchanged is P_0 Portfolio balance (equality of return rates) requires that the mineral lease should be rising in expected value at the rate of interest. Thus the future lease exchange price P_i will be determined by the term $P_0(1 + r)^t$ where r is the market rate of interest. This means in turn that mineral prices net of extraction costs (net price, royalty) should also be rising at the rate of interest.

According to Solow[22] this link between the resource royalty and the rate of interest is the fundamental principle of the economics of exhaustible resources "if the net price were to rise too slowly, production would be pushed nearer in time and the resource would be exhausted too quickly because no one would wish to hold resources in the ground and earn less than the going rate of return. If the net price were to rise too fast, resource deposits would be an excellent way to hold wealth, and owners would delay production while they enjoyed supernormal capital gains." The market prices of the minerals grow exponentially over time restricting demand and encouraging supplies. When a shortage of a particular mineral is forecast at some future time t the expected future mineral lease exchange price P_t will rise, it is then necessary for the current lease exchange price P_0 to rise to maintain the identity $P_t = P_0(1 + r)^t$. This will mean a rise in the market price of the mineral consequently restricting current demand. Given a known stock of minerals, of uniform quality but different extraction cost structures, the lowest cost mineral deposits (most profitable) will over a period of time be extracted first then successively more costly deposits as the mineral price rises. As Fitzgibbons and Cochrane[23] conclude, "if the market foresees the future correctly, this process will continue until eventually the highest cost field will be exhausted and simultaneously quantity demanded will have fallen to zero. The deposits will be used up when the price has reached the maximum that buyers are willing to pay."

The economists who advocate this type of free-enterprise (market) approach to resource depletion problems also take a particular (largely optimistic) view of technological progress both in terms of the likelihood of the continued development of natural-resource-saving technology and the prospects for substitution of exhaustible resource production inputs by labour and reproducible capital inputs. Empirically, a great deal remains to be learnt about the various elasticities of substitution, i.e. the measure of the ease or difficulty of replacing an exhaustible resource with other inputs. Taking a long-run view, the elasticity of substitution concept can be illustrated diagramatically as shown in Figure 7.1.

The position X is assumed to represent the current input mix used to produce a given level of some particular total output. Lines (constant output curves) drawn through X indicate alternative combinations of inputs that could be utilized to produce the same level of total output. The two lines drawn indicate the two extremes of zero substitutability and infinite substitutability both of which are unrealistic. The real division of opinion concerns the space between these two lines and whether in the future society will be able to remain closer to the infinite substitutability end of the spectrum than to the zero substitution position.[24]

Nordhaus,[25] in the context of energy resources, has hypothesised the

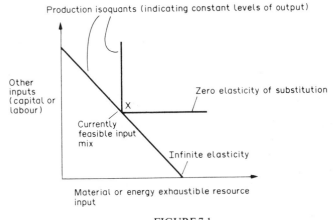

FIGURE 7.1

Substitution elasticities.

existence of what he terms a "backstop technology". This technology is capable of producing or substituting for a mineral resource at relatively high cost but on an effectively inexhaustible scale. The breeder reactor using plutonium fuel, he argues, would be a close approximation to this "backstop" concept; although Lecomber[26] argues that much depends on the growth rates assumed for energy demand. Large-scale utilisation of nuclear fusion or solar power technology if available would in Nordhaus's terms provide the ultimate energy "backstop". In the neoclassical resource-depletion model developed above the "backstop technology" would provide a ceiling for the rising resource prices. The prospect of an infinite or near infinite resource plateau would cause resource prices to level out and depletion policy debate to dwindle into insignificance.

Limitations of the Free Enterprise Depletion Model

The basic assumptions of the model—perfect competition and the absence of uncertainty—are not realistic and various real world market imperfections influence the actual rates of resource depletion, some causing actual depletion rates to diverge from the Pareto optimal rates. Advocates of the neoclassical approach have recognised and analysed some of the imperfections and their likely impact on depletion. Critics[27] argue, however, that even the modified neoclassical model still does not provide a very meaningful analysis of the long-run problems of resource depletion. Fitzgibbons and Cochrane, in the reading below, argue that the prevailing system of mineral tenure is a critical variable which the free enterprise school of thought treats as uniform in all markets. In fact the closed-tenure system assumed (ownership of mineral resources being vested in the owners of the land containing the deposit) is not typical of countries outside the USA.

Monopoly or oligopoly market structures

Many modern large-scale industries, especially those concerned with resource extraction, do not operate in competitive market structures but rather a small number of massive, often multinational, corporations effectively dominate the market. In the case of oil and bauxite, for example, current resource owners (the governments of the countries within whose borders the resource deposits are located) have increasingly sought to create international cartel (monopoly) supply conditions after initially nationalising the resource assets previously controlled by multinational companies. The Organisation of Petroleum Exporting Countries (OPEC) cartel has had a major effect on world oil prices since 1972–73.[28] Economic theory predicts that monopoly market structures will result in higher prices and lower outputs than would be the case under conditions of perfect competition. Could it then be argued that the observed rates of resource exploitation are less than the economically optimal rate? Kay and Mirrlees[29] and Heal[30] have indeed argued that from an efficiency point of view rates of resource depletion may be too low. It is questionable, however, whether the OPEC cartel, for example, is operating on textbook principles. Rather, a range of complementary and conflicting influences — strategic, religious, political and economic — all have some effect on OPEC production and pricing policy. Whether the end result is Pareto optimal or not is difficult if not impossible to judge.

The discount rate

As we outlined above the fundamental principle of the economically-optimal intertemporal resource depletion model was that resource prices increase at the same rate over time as the rate of interest. The discounting process is necessary in order to integrate resources policy criteria with efficiency criteria for the economy as a whole. Intertemporal optimality requires that the market discounts future profits at the same rate as society as a whole prefers to discount the welfare of future generations. The prevailing rate of interest is, however, the private discount rate (opportunity cost of capital rate — see Section 2) and there are several reasons why this private rate might be systematically higher than the correct social time preference rate. Two such reasons that have been identified are individuals' perception of risk and the existence of taxes on income from capital.[31] But over and above these reasons other writers have questioned the legitimacy in social decision-making of utilising private time preference as the basis for intertemporal decisions given the possibility of individual myopia and the consequent neglect of the long-term future.[32] Thus the argument runs that the market-determined resource-depletion rates will be too high and production biased in favour of the current generation because of the high discount rate. Fitzgibbons and Cochrane[33] argue that if a society were experiencing a decline in its economic growth rate or was in a "stationary state" then the proper discount rate would be zero or negative. A critical assumption underlying positive interest-rate discounting is that physical limits to growth do not present intractable problems. Discounting is invalid, they argue, unless it is already known that the impending resource limits will not constrain economic growth. Yet it is in this very area that current empirical data is deficient. The anti-growth commentators would wish to stress here that seemingly large additions to resource stocks will make only a minor difference to resource lives in a world of exponential growth rates. More optimistic analysts would then counter that empirically it has not been proved that the crucial equations are exponential growth equations.

Forward markets

Solow and Heal[34] among others have demonstrated that perfectly competitive markets will achieve optimal intergenerational rates of resource consumption only if there exist a set of perfectly functioning futures markets for resources. These markets are supposed to ensure that resource owners can forecast future resource prices with certainty. They would then be able to sell, on the futures market, a claim today on a unit of the resource which will actually be delivered x years in the future. Again Fitzgibbons and Cochrane[35] argue that even with futures markets the market operators would still require the knowledge to enable them to set the correct rate of discount when they linked their forecasts of future prices to present prices. How is such knowledge obtained?

Long-term forward markets do not currently exist and thus future resource prices are uncertain and are therefore expected prices. Failure to predict these future prices correctly can bring about cyclical movements in prices. So-called precautionary (the buying of materials for inventory-stock purposes) and speculative demands can have complicated effects on resource prices.[36] Taking speculative demand as an example we can illustrate in a simplified fashion, following Banks' analysis,[37] the role that expectations can play. If we assume demand (D_t) to be a function of the current resource price (P_t) and also a function of the price expected in the next time period $(P_t^e + 1)$ we derive the following equation:

$$D_t = D_t(P_t, P_{t+1}^e) = a_0 + a_1 P_t + a_2 P_{t+1}^e$$

where $\qquad a_1 < 0, a_2 > 0.$

Now the expectations that market operators form could be extrapolative expectations. Thus if the resource price increased from the last period to the current period a price increase is expected in the next period so that:

and

$$P^e_{t+1} = P_t + \lambda(P_t - P_{t-1}), \text{ with } \lambda > 0$$

$$D_t = a_0 + [a_1 + a_2(1 + \lambda)]P_t - a_2\lambda P_{t-1}$$

where

$$\lambda > 0.$$

On the other hand, reverse extrapolation expectations may exist, where in terms of our equations $\lambda < 0$. In reality λ would probably be a non-constant term that was positive (extrapolative expectations) on some occasions and negative (reverse extrapolation) on others.

In terms of precautionary demand the relation of inventories (stocks) to demand plays a key role in determining the market price of a commodity. Statistically it would appear that the price of most industrial raw materials is a function of the ratio of stocks to demand. Often what appears to happen is that if stocks are falling very rapidly in relation to current consumption, price has a tendency to rise. Given these complications the level of future prices may be *overestimated* in which case too low a rate of resource depletion will be sustained (it being apparently attractive for resource owners to leave resources in the ground and let their value appreciate). On the other hand, if the level of future prices is *underestimated* too high a rate of resource depletion will be sustained (resource owners finding it apparently more attractive to exploit and sell their resource holdings).

Insurance markets

Because of the lack of insurance markets in natural resources if resource owners are risk averse they will tend to discount the future heavily with the implication that depletion rates will be above socially optimal levels. On the other hand, resource owners may also be risk averse when it comes to further exploration of potential new sources of supply. More potential resources left *in situ* would of course be to the benefit of future generations.[38]

The neglect of common property resources

Krutilla and Smith[39] have recently emphasised that conventional (neoclassical) methods for modelling the role of natural resources in economic activity are incomplete. They conclude, "Past theoretical and empirical studies have considered only industrial raw materials using arguably challengeable assumptions and, in so doing, implicitly ignored the role of the services of environmental common property resources that are used in economic activity". In particular the residuals-disposal and life-support services of the environment have been subject to cumulative depletion as economic growth has proceeded. Thus the optimistic view of future technological advance typical of neoclassical resource models must be tempered by a more detailed analysis of the implications for the environmental common property services. Randall[40] in the reading below reminds us that the role of technology should be given an entropy perspective. Technological advance has enabled mankind to consume and otherwise exhaust our universe at an exponential rate transferring wealth from future to present generations. Careful consideration of thermodynamic laws would appear to magnify the importance of the pessimistic growth model findings reviewed earlier.[41] Nevertheless not all technologies are equally destructive to low entropy per unit of value produced—"the search for and implementation of technologies which are less destructive of low entropy would seem to be a potentially rewarding activity."[42] Policymakers ought to be thinking about channelling investment into a search for modes of production and consumption which increase entropy efficiency, i.e. ones which produce a greater value of output per unit of entropic degradation.

A number of commentators have also warned that the substitution of scarce resources for synthetic substances made possible by technological advances may only serve to increase ecological risks.[43] Some economic activities such as, for example, the burning of fossil fuels may well reach a level that poses a threat to the life-support services provided by the biosphere. Both local and global increases in atmospheric temperature will be stimulated by waste heat from the increasing use of coal and nuclear energy. The burning of fossil fuels produces carbon dioxide emissions which together with the discharge of fine heat-absorbing particles can result in the so-called "greenhouse effect". The consequent increase in mean global temperatures has potentially catastrophic impacts associated with it.[44] Smith and Krutilla[45] conclude that "even if the early analyses [Barnett and Morse] suggesting that there has been relaxation of the private property resource constraints are accepted as correct, there is still reason to question these conclusions because their analytical framework fails to recognise that such gains may have been achieved at the expense of reductions in the stock of common property resources potentially yielding life-support services. Thus, continued faith in the cornucopian promise of technology may need to be modified in important respects."

Resource Availability and Demand: The Information Gap

A recurring problem that surfaces in critiques of both the pessimistic and optimistic resources and growth arguments is the limited quality and quantity of the empirical data available to substantiate crucial assumptions. There is little scientific validity in assuming either an optimistic view of resources availability and growth or assuming that global disaster is imminent if neither view can be substantiated with currently available knowledge. Much of the Limits to Growth debate has been a debate over theoretical models. What has been demonstrated is that different models and assumptions yield different theoretical possibilities for future economic life. In the light of current data deficiencies it could be argued that present resource policy ought to incorporate a safety margin mentality. Given that future generations would be faced with severe costs if the more pessimistic scenarios of rapid and sudden resource exhaustion actually proved correct, perhaps resource policy ought to be based to some extent on a "worst possible" scenario which cannot yet be discounted given current knowledge. Landsberg[45] concluded that the debate over global materials exhaustion had reached a standoff by 1976. The technical deficiencies of the Club of Rome's models had severely limited their relevance to policymaking but, on the other hand, the optimistic technological expectations of the neoclassical economic models remained speculation: "no technological breakthroughs of the kind that would give the argument that depletion continues to be shifted forward in time a winning edge have occurred".

If we also take into account the neglect of cumulative depletion of common property resources by the neoclassical economic modelling approach to resource depletion; and take seriously the possible ecological risks that continued economic growth brings with it then the "safety margin" policy mentality seems to have much to commend it. We saw in Section 5 that Daly's "SSE" approach, although lacking precision, did clearly identify the general policy goal of flexibility and maintenance of "safety margins". Howe[46] has expanded this line of reasoning and outlined what he terms "a responsible natural resources policy" based on a sustainable level of aggregate production and a liveable environment over the very long-term future. In his terms the long-term policy goal should be "A responsible natural resources policy . . . consisting of a set of rules, inducements, and actions relating to natural resource use that are sufficient to move the economy to an efficient indefinitely sustainable, nondeclining pattern of aggregate consumption, with no irreversible deterioration of the physical environment, and without the imposition of significantly greater risks on future generations".

Supply: Resources and Reserves

On a global basis *resources* can be defined as the total amount of an element that exists down to some defined grade that is higher than crustal abundance but lower than currently mineable grades.[47] As far as minerals are concerned resources represent the ultimate amount available for useful extraction. Resources therefore do not include all minerals, some are present in such small amounts in crustal rock that they are not feasible recovery options, at least on any foreseeable timetable. Recovery would present overwhelming energy requirements and extensive environmental damage. Not many attempts have been made so far to determine global mineral resource bases. Durham[48] highlights three particular studies: First, the US Bureau of Mines Study 1970, which served as the basis for the Limits to Growth Study and the Ecologist's "Blueprint for Survival" Studies (1972).[49] Second, the US Geological Survey 1973, which contained decidedly more optimistic estimates than those of the Bureau of Mines study. For example, copper estimates (in terms of renewable metal) are 308 million tons in the Bureau of Mines study but some 344 million tons (plus a further 1445 million tons, categorized as hypothetical, speculative or sub-economic) in the 1973 survey. Third, the United Nations World Iron Ore Resources Study 1970, which also presented a more optimistic picture.

It is important to stress that various geological constraints make such estimates uncertain and all such estimates should be viewed in light of the constraints. Four broad environments of mineral concentration can be distinguished. The superficial cover of the continental crust contains small highly concentrated mineral deposits but in the northern hemisphere an overcover of glacial deposits presents a major obstacle to the exploitation of such deposits. In wet tropical climates, laterite cover is the problem but it does have a compensation, in that aluminium ore (bauxite) is found concentrated in pure deposits. Secondly, the solid rocks of the continental crust provide the principal source of useful minerals. The estimates of resource potential in this environment are unfortunately far from being totally accurate. The geological conditions that have controlled ore genesis are very complicated and thus difficult to predict. Guild[50] argues that systematic exploration should be based on a genetic model and as deposits become more difficult to detect it is inevitable that the discovery record should correlate positively with the correctness of the model. The third environment is provided by the sediments of the ocean floors which incorporate deposits of so-called manganese nodules containing amounts of copper, cobalt and nickel besides manganese and iron. Currently, these resources must be judged potential rather than identified resources.[51] Ford and Gibbons[52] have summarised the complex technical and economic problems involved and have alluded to the political and legal issues that remain to be settled. The United Nations Conferences on the Law of the Sea have yet to settle who owns the nodule deposits. Finally, the solid oceanic crust must potentially contain mineral deposits but whether mining will ever prove to be feasible is unknown.

One of the hypotheses put forward to explain the optimistic resource scarcity findings of the Barnett and Morse study, mentioned earlier, was the geological one that when higher-grade sources are exhausted, lower-grade sources are found in greater abundance and that the latter are qualitatively not greatly dissimilar. But this is, however, by no means an unchallenged thesis in the light of currently available knowledge. Brobst[53] presents evidence that suggests there may be significant differences in the distribution of the geochemically abundant metals compared with the scarce elements. The less geochemically abundant materials may well decline quantitatively at lower-grade levels after the richest grades have been exhausted.[54]

Reserves, whether they are proved, probable or possible, are deposits known to provide feasible extraction options under current economic and technical conditions at any particular place.[55] The size of the reserves either at the individual mine level or at the global level is a function of exploration and development decisions taken in the past. Reserve bases are dynamic rather than static changing as prices, technology, exploration and development work take place.[56] Nordhaus[57] utilising the US Geological Survey 1973 data identifies three important resource availability ratios, the R–C ratio, the ratio of proved reserves to current consumption, which a number of empirical studies have shown to be low for most minerals; the CA ratio, total crustal abundance of different materials, which represents the opposite end of the availability spectrum; and the URR ratio, ultimately recoverable resources. This latter ratio is the economically relevant measure dependent on technological changes (in discovery technology, exploration technology, recovery technology and use technology) and on the level of prices. Nordhaus has compared the ratio of energy reserves to 1970 levels of consumption in the USA under differing technology scenarios. With current technology the utilisation of fossil fuels and nuclear power apparently gives us 8400 years of supply at 1970 consumption levels while the addition of breeder reactors and fusion technology gives us virtually unlimited supplies.

Resource Demand

Having briefly examined the difficulties of estimating resource availability we turn from the supply side of the equation to the demand side. We need to look at the equally hazardous problems of forecasting likely future demands for resources rather than merely assuming some constant level of demand as the Nordhaus model does. Ideally, to forecast world demand for resources we require a combined macro-economic/input–output model containing detailed data on growth rates, individual economy product-mix information over time and technical input–output coefficients. Future price levels will also need to be forecast and the feedback effects of rising prices on forecast demand identified. Needless to say such models do not currently exist. In the past most forecasts used the trend extrapolation technique which basically reduces to an assumption that past trends will continue into the future. The so-called materials consumption/gross national production (GNP) ratio or the energy consumption/GNP ratio have been derived from past statistics and then used as the basis of forecasts. Projections of GNP, assuming unchanged coefficients between GNP and minerals or energy consumption produce estimates, of a sort, of demand in the future.

Energy forecasting

Long-term trend projection models were commonly used in the field of energy forecasting up to 1970 but objectively they should be regarded not as forecasting methods but as providing benchmarks against which more sophisticated forecasts can be compared. Economists prefer the so-called model building approach to forecasting in which a theory is constructed and tested to explain the behaviour of the variable to be forecasted. One step removed from the trend projection models are the partial equilibrium models which attempt to relate fuel demand to independent predictor variables such as, the price of the fuel concerned, income and the price of substitute fuels. Both the trend projection and rudimentary partial equilibrium models have to be handled with great caution and often produce misleading results. Such models imply a relatively fixed GNP/energy consumption ratio and thus if energy supplies become short economic growth rates would collapse. From a policy point of view the implication is that the critical strategies are those concerned with increasing future energy supplies since demand cannot be altered very much. Energy use is, according to these models, likely to continue to increase as rapidly in the future as it did in the past despite price increases.

Typical of the above approach to energy forecasting are the methods used in the official UK demand forecasts for the period up to the year 2000.[58] A number of writers[59] have pointed out the drawbacks of this official forecast and policy review including the critically important point that the year 1973/74 marks a major discontinuity in the world energy market. The global shift from an era of relatively low energy prices to one of relatively high and rising prices makes forecasting on the basis of historical experience (pre 1973) much more uncertain. Papadopoulas[60] points out that in the five years up to the 1973/74 energy crisis the average annual growth in primary energy consumption in the UK was 2·2 percent against a 3 percent growth in GDP. Electricity sales grew at an average annual rate of 4·7 percent with non-domestic electricity sales averaging 4 percent per annum. Since 1973/74 primary energy consumption has fallen by 1 percent per annum on average against a 0·5 percent average annual growth in GDP. Electricity sales show an average annual growth of 0·4 percent with the non-domestic sales growing by 1·2 percent per annum. Now the official UK energy policy consultative document recognises that high energy prices will reduce the ratio between percentage increases in primary energy consumption and economic growth yet the officially favoured scenario has primary energy consumption growing by on average 2 percent per annum, and electricity sales and economic growth growing by 3 percent. These figures suggest a situation much closer to the pre-1973 period than the post-1973 period characterised by a tight energy market and government-sponsored energy-conservation measures with their consequent inhibiting effects on electricity sales growth.

Since the early 1970s more sophisticated energy-forecasting models have been constructed on a general equilibrium basis. These models attempt to incorporate the two-way interdependencies that exist between GNP growth rates and energy consumption. The previously neglected reverse effects that high energy prices might have on energy consumption and conservation are modelled. The models utilise the long-run price elasticity concept which is taken to represent the elasticity of substitution possibilities between energy and other inputs into the economy. The models predict that, with substitution possibilities appearing to exist at least on the basis of the short run of data available since 1973, over the long run economic growth can be separated to some extent from energy growth. Other modellers[61] have utilised physical models rather than traditional economic extrapolations. The physical models contain estimated sectoral end-use energy requirements (based on post-1973 data) in the economy taking into account energy-conservation technologies currently available. A range of energy-consuming activities related to each sector of the economy are then projected (via linkages to forecasted future GNP) into the future. Energy requirements are then computed by forecasting the amounts of energy used per unit of activity, i.e. the energy intensity.

Most informed commentators agree that data constraints remain formidable obstacles to the rapid refinement of the art of resource forecasting. Calculating the area under the mineral-depletion curve presents a continuing problem. Schanz,[62] in a survey of minerals economics, concludes "the combination of the physical unknowns of the earth's geology and the economic puzzle of the future supply/price relationship is still the monumental stumbling block". We should also remember that the costs of improving our resource inventory data are large and diminishing returns could well set in fairly early in the process of data base improvement. It is difficult to know exactly how far down this road it would pay society to go. As we have tried to emphasise, reserve estimates only provide the lower limits of resource availability and are therefore only useful over a limited planning horizon. Reserve estimates are most valuable if they in fact indicate the likelihood of supply constraints and by implication rapid price escalation and forced alterations in consumption habits in the near future.

Policies to Reduce Resource Depletion

It has become clear over time that the largely academic growth–no growth debate began to be paralleled by increasing governmental interest. The year 1973 marked a watershed in the economic history of western nations, the result of the dramatic rise in oil prices announced by OPEC in that year. The OPEC action somehow formalised and empiricised the momentum already established intellectually in the growth debate. The later stages of the intellectual debate were thus paralleled by increasing governmental interest in resource-conservation policy. Fears began to be expressed in government circles that certain other materials, notably copper, bauxite and perhaps phosphates, could equally well be "cartelised". The prospects for successful mineral cartels are, nevertheless, more difficult to predict and will vary from commodity to commodity. But probably the overriding effect of the oil crisis as far as Western governments were concerned was the balance of payments effect and it has led them to think of ways of reducing the materials and energy import bill.

In some countries fairly dramatic rethinking has occurred as with the substantial research initiatives in the USA into new energy sources and alternative energy consumption scenarios as well as into the complete spectrum of resource use, conservation and recovery. The US Resource Conservation and Recovery Act of 1976 is just one piece of legislation in a line of environmentally-orientated measures that followed, in piecemeal fashion, the passing of the National Environmental Policy Act of 1969. The 1976 Act defines resource conservation as "reduction of the amounts of solid wastes that are generated, reduction of overall resource consumption and utilization of recovered resources". By contrast, the UK reaction has been lukewarm, especially on the materials front. The initial British governmental reaction was the production of a green paper entitled "War on Waste"[63] and this promised "a new national effort to conserve and reclaim scarce resources" and a "war on waste involving all sections of the community". The green paper referred to the recently formulated, but not then implemented, Control of Pollution Act, 1974 which for the first time, in part one, sections 20 and 21, required local authorities to examine ways of promoting the reclamation (a generic term encompassing a number of different types of resource recovery) of waste and the necessary powers for this purpose. A further move was to establish the Waste Management Advisory Council (WMAC) in 1975 which in turn struck a number of sub-committees to establish policy guidance in individual resources. The WMAC has since published a number of reports[64] but the reclamation sections of the 1974 Act still have not been fully implemented.*

A number of policies that have been suggested are aimed at specific sources of market failure (see essay in Section 2) in the resource industries themselves. Thus policy instruments such as effluent charges and numerous forms of regulations have been suggested and implemented (though in the case of the former instrument only in restricted fashion) particularly in the context of pollution control. We examine a range of pollution-control instruments in Section 9. Making industry's residuals disposal activities more expensive should stimulate increased recycling of residuals as well as product and process changes beneficial to the environment. Taxes on the production and consumption of virgin raw materials could also provide an incentive through the market mechanism to reduce the consumption of these materials and increase the rate of recycling secondary materials by pushing up the former's costs closer to their true social values. A variety of taxes are available but one popular candidate is the so-called severance tax, which is a tax levied per unit of a non-renewable resource extracted by a company.[65] Lecomber[66] has suggested that the pollution-rights concept[67] could be applied both to renewable and non-renewable resource industries. The aim would be to create artificial markets in transferable residuals discharge rights, or extraction licences for non-renewable resources or in fishing rights. Such measures, however, would not go far enough to satisfy the general anti-growth school of thought. We reviewed in Section 5 the arguments calling for a paradigm shift in the science of economics and the suggestions for a steady-state economic system better adapted to ensure the long-term survival of mankind. Randall[68] in the reading below has serious reservations about current resource policy in the industrialised world. He sees the long-run state of society as being largely the result of a long sequence of short-term policy decisions usually taken in a "crisis" atmosphere. The result is a myopic set of policies which do not go very far in providing for a long-term solution based on

---

* In 1981 the Conservative Government abolished the WMAC along with a number of other environmental quangos (quasi public bodies)—see pp. 460–461.

a reduction in the prevailing rate of time preference, the development and use of entropy-efficient technologies and flow resources, and a reorientation in consumption habits. O'Hearn[69] explores the social and political changes he believes are needed in order to attain a stable long-term future for the human race.

The Desirability of Future Economic Growth

In the more recent stages of the growth–no growth debate a number of writers have attempted to analyse the underlying issues in a wider context and claims concerning the utility of either optimistic or pessimistic long-term forecasts have become more cautious. Support for comprehensive (global) long-term forecasting models seems to have waned considerably. It has become apparent that such general models yield minimal information at a prodigious cost. It has now become fashionable to engage in scenario-building exercises which rather than forecast the future merely identify the various choices available to society. Choices are then combined to produce a set of consistent futures for presentation to the policymaker. With limited funds available detailed analysis is better directed at crucial sub-problems, currently energy utilisation would seem to be a primary candidate, rather than on grandiose global computer simulation exercises. Gordon's[70] reading below is a good survey of the growth debate in its wider context. Much of the debate was concerned almost exclusively with the question of the feasibility of future growth and the equally important question of the desirability of growth was perhaps neglected. A consistent critic of the pro-growth school Mishan,[71] has attempted to focus attention on the issue of whether in an already affluent society continued economic growth is in fact producing a more satisfying life for ordinary people. For Mishan the dominant issue is

"whether we are ready seriously to recognise that the collective pursuit of economic growth, which depends, in the main, on scientific advance and technological progress, has begun to have complex and far-reaching consequences both on the biosphere and on the 'sociosphere'. For it is now reasonable to believe that, despite the abundance of man-made goods produced by continued economic growth, its net effect on human health and happiness could be adverse and possibly disastrous, a continuation of economic growth, as conventionally understood, and assuming it to be possible, could not be counted upon to improve social wellbeing. If wellbeing is society's objective, we should do better to think more directly and carefully about the ways in which this might be improved rather than to allow ourselves to be guided by orthodox doctrine and put our trust in economic growth."

It now seems plausible to argue that in some affluent countries, at least for a large percentage of their populations, levels of satisfaction derived from the consumption of goods and services have, or are likely very soon to, levelled off. The reasons for this would appear to be both that a satiation plateau has been reached and because satisfaction has less to do with absolute income and more to do with relative incomes in these different societies. The relative income hypothesis was first propounded by Dusenberry in 1949 to highlight what he saw as a growing concern individuals had with position in the overall structure of incomes. In addition we examined in Section 6 Hirsch's[72] thesis that competition to possess what he terms "positional goods" bids up their prices and eventually impedes economic progress. Because both conspicuous consumption (expenditure to display how wealthy an individual is) and positional good consumption are relatively costly they are available only to a privileged wealthy elite. Thus it is not possible to make everybody in society relatively better off over time despite positive rates of economic growth.*

We mentioned earlier the fears expressed by some analysts concerning the possible increased ecological risks that are posed by modern technological advance. Mishan[73] also emphasises these growing risks and identifies a number of broad categories of technologically-induced environmental hazard and sources of social instability. Worldwide transport and communications networks have increased the risk of large-scale epidemics and may have served to increase resentment between the "have" and "have not" countries of the world. The development of synthetic substances may have complicated long-term damage effects on the biosphere if released in sufficient quantities. Finally, advances in weapons technology and the growth of urban conurbations have served to increase the vulnerability of large population groups to catastrophe induced by systems breakdown or direct sabotage. Technological advance brings with it a range of worrying social issues not the least of which would appear to be an extension of government surveillance and controls. The growing threat to individual freedom of action and speech is becoming increasingly apparent.

Notes and References

1. McInerny, J. (1976) The Simple Analytics of Natural Resource Economics, *Journal of Agricultural Economics*, vol. 27 (1). Unfortunately, the analysis on pp. 45-47 of the original article contained an error and a corrected version of this section can be found in McInerny, J. (1978) On The Optimal Policy For Exploiting Renewable Resource Stocks, *Journal of Agricultural Economics*, vol. 29.
2. See Pearce, D. W. and Walter, I. (1977) *Resource Conservation: The Social and Economic Dimensions of Recycling*, New York University Press and Longmans; and for a detailed study of one city's (Norwich) local recycling market see O'Riordan, T. and Turner, R. K. (1979) Recycling and Householder Attitudes: A Survey of Norwich, *Resources Policy*, vol. 5 (2).
3. Quimby, T. (1975) *Recycling. The Alternative to Disposal*, Johns Hopkins University Press.

* Some public opinion surveys have yielded evidence of a contradiction in the reported association between increasing income and happiness (known as the "Easterlin Paradox"). For a good analysis of this paradox and the 'Limits' philosophy see: Abramovitz, M. (1979) Economic Growth and its Discontents; and David, P. A. (1979) From Growth to the Millenium; Economics and the Transformation of the Idea of Progress, in Boskin, M. J. *Economics and Human Welfare*, Academic Press.

4. Bower, B. (1975) Studies In Residuals Management in Industry, in Mills, E. S. (ed.) *Economic Analysis of Environmental Problems*, Columbia University Press.
5. For a discussion of natural resource economics in general see Pearce, D. W. (1976) *Environmental Economics*, Longmans; Lecomber, R. (1979) *The Economics of Natural Resources*, Macmillan; and Howe, C. W. (1979) *Natural Resource Economics*, John Wiley.
6. Hector, M. (1979) Overfishing; An Economic Analysis, *Journal of Agricultural Economics*, vol. 30.
7. Butlin, J. A. and Tomkins, J. M. (1975) A Theoretical and Empirical Approach to Fisheries Economics, *Journal of Agricultural Economics*, vol. 25.
8. Freeman, C. and Jahoda, M. L. (eds.) (1978) *World Futures; The Great Debate*, Martin Robertson.
9. Wilson, K. D. (ed.) (1977) *Prospects For Growth; Changing Expectations For The Future*, Praeger.
10. See, for example, Mishan, E. J. (1967) *The Costs of Economic Growth*, Penguin; Schumacher, E. F. (1973) *Small Is Beautiful*, Blond and Briggs; Meadows, D. *et al.* (1972) *The Limits To Growth*, Earth Island; Mesarovic, M. and Pestel, E. (1975) *Mankind at the Turning Point*; Hutchinson, Erlich, P. and Erlich, A. H. (1970) *Population, Resources Environment: Issues in Human Ecology*, Freeman.
11. Mishan, E. J. (1967) *op. cit.*
12. Meadows, D. L. *et al.* (1972) *op. cit.*
13. Meadows, D. L. *et al.* (1972) *op. cit.*, and Mesarovic, M. and Pestel, E. (1975) *op. cit.*
14. Erlich, P. and Erlich, A. H. (1971) *op. cit.*
15. Heilbroner, R. L. (1974) *An Inquiry Into The Human Prospect*, Norton.
16. For a summary and some original forecasts see Freeman, C. and Jahoda, M. (eds.) (1978) *op. cit.*
17. Kahn, H. *et al.* (1976) *The Next 200 Years*, William Morrow & Co.
18. See Cole, H. S. D. *et al.* (eds.) (1973) *Thinking About The Future*, Chatto & Windus; Beckerman, W. (1972) Economists, Scientists and Environmental Catastrophe, *Oxford Economic Papers*, vol. 24 (3); Beckerman, W. (1974) *In Defence Of Economic Growth*, Jonathan Cape; Nordhaus, W. (1973) Word Dynamics: Measurement Without Data, *Economic Journal*, vol. 83 (4); Solow, R. M. (1974) The Economics of Resources or the Resources of Economics, *American Economic Review*, Paper and Proceedings, vol. 44; Ridker, R. (1973) To Grow or Not To Grow: That's Not The Question, *Science*, vol. 182.
19. Barnett, H. J. and Morse, C. (1963) *Scarcity and Growth: The Economics of Natural Resource Availability*, Johns Hopkins University Press.
20. There is, of course, nothing sacred about the Partisan approach as the reading by Fitzgibbons and Cochrane in this Section emphasises.
21. Page, T. (1977) *Conservation and Efficiency*, Johns Hopkins University Press.
22. Solow, R. M. (1974) *op. cit.*
23. Fitzgibbons, A. and Cochrane, S. (1978) Optimal Rate of Natural Resource Depletion, *Resources Policy*, vol. 4 (3).
24. For a discussion of the concept of the elasticity of substitution in the context of energy resources see: Hitch, C. J. (1977) *Modelling Energy — Economy Interactions: Five Approaches*, Resources For The Future; Lecomber, R. (1977) *op. cit.*; and Darmstadter, J. (1979) *Economic Growth and Energy Conservation: Historical and International Lessons*, Resources For The Future, Reprint 154.
25. Nordhaus, W. D. (1973) *The Allocation of Energy Resources*, Brookings Papers on Economic Activity.
26. Lecomber, R. (1979) *op. cit.*
27. Fitzgibbons, A. and Cochrane, S. (1978) *op. cit.*
28. See Darmstadter, J. and Landsberg, H. H. (1975) The Economic Background of the Oil Crisis, *Daedalus*, vol. 104 (4); and Banks, F. E. (1977) *Scarcity, Energy and Economic Progress*, Lexington Books, D C Heath.
29. Kay, J. A. and Mirrlees, J. A. (1975) The Desirability of Natural Resource Depletion, in Pearce, D. W. (ed.) *The Economics of Natural Resource Depletion*, Macmillan.
30. Heal, G. (1975) Economic Aspects of Natural Resource Depletion, in Pearce, D. W. (ed.) *The Economics of Natural Resource Depletion*, Macmillan.
31. Solow, R. M. (1974) *op. cit.*
32. For a survey of such views see Page, T. (1977) *op. cit.*

33. Fitzgibbons, A. and Cochrane, S. (1978) *op. cit.*
34. Solow, R. M. (1974) *op. cit.*, and Heal, G. (1975) *op. cit.*
35. Fitzgibbons, A. and Cochrane, S. (1978) *op. cit.*
36. Banks, F. E. (1976) *The Economics of Natural Resources*, Plenum Press.
37. Banks, F. E. (1976) *op. cit.*
38. See Heal, G. (1975) *op. cit.*
39. Smith, V. K. and Krutilla, J. V. (1979) Resource and Environmental Constraints to Growth, *American Journal of Agricultural Economics*, vol. 61 (3).
40. Randall, A. (1975) Growth, Resources, and Environment: Some Conceptual Issues, *American Journal of Agricultural Economics*, vol. 57 (4).
41. Georgescu-Raogen, N. (1976) *Energy and Economic Myths*, Pergamon Press.
42. Randall, A. (1975) *op. cit.*
43. See Mishan, E. J. (1976) Extending the Growth Debate, in Wilson, K. D., *Prospects for Growth: Changing Expectations for the Future*, Praeger; Commoner, B. (1971) *The Closing Circle*, Jonathon Cape; and Page, T. (1978) A Generic View of Toxic Chemicals and Similar Risks, *Ecology Law Quarterly*, vol. 7 (2).
44. Nordhaus, W. D. (1977) Economic Growth and Climate, *American Economic Review*, Papers and Proceedings, vol. 67.
45. Landsberg, H. (1976) Materials: Some Recent Trends and Issues, *Science*, vol. 191.
46. Govett, M. H. and Govett, G. J. S. (1977) Scarcity of Basic Materials and Fuels: Assessments and Implications, in Pearce, D. W. and Walter, I. (eds.) *Resource Conservation*, New York University Press and Longmans.
47. Howe, C. W. (1979) *op. cit.*
48. Durham, K. (1978) World Supply of Non Fuel Minerals: The Geological Constraints, *Resources Policy*, vol. 4 (2).
49. Editors of the Ecologist (1972) *A Blueprint For Survival*, Penguin.
50. Guild, P. (1976) Discovery of Natural Resources, *Science*, vol. 191.
51. Hammond, A. L. (1976) Manganese Nodules: A Mineral Resource on the Deep Seabed, *Science*, vol. 191.
52. Ford, G. and Gibbons, M. (1979) Whose Nodules Are They?, *New Scientist*, May.
53. Brobst, D. A. (1979) Fundamental Concepts for the Analysis of Resource Availability, in Smith, V. K. (ed.) *Scarcity And Growth Reconsidered*, Johns Hopkins University Press.
54. See Howe, C. W. (1979) *op. cit.*, for a survey of these geological theories.
55. Govett, M. H. and Govett, G. J. S. (1977) *op. cit.*; and Govett, G. J. S. and Govett, M. H. (1979) Geological Supply and Demand: The Unresolved Equation, *Resources Policy*, vol. 4 (2).
56. Robinson, C. (1975) The Depletion of Energy Resources, in Pearce, D. W. (ed.) (1975) *The Economics of Natural Resources*, Macmillan.
57. Nordhaus, W. D. (1974) Resources as a Constraint on Growth, *American Economic Review*, Papers and Proceedings, vol. 64.
58. UK Department of Energy (1978) *Energy Policy: A Consultative Document*, HMSO.
59. See, for example, Papadopoulas, R. (1979) The UK Consultative Document on Energy Policy, *Energy Policy*, vol. 7 (3).
60. Papadopoulas, R. (1979) *op. cit.*
61. See, for example, Lewis, C. (1979) A Low Energy Option for the UK, *Resources Policy*, vol. 7 (2).
62. Schanz, J. J. (1977) *Minerals Economics — Prospectives of the Past, Present and Future*, Resources for the Future, Reprint No. 138.
63. UK government (1974) *War on Waste: A Policy for Reclamation*, HMSO.
64. The first report was published in 1976, see UK Waste Management Advisory Council (1976) HMSO.
65. For a thorough analysis of this fiscal instrument in the context of US minerals industries see Page, T. (1977) *op. cit.*
66. See Lecomber, R. (1979) *op. cit.*
67. The original idea was first published in Dales, J. H. (1968) *Pollution, Property and Prices*, University of Toronto Press.
68. Randall, A. (1975) *op. cit.*
69. O'Hearn, J. (1978) Beyond the Growth Controversy: An Assessment of Responses, *Alternatives*, vol. 7 (3).
70. Gordon, L. (1976) Limits to the Growth Debate, *Resources*, vol. 52.

71. Mishan, E. J. (1977) *The Economic Growth Debate: An Assessment*, Allen & Unwin.
72. Hirsch, F. (1976) *Social Limits To Growth*, Routledge & Kegan Paul; for critical reviews of the Hirsch thesis see Smith, V. K. (1978) Economic Growth—Meritorious or Meretricious: A Review of Social Limits to Growth, *Socio-Economic Planning Sciences*, vol. 2 (2); and Juster, F. T. (1978) A Review of Hirsch, *Science*, vol. 200.
73. Mishan, E. J. (1977) *op. cit.*

READINGS

OPTIMAL RATE OF NATURAL RESOURCE DEPLETION*

Athol Fitzgibbons and Stuart Cochrane

At the vociferous ends of the debate about the proper rate of depletion of natural resources, there are two major schools of thought – a doomsday school and a school of free enterprise. Followers of the doomsday doctrine stress impending resource and environmental constraints, and predict calamity if the present rates of economic growth continue. Soldiers for the other doctrine believe that the ultimate constraints on resources are so distant that they can be disregarded, and that the rate of resource depletion is best determined by the free market system.

The debate is an old one, and the advocates of unlimited growth can refer to failed doomsday writings much earlier than the pessimistic predictions of Thomas Malthus in the early nineteenth century. We have nothing to add to the criticisms of the doomsday writers. Their specific claims that resource exhaustion is impending have been advanced by the cavalier use of inadequate data, by the simplistic extrapolation of uncritically selected trends, and by the obscurantist use of quantitative scientism. In particular, the inadequacy of future technological changes and the limits to resources have been implicitly assumed rather than demonstrated, and the indefinite exponential growth in demand for minerals assumes that the new technology, implicitly assumed in the demand function, will not significantly affect minerals supply.

Nevertheless, an erroneous methodology in one doctrine does not suggest the validity of the methods of its detractors. The doctrines of doomsday and the doctrines of free enterprise are not full contradictories – to the contrary, there are some basic methodological similarities between the rivals.

Discounting

Critics argue that Forrester, Meadows, and others[1] reach pessimistic results because they adopt pessimistic assumptions. But it has not been so well remarked that the rival free enterprise school begins with the assumption of optimism, and after complex and obscuring economic analysis reaches optimistic conclusions.

The circularity of optimism is typically effected through the free enterprise theory of interest and discounting. The process of discounting is compound interest worked backwards. For example, if $100 could be invested at 10% per annum it would be worth $110 after a year and $121 after 2 years. The $121 received in 2 years time can be said to have a present value of $100, the future sum being 'discounted' at the rate of 10%.

*Reprinted with permission from *Resources Policy*, Vol. 4, No. 3, 1978, pp. 166–171. The authors are with the Department of Economics, University of Queensland, Australia.

Discounting effectively shortens the time horizon. Assuming still that the discount rate is 10%, $100 in 30 years time would be worth only $6. Conservationists who think that a high value should be placed on resources for future generations should therefore reject a discount rate in the region of 10%.

The free enterprise school view the discount process as necessary to integrate mineral resources policy criteria with efficiency criteria for the rest of the economy. A resource in the ground is seen as an investment, in that it involves a current sacrifice of consumption with a view to a greater future consumption. Economic efficiency requires that the rate of return on all forms of investment, natural and man made, should be the same. In the sense of economic efficiency, depletion is not a loss of wealth if the value of the resource is replaced, although the value need not be replaced in kind. The free enterprise advocates conclude that rather than wait, it is more efficient to extract any resource today provided only that the extraction is profitable. Naturally the more high grade the resource the more likely it is that extraction is profitable, but profits could be reinvested at interest, and in this way the original resource could be transformed into machines or into other capital for the *future*. Rather than leave posterity a mountain of high grade ore, the advocates of market determined growth would leave behind a beneficiation plant which could process low grade ore – that is, if the market so decreed. The extraction of the more profitable ores today would make the present more happy and the future more wealthy.

No doubt some readers would reply that they would be not more but less happy if the market were allowed unmitigated sway, and that they would also be pleased to forfeit the prospect of their promised future wealth. From the nature and purpose of society in the free enterprise doctrine, dissident views are already accounted for, but minorities do not prevail. According to doctrine, the purpose of society is the satisfaction of peoples' desires. Subject to secondary qualifications, markets are as though competitive, so that the cost of satisfying any desire is equal to the price of it. Prices of course are values. Therefore the discount rate measures both the cost and the value of satisfying present desires against future desires, and all dissident views have been recognized by the market. It does not matter if the dominant motivations are ignorance, frailty and greed. Values other than the satisfaction of desires through the market are subordinate at best. This is the perspective which we first adopt, to see how the logic of free enterprise doctrine is to be applied to guide society over the centuries to come.

There is a free enterprise theory of conservation. The economists interpret the system as though it were dominated by many small markets. Each person has to choose between holding mineral leases or holding other assets. Portfolio balance requires that the mineral lease should be rising in expected value at the standard rate of interest. This means in turn that mineral prices net of extraction costs should also be rising at the rate of interest. Therefore mineral prices grow exponentially, restricting demands and encouraging supplies, unless an infinite resource plateau is reached.[2],[3] At the infinite resources plateau, mineral prices level out, resource demand grows in proportion to the rest of the economy and conservation is to be forgotten.

To illustrate how the competitive market will yield the optimum time distribution of use, consider a known stock of deposits of differing cost structures but with uniform quality and constant unit costs within each field. The lowest cost deposit will be worked first. Price will rise until the lowest cost deposit is depleted and price has reached a level at which it pays the next lowest cost producer to enter the market. If the market foresees the future correctly, this process will continue until eventually the highest cost field will be exhausted and simultaneously quantity demanded will have fallen to zero. The deposits will be used up when the price has reached the maximum that buyers are willing to pay.

At a common level some free enterprise economists are unaware of the significance of the relation between the rate of discount and the rate of economic growth. If the wealth of society were stationary or declining, the proper discount rate would be zero or negative – at least unless some lack of control, such as the greed of parents against children, were to prevail. A critical assumption underlying positive interest rate discounting is that resource limitations do not constrain economic growth – that $100 today really does have to be worth more in the future. Discounting is invalid unless it is already known that impending mineral resource limitations do not constrain economic growth, and it is circularity based upon unwarranted optimism to proceed with a positive discount rate argument with the corollary that the time horizon is severely curtailed, only to conclude that resource depletion will not be a problem. Though today a beneficiation plant might be a more valuable asset than a mountain of high grade ore, that might be because the ore is artifically cheap due to excess depletion today.

To show the incapacity of the market system to determine resources policy, we describe the elementary economics of a finite resource system. Some sailors have been shipwrecked on an island. There is no opportunity to grow food on the island, and there is no prospect of rescue. Each sailor has only a supply of hard tack, which, with careful husbanding, will last his life. The growth rate of the hard tack economy is therefore zero, and the resource stock is finite. Both borrowing and the interest rate should also be zero, since if either sailor paid a positive interest rate for borrowing from the other he would pointlessly shorten his own life.

But suppose that the amount of hard tack was unknown to the sailors. Each sailor has his supply in a dark box from which it is extracted only with difficulty. If some sailors had less foresight than others, there could develop a high consumption economy together with borrowing and lending of hard tack, naturally at a positive interest rate. If the sailors were economists, they could develop formal rules of discounting to justify their prodigality. If they engaged in the optimistic circularity of thought which characterises Kay and Mirrlees,[4] and many other free enterprise writers, they might deduce from the positive discount rate that their economy should be even further accelerated – to their evenutal and mutual detriment.

This story does not assert the actuality of a finite resource system, but it is a guide to the logic of the common free enterprise theory of the supremacy of market wisdom. The problem of resource depletion that besets the sailors cannot be abolished if they decide to form a capital market and a futures market for hard tack among themselves.

A high discount rate implies a short time horizon, which in turn implies a fast rate of extraction. But then the wheel turns full circle. The faster the rate of extraction the higher the rate of economic growth, and so the higher again is the rate of discount. This logic still does not tell us in what form, if at all, the faster growth can be maintained. Futuristic extrapolation is more than dubious, but an answer to resource problems based on economic principles merely obscures our ignorance. There is a second limit to the scope of free enterprise theory which is taken up again in the last section, and which suggests the proper direction of investigation. Though it is only moral morons who want to pauperize the flow of generations to come, we cannot know the nature of the future societies to which we bequeath our resources, and we cannot know how the resources will be valued by them. They may choose to squander or to forget their heritage, and perhaps this will happen again and again in the long eons of time. We are ignorant of the future, and we cannot choose for it. All that we can decide now is how resources would be evaluated by a good and wise society, and what should be properly left to such a society. But to know the nature of the good and the wise, we must try to understand the nature of man. It will be necessary to think beyond mechanistic stimulus and response, beyond the free enterprise utility maximizing calculus, which is either blindly hedonistic or else merely vacuous.

Futures markets

At a more sophisticated level some free enterprise economists are aware that the market discount rate is not necessarily correct, but they more subtly build optimism into their conclusions through an implicit optimistic extrapolation. When the market price of an ore is steady, the past may generate strong expectations of price constancy in the future. If these constant price expectations were to predominate over expectations of price increases, then rather than leave ore in the ground, some firms could bring forward their production decisions, while others could extract at a faster rate than they might otherwise choose. This in turn would put further downward pressure on mineral prices. Through ignorance reinforced by optimistic extrapolations, a market system could proceed upon an arbitrary though long self-justifying depletion rate, with ultimately disruptive consequences.

The possibility of arbitrary market behaviour is discussed by Solow, but he dismisses it with an assumption. He supposes that 'producers do have some notion that the resources they own has a value anchored somewhere in the future, a value determined by technological and demand considerations'.[5]

If producers really did have such information about the future, the debate on possible resources constraints could be resolved by reference to them. But Solow does not say what is to be the basis for the long view that producers are to take, and though he says that 'professional standards' are to prevail, this is inadequate. For example, it is clear that Solow could not admit that professional standards would be met by forecasting on the basis of Forrester's pessimistic assumptions.

A similar difficulty arises for Solow, Stiglitz[6] and others who believe that the correct rate of resource depletion would be followed in an economy with a hypothetically full set of futures market for resources. Even if there were full futures markets, speculators and others who operate in the futures market would have to decide on the correct rate of discount when they tied their estimates of future prices to present prices. This in turn means that they would have to know the extent to which resource limits would constrain future economic growth. But this again raises the question at issue, for the speculators must derive their knowledge somehow. The resources problem should be pursued by rational thought, and it is misleading to refer to a hypothetically omniscient market. The market system can long transmute the speculations of buyers and sellers into profits, but it is to ask too much that it should transmute common ignorance into social wisdom.

Tenure system

In their emphasis of the excellence of the market, free enterprise economists are often charged with neglecting the legal and social systems that underlie the market. Consistently, no free enterprise writer has analysed the system of mineral tenure, or how it might affect resource depletion. Having come to a bridge between economic and political analysis, they resolutely turn their heads and refuse to cross. Yet the form of tenure system which they assume unawares is at least as critical as their assumption of perfect competition.

The free enterprise economists have implicitly but erroneously assumed that the tenure institutions controlling mineral resources rights are akin to a closed tenure system, ie the ownership of mineral resources is vested in the owner of the land containing the resources. Under a closed or perfect tenure system, there are many sellers of privately owned subsurface minerals, and an explorer must buy his lease on an active lease market. But with the notable exception of the USA, the dominant tenure system in the non-socialist world is the open tenure system, under which the formal ownership of minerals is vested in the Crown. In practice the Crown transfers the beneficial ownership to the discoverers of the resources, provided that the Crown is satisfied that mineral production will begin at an acceptable rate. Production is usually one of the conditions of lease tenure.

The erroneous assumption that the dominant tenure system is closed is critical, since it is not meaningful to advocate a competitive market structure divorced from the associated form of lease tenure. Market behaviour depends upon the lease tenure system to such an extent that a competitive exploration industry under one tenure system is identical in behaviour to a monopoly industry under a different tenure system.

Given a hypothetical competitive exploration industry, the difference between the closed and open tenure systems are as follows. Under the closed tenure system, the owner of a lease would act to maximize its value. Production would begin around the point of time when the value of the minerals left in the ground was not rising more rapidly than the interest rate. This has been called the 'fundamental rule of resource economics'.

But under the open tenure system, minerals would be explored for, and the lease developed, at an earlier date when the expected value of the lease was equal to the cost of exploration.[7] Any firm which delayed exploration would find itself pre-empted by another firm operating under the hypothetical competitive stimulus. Under the closed system production begins at a time that maximizes the value of the lease, whereas under the open system, production begins at an earlier time when the lease value is merely positive. Only a regional monopoly industry under an open style tenure system would cause exploration to begin at the same time as a competitive industry under a closed tenure system. Free enterprise complaints against the OPEC nations, and other resource monopolies, may be quite unfounded since both a monopolist under open tenure and a competitive industry under closed tenure would explore at the same rate that maximizes lease values. Similarly, the conclusion by Kay and Mirrlees that 'there is a real danger that the world's resources are being used too slowly',[4] is implicitly based upon a misunderstanding of the most common tenure system.

Actual rate of depletion

Over the past century the rate of mineral discoveries has not progressed smoothly, but outside North America it has been concentrated in two great waves – that of the 1890s and the post-war wave, most of which occurred in the 1960s. Admittedly, any chronological account of the mining industry is inevitably fuzzy, since decades may elapse between a decision to explore and production from the final discoveries. Our meaning may be made more clear by giving Australia as an example. In Australia, at the end of the nineteenth century, there were world scale discoveries of gold, silver, lead, zinc and copper. In the 1960s there were discoveries of iron ore, bauxite, and coal, followed by rich discoveries of nickel, phosphate rock, petroleum and uranium. With one partial exception, there were no significant mineral discoveries in Australia during the first half of the twentieth century.

This is the pattern which seems to have been general outside the USA, and is consistent with Canada's experience. As another, very important example, the major world petroleum discoveries were made within the two decades before the First World War in Iran, in Venezuela, and in Indonesia. The next major wave of discoveries followed the Second World War. Mineral resources have not increased smoothly with the market, but have been determined in great discontinuous waves.

Mineral discoveries require enterprise and exploration expenditure, but it is shallow to leave the matter there, since peripheral enterprise and exploration expenditure are highly variable over time. Immediately behind the enterprise and the exploration is a set of technical changes, partly in modes of transport and communication. In the 1890s the new applied technologies included the steamship, the wireless, and electricity generation. The boom of the 1960s coincided with the development of the world bulk carrier fleet, the mechanization of port facilities, and a wide range of advances in exploration and extraction technologies. Without the bulk carrier, for example, the boom in bulk minerals in the 1960s would have occurred, if at all, in a radically different character.

The diffuse nature of the new technologies suggests that they in turn were brought about by other changes. Both recently and at the end of the nineteenth century there was a sharp rise in the scale of international economic organisation. Most recently there has been the development of the Eurodollar market and 20 years of rapid expansion by the mining and non-mining multinationals. Similarly, in the 1890s there was rapid growth of the international capital market, and an associated rise of multinationalism, again in the natural resources industries as well as in other industries. Without these institutions, major mineral developments would have taken on very different characteristics if they could have occurred at all. In the 1960s the continued acceptance of US dollars as international money removed a balance of payments constraint on US foreign investment. In different strategic situations other nations might have refused to admit US multinationals while simultaneously accumulating US dollar balances – as eventually did the French. The rate of mineral extraction may depend especially upon strategic factors at the time of the extension of the periphery.

There are two other factors associated with the scale of economic organization and which affect the timing of the world mineral booms. Massive capitals cannot be transmitted into peripheral areas unless there is a reasonable expectation of security of tenure. This means that the military and diplomatic strength and the cultural ties of the investing nation must be adequate to secure tenure against possible nationalism in the periphery. For example, the British ceded large tracts of valuable Middle East oil land to the USA after the First World War.[7]

The second factor is that the bulk of reserves of each mineral is usually located in a few countries, and within each major producing country again the bulk of reserves of each mineral is from three or four mineral basins.[8] Most mineral output usually comes from a limited number of sources, and evidence shows a high skew in the distribution of both petroleum and non-petroleum reserves. The actual rate of resource depletion therefore depends substantially upon the rate of exploration for potential giant peripheral basins, and on the rate of extraction from them.

To sum up so far, resources development is related to expenditure on resources exploration, which in turn has been stimulated by new technology, which has been aided by the growth in economic scale, which has been associated with military strength and the force of cultural transmission. This story is oversimplified, and has left out many interactions. Nevertheless, it is reasonable to say that to the extent that changes in economic, military and cultural scale reflect changes in population and economic growth, there is a supply relationship between resources development and growth. The various components of the system – cultural, military, economic and technological – are interlocking and mutually reinforcing.

However, it is not meaningful to ask if the rate of resource depletion has been economically optimal. The course of events has had little connection with the properties of the competitive market system. The influencing factors have included factors such as strategic national position and strategic incident, technological drive and technological incident, cultural vigour, and the factors which underlie mighty economic scale such as the inequality of incomes and the force of social hierarchy in the central nations. Neither have we mentioned the important influence of ideology. No doubt all these matters are influenced by market structure as well as being influences upon it. Yet it is to put too much weight upon pure economic matters to ask what is the optimal rate of depletion over any but relatively short periods of time.

An economic efficiency theory of depletion

We will therefore sketch a possible economic efficiency theory of resources depletion, to show how it relates to the deeper matters that determine historical movement. We begin in a tangible historical circumstance. Assume first that there has been a recent outwards movement of the resources periphery, which we will call the extensive margin of production. The state of technology is given. The new periphery is largely unexplored, or at least only basic geological knowledge is available, but there are reasonable expectations of rich resource basins. There is a limited set of exploring firms which have some degree of monopoly power, owing to their advantages with respect to capital market access, geological information and access to output markets. The tenure system is open and the peripheral political system requires that tenure is followed by production. The economic problem is whether the rate of resources discovery is economically correct.

Initially each firm tends to defer exploration, and waits for the production of additional basic geological information. Perhaps some firms anticipate that there could be an informative success or failure by a neighbour, or perhaps a discovery elsewhere will be indicative. In any event, there is still much potential area to be explored, and exploration proceeds at a slow rate.

Over time the prospects become more specific, basic geological information becomes more complete, and potential resource bearing land becomes more specific. Now each firm must move quickly to avoid being pre-empted by a rival. As land becomes more valuable, and more limited in extent, there develops an exploration race. The race is faster the higher the level of potential profits and the keener the rivalry between firms. Finally all reasonable prospects are taken up, and the exploration crescendo comes to a sudden end.

There are therefore two sequential factors. Initially the rate of exploration is too slow for economic efficiency, because of exploration externalities caused by each firm waiting for the others. Later the rate of exploration is too fast for efficiency, because firms compete to gain the limited free lease tenure. Judging from experience, the combined time period of the two phases of economic inefficiency has been about 20 years, which is about the time from the shift of the extensive margin to the final exploration boom.

In principle the economic inefficiencies we describe could be corrected by various tax subsidy devices. Abstracting from political and other limitations, our descendants could gain some possible economic advantage from a more controlled rate of exploration of the Antarctic or the oceans.

Concluding comments

We have concentrated on the determinants of the extensive margin because that is the critical variable. The rate of extraction from each new basin will be determined especially by the applicability of large capital intensive technology, and by security of tenure, which are again dependent upon even more basic factors.

Yet clearly free enterprise theory can only describe how to operate efficiently within a given framework. The economists' optimal rate of depletion can only be a limited short-run concept, in which the important underlying determinants of depletions are implicitly assumed to be unchanging. In our particular account the determinants of the resources periphery lie beyond the confines of demand and supply analysis, and a free enterprise theory can only consider the cheapest rate of exploration within the periphery. This is the less significant matter, for the perspective of the free enterprise economists is too cramped for a meaningful pursuit of the wider resources problem.

The same cramped perspective underlies the assertion about the potential for substitution between commodities. This school says that to the extent that commodity substitution is available, the exhaustion of any one mineral resource is unimportant. For example, petroleum could be substituted by the liquification of coal, or plastic conduit pipes could replace metal pipes.

The role of commodity substitution is central in free enterprise thought, and yet in a purely scientific study it is futile to assert or to deny its likely scope. The degree of human inventiveness with respect to commodities or in general has been variable in the past, and certainly a non-dialectical analysis will not tell how creative or inventive human minds will become in the future. What can be said is that the exclusive emphasis on commodity substitution relies on a hidden hedonistic interpretation of the nature of man. A method which abstracts from the factors that give rise to inventiveness and creativity does not have the scope to analyse even pure commodity substitution in the future.

In another sense the application of the doctrine of commodity substitution goes too far, when it implies that the relation between commodities and states of mind in general can be ignored. There may be many ways of getting from one place to another, but if travel is an aid to emotional refurbishment, or to the aquisition of wisdom, rather than an end in itself, then some ways are different in essence to others. A catalogue of the hedonistic possibilities of substitution does not say much, for the matters of true concern are the mind states which the commodities are properly to facilitate.

Conservationists and economists too often conduct the analysis in the wrong units. What matters is not the rate of depletion but the underlying factors which are manifested in the rate. Natural resources are important to the extent that they help to develop human resources. Except in the limited economic sense, the rate of resource depletion is an intermediate concept and not a fundamental goal.

Acknowledgements

The authors are indebted to Dr Lesley Cook of the University of Sussex for her valuable comments and criticisms of an earlier draft of this paper. The entire responsibility for the paper, however, rests with the authors.

References

1. J. Forrester, *World Dynamics*, Wright-Allen Press, Cambridge, Mass., 1971: D. H. Meadows, *et al., The limits to Growth*, Earth Island, London, 1972: M. Mesarovic and E. Pestel, *Mankind at the Turning Point*, Hutchinson, London, 1975.
2. Orris C. Herfindahl and Allen V. Kneese, *Economic Theory and Natural Resources*, Resources for the Future, Washington, 1973.
3. William D. Nordhaus, 'The allocation of energy resources'. *Brookings Papers on Economic Activity*, No 3, 1973, pp 529–70.

4. John A. Kay and James A. Mirrlees, 'The desirability of natural resource depletion', in D.W. Pearce. ed, *The Economics of Natural Resource Depletion*, Macmillan, London, 1975, pp 140–176.
5. Robert M. Solow, 'The economics of resources or the resources of economics', *American Economic Review*, vol 64, 1974, pp 1–14.
6. J.E. Stiglitz: 'Growth with exhaustible natural resources', *Review of Economic Studies*, Symposium 1974, pp 123–152.
7. Mason Gaffney, 'Editor's conclusions', in Mason Gaffney, ed. *Extractive Resources and Taxation*, University of Wisconsin Press, Milwaukee, 1967, pp 333–419.
8. M. Allais, 'Methods of appraising economic prospects of mining exploration over large territories: Algerian Sahara case study', *Management Science*, vol 3, No 4, 1957, pp 285–347.

GROWTH, RESOURCES, AND ENVIRONMENT: SOME
CONCEPTUAL ISSUES*

Alan Randall

Fundamental limitations on resource availability will become increasingly important, as present and future generations attempt to satisfy their demands for goods, services, and amenities. The prognosis for the future of civilization is uncertain, but the more pessimistic predictions paint an ugly picture (Meadows *et al.*; Heilbroner). The production and consumption of material goods and services (MGS) and environmental amenities are subject to resource scarcity. Choices must be made as to the mix of MGS and environmental amenities to be produced in any time period and the relative size of the total consumption bundle in each time period. What kinds of things will each generation consume, and how much will each generation consume relative to preceding and future generations?

Intertemporal allocation

Let us examine first what economic theory suggests about the problem of intertemporal allocation and, second, what some fundamental laws of physics indicate. Are our economic growth models consistent with the physical laws governing the operation of our universe?

The problem of economic growth has often been analyzed as one of determining the optimal rate of capital accumulation in a world where resources are inexhaustible. The results obtained by Dorfman are typical. If social welfare is maximized in the long run by maximizing the present value of consumption over time, the rate of consumption in each time period must be chosen so that the marginal productivity of capital is equal to the sum of the social discount rate, the rate of physical deterioration of capital, and an expression representing the additional psychic cost of saving a unit of capital at the beginning of each time period rather than the end. From Dorfman's model, the optimal growth paths under many conditions approach the situation in which consumption and the capital stock grow exponentially at a rate determined by the rates of population growth and technological change. Once an optimal growth path is attained, any further growth in per capita consumption is wholly dependent on technological change. "Plateau" consumption depends on the social discount rate, higher discount rates resulting in lower steady state consumption per capita.

*Reprinted with permission from *American Journal of Agricultural Economics*, Vol. 57, No. 4, 1975.

Turnpike models such as Dorfman's are highly unrealistic. Nevertheless, they enable identification of several key variables: the social discount rate, the rate of population growth, the rate of technological change, and the rate of physical deterioration of capital.

Solow, and Dasgupta and Heal have constructed more sophisticated models which permit the inclusion of exhaustible resources. They show that, even with the optimistic assumption that technological progress and the resource base are adequate to permit a high steady state level of consumption, the application of a positive social discount rate may result in per capita consumption tending asymptotically to zero. In other words, a society may choose eventual extinction.

Solow takes us one important step further by considering the possibility of substitution of inexhaustible inputs for exhaustible resources. His conclusion is that if the elasticity of substitution between exhaustible resources and other inputs is one or greater and if the elasticity of output with respect to reproducible capital exceeds the elasticity of output with respect to natural resources, then a constant population can maintain a constant level of per capita consumption into the very long-term future. If either of these conditions fails to be satisfied, the highest level of consumption which can be maintained into the long, long term is zero. Neither Solow nor this author can offer much empirical guidance as to the likelihood of fulfillment of these necessary conditions. However, their fulfillment in the long term will require considerable and continued human ingenuity.

The laws of thermodynamics provide knowledge about the functioning of the universe which economics cannot ignore. The second law (the entropy law) states that the entropy of a closed system continuously increases or that the order of such a system turns steadily to disorder. It indicates that our universe will inexorably "run down" or exhaust itself in the very long run, even in the absence of man's activities. The activities of man in increasing the rate of entropic degradation bring the inevitable end closer in time (Georgescu-Roegen). Thus, the long-term economic problem is best analyzed in terms of adjusting the rate of conversion of low entropy to high entropy or, perhaps more graphically, the rate of exhaustion of our universe.

The entropy law has great value in clarifying several of the issues pertinent to intertemporal allocation and growth theory. First, it places the role of technology in perspective. For the most part, technology does not expand the size of space ship earth along those dimensions that are most significant for human existence, as Ruttan (p. 708) and Schultz (p. 238) would have us believe. Rather, the technologies of the industrial and postindustrial revolutions have mostly enabled us to consume and otherwise exhaust our universe at an ever increasing rate, making massive transfers of wealth from future to present generations. However, not all technologies are equally destructive to low entropy per unit of value produced. The search for and implementation of technologies which are less destructive of low entropy would seem to be a potentially rewarding activity.

Second, this law enables us to perceive the "dichotomy" of reversible versus irreversible change as really a continuum.[1] The nonexistence of reversible change emphasizes the need for "with" and "without" project analysis and the inclusion of preservation values in project evaluation. It also provides a useful warning that recycling has inherent limits. The kind of partial recycling which is possible is not sufficient to make any exhaustible resource inexhaustible. The determination of the efficient degree of recycling is itself an economic problem.

Third, the entropy law focuses our attention on the use of flow resources as a means of increasing the value of output per unit of entropic degradation, at the same time warning us that flow resources do not quite offer a panacea in the ultimate sense.[2]

The First Law of Thermodynamics (the principle of conservation of matter-energy) is also pertinent. Since neither production nor consumption is a waste-free process (Ayres and Kneese) and since waste disposal is costless in neither money nor entropy terms, increasing consumption and/or investment increases the rate of entropic degradation by increasing the demand for low entropy for waste disposal (as well as in the ways discussed above).

Careful consideration of these two laws of thermodynamics magnifies somewhat the pessimism of the more pessimistic findings presented by the growth theorists. Our current policies emphasize the development and implementation of technologies which make us more effective in the exhaustion of exhaustible resources and appear to be based upon a social discount rate somewhere near the opportunity cost of capital in the private sector (which is positive and relatively high). Continuation of these policies into the long term seems certain to result in Solow's case where consumption eventually declines to zero. It is left to others to estimate or guess how far in the future this will occur. However, it is not unrealistic to suggest that the intervening time may be measured in hundreds rather than millions of years.

It is useful, however, to consider the kinds of policy changes which may prolong the span of human civilization. In research and development, emphasis could be placed on finding modes of production and consumption which increase entropy efficiency. A more entropy-efficient process is simply one which produces a greater value of output per unit of entropic degradation. The use of flow resources and the development of more entropy-efficient technologies (e.g., those which reduce friction, genetic improvements in plant and animal species, etc.) are potential methods of increasing entropy efficiency. And, it seems that the maximization of the long-run welfare of the human species requires a high level of entropy efficiency.

The social rate of time preference, made effective through the social discount rate, determines the rate at which we on the one hand, invest for future generations and on the other "sell out" future generations by exhausting their universe. Further, where exhaustible resources are privately held, in the absence of policies to the contrary, the decision to hold or to extract these resources will depend on the market rate of interest, that is, the price of capital. For a private holder to continue holding, he must expect the net price of the resource (i.e., net of extraction and marketing costs) to continue growing exponentially at a rate at least equal to the rate of interest in the private sector (Hotelling, Solow).

One may express the pious, but perhaps futile, hope that some combination of altruism and survival instinct of humanity will result in some reduction of the social rate of time preference expressed in reduced social discount rates. Those who find the outcome of capital markets acceptable for the short-term allocation of capital but not for the intergenerational allocation of exhaustible resources will perhaps opt for policy solutions such as a system of graduated severance taxes, falling through time, on exhaustible resources (Solow).

Long-term solutions will require not only some adjustments in total consumption (and it should be noted that the prospects for per capita consumption can be improved by stabilizing population) but also adjustments in the consumption mix. As entropic degradation continues, it can be expected that relative scarcities will change. These changes will be reflected sooner or later in changing relative prices and/or shadow prices. Adjustments in the consumption habits of consumers will be necessitated.

Resource allocation for the near future

So far, this paper has considered aggregate consumption over the long term. Now, let us consider resource allocation and the mix of goods and amenities to be produced in the short term.

The static theory of resource allocation is most instructive, not only in the conclusions it generates but also in the assumptions required to achieve those conclusions. These assumptions can be interpreted as warnings as to how real world outcomes might vary from the theoretical optimum. If actual distributions of income, wealth, legal rights, etc., coincide with the distributional preferences of society, if all rights are nonattenuated,[3] and if all of the requirements of pure competition are satisfied, unfettered markets will result in socially optimal production and consumption patterns, given resource scarcity and the existing tastes and preferences of the participants in those markets.

It would be an arduous task to compile an unabridged compendium of the ways in which the essential conditions are violated in the real world. However, some violations which are especially pertinent to the resource issue will be enumerated below.

There is no evidence that the distributional variables are coincident with social preferences. Resource markets, particularly in energy and mineral resources are especially susceptible to noncompetitive influences. International cartels of resource-exporting nations have arisen. Corporate oligopoly is no longer confined to individual resources, and energy conglomerates threaten to modify substitution patterns by changing long-established price cross elasticities on the supply side. Attenuation of property rights is not unknown in the markets of MGS and seems almost the rule rather than the exception in markets for environmental amenities.

Economists, led by Ayres and Kneese, have rediscovered the First Law of Thermodynamics. The myths of waste-free production and total consumption have been exploded. Waste disposal is an integral part of production and consumption processes. In effect, the production and consumption of MGS tends to use environmental resources and reduce the flow of environmental amenities.

Where the expense of waste disposal is external to the private economic calculations of producers and consumers, externality is pervasive rather than unusual and empirically insignificant. Without corrective social action in the form of regulation, price modification, or redefinition of property rights, the market will underprovide environmental amenities.[4] The problem is broader than indicated by the more restrictive definitions of externality in that environmental resources are often of the common property variety and environmental amenities are often public goods. Attenuation of property rights often results from government action, particularly in the regulatory field. Thus, government is a major contributor to the list of market imperfections.

Even in the absence of the kinds of market imperfections discussed above, some serious adjustment problems would face our society in the near term. The changes in relative scarcity and prices which we are now experiencing are not entirely due to market imperfections. The immense production of MGS in aggregate and the particular kinds of MGS we are producing (i.e., kinds which are often highly destructive of low entropy) suggest that depletion of at least some resources is well under way. Thus, some relative and absolute changes can be expected in resource prices, necessitating adjustments in consumption habits.

Sharp changes in the patterns of relative and absolute scarcity are likely to have major distributional consequences. Thus, it is important to ensure that the costs of dislocation and adjustment are not borne disproportionately by the poor. The short-term needs, in the most general terms, are for policies aimed at promoting distributional justice, promoting competitive structures (or structures which perform in the manner of competitive structures) in resource markets, eliminating, to the extent possible, market imperfections attributable to attenuated structures of property rights,[5] and assisting, or at least not impeding, the process of market adjustment to changing relative scarcity.

Reconciling the immediate and long-term solutions

The long-run outcome will be largely the result of a long sequence of short-term policy decisions to solve short-term problems or "crises", as we typically call them. However, I have serious reservations about some of the policy directions in which our crisis mentality seems to be leading us.

If it can be agreed that the long-term problem can best be attacked by the reduction of prevailing rates of time preference, the development and use of entropy-efficient technologies and flow resources, and the adjustment of consumption habits to the emerging realities of scarcity, then the policy question, in simplistic but nevertheless useful terms, is to find ways to make the necessary adjustments without causing excessive dislocations and demanding excessive sacrifices from present generations. Policies for the near future must start us moving in directions compatible with and contributory to the long-term solution.

Economists are long accustomed to using prices as the best indicators of the interactions of scarcity and consumer demands. However, in analyses designed to identify long-run solutions, the uncritical use of existing prices is dangerous for the reasons discussed below (in addition to those suggested by market imperfections). Crucial prices can be expected to change drastically as our uncertain future unfolds. Technological developments will change cost ratios in production while future demands of MGS and environmental amenities are most uncertain. Human values are fundamental to utility functions, which are fundamental to the price ratios of goods, services, and amenities. Yet value systems can be expected to change, as a result of propaganda, in accommodation to new views of reality (we are already seeing some of this reflected, for example, in the market for automobiles), and in other ways not well understood. And if, as some believe, the present value system of our culture is incompatible with the long-term survival of our civilization, the process of changing value systems might fruitfully be encouraged. All of this provides a warning that the implementation of solutions (particularly those involving massive and perhaps publicly subsidized capital investment) based on current prices may perpetuate our problems by delaying essential adjustments in technology and human demands.

These considerations suggest that research to identify and evaluate policy solutions must incorporate materials flow analysis and energy budgeting (better yet, entropy budgeting, if techniques can be made applicable) into economic analyses.[6] Energy budgeting, for example, is potentially helpful in providing early warning of coming changes in scarcity and price relationships.

One suspects that some of our current policies are quite myopic, viewed from the perspective suggested above. Policies aimed at simply substituting somewhat less scarce fossil fuels for the very scarce ones may fall in that category. It is easy to see why coal gasification and liquefaction are receiving encouragement: the final products are compatible with existing systems for distribution, marketing, and end use. In that sense, the process of short-term adjustment to scarcity of oil and natural gas is eased. Yet, supplies of coal will not last forever and in the interim preceding exhaustion (a period of perhaps no more than a few hundred years, at current rates of use), expanded rates of extraction will come at increasing costs in terms of both money and environmental amenities.[7] Nuclear energy production based on breeder reactor technology would enable us to utilize an exhaustible resource which is expected to last hundreds and possibly thousands of years. However, future generations would be left with the burden of the perpetual care of plutonium, which is both extremely toxic and a prime weapon material (Krutilla and Page). Shale oil appears to be available in large quantities, but its extraction appears to be both environmentally devasting and of relatively low energy efficiency (i.e., the amount of energy used in extraction approaches the amount produced).

One wonders why flow sources of energy, the sun, the winds, and even the tides, have received research and development expenditures which are only a small fraction of those devoted to these exhaustible resources. One answer may lie in the area of property rights. Private sector entrepreneurs could expect to capture the patents to technologies they develop but not the ownership rights to the resources whose value is suddenly increased. Regardless of any institutional reasons for our current low level of effort in developing flow energy sources, one suggestion emanating from the logic developed herein is that more effort should be made.

These arguments are not intended to deny the need for continued exploitation of exhaustible resources. That is essential, if for no other reason, to ease the burdens of adjustment placed on present generations. However, a shift in emphasis toward utilization of flow resources seems called for, starting immediately.[8]

One may also be critical of policies which seem aimed at slowing the adjustments of consumers to the emerging realities. Continued and substantial public expenditure on highway development is one example. It seems that adjustments in the use of petroleum products (not only as energy sources, but also in the production of a wide range of goods including pesticides, fertilizers, and plastics) must be made eventually, if not immediately.[9]

There are indications that it is current policy to allow the underprovision of environmental amenities in general (occurring in the first instance as a result of pricing problems in externality and public goods situations) relative to MGS to continue.[10] Even if this is consistent with current voter preferences (and I do not concede that it is), it seems inconsistent with any acceptable long-run solution.

The above comments are directed primarily at American society, yet an international perspective is also essential. Population pressures, if unchecked, combined with the traditional use of less developed countries as suppliers of raw materials (often exhaustible resources) to more prosperous countries, seem to guarantee that per capita consumption in many of the LDCs will not rise to the levels enjoyed in western Europe and North America.[11] This suggests the need for stringent population control in many LDCs. It may even be desirable to encourage this process by offering some international redistribution of income and wealth as a quid pro quo.

In the more prosperous nations, population growth seems to be slowing down. Considering, particularly, the impact of population in reducing the level of environmental amenities, it seems there is nothing to gain from a reversal of this trend.

Concluding comments

The doomsday predictions, perhaps typified by the Club of Rome report (Meadows *et al.*), seem to have been largely discounted. However, there is no serious disagreement that, if the world economy were to maintain its present course, disaster would strike in a relatively few years. On the contrary, the prevailing argument is that the doomsday theorists have grossly underestimated the human ability to make adjustments in technology, resource substitution, and consumption habits.

Even the so-called "optimistic" studies such as the Ridker report amplify the need for such adjustments.[12] Public policy must be directed at encouraging the essential adjustments without placing excessive burdens on present generations. Some directions for public policy can be suggested.

The rate of resource exhaustion and, more generally, entropic degradation, which has been increasing apace, must be decreased. Appropriate policies include the reduction of the social rate of time preference; a system of graduated severance taxes, falling through time, on exhaustible resources; a conscious policy of risk aversion where disastrous outcomes reversible at great expense, if at all, are possible; and conscious efforts to control population growth. The development and implementation of technologies to use flow resources should be encouraged through ingenious modifications of the system of property rights and direct public investment, to the extent that efforts through the former route fall short of achieving the goal. Efforts to end the systematic underprovision of environmental amenities (resulting from market imperfections), begun in earnest in the first few years of the current decade, should be continued without interruption.[13] Increasing scarcity (perhaps with the exception of that attributable to monopoly influences) should be allowed to be reflected in market prices. Sudden, shocking, and perverse distributional consequences should be alleviated through lump sum transfers.

No policy can repeal the entropy law. However, the kinds of policies suggested above will allow us to live with that law as best we can, and that seems eminently desirable.

References

Ayres, R. and A. Kneese. "Production, Consumption, and Externalities." *Amer. Econ. Rev.* **59** (1969):282–97.

Boulding, K. "Fun and Games with the Gross National Product." *The Environmental Crisis*, ed. H. W. Helfrich, Jr., pp. 157–70. New Haven: Yale University Press, 1970.

Dasgupta, P. and G. Heal. "The Optimal Depletion of Exhaustible Resources." *Rev. Econ. Stud.* **41** (1974):3–28.

Dorfman, R. "An Economic Interpretation of Optimal Control Theory." *Amer. Econ. Rev.* **59** (1969):817–31.

Georgescu-Roegen, N. *The Entropy Law and the Economic Process.* Cambridge: Harvard University Press, 1971.

Heilbroner, R. *An Inquiry into the Human Prospect*, New York: W. W. Norton & Co., 1974.

Hotelling, H. "The Economics of Exhaustible Resources." *J. Polit. Econ.* **39** (1931):137–75.

Krutilla, J. and R. T. Page. "Towards a Responsible Energy Policy." *Policy Analysis* **1** (1975):77–100.

Meadows, D. H., D. L. Meadows, J. Randers, and L. Behrens, III. *The Limits to Growth*, New York: Universe Books, 1972.

Ridker, R., ed. *Population, Resources, and Environment.* Washington: Commission on Population Growth and the American Future, 1972.

Ruttan, V. "Technology and the Environment," *Amer. J. Agr. Econ.* **53** (1971):707–17.

Schultz, T. "Is Modern Agriculture Consistent with a Stable Environment?" *Papers and Reports, International Conference of Agricultural Economists* **15** (1973):235–44.

Solow, R. "The Economics of Resources or the Resources of Economics." *Amer. Econ. Rev.* **64** (May 1974):1–14.

Notes

1. Since all change involves some entropic degradation, no change is completely reversible. However, many changes are partly reversible, i.e., they may be reversed at some finite cost or, in other words, if some finite amount of low entropy is introduced into the system. The polar cases of the continuum will seldom (irreversible) and never (reversible) be observed.

2. The characteristics of flow resources place some limitations on their potential uses. No resource will continue to flow at an undiminished rate forever. The flow of solar energy, however, is expected to continue for a very long time. The rate of flow of a flow resource is for the most part unresponsive to man's attempts to control it. A flow resource must be used when it is provided. If not used today (or at least captured and stored), today's flow cannot be used tomorrow. Flow resources tend to flow into stocks. Thus, all of a flow cannot be used without lowering a stock. Capture of a substantial proportion of the flow of solar energy may lower the temperature of the earth. All but the most primitive production processes using flow resources seem to require the simultaneous use of some exhaustible resources.

3. This means fully specified, rigidly enforced, exclusive, transferable, and in no way inconsistent with the marginal equalities necessary for efficiency.

4. The author prefers this latter approach to the extent that it is feasible. He is aware of some of the limits to its feasibility.

5. This implies elimination or modification of many existing public policy and regulatory instruments.

6. Energy budgeting alone, however, is also misleading. Some forms of energy and low entropy can be used more cost-effectively than others. Outputs are not all of equal value.

7. There is another, short-term reason to be wary of immense investments in coal conversion. The current price of oil contains a large element of monopoly profit which could be reduced at will. Oil substitutes produced from coal could overnight become the higher cost alternative.

8. A major problem facing the policy analyst is the scheduling of the depletion of each exhaustible resource and the implementation of technologies to bring flow resources on line. The risk averse will apply the principle "better too soon than too late" to the latter.

9. The monopoly element in current petroleum prices makes all policy pronouncements subject to revision at short notice.

10. On the other hand, particular goals proposed by public agencies (e.g., "zero discharge" into the nation's waterways) go beyond the efficient level of internalization and, if doggedly pursued, would result in overprovision of some kinds of environmental amenities.

11. The exceptions occur where it is possible to extract huge monopoly rents on raw materials for a long and continuing period (as the OPEC nations have done for a few years, as of now). At any rate, "if the whole world developed to American standards overnight, we would run out of everything in less than 10 years" (Boulding, p. 166).

12. Ridker estimates that resource scarcity will cause few severe shortages in America during the next thirty to fifty years. However, his definitions and assumptions suggest some cause for concern. Severe shortage is defined as a situation leading to a relative price increase of 50% or greater for any raw material. Thus, Ridker's conclusion could be consistent with sharp relative price increases for many resources. That study assumes continued technological progress and resource substitution, and continued unimpeded imports of raw materials. The possible impacts of increased monopoly influences and rising resource demands in the rest of the world are ignored. Thus, it is possible to read Ridker's "optimistic" study as suggesting less than unrestrained optimism.

13. And, perhaps, efforts should be redirected toward making fuller use of the inherent efficiencies of the market system. Total reliance on the market, however, would be naive.

LIMITS TO THE GROWTH DEBATE*

Lincoln Gordon

FOUR years after the worldwide debate on "limits to growth" was launched by the Club of Rome, supporters and opponents are still fighting over the wrong question. That there are ultimate limits to economic growth is incontrovertible. That there are imminent and stringent physical limits is unproven and unprovable. So the debate in these terms—limits or no limits—is sterile. It is of far less consequence than the issues arising from changing *directions* of growth.

We can now reassess with some perspective the first two major studies sponsored by the Club of Rome: the report of the Meadows team at MIT, *The Limits to Growth*, published in 1972, and the Mesarovic and Pestel report, *Mankind at the Turning Point*, published in 1974. When the Club of Rome met in Philadelphia in April of this year, its pronouncements reflected a frame of mind quite different from that of 1972. Still more recently, Herman Kahn and his colleagues at the Hudson Institute have favored us with *The Next 200 Years*, a book evidently inspired as much by antagonism to the limits-to-growth school of thought as by affirmative faith in its own vision of technological optimism.[1]

Before entering into detail, let me summarize my own position in four points:

1. While no trend of growth of anything can continue indefinitely in the real world, there are not global physical limits to economic growth within a time frame susceptible to plausible foresight or relevant to policy making.

2. In some world regions, notably South Asia and tropical Africa, popula-

*Reprinted with permission from *Resources*, No. 52, 1976, pp. 1–6 (Resources for the Future, Washington).

tion growth rates do indeed threaten to create a kind of Malthusian trap, and the rapid reduction of fertility is critically important to their development prospects and urgent in time.

3. For other parts of the world, both rates and directions of growth will be more influenced by changes in preferences for consumption and in attitudes toward production than by physical constraints, although higher energy costs and environmental pressures will also be important influences in generating such changes in growth patterns.

4. Probable changes in directions of growth will generate new and important issues in international economic and political relations, with both dangers and opportunities for the evolving world order.

This kind of middle-of-the-road position is not as exciting as the extremes. It requires one to be constantly leaning against any prevailing popular wind. It contests the fictitious data and dubious methodology of the Meadows team, rejects the kind of historical determinism introduced into this debate by Robert Heilbroner on the pessimistic side and Walt Rostow on the optimistic side, and is skeptical of the almost undiluted technological optimism of Herman Kahn. It also reflects amazement at the didactic arrogance of the would-be prophets— whether of doom or utopia. Even a nodding acquaintance with past projections and prophecies should generate more humility in face of the future. There is nothing in recent methodological advances in futurology, computer simulations included, which warrants the abandonment of that humility.

It is amusing to pick up Kahn's new book and to see his sweeping curves from 1776 to 2176, with the critical points of inflection exactly coinciding with this, our bicentennial year. Meadows was more modest in his time horizons, cutting off his charts at the year 2100, a mere century and a quarter hence. But the only thing one can say with certainty about economic and technological projections over one or two centuries is that they will turn out to be wrong. The future at that remove is literally unknowable, because it depends so heavily on discoveries not yet made.

Over the whole sweep of recorded history, there was probably sufficient stability for century-long projections only in early Egypt or China. There was not in classical Greece or Rome, nor in feudal Europe, and still less anywhere in the world since the age of discovery in the sixteenth century, the agricultural and industrial revolutions of the seventeenth and eighteenth centuries, the scientific and technological revolutions of the nineteenth century, the wars and decolonizations of the twentieth century, and the pace of change which is visibly around us today. The most sober scholar of modern economic growth, the Nobel prize winner Simon Kuznets, gives the greatest weight in major economic changes to what he calls "epochal inventions"—events which are unforeseeable by definition. The great ideological movements—Christianity, Islam, the American and French revolutions, or Marxism— are equally unforeseeable, as are basic institutional changes like the formation and dissolution of empires. Even simple relationships, such as the correlations between amounts of capital investment and rates of growth, turn out to be enormously variable from country to country and from time period to time period. How much more so the great discontinuities in human affairs traceable to major technological, ideological, or institutional changes.

Physical Limits in Perspective

On March 2, 1972, the day the Meadows study was unveiled with great cere-mony at the Smithsonian Institution, a polite but very critical review appeared in the *Washington Post* by two senior staff members of Resources for the Future. To quote one paragraph from that review by Allen V. Kneese and Ronald G. Ridker: "The model results are very sensitive to particular assumptions about highly uncertain and ill-defined relationships, and the uncertainty increases (probably exponentially) as the simulation rolls out into the distant future. Any reflection of reality which may be in the model soon fades away, but the com-puter keeps right on charting precise lines for nearly 150 years."

I had to give a talk about the Meadows study within two weeks of its publica-tion. Even at that early stage, I referred to "strong evidence that the Meadows study overrates the pollution hazards and the costs of pollution abatement, and underrates the possibilities of materials substitution." I felt, however, that the general thrust of the book should be taken seriously and that some of its con-clusions might be right even if for the wrong reasons. I had in mind especially the urgent need for population control, for greater emphasis on internalizing en-vironmental costs, and for what I called "giving history a push by devising in-centives to shift economic growth more into services and other forms of qualitative growth, instead of simply into material-consuming quantitative growth." The Meadows contention that "overshoot and collapse" were built into the very structure of modern economic growth patterns was not persuasive. Even less believable was the notion that all growth must be stopped within the next two or three decades to avoid "overshoot and collapse" for mankind as a whole.

With four years' perspective, the scientific foundations of the Meadows study look even weaker than at the time. The study was seriously wrong in its data on resources, wrong in its assumptions on the costs of environmental control, faulty in its modeling methodology, defective in its neglect of prices as an allocator of scarce resources, and strikingly oblivious to known technological possibilities, to say nothing of plausible new technologies. There were convinc-ing scholarly refutations in scientific and popular journals, in an early analysis by the World Bank staff, in the excellent book by the Sussex University (Eng-land) Science Policy Research Unit entitled *Models of Doom*, and more recently in books by the British economist Wilfred Beckerman and by Herman Kahn.[2] Although it was not the central point of their "Second Report to the Club of Rome," the Mesarovic–Pestel study also contained very sharp criticisms of the Meadows data and methodology.

Yet none of these rebuttals has had remotely the resonance of the Meadows book. According to the original publisher, Potomac Associates, there are now over 2·4 million copies of the Meadows book in print in various languages. One hears echoes of its theses in this season's campaign speeches by Congressman Udall, Governor Brown, and others. There is evidently a widespread will to believe in limits to growth, a phenomenon more suitable for diagnosis by a social psychologist than by a political economist. Speculating as a layman on the motives, I would guess that they contain a healthy element of concern at mankind overplaying the Faustian hand: setting in motion forces approaching those of nature in magnitude, risking major environmental crises, permitting the scale of institutions and technologies to grow seemingly beyond control of individuals or even nations, and converting technological advance and economic growth into ends in themselves instead of instrumental means for greater human satisfaction.

Those are all concerns which I share, but they have to do with *directions* of growth rather than *limits*. In fact, coping with most of the visible social and economic problems of the coming decades will require more rather than less growth, provided that it is the right kind of growth. Because of its grossly over-simplified structure, treating the world as a single unit and most forms of economic growth without differentiation, the Meadows study must be regarded more as a distraction from the real issues than a contribution to their solution.

From the viewpoint of style, however, the Meadows book was a model of lucid and persuasive exposition. Its way of presenting the power of compound interest evidently made a deep impression on reviewers and readers. Yet that may tell us more about the naïvete of these readers than about the soundness of the "limits" thesis. To any thoughtful person with even a modicum of mathematical training, it is an elementary truism that neither exponential growth nor even linear growth can continue indefinitely if there are any relevant finite limits, such as space on the surface of the earth or the amount of incoming solar radiation. To cite one simple example, continuation of recent world population growth rates of 2 percent a year would bring today's figure of about 4 billion to 6·6 billion by the end of this century (about the UN medium projections), 18 billion by the middle of the next century, 48 billion by the year 2100, and 344 billion by the year 2200. Obviously population growth will be checked somehow before the year 2100, with a slowing down of growth rates and an ultimate stabilization or decline. The interesting question is not whether there must be some limit to population growth; it is when and how and at what level, and with what differential effects on the various regions of the world.

Equal absurdities come from long-term projections of constant growth rates on the positive side. Two years ago, according to World Bank estimates, total economic output in the world averaged about $900 per capita (at price levels of the late 1960s) and had been growing for seven years at 3·1 percent a year in real terms, excluding inflation. Projecting such economic growth at a constant rate brings per capita incomes by the year 2000 to about $2,000, just about the average in the richer industrialized countries of the world in 1972. An additional century moves the figure up to $42,000; a further century to $900,000; and by our national fifth centennial in 2276 it hits over $9 million per capita at prices of the late 1960s. What would or could incomes of those magnitudes mean? Here again, entirely disregarding possible resource or environmental constraints, somewhere between the $2,000 and the $42,000 figure per capita — that is during the course of the twenty-first century — attitudes and preferences toward income and the uses of money would change radically.

It follows that, in a sufficiently long-term perspective, the logistic or S-shaped curve is a far more likely growth path than either exponential or linear projections. In some fields, there are also cyclical patterns of repeated ups and downs. Some climatologists believe that the past record implies the imminent return of at least a mini-ice age, if not another major glaciation. Walt Rostow and Jay

Forrester are both reviving interest in the idea of fifty- to sixty-year business cycles, first identified by the Russian economist Kondratieff. Without some persuasive causal mechanism, however, it is hard to take such projections seriously.

Another and less admirable factor in the enormous response to the Meadows report doubtless resulted from the combination of spurious scientism, generated by computer printouts, with the doomsday concept of "overshoot and collapse" and the prescription calling for economic and population growth cessation before the end of this century. Since that prescription could not be accepted in the real world, least of all in the poorer countries of the world, a reader taking Meadows seriously should have followed one of two courses: either to "eat, drink, and be merry" for the next few decades, before "overshoot and collapse" set in, or else to commit suicide, since "overshoot and collapse" were unavoidable. Perhaps the experiments in existential mind expansion and in "dropping out" by some of our younger generation in recent years were the moral equivalents of those courses of action. I doubt that they were the consequences that either the Club of Rome or the Meadows team wished to promote.

It would be beating a dead horse to devote more time to the errors of the Meadows book on depletable resources and pollution control costs. If anyone remains in doubt on the first point, I recommend consulting the Goeller and Weinberg article on "The Age of Substitutability" in the special "Materials" issue of *Science* for last February 20. On this subject, in contrast to most of Kahn's book, I would also endorse without reservation the criticisms of Meadows in chapter IV of *The Next 200 Years*.

Another cardinal defect of the Meadows study was its treatment of the world as a single unit. In reality, one of the most striking features of today's world with respect to problems of growth is the bipolarity between rich countries and poor (what the current UN jargon calls developed and developing countries). That bipolarity extends to birth rates and population growth, income levels, resource consumption, and capacity for technological innovation. Only a surprisingly small number of countries are in an intermediate position, with possibilities of jumping the gap from developing to developed within the reasonably near future.

Mesarovic and Pestel: Mankind at the turning point

That brings us to the second Club of Rome study, the Mesarovic–Pestel volume on *Mankind at the Turning Point*. From the technical viewpoint, it represented a major advance over the Meadows book, partly because of its disaggregation of the world into ten reasonably homogeneous regions and part-ly because of much greater economic and technological sophistication in the modeling structure. Perhaps because these two aspects of the study brought it much closer to the real world, it failed to evoke anything like the enormous public response to the Meadows study. It, too, suffers from serious technical handicaps, notably in its nonincorporation of plausible technological change. Moreover, many of the striking conclusions of the authors do not flow from the analysis in the model. They are rather the reactions of sensitive world citizens concerned with relations between rich and poor countries, population pressures in food-deficit crowded countries, and the dangers of nuclear proliferation. Those are all entirely legitimate concerns, but they do not need the analytical apparatus to justify them.

As to the prescription, summarized in the phrase "from undifferentiated to organic growth," even a very friendly critic must take issue with the terminology. Many things are wrong with the growth. Those patterns have obviously tried over the last quarter century—or ever since the industrial revolution for that matter—but they cannot realistically be described as "undifferentiated growth." Those patterns have obviously disregarded some important external costs, failed to deal adequately with the community's interest in common property resources, and possibly—although here the evidence is much less convincing—given too little attention to the interests of future generations in relation to the present. There are also good reasons in many developing countries, especially in the more densely crowded ones which are poor in natural resources, to seek development strategies quite different from simply following the path of Western Europe, North America, and Japan. But both terms of the Mesarovic–Pestel phrase are confusing: "undifferentiated growth" because it is a caricature of the past and present, and "organic growth" because it is a very imprecisely defined prescription for the future.

Club of Rome in Philadelphia

Not having been able to attend the Club of Rome meetings in Philadelphia in April, I must judge them from press reports and some brief summary documents. Their new consensus appears to reject explicitly the notion of insurmountable physical limits to growth and to give far more attention to North–South questions between rich and poor countries, directions of growth compatible with environmental constraints in rich countries, and efforts to plan the broad directions of structural change at both the national and international levels.

I find these shifts much in accord with my own thinking and a great improvement over the Club of Rome's previous identification with the blind alley of rigid limits to growth. In the reports of the third day of the meetings, however, there is a disturbing new theme, with serious potential pitfalls, in the emphasis on cooperative action by developing nations *independently* of the developed countries in order "to correct the world's economic imbalances.' That is a reflection of the line of thought developed by the 'Third World Forum' and much in evidence in the recent Nairobi meetings of the UN Conference on Trade and Development (UNCTAD) under the rubric of "collective self-reliance".

Insofar as it implies more intensive mobilization of domestic capital and skills for accelerating development in poor countries, either singly or in groups, this theme of collective self-reliance is much to be welcomed. Insofar, however, as it implies decoupling from the markets and technology of the industrialized world (and that is precisely the objective of some of its advocates), it risks forfeiting a major potential force for accelerating economic development. And insofar as it reflects a desire for aggressive confrontation with the developed world, in the hope of emulating the massive income transfers to the oil producers, it is almost certainly counterproductive. To quote from a recent paper of my own on the Third World, 'Except in the case of oil, the Third World's potential for successful economic aggression against the economic order generally, or the First World in particular, is not very great; . . . and, if there is a threat, it is largely one to the Third World itself, while the asset could bring gains to the world at large.'

Herman Kahn's two-hundred-year scenario

As always, it is a breathtaking but baffling experience to read a new book by Herman Kahn. His technological optimism is just enough qualified so that, whatever happens, a sentence can be pointed to somewhere in the pyrotechnics which will have anticipated that contingency. In general, the distant future—which none of us will live to see—is glowing with promise, while the near-term future is full of hazards and uncertainties. His discussion of technological assessment presents quite persuasively the difficulties of anticipating even the first-order, medium-term effects of important new technologies, to say nothing of their indirect consequences. But how this appreciation is to be reconciled with the uninhibited sweep of the charts to the year 2176 confounds logical analysis. Perhaps one should relax and recognize that the brilliant logician inhabits the same human envelope as the even more brilliant showman.

Whatever his other ambiguities and internal contradictions, there is no doubt that Kahn rejects the thesis of significant physical limits to growth, even in low-income and resource-poor countries. A brief comment on each of the major factors should help to illuminate my own views as well as his. I will follow the now familiar litany of population, food, raw materials, environmental quality, and energy.

Population. On population, I differ sharply from Kahn, who takes the complacent view that reduced birth rates will follow automatically from growing affluence. He believes that the world is just passing through the point of most rapid population growth, and that world numbers will stabilize within the coming two centuries at around 15 billion, or just under four times present levels.

In the fine print, however, his estimate of 15 billion is qualified by the phrase "give or take a factor of two (that is, a range of 7·5 to 30 billion)"! I agree that such a range does encompass the probable level of ultimate human numbers on the globe but also believe that it makes the most profound difference to the prospects for human dignity and world peace whether the figure is closer to the bottom or the top of the range. Moreover, Kahn does not discuss at all the grim regional implications, even of his 15-billion figure. The UN projections indicate that, with a fourfold growth in total world numbers, the population in South Asia would grow almost six times, in Latin America over seven times, and in Africa almost ten times.

Kahn relies on the income gap between rich and poor countries somehow to suck the latter up toward the former, and then applies his calculating machine to the effects of a 2·3 (or even a mere 1) percent per year growth in India's per capita incomes over the next two hundred years. Indians become prosperous; birth rates fall; Q.E.D., Mr. Pangloss. The historical evidence, however, suggests that the developmental effects of income gaps work best with middle-class countries which are not far behind the leaders, while the poorest ones may stagnate in poverty indefinitely. Unless birth rates in South Asia are brought down quite rapidly, such stagnation in a Malthusian trap seems to me more probable than Kahn's scenario. In some ways, the case is even worse in tropical Africa, where current low population densities make governments very complacent about the absence of population pressures. What they fail to recognize is that their mortality rates are still very high and will almost certainly be greatly reduced through public health measures in the next decade or two. They consequently have the prospect of substantial increases in population growth rates before the curves turn around. They would be well advised to lose no time in attending to the birth rate side of the demographic equation.

Governments in South Asia, and especially in India, are evidently increasingly conscious of their population problems, as witnessed by the current discussions of compulsory sterilization for couples with three children or more. How much better than such an extreme measure, whose political acceptability and practical workability remain in doubt, would have been a series of selective developmental efforts focused on birth-rate reduction.

Food. The food prospects are closely related to those for population. I agree with Kahn that, barring an unlikely chain of weather disasters in several important producing areas year after year, the technical potential exists for meeting minimum needs and somewhat improving nutrition over the next generation, even in the largest food-deficit and overcrowded countries of South Asia. Yields of rice in India, for example, could be greatly expanded with known methods of water control, fertilization and cultivation. When one looks beyond a doubling of the Indian population, however, the task becomes much more formidable, with the limitations of land and water increasingly severe. The population ratios are such that surpluses from North America are sharply limited in their capacity to meet potential Asian shortfalls, even if the transfers were financed as free food aid. New breakthroughs in agricultural technology may provide solutions, but Kahn is far too glib in his easy assertions of unconventional food factory production as a solution already in sight for the early twenty-first century.

Raw Materials. As already indicated, I fully agree with Kahn's finding that there is no early or even remote problem of depletion of minerals, other than the fossil fuels. In fact, contrary to the popular position among environmentalists, I am more concerned about shortages of some renewable materials than about the minerals. The adverse environmental effects of deforestation in many countries, especially through soil erosion and river siltation, make one wish that "depletable" mineral fuels and construction materials were being used in place of the theoretically renewable wood.

Environmental Quality. Here again, I am generally in agreement with the thrust of Kahn's arguments. They distinguish among (1) long-term global hazards, such as inadvertent climate modification or destruction of the ozone layer, (2) local or regional air or water pollution, and (3) environmental esthetics involved in many land use controversies. The first of these categories requires more monitoring and analysis. On the second, where most of the public attention and expenditure is focused, there is strong evidence that reasonable protection against major health hazards and impairment of productivity can be achieved at costs not exceeding 2 or 3 percent of the gross national product of the richer countries, including our own. The third category, in which environment appears as a kind of consumption good, is a matter of social preferences—a form of luxury consumption which the richer societies logically add to their preference schedules.

My colleagues at Resources for the Future have been pioneers in developing the theoretical and applied literature on environmental economics and the relationship between environment and development. Without seeking to underrate the importance of water and air quality and land use problems which have aroused so much attention over the last decade, they have persuaded me that these problems are manageable within readily affordable costs, and that the environmental problems of agriculture in poor countries should be much greater causes for concern.

Energy. Except for food, energy is the most important of the natural resources, being in large measure the agent for substitution of the scarcer ones as well as the indispensable ingredient of increased human productivity and higher living standards. The coming and going of the age of petroleum, within the life span of people now living, is one of the great discontinuities in human history. Here again, Kahn's presentation is a cornucopia of technical possibilities, sometimes without cost estimates and sometimes with cost statements which are already obsolete on the low side.

Kahn is certainly correct in stating that coal can be a principal reliance for American energy needs for many decades. That is not so clear for the world as a whole. He probably exaggerates the imminence and cost-competitiveness of solar electric power generation. In general, his technological optimism emerges most strongly in the discussion of energy. Only on nuclear fission does he acknowledge some doubts, which he would not have done five years ago. He does not recognize the quite different perspective on nuclear fission in countries without substantial oil, coal, and shale deposits. Nevertheless, his basic point is sound that alternatives to oil and gas do exist and that one or several of them will be developed at whatever cost it takes. If mankind has to fall back on the ultimate reliance of solar energy, and if its costs turn out to be several times even the current price of oil, there would be a considerable drag on economic development prospects, especially in the poorer countries. That point requires greater analysis than anyone has yet given it. What can be said with certainty, however, is that zero energy growth makes no sense whatever for the poorer countries and makes sense in the United States only for a limited period during which progressive measures of conservation are being implemented.

The issues of energy supply are among the most difficult facing our own and other countries. No doubt that is why we have made so little progress in finding answers after two and a half years of declarations of energy independence and frenetic debate. The related questions of nuclear proliferation and safeguards are gaining increasing attention, but by no means as much as they deserve. An era of higher energy costs will certainly affect rates and patterns of growth. Unless, however, the global climate heating problem turns out to be much more imminent than present evidence suggests, energy availability need not be an insuperable limit on growth in general.

Problems of changing directions of growth

So much, then, for physical constraints and limits (or nonlimits) to growth. At the start, I mentioned my own conclusion that both rates and directions of growth, outside the most crowded world regions exposed to the Malthusian trap, will be more influenced by changes in values and attitudes toward both consumption and production than by physical constraints. That conclusion is strongly reinforced by the preliminary findings of an RFF study on relations among population, resources, and environment in the United States up to the year 2025, which includes a fairly detailed disaggregation by both economic sectors and geographic regions. From some discussion with Wassily Leontief, it is also my impression that this conclusion is in line with his new studies for the United Nations.

If that view is correct, it would be well for us to close the book on the growth-limits debate and to start exploring the more difficult but more relevant terrain of social adaptation to changing consumption preferences and changing attitudes toward employment preferences and job satisfactions. In the richer countries, for example, what are the educational, employment, and life-style implications of a further shift toward services—one which substantially affects the composition of output as well as the occupational distribution? In the poorer countries, what alternative development strategies are really viable, whether focused on basic necessities, on different degrees of integration into the world economy, or on ways of avoiding some of the historical errors of the development experience of the presently rich countries while securing the benefits of high technology and high productivity?

Of special interest to me is the question of how changing growth patterns in the rich and poor countries can be geared together in some kind of world order without intolerable strains and fissures. Like Kahn, I believe that for the poorer countries, closing the income gap with the rich is much less important than making absolute advances in their levels of food, shelter, and education, and in their conditions for human dignity—in which I would give greater weight to the importance of liberty than most current writers on this subject. But I disagree with the implication — sometimes stated explicitly by American officials at international meetings—that since the gap is itself a great force for development, the best thing the North can do to promote development in the South is to focus exclusively on our own prosperity. There is a ring of Victorian upper-class smugness about that proposition—a kind of international "Upstairs, Downstairs" philosophy, which is unlikely to carry conviction below the stairs.

At the same time, there is a close linkage in the present world economy between high growth rates in the industrialized world and developmental opportunities for much of the developing world—a linkage through markets for raw materials, tropical foodstuffs, and labor-intensive manufactured goods, and through capital transfers. That linkage will not be altered by UN resolutions or by unilateral action of the developing countries alone. What kinds of trade and investment and resource policies might help to modify it in ways acceptable to all concerned is a question on which I plan to initiate a substantial research project early next year. I hope that it can be paralleled by realistic future-looking studies in both rich countries and poor.

Notes

1. Donella H. Meadows and others, *The Limits to Growth*, Universe Books for Potomac Associates, New York, 1972; Mihajlo Mesarovic and Eduard Pestel, *Mankind at the Turning Point*, E. P. Dutton, New York, 1974; Herman Kahn and others, *The Next 200 Years*, William Morrow & Co., New York, 1976. The Philadelphia meeting of the Club of Rome was reported in *The New York Times* of April 13, 14, and 15, 1976; there were also several press releases distributed at the meeting. An article summarizing the discussions is in preparation.
2. H. S. D. Cole and others, *Models of Doom: A Critique of the Limits to Growth*, Universe Books, New York, 1973; Wilfred Beckerman, *Two Cheers for the Affluent Society: A Spirited Defense of Economic Growth*, St. Martin's Press, New York, 1975; Kahn, *op. cit.*

SECTION 8

Environmental Education

INTRODUCTORY ESSAY

In Section 6 we discussed some of the factors that cause people to behave in an environmentally irresponsible manner. The phrase "environmental irresponsibility" is a pejoritive one so we should define it. Basically it means indulging in activities which on their own or in concert with others result in consequences that reduce the quality of the living environment for fellow human beings and other living creatures. We recognise that almost any act will have negative environmental consequences, given the complex interacting nature of both human and natural ecosystems, so in practical terms we have to circumscribe the definition a little to incorporate the fact that inadequate compensation (of whatever kind) is made to those who suffer. In economic parlance, environmentally irresponsible behaviour results in a reduction in net social welfare. Now there are many who accept that most kinds of conventional economic development will reduce various aspects of environmental quality, most particularly for those who are unable to protect their environmental interests, but that the social and economic gains of such development outweigh the losses. In Section 1 we discussed the arguments that refute this optimism so we have reservations that this kind of argument can continue indefinitely. Thus we think it appropriate that we should look at how our educational institutions deal with the problem of environmentally irresponsible behaviour. However, before they are condemmed or praised we must place the opportunities for environmental education in a general context.

The Context of Education in the Promotion of Environmentally Responsible Behaviour

First of all, one must bear in mind some of the arguments already presented in Sections 1 and 6, namely that centralised, urbanised, technically specialised and administratively controlled capitalistic political economies create an interacting web of incentives that discourage the free and spontaneous expression of environmental responsibility. The price mechanism does not deal with environmental bads when it allocates economic goods, the pattern of legal rights is inappropriately developed to cope with rights to environmental quality in commonly owned property, and few pathways are available in most countries for citizens to challenge administrative actions to ensure that certain environmental resources are protected or at least to be sure that the loss of such resources is properly balanced against any gains made. Capitalist economic enterprises are not noted for their environmental sensitivities and consumer-oriented cultures often lose a sense of perspective when they see the price or availability of valued goods and services altering in such a way as to make acquisition of them impossible.

What we are implying here is that our education content is to a large degree a reflection of existing cultural values. In the so-called "great education debate" initiated by the Labour Government in 1976, the palpable aim was to discover why UK schools and universities did not produce more engineers, computer technologists and business managers so that private enterprise industrial manufacturing, regarded as vital to the national economy, could flourish. The concern was to try to keep the old growth pattern firmly in place, making only relatively minor adjustments to meet the needs of modern times.

Many environmentalists of the liberal ecocentric variety would claim that this debate was misdirected, but what is revealing is that it is not new. Kumar[1] notes that this litany for technological and business literacy in education began 100 years ago, but that the captains of Victorian industry were not anxious to see their sons and daughters follow their example. They preferred that they train themselves for public service and commerce. In the twentieth-century version of this debate, few people talked about preparing the nation's future citizens for a radically different approach to living of the kind outlined by Hall in Section 1 and nowadays widely discussed across a wide range of political ideologies.[2] Here, for example, is how Kumar[3] believes our future education should be directed.

"Exhortations to 'get manufacturing industry going again', or attempts to bribe students to do science and engineering, seem to me beside the point — not to mention going against the forces of history and the grain of the national culture. What we need to do is strengthen the new growth points in society, not prop up the old decrepit structures. There is the prospect here of a society in which, matched with appropriate technology, human skills can once more be encouraged in the context of a locally based household economy . . . We could do a lot more of our own repair and maintenance of goods, and perhaps even a lot more of the repair and maintenance of people, . . . We would all be 'semi-employed' in the formal economy. This would leave us time to attend to production within the informal household economy, which could also be the basis of many of the activities of child rearing, education and social welfare."

Since our educational thinking is largely bound up with our political ideologies, it seems that only when economic circumstances change drastically will educational curricula effectively respond. While one sometimes gets a little disheartened at the content of many so-called environmental education courses in this country and elsewhere, one must always bear in mind the very powerful forces of conservatism that circumscribe innovation in education. Certainly the training of tomorrow's citizens for greater individual and communal self-reliance is not exactly at the heart of modern GCE syllabuses, but one suspects that it will steadily be included over the next generation. Also to come is a shift towards better understanding of how socio-political systems operate and how to manage diplomatically the transition into redistribution with the context of nearly static growth. Lord Ashby,[4] making use of one of his many biological metaphors, argues this point as follows:

> "How will those nations ... which practice Western democracy and repudiate dictatorship, build into their human ecosystems ... *gyroscopes*; to stabilise their interdependence, to confer a stability commensurate with the complexity of their social structure? ... If my reflections have a message, it is this. Geopolitics, social psychology, social anthropology, political science (despite its name): these are still regarded as second class citizens in the hierarchy of the sciences. But if my thesis is correct, these are the disciplines which will help us to understand, and to influence even if we cannot control, the destiny of Industrial Man."

Ashby is talking not just of a need for training in global environmental understanding, but also of a necessity to be familiar with the difficult choices with which modern democratic governments are faced and the many factors that limit their room for manoeuvre, especially in foreign-policy matters.

Secondly, one must not ignore the very complex relationships which influence actual behaviour and which can cause a well-meaning, environmentally responsible person to behave in an environmentally irresponsible manner. This line of reasoning emerges from the "commons" argument already presented in Section 6 where, for example, it was noted that people who preferred to consume products that require less energy in manufacture and use, and who otherwise behave in an energy-conserving manner, find that they have to pay more for the product, or have to go to great lengths to find it, or have to spend a fair amount of time in tedious chores which often accompany the use of such products. In short, they are faced with a choice of saving effort and money and consuming energy or spending effort and money and saving energy, a choice that does not exactly encourage busy people to adopt energy-conserving behaviour. Meanwhile they see their neighbours enjoying the spare time and money available to them because of their energy-intensive behaviour and are caught in the famous "double-bind" described by Hardin in Section 6.

Equally perverse is the behaviour which in microcosm looks environmentally sound but which when copied by millions can have disastrous consequences. For example, environmentalists tell us that we should wear clothes made of natural materials rather than synthetics which are environmentally damaging to produce.[5] But imagine the impact on a country like Egypt to say nothing of the repercussions on the domestic synthetic fibre and chemical industries, if the western world began exclusively to purchase cotton shirts or leather belts and handbags, given the severe pressures on basic food resources caused by an excessively high population that is bound to double in size within the next 25 years and the disappearance of leather-hided species. Apart from the sheer shortage of land, one can readily comprehend the social and economic effects of such a massive reorientation of demand upon income distribution and political stability unless fairly major social democratic reforms accompany these economic developments. A similar line of reasoning follows from the plea that every western family should eat one meatless meal per week, the argument being that animal food products are very energy intensive and require many precious grains that otherwise would be available to the starving millions in the poor countries. Apart from having a fairly drastic effect on the hill farmers and other meat producers, one cannot be sure that much of the released grain would actually get to those who really need it, and in any case there are good reasons to believe that the real shortage in the developing world is animal protein coupled with sufficient carbohydrates intake to ensure that the animal protein is being fully utilised.[6] Eating one meatless meal per week may salve the conscience but, given the existing pattern of agricultural activity, population densities, income distribution and political jerrymandering of land ownership, it is probably irrelevant in terms of serving its intended purpose. It might even prove counterproductive for it could reduce much needed incentives for grain production in the developing world.

Again there is a lesson for environmental education here. Preaching environmental responsibility in a narrow, western-oriented context, can be dangerous because the forces that operate global socio-political systems cannot be tinkered with in a facile manner. Reform in educational curricula is only a small part of the change that is required and should be carefully phased in concert with other developments.

The third point relevant to the educational aspects of promoting environmentally responsible behaviour arises out of the diagrams illustrated as Figure 8.1 a, b and c. These have been developed out of the voluminous social psychology literature which looks at the relationship between attitudes and behaviour. This is a tremendously extensive and in many respects inconclusive literature which is largely too technical and abstruse to be included in a publication of this kind. Broadly speaking, however, the conclusion is that attitudes (a combination of beliefs about an object or situation and a positive or negative disposition toward that object or situation) by and large lead to certain behaviours

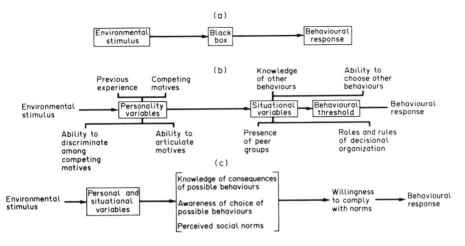

FIGURE 8.1

Relationships between attitudes and behaviour. This diagram presupposes a one-way relationship between attitudes and behaviour. In practice the two may interact in a rather complicated manner but this hypothesis remains to be satisfactorily tested. Figure 8.1a illustrates the basic premise that knowing attitudes helps to predict behaviour. Figure 8.1b points out some of the variables in the "black box" especially those relating to personality and the circumstances in which the relationship is being analysed. Figure 8.1c emphasises that there must also be "knowledge (awareness of consequence) and sense of culpability (sense of blame and understanding of alternative behavioural options) before behaviour responds to societal norms. In the context of environmental issues and in the light of the relationships depicted in Figure 6.3, these three components (knowledge, culpability and societal norms) may well be ill-developed.

(actual deeds or at least dispositions to support or oppose certain happenings), but that there are many intervening variables that affect this relationship. Furthermore, there will be an interactive relationship between attitudes and behaviour, for in many cases because particular behaviours are followed, attitudes and the awareness which is thereby developed are altered to suit.[7]

This last point awaits more intensive research, but it can be postulated that if someone, for whatever reason, embarks on environmentally responsible behaviour that involves a shift from past behaviours and which in turn involves the expenditure of time and effort rather than money, then he might well search for confirmation that this shift is personally and socially worth while. This search may involve talking to various people or reading up relevant material in the newspapers or journals, but however it is done it should produce an alteration in the person's beliefs about what is responsible or irresponsible behaviour. For example, during the great British drought of 1976, British people cut their consumption of water by up to 20 percent and undoubtedly became aware, through many changes in behaviour, of the importance of water and the need to conserve it. Both behaviour and attitudes shifted to suit a new set of circumstances. The fact that water consumption reverted to its old pattern once the drought scare was over either reinforces the point or simply indicates that during the shortage people conserved simply because they realised this was only a short-term problem. The test of the theory on the effect on energy-conservation behaviour and related beliefs will come if real energy prices continue to increase in such a way as to be obvious to the consumer.

This research remains to be done. Let us return to the diagrams and look at some of the points illustrated there in more detail. Figure 8.1a illustrates the new rejected thesis that attitudes directly influence behaviour. For example: "I don't think it is right that people should cause air pollution because air pollution is injurious to public health therefore I shall not drive a car." This kind of relationship is too simplistic and unreal. So the next stage is described in Figure 8.1b where it will be observed that lying between the environmental stimulus "should I place on my car an emission control device?" (in countries where such things are not compulsory) or "should I disconnect my emission control device?" (in countries where they are mandatory), and the actual behaviour (answer to the question) are two major intervening variables and a behavioural threshold. One set of variables relates to the individual himself, whether he has had any previous experience of emission-control devices, whether he is aware of what adding one on or taking one off does, how much he is prepared to balance the moral (and legal) arguments for putting (or keeping) the device are against the known costs of extra petrol that it will require, etc. Not only does he have to know all these factors (and there are many more even in this simple example) but he has to be able to think through them in a rational and logically consistent manner.

Then there are the situational variables, the factors that occur by virtue of the circumstances in which he asks the question. Does he know what other people, especially his friends are doing? What would they think of him if he bought or disconnected the device whatever the case might be? Are there other ways in which he could reduce the air pollution his car causes (e.g. by cycling more, joining a car pool, living closer to work, changing jobs) and what would be the likelihood that he might be subsidised or caught (again depending on the case) by the regulatory authorities involved? Again all this involves a fairly complicated trade-off arrangement where the poor soul caught up in the middle is supposed to weigh up all the relevant arguments.

But he is not off the hook, because we find from Figure 8.1c that the behavioural threshold, namely where an actual decision to do one thing or another, or to switch from an existing pattern of behaviour occurs, is influenced by three further factors which in our view are quite central to good environmental education. First of all he is supposed to be aware of the consequences not only of his proposed behaviour (in this case to connect or disconnect the emission-control device), but of all other possible behaviours which are relevant to the air-pollution issue. We have already stressed that in practical terms this is very difficult without a very extensive training in the environmental sciences and in any case on many environmental matters scientists are in violent disagreement about the consequences of certain activities. The case of aerosol sprays is an obvious one.[8] There are those who simply do not believe that chlorofluoromethane gases do deplete ozone in the atmosphere to a degree that could be harmful, then there are those who believe that the aerosol propellant spray is not the main culprit for refrigerators and air conditioners produce roughly equal quantities of chlorofluoromethanes. Since disputes among so-called experts abound in many areas where toxic substances are involved it is hardly surprising that ordinary people either do not know or are not certain what precisely are the consequences of particular behaviours. Given that this kind of thinking must always take place in the "commons" context where the balance of gains against losses generally favours the continuation of mildly damaging behaviour, it is clear that only those who are genuinely environmentally concerned will arm themselves fully with the necessary understanding.

Then we come to the second stumbling block, namely awareness of choice that other behaviours exist. As we have already discussed this in Section 6, it shall not be developed here; suffice it to say that more often than not our economic and social arrangements make it difficult for more environmentally safe behaviours to be adopted. Finally, there is the matter of what the individual, faced with a choice between environmentally responsible and environmentally irresponsible behaviour, perceives to be prevailing social morals. People generally may pay lip service to antipolluting behaviour but in practice may ignore the kind of moral code that Leopold was talking about in Section 6. Thus if societal norms are not powerful, and again we judge this to be an important educational matter, they may not encourage the individual to conform—especially in those critical situations when he is unobserved and the environmentally responsible alternatives involve various kinds of additional "costs" most of which have to be absorbed personally. These pressures therefore all influence the individual's willingness to comply with the social norms, or to put it in another way, cause him to interpret the social norms differently so as to justify his final actions. Given all these inherently conflicting forces and the fact that environmentally responsible behaviour often means a struggle against the prevailing economic and social "tide", it is hardly surprising to discover that most people in modern industrial societies who profess to be committed environmentalists indulge in day to day behaviour which, particularly when multiplied by the actions of many millions of others, is environmentally destructive.

Where then does environmental education come in to all this? Let us look at four commonly accepted objectives of environmental education:[9]

1. Integration of environmental concern knowledge and skills into all relevant areas of learning.
2. An environmentally literate citizenry.
3. The preparation of experts qualified to deal with specific environmental problems.
4. A deeper understanding of environmental matters by a large number of groups—politicians, planners, civic leaders, teachers at all school levels.

Clearly a combination of wider awareness and improved skills is a primary focus for environmental education, and there are a number of ways in which this can be achieved. Because of shortage of space we shall look mainly at developments in conservation education and urban studies. In the reference notes we direct readers to the sources of more information.

Outdoor Skills and Field Studies

Environmental education in Britain began with the concept of providing a basic ability to cope with the out of doors. This generally meant improving physical fitness and developing skills in activities such as long-distance walking, mountain climbing, nature observation and camping. But equally significant was the belief that such activities undertaken with others improved the students' ability to interact socially, upgrade his organisational capabilities and generally improve his self-confidence and self-esteem. Indeed there are many educators who are convinced that delinquency and other forms of social deviance can best be corrected by taking miscreants on outdoor expeditions where they have to work closely with others in order to survive and where frequently their physical fitness and outdoor skills are tested to their limits—the point being that these limits are extendable given particular circumstances and attitudes of mind. The outward-bound programme and the Duke of Edinburgh's award scheme, both highly praised and increasingly popular, are based on these principles and appear to work well so long as they are handled by experienced and sensitive leaders.

By taking young people out of their urban settings, away from their homes where there may be poor family relationships and away from their fellows who may encourage socially undesirable behaviour, these schemes serve a valuable purpose in providing a learning environment, based largely in the out of doors, which is conducive to personality development and public spiritedness. Co-operating with and helping others is an essential ingredient in such programmes, and this in turn breeds a sensitivity to the needs of others and a satisfaction in the sheer joy of doing a good turn for someone else. In short, such courses encourage the skills of altruistic behaviour, because they are conducted in settings in which altruism is rewarded, which hopefully may spill over to circumstances where, as Hardin frequently observes, pure altruism is discouraged.

But there is another element to this kind of education, apart also from the physical fitness and sociability aspects, and that is an association with nature in a more immediate form than is commonly experienced by most urban youngsters. The aim here is to give people a more realistic sense of what nature is all about, a greater respect for natural forces that are more powerful than man's abilities to conquer them, and in essence, a feeling for the bioethic and biorights notion that were discussed in Section 1. We are careful to stress the notion of "feeling for" here for it would be wrong to claim that outward-bound education courses are primarily devoted to instilling an ecological ethic: an ecological awareness, possibly, but an ethic only tangentially.

Understanding of, and sensitivity to, the wonders of ecological processes is the principal objective of the field studies centres. The idea in terms of formal environmental education originated in the mid-sixties (for the practice has a longer heritage—the Council for the Promotion of Field Studies being formed in 1943) following the publication of the Buchanan report[10] which revealed how much the conservation of the urban fabric was desperately needed and thus how much an aesthetically aware citizenry was required, and the series of conferences known as *The Countryside in the 1970s*.[11] These meetings, inspired by the initiative of the Duke of Edinburgh, brought together all the key landscape protection and conservation interests in the country, and out of their discussions emerged the idea of an ecology-based curriculum to help young people understand and participate in the problems of conservation. The specific phrase "environmental education" emerged at a Study Conference on Education held in 1965 and was supported in principle, though not much in practice, by the government of the day. This resulted in the modest proliferation of field studies centres in a number of local education authority areas where school children could spend a week or so studying the environmental sciences in practice, becoming sensitised to the concept of an environmental ethic, recognising the importance of interdisciplinary research and enjoying all the fun that these courses in such settings provide. Though in general these courses are of great educational importance, when applied to practical case studies, for example looking at the causes and consequences of river abstraction or water pollution, they can be of particular value as was demonstrated when the Advisory Centre for Education in Cambridge joined forces with the

Sunday Times to promote a children-run survey of water pollution and beach litter throughout the country. Today field study courses form the basis of the A level curriculum in environmental studies as set by the London University Board, the objects of which are (a) to identify the inter-relationships of the physical and biological factors that make up the environment, (b) to analyse ways for control and values for guidance, and (c) to establish a set of personal values towards the place of man in the environment.

Both the outdoor skills and field studies programmes are thoroughly successful components of environmental education in the UK today because they have an obvious practical significance and because they take pupils out of the classroom setting where social interaction is constrained and the authoritarian image of the teacher is enhanced. Unfortunately to the more conservative elements in education administration these fairly costly exercises are viewed with suspicion, partly because they fall outside the highly traditional view of "education" so tend to fall foul of a cost-cutting programme. During the round of education cuts that took place in the late seventies and early eighties these programmes became very vulnerable, though in educational terms this may turn out to be quite a serious false economy.

Urban Environmental Education

The great town planner Sir Patrick Geddes was probably the first real environmental educator in Britain. At the turn of the century he wrote powerfully about the need to regard the city as a functioning organism in which work, play and social development all fused.[12] He was a great believer in encouraging school students to undertake their own surveys of urban processes and aspects of environmental quality and saw the advantages in getting young people out of the classroom. His initiative was, in part, instrumental in the setting up, in 1899, of the Town and Country Planning Association, a voluntary organisation dedicated, among other things, to improving the quality of urban living. Following up one of the recommendations of the Skeffington Report[13] on citizen participation in planning, namely that citizens should be encouraged to become more familiar with the forces that shape the urban environment, and become part of the processes of change, the TCPA established, in 1971, its own Education Unit and launched the monthly magazine for teachers, *Bulletin of Environmental Education*. This is an excellent source of all sorts of practical ideas about how to encourage youngsters to become aware of their urban surroundings, and is the sponsor of the imaginative programme entitled Art and the Built Environment in which children of all ages are encouraged to portray and describe the townscape as it is and as it is being changed. Nicholson and

Schreiner[14] sum up the objectives of the modern breed of urban educator:

> "One of the main problems facing community involvement is the present lack of awareness among people, of the environment itself. The majority of people are relatively unaware of the parts and wholes which make up their surroundings, and are unaware of the reasons for the existence of the built environment and of how they themselves interact with the built forms....
> If the psychological barriers are removed, frustration may increase if people are powerless to actively change anything and construct a better environment for the future. Passivity toward the environment is, therefore, first of all environmentally conditioned from childhood, and subsequently reinforced by lack of access to decisionmaking. It is only with considerable effort that individuals can escape this."

There are three themes which interact in present-day urban environmental education—a heightened sensitivity to the townscape, an understanding of the forces that shape urban form and functioning, and a preparation for constructive participation in urban planning. As regards the first, promoting a sense of perceptual awareness of the townscape, the lead was taken by the architect Gordon Cullen[15] who demonstrated with words and pictures why collections of buildings and streets as opposed to individual structures were so important. His ideas were followed up by Keith Wheeler[16] who made a number of practical suggestions as to how young people could be encouraged to look about them and evaluate their urban surroundings in a constructive manner. O'Riordan[17] has followed up Wheeler's proposals by devising a scheme of small-group evaluation exercises that not only help the student to be a better judge of what he is perceiving but to recommend where parts of townscapes (or indeed countryscapes) could be improved. The aim of the exercise is to encourage the student to be a planner, for the technique is designed to relate a knowledge of function to a sense of the aesthetic, and to integrate personal judgement with small group decisions. Three years of testing the method has demonstrated that it enhances the inherent creativity of the individual, stimulated by working in small groups, and that it can be practicably attuned to real planning problems. There is always the danger, of course, that such exercises will become quite irrelevant to the kinds of constraints under which planners have to work (budgetary limits, pressures from various interests, co-operation from elected members). There is no easy answer here except to point out that the teacher should try as far as possible to gain the confidence of local officials, seeking their support, but not necessarily confining the task precisely to their requirements.

An article by Michael Storm[18] stimulated a number of educators to consider a more problem-based approach to urban studies. The aim, albeit still rather vague in practical terms, is to develop curricula which make the student aware of how the city functions, what the forces are that shape its growth and how actual decisions are made both in terms of regional structure plans and specific planning proposals. In a more recent article, Storm[18] reassesses the reasons why urban studies are so important. First, he emphasises the instrumental component of developing skills in interpretation, aesthetic judgement and map understanding. Second, he stresses the analytical component, the use of integrated urban studies for practical access to various curriculum topics ranging from geology and ecology, to art and social studies. Third, he considers the important matter of activism, the direct participation of students in urban-planning issues, which in turn requires high development of both the instrumental and inquiry approaches. He also warns against too much emphasis on urban history and a myopic parochialism which inhibits students from looking at the wider array of forces which shape urban-planning decisions.

One organisation that is taking urban studies very seriously is the Schools Council Curriculum Development Project, Geography 16–19,[19] which is preparing a number of teaching aids on how to prepare a study of local planning issues. The Project's new A level syllabus includes a decisionmaking exercise as part of its papers. The candidate is presented with a case study plus adequate background data, and then has 2 hours in which to consider the evidence and to make and justify a final decision. Needless to say, the object of the exercise is as much to develop skills in assessing the problem as determining a final solution. In the actual course work, much emphasis is placed on role playing and direct contact with local officials and the main interested parties. In practice, a close understanding of a specific problem may be difficult to arrange, but given diplomatic skills and much motivation, a dedicated teacher can work wonders.

A more controversial aspect of urban education is the direct involvement of school students in participatory activities. Vicarious studies of planning issues is one thing, but attending public meetings, organising protests, and, *in extremes* taking part in direct action tactics, is quite another. The Schools Eco-Action Group is quite enthusiastic about this aspect of direct learning, though it does not confine its interest to the urban scene:[20]

> " 'Doing' is the most effective way of learning. Nothing brings to life the problems of industrial waste, the clash of economic and community interests, biological investigations and pollution control as monitoring oil spillages and getting them stopped. You learn about the issues and also about the techniques of activism—whether or not you succeed in your main aim. Society is so complex that most people are bewildered by the number of committees, forms, officials and restrictions that seem to stop them expressing their views about local problems. Education fails if it doesn't enable you to thread your way through the maze and achieve the changes you want; but it is not something that can be learnt in the classroom."

The educational establishment is understandably cautious about direct participation. For one thing, it may provoke a resentment from

among the more conservative minded members of education committees who believe that education takes place in the classroom and not in
the streets. For another, direct action involves a lot of preparation on the
part of the teacher, which may absorb some of his more "conventional"
teaching duties, and could mean that students are away from the school
premises when they should be attending other classes, for public inquiries and committee meetings of the local council are usually held
during school hours. In addition, direct involvement in particularly
controversial public issues can be dangerous in educational terms, unless
very carefully handled, because lobbying by student groups rarely has
specific political value in comparison with lobbying from other vested
interests (unless the issue involves some aspect of the school or its neighbourhood), and students may obtain an unfairly jaundiced view if the
political process of their expectations about their political influence are
naïvely raised only to be dashed when their efforts are ignored or lost in
the general controversy.

Nevertheless, it would be equally foolhardy to reject the idea of
direct involvement in community affairs as part of environmental
education. Young people are genuinely enthusiastic about working on
topics that are currently exercising the minds of local planners and elected members, and frequently approach the task with more commitment
than might be the case with pure simulation. The need is to place any
kind of involvement in its political and social perspective and to consider carefully how the participation of school pupils can be most constructive and effective. For involvement undoubtedly generates a sense
of real-world immediacy, it gives pupils a sense of purpose, it often encourages a genuine search for a multidisciplinary perspective that even
the vicarious case study cannot always engender, and, above all, it
brings to life the often meaningless symbols of political and bureaucratic organisational charts and decisionmaking flow diagrams. One
feature of environmental education that has still to come of age is a
greater emphasis on how the political system actually works, how the
forces of power operate, how the various interests marshall their arguments and interact with the really important power brokers, how the
law helps or hinders, what rights various people have in various circumstances and how these can be exercised, and what are the conventions of
policymaking and decisiontaking, including the various roles of selective consultation, official secrecy, ministerial discretion and
bureaucratic and otherwise expert advice. These are the major strands
of the British policymaking system which can best be unravelled in the
context of live public issues in which the school plays a constructive
part.

Chris Webb, director of the Notting Dale Urban Studies Centre, is,
however, not too optimistic about these developments. Noting the

intransigent bureaucracy of much of modern planning and the tokenism officials pay to participation he bemoans the possibilities that environmental education will simply become slotted comfortably into the traditional school curricula. He reaches three conclusions:[21]

> "One, that if one is going to develop local or urban studies into the political (economic/social) realms which are the natural progression on from perception studies/trails and the rest, then the resources themselves present an enormous pedagogic problem. They *are* inherently complex, difficult and often incomplete. Given the traditional wet Friday afternoon how can they be made to work.
>
> "Two, assuming that the above can happen, they must surely be approached through an eclectic medium . . . as opposed to the odd, subject based notions of schooling and higher education.
>
> "Three, these will only fuse into an effective experience if the ethos is right. By this I mean that Urban Studies must be participatory and generative, in line with the adult experiences, if it is to be important in any way . . ..
>
> "The experience of being taught in schools is a tepid one compared with the agonies, frustrations and learning of many deprived inner city residents. Unless some of that intensiveness can be found in the school or educational experience, we doubt the effectiveness of such studies in transforming people's views of their life chances."

An intermediate form of more direct involvement in urban studies is the construction of a town trail, one of the earliest developed and still most popular forms of environmental education.[22] The trail itself may not actually be a path or route but a series of foci to stimulate sensory awareness of different aspects of the townscape and to set the scene for discussion about a range of topics ranging from urban history to current planning controversies. The trail concept is adjustable in a number of ways, the most imaginative schemes deploying it for a number of educational purposes. Sometimes the trail can be designed to be self-guiding or it may be prepared for small groups to travel through and comment upon. Often a lot of background information is required but again good trails may excite the students to prepare their own material. Here is where the Art and the Built Environment programme could be linked to the town trail as is indicated by a number of more adventurous reports published in the *Bulletin of Environmental Education*.[23] Also, the town trail idea can become closely associated with direct involvement, since local community groups are often willing to co-operate with teachers in providing relevant information on topical issues, and sometimes helping out in the leading of student groups. However, there is always a danger in "politicising" a trail, that is, making it a device to promote a particular interest group objective without providing a reasonable balance of interpretations. Nevertheless, there are occasions when a trail should be used to heighten student awareness of the quality of a townscape or the threat to a particular landmark and to encourage students to become more interested in the processes that influence the enjoyment of their urban surroundings.

The Future of Environmental Education

Ever since the Stockholm Conference in the Human Environment the twin UN organisations UNESCO and UNEP have become very interested in environmental education as a means for improving both citizen understanding of global environmental problems and instilling some sense of a bio-ethic. These efforts culminated in two declarations arising out of important international gatherings, the so-called Belgrade Charter which emanated from an International Environmental Education Workshop held in Belgrade, 13–22 October 1976, and the Tbilisi Declaration, the result of the meeting of the First Intergovernmental Conference of Environmental Education convened in Tbilisi, USSR, 14–22 October 1977. We publish the latter statement in the readings that follow, not just for what it says, as to indicate how the international environmental education community envisages the future development of the idea.

Clearly there is much noble rhetoric in these ringing declarations and it remains to be seen how supportive the various governments will be. In Britain, the Department of Education and Science has been notable for its verbal support but inadequate commitment of resources.[24]* The late seventies concern with public spending cuts does not inspire much optimism that either the necessary teachers will be hired or that improved training programmes will be developed. As is so often the case, much will depend on how teachers can "make do" with their present inadequate resources and how much support they will get from within their school and local community. A lot, too, will depend on motivation and sincere commitment when curricula and timetables are not always conducive to encouraging out-of-classroom activities and an interdisciplinary (multiclass and hence multiteacher) approach to problems and to themes. For genuine interdisciplinarity is often very difficult to achieve in practice even on a problem-focused basis, as it requires much cooperation and considerable preparation among many people not all of whom may be so committed to the environmental education ideals outlined in the declaration that follows, and whose promotion prospects are not always improved by what might be loosely termed a collective approach to education. At present, the Council for Environmental Education, the coordinating organisation in the UK, is attempting to restructure its effort to grapple with these difficult practical problems and is still in the process of working out its future operations and organisational aims. It will be a little time yet before the Council is as

---

* For an up-to-date review of the British view on environmental education, see Department of Education & Science (1981) *Environmental Education: A Review* and *Environmental Education: Sources of Information 1981.* Both documents are available from HMSO, London.

influential as it would like to be in guiding the future of environmental education in the UK.[25]

An aspect of environmental education that awaits development is the training of both development officials and teachers in developing countries to incorporate an awareness of environmental sustainability (as developed in Section 4) into the strategy of development. This is not an easy task partly because no-one is sure what environmentally sustainable development really means in practice,[26] and how far it should permeate the social repercussions of development, and partly because it is an understandably delicate matter for so-called developed nations to suggest how to put other people's environmental houses in order when their own quality of life continues to deteriorate. In any case, most environmental problems in the Third World are a product of poverty and inequality, themselves partly an outcome of colonialism, and the consequence of social and political factors that are far more difficult to change than some of the attitude shifts aimed at in the UN-based declaration that follows.

Nevertheless, there is a good case for stimulating a greater awareness of the wider environmental consequences of development schemes and programmes as indicated in Section 4, and consequently a need to improve the training of those directly involved in both the development process and environmental protection. (In many developing countries these two functions are not always as integrated as they ought to be.) It may well be that such a training programme should be divided into three parts — one aimed at senior administrators who advise development and environment ministers, one at people who prepare development programmes and design the actual schemes, and one reaching those who would be environmental educators in their own countries both for the groups already mentioned and also more generally in the schools. This is a tall order that awaits much thought and careful preparation, but there is little doubt that there will be initiatives in this area as environmentally sustainable development becomes a more urgent task.[27] Already the US Agency for International Development is sponsoring a number of training schemes for its own officials and it has indicated that it will extend those to developing country personnel as circumstances permit. The UK Overseas Development Administration is also showing considerable interest in this idea as indeed are a number of other bilateral and multilateral development assistance agencies.

Despite all this optimism for the future of environmental education, the fact remains that is still in its infancy in terms of the total educational effort despite at least 10 years of existence of the work of many dedicated individuals. Like all things which are "environmental" it falls uneasily between current ways of doing things and changing attitudes of mind. It seeks to challenge commonly accepted practices without always being clear as to why its approach is better. It aims to tackle social ills that are the product of persuasive influences that in turn are perpetuated by inertia. Chris Webb of the Notting Dale Urban Studies Centre asks the relevant rhetorical questions.[28]

"If one wants today's children to become tomorrow's potent adults, then can traditional school-based or less traditional issue-based urban studies be the effective medium?... If it is consigned to yet another commodity in the educational market place, will it raise itself above packaged 'controversiality'?... Will perceptions studies and that interesting celebration of self become ingredients in yet more taxonomies, through which coarse grained net slip the real energies and complexities of social beings?... will the link be made between the existential and perceiving human and the implications of this for action in the real world?"

Notes and References

1. Kumar, K. (1979) First In, First Out: Will Britain Pioneer the Post-Industrial Future? *New Ecologist*, vol. 9(3), pp. 86–91.
2. Reference has already been made to a selection of books and articles on what might loosely be called the alternative society in Section 1.
3. Kumer, *op. cit.*, p. 91.
4. Ashby, E. (1976) A Second Look at Doom, *Encounter*, January, pp. 16–27. The quotation is from page 27.
5. This statement is probably most forcefully argued by Barry Commoner. See his *The Closing Circle* (1972), Knopf, New York, and *The Poverty of Power* (1977), Viking, New York.
6. This is a controversial topic. A good reference is Allen, G. (1976) Some Aspects of Planning World Food Supplies, *Journal of Agricultural Economics*, vol. 27, No. 1, pp. 97–120. See also Tarrant, J. R. (1980) *Food Policies*, Wiley, Chichester, pp. 192–195 and pp. 218–219.
7. These points are further explored in O'Riordan, T. (1978) Attitudes, Behaviour and Environmental Policy Issues, in I. Altman and J. F. Wohlwill (eds.) *Human Behaviour and the Environment Advances in Theory and Research*, Plenum, New York, pp. 1–36.
8. For a convenient summary, see Reprint of the Federal Task Force on Inadvertent Modification of the Stratosphere (1975) *Fluorocarbons and the Environment*, Council on Environmental Quality, Washington, DC.
9. This comes from L. Emmelin (1977) Environmental Education Programmes for Adults, in *Trends in Environmental Education*, UNESCO, Paris. UNESCO has published another series of relevant papers in 1982 entitled *New World Trends in Environmental Education*.
10. Buchanan, C. (1965) *Traffic in Towns*, Penguin, Harmondsworth.
11. The Countryside in the 1970s consisted of three conferences held in 1963, 1965 and 1969.
12. The history of environmental education in the UK is described by K. Wheeler (1975) The Genesis of Environmental Education, in K. Wheeler and G. C. Martin (eds.) *Insights Into Environmental Education*, Oliver & Boyd, Edinburgh, pp. 2–19.
13. Skeffington, A. (1969) *Citizen Participation in Planning*, HMSO, London. There have been many reviews and critiques of the Skeffington Report, but for a good comprehensive statement see Fagance, M. (1977) *Citizen Participation in Planning*, Pergamon, Oxford.
14. Nicholson, S. and Sheiner, B. K. (1973) *Community Participation in City Decision Making*, Open University, Urban Development Course D7201, Unit 22, Milton Keynes. The quote is from page 32.
15. Cullen, G. (1971) *The Concise Townscape*, Architectural Press, London. This is a revised edition of the original which appeared in 1961.
16. Wheeler, K. (1976) Experiencing Townscape, *Bulletin of Environmental Education*, No. 68. See also Goodey, B. (1977) Sensing the Environment, *Bulletin of Environmental Education*, No. 72, and Bishop, J. (1977) Building Appraisal, *Bulletin of Environmental Education*, No. 73 for related developments in the techniques of sensing awareness.
17. O'Riordan, T. (1977) Putting Experiencing Townscape into Practice, *Bulletin of Environmental Education*, No. 79, pp. 4–6;
   O'Riordan, T. (1978) An Example of Environmental Education, *Journal of Geography in Higher Education*, vol. 2, pp. 3–16;

O'Riordan, T. and Walmsley, M. (1979) Evaluating Environmental Potential, *Bulletin of Environmental Education*, No. 95, pp. 6–12.
18. Storm, M. (1971) Schools and the Community: An Issue-based Approach, *Bulletin of Environmental Education*, No. 1.
    Storm, M. (1979) Why Study the Urban Environment, *Bulletin of Environmental Education* Nos. 100/101, pp. 24–26.
19. This project is run through the Institute of Education, University of London, 20 Bradford Way, London WC1 0AL. The project director is Michael Naish. Its aims are broadly to focus on the man–environment relationship, characterised by an emphasis on the examination of questions, issues and problems arising from man's interrelationship with his environment. Geography is seen as an educational medium through which 16- 19-year-olds can be helped to understand the environment within which they live, rather than as an academic end in itself.
20. Schools Eco-Action Group (1978) Guide to Secondary School Environmental Action, 1a Glenlyon Road, London SE 9.
21. Webb, C. (1978) More Passion and Urgency Needed, *Bulletin of Environmental Education*, No. 87, pp. 10–12.
22. The idea of the town trail is part of general discussion on practical urban studies discussed by Ward, C. and Fyson, T. (1973) *Streetwork: The Exploding School*, Routledge & Kegan Paul, London.
23. For a summary of the Art and the Built Environment Project, see *Bulletin of Environmental Education*, No. 78 (October 1977) and No. 98 (June 1979). The basic aims of the project are: (a) to enlarge the students' environmental perception and enable them to develop a "feel" for the built environment; (b) to enhance their capacity for discrimination and their competence in the visual appraisal of the built environment; (c) to evolve generally applicable techniques for (a) and (b); and (d) to disseminate these in a form suitable for teacher training and guidance.
24. For a sense of the present official attitude to environmental education see UK Department of Education and Science (1977) *Environmental Education in the UK*, and UK Department of Education and Science (1979) *Curriculum 11–16: Environmental Education, Environmental Education in Further and Adult Education, Post Tbilisi Document*, and *Initial and In Service Training for Teachers in Environmental Education*.
25. The Council of Environmental Education is based in the School of Education, University of Reading, Reading RG1 5AQ. It publishes a quarterly newsletter with up-to-date information on its activities and relevant developments, and is regarded now as the national spokesbody for environmental education in Britain.
26. This subject has been explored by the UN Environment Programme (1970) *Ecodevelopment* UNEP/GC/80, Nairobi. See also International Institute for Environment and Development (1978) *Banking on the Biosphere?* 10 Percy Street, London W1V 0DG.
27. This is one of the principal recommendations of a six-nation study of bilateral aid agencies undertaken by the International Institute for Environment and Development.
28. Webb, C. (*op.cit.*), p. 12.

READING

THE TBILISI DECLARATION, 1978*

IN THE last few decades, man has, through his power to transform his environment, wrought accelerated changes in the balance of nature. The result is frequent exposure of living species to dangers which may prove irreversible. The Declaration of the United Nations Conference on Human Environment organized in Stockholm in 1972 proclaimed: "to defend and improve the environment for present and future generations has become an imperative goal for mankind." This undertaking urgently calls for new strategies, incorporated into development, which particularly in the developing countries is a prerequisite for any such improvement. Solidarity and equity in the relations

*Reprinted by permission from *Connect* (Unesco-UNEP Environmental Education Newsletter) Vol. 3, No. 1, pp. 1–8.

between nations should constitute the basis of a new international order, and bring together, as soon as possible, all available resources. Education utilizing the findings of science and technology should play a leading role in creating an awareness and a better understanding of environmental problems. It must foster positive patterns of conduct towards the environment and nations' use of their resources.

Environmental education should be provided for all ages, at all levels and in both formal and nonformal education. The mass media have a great responsibility to make their immense resources available for this educational mission. Environmental specialists, as well as those whose actions and decisions can have a marked effect on the environment, should be provided in the course of their training with the necessary knowledge and skills and be given a full sense of their responsibilities in this respect.

Environmental education, properly understood, should constitute a comprehensive lifelong education, one responsive to changes in a rapidly changing world. It should prepare the individual for life through an understanding of the major problems of the contemporary world, and the provision of skills and attributes needed to play a productive role towards improving life and protecting the environment with due regard given to ethical values. By adopting a holistic approach, rooted in a broad interdisciplinary base, it recreates an overall perspective which acknowledges the fact that natural environment and manmade environment are profoundly interdependent. It helps reveal the enduring continuity which links the acts of today to the consequences for tomorrow. It demonstrates the interdependencies among national communities and the need for solidarity among all mankind.

Environmental education must look outward to the community. It should involve the individual in an active problem-solving process within the context of specific realities, and it should encourage initiative, a sense of responsibility and commitment to build a better tomorrow. By its very nature, environmental education can make a powerful contribution to the renovation of the educational process.

In order to achieve these goals, environmental education requires a number of specific actions to fill the gaps which, despite outstanding endeavours, continue to exist in our present education system.

Accordingly, the Tbilisi Conference:

Appeals to Member States to include in their educational policies measures designed to introduce environmental concerns, activities and contents into their education systems, on the basis of the above objectives and characteristics;

Invites educational authorities to promote and intensify thinking, research and innovation in regard to environmental education;

Urges Member States to collaborate in this field, in particular by exchanging experiences, research findings, documentation and materials and by making their training facilities widely available to teachers and specialists from other countries; and lastly,

Appeals to the international community to give generously of its aid in order to strengthen this collaboration in a field which symbolizes the need for solidarity of all peoples and may be regarded as particularly conducive to the promotion of international understanding and to the cause of peace.

The role, objectives and characteristics of environmental education

The Tbilisi Declaration together with two of the recommendations of the Conference constitutes the framework, principles and guidelines for environmental education at all levels — local, national, regional and international — and for all age groups both inside and outside the formal school system.

I. The Conference *recommends* the adoption of certain criteria which will help to guide efforts to develop environmental education at the national, regional and global levels:

– Whereas it is a fact that biological and physical features constitute the natural basis of the human environment, its ethical, social, cultural and economic dimensions also play their part in determining the lines of approach and the instruments whereby people may understand and make better use of natural resources in satisfying their needs.

– Environmental education is the result of the reorientation and dovetailing of different disciplines and educational experiences which facilitate an integrated perception of the problems of the environment, enabling more rational actions capable of meeting social needs to be taken.

– A basic aim of environmental education is to succeed in making individuals and communities understand the complex nature of the natural and the built environments resulting from the interaction of their biological, physical, social, economic and cultural aspects, and acquire the knowledge, values, attitudes and practical skills to participate in a responsible and effective way in anticipating and solving environmental problems, and in the management of the quality of the environment.

– A further basic aim of environmental education is clearly to show the economic, political and ecological interdependence of the modern world, in which decisions and actions by the different countries can have international repercussions. Environmental education should, in this regard, help to develop a sense of responsibility and solidarity among countries and regions as the foundation for a new international order which will guarantee the conservation and improvement of the environment.

– Special attention should be paid to understanding the complex relations between socio-economic development and the improvement of the environment.

– For this purpose, environmental education should provide the necessary knowledge for interpretation of the complex phenomena that shape the environment, encourage those ethical, economic and esthetic values which, constituting the basis of self-discipline, will further the development of conduct compatible with the preservation and improvement of the environment; it should also provide a wide range of practical skills required in the devising and application of effective solutions to environmental problems.

– To carry out these tasks, environmental education should bring about a closer link between educational processes and real life, building its activities around the environmental problems that are faced by particular communities and focusing analysis on these by means of an interdisciplinary, comprehensive approach which will permit a proper understanding of environmental problems.

– Environmental education should cater to all ages and socio-professional groups in the population. It should be addressed to (a) the general non-specialist public of young people and adults whose daily conduct has a decisive influence on the preservation and improvement of the environment; (b) to particular social groups whose professional activities affect the quality of the environment; and (c) to scientists and technicians whose specialized research and work will lay the foundations of knowledge on which education, training and efficient management of the environment should be based.

– To achieve the effective development of environmental education, full advantage must be taken of all public and private facilities available to society for the education of the population: the formal education system, different forms of nonformal education, and the mass media.

– To make an effective contribution towards improving the environment, educational action must be linked with legislation, policies, measures of control and the decisions that governments may adopt in relation to the human environment.

II. The Conference *endorses* the following goals, objectives and guiding principles for environmental education:

The *goals* of environmental education are:

– to foster clear awareness of, and concern about, economic, social, political and ecological interdependence in urban and rural areas;

– to provide every person with opportunities to acquire the knowledge, values, attitudes, commitment and skills needed to protect and improve the environment;

– to create new patterns of behaviour of individuals, groups and society as a whole towards the environment.

The categories of environmental education *objectives* are:

Awareness: to help social groups and individuals acquire an awareness and sensitivity to the total environment and its allied problems.

Knowledge: to help social groups and individuals gain a variety of experience in, and acquire a basic understanding of, the environment and its associated problems.

Attitudes: to help social groups and individuals acquire a set of values and feelings of concern for the environment and the motivation for actively participating in environmental improvement and protection.

Skills: to help social groups and individuals acquire the skills for identifying and solving environmental problems.

Participation: to provide social groups and individuals with an opportunity to be actively involved at all levels in working toward resolution of environmental problems.

Guiding principles—environmental education should:

– consider the environment in its totality — natural and built, technological and social (economic, political, cultural-historical, moral, esthetic);

– be a continuous lifelong process, beginning at the pre-school level and continuing through all formal and nonformal stages;

– be interdisciplinary in its approach, drawing on the specific content of each discipline in making possible a holistic and balanced perspective;

– examine major environmental issues from local, national, regional and international points of view so that students receive insights into environmental conditions in other geographical areas;

– focus on current and potential environmental situations while taking into account the historical perspective;

– promote the value and necessity of local, national and international cooperation in the prevention and solution of environmental problems;

– explicitly consider environmental aspects in plans for development and growth;

– enable learners to have a role in planning their learning experiences and provide an opportunity for making decisions and accepting their consequences;

– relate environmental sensitivity, knowledge, problem-solving skills and values clarification to every age, but with special emphasis on environmental sensitivity to the learner's own community in early years;

– help learners discover the symptoms and real causes of environmental problems;

– emphasize the complexity of environmental problems and thus the need to develop critical thinking and problem-solving skills;

– utilize diverse learning environments and a broad array of educational approaches to teaching/learning about and from the environment with due stress on practical activities and first-hand experience.

Environmental Pollution Control

INTRODUCTORY ESSAY

The Information Gap

According to Baumol and Oates[1] the damage function that characterises a particular type of polluting activity may be of central importance in determining the policy instrument appropriate for its control. Pollutants have typically been divided into two general categories. The so-called *flow* pollutants present less intractable environmental problems since they are bio-degradable and the nature and extent of their damage is somewhat easier to chart. In developed countries the damages are usually (but not exclusively) confined to amenity losses (such as eutrophication) and "mild" health effects. In developing countries, however, flow pollutants present a serious health hazard. On the other hand, the *stock* pollutants are typically non-degradable (except in the very long term) and are much more difficult to track down, usually accumulating in the environment over time until a critical "threshold" level is attained and significant human health damages become apparent.

The exact form of the damage function is therefore very important. Many pollutants involve complex damage functions especially when synergistic (interactive) effects are present (which they often are). If major discontinuities in the damage functions or "threshold effects" can be determined then an ambient environmental quality standard could be based on such a level. Unfortunately, as we stressed in the essay in Section 2 little is yet known about the shape of these damage curves and abatement costs. Indeed the informational deficiencies are such that it is not yet possible empirically to derive the damage and abatement cost functions for a great many pollutants and therefore not possible to determine the economist's "Pareto optimal" level of pollution (as indicated in Figure 2.9). Burrows[2] states that the determination of the optimal pollution level "presumes a great deal of information, much of which is costly to obtain in reality and some of which, such as the ecological and psychic components of the damage function, may be unobtainable in money terms at any price".

The "Environmental Risk" Problem

Page[3] has recently pointed out that society now has to face a degree of "environmental risk" (often involving stock pollutants) which has increased rapidly in importance over recent decades. This type of problem is exemplified by "the risk of leakage and contamination in the disposal of nuclear wastes; the production of synthetic chemicals which may be toxic, carcinogenic, mutagenic, or teratogenic; the risk of ozone depletion due to fluorocarbon emissions by supersonic transports; and the danger presented by recombinant DNA of the creation and escape of a new disease against which mankind has no natural defence". Controlling the risks of toxic substances is especially difficult both because the exact nature of the hazard has yet to be fully recognised by regulatory authorities and becauses of certain characteristics displayed by such pollutants which make control by traditional policy instruments (some of which are reviewed below) fairly ineffective. According to Page these characteristics are: (a) a general lack of data on pollution generation, transfer functions and dose-response relationships (see Figure 2.10) but with the data deficiencies being probably most severe in this "risk" context identified by Page; (b) the potential for catastropic costs and relatively modest benefits in terms of the environmental risk gamble; (c) very great uncertainty surrounding the potential costs, benefits and probabilities; and finally (d) severe institutional problems created by the characteristics of collective risk-bearing (accepted by large numbers of people simultaneously), latency (the extended delay between the hazard occurrence and the manifestation of its damage effects), and irreversibility of effect. The essay in Section 3 reviewed the literature dealing with considerations such as the fair distributions of costs and risk over time (intergenerational equity) and the ethical and institutional implications which are raised because of latency and irreversibility characteristics. In this essay where we are principally concerned with the management of pollution and environmental risk we should note Page's call for the redesign of pollution-management institutions. The redesign is necessary, he argues, in order to be able to anticipate adverse effects rather than merely to react to existing, known effects.

"Acceptable" Ambient Quality Standards and Environmental Risk

Despite the dimensions of the quantification problem and the shortage of good empirical data evident in cases of both flow and stock pollution flows, it is clear that in practice some kind of exogenously determined "acceptable" environmental quality standards have to be set either explicitly or implicitly as a "second-best" alternative to the unknown optimal standard. The objective of the policymaker when dealing with the more familiar pollution problem (involving flow pollutants) would probably be to maintain average level of ambient quality for most of the time. One should seek to avoid letting ambient quality fall below the minimum threshold level (if known) where a discontinuity in the damage function occurs and where consequently damage costs escalate rapidly.

In the context of environmental risk problems, however, policymakers must decide what degree of risk is acceptable. Frankel[4] has summarised the procedures used (and their limitations) in the UK to set acceptable — in official terminology "practicable" — standards for toxic substances as well as for the more traditional air and water pollutants. He stresses that no toxic substance can ever be produced to completely "safe" levels, that much experimental evidence is subject to wide margins of statistical error which is not always taken into account, and that some experiments have only been conducted on animals under laboratory conditions and therefore may not be relevant for humans in a variety of circumstances. The UK Council for Science and Society[5] has also produced a critique of the UK approach to risk management. The Council argues when weighing acceptable risk against the anticipated benefits from new technologies "that while scientific methods and scientific rigours are essential for proper analysis of risk, the human factor is always present and must be respected and utilised in all analysis, decisions and controls, for risks to be genuinely acceptable to the people concerned".

Page[6] notes that the legal and regulatory methods that have been developed to manage the more familiar pollution problems are inadequate for the management of environmental risks because they are based on what he terms the "limiting of false positives"—i.e. starting with the assumption that there is no risk, since for a hazard to exist, it has to be proved beyond some standard. It follows therefore that if that standard of proof is not met, then the risk is acceptable. What worries Page is that under this procedure sometimes the distinction between the failure to find an effect and the finding of no effect is ignored and hence the latter case can be interpreted as the non-existence of an effect (the "fallacy of false negative"). For example, suppose a certain dose of a chemical caused cancer in 0.1 percent of people exposed to it. Cancer would then be expected in one out of every 1000 animals or persons exposed. But in statistical terms many thousands of subjects must be exposed before this relationship is proven: if no animal (person) appears affected out of a thousand exposed, to say that there is "no effect" is preposterous.

The implication here is that efforts should be made to limit "false negatives" as much as possible in the decision-making process assuming that is, that society really wants to reduce involuntary exposure to toxic substances, and is prepared to pay in terms of more expensive products and very costly and time-consuming regulation. It is now estimated that up to 25 percent of the research and development cost of a modern pesticide is devoted to limiting toxic hazard, while in the US, the Toxic Substances Control Act requires that every chemical known to be potentially dangerous (and this could be 30,000 formulations) must undergo exhaustive tests before each is pronounced safe. This exercise could cost well over $1 billion. Despite these costs, there is now a much more precautionary approach towards environmental risks and the consequent setting of a lower level of "acceptable" risk. Page nevertheless recognises that in reality "for many environmental risks it is difficult to define a candidate which might or might not become a false negative, much less to design an institutional structure which would take the chance of a false negative into account as well as the chance of a false positive". Thus caution may not necessarily lead to safety.

Because the benefits of pollution control (savings in health costs, damage to property and the environment generally) cannot be quantified accurately, society has to set the level of "acceptable" risk in relation to the likely costs involved in reducing hazard. It follows that there is no such absolute as "acceptable" risk since as more scientific and medical information becomes available, and the public become less willing to tolerate harm, so acceptable exposure to risk is altered. For example, in 1925 the permitted dose of ionizing radiation for workers was 52 rems per year (a rem is a measure of the intensity and quality of radiation per area of tissue exposed). This has fallen steadily to 36 rems in 1934, 15 in 1950 to the present allowable level of 5 rems per year. The permitted dose to the public has undergone a similar decline from 1.5 rems per person per year in 1952 to 0.5 rem per person per year today. However, there is plenty of evidence to suggest that even these levels are too high if society really is serious about eliminating involuntary exposure to cancer.[7]

The problem of setting acceptable levels of risk is twofold. One relates to the question of whom to believe. In the past scientists were regarded as experts and the repository of truth. Now it is recognised that scientific analysis cannot be separated from a set of values which determine not only how experiments are conducted but also how scientific evidence should be interpreted. So there are equally respectable scientists who dispute not only each other's findings but the implication of their analyses for public health and safety. This means that the politician, or more precisely his regulatory adviser, is placed in a more vulnerable position when setting acceptable standards, for usually he likes to be guided by clear-cut scientific advice.

The related problem is how far to take this debate out to the public. In most European countries (including the UK) the custom has been to leave this matter to scientific advisory committees composed of distinguished experts well known for their impartiality and knowledge of the subject under discussion. This is now regarded by many environmentalists as an unsatisfactory arrangement because "impartiality" requires public accountability. So the pressure is on to bring the whole matter of acceptable risk into the democratic arena of adversary politics and reasoned discussion. On the face of it this appears to be a very reasonable request, but in practice too much democracy could make matters worse, since compromise may just not be possible. Behind much of the dispute is a major schism of values about the kind of society that is desirable, the use of synthetic products, the dependence on regulation and expertise, matters that simply cannot be resolved by numbers. As we have stressed a number of times before in this book, the challenge here is to improve political institutions for allowing this debate to be opened up so that these deeper values are more fully thrashed out and proponents on both sides shown to be accountable for the full implication of their demands. Standards requiring zero levels of toxic emissions are economic nonsense and may be medically unnecessary.

Meanwhile what is "acceptable" is often defined not by medical science but by what can be afforded by industry. For example, after many disclosures that many workers associated with asbestos were dying or suffering the agonies of asbestosis, the UK government set up an Asbestos Advisory Committee in 1976. This Committee reported that the levels to which workers should legally be exposed should be cut by half (from 2 million to 1 million fibres of chrysolite (white) asbestos per cubic meter and for 1 million to 0.5 million fibres of amosite (brown) asbestos per cubic meter) over a period of 18 months.[8] These figures are over twice the levels believed safe by the trades unions involved, but the Asbestos Information Centre, the public relations part of the asbestos industry, claims that the industry "cannot afford" to meet higher standards. Yet the Advisory Committee regards these levels as maximum tolerable rather than acceptable.*

Risk management basically involves four phases, which by necessity are closely related. Scientific expertise (value judgments included) is necessary to identify and monitor specific pollutants and hazards, while a combination of political and scientific judgement is required to evaluate these risks (as already discussed) to weigh up the ramifications of setting particular standards for different groups of people and hence to set guidelines for actual regulation, including enforcement and prosecution. Generally speaking, research and information is well developed in the first two phases, but institutions and analysis are still ill-equipped for the latter two phases. This bias is in part the cause of the

* In 1982 the asbestos issue, like the lead-in-petrol issue blew up into a major political controversy in the UK.

present tension because judgemental institutions have not yet learnt to wrest themselves totally from the confinement of expertise.

Pollution-control Policy Instruments

The general aim of pollution-control policy is, by a number of alternative means, to induce residuals dischargers to implement residuals reduction and/or modification (including recycling programmes) activities. It has been pointed out that these incentives can be both positive or negative, direct or indirect, prescriptive or proscriptive.[9] The practical policy problem is which of a range of policy instruments available will provide the best means of attaining some given "acceptable" ambient quality standard for most of the time. To operate efficiently all the devices that have at one time or another been proposed require complete information about the costs and benefits of pollution abatement and damage. Further, they all involve *transactions costs*, which include data collection costs, costs of establishing bargaining positions and administrative and enforcement costs. It has become clear, as Marin[10] has admirably demonstrated specifically in the case of sulphur dioxide pollution in the UK, that no one approach to pollution control is likely to provide a panacea. Roberts[11] surveys the available instruments and presents a list of criteria by which any can be evaluated. Ideally the policymaker will need to adopt a politically feasible pollution control strategy that minimises transactions costs; is reliable, efficient and flexible; and takes into account distributional equity and environmental risk aversion. Roberts rejects the "economic optimum solution" approach as a useful way of portraying the problem. Rather he argues "we are simply trying to discover and arrive at a set of arrangements which make enough people better off to make those conditions preferable to current circumstances". The structure of the decision process is then a "satisfising" rather than a maximising one.

Now the effect of any particular incentive or set of incentive instruments will depend on their location in the economic system. In Figure 9.1 we present the partial materials balance model including the throughput flows in a simple economic system and additionally some possible incentive measures and their location with the system. We will now outline briefly the main policy instruments that have either been used in an operational setting or that have been suggested in the academic literature.

Market Solutions

The basic idea underlying the market approach is that no public (government) intervention is necessary for a large class of pollution

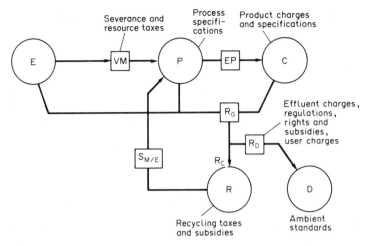

FIGURE 9.1

A partial materials balance model. This diagram illustrates the processes of raw material extraction, processing, manufacture, and consumption and the points where various policy instruments to discourage waste and encourage product longevity and materials recycling could be introduced.

problems. The free play of the market mechanism can be relied upon to regulate any externalities. The Coase Theorem[12] seeks to show that under certain conditions and given certain assumptions it is possible to achieve an efficient pattern of resource use through private negotiation between affected parties that internalises all social costs and benefits. The implication of the analysis is that many pollution problems are best left to negotiation among the affected parties with no government intervention. Nevertheless, efficient negotiation does require the existence of a defined and rigidly enforced system of property rights including some liability law for damages associated with any externalities.

Randall[13] illustrates two extreme cases. The first is the case of an L^z or zero liability rule—negative externalities carry no liability and thus affected parties have an incentive to *bribe* the acting party to abate his output of the externality. Mishan[14] has contended that current Anglo-

Saxon law is, in general, the L^z type law which he terms "permissive"; thus it would seem that although in principle at common law all individuals have the right to a clean environment, these rights are relative not absolute rights, with the one exception of riparian owner rights.[15] The second is the case of an L^f or full liability law—no negative externalities without the consent of the affected party. Mishan[16] has proposed an "amenity charter" for all citizens which can be encapsulated in the phrase "no pollution without compensation". Here the onus rests with the polluter not to damage the well-being of the polluted without satisfactory compensation, as opposed to the L^z case where the burden of proof rests with the victim of the pollution.

In practical terms Mishan is correct in observing that the L^z rule applies, for it will readily be appreciated that unless a pollution damage is serious or of such a nature as to be noxious to a number of people, it is unlikely that polluted parties will organise themselves to protest or take legal action. Neither industry nor statutory authorities (e.g. the regional water authorities responsible for sewage-treatment works) would ever contemplate the L^f state, since this would open them up to all manner of prosecutions and claims for damage which they could not possibly meet. Unless, of course, the courts applied the "reasonableness test"[17] in which case the rulings would not differ much for those if the L^z rule applied.

According to the Coase analysis, the allocation of resources is the same when there is no liability for damage as it is when the polluter is liable for the damage inflicted on others, if the parties concerned (sufferer and polluter) can bargain costlessly, i.e. with no transactions costs, and if they behave competitively. If these assumptions of perfect competition and zero transactions costs are accepted then it is irrelevant whether an L^z or L^f rule operates and negative externalities would be modified by private negotiation. Critics of the theorem have pointed, however, to the unreality of the world assumed to exist in the Coasian model and also question the theory itself. On the former grounds Coase's analysis is relevant for producer-to-producer externality situations where because of the small numbers involved (in Coase's examples only two parties are involved) transactions costs are low. Many real world externality problems involve large diffuse groups of consumers and single or small groups of large-scale polluters with consequent prohibitively high transactions costs. In a survey of the "anti-Coase" literature Dick[18] concludes that: "it cannot realistically be maintained that there are both large numbers and zero transactions costs; nor can it be maintained with any more realism that there are both small numbers and competitive behaviour. While Coase is aware of the first limitation, he proceeds as if he is not aware of the second." Even in the case of only two bargainers, the outcome of the negotiations is likely to be indeterminate and only optimal by chance. There is also the distinct possibility of the use of threats which can distort a "free" bargaining outcome. Since to be effective the bargainers would not wish to disclose to the "opposition" what their actual bargaining limits are there is every incentive to use threatening behaviour at the start of negotiations. With threats there is no guarantee that the outcome of the negotiations will be optimal.

Even on theoretical grounds in some cases it does matter (as Randall[19] shows) which liability rule is in operation. He argues that because of income effects the L^f rule will result in a higher degree of pollution abatement than the L^z rule. It is also questionable whether the ethical neutrality implied by the Coase analysis is acceptable. To the Coasians it makes no sense to separate polluter and victim for the situation is reciprocal. But one could argue why should a polluter increase his welfare because he happened to be in a position to place involuntary burdens on others. Further, should we ignore the timing element if the pollution sufferers were the inhabitants of a particular area before the arrival of a pollution source.

The Status of Common Law and Pollution Control

Common law is the body of case law defined by rulings in the courts based upon the evidence from particular cases, as opposed to statutory law which is determined by parliamentary legislation. As we have already indicated there is really no common law relation to environmental quality: ordinary citizens have no absolute rights to peace and quiet or pure air or clean water, nor (at present) do they have any legal access to the courts to pursue such a right. This is a complicated matter so let us be a little more specific. When someone owns property, such as a house or a farm or a factory, and damage caused by a pollution discharge harms either his person or his business or his well-being, then he does have a case at common law to take proceedings against the polluter so long as he can be sure that the defendant can be identified, that his discharge did undoubtedly cause injury and that he (the plaintiff) suffered harm that was unreasonable even though shared by society at large. Such a prosecution can proceed even where the polluter was meeting his statutory obligations as, say, laid down by regulations associated with various pollution-control acts.

However, where the individual suffers harm when he is not on his own property, but on common property (in the street, a wilderness area, etc.) and where the nuisance is suffered by many, then there is normally no privately-initiated legal recourse unless the source of the trouble can be shown to have exceeded statutory regulations. This of course requires careful monitoring over a long period of time, for many regulations permit some flexibility in individual discharges so long as a statistically derived mean discharge is not exceeded. We emphasise the adjective legal, because there is always the avenue of complaint to the regulatory body (the local district environmental health department, the Alkali or Factory Inspectorates, the regional water authorities, etc.). And, if a person is dissatisfied with the way these officials handle or appear to be handling his complaint, he can always take political action and press his local councillor, or MP. The point here, however, is that while legal action is based on an accepted premise of rights and duties which are clearly defined and (in theory at least) independent of the political or social status of plaintiff and defendant, complaints to administrators or politicans are effective according to their perceived legitimacy or political respectability. Rights and wrongs may therefore be interpreted differently.

A number of lawyers[20] have advocated an L^f arrangement where there are definable rights to certain democratically determined levels of environmental quality which would not only allow individuals to prosecute polluters in their own right but would permit them to take action against regulators if they were in dereliction of their statutory duties. This arrangement, for example, does now exist in the US State of Michigan where it seems to have been used by regulatory agencies with much effect when prosecuting offenders. Far from encouraging a large number of "frivolous" prosecutions, the Michigan Environmental Protection Act seems to have given new life to the regulatory officials who now have the threat of citizen-initiated prosecution to aid their bargaining position with polluters. Nevertheless, a general common law right to environmental quality is viewed with suspicion even in the US, where the law is a far more effective weapon in the politics of environment than it is in Europe. This caution is partly due to the fear that it could open up a Pandora's box of prosecutions for liability and compensation across a wide range of third parties which might cripple polluters financially, but it is also due to the belief that regulatory agencies are really the only competent authorities to deal with pollution and related damage. In general they have the tools, the expertise, the experience and the residual authority: to place pollution control in the hands of the law could well lead to a state where the courts become the arbiters of public health and safety.

Such an arrangement would be inconceivable in the UK where the courts are generally subservient to Parliament, where the law is couched in vague and discretionary terms and where there is still a presumption of administrative expertise. Nevertheless the system is by no means perfect, and there are growing doubts about the wisdom of leaving what in part are political judgements to cabals of scientists and administrators who are closely advised by the very organisations they are supposed to regulate. This is a matter we have raised a number of times already: so we leave it to a very distinguished lawyer, Lord Justice Scarman, to outline his views.

A number of writers have examined the question of damage liability placement and its use as a pollution-control policy tool. Ogus and Richardson[21] have presented an analysis of the efficacy of the nuisance action (private and public) as an instrument of pollution control. In terms of private property rights, actionable pollution can be defined as any adverse change in the environment which the purchaser might not reasonably anticipate when he buys his interest in land. The traditional private action can both compensate victims (by obtaining damages in tort) and enforce environmental quality standards by an injunction. Roberts[22] points out, however, that all proposals to use liability rules and damage suits either as a substitute for possibly protracted bargaining processes or in order to stimulate a bargaining process suffer from several deficiencies. In the first place it appears to be very difficult to encompass aesthetic and ideological benefits by such a process. Ogus and Richardson also note that English law has persistently refused to condemn aesthetic nuisances, that is visual intrusion or eyesores. Secondly, the plaintiff in English law must prove interference with the enjoyment of his interest. In cases of physical damage proof of actual damage is not always required but as far as amenity damages are concerned the plaintiff must "prove" that the defendant's activities have inflicted harm on the plaintiff and therefore constitute an unreasonable use of his land. This is clearly not an easy task if the damage is more of a psychological kind than something that can medically or financially be assessed. In amenity damage cases English courts have limited themselves only to the rather crude "neighbourhood test". The plaintiff must expect only environmental quality standards considered appropriate for his particular neighbourhood. Thus what would be a nuisance in, say, Kensington, would not necessarily be so in, say, a working-class district of Preston. In Britain, the common law of pollution reflects social class, and, by implication, the inequalities enshrined in the current distribution of nuisance.

Ogus and Richardson's[23] primary conclusion is that the nuisance action can play at least only a subsidiary role in any system of pollution control having as its objective general social welfare. They present three main reasons for this conclusion.

"The first is the principle of justice which postulates that existing property rights must be protected even where the result will impose greater costs on society at large. The second is the private law's limited ability to deal with generally inferior environmental conditions, both because it can intervene only where there has been a perceptible change (damage) and because the system of control presupposes an interest in neighbouring land. Finally, enforcement of standards created by the private law is likely to be only selective. The system assumes that holders of property rights will be aware of their entitlement and will be willing and able to enter into appropriate market transactions to secure the necessary protection."

Effluent charges and user charges

Section 52 of the UK Control of Pollution Act provides for the charging of effluent discharged directly to rivers and coastal waters. This section basically applies to sewage and trade waste discharges similar rules as are now applied to other water services as legislated in Sections 29–31 of the Water Act, 1973. Under Section 29 of that Act all water authorities now have a duty "to discharge their functions so as to secure that, taking one year with another, their revenue is not less than sufficient to meet their total outgoings properly chargeable to revenue account". In short, water authorities are expected to charge users for services rendered so as to recover costs of providing that service including, at least, costs of debt financing. There is some doubt whether water authorities can also charge for interest payments on capital expenditures designed to improve their service in the future.[24] Nevertheless this discussion is somewhat academic as Section 52 has not formally been ratified as law nor does it appear likely that it will become law in the foreseeable future as there continues to be much opposition from industrial interests. However, effluent charging systems have been operating in a number of European countries since the 1960s and have been analysed at some length in the academic literature.[25]

In principle an effluent charge is a financial obligation imposed on a residuals discharger, the size of the charge varying with the marginal damage costs inflicted on the environment by the effluent. This device should, therefore, not be confused with the so-called *user charge* approach which is widely used in industrial countries. Industrial dischargers in the UK have to pay what is known as a trade effluent charge for the discharge of residuals into the foul sewer system for treatment by water authority-owned sewage works. This particular user charge is based on a generalised "average" cost for treating all effluent (domestic and trade) in a region. The formula that is applied is known as the Mogden formula, namely

$$A + B + \frac{MC}{M_1} + \frac{SD}{S_1}$$

where A = average costs of receiving all effluent into the sewerage system (per 100 litres),

B = average cost of primary treatment (per 1000 litres),

C = average cost of secondary and biological treatment (per 1000 litres),

D = average cost of the treatment and disposal of sludge (per 100 litres),

M = the strength of the settled trade effluent,

M_1 = the mean strength of all settled sewage,

S = the suspended solids content of the trade effluent in milligrams per litre,

S_1 = the mean suspended solids content of all sewage also in milligrams per litre.

The interpretation of the formula by each RWA is, however, not very consistent. A number of criticisms have been levelled at this approach. To begin with there is too much emphasis upon average costs across a region and the charge itself is based on historic cost accounting (based on capital costs and inherent payments made in the past, not necessarily being made currently, and certainly not based on future investments). Ideally the charge should be based on current cost accounting as implied by Sections 29–31 of the 1973 Water Act, but there would have to be a fairly long period of transition before this arrangement was attained because of the severe distortions placed on individual dischargers that reflect averaging. In short, a current cost accounting scheme would mean that dischargers would have to pay in proportion to the demands they make to sewerage provision and sewage treatment: at present there is much cross-discharger subsidisation. A related criticism is that the costs of treating sewage do not vary linearly with the quantity of flow received. Though there is as yet little hard evidence, the cost curve may have a number of thresholds on it depending on what else is in the sewer pipe and the variability of the total flow. This relationship needs to be looked at much more carefully if Sections 29–31 of the Water Act (and eventually Section 52 of the Control of Pollution Act) are really to be observed. As things stand now, some dischargers undoubtedly pay more than they should (and therefore may invest in costly on-site removal facilities) while others are subsidised and should pay more.

Baumol and Oates[26] have proposed a scheme whereby all plants (assumed to be cost minimisers) discharging residuals into, say, a watercourse would be charged at a rate of $t(b)$ pence per gallon, where t is the charge rate and b might represent the Biological Oxygen Demand (BOD) or Chemical Oxygen Demand (COD) value of the residuals. The charge provides a stimulus to the plants in question to search for the least-cost (in terms of the costs and benefits perceived) combination of pollution-abatement measures (including recycling) and charge payments. Each firm would thus seek to reduce residuals discharges up to the point where the marginal cost of the pollution-control measures undertaken just equals the charge. The charging system, being flexible, should be able to take into account the variety of abatement costs faced by different firms.

There is, however, a problem of setting the correct initial charge, sufficient to reach the predetermined ambient quality standard required in the particular watercourse in question. Baumol and Oates believe that initially the charge should be set at a relatively low level and subsequently raised until the general water quality was regarded as satisfactory. They and other economists claim that the charging mechanism provides the least-cost method (in terms of transactions costs) of attaining a "given" ambient quality standard and that it has the added advantage of exerting continuous pressure of the residuals discharger to improve his abatement technology.

A number of criticisms of the effluent-charge approach have been put forward. Most of these concern not the theory itself but the reality of the assumptions upon which the theory is based and its subsequent practicability. The implications of the trial-and-error iterative charge adjustment process suggested for the charging scheme has stimulated considerable debate. Baumol and Oates make the intuitive judgement that the information necessary for the adjustment process would be easy to obtain and that experience would soon permit the authorities to estimate the appropriate charge levels. Orr,[27] however, cites other writers who argue that the iterative process could lead to the very sort of protracted bargaining problems from which effluent charges are supposed to provide an escape. Burrows[28] has argued that as the process of installing abatement capital is only reversible at a cost and technological "lock-in" effect is likely to occur. If firms get locked into expensive and "lumpy" abatement investment they cannot respond efficiently unless the changes in the charge are very great and then the response could well be very inefficient. His argument illustrated in Figure 9.2 where it can be seen that a firm may be forced to adopt a partial abatement technology early on, rather than a more comprehensive abatement scheme (often allied to a change in production technology generally) which, though initially expensive, would prove a better investment as charges were raised. Firms require very long warning periods of price changes before lumpy investments are regarded as practicable, particularly so when pollution-control facilities (which are not normally profit-creating) are involved. Walker and Storey[29] support this point by noting that there are likely to be serious adjustment cost and time-lag problems connected with the iteration procedure. Any charge system would have to be enforced for at least 3 to 5 years (or more) before one could hope to observe the equilibrium response.

Mäler[30] has also commented that a charge might not work efficiently where the aggregate marginal cost of abatement curve is "flat" in a region around the desired quality standard. Indeed Dorcey[31] has collected some empirical evidence to suggest that this may be a real problem in municipal sewage treatment and in the pulp and paper industry. In both these cases average residuals treatment cost functions appear to be remarkably insensitive to price over a wide range. Dorcey concludes that, given this evidence, it would be difficult for pollution-control authorities to use a charging device without resort to bargaining with each firm involved. He suggests that this could reflect the transactions costs already referred to, but rarely considered in the effluent charge literature, and that the onus of proof (i.e. the cost of providing the evidence) should rest with the polluter to show why a particular charge should be lowered.

Work carried out at Resources For The Future[32] has included surveys of the technical and economic options for residuals discharge reduction which are theoretically available for selected industries. The studies have paid particular attention to the response that assumed cost-minimising plants would make to effluent charges. In the petroleum-refining study model airborne residuals, because they often required costly process changes, were difficult to modify through the charging mechanism. Waterborne residuals, on the other hand, could apparently be significantly reduced through the imposition of a charge. But one should not forget that these are theoretical models and not observations of actual responses by polluters. The assumption of cost minimisation in the charging model is open to criticism. Other economic schools of thought believe that sales revenue maximisation or "satisfising" criteria are more representative of actual industrial decision-making strategy. Storey[33] concludes that some firms starved of investment funds (especially during periods of high interest rates) will tend to under-invest in pollution abatement and pay higher charges out of current cost budgets (which are easier for their management boards to accept) rather than face boardroom hostility toward proposals for long-term capital financing of major pollution-control facilities and pay lower (current account) charges. However, where credit is easy and the water authorities appear to want far higher user charges, clearly it makes sense to invest in capital equipment.

It is thus no wonder that British industry want nothing to do with charges for direct emissions into UK watercourses. They regard this as a waste of money since they believe that the license to discharge (which in effect is the result of a negotiated settlement between polluter and regulator) should result in an effluent that does no real damage. In short, firms believe that they meet their consent (license) conditions, there is no pollution, and hence no charge should be levied. In practice, of course, there is pollution, even though much of it may be of a fairly benign kind in terms of human health. Nevertheless most of the lower stretches of UK rivers and all her industrial estuaries are recognised officially as grossly or severely polluted, though this is mainly of a kind that does not damage seriously either human health or, where there is any recreational use, aesthetic enjoyment. The consequences to aquatic life, including fish, may be quite severe and these losses are not reflected in pollution-abatement costs.

The Baumol and Oates charging model also assumes that the location of the residuals discharge is not important and thus that there are no variations in the assimilative capacity of the receiving water. This is a most unrealistic assumption as the dilution capacity of waterbodies does vary, particularly in estuaries. The level of pollution abatement correspondingly varies with location. A varying schedule of charges rather than a single regionwide charge will of course mean increased transactions costs. In addition, Russell and Vaughan[34] point out that in the real world marginal abatement cost curves may exhibit a number of discontinuities, depending on the residual discharged and the number of abatement options available for its removal. If technological options are limited some kind of emission regulation as opposed to a charge may well prove to be the more precise control mechanism.

We have tried to show that even at the theoretical level the choice between an effluent charge or standards (regulatory) approach to pollution control is far from clear cut. Actual charging systems are much simpler constructions than the textbook versions. The number of pollutants included is small (varying from two to four in the French, Dutch or German systems) and the pollution per unit of output is assumed constant for each firm in each major industry. While empirically these charging systems are not obviously superior in any significant respect to actual effluent standard systems, they do have the advantage of resulting in a fund which can be used by the more imaginative authorities to finance regional waste-disposal facilities and compensate victims who suffer for no fault of their own.

Pollution Rights

A policy option that, in principle, seems to combine some of the desirable features of both the effluent charges and standards approaches involves the creation of new artificial markets in transferable residuals discharge rights. Dales[35] has suggested that a pollution-control board could establish an "acceptable" standard for the total residuals emissions into a watercourse or airshed. The board would then issue "dumping rights" that would allow the owners of such rights to discharge a certain amount of residuals over a given period of time. The rights would be saleable commodities on an open market, but the total number of rights available would be determined by the level of total residuals discharge to be allowed, which in turn would be a function of the assimilative capacity of the particular airshed or watershed in question.

Marr[36] has modified the original rights model in order to increase its general applicability. In Marr's scheme the right has a spatial dimension. Discharge is only possible at specified locations along, say, a river. The rights itself is also defined in terms of changes in water quality rather than allowable amount of discharge. He argues that the transferable nature of the rights lessens the possibility of an inefficient allocation of residuals-abatement effort. The voluntary transactions that will be stimulated will thus tend to minimise control costs so that only firms faced with relatively expensive abatement procedures would find it in their interests to purchase rights. The transferability characteristic also enables the system to cope with economic growth. New residuals dischargers could buy a share of the existing stock of permits thereby increasing the general price level and providing an extra incentive to all dischargers to institute process and/or product changes or recycling measures. The rights option is, of course, not without its drawbacks. Some writers believe the costs of administering the scheme would be prohibitive,[37] others stress the difficulties of calculating the so-called dose–response relationship, linking discharges to ambient concentrations. Marr himself notes that enforcement costs could be high and the likelihood of legal challenges to pollution board fines very great.

For any pollution discharge-rights scheme to work relatively efficiently (i.e. for it to provide a superior control system to the conventional standard setting approach or possibly a charging arrangement) two basic conditions need to be met. First, there must be enough residuals dischargers present to enable the artificial market to function smoothly while not numerically overloading the system and forcing up administration costs. Second, the kind of discharges and the nature of the watercourse (or airshed) should be such that by using only a small number of different kinds of rights certificates (for different residuals) it is still possible to approach the required ambient standard.

In the reading below, Ackerman[38] presents a detailed examination of the rights option and concludes that it could fit into the current regulatory US pollution control strategy with the minimum of difficulties. The US Clean Air Amendments of 1970 gave the US Environmental Protection Agency (EPA) the responsibility of setting ambient air-quality standards which individual states had to meet by no later than 1977. These standards were of two kinds: national primary standards to protect public health, and national secondary standards to safeguard the public welfare from any unknown or anticipated adverse effects. In 1977, however, most states had still failed to meet at least one of these two standards, the legal implication being that no new industrial growth could be permitted in these "non-attainment" areas. The EPA responded by introducing an "emission offset policy" which allows new plants to locate in a non-attainment area provided that its residuals emissions are more than offset by concurrent emissions reductions from other plants in the same airshed. The new emission source also has to meet some additional conditions that ensure it operates with the lowest achievable emission rate and that there will be a positive net air-quality benefit in the area due to the arrival of the new plant. In other words, the emission reductions achieved must exceed the emissions resulting from the new source.

Yandle[39] discusses the Sohio Oil and other cases where negotiations between polluters on the transfer of emission rights are involved. Yandle argues that there is evidence in the US of an embryonic but perhaps persistent air-pollution rights market. Standard Oil of Ohio (Sohio) had been seeking permission to build a pipeline terminal near Long Beach, California, in order to bring Alaskan Slope oil to the US market. The California state legislature blocked the move, on the grounds that increases in hydrocarbons, sulphur dioxide and suspended particulates would result in aggregate levels of these pollutants that exceeded the primary standards set for the region. Sohio then offered to purchase an old plant in the area, close it, and build the new (cleaner) pipeline terminal. The oil company began to look for offsets for hydrocarbons, sulphur dioxide and other residuals that the proposed terminal would generate. In August 1978 Sohio undertook to pay up to $78million towards the cost of constructing and operating air-pollution-control facilities at an electricity generating plant in Long Beach. Sohio has been instructed to work on an offset ratio of 2 to 1 exchange on sulphur dioxide and a ratio of 7·2 to 1 for hydrocarbons.

The pollution-rights approach could be accommodated into proposals for changes in water-quality now being considered in Britain. At present the regional water authorities (RWAs) issue consents (licences) to each discharger representing a permit to emit a certain quantity and quality of effluent directly into a watercourse. In general the consent is tailored to suit the particular circumstances of the firm, other discharges in the region and the level of pollution already present. The actual negotiations leading up to agreement over a consent are normally confidential and not even a neighbouring landowner is privy to the consultations, though he may have a right to object. For a long time there have been criticisms of the undue secrecy involved in all of this and consequently suspicion that both the polluter and the regulator may have something to hide. Nevertheless, before the passage of the 1974 Control of Pollution Act, strict penalties were available if pollution-control officers divulged any information about a particular discharge (either as to the consent granted or to actual flows) without the permission of the polluter. Indeed, these fines were greater than the penalties for contravention of the consent conditions.

Under Section 41 of the 1974 Control of Pollution Act, RWAs must make public a register of all consents and actually monitored discharges for direct emissions into the watercourses under their jurisdiction. In practice this section has yet to be implemented, and in the late 1970s hostility to "unnecessary public spending" this provision could be delayed until well into the 1980s.* However, when it does become law it will make it possible for the first time for an interested citizen (either a landowner or an environmental group) to prosecute a discharger where his actual emission was exceeding his consent. It is well known that in practice many consents are being exceeded, the most serious offenders being the RWAs themselves who operate all sewage-treatment works,[40] many of which are overloaded and ill-maintained. So the RWAs, faced with the threat of prosecution, and badgered by industry anxious not to be penalised, considered two options. One was simply to vary the consents, which legally they are able to do; in effect to lower them so as to match them with existing discharge practice. This is their short-term strategy but one that is fiercely criticised by environmental groups as an indication of failure. To quote a statement from the Committee on Environmental Conservation[41]: "at best the proposed review is no more than a cosmetic exercise, and at worst it will lead to a lowering of standards. The best rivers will not measurably improve; the worst will remain as chemical conduits."

The longer-term strategy is to relate discharge consents to receiving water-assimilative capacity. The RWAs are now in the process of devising "river quality objectives" (RQOs), namely targets of watercourses quality that should shape pollution-control policy in the future. In practice the RQOs should help the authorities to stave off threats of public prosecution for they will be regarded as long-term objectives that need not be met at any particular time. This will get the RWAs off the hook as it were for at present they simply cannot afford to upgrade all sewage-treatment works to an acceptable standard, public expenditure ceilings being what they are.

However the RQO could be a very exciting innovation in pollution control in the UK for it could be used to relate planning to water-quality management (see Figures 9.2 and 9.3). Generally speaking at present planners grant permission for development and pollution control officers seek to obtain the best consent for discharge reasonably attainable through negotiation. If RQOs become established, then it may be possible for pollution-control officials to work more closely with planners before the final locations of actual discharges are decided upon and for them to insist on the best practical means for waste disposal. It is also possible that planners and pollution-control officers would co-operate in the "offset" arrangement already described as working in the US, where much needed, but polluting industry could be encouraged not only to adopt the best available pollution-control technology, but also to improve the waste discharge of another emitter in the watercourse (or

*It will come into force in stages between 1982 and 1986.

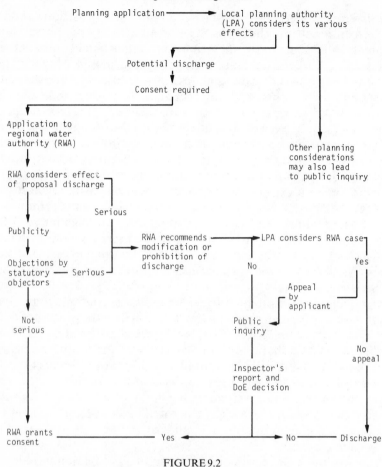

FIGURE 9.2

The relationship between planning and water-pollution control. This diagram simplifies the consultative procedures that are supposed to operate when a local planning authority considered a planning application that could result in a polluting discharge. Only very rarely does a planning inquiry involve discussion of a proposed discharge: mostly it deals with matters of amenity and community impact.

watershed zone) so as to retain the RQOs where otherwise it would be breached.

Unfortunately, it is most unlikely that this imaginative and potentially very efficient (in economic terms) arrangement will become widespread practice in Britain despite the availability of RQOs. To begin with, the concept of genuine economic efficiency is still not at all well developed in pollution-control practice, and the idea of firms helping each other to clean up is too novel to be acceptable to dischargers. In any case, it is not at all clear how effective the RQOs will be. The idea in principle is for them to reflect the desirable mix of uses for the watercourse: if

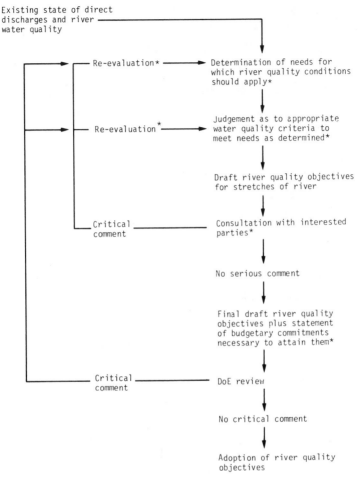

Existing state of direct
discharges and river
water quality

Re-evaluation* ————→ Determination of needs for
which river quality conditions
should apply*

Re-evaluation* ————→ Judgement as to appropriate
water quality criteria to
meet needs as determined*

Draft river quality objectives
for stretches of river

Critical ———————— Consultation with interested
comment   parties*

No serious comment

Final draft river quality
objectives plus statement
of budgetary commitments
necessary to attain them*

Critical ———————— DoE review
comment

No critical comment

Adoption of river quality
objectives

FIGURE 9.3

Setting water-quality objectives and public consultation. This diagram illustrates the consultative procedures which are supposed to be followed by water authorities when determining river quality objectives. The * marks points where planning and water-quality management should be closely coordinated.

high amenity is required, for example, then all emissions should have any nutrients that might lead to eutropic enrichment stripped away, otherwise the waterbody will become polluted with algae that will give it an unappealing murky appearance and most of the interesting large-leaved water plants which harbour insects such as mayfly and dragonfly will disappear. In practice, however, shortage of cash, the need to protect jobs, and the overwhelming desire to keep Britain's balance of payments deficit to a minimum will probably mean that any RQO that could affect industrial performance and location will be lowered. If this is the case, then the possibility of attaching a pollution-rights policy to regional planning procedures will be lost.[42]

Pollution-abatement subsidies

Another approach to pollution abatement is to help dischargers to construct appropriate treatment facilities through subsidies such as grants, and low-interest loans on tax concessions. This policy approach has often been criticised on the grounds that it would make it profitable for a firm to pollute more than it might otherwise have done, in order to qualify for a larger subsidy. Nevertheless, a large number of countries operate some kind of subsidy programme.[43] In practice it is often very difficult to disentangle pollution-abatement subsidies from a host of other subsidies (for locating in depressed areas, taking on additional labour, investing in particular kinds of production lines) some of which mean an alteration of manufacturing processes (or the encouragement of linked industries that utilise the by-product of a parent industry) which in turn lead to overall pollution abatement. It must not be forgotten that however much environmentalists may moan, pollution control is still subservient to growth and regional economic development. So it may be necessary to subsidise a firm's pollution-control facilities just to help it stay in an area rather than shut down or locate in an area where pollution regulations are less strict. The troublesome issue here is to be sure that a firm which is threatening to close really means it, and really can prove that no cost-effective abatement technology is available. Some subsidiaries of multinational firms have an annoying habit of exploiting the relative ignorance of local pollution-control authorities over such matters. However, deployed effectively, subsidies can help pollution-control effects: in Scandinavia, for example, selective subsidies (in the pulp industry) have resulted in increased research and development in pollution-abatement technology.

Recycling Taxes and Subsidies

Anderson and Spiegleman[44] have documented a number of legislative proposals containing specific measures designed to encourage increased levels of recycling (which in general, though not in every case, can be regarded as an overall reduction in pollution[45]) that have come before the US Congress in recent years. A scheme to grant investment tax credits for the purchase of equipment to recycle materials for energy conservation was given congressional approval in 1978. Another suggestion is for the federal subsidy of a major regional recycling facility so that a number of firms can offload residuals at a scale which could prove economic.

Product charges

The effluent charge concept would seem to be well suited to solid-waste-management problems. For example, the so-called product charge (a sales tax levied, for administrative ease, at the point of product (or package) manufacture) could be related to the full social costs of collecting and disposing of the products concerned. It is argued that such a charge is necessary because those who generate residuals (both producers and consumers) do not currently bear the full marginal social cost of disposal.[46] In the UK, householders pay rates to local authorities part of which are used to pay for solid-waste collection and disposal. The rates payment is based not on the local services (including waste collection and disposal) actually consumed by the household but on the rateable value of the property, so there is no incentive for householders to reduce their waste-generation rates.

Packaging products would seem to be ideal candidates for the product charge device. The imposition of the charge, based on the full social costs of disposing of packaging, will serve to increase packaging product prices and reduce final demand. Recycled products, however, must be exempted from any product charges, and there will be a consequent relative price decrease for recycled materials in terms of virgin materials. There should then follow a substitution from virgin to secondary materials and increased recycling rates. Overall, in principle, the imposition of a product charge will produce a twofold effect in the economy, an increase in recycling activity rates[47] and also a general reduction in waste generation and disposal rates.[48] As yet the product charge remains a theoretical concept. Considerable discussion and analysis of the device has taken place in the USA both in academic and official government circles. Interest in such a device in the UK, however, has been negligible despite the existence of the UK Waste Management Advisory Council and government policy supposedly directed at the problems of waste recycling and disposal.

Standard Setting and Regulation

The customary practice in pollution control throughout the world is for administrators to set regulations as to the appropriate level of a particular discharge (the emission standard) or as to an acceptable level of cleanliness or peace and quiet (ambient quality standard). This approach does not usually involve the economic concepts of taxes and subsidies already outlined but is based on negotiations between the polluter and the regulator in the case of emission standards and many polluters and other interested parties together with the regulators in the case of ambient quality standards. Generally speaking the practice of pollution control is evolving from a case by case approach to a regulatory regime based on claims of discharges and ambient quality standards (see Figure 9.4).[49]

The principle upon which these standards are set is that of best practicable means (bpm) in the UK and best available control technology (bact) in the US. While there is little distinction between the two approaches in terms of concept, for both relate to balancing the costs and technologies of pollution control to the implications on the firm's economic viability, competitiveness and the relevant environmental circumstances of the actual discharge (i.e. the assimilative capacity of the receiving medium and the tolerance to nuisance acceptable to the local public), they are applied in practice in very different ways.

The British bpm approach is described in some detail in the extract from the Alkali Inspector's report that follows. The Alkali and Clean Air Inspectorate have used this concept for over 100 years in the regulation of noxious air pollutants from certain classes of industry and while the bpm idea is still officially limited to the Inspectorate's work, in practice it is applied to the control of all pollutants in the UK.[50] Its proponents assert that its advantages lie in its flexibility, its adaptability to particular circumstances and its gradualness (see Figure 9.5). Here is an extract from

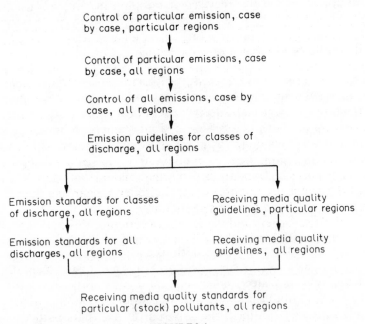

FIGURE 9.4

The evolution of pollution control. This diagram is discussed in the text. Basically it illustrates the point that pollution control is moving from a case-by-case facilitative process to a much more interventionist activity involving broad considerations of quality levels and regional development needs. This is a trend only: there are many hiccups along the way.

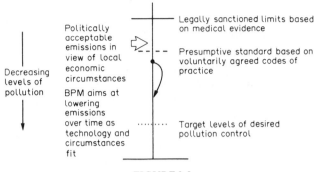

FIGURE 9.5

The UK approach to air-pollution control. This diagram illustrates the arguments presented by the Chief Alkali Inspector in the reading that follows. Below danger levels, air-pollution control is a persuasive business involving close co-operation between the inspectorate and the polluter. So long as the polluter is willing to comply, prosecution is avoided.

the Twenty-fourth Annual Report of the Inspectorate published in 1887.

"It would I think be found that the injunction to use the 'best practicable means' for preventing the emission of noxious gases would prove an elastic band, tightening as chemical science developed and placed greater facilities in the hands of the manufacturer. When necessary it could be shown that this phrase would give a greater security to the public *than would the adoption of any fixed standards*, at the same time pressing with less severity on some of the manufacturers, but more equally on all" (emphasis added).

A number of critics have argued that this method is too flexible, that there are insufficient guidelines to help regulatory officials to judge the merits of a particular case (especially as they may not be so well informed as the discharger both as to the possible abatement technologies available and to the effect on the economic competitiveness of the firm) and that all the discussions are too confidential. We have already noted that secrecy is legally sanctioned in such discussions and that interested members of the public are not able to air their views regarding the possible nuisance arising from a proposed discharge.

Both the dischargers and the regulators counter this criticism on the grounds that confidential discussions conducted on an amiable basis are most likely to achieve the best results, for an antagonised polluter will only grudgingly respond and much costly litigation may be necessary. Furthermore, the regulatory officials are proud of their record in improving the quality of the nation's air and water and enjoy the trust granted to them by local authorities and central government by allowing them discretion in making final recommendations about standards and in deciding how to deal with an offender. Consequently, prosecutions are rare even when offences are committed, as can be seen from Table 9.1, because prosecutions are regarded as a means of last resort and an admission of failure in the conduct of regulatory negotiation. One must remember that in Britain most pollution-control officers do not regard themselves as policemen or even as regulators, but more as technical specialists whose job is to help and advise the polluter, not to threaten him.

The problem arises when people not privy to this pleasant arrangement become suspicious that there is too much of the carrot and not enough of the stick, especially with regard to the matter of enforcement. For despite its name, the bpm approach generally results in fairly similar conditions being set against emission of a similar nature unless the circumstances are quite unusual. In their annual reports, for example, the Alkali Inspectorate publish what they term "presumptive standards" for emissions from a variety of processes. They regard these as the model discharges which should be produced by a firm which is using the best technology currently available, which is keeping its equipment in good working order and which is ensuring that its engineers are suitably trained. Bpm relates as much to operation and maintenance as it does to the design of abatement technology. With respect to the enforcement matter, we have already noted how the Control of Pollution Act, 1974 will alter the nature of possible legal action and how the authorities have responded with respect to water pollution.

In the case of air and noise pollution and solid-waste disposal, the Act also provides for the publication of registers and for the right of interested individuals to comment on proposals for regional waste-disposal plans. However, in day to day operations, enforcement of air and noise pollution is based on a combination of discretionary initiative on the part of the pollution-control officers in relation to certain statutory regulations and in response to complaints from neighbours. The whole matter of complaint is, however, dependent upon nuisances that can be smelt, seen or heard, so some toxic hazards could remain undetected. Yet most local public health authorities neither have the budgets nor the manpower to monitor air and noise pollution so the fact remains that they do rely on the complaint mechanism as a means for identifying offenders. Despite its curious ad hocery this arrangement is likely to remain. In The Netherlands it has even been institutionalised, for the authorities in Rotterdam have provided a free phone telephone number to allow residents to complain when pollution becomes a nuisance (particularly smell where there is always a sensitive public nose and where there are really no effective guidelines for emission control). This arrangement is obviously particularly helpful when there are accidental discharges and the pollution-control authorities have to deal with the matter quickly.

The Americans are much more formal about pollution control and hence create more antagonism, more litigation and more expense. The

TABLE 9.1

Infractions and Prosecutions under the Alkali and Clean Air Acts in England and Wales. Note that only about half the local public health authorities reported so there may be a bias of self-selection. In general prosecutions are avoided as they are costly and may lead to bad feeling.

Year	Alkali Inspectorate				Local Public Health Authorities			
	Infractions	Prosecutions	Prosecutions as % of infractions	Successful prosecutions	Contraventions	Prosecutions	Prosecutions as % of contraventions	Successful prosecutions
1970	25	2	8	2	2417	88	4	81
1971	38	3	8	2	2527	133	5	123
1972	58	3	9	3	2928	94	3	84
1973	59	5	5	4	2452	60	3	52
1974	57	2	7	2	2656	50	2	43

Source: Royal Commission on Environmental Pollution Fifth Report (1976) Air Pollution: An Integrated Approach, Cmnd. 6371, pp. 63 and 64. Permission by the Comptroller, HMSO.

application of bact, especially in the case of water pollution, often does not make economic sense. For example, some local authorities have to spend many millions of dollars upgrading sewage treatment plants when the assimilative capacity of the receiving waters is already very high. The setting of national primary and secondary ambient quality standards for various air pollutants required numerous public hearings and much controversy between scientists employed by industry and environmental groups. Even now there is much suspicion that the levels finally determined are unnecessarily strict and a burden on industry. Likewise the Americans have taken the meaning of best available control technology very seriously despite the rider in the definition of bact that it must also be economically the most feasible technology. Thus industry moving either into areas where the primary or secondary air quality standards are already breached (the non-attainment areas) or where existing high-

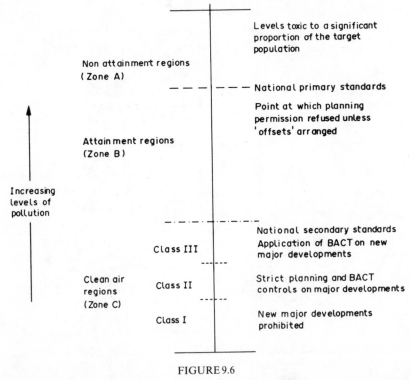

FIGURE 9.6

The US approach to air-pollution control. In the US air-quality standards are legally defined and thus legally enforced. Regulatory officials must justify in public why they set the receiving quality levels and face cross-examination. Because of the importance of the law in the US, environmental groups are active in ensuring that the highest standards of pollution control are met both in clean-air regions (espcially zones 2 and 3) and in the non-attainment regions. The latter are generally urban areas where primary air-quality standards are not met and where new industrial activity which would add to the existing pollution burden, are discouraged.

quality air is to be protected (the so-called non-degradation zones) must meet the most searching examination of their pollution-control technology and operation (see Figure 9.6). This has undoubtedly put a lot of strain on the regulatory process, bearing in mind the constant threat of litigation by environmentalist groups if the regulators appear to default, and has showed up industrial development in many areas. Now there is a bit of a backlash as Americans face more recession, higher inflation and unemployment and grumble loudly about the cost of bureaucracy. So the option of "variance" or flexibility is now being more freely applied which in part makes nonsense of the rigidly defined procedures laid down in the US pollution-control regulations, both for air and for water.

It is thus likely that there will be a convergence in pollution-control practice in the US and the UK where authorities will attempt to adopt the best of the approaches used by each to suit their circumstances. The British, prodded by the European Commission, are reluctantly being forced to adopt ambient quality standards and more precisely defined emission standards,[51] and, as we have noted, will eventually allow more direct public participation. The Americans will probably accept more of the flexibility and discretion that works so well in the UK, though they will retain the measures of openness and accountability that are still missing in the UK. In the final analysis, however, pollution control is where environmentalism comes most directly into conflict with economic decline, for a static economy cannot easily devote resources to pollution abatement without recognisable sacrifice. In this context the decade of the eighties may well provide an important indicator of how far society is willing to go to protect its environmental quality.

Notes and References

1. Baumol, W. J. and Oates, W. E. (1975) The Instruments for Environmental Policy, in Mills, E. S (ed.) *Economic Analysis of Environmental Problems*, Columbia University Press.
2. Burrows, P. (1974) Pricing Versus Regulation for Environmental Protection, in Culyer, A. J. (ed.) *Economic Policies and Social Goals: Aspects of Public Choice*, Martin Robertson, pp. 273-283.
3. Page, T. (1978) A Generic View of Toxic Chemicals and Similar Risks, *Ecology Law Quarterly*, vol. 7 (2), pp. 207-244.
4. Frankel, M. (1977) *The Social Audit Pollution Handbook*, Macmillan.
5. The Council For Science and Society (1977) *The Acceptability of Risks*, Barry Rose (Publishers) Ltd.
6. Page, T. (1978) *Op. cit.*
7. For a discussion of the continuing over "acceptable" levels of emitting radiation, see Bunyard (1978) Radiation Risks: How Low Can One Get?, *New Ecologist*, vol. 2 (5), pp. 161-166, and Ryle, C. and Garrison, J. (1979) Radiation Risks, *Vole*, vol. 3 (1), pp. 8-12.
8. Report of the Asbestos Advisory Committee (1979) Health and Safety Executive and HMSO, London. See also Singer, A. Report on Asbestos Safety Attacked, *The Guardian*, 25 October, p. 1.
9. Bower, B. T., Ehler, C. H. and Kneese, A. V. (1977) Incentives for Managing the Environment. *Environmental Science and Technology*, vol. 11 (3).
10. Marin, A. (1978) The Choice of Efficient Pollution Policies: Technology and Economics in the Control of Sulphur Dioxide, *Journal of Environmental Economics and Management*, vol. 5 (1).

11. Roberts, M. J. (1976) Environmental Protection: The Complexities of Real Policy Choice, in Swainson, N. A. (ed.) *Managing The Water Environment*, University of British Columbia Press.
12. Coase, R. H (1960) The Problem of Social Cost, *Journal of Law and Economics*, vol. 3 (1).
13. Randall, A. (1972) Market Solutions to Externality Problems: Theory and Practice, *American Journal of Agricultural Economics*, vol. 54.
14. Mishan, E. J. (1974) On the Economics of Disamenity, in Marris, R. (ed.) *The Corporate Society*, Macmillan.
15. Riparian rights are common law rights pertaining to the enjoyment of water "undiminished in quality or quantity" which are enjoyed by landowners whose property abuts a watercourse. In practice the absoluteness of the right is modified to allow other users of the water a reasonable degree of pollution and abstraction so long as the riparian interests are not unduly harmed.
16. Mishan, E. J. (1974) *op. cit.*
17. The reasonableness test is based on the dictum "sic utere tuo et alienum non laudes" which means "use your own property in such a way as not to injure that of another". Thus nuisance can be tolerated so long as each party shows that it is being reasonable in abating the worst of the damage and is not demanding such a level of environmental quality as to put the polluter out of business.
18. Dick, D. T. (1976) The Voluntary Approach to Externality Problems: A Survey of the Critics, *Journal of Environmental Economics and Management*, vol. 3 (2).
19. Randall, A. (1972) *op. cit.*
20. Most of this literature is American because the US Constitution permits much freer use of the courts than is the case in the UK. See especially Sax, J. (1970) *Defending the Environment*, Knopf, New York.
21. Ogus, A. I. and Richardson, G. M. (1977) Economics and the Environment: A Study of Private Nuisance, *Cambridge Law Journal*, vol. 36 (2).
22. Roberts, M. K. (1976) *op. cit.*
23. Ogus, A. I. and Richardson, G. M. (1977) *op. cit.*
24. This matter is discussed in some detail in the Third Report of the Jukes Committee (1974) *The Water Services: Economic and Financial Policies*, HMSO, London.
25. See Baumol, W. J. and Oates, W. E. (1975) *op. cit.* and Anderson, F. R. *et al.* (1977) *Environmental Improvement Through Economic Incentives*, Johns Hopkins University Press; McIntosh, P. T. and Wilcox, J. (1979) Water Pollution Charging Systems in the EEC, *Water Pollution Control*, vol. 78 (2); and Johnston, R. W. and Brown, G. M. (1976) *Cleaning Up Europe's Waters*, Praeger.
26. Baumol, W. J. and Oates, W. E. (1971) The Use of Standards and Prices for Protection of the Environment, *Swedish Journal of Economics*, vol. 73 (1).
27. Orr, L. (1976) Incentive Versus Grant Transactions. In Environmental Models, *American Economic Review*, vol. 66, (2).
28. Burrows, P. (1974) *op. cit.*
29. Walker, M. and Storey, D. J. (1977) The "Standards and Price" Approach to Pollution Control: Problems of Iteration, *Scandinavian Journal of Economics*, vol. 79 (2).
30. Mäler, K. G. (1974) *Environmental Economics*, Johns Hopkins University Press.
31. Dorcey, A. H. J. (1973) Effluent Charges, Information Generation and Bargaining Behaviour, *Natural Resources Journal*, vol. 12 (2), pp. 113-132.
32. Russell, C. S. (1973) *Residuals Management in Industry: A Case Study of Petroleum Refining*, Johns Hopkins University Press; and Russell, C. S. and Vaughan, W. J. (1976) *Steel Production: Processes, Products, and Residuals*, Johns Hopkins University Press.
33. Storey, D. J. (1978) Market Structure and Externalities: The Case of Water Pollution in England and Wales, *The Journal of Industrial Economics*, vol. 27 (20).
34. Russell, C. S. and Vaughan, W. J. (1976) *op. cit.*
35. Dales, J. H. (1968) *Pollution, Property and Prices*, University of Toronto Press.
36. Marr, B. W. (1971) A System of Waste Discharge Rights for the Management of Water Quality, Water Resources Research, vol. 7 (5).
37. For example, Baumol, W. J. and Oates, W. E. (1975) *op. cit.*
38. Ackerman, S. (1977) Market Models for Water Pollution Control, *Public Policy*, vol. 25 (3).
39. Yandle, B. (1978) The Emerging Market in Air Pollution Rights, *Regulation*, July/August, and Yandle, B. (1979) Alternative Systems for Allocating Air Quality—The Prevention of Significant Deterioration, US Council on Wage and Price Stability Staff Paper, Washington, DC.

40. See, for example, the Report on the Advisory Committee on Sewage Disposal (Lady Jeger, Chwm) (1970), HMSO, London.
41. Committee on Environmental Conservation (1978) Response to the Consultation Paper issued by the National Water Council on River Quality Objectives.
42. For a discussion of the general issues raised here, see O'Riordan, T. (1979) The Role of Environmental Quality Objectives in the Politics of Pollution Control, in T. O'Riordan and R. C. d'Arge (eds.) *Progress In Resource Management and Environmental Planning*, vol. 1, John Wiley, Chichester, pp. 221-257.
43. Johnston, R. W. and Brown, G. M. (1976) *op. cit.*
44. Anderson, R. C. and Spiegleman, R. D. (1977) Tax Policy and Secondary Material Use, *Journal of Environmental Economics and Management*, vol. 4.
45. Turner, R. K., Grace, R. G. and Pearce, D. W. (1977) The Economics of Waste Paper Recycling, in Pearce D. W. and Walter, I. (eds.) *Resource Conservation, Social and Economic Dimensions of Recycling*, New York University Press, and Longmans.
46. Irwin, W. A. (1977) Alternative Institutional Approaches to Recycling Used Oil, in Pearce, D. W. and Walter, I. (eds.) *op. cit.*
47. For a detailed analysis of how the secondary market works for one town in the UK see O'Riordan, T. and Turner, R. K. (1979) Recycling and Householder Attitudes: A Survey of Norwich, *Resources Policy*, vol. 5 (1), pp. 42-50.
48. Miedema, A. K. (1977) Preliminary Analysis of a Product Charge on Major Components of Past Consumer Solid Waste, Research Triangle Institute, prepared for the US Environmental Protection Agency; & Smith, F. E. (1977) Pollution Charges: The Practical Issues, in Pearce, D. W. and Walter, I. (eds.) *op. cit.*; and Bigham, T. H. (1977) Alleviative and Distributive Effects of a Disposal Charge on Product Packaging, in Pearce, D. W. and Walter, I. (eds.) *op. cit.*
49. For a detailed discussion see O'Riordan T. (1979) *op. cit.*
50. For a detailed review of pollution-control administration in the UK see Bennett, G. (1979), *Polluter Control in England and Wales: A Review*, *Environmental Policy and Law*, vol. 5 (2), pp. 93-100. For an excellent analysis of a bpm concept see The Royal Commission on Environmental Pollution (1976) *Air Pollution Control: An Integrated Approach*, Cmnd. 6371, HMSO, London. For a critique, see Frankel, M. (1974) *The Alkali Inspectorate*, Social Audit, 9 Poland Street, London.
51. See O'Riordan, T. (1979) *Op. cit.*

READINGS:

MARKET MODELS FOR WATER POLLUTION CONTROL: Their
Strengths and Weaknesses*

Susan Rose-Ackerman

I. Introduction

The 1972 Amendments to the Federal Water Pollution Control Act represent the strongest stand on water pollution likely to emerge from the Congress in the years ahead. Soon after the bill was passed, concern for energy supplies tempered the political appeal of environmentalism. Given the growing recognition of the high costs of pollution control, two policy options are open. On the one hand, quality goals may be lowered; on the other, cheaper means of achieving the 1972 goals may be designed. This paper takes the second approach,[1] and proposes the selective introduction of market mechanisms to achieve substantial cost reductions. The market proposal advanced, however, is not the "effluent charge" most frequently recommended by economists as a policy

*An earlier version of this paper was prepared for the National Commission on Water Quality. The paper has not, however, been reviewed by the Commission. The author acknowledges the helpful suggestions of the Journal's anonymous referees.

response. Instead, we propose the introduction of a "pollution rights" scheme,[2] under which dischargers bid for the right to emit wastes to the extent permitted under the 1972 standards. Section 1 establishes the framework for the comparison of effluent charges with pollution rights that is the principal concern of Section II. The paper concludes in Section III with an exploration of some of the differences between market schemes and non-market regulatory plans that seek to assure compliance through the legal enforcement of specified clean-up orders.

A. *Necessary revisions of the 1972 Act.* Even if the 1972 Act's goals are to remain intact, the underlying statutory scheme must be amended before a market mechanism can have an important allocative function. At present, the Act barely concerns itself with ambient water quality,[3] and instead requires individual dischargers to construct waste treatment facilities of certain approved types. If this system were left intact, the introduction of an effluent charge would serve only a modest function. Charging a polluter per unit of discharge and *also* requiring him to build a treatment plant of a particular sort is redundant. The only economic function of a fee in this case may be to speed up the discharger's compliance with the required standards.[4] Of course, a fee system of this sort will raise revenue for whatever agency imposes the charge. And if the agency requires funds for its pollution control activities, this system may appear to provide an equitable way of distributing the tax burden.[5] Except in extreme cases, however, this fee system has none of the efficiency characteristics of a pricing mechanism. The level of each polluter's discharge has been set *a priori* and the fee has no allocational consequences unless it induces some dischargers to leave the area,[6] or unless the discharge standard is so lax relative to the fee that the fee is a binding constraint on the dischargers.[7]

Therefore, in order to discuss situations where the pricing system plays a fundamental allocative role we shall assume that the current method of mandating polluter-by-polluter standards is changed to one where ambient standards are set for different bodies of water. While the latter approach seems a realistic description of the way voters and politicians think about pollution, it limits the possible role of a pricing mechanism. Prices cannot by assumption determine "how much" clean water is produced but only how costs are allocated among dischargers. In a competitive market, of course, the role of prices is much broader, with both the total quantity of a good and its distribution among suppliers determined by the market. While some theoretical discussions of effluent charges envisage this dual role for a fee system,[8] such a strong commitment to the market system seems unjustified in view of the difficulties—to be discussed below — of creating a "pollution market" that resembles the economist's competitive ideal.

Having sketched the kind of market system that seems operational, it remains only to note the difficulty of designing governmental units that might implement the scheme. For present purposes, we shall assume the existence of functioning basin-wide agencies. While regional, basin-wide agencies have an obvious appeal, those that exist have not been notably successful, particularly where interstate cooperation is required.[9] Unfortunately, however, a discussion of alternative institutional structures is beyond the scope of this paper.

B. Defining pollution. People speak glibly of "water pollution" as if they knew what it was. Actually, it is not at all clear how a "unit of water pollution" ought to be defined. Many different substances are dissolved or suspended in water. Much of the material is oxygen-demanding waste, but other substances include suspended solids, acids, poisons, heavy metals, nutrients that can generate algae blooms, and so on. Thus a market system cannot simply levy a single price on pollution but must deal with a number of different substances, recognizing that the relative prices that prevail may affect the type of treatment or process change chosen by dischargers.[10]

Even if the different physical pollutants can be easily identified for the purpose of pricing them, a second definitional difficulty arises because nobody consumes pollutants directly upon discharge. Individuals are concerned about the quality of drinking water, the presence of poisons in fish and shellfish, the healthfulness and beauty of the water for swimming, its hospitality to fish and wildlife, and its appearance. The relationship between these water uses and the waste emitted by any single discharger is not a simple one. It depends on the characteristics of the stream, the season of the year, the location of dischargers relative to users of the water, and the location and waste discharges of other polluters. Of particular importance to an economist is the fact that benefits to users do not increase continuously as emissions are reduced. At a certain point, a river becomes overloaded with biological waste, causing the water to smell like rotten eggs. If, however, a relatively small quantity of waste is treated, this serious condition may be completely eliminated. Other less dramatic thresholds are also important. Fish species require different amounts of dissolved oxygen in order to survive. States set water quality standards for swimming. These standards are quite arbitrary and vary widely across states, but they are threshold nonetheless.[11] As we shall see, the existence of these thresholds is an important reason for favoring a pollution rights scheme over an effluent charge sytem.

II. Effluent charges versus pollution rights

In order to analyze government-established market mechanisms for the control of water pollution we must understand why a free market fails to arise independently of a public policy initiative. This perspective is important because any attempt to use monetary incentives in pollution control must face squarely the inevitable difficulty of legislating a market into being when the preconditions for a private market do not exist. Problems arise because (1) liability for pollution damage may be unclear, (2) the relationship between ambient water quality and waste discharge is not simple, and (3) while many people use the water for swimming, boating, fishing, and nature study, the marginal cost of an additional user is close to zero. These three difficulties are distinct. Suppose the water in a particular river were only used by one downstream town for drinking and waste disposal and by one upstream industry for waste disposal. Then only the first problem would arise. Without a clear liability rule each side may believe that, if no agreement is reached, the other side will bear all the costs. Hence the water users may have no incentive to strike a mutually satisfactory bargain. If either the upstream or downstream discharger were assigned property rights to the river waters, however, the water users could more easily negotiate a cost-sharing arrangement.[12] This solution is, of course, a bargaining rather than a market solution, since only two dischargers are involved. The use of an impersonal price system implies that at least one side of the market is not monopolized and hence takes prices as given.

If there are many upstream dischargers and only one downstream user who is assigned "ownership" of the river, then the second problem arises. The downstream user cares about the quality of the water near his intake pipe, but all he can accomplish through a price system is a reduction in upstream waste discharges. In order to set a price on these discharges he requires an engineering model that relates discharges at several locations to water quality at his intake pipe. Constructing such a scientific model is not a trivial problem[13] and places the downstream user in the position of a buyer who cannot evaluate product "quality" or of a businessman with a production function that includes poorly defined functional relationships and uncertain parameters. Yet in order for a market to function, buyers and sellers must know something about the product being traded. Markets where information about product characteristics is imperfect are notoriously inefficient.[14] Given the capital intensity of both waste treatment and water purification technology, "discovering" the relationship between upstream discharges and downstream water quality by the trial and error procedure of setting different prices and observing polluter responses may not be a feasible response to uncertainty.

The third difficulty arises when there are numerous water users, including some who physically remove the water from the stream only to return it dirtier or hotter than they obtained it, and others, mostly recreationists, who use the water without moving it anywhere and without interfering with others who wish to use it for the same purpose.[15] Use of water for sewage disposal, for example, is generally incompatible with in-stream uses such as swimming and fishing.[16] Nevertheless, using a price system to exclude swimmers and fishermen is inefficient because the marginal cost of an additional user is often zero. While charging in-stream users may be inefficient, if they are not charged the water may remain dirty because no one will pay voluntarily for a clean-up that everyone else can obtain at no charge.[17]

The implication of this discussion is that an efficient free market in water quality will not arise through the simple expedient of assigning property rights to one or another water user. Instead, government must take a more active role in specifying either prices or quantities and, as we shall argue in Section III, supplementing any market scheme with certain more direct regulatory tools.

We turn now to consider two alternative methods by which market incentives might be introduced. Under the first, effluent charge, system, a central authority sets prices, and dischargers can "buy" as much pollution as they wish given these prices. Under the second, pollution rights, system, the amount of discharge that is permitted in a given region or body of water is fixed by the central authority and dischargers (and environmental groups) bid for the discharge rights. While the distinction between setting prices and setting quantities might seem at first a merely technical detail, we shall argue that it is of the first importance in the practical design of a market program.

A.' Time and uncertainty. In a static world of perfect certainty an effluent charge system, a pollution rights program, or direct regulation by legal orders could all lead to identical results. Given a level of ambient water quality, a model relating ambient quality to discharges, and information about least cost waste removal techniques for each discharger, the method of obtaining compliance would be a matter of indifference from the point of view of efficiency. Questions concerning the equity of requiring dischargers to pay for their pollution would predominate.

Unfortunately, information is far from perfect in the real world. While reasonably accurate engineering models exist relating discharges to ambient water quality, cost data are generally weak and fragmentary. Given these facts, the biology of the water pollution problem leads one to recommend a pollution rights plan over an effluent charge, for (as we have seen) a rights plan can deal with the problem posed by biological water quality thresholds far more readily than its effluent charge competitor.[18] Under a charge approach, an agency whose objective is to eliminate stench or prevent fish-kills runs the risk of setting "too low" a charge on the basis of underestimates of true treatment costs. Polluters, in response, may invest large sums in treatment facilities that fail, however, to achieve any important water quality goal. For example, suppose the agency sets a fee of 10 cents per pound of biological waste discharged because it mistakenly believes that, given this fee, dischargers will cut back their pollution enough to prevent fish-kills. If the actual marginal costs of waste removal are higher than expected costs, discharges will be higher than predicted and the water quality threshold will be violated. Of course charges can be adjusted if they prove to be erroneous. But given the capital intensity of most waste treatment technology and process changes, adjustment to prices will not be rapid and may not occur at all if polluters adopt a wait-and-see attitude in the face of frequently fluctuating fees. Hence, in order to induce dischargers to invest in treatment technology, the authority might have to promise that fees will remain unchanged for fixed periods of time, and seek to avoid violating thresholds by setting a fee that could well prove "too high".

With a rights plan the threshold difficulty may be readily accommodated. The agency issues no more rights than are required to maintain the desired threshold level. Prices adjust instead of quantities. If the agency has underestimated the treatment costs of dischargers, then a fee will generate water that is dirtier than expected, while under a rights system, the price of rights will be higher than expected and the mandated level of water quality will be reached.[19]

In this context it is difficult to understand the contention of Kneese and Schulze (1975) that effluent fees dominate pollution rights because of the imprecision of engineering models that relate discharges to ambient water quality. Even granting Kneese and Schultze's assessment of current scientific efforts, so long as one is at all concerned with ambient water quality, imperfect models complicate *both* fee and rights sytems. The use of charges simply involves an additional uncertainty. The agency is uncertain not only about the relationship between discharges and water quality but also about the relationship between its fee schedule and discharges.

Long-run economic growth can also be accommodated more easily by a pollution rights system than an effluent charge plan. The difficulties of an effluent charge in the face of economic growth are well known (Roberts, 1976;

Rose-Ackerman, 1973). If water quality thresholds are important and if the agency is sluggish in responding to changed conditions,[20] the medium-run consequences of growth for water quality may be serious. In contrast, under a pollution rights scheme, water quality will not deteriorate *unless* the agency acts. The prices of a fixed number of pollution rights will automatically rise over time in a growing environment with new entrants purchasing rights from exist-ing dischargers.[21]

Furthermore, a rights plan has the advantage of placing the burden of affir-mative action on polluters, a rather small and easily organized group, each of whom individually has a great deal at stake. Alternatively, under an effluent charge plan, this burden is imposed upon a diffuse group of river users whose individual interest in water quality is often relatively small.

B. Emergencies. In spite of a generally high level of waste treatment, emergen-cies can arise that require immediate, drastic measures to prevent the violation of ambient water quality standards.[22] An effluent charge system is a cumber-some tool in an emergency. Prices must be raised for a short period to very high levels in order to induce dischargers to hold back their waste until the abnormal situation has been corrected. Since in an emergency the agency generally knows what it wants in quantitative terms, direct orders rather than indirect price sig-nals are likely to be more quickly effective.[23] Orders of this type can, however, be incorporated within the framework of a pollution rights system more easily than they can if an effluent charge plan is in effect. The agency, for example, might follow. Tietenberg's (1974, p. 289) proposal and offer two different types of rights for sale. The first type, issued in relatively large numbers, would permit discharge of a specified amount of waste under "normal" conditions. The second type, issued in very small numbers, would permit discharges in "emer-gencies" defined either in terms of particular events or by the violation of certain ambient water quality thresholds. Dischargers able to store their wastes for short periods of time would not purchase any emergency discharge rights. Others would pay a high price to obtain some of the scarce supply.

C. Simple versus complex systems. Many of the practical proposals for market schemes envisage a single basin-wide pollution market. (Some, in fact, envisage uniform national fees but we defer discussion of this more extreme proposal until Section G.) Simple, basin-wide schemes may not dominate the method of legal orders, however, if dischargers are spread out along the river's banks.[24] With geographical dispersion, each discharger's impact upon water quality depends on its location, and full cost minimization requires taking this variable into account. Tailor-made charges or rights, however, essentially convert mar-ket mechanisms into legal order systems, as well as being very complicated and difficult to administer. It is possible, nevertheless, for a basin agency to design an administratively feasible effluent charge scheme that is more efficient than a single-fee system. The most plausible approach divides the river into a number of geographical zones and levies an identical charge on the wastes of all polluters located in the same general river area, while charging different fees in different zones. The difficulty with zoning schemes, however, is that if interzonal dif-ferences in fees are substantial, dischargers located on the "wrong" side of an arbitrarily defined zonal boundary will feel unfairly treated. These complaints will generate a tendency toward uniformity in interzonal fees.[25]

While these pressures toward uniformity will be felt under a zoned rights regime as well, there is reason to believe they can be controlled more readily in this regulatory context. Imagine, for example, that the authority divides the river into several zones and allocates a fixed number of rights to each. If zonal prices vary considerably, polluters can be given the freedom to pipe their wastes to low-cost zones and purchase discharge rights there.[26] Thus, a polluter near a zonal frontier has little cause for complaint since he can cheaply transfer his waste to a neighboring zone. This flexibility in piping, however, cannot be reasonably accorded to polluters under an effluent charge approach. The critical problem, once again, is posed by the existence of water quality thresholds. If, for example, the authority establishes a set of effluent charges in the hope of preserving aquatic life throughout the river, clearly this expectation will be disappointed if waste dischargers respond to the zonal variation in fees by concentrating their wastes in a few low-fee zones. Instead, before piping can be permitted, the authority must determine the extent to which these interzonal transfers are inconsistent with the agency's water quality goals and alter effluent fees accordingly. In contrast, interzonal transfers do not endanger the agency's water quality objectives since the number of rights in each zone remains fixed and prices adjust automatically in response to polluters' decisions.

D. Municipalities and market schemes. Market schemes generally place much heavier financial burdens on dischargers than do legal orders systems in which dischargers' clean-up obligations are directly specified by the central authority. Because added costs appear particularly difficult for municipalities to bear, many effluent charge proponents would exclude municipalities entirely. Others recommend that municipalities pay fees but that this expense be offset by heavy subsidies. We shall show, however, that a pollution rights plan can be administered so that municipalities benefit without the necessity of designing such an "offsetting subsidy" program.

It is important to recognize that a complex plan that combines charges with subsidies runs the risk of distorting a town's clean-up incentives. To resolve this difficulty, one of two subsidy approaches must be considered. First, the subsidy can be a lump-sum transfer, designed to be independent of the locality's spending on pollution control. While general revenue sharing of this kind has a clear efficiency advantage, it may seem inequitable to some precisely because it subsidizes towns independently of their differing clean-up efforts. If these doubts are given weight, however, a much more complex alternative to lump-sum tranfers must be considered. Under the second approach, towns are offered a subsidy that covers a percentage of total treatment costs, but the perverse incentive effects are counteracted by devising a charge system that levies different fees on firms and on municipalities.[27] For example, if a federal subsidy covers 50 percent of municipal waste treatment costs, then municipalities must be charged a fee that is one-half that levied on firms. Of course, this approach not only requires good cost data, but will also create an incentive for firms to enter municipal systems even when the firms could in fact have treated at lower social cost if they had acted independently.[28] In response to these difficulties, drastically truncated versions of the charge strategy are often offered for serious public consideration. In the effluent charge bill proposed by Senator Proxmire, for example, municipalities are not required to pay a tax on any waste generated in the course of ordinary domestic living, although commercial and industrial effluent is subject to the proposed tax.[29] This bill has the advantage of removing any incentive for a firm to enter a municipal system, but its effort to regulate domestic waste through legal orders has most of the disadvantages generally associated with this mode of control.

In contrast, it is a rather straightforward matter to design a pollution rights system that will avoid the difficulty presented by perverse revenue flows. The problem may be solved through the simple expedient of initially assigning discharge rights in an equitable fashion to the cities bordering the estuary and authorizing them to sell off as many rights as they believe proper at an auction to be held under the authority's auspices. At such an auction private firms will, of course, bid varying sums for varying quantities of rights, leaving it up to the representatives of the municipalities to determine the extent to which it will minimize their costs to see the rights at the bid prices and treat municipal wastes instead. At the end of the auction both the public and private polluters will have redistributed the rights in the way they believe will generate the cheapest pattern of clean-up, given the pollution authority's quality objective. If at a later time one of the polluters finds it has misjudged costs, it remains free to buy or sell rights at the regular markets the control authority will hold for this purpose. Thus the rights system, properly structured, may generate both a solution to the pollution problem that moves in the cost-minimizing direction and a new source of income for the revenue-starved cities.

E. Collusion by dischargers. A general objection to market schemes for pollution control is the possibility that dischargers may collude to produce inefficient results. This objection has force only if an effluent charge system is used and if the central authority uses polluter responses to determine whether to raise or lower the initial level of the fee. For example, if total marginal costs are rising, a cartel of dischargers might treat their wastes to a point where marginal costs *exceed* the fee since they realize that lower levels of treatment will induce an increase in the fee in the next time period.[30] Thus the authority may obtain false signals about the relationship between treatment costs and various levels of water quality.

In contrast, under a pollution rights scheme, the collusion of discharges is unlikely to have any efficiency consequences if the number of rights has been set to capture an important water quality threshold. Hence the authority does not use the bidding process to obtain information about its subsequent behavior. If dischargers collude and make a single low bid, the only result is less revenue for the agency. The colluding dischargers still have an incentive to divide the rights among themselves in a least-cost manner. The only difficulty with rights in this context is the possibility that they could be used to block entry. For example, if a river basin's dischargers consist entirely of large paper mills, the mills might refuse to sell rights to another paper mill seeking to locate on the same river.[31] An effluent charge could not usually be used for this purpose since a fee high enough to deter entry would also impose a high cost on existing firms. Of course, the anti-trust laws should prevent entry-blocking behavior even with a pollution rights scheme, for the refusal of the cartel to sell to the potential entrant would be relatively easy to document.

Collusion does seem a greater threat to the program's pollution control objectives, however, under a rights approach in which it is the cities, rather than the authority, that obtain the revenues from the rights sale. In this case, the supply of rights is not fixed to the cartel but depends positively on the price they are willing to pay; it can be easily shown that if the marginal cost of treatment for municipalities rises with an increase in treatment levels, then the cartel will buy too few rights and treat to too high a level while municipalities will undertreat. Thus, under the variant of the rights scheme that seems to us most desirable, collusive behavior may to some extent undermine efficiency objectives. The seriousness of this point, however, depends upon the likelihood of cartelization, which in turn will depend on the number and size of industrial dischargers.

F. Enforcement. While the preceding arguments suggest the superiority of the rights plan, there are of course factors that point in the opposite direction. The most important point involves the costs of policing the two schemes. Under either approach, the agency must recruit a staff of inspectors to undertake a regular series of unannounced site visits to each pollution source. Under the rights approach, however, the policing task will be more complex. It will be necessary for the agency not only to determine the amount of various effluents discharged, but also to levy penalties for each pound of waste emitted beyond the quantity authorized by rights. If these penalties are substantial, as they should be, it is likely that the inspector's findings will often be challenged by the penalized discharger, and both fairness and the Constitution require that protesting polluters be given the right to a hearing. In contrast, the likelihood of hearings seems much less under the effluent charge system, where a discharger plays a rather small sum in tax for each pound, no matter how much he chooses to emit. The difficulties of enforcing any scheme that relies upon the voluntary compliance of dischargers are substantial, however, because monitoring polluter discharges is not yet a trivial operation.[32]

G. Uniformity and market schemes. A final argument ostensibly favoring effluent charges over pollution rights concerns the supposed benefits of national uniformity. A single effluent fee would be simple to administer and would be "fair" in the sense that no discharger would be disadvantaged by his geographical location. A national market in pollution rights also seems "fair" but requires a nation-wide rights auction that would be relatively difficult to administer. Furthermore, permitting rights to be exercised anywhere in the nation would forfeit the major efficiency advantage of the program, since the integrity of regional water quality thresholds could no longer be guaranteed. It is true, of course, that a uniform effluent charge suffers under the same difficulty. While a single fee assures that marginal treatment costs will be equalized across river basins, it will *not* produce either a *uniform* level of water quality throughout the nation or assure the achievement of important regional thresholds. Stream hydrologies, present water quality, and total discharges from point and non-point sources all vary so widely that wide variability in stream quality is inevitable.

It follows that even if uniform national levels of stream quality continued as the national goal,[33] neither a single effluent charge nor a single rights market could be plausibly recommended as a policy instrument. Once interregional variation in regulatory tools is recognized as necessary, however, a pollution rights plan dominates an effluent charge system for all of the reasons presented above.

It should be noted that interregional variations in marginal treatment costs may well compel some industrial plants to shut down, change location, or choose alternative sites for expansion. This result is not a problem to be deplored but a hopeful sign that the pollution control program has had some concrete effects. Since in the absence of legislation, industry and households choose their locations without taking the relative costs of waste discharge at different locations into account, there is no reason to think that the existing pattern of development is efficient once the externalities of waste disposal are considered.[34] It is likely, however, that a program that contemplates very unequal treatment of dischargers would, to find political acceptance, require subsidies rather than fines as a way of mitigating severe dislocations.

III. Market mechanisms in perspective

While market devices promise substantial savings in cost, their advantages over more traditional regulatory tools should not be overstated. In the present section we shall critically assess certain arguments sometimes made in favor of market mechanisms and then turn to consider situations in which non-market modes of control seem required to achieve agency goals. This will prepare the ground for a final recommendation, suggesting the introduction of a pollution rights program supplemented by a selective set of direct controls.

A. Some overemphasized advantages of market mechanisms

1. Market systems as revenue raising devices. Market schemes are sometimes proposed as revenue raising techniques. If, however, the pricing system is designed to induce a cost minimizing allocation of pollution loads, its revenue raising function must be of secondary importance. On the one hand, as soon as the agency has a "budget" that must be balanced through the levying of fees or the issuance of rights, the regulatory scheme can no longer be geared to achieving a particular level of water quality. On the other hand, if the agency has no large budget and returns the bulk of its revenues to polluters in the form of subsidies, it must avoid structuring its transfers so as to defeat the cost minimizing purpose of the market scheme.[35] Perhaps the easiest way to dispose of fee receipts is simply to divide them among the riparian states or send them to the Federal Treasury, thus effecting a redistribution from those who produce water pollution to those who do not.[36] Fee revenues ought, in fact, to be something of an embarrassment to the central authority. The agency can spend them as it wishes on incentive free transfers, regional treatment facilities, recreation sites, the clearing of debris, and the like, but it will defeat the purpose of any pricing system if the agency is required to balance its budget with fee payments.

2. Innovation. One frequently cited benefit of market models is the incentives for innovation that they provide to individual dischargers. There are several reasons for believing, however, that those incentive effects have been overemphasized. In the first place, many dischargers are municipalities, operating under such severe budgetary limitations that research is unlikely under any regulatory scheme. Second, even so far as firms are concerned, a price system may not produce much additional research activity. The relationship between firm research and development decisions and the financial benefits of innovation is poorly understood but seems to depend as much upon the structure of the industry and its suppliers and customers as upon the relative costs of inputs.[37] Furthermore, recent studies of industrial process changes suggest that the source of a high proportion of innovations is suppliers rather than users.[38]

In the third place, at least some legal orders regimes—in which a polluter is allowed to discharge only a fixed quantity of waste—can be more of a spur to innovation for a growing firm than a market scheme. A growing firm can pay higher fees or purchase more rights, but a fixed quota will require higher and higher levels of treatment as time passes. It is true, of course, that other forms of non-market regulation provide fewer incentives to innovate,[39] but this fact does not permit a general indictment of non-market techniques.

Finally, neither administrative orders, fees, nor rights should be regarded as fixed by dischargers. Any polluter-specific method of control can be equally effective at generating innovations so long as dischargers predict that the agency will increase the stringency of its regulations over time. However, if firms assume that technical changes will *cause* the agency to raise its fees, retire some rights, or raise standards, all three allocation methods will discourage innovation. Only small discharges who have little impact on the body of water will continue to have an incentive to innovate.

Therefore, because the indirect incentives to engage in research and development activity may not be large under any regulatory scheme, basin-wide agencies or the federal government ought to consider the direct sponsorship of research on new methods of pollution control. A research program of this sort could well have a higher payoff than one that expects innovation to arise as a side benefit from either a pricing system or the use of legal orders to regulate the discharges.

B. The remaining uses of direct regulation

1. General remarks. Even though a regional pollution rights system appears to promise a number of beneficial results, at least four situations in which direct regulation must replace or supplement any market scheme should be noted. First, direct action may be required in emergencies. Second, toxic substances believed to produce serious effects if consumed even in small quantities should simply be prohibited. The difficulty with prohibitions, of course, is that they may produce locally severe damages to a few dischargers. Hence a good case can be made for achieving poison control through prohibitions combined with subsidies to the owners and employees of hard-hit firms.[40] Third, the agency may find it worthwhile to control pollution after it has entered the stream through devices such as in-stream aeration of the cultivation of water hyacinths. Finally, economies of scale may suggest the desirability of constructing joint treatment plants. The agency's role in supervising the regionalization of waste treatment requires a more extended discussion, to which we now turn.

2. Location of regional plants. Market schemes have only a limited usefulness when economies of scale in waste treatment are so large that regional treatment plants are the most efficient means of reducing waste loads. In principle, dischargers who would benefit from cooperative arrangements have an incentive to construct joint treatment plants under either a pollution rights or an effluent charge system. In practice, however, two difficulties are likely to arise. First, cooperation between firms and communities who are not used to working together may be difficult to achieve. Firms may be suspicious of each other and of nearby municipalities, and local governments may be unwilling to sacrifice the patronage provided by having their own sewage treatment plants.[41] Second, even if cooperation can be achieved, market schemes cannot, in principle, provide accurate signals about the location of the regional treatment plant. The dischargers will seek to minimize the sum of treatment costs plus piping costs plus total *payments to the authority* while the socially efficient solution minimizes the sum of treatment costs plus piping costs plus *residual damages*. So long as total charges or rights payments do not equal the value of damages, the regional plant may not be located efficiently.[42] Similar problems arise under a rights system if the location of the plant affects ambient water quality. Hence if joint treatment appears to minimize costs, the central authority should choose the locations of regional plants.

As a more activist alternative, the central authority could build and operate regional plants.[43] In the context of government operated plants an effluent charge can have limited applicability, especially if the plant is not required to cover its costs through fees. If this is the case, the authority can set fees equal to the marginal cost of treatment plus piping costs,[44] thus inducing an efficient division of treatment activity-between the point-source dischargers themselves and the regional plants.[45] A regional plant that must use fees to cover all costs will not generally be able to set prices that induce an efficient division of treatment between regional plants and individual dischargers.

IV. Policy recommendations

We are, in short, proposing a mixed market non-market approach to implementing water quality goals.[46] On those river systems where joint treatment will produce substantial economies of scale, basin-wide agencies must play an active role in determining the location of regional facilities. On this important question of treatment plant location, no market scheme seems feasible. Once regional plants are in operation, however, a fee system can be used to allocate treatment responsibilities efficiently between regional plants and individual waste-producers.

In cases where joint treatment is not efficient, a rights system seems superior to other alternative regulatory schemes. In particular, pollution rights seem superior to a system of effluent charges because they (1) assure the early attainment of water quality thresholds; (2) minimize the inequities involved in setting zonal boundaries within river basins; (3) provide a simple means of subsidizing municipalities without sacrificing the efficiency benefits of market schemes; (4) permit growth and new entry to occur without burdening existing dischargers; and (5) provide a regulatory structure in which emergencies may be readily resolved. In addition, the rights scheme would permit the EPA to remain within the spirit of the 1972 Act's insistence on the attainment of uniform national standards of water quality while recognizing that the efficient attainment of this objective demands variations in the clean-up efforts of dischargers, depending on their location and abatement costs.

Finally, the rights plan may be incorporated into the existing legislative structure without altogther revolutionizing the approach taken by the Water Pollution Control Act of 1972. Under the present law, each polluter is given a permit that specifies the quantity of waste that may be legally discharged without incurring criminal and civil penalties.[47] Instituting a rights plan would not require the revision of this basic enforcement structure but would simply make it legal to sell pollution rights to others. In contrast, introducing an effluent charge at this time would require the elimination of the existing permit system that was so laboriously established under the 1972 Act, since it is an essential feature of a charge scheme to allow each polluter to discharge as much as he is willing to pay for. The fact that the rights plan can be easily adapted to current practice is especially important, since Congress is now attempting to revise the Act without altogether abandoning its past initiatives.[48] While policy makers are not willing to retreat from the Act's insistence that *all* polluters install the "best practicable" treatment within the near future, much more doubt is expressed regarding the Act's further demand that all dischargers improve their treatment to the "best available" level by 1983. Implementing a rights plan would permit Congress to adopt a sophisticated approach to water quality in the 1980s without retreating from its present commitment to the "best practicable" standard. In each river system, the Environmental Protection Agency could be charged with determining whether a new higher ambient threshold may be achieved by the use of the "best available" technology. If the EPA decides to seek a water quality improvement, rights could then be issued in amounts necessary to achieve this goal, and dischargers could bid for the right to avoid further treatment. High cost dischargers could purchase large numbers of rights, but everyone would be required to meet the "best practicable" standards.[49]

Bibliography

Ackerman, Bruce, Susan Rose-Ackerman, James Sawyer, and Dale Henderson. *The Uncertain Search for Environmental Quality*. New York: Free Press, 1974.
Akerlof, George A. "The Market for Lemons." *Quarterly Journal of Economics* **84** (1970):488–500.
Baumol, William, and Wallace Oates. *The Theory of Environmental Policy*. Englewood Cliffs, N.J.: Prentice-Hall, 1974.
Bohm, Peter. "Pollution Purification and the Theory of External Effects." *Swedish Journal of Economics* **72** (1970):153–166.
Brown, Gardner, and Ralph Johnson. *Cleaning Up Europe's Waters: Economic Management Policies*. Manuscript, 1975.
Brown, M., and A. Conrad. "The Influence of Research and Education on CES Production Relations." In M. Brown (ed.), *The Theory and Empirical Analysis of Production*. New York: Columbia University Press for NBER, 1976.
Coase, Ronald. "The Problem of Social Cost." *Journal of Law and Economics* **3** (1960):1–44.
Council on Environmental Quality. *1971 Annual Report*. Washington, DC.: Government Printing Office.
Council on Law-Related Studies. *Effluent Charges on Air and Water Pollution: A Conference Report, October 15 and 16, 1971*. Summary of Proceeding with Reporter's Notes by Edward I. Selig, Environmental Law Institute, 1973.
Dales, John H. *Pollution Property and Prices*. Toronto: University of Toronto Press, 1968.
Klevorick, A. K., and G. H. Kramer. "Social Choice on Pollution Management: the Genossenschaften." *Journal of Public Economics* **2** (1973): 101–146.

Kneese, Allen V. "Discharge Capacity of Waterways and Effluent Charges." In Selma Mushkin (ed.), *Public Prices for Public Products*. Washington, D.C.: The Urban Institute, 1972, pp. 133–151.

Kneese, A., and B. Bower. *Managing Water Quality: Economics, Technology Institutions*. Baltimore: Johns Hopkins, 1968.

Kneese, Allen V., and Charles L. Schultze. *Pollution, Prices and Public Policy*. Washington, D.C.: The Brookings Institution, 1975.

Meta Systems Inc. *Effluent Charges: Is the Price Right?* Mimeo prepared for the Environmental Protection Agency, Cambridge, Mass., 1973.

Montgomery, W. David. "Markets in Licenses and Efficient Pollution Control Program." *Journal of Economic Theory* 5 (1972): 395–418.

National Academy of Sciences, Commission on Natural Resources. *Air Quality and Stationary Source Emission Control*. Report prepared for the Committee on Public Works, U.S. Senate, March 1975.

National Commission on Water Quality. *Staff Draft Report*. Washington, D.C.: Government Printing Office, 1975.

Nelson, Richard R. "In Search of a Useful Theory of Innovation." *Research Policy* (forthcoming).

Nelson, Richard, Merton J. Peck, and Edward Kalachek. *Technology, Economic Growth and Public Policy*. Washington, D.C.: The Brookings Institution, 1967.

Olson, Mancur. *The Logic of Collective Action*. Cambridge, Mass.: Harvard University Press, 1965.

Roberts, Marc. "Environmental Protection: The Complexities of Real Policy Choice." In Neil Swainson (ed.), *Managing the Water Environment*. Vancouver: University of British Columbia Press, 1976, pp. 157–234.

Roberts, Marc. "River Basin Authorities: A National Solution to Water Pollution." *Harvard Law Review* 83 (1970): 1527–1556.

Rose-Ackerman, Susan. "Effluent Charges: A Critique." *Canadian Journal of Economics* 6 (1973): 512–528.

Starrett, David, and Richard Zeckhauser. "Treating External Diseconomies — Markets or Taxes?" In John Pratt (ed.), *Statistical and Mathematical Aspects of Pollution Problems*. New York: M. Dekker, 1974.

Terleckj, N. *Effects of R and D on the Productivity Growth of Industries*. Washington, D.C.: National Planning Association, 1974.

Tietenberg, Thomas. "The Design of Property Rights for Air Pollution Control." *Public Policy* 22 (1974): 275–292.

Weitzman, Martin L. "Prices vs. Quantities." *Review of Economic Studies* 61 (1974): 477–492.

Notes

1. By taking this approach I do not mean to imply that I find the Act's provisions satisfactory. For critiques of the 1972 Act, see Ackerman *et al*. (1974), Chap. 20, and Kneese and Schultze (1975).

2. The outlines of this alternative originated with Dales (1968). The discussion in the present paper is an elaboration of Ackerman *et al*. (1974), Chap. 18. For other recent work that analyzes pollution rights schemes see Henry Jacoby and Grant Schaumberg, in Council on Law-Related Studies (1973), pp. 36–43; Montgomery (1972); Roberts (1976), pp. 193–197; and Tietenberg (1974). Tietenberg provides references to other literature on this and similar proposals.

3. Ambient quality becomes important only after the "best available" treatment technology has been installed. If at that point the water cannot support a "balanced population" of wildlife or permit recreation, then the Environmental Protection Agency can calculate the costs and benefits of requiring treatment levels that exceed the "best available," see U.S.C.A. 1312 (a) and (b) (Suppl. 1973) and Ackerman *et al*. (1974), Chap. 20.

4. Many examples of functioning "effluent charges" are, in fact, schemes of this type. Thus the charging schemes in Vermont, in the Ruhr Valley in Germany, and in Hungary are all tied to programs of direct regulation. See Brown and Johnson (1975) for case studies of the European experience; the Vermont Act is summarized in Council on Law-Related Studies (1973), pp. 16-17. The Vermon Act was specifically designed to speed compliance with regulations since the charges terminate when the polluter has treated his waste stream to the required level. Effluent charge bills introduced by Senator William Proxmire also fall into this class since the fees are designed to supplement existing regulations rather than supersede them [Council on Law-Related Studies (1973), pp.45–52].

5. This is the system followed in the Ruhr where the equity rationale appears to be the decisive one. See Brown and Johnson (1975). Klevorick and Kramer (1973) explore the implications of this taxing scheme on the political behavior of participants.

6. The fundamental discontinuity introduced by a firm's shutdown point is analyzed by Bohm (1970), Starrett and Zeckhauser (1974), and Rose-Ackerman (1973). As these authors show, shutdown of a firm in response to effluent charges may or may not be efficient depending on the relationship between the firm's total charge liabilities and the total residual damages caused by its discharge.

7. In other words, the fee will be binding if the marginal cost of treating to higher levels than required by the standard is less than the fee.

8. For example, Rose-Ackerman (1973), Kneese (1972).

9. Kneese (1975) and Roberts (1970), among others, support the establishment of regional agencies. For a critique of basin agencies in the context of the experience of the Delaware River Basin Commission see Ackerman et al. (1974), Chaps. 11–14.

10. This complexity has, of course, been recognized by all serious students of the environment. For instance, see Kneese and Bower (1968), and Roberts (1976), pp. 167–171. Nevertheless, Kneese and Schultze (1975) have proposed levying fees on biological oxygen demand alone. Fees in most European countries are based on a weighted average of various components. See Brown and Johnson (1975). Meta Systems, in a report to the Environmental Protection Agency (1973), recommend setting the fee on units of a composite measure that they call "bio-mass potential."

11. Discussions of the biology of water pollution written for lay audiences are found in Kneese and Bower (1968), and Ackerman et al. (1974), Chaps. 3 and 4.

12. See Coase (1960). Coase's contention that, in the absence of transactions costs, liability can be assigned to either actor with equivalent results holds only if the marginal value of money is constant for both bargainers and if neither is close to his shutdown point. The potential of liability rules and citizens' suits is summarized in Roberts (1976), pp. 207–215.

13. For a discussion of engineering models that attempt to solve this problem, see Ackerman et al. (1974), Chaps. 2–5.

14. A good discussion of the problems that arise can be found in Akerlof (1970). His argument can be translated into a critique of effluent charges as a means of improving ambient water quality.

15. Of course, it is not strictly true that recreationists do not interfere with each other. Beyond some point congestion occurs with each additional user, lowering the benefits obtained by existing users.

16. A body of water can, however, cleanse itself of oxygen-demanding waters such as domestic sewage so long as the volume is not excessive. Thus a sewage discharge upstream may not affect recreational opportunities several miles downstream.

17. For a discussion, see Olson (1965).

18. A rights plan can, of course, also respond well to legislatively mandated threshold like those established for swimmable water by Public Health authorities. It should be emphasized, however, that many of the discontinuities in the water pollution benefit schedule are not merely the products of legislative fiat but are well recognized by competent biologists. For accessible discussions, see ftn. 11. In contrast, the thresholds discussed by Tietenberg (1974) in his analogous air rights proposal are those created by the new federal statute's demand that each air pollutant be reduced to a specific threshold level. It is not clear, however, that the marginal damage curves actually caused by air pollutants display discontinuities at the "legal" thresholds [see National Academy of Sciences (1975), Chaps. 4 and 5]. And if this is so, it is not clear that even the draftsmen of the Air Pollution Act would place a high value on small deviations from the legal threshold, making the case for a rights system more compelling in the water case than in the air case.

19. For a mathematical statement of some of these points in a more general context, see Weitzman (1974).

20. River basin authorities in the Netherlands seem, in fact, to have had no difficulty in steadily increasing fees over time [see Brown and Johnson (1975)].

21. Roberts (1976), p. 194) also makes this point. If predictable seasonal changes in the severity of pollution are the only sources of instability, however, rights seem to have no special advantages over charges in addition to those catalogued in the text. Fees can be adjusted seasonally, and as Tietenberg (1971), p. 289 suggests, rights can also be differentiated by season of the year.

22. In this context it is worth noting an extremely common pollution "shock" experienced by bodies of water adjacent to old population centers. Most large cities in the northeast and mid-

west have combined sanitary and storm sewers. When it rains heavily their treatment plants cannot handle the volume of water generated, and both storm water run-off and sewage are dumped untreated into the watercourse. Although this storm water overflow may only occur during ten or twelve days a year, it can represent an important drop in oxygen levels that is damaging to fish life.

23. This issue is treated very briefly here since it has been exhaustively analyzed by Baumol and Oates (1974).

24. This is shown in Rose-Ackerman (1973).

25. In the Delaware Estuary the same trend towards uniformity was present in administering a zoned legal orders regime with equal levels of percentage removal required in each zone. The pressures were so strong that the end result was close to uniform percentage treatment. See Ackerman *et al.* (1974), pp. 240–243.

26. Since they are superficially similar in form, it is important to recognize the differences between Tietenberg's air rights plan and my zoned pollution rights proposal. Tietenberg envisages a system with one critical zone of poor air quality. A technical model then relates discharges at any point to marginal changes in ambient quality in that zone. Rights are calibrated in terms of ambient quality in the critical region. A table of coefficients then tells a firm how much waste he can discharge given his location and the number of rights purchased. The proposal has the advantage of making it possible for all point-source dischargers in a region to come together in a single rights market. This advantage, however, depends crucially upon the existence of a single "critical" zone. When several critical zones exist, the proposal is less attractive. As Tietenberg himself points out, a discharger who has purchased rights for zone one now must purchase some fixed number of rights in zone two if he wishes to be able to use all of his rights. [Cf. Montgomery (1972) for a sophisticated treatment of this issue.] When water quality must be improved in specified ways everywhere in a river or air basin, the zonal scheme in the text must be substituted for Tietenberg's. Rights are then not expressed in units of *ambient* quality at particular locations but instead are expressed in units of waste *discharged* in various zones. A technical engineering model can be used to determine feasible rights assignments sufficient to guarantee that standards are met throughout the region.

27. In reality, the problem of designing such a system is complicated by the existence of subsidies for firms in the form of special tax treatment for pollution control equipment [Int. Rev. Code of 1954, p. 169; Treas. Reg. 1. 169-1 to 1. 169-3, 602, 1 to 602. 10 (1973)]. The 48 percent corporate tax rate also implies that every dollar of pollution control expenditure "costs" only 52 cents. However, since effluent fees would also be considered tax deductible expenses, this will have no incentive effects.

28. Finally, a third approach would exempt municipalities from the charge and instead pay them a bounty for each pound treated. See Baumol and Oates (1974), Chap. 12, for a detailed discussion of this case. Since opportunity costs are not distorted, it appears that although firms will wish to join municipal systems, cities will not accept them unless the marginal cost of treating any firm's waste is less than the bounty paid per pound treated. Firms, however, would be willing to pay municipalities bonuses (or bribes) for being permitted to use municipal systems since municipal treatment, under a bounty plan, will generally be cheaper for the firm than the sum of individual treatment and fee costs imposed upon it if it chooses to treat independently of the system.

29. See Senate Bill 3181, 91st Cong., 1st Sess. (1969), 4(a) and 5(a).

30. This is formally argued in Bohm (1970) and Rose-Ackerman (1973).

31. Tietenberg (1974) also raises this possibility. However, it should be noted that collusion may not deter new entry completely since the mill can, of course, locate along the shores of a different river.

32. Five-day biological oxygen demand, a standard measure of organic waste, has been rejected in many applications because of the difficulty in monitoring this variable. See Brown and Johnson (1975), and Meta Systems (1973).

33. We do not, in fact, believe that this simple goal is justified. Rivers differ widely in their potential for in-stream uses. Thus pollution policy should be explicit about these stream differences by enacting stringent controls in those that are currently quite clean, initiating a holding action in other heavily polluted rivers, and cleaning up some bodies of water near population centers to produce recreational facilities for city dwellers.

34. Although interregional variations are to be expected and encouraged in setting fee levels, or in issuing rights, national policy must choose the *instruments* available to local authorities. Every

basin should be required to use the same set of tools, be they rights or administrative standards. Cost differences generated only by differences in administrative devices will produce inefficient results, i.e., firms moving from basins with effluent fees to basins with legal orders regimes even though the actual amount of clean-up performed by the firm is identical in both basins.

35. Tietenberg's (1971, p. 237) suggestion that some of the revenues from an air rights program be returned to municipalities in proportion to their payments for rights suffers from this difficulty.

36. Actually, of course, people cannot be divided up so simply into polluters and non-polluters. Everyone produces domestic sewage, and everyone consumes goods whose production creates water pollution.

37. See Nelson (1976) for a critique of past efforts. Nelson, Peck, and Kalachek (1967) provide the basic information on industry structure and research spending. In addition, in pollution control the underlying waste treatment technology often contains important discontinuities. If this is true, and if the expected cost of generating successful innovations is high, the added incentives produced by market schemes may not be sufficient to generate any additional investment.

38. See Brown and Conrad (1967); Nelson, Peck, and Kalachek (1967, pp. 29–34); and Terleckj (1974).

39. For example, a regulatory scheme in which a firm is ordered to remove a fixed percentage of its waste provides little incentive to innovate so long as the technology exists to enable the firm to remove this percentage of its waste at any level of operations. The only incentive the firm has is to find cost-saving ways of removing the mandated percent of its waste.

40. This is, in fact, similar to the approach taken by the 1972 Act. The Environmental Protection Agency has, however, been slow to implement this portion of the act.

41. This problem is also discussed in Roberts (1976), pp. 201–202. The phenomenon has been documented in Camden County, New Jersey [see Ackerman et al. (1974), Chap. 19].

42. The central difficulty here is the attempt to use a single tool, the effluent charge, to resolve two distinct allocation problems, that of plant location and that of treatment level. Since the marginal benefits obtained from different levels of clean-up will vary depending upon the location of the regional plant, the fee should vary with plant location. For example, if at each location marginal damages fall as treatment levels increase, then the total fee paid will exceed marginal damages for all sites, and polluters acting will not choose the optimal plant location. See Rose-Ackerman (1973, p. 521) for a demonstration of this point. The agency could, however, adopt a complex scheme under which it first establishes a schedule of effluent fees set at the level where marginal costs equal marginal benefits at each location. It next announces that at every location it will pay lump sum subsidies calculated to equal the difference between total fees paid and total residual damages actually caused by the dischargers. If this combination charge and subsidy procedure were followed, polluters would locate their joint treatment plant optimally. But of course the amount of information required to undertake such a regulatory scheme would be immense, and it is thus unlikely that the charge and subsidy plan would be preferable to one in which the central authority simply chooses the location of the regional plant.

43. This is done, for example, in the Ruhr Valley in Germany. See Brown and Johnson (1975), and Kneese and Bower (1968). A detailed discussion of the role of river basin agencies in water pollution control is found in Roberts (1970).

44. Assessing piping charges will not be easy if several dischargers can use the same pipe. Marginal costs for any discharger would then depend upon the order in which dischargers join the system. One way out of this problem is to calculate piping costs with and without any particular discharger, assuming that everyone else joins the plant. The discharger would then pay the difference between the two cost estimates.

45. This alternative is analyzed with care by Bohm (1970). In his model, fees also determine only the division of waste between dischargers and regional plants, not the location of these plants. He does, however, note the importance of considering how marginal benefits vary with plant location.

46. Other proposals for mixed systems of various sorts can be found in Baumol and Oates (1974), Kneese and Schultze (1975), Meta Systems (1973), and Roberts (1976).

47. See National Commission on Water Quality (1975), V-14 to V-34.

48. National Commission on Water Quality (1975), Chap. 1.

49. Because of the substitution of rights for fees this proposal appears superior to Meta Systems' (1973) proposal that regulations be used to achieve "best practicable" treatment, with fees used to attain higher quality levels.

THE CHALLENGE OF THE ENVIRONMENT*

Leslie Scarman

FOR environment a traditional lawyer reads property: English law reduces environmental problems to questions of property. Establish ownership or possession and the armoury of the English legal cupboard is yours to command. This is not to say that English law is, or has ever been, helpless in the face of a threat to the environment. Trespass and nuisance have proved over the centuries potent causes of action enforceable by the effectual remedies of injunction and damages; and, on occasion, the law permits self-help as well, *e.g.* in the abatement of nuisance by going on one's neighbour's land and rooting it out. But, as ever, the law operates only when set in motion by litigants with the necessary means and determination: for instance we owe to the determined use by anglers of the law of nuisance the arousing of national interest in the pollution of our rivers and the emergence of action to diminish it.[1]

Nor was the common law helpless in face of the threat to the environment presented by the industrial and technical developments of the nineteenth century, though it has to be conceded in retrospect that Parliament, not the courts, must be given most of the credit. I take two examples well-known to every law student, the development by the judges of a remedy in damages for damage done to one's property by the non-natural use of land—the familiar Rylands versus Fletcher principle — can be seen as a significant attempt to protect the environment against the consequences of industrial and technological development. Like so many judicially-created rules, it contains its own obscurities and raises new problems: but the cynic may say that is one of the strengths of the common law. The illumination of obscurity and the process of first asking and then perhaps years later, answering fresh questions has given, and still gives, the law, and the judges, a degree of flexibility and the room for manoeuvre, which in turn bring the gift of survival. What is a non-natural use of land? Does what was unnatural in a pre-industrial society become natural as the technological revolution takes over? Does the principle apply to personal injury or financial loss, as it admittedly does to damage to property? These questions have enabled the judges to flex their muscles, and their answers have shown the common law adjusting itself with ingenuity and a measure of success to a particular sort of environmental threat. By second example is the development of the law of negligence. Its classic exposition is to be found in the famous words of Lord Atkin:

"... English law there must be, and is, some general conception of relations giving rise to a duty of care ... The rule that you are to love your neighbour becomes in law, you must not injure your neighbour; and the lawyer's questions, Who is my neighbour?, receives a restricted reply."[2]

The judges have done wonders with the principle of the duty of care. It lies at the root of the defences erected by judges and Parliament for the safety, health and welfare of society at work and play, in the factory, on the roads, and at home. As with the principle of strict liability, so also the principle of negligence has owed much of its value to its own inbuilt imprecisions and obscurities: they have given

*Reprinted with permission from *English Law – The New Dimension*, Stevens, London, 1976, pp. 51–60.

the judges the opportunity they needed to develop it to meet changing conditions.

But the truth has to be faced. The judicial development of the law, vigorous and imaginative though it has been, has been found wanting. Tied to concepts of property, possession, and fault, the judges have been unable by their own strength to break out of the cabin of the common law and tackle the broad problems of land use in an industrial and urbanised society. The challenge appears, at this moment of time, to be likely to overwhelm the law. As in the area of the social challenge, so also the guarding of our environment has been found to require an activist, intrusive role to be played by the executive arm of government.

The state with its money and managers has marched into an area where until the last hundred years it was unknown. At first it used the existing legal system. The Factory Acts, which the courts have interpreted as giving a right to damages to an employee injured by their breach, are an illustration of the early intrusion. But they brought with them an inspectorate, the exercise of whose discretion lies outside the effective control of the law. The Factory Acts have, therefore, fallen between two stools and are themselves suspect today. Should they be concerned at all with financial compensation for injury? Should not their object be, to the exclusion of all else, the maintenance of safety and health at work? They have been used by the legal profession and the courts for one purpose, by the inspectorate for the other. In so far as they have been latched on to the common law by the lawyers, they are a compensation code operating only indirectly to protect the environment: in so far as they have been concerned directly to protect the workers' environment, the inspectorate has relied almost exclusively on extra-legal action, remaindering the law to the abnormal situation of prosecution when all else has failed.[3]

But the Factory Acts have had other, very serious consequences for the common law. They have cast a shadow upon the whole system of compensation for fault. Is the factory the only environment in which man should be entitled to the remedy of damages, *i.e.* full compensation notwithstanding his inability to establish any fault on the part of another? True, he has to prove a breach of statutory duty, *i.e.* a breach of the Factory Acts: but such breaches frequently occur without fault or negligence on the part of the factory owner. If a safe environment be seen, as increasing numbers of people now regard it, as one of the human rights, why should compensation be available only to those who are fortunate enough to have the evidence to prove fault on someone's part? Yet, why should some other person (or his insurance company) pay if there be no fault? These questions, as is well known, are being considered by a Royal Commission under Lord Pearson. Their relevance to my theme is that the law, left to itself, cannot solve them. New principles will have to be accepted, old concepts and classifications discarded: and everywhere room will have to be found for the busy, intruding government deploying its money and its managers. Will they be subject to effective control within the general legal system, or will some extra-judicial, administrative control take its place?

Modern man demands not only a safe and healthy but a pleasant and economically viable environment. He sees this as a human right independent of the ownershp or possession of property. Individually, men have relied on the acquisition of property to protect their environment. But the property law, the most elaborate, and if I may say so, without offence, the most astonishing creation of the English legal profession,[4] cannot meet the modern requirement. If land were always to be controlled by land owners who were enlightened and prepared to plan their land use with an eye to the needs of the unborn generations, the law could do an excellent job: easements, long leases, restrictive covenants, stand as historical monuments to the law's endeavour to meet the wishes of land owners eager to protect the environment of themselves and their families. Since the land owner's environment is part and parcel of that of the rest of us, his protection also happens in some respects to be ours. But it has proved not to be enough. A bad land owner could not be prevented from doing irreparable harm: and there were interests besides those of the environment which the law had to accommodate—freedom to buy and sell, to develop, and to use one's own property as one wished. In the clash of interests which the law had to reconcile there was one major casualty—society's interest in land use. This interest the law could not directly protect, because of its starting-point in the law of property. And so, beginning in 1909,[5] came the now familiar sequence of Town and Country Planning legislation. But this legislation achieved little until 1947, when the real break with the legal system came. In that year the Town and Country Planning Act was enacted, ensuring that no one could thereafter ignore or avoid government policy in the use of land. Any material change in the use of land required planning permission from the local planning authority: county councils and county boroughs were required to prepare and publish development plans, the object of which was to establish the policy for land use in their areas. The citizen who found himself denied planning permission could appeal on the merits only to the Minister. Citizens were also entitled to raise objections to a development plan which affected them and their objections were to be considered by the Minister before he approved or modified the plan. The machinery established for hearing appeals and objections was the local public enquiry conducted by an inspector, who was the Minister's man—appointed by him, reporting to him. The Minister was free to accept or reject, in whole or in part, his inspector's report. In the early days the citizen never saw the report —but only the Minister's decision: that has now been changed and the report is normally made available. The inspectors, who over the years have earned the respect of the professional lawyers and surveyors who attend their enquiries and read their reports, are not lawyers, but are usually drawn from the architects, surveyors, and, less frequently, the civil engineering professions: by now, many of them have a qualification in the new profession of Town and Country Planning. It would be unreal to pretend that the public has anything like the same confidence as the professionals have in the merits and justice of the local public enquiry. The inspector lacks the independence and power of a judge in his court: the public are only too well aware that he does not make the decision: they feel they are never face to face with whoever it is—Minister or civil servant—who does. The law is kept at arm's length from the process: it is there only to ensure that the statute, and the statutory rules for conducting the process, are obeyed, but is not concerned with any of the problems of land use with which the process has been established to deal, and which are the problems that interest the citizen.

The Town and Country Planning legislation is, therefore, a code regulating land use largely by extra-legal means. It goes much further than the practice of compulsory acquisition of land with which our society has become increasingly familiar since the middle of the nineteenth century. Compulsory purchase of land by a public authority for a specific purpose defined by statute has emerged as the legal weapon for changing the environment, *e.g.* constructing a railway, road, or airport, building a school, clearing a slum, or comprehensively redeveloping a decayed urban area.[6] It is an important instrument in the hands of the state for the development and protection of our environment and, like planning control, is subject to the process of the local public enquiry, and only marginally subject to any direct legal control: the merits of acquisition are kept away from the courts. Nevertheless, compulsory acquisition remains the exceptional case: but planning control of land use is universal, affecting the citizen in the every day use of what belongs to him.

In the protection of our environment as in the provision of social security, government with its money and managers has moved, a welcome intruder, into the empty spaces of the law. Dirigism has never been a feature of the common law: on the contrary, it has been regarded as a theory and a practice likely to undermine freedom. But, faced with new problems and accepting a new scale of values near the top of which one finds such newly-formulated freedoms as the "Roosevelt freedoms" from want, poverty, and disease and a whole new code of human rights, society has decisively accepted the dirigist activities of government in the use of land, a field of the law hitherto dominated by private property and private right. Thus the protection of the environment has come to be another administrative task undertaken by the executive arm of government. The common law concepts of trespass and nuisance, being rights of action available to the owner or occupier of land, the founding of rights upon property and possession, and the elaborate apparatus of the property law with its easements, restrictive covenants, long leases, and building schemes have failed because they have been ultimately no more than means for protecting private right and enforcing private obligation: the law has never understood or accommodated a public right or obligation in the environment save, perhaps, for the right of passage along the King's highway. Society has now broken into this private world of land ownership, and for the moment its weapons are administrative and extra-legal. When analysed, the challenge is similar in character to the social challenge, raising the same, so far unanswered questions. The law can now be directed along one of two routes. The problems of the environment can be left to administrative control or an attempt can be made to use the legal system so as to ensure that the merits of decisions taken are subject to a measure of review. The difficulties in reconciling the requirements of the policy with effective legal principle should not be allowed to obscure the fact that there are rights to be supported, obligations to be enforced, in a conflict between citizen and government over land use. It is a world of law as well as of administration, and there is a requirement for the rule of law as well as for the implementation of policy. How is the needed regulation of conflict to be provided—by the legal system as we know it, or by some specialist system, administrative in emphasis and remote from the general law? If the law and lawyers are to retain a relevant role in environmental law, they must find an answer to these questions. And it must be an answer which society finds helpful.

References

1. Sustained pressure by litigation or the threat of litigation was exerted by anglers upon local authorities, river boards, and industrial undertakings.
2. *Donoghue* v. *Stevenson* [1932] A. C. 562, 580.
3. See Law Commission Working Paper 1970, No. 30.
4. "One of the most brilliant creations of English law," *The Rational Strength of English Law*, F. H. Lawson (London, 1951) (Hamlyn Lecture).
5. Part II of the Housing, Town Planning etc. Act 1909: Pt. I, significantly, was concerned with the "Housing of the Working Classes".
6. See *Statutes in Force, sub tit.* "Compulsory Acquisition".

BEST PRACTICABLE MEANS: AN INTERPRETATION*

Frank Ireland[1]

LAST year I said that I would attempt to describe best practicable means in some detail, because it is so often misunderstood by its critics. The policy of the alkali inspectorate has evolved round "best practicable means", but one needs to live with it and use it regularly, like a good system of contract bridge played with a co-operative partner, in order properly to understand all its nuances. The concept of best practicable means is ageless and I submit that those who criticise it as being out-of-date because it was conceived many years ago, are really criticising the standards and requirements which have been set under it and the toughness of their implementation by the inspectorate. Best practicable means—or to give it its abbreviation of "b.p.m."—can always be modern if it is used properly ... The expression "best practicable means" was first used in The Alkali Act, 1874. After specifying an efficiency of condensation of hydrochloric acid gas, Section 5 continued "the owner of every alkali works shall use the best practicable means of preventing the discharge into the atmosphere of all other noxious gases arising from such work, or of rendering such gases harmless when discharged" ... The basic needs for good control of emissions are (*a*) the setting of standards and other requirements, (*b*) prior approval of appliances, (*c*) continuing routine inspection and testing, and (*d*) recourse to legal action when works misbehave in a way that deserves public punishment. B.p.m. under the Alkali Act contains all these elements and more, as we can see from study of the main provisions ... The expression "best practicable means", where used with respect to the prevention of the escape of noxious and offensive gases, has reference not only to the provision and the efficient maintenance of appliances adequate for preventing escape, but also to the manner in which such appliances are used and to the proper supervision, by the owner, of any operation in which such gases are evolved.

The Act only contains four statutory standards of emission, which cannot be changed without having an amending Act of Parliament. B.p.m. also apply to these cases as an additional control measure. In order to guide works managements in the design of plant and to assist inspectors in the execution of their duties, chief inspectors have set their own standards of emission, where possible, as interpreting the results of applying the requirements of b.p.m. These have the force of law behind them, because works which do not meet these stan-

*Reprinted with permission from *Annual Report of the Chief Inspector*, HMSO, London, 1973, pp. 8–15. Crown copyright.

dards, known as presumptive standards, are presumed not to be using b.p.m. As will be seen from Annual Alkali Reports, infraction letters are sent to works on these occasions, such letters being the first step to legal action, if it is decided to go to Court. Presumptive standards have been published in Annual Alkali Reports.

There are many scheduled works and parts of scheduled works with potential sources of emission, but where standards of emission cannot be set and, in these cases it is the policy to write codes of practice. Coke ovens are a prime example where b.p.m. consists of good teamwork in charging and discharging, use of efficient steam ejectors to contain "green gas", attention to the sealing of doors, good housekeeping and similar factors; see the "Notes on Code of Practice for Coke Ovens" described in Appendix VI of the 109th Annual Report for 1972. In other cases b.p.m. includes the covering of conveyors, suppression of odours, or efficient dispersion, etc. In other words, every possible source of an emission of noxious or offensive gas or particulate matter is assessed and controls are applied in the most practicable way.

On the subject of dispersion, it will be seen that b.p.m. must be used, firstly, to prevent emissions of noxious or offensive gases and particulate matter, and, secondly, to render harmless and inoffensive those necessarily discharged. The second of these is usually effected by suitable dispersion from tall chimneys. The alternatives of prevention or dispersion are not offered to industry. The inspectorate only considers dispersion when the best practicable means of prevention have been fully explored. There are many examples, such as gaseous products of combustion, where practicable means of prevention have not yet been developed. We must not forget the siting of works and commercial or domestic premises in relation to each other. Some industries will always be uncomfortable neighbours and we should be able to rely on good planning to keep them reasonably isolated.

The definition of b.p.m. in Section 27 is important, because it gives the inspectorate powers to control the processes giving rise to emissions. The inspectorate is not merely interested in what leaves the chimney or other source; it has to ensure that operations and maintenance are properly conducted, that instruments are used to control reactions, that routine tests are carried out by the owner, that suitable materials of construction are used and spares are kept in stock, that operators are correctly trained and instructed by the owner, and any other means are used which will help to minimise emissions to air. These powers are unusual in international control statutes and involve inspectors in an intimate knowledge of scheduled industrial processes to a greater extent than many other control agencies. The emphasis is on prevention rather than cure.

One of the great advantages of b.p.m. is that it can be altered at will by the chief inspector to take account of technological advances or the changing demands of the public for better amenities, not that we can always meet these demands even with new plants, nor have existing plants brought up to modern standards. Although the word "practicable" is not defined in the Alkali Act, over nearly 100 years there has evolved the acceptance that this includes both technology and economics. In the parallel legislation of the Clean Air and Public Health acts, the word "practicable" is defined and it would be unreasonable to interpret the Alkali Act differently. In the Clean Air Act 1956, "practicable" means reasonably practicable having regard, amongst other things, to local conditions and circumstances, to the financial implications and to the current state of technical knowledge.

Determination of best practicable means

I have often said, and been criticised for it, that if money were unlimited there would be few problems of air pollution control which could not be solved technically. In this statement can be included the supply of manpower and material resources. We have the technical knowledge to absorb gases, arrest grit, dust and fumes, and prevent smoke formation. The chief reason why we still permit the escape of these pollutants is because economics are an important part of the word "practicable". A lot of our problems are cheque book rather than technical, and attitudes which take little account of the economics of scarce resources, on which there are many claims, can so easily get priorities out of perspective. The inspectorate strives for perfection in prevention, but the further one goes along this path the more difficult it becomes to gain significant improvements at practicable cost, because we reach the area of diminishing returns.

The first step in determining b.p.m. is to set a goal, where possible, for the allowable effects of emissions on the environment. For example, that there shall be no visible emission, that it shall not be coloured, that it shall not smell, that there shall be no significant deposition of liquid or solid particles, that vegetation and farm animals shall not suffer, and so on. Rarely can zero standards or effects be achieved and for design purposes limits have to be put on emissions and dispersion techniques. The available information on toxicity to humans, vegetation and animals, and damage to materials of construction are studied, together with amenity effects, and the most significant is taken as the goal. Public health is naturally the most important aspect and the inspectorate could not permit an emission to be a demonstrable public health hazard; indeed we aim at atmospheric concentrations with a large margin of safety. Inherent in our policy is the thesis that there are no such things as harmful materials, there are only harmful concentrations. Unfortunately, whilst the inspectorate attempts to make emissions to air completely acceptable, it does not always succeed. It has already been said that b.p.m. is in two parts, prevention and dispersion, in that order. There is a long history of co-operation between industry and the inspectorate in finding solutions to difficult technical problems, industry being offered a partnership with the inspectorate. Working parties and discussion groups are set up, consisting of representatives of the industry, its research organisation, if any, and the inspectorate. Outside specialist bodies are consulted when necessary and when available. The emissions are investigated by the partners, including the routes by which pollutants reach their targets, research and development being carried out by the industrial side with their own specialists and at their own expense and with inspectors holding a watching brief. The inspectorate frequently travels abroad, sometimes in company with industry representatives, to examine foreign technology. Results are reported to both the industry and the inspectorate. The chief inspector makes the final decision on any standards and other requirements, for he is ultimately responsible, but this only follows mutual discussions with industry representatives whose approval is gained if possible. Decisions are circulated within the industry and the inspectorate and are published in Annual Alkali Reports. This participation by the trade associations is a good guarantee of their support in gaining implementation by their members, for they are anxious that all similar works in the country should have to meet the same requirements, with due allowance for adjustments to meet special local circumstances. Frequent, usually annual, meetings are held between trade associations and the inspectorate to note progress, discuss new technology, review research and development and generally re-assess situations with the object of gaining further improvements and possibly setting tougher standards and requirements for b.p.m . . .

The implementation of best practicable means

From what has been written above, it might be thought that we should be well on top of all our problems, but this is not the case. The inspectorate is a team of troubleshooters, only dealing with technically difficult problems of control, or trying to find practicable answers to unsolved problems. Not to have achieved that degree of perfection currently being demanded by the public is not failure to do our duty. It would indeed be strange if we had solved all our problems.

In the case of new plants, where prior approval is required, designers and engineers consult with inspectors at the blue-print stage, when they learn by an interchange of information the basic requirements for emission standards, the type of prevention apparatus which will be acceptable, what instrumentation and control mechanisms will be needed, codes of good practices to be adopted, final height of dispersion, safeguards, and the like. Where corrosion and erosion are to be expected and overcome, should costly impervious materials of construction be used, or should cheaper replaceable units be made? How far should equipment be duplicated in case of breakdowns, e.g. fans, pumps and electrical precipitators, and what spares should be kept in stock? What extra provisions should be made to prevent or disperse excessive emissions during start-up and shut-down? These and other similar considerations are discussed. Much will depend on the value of the product and the consequences of failure. A breakdown which interferes with the amenities by producing black smoke or releasing inert dust is by no means so serious, as a breakdown which might result in the massive release of highly toxic materials, such as chlorine, phosgene, hydrogen sulphide or tolylene di-isocyanate. The design problems facing the industrialist and the inspectorate are concerned with how far we can go along the road to perfection in protecting the public without causing financial embarrassment to the industry, or individual works, a small community, or even the nation, for in the long run it is the public which pays, directly or indirectly. Despite all the care taken in planning and designing new plant, we all know that performances do not always come up to expectations, especially when a new step forward is being taken, that excessive teething troubles can be experienced, or that unforeseen weaknesses develop. The consequence is that local amenities suffer. Shutting the plant down rarely provides an answer. Only by continuous operation, diagnosis and modification can the troubles be overcome. These are difficult decisions to take and the inspectorate comes in for much criticism during these unsettled times. Continual stopping and starting of process plant never gives the arrestment plant or other control units a fair opportunity to work effectively and we have been faced with many such problems as process units have been scaled-up and/or become more complicated.

In practice, inspectors make routine, unannounced visits to inspect registered processes and to carry out their own emission tests where necessary. At least 2 visits per year are made to even the smallest, least offensive works under the inspectorate's control and at least 8 visits per year to what are known as "major potential offenders". Usually far more visits than the minimum are carried out, many of a special nature by appointment to discuss developments and improvements with top management officials. All inspectors carry with them fairly simple sampling and analysing equipment which is used to check emissions and to compare results with those of the works, for it is a requirement of b.p.m. that owners shall carry out an agreed procedure of routine testing in order properly to control the process. Their results are examined by inspectors on routine visits. There are certain types of analyses which cannot be carried out without the use of complicated, expensive and non-transportable apparatus and it is the inspectorate's practice to collect samples and send them away to specialist laboratories for examination. During 1973, 1,790 such samples were sent to the Government Chemist's Laboratory for determination of 2,694 metallic constituents. In the last two years, four sampling teams, each of two men, have been strategically placed round the country to act as a service section to inspectors in the field. Already they have shown themselves as a valuable asset.

The chief inspector, with the help of his deputies, lays down the broad national policies and provided they keep within these broad lines, inspectors in the field have plenty of flexibility to take into account local circumstances and make suitable decisions. They are given plenty of autonomy and are trained as a team of decision-takers with as much responsibility and authority as possible. Nonetheless, they keep the head office staff well informed about the works under their control, so that the information can be assessed, compared and disseminated as necessary. It helps to formulate new policies, which are regularly discussed at annual staff meetings when all the inspectors from the United Kingdom gather for a 3-day meeting and exchange notes. Even if inspectors had works under observation all the time, there would still be incidents and breakdowns which could not be prevented. The inspectorate relies on managements and local authorities reporting such incidents to them. When incidents repeat themselves excessively, the inspectorate seeks permanent solutions and there is always a search for general improvements during routine visits. There is, of course, controversy over the severity with which the inspectorate carries out its duties and deals with offences. We do not hesitate to take legal action when we believe it to be deserved, but legal action will not solve technical problems or breakdowns, teething troubles or the occasional results of industrial action.

There is no finality about the best practicable means for controlling emissions from industrial processes. Industry cannot stay still; it is either progressing or declining and presenting new problems. Revolutions are occurring continually and there are many examples of new processes being invented, dominating the production scene and then being supplanted by newer processes or cheaper routes to the same end-product. This results in a constant battle for the inspectorate to cope with new situations and to satisfy the ever more stringent requirements of the public for cleaner air. Pressures and criticisms often come from groups with a narrow interest. The inspectorate has to take a broad view, but never does it forget that its job is to protect the health and well-being of the public. Much progress has been made and much has yet to be done.

There are important facets of the alkali inspectorate's work which cannot be described as part of b.p.m., but which contribute enormously to the smooth running of the system and are worth mentioning again even though they have been described more fully in earlier reports.

One of these is the education of industry in its environmental responsibilities to the community and the organisation of control, maintenance, supervision, training and testing on a proper footing. Some quite sophisticated internal systems have been set up by large and small organisations, companies and individual works, in which the new staff act as self-imposed alkali inspectors, critical of their own methods and ensuring that statutory requirements are met. The inspectorate has preached to industry the appointment of these environmental control officers, not only to look at works effluent problems broadly, but to act as a communications link with the public. There has been a good response and industry is learning to speak far more freely to the public about its operations and emissions than ever before.[2]

Another important facet is the long history of co-operation between the alkali inspectorate and local authorities, now being joined by local industry to make the third partner. Since 1958, inspectors have been instructed to visit at least twice yearly as a routine all those public health departments of local authorities in which registered works are sited. During these routine discussions, frank exchanges are made and a good teamwork has built up between the two parties. A much better understanding of each others problems has developed and local authority officers are kept informed about what is happening at registered works. Arrangements have been made in many instances for local public health inspectors to contact works direct and immediately when complaints are received or unusual emissions are noted. This allows works managers to take corrective action straight away instead of having to deal with past history if the complaints are routed only through the alkali inspector, who always makes his own follow-up visit of investigation. It is also our policy to encourage the managements of registered works to advise the inspectorate and the local authority immediately they run into trouble, so that the public can be reassured that control authorities are wise to the situation and corrective action is being taken. Each works has its own impact on the local environment and it is with the local people that works must communicate when necessary. The inspectorate has tried hard in recent years to draw works, local authorities and local residents closer together into united and closely-knit communities, helped sometimes by local liaison committees. We must try to eliminate gulfs and adversary attitudes where they exist and reap the full benefits of best practicable means.[3]

Much has been said and written about the Polluter Pays Principle as though it were a newly-discovered control policy, especially when allied to the imposition of charges. It has long been the inspectorate's policy to have works and industries use their own specialists, at their own expense, to carry out research, investigation and development to find solutions to their air pollution problems to continue to search for better methods of control and to pay the costs of pollution control and prevention methods. It is inevitable that the producer will pass on these costs to the consumer, the public. So it is the public that pays in the long run. If the extra cost of pollution control is excessive, the works will not be able properly to compete with similar works in other areas or countries not subject to such controls, nor with rival commodities competing for the same market. The result could be that works would have to reduce production or even close permanently, with a consequent loss of jobs, taxes and rates. It is still the public that pays, and let us not overlook the fact that the loss of, say, 100 jobs in a works could effect perhaps up to 1,000 people dependent on those jobs. In an indirect way, the inspectorate is being responsible for the spending of public money and it has to be careful not to unbalance the system in a manner harmful to the public. Frequently we receive requests to make industry pay unlimited sums of money to remove the last traces of pollutants from the atmosphere, but those making the requests rarely take into account the overall cost to the local community or the nation. The inspectorate has to take a broad view and must ensure that the word 'practicable' is properly interpreted as including economics in its requirements. The object of applying a charge to waste disposal is to reduce the effect on the environment to a pre-determined optimum. The charge is on a sliding scale according to the amount of pollutant being discharged, so that owners are encouraged to treat their wastes to the point at which further reduction increases the cost of treatment beyond the optimum. This may be an acceptable method of control for certain types of waste such as solids or liquids. It is claimed that such a system would be self-regulating and need only a token enforcement staff. In the case of air pollution control, such a system would be over-complicated and it pre-supposes that an optimum point can be pre-determined. From what has been said already under "best practicable means" it will be obvious that we are dealing with a complicated emission system and that controls must embrace imponderables such as meteorological variations, indirect emissions such as leakages, breakdowns, wind-whipping, good housekeeping, maintenance and all the other items previously described which cannot be measured. One's mind boggles at the thought of applying charges generally to air pollution control and I feel sure that some owners would prefer to pay the charge when they fell short of the optimum rather than spend more money to correct or replace an imperfect unit. Why replace the existing simple, effective system with complicated, unproven theory?

Editorial Notes

1. Chief Alkali Inspector at the time of writing (1973).
2. The 1974 Control of Pollution Act contains a section (41) which requires that local authorities publish a register of all emissions into the atmosphere. Due to public expenditure restrictions and other considerations this section is not yet in force.
3. At present there are only three local liaison committees in the UK. They are very much an *ad hoc* arrangement but at least they keep various interests in communication with each other.

Postscript

THE linking chapters to this reader were written in 1979 since when there have been a number of important developments so, we feel it would be wise to add this contemporary commentary.*

Environmentalism and Recession

There seems little doubt that throughout much of the eighties, and possibly well beyond, the wellbeing of the globe will be influenced by economic recession. Though this will probably get more publicity in the developed countries, recession being somewhat novel to the post-war generations, the effect of global economic decline will be far more acutely felt in the non-oil least-developed nations whose populations embrace more than half the world's people. While some in the west regard their plight as merely an extension of generations of destitution, it is becoming increasingly evident that, unless there are major changes in policy and political economy in these nations, their poverty will have repercussions on Western economic growth and global environmental systems. Both the World Bank (1979) and the OECD (1980) warn of the threat to international money markets should the non-oil least-developed nations default in the $300 billion debts which they have accumulated.

OPEC Oil Revenues and the International Economy

The oil-exporting OPEC economies as a group built up a huge current account revenue surplus in 1974 in the wake of the oil-price escalations engineered by the cartel. The period between 1974 and 1979 saw a marked decline in the real price of oil and the inevitable cartel response came in 1979 and 1980 with further large price increases. In the immediate aftermath of the first oil-price escalation the OPEC countries accumulated foreign assets of around $67 billion. After the 1979 price increases the total assets held by OPEC exporters totalled some $240 billion. The important question is what happened to this vast surplus of

*This postscript was completed in April 1981.

funds. In particular, did the non-OPEC developing countries derive much in the way of assistance from OPEC? In 1974 over half of the funds went into deposits located in the banking system of the "North", and only some $5 billion went directly into loans and aid to non-OPEC developing countries. The banking system then proceeded to recycle the OPEC funds largely by means of capital investment loans to the developing countries. The same recycling process has, however, been made more difficult in the post 1979 oil price-rise period because of the debts that the non-OPEC countries have accumulated.

If the banking system in the North is more constrained what other mechanisms are available to facilitate a transfer of funds to the oil-deficient developing world? The established international financial institutions, the International Monetary Fund (IMF) and the World Bank were not originally designed to cope with the sort of severe long-term balance of payments difficulties that the non-OPEC developing countries are now experiencing. A current account deficit of some $50 billion was recorded by these countries in 1979, a third of which was due to oil-import bills. The IMF, in particular, seems reluctant to make any major changes in its mode of operation in order to facilitate a much larger and swifter transfer of resources between the North and South. While direct aid flows from OPEC to the other developing economies remained fairly static between 1975 and 1980 a long-term OPEC special fund has been established which could be extended significantly to cover the financing of oil imports by developing countries. One should also bear in mind, however, that the wealth of individual OPEC countries is still not comparable with the major Western industrialised economies.

Economic growth in poor countries cannot easily be attained without potentially catastrophic environmental damage especially through the loss of tropical forests, widespread soil erosion, desert margin dessication, salinisation of irrigated soils and massive loss of plant and insect species. These conclusions are reached by two independent yet penetrating reports (International Union for the Conservation of Nature, 1980; US, Interagency Committee, 1980) which show clearly the link between poverty, environmental ill-health, and ecological destruction. The rate by which damage is apparently increasing is very alarming, yet world governments appear impotent to cope. Even a top-level commission (Brandt Commission, 1980) which also documented these problems and which argued in favour of joint North–South economic development, a most conventional Keynesian solution, has had very little impact on World leaders. (See also Pearson and Pryor (1978) for a similar type of analysis and conclusions.) Nevertheless, the identification of global trends from the available aggregate data on population growth, per capita income growth, arable land and food production and environmental quality remains a very imperfect art. Simon (1980, 1981) has recently reiterated the optimistic technocentrist (see Sections 1, and 7) arguments about future levels of economic growth and welfare. Simon's article stimulated a series of responses challenging both his interpretation of the available statistical data and his faith in benign technological advance (Science, 1980). Daly (1980) has brought together a new expanded set of readings grouped around the theme of steady-state economics which provide a useful contrast to Simon's analysis. In the absence of new North–South co-operative effort it appears that the poor will either have to learn even better how to cope for themselves in their own development mode coupled with infusions of appropriate technology (McRobie, 1981), or else a major environmental calamity coupled with massive human tragedy will bring the West to its senses. That may take another 20 years or more by which time the damage may be irreparable.

Meanwhile, in the Western world, recession has brought with it a paradox. Governments pursuing right-wing monetarist policies are cutting back on public sector investments such as major energy developments and other large construction schemes that have always been such an anathema to resource-conservation-minded environmentalists. Yet the same policy of public sector expenditure reduction has meant that any of the regulatory agencies responsible for health and safety, including risk assessment and pollution control, are starved of research and administrative funds, are suffering from a loss in morale and are being told to ease off on controls which appear unnecessarily to hamper industrial regeneration. Thus the UK government (1980) has told its inspectorates to be more cost effective in regulatory practices, yet it is now so underpaying its inspectorates that recruitment is impaired, and senior experienced people are leaving to join the private sector. The British government has also recently axed two environmental quasi-autonomous, non-governmental organisations (quangos), the Waste Management Advisory Council and the Noise Advisory Council,* both of which provided useful background information and constructive criticisms and recommendations. Their disappearance has left a serious gap in policy advice in these two important areas of environmental protection.

In the US, the Reagan administration has begun to relax clean air and clean water regulations, so carefully built up during the seventies, and has placed the formerly independent and much admired Council on Environmental Quality within the budgetary aegis of the Environmental Protection Agency. This action is regarded by many as the kiss of death for the Council. Previously protected US federal land is now being opened up to logging, mining and petroleum exploitation. Funding for national parks has been reduced and sales of offshore oil and gas leases has often been stimulated against the wishes of state governments.

*In mid-1982 the National Water Council and the Water Space Amenity Commission were also scheduled to be closed down.

In this new generally antiregulatory mood the US Environmental Protection Agency (EPA) has been searching for new regulatory approaches. The so-called "bubble" programme has been designed to reduce corporate costs while preserving environmental standards (Smith 1981). Under this bubble approach strict process standards have been replaced by a far more flexible form of control which treats an entire plant as a single polluter and requires a cutback in, say, the total air-pollution discharge. It is largely up to the company concerned how the reduction in discharges should be achieved and in this sense the approach is similar to the best practicable means procedure operated in the UK by both air and water pollution-control agencies. The promising initial results achieved after one year of operating the bubble programme has apparently stimulated EPA to develop additional regulatory innovations such as a futures market in pollution rights and saleable permits to pollute with asbestos or chlorofluorocarbons. Many of the firms in the bubble programme have been able to reduce discharges to below that required by the control legislation. In these cases credits have been granted to the firm toward added pollution in future. EPA plans to establish a brokerage network for selling these credits between firms and such systems have already been established through local governments in Louisville, San Francisco and Seattle.* We surveyed pollution-control policy and instruments in Section 9, and Burrows (1979) and Lowe and Lewis (1980) have also recently reviewed these matters.

Control of pollution externalities continues to be as difficult a problem in the industrialised economies of the Soviet Union and Eastern Europe as it has proved to be in the West. Komarov (1980) criticises the environmental record of the Soviet authorities and finds it severely wanting despite the existence of a great deal of formal legislation. In fact his treatment shows how centralist institutions geared to economic growth are often quite insensitive to possible environmental dangers even in the face of authoritative scientific caution.

It is difficult to forecast the long-term effects of this shift in policy away from tough environmental protection measures as a major public policy objective. Much will depend upon the nature of economic growth and in particular associated levels of unemployment over the next generation and upon the legacy of the seventies when major improvements in manufacturing processes led to better pollution control and energy/materials conservation technologies. These developments tend to indicate that the picture is not as serious as it appears. Much depends

---

*For a survey of these issues, see Tietenberg, T. H. (1980) Transferable Discharge Permits and the Control of Stationary Source Air Pollution: A Survey & Synthesis, *Land Economics* 56 (4) ; and Batey Blackman, S. and Baumol, W. (1980) Modified Fiscal Incentives in Environmental Policy, *Land Economics* 56 (4).

too on the "environmental-mindedness" of the productive sector of society and its interactions with environmentalists who really believe in a totally different kind of political economy. Sandbach (1980), Schnaiberg (1980) and Cotgrove (1982) have tackled this issue bravely. They are convinced that society will divide into two classes, broadly along the ecocentrist-technocentrist line already outlined in Section 1, and that there will be a constant struggle between those described as environmental managers (who are really accommodators between the requirements of environmental protection and economic growth without recognising any adjustment in the pattern of economic and political power) and those regarded as federalists and "soft technologists" who seek a more decentralised political economy based upon the principles of materials conservation, appropriate technology and human scale communities.

While Sandbach, Schnaiberg, Cotgrove and to a lesser extent the authors in the anthologies edited by Dunlap (1980) and Mitchell (1980) do not believe that ecocentrism will prevail outside of some fairly serious economic and/or environmental distress afflicting a specific minority, a new breed of authors such as Shankland (1980) and McRobie (1980) argue that the pattern of economic development is already changing in favour of so-called "alternative" pioneering experiments and the proliferation of the informal economy (where transactions take place outside of the formal "tax" economy and where services can be exchanged for kind, not money). These writers plus various other neo-Fabians provide some optimistic conclusions, namely that out of distress will emerge the elements of a new renaissance along the lines already discussed by Hall in the readings but with much more emphasis upon informal economies and technologies. These, they claim, are already what make the "destitute" Third World tick, so the principal is well tried. The aim now is to fashion it to the modern world and to particular societies.

How all this will affect the environmental lobby is also uncertain. Private interest environmental groups struggling to protect their own local environmental amenities will undoubtedly continue to form, flourish and decay as particular issues rise and fall. Currently there is much furore in the UK over the distribution of wildlife habitats and heritage landscapes by farming and urban development (Mabey, 1980; Shoard, 1980; Goode, 1981) and doubtless skirmishes in particular trouble spots will continue throughout the decade.

The public interest or cause groups have a more uncertain future. Their seventies-style "shock" treatment has now worked to the point where environmental protection to a degree is now part of the subconscious of the nation. Really fundamental reform coupled to major policy shifts are not forthcoming yet the groups are getting tired, they are starved of funds, their personnel are changing too rapidly to maintain continuity and they have not passed through the transition between fighting for principles and putting into action at grass-roots level the kind of technologies and social relations they believe to be suitable for the twenty-first century. It may well be that a new revolution in the structure and activity of British environmental groups is in the offing, in favour of a more loose confederation of local groups committed to the enhancement of social and environmental wellbeing more closely linked to the establishment. If so, it would be very much in line with the evolution of environmental pressure groups in the UK (Lowe *et al.*, 1980). In the US, funds are also becoming tight for the major environmental organisations, so they will have to rely on a small number of highly competent experts, will probably have to programme their issues even more and will seek to establish a new trust with senior administration officials who will be appointed to keep them at bay. The outlook is tough, but not desperate.

References

Brandt Commission (1980) *North South: A Programme for Survival* (London: Pan Books).
Burrows, P. (1979) *The Economic Theory of Pollution Control* (Oxford: Martin Robertson).
Cotgrove, S. (1982) *The Environment: Catastrophe or Cornucopia?* (Chichester: John Wiley).
Dunlap, R. E (ed.) (1980) Ecology and the Social Sciences: An Emerging Paradigm, *American Behavioral Scientist*, **24**, 3-151.
Goode, D. (1981) The Threat to Wildlife Habitats, *New Scientist* **89** (22 January), 219-223.
International Union for the Conservation of Nature (1980) *World Conservation Strategy* (Geneva: IUCN); see also Allen, R. (1980) *How to Save the World* (London: Logan Page).
Komarov, B. (1980) *The Destruction of Nature in the Soviet Union* (London: Pluto Press).
Lowe, J. and Lewis, D. (1980) *The Economics of Environmental Management* (Oxford: Philip Allan).
Lowe, P., Clifford, J. and Buchanan, S. (1980) The Mass Movement of the Decade, *Vole* 3 (4), 26-28.
Mabey, R. (1980) *The Common Ground: A Place for Nature in Britain's Future* (London: Hutchinson).
McRobie, G. (1981) *Small is Possible* (London: Jonathon Cape).
Mitchell, R. C. (ed.) (1980) Whither Environmentalism?, *Natural Resources Journal*, **20**, 217-359.
OECD (1979) *Facing the Future: Mastering the Probable and Managing the Unpredictable (Paris: OECD)*.
Pearson, C. and Pryor, A. (1978) *Environment North and South: An Economic Interpretation* (Chichester: Wiley).
Pye-Smith, C. and Rose, C. (1981) Lost in A Fool's Paradise, *Vole* (4 April), 5.
Sandbach, F. (1980) *Environment, Ideology and Policy* (Oxford: Basil Blackwell).
Science (1980), Letters 210, 19 Dec., 1296-1306.
Schnaiberg, A. (1980) *The Environment: From Surplus to Scarcity* (New York: Oxford University Press).
Shankland, G. (1980) *The Secret Economy* (London: Anglo-German Institute).
Shoard, M. (1980) *The Theft of the Countryside* (London: Maurice Temple Smith).
Simon, L. (1980) Resources, Population, Environment: an oversupply of false bad news. *Science* **208**, 27 June, 1431-437.
Simon, L. (1981) *The Ultimate Resource* (Princeton, N.J.: Princeton University Press).
Smith, R. J. (1981) EPA and Industry Pursue Regulatory Options, *Science* vol. 211, Feb., 796-798.
UK Government (1980) *Non Governmental Bodies* (London: HMSO).
US, Interagency Committee (1980) *Global 2000* (Washington: US Government Printing Office).
World Bank (1980) *Second Development Report* (Washington: World Bank).

Other titles in the series

HOYLE, B. S. & PINDER, D. A.
Cityport Industrialization and Regional Development (Volume 24)

TAYLOR, J. L. & WILLIAMS, D. G.
Urban Planning Practice in Developing Countries (Volume 25)

SPENCE, N. *et al.*
British Cities: An Analysis of Urban Change (Volume 26)

PARIS, C.
Critical Readings in Planning Theory (Volume 27)

STARKIE, D.
The Motorway Age (Volume 28)

The terms of our inspection copy service apply to all the above books. A complete catalogue of all books in the Pergamon International Library is available on request. The Publisher will be pleased to consider suggestions for revised editions and new titles.